THE ARCHAEOLOGY OF OXFORD IN THE 21ST CENTURY

THE ARCHAEOLOGY OF OXFORD IN THE 21ST CENTURY

INVESTIGATIONS IN THE CITY BY OXFORD ARCHAEOLOGY, 2006–16

Edited by ANNE DODD, STEPHEN MILESON and LEO WEBLEY

With contributions by Steven Teague, Leigh Allen, Martin Allen, Enid Allison, Robin Bashford, Edward Biddulph, Paul Blinkhorn, Sheila Boardman, Kate Brady, Lee G. Broderick, Richard Brown, Carl Champness, John Cotter, Geraldine Crann, Michael Donnelly, Julie Dunne, Richard P. Evershed, Ben M. Ford, Deirdre Forde, John Giorgi, Lee Grana, T.G. Hassall, David A. Higgins, Lynne Keys, Toby Martin, Julia Meen, Julian Munby, Rebecca Nicholson, Chris Pickard, Cynthia Poole, David Radford, Alice Rose, Ian R. Scott, Ruth Shaffrey, Andrew Simmonds, Mike Sims, Kirsty Smith, Wendy Smith, Lena Strid, Gerry Thacker, John Tibbles, Alison de Turberville, Ken Welsh, and Hugh Willmott

Illustrations by Charles Rousseaux, Markus Dylewski, Lucy Gane, David A. Higgins, Victoria Hosegood, Gary Jones, Hannah Kennedy, Wendy Morrison, Conan Parsons, and Magdalena Wachnik

OAHS Occasional Paper, 1

First published 2020

ISBN 978-1-78327-613-4

A Oxfordshire Archaeological and Historical Society publication
Published by The Boydell Press
an imprint of Boydell & Brewer Ltd
PO Box 9, Woodbridge, Suffolk IP12 3DF, UK
and of Boydell & Brewer Inc.
668 Mt Hope Avenue, Rochester, NY 14620–2731, USA
website: www.boydellandbrewer.com

A CIP catalogue record for this book is available
from the British Library

This publication is printed on acid-free paper

Printed by TJ Books Limited

Contents

Abbreviations

BAR	British Archaeological Reports (Oxford, 1974–)
BAR BS	British Archaeological Reports, British Series
Bodl.	Bodleian Library, Oxford
CBM	ceramic building material
EVE	estimated vessel equivalent
Ctx	context
Dodd, *Oxford*	A. Dodd (ed.), *Oxford Before the University: The Late Saxon and Norman Archaeology of the Thames Crossing, the Defences and the Town*, Thames Valley Landscapes Monograph, 17 (2003)
EETS	Early English Texts Society
Hassall, 'St Ebbe's, Part I'	T.G. Hassall et al., 'Excavations in St Ebbe's, Oxford, 1967–1976: Part I: Late Saxon and Medieval Domestic Occupation and Tenements, and the Medieval Greyfriars', *Oxoniensia*, 54 (1989), pp. 71–277
Hassall, 'St Ebbe's, Part II'	T.G. Hassall et al., 'Excavations in St Ebbe's, Oxford, 1967–1976: Part II: Post-Medieval Domestic Tenements and the Post-Dissolution Site of the Greyfriars', *Oxoniensia*, 49 (1984), pp. 153–275
JMHS	John Moore Heritage Services
Mellor, 'Synthesis'	M. Mellor, 'A Synthesis of Middle and Late Saxon, Medieval and Early Post-Medieval Pottery in the Oxford Region', *Oxoniensia*, 59 (1994), pp. 17–217.
Munby, *Oxford Castle*	J. Munby et al., *Excavations at Oxford Castle, 1999–2009*, Thames Valley Landscapes Monograph, 44 (2019)
n.	note
ns	new series
OA	Oxford Archaeology
OA Library	Oxford Archaeology online repository for client reports: https://library.thehumanjourney.net (specific urls given in footnotes for available reports)
OHS	Oxford Historical Society
ORS	Oxfordshire Record Society
Poore, *Beaumont*	D. Poore and D.R.P. Wilkinson, *Beaumont Palace and the White Friars: Excavations at the Sackler Library, Beaumont Street, Oxford*, Oxford Archaeology Occasional Paper, 9 (2001)
Poore, 'No. 4A Merton St.'	D. Poore et al., 'Excavations at No. 4A Merton St., Merton College, Oxford: The Evolution of a Medieval Stone House and Tenement and an Early College Property', *Oxoniensia*, 71 (2006), pp. 211–341
Roth, *Jews*	C. Roth, *The Jews of Medieval Oxford*, OHS, ns 9 (1951)
Salter, *Oseney*	H.E. Salter (ed.), *Cartulary of Oseney Abbey*, 6 vols., OHS, 89–91, 97–8, 101 (1929–36)
Salter, *Survey*	H.E. Salter, *Survey of Oxford*, ed. W.A. Pantin and W.T. Mitchell, 2 vols., OHS, ns 14, 20 (1960 and 1969)
SMidlA	South Midlands Archaeology
TVAS	Thames Valley Archaeological Services
VCH	*Victoria History of the Counties of England* (London, 1900–)
vol.	volume

Preface

This volume presents the results of eleven excavations carried out by Oxford Archaeology within the historic walled city (a town until 1542) and in the extramural area just to the north. These investigations were carried out as separate projects undertaken in advance of development on behalf of different clients, but it was decided to bring the reports together in this volume – the first in a new series of OAHS Occasional Papers – because they address common research questions. In particular, they shed fresh light on the character of medieval Oxford (both before and after the Norman Conquest), and, taken together, they represent a significant contribution to knowledge of Oxford's archaeology and history.

In terms of the Anglo-Saxon period, the excavation at the Ashmolean Museum was notable in uncovering rare eighth- to ninth-century Ipswich ware pottery which, along with earlier finds at the Sackler Library, suggest connections with wider trading networks, and also raise the tantalising possibility that Henry I's nearby early twelfth-century Beaumont Palace was located in an area with much earlier high-status occupants. The St Aldate's/Queen Street investigations add to the evidence for eighth- to ninth-century activity close to Carfax, which perhaps then as in later periods was the town's central crossroads. New data are also supplied (from St Peter's and Queen's) which add to ongoing debate about the date and extent of the defensive enclosure (or *burh*) created in the late ninth or early tenth century, while small pits found at St Aldate's/ Queen Street give clues about the character of buildings within the *burh*, at least some of which may actually predate its establishment. The pottery found in these pits and later cellars yield insights into what may have been differences in social character between zones within the late Anglo-Saxon town.

The excavations also tell us much that is new about the post-Conquest medieval period. There is rich data about diet and economic activity, including in the town's northern suburb, and about the development of the medieval university halls and colleges, including Merton and Queen's colleges. Finds from this period bring us close to some of Oxford's well-known activities, including the scholarly life reflected in writing materials and book clasps, but they also offer glimpses into a wider range of people and lifestyles, including the craftspeople involved in metal-working and even those who left finger prints on freshly made roof tiles (found at Merton), at least one of whom was probably a child. Most exciting of all is the evidence from the town's twelfth- to thirteenth-century Jewish quarter. The bone remains and organic residues on pottery from St Aldate's/Queen Street reveal the first (very likely) medieval Jewish signature in British zooarchaeology in a striking absence of pig bones and fats, as well as eel and shellfish, a picture in clear contrast to that in the site's earlier and later phases.

Late-medieval and early modern developments are also well represented, with evidence of changes in building layout (again at St Aldate's/Queen Street) and shifts in food consumption as diets apparently became more varied (as the Ashmolean excavation shows). A reduced population allowed colleges to acquire land for their gardens, including St John's in 1600. Growing domestic comforts are suggested by the increased presence of window glass, and by the rare find of pieces of a sixteenth-century tiled stove (again at St John's) which was probably imported from Germany. Finally, the physical impact of the Civil War on the city is indicated by finds of musket balls and a powder holder at the Ashmolean and, above all, by remains of several phases of defences dug in the 1640s (at Mansfield College).

The volume is divided into three parts, the first of which (Part I) includes an overview of the key findings from the excavations (by Anne Dodd), as well as a valuable new synthesis of current knowledge of Oxford's archaeology by David Radford, which places the findings presented here in a larger context, including that of discoveries from other parts of the city – notably from the Westgate and the castle in the west, the Radcliffe Observatory Quarter in the north, and

Magdalen College in the east – and from its suburbs and surrounding villages. A chapter by Tom Hassall (founding director of the Oxford Archaeological Unit, now Oxford Archaeology), fills out the context in a different way, by laying bare the changing aims and methods of archaeology carried out in the city over the last fifty years. Hassall's contribution also tells the human story of those involved in Oxford's archaeological research, and how they have helped to shape the modern city's identity and sense of its past. Parts II and III are the meat of the book, the former reporting on those sites which mainly yielded information about the medieval and early urban centre and university, the latter on the northern suburb (around St John's, the Ashmolean, and St Cross) and the Civil War defences (at Mansfield and the Tinbergen Building).

Stephen Mileson

PART 1

Introduction and Synthesis

1.

The Archaeology of Oxford: Current Knowledge and Future Prospects

DAVID RADFORD

SUMMARY

This chapter offers a summary of present knowledge of Oxford's medieval and later archaeology, and, just as importantly, sets out what archaeological data can tell us about the city's development over time. Consideration is given to the strengths and weaknesses of the archaeological record, its value alongside documentary evidence, and the tension between excavation and preservation in the hope of future advances in archaeological techniques. Particular attention is paid to areas for future research and the ways in which archaeological findings can be shared with the wider public.

In an era of transnational genome studies, extensive LiDAR surveys and big data processing projects, the ongoing study of a south Midlands Anglo-Saxon town may seem to some a rather parochial activity. Surely, one might ask, we have resolved by now all the big questions relating to Oxford after almost 150 years of investigation and with urban archaeology taking centre stage in the national archaeological awakening of the post-war rescue era?[1] The reality is that despite major advances in our understanding of the town's material culture the reactive nature of investigation under the current development-led planning framework has left open a number of key 'building block' questions relating to Oxford's early development. For example, when and how did a middle Anglo-Saxon settlement emerge? Was it centralised or polyfocal in character? When and how was the settlement more formally laid out, extended and defended? Thus, whilst the large body of data recovered from past excavations has opened up many possible avenues of study relating to urban development, consumption, trade, wealth, health, mortality, social relations, cultural difference and so on, many of the key processes relating to the town's emergence and early evolution remain unresolved. For the late Anglo-Saxon period, long-established interpretations have been called into question by recent discoveries. For later periods the sheer volume of information being recovered presents us with major challenges in terms of synthesis and requires us to constantly refocus our enquiries, taking into account developments in medieval and post-medieval studies.[2]

1 For an overview of the post-war and later periods: C. Gerrard, *Medieval Archaeology: Understanding Traditions and Contemporary Approaches* (2003), pp. 95–9, 133–8.

2 An extensive overview of developments in later-medieval archaeology is provided by C.M. Gerrard and A. Gutiérrez (eds.), *The Oxford Handbook of Later Medieval Archaeology in Britain* (2018). A regional overview of the post-medieval period is provided by J. Hind, 'The Post Medieval and Modern Period (AD 1540 Onwards): Resource Assessment', in G. Hey and J. Hind (eds.) *Solent-Thames Research Framework for the Historic Environment Resource Assessments and Research Agendas*, Oxford Wessex Monograph, 6 (2014).

WHY IS OXFORD OF INTEREST?

The question of why we should continue to expend resources investigating Oxford can be addressed directly. The location of the town on a crossroads, on a major river, in a central location within the landmass of central-southern England should provide geographical clues to its capacity to preserve a thorough cross-section of local and imported material culture from the middle-Anglo-Saxon period onwards. Oxford remains significant and worthy of study as a border settlement influenced by the state forming processes taking place in the middle Anglo-Saxon kingdoms of Wessex and Mercia. It was a favoured central meeting point for late Anglo-Saxon, Danish and Norman royalty, an important cloth town in the early Middle Ages, and subsequently a university town that was European in terms of its intellectual reach and intake, even if the bulk of the student body remained predominantly 'local' in background.[3] Oxford attracted the full medieval urban package of defences, peripheral abbeys, mendicant friaries and hospitals with many of these institutions gaining additional complexity through their relationship with the developing university.

With its tradition of modern crime fiction, it is fitting that Oxford has been used alongside London as an exemplar of high medieval murder rates.[4] Such distinctive interpersonal conflict being in part a reflection of the power struggle commonly referred to as 'town versus gown', a conflict that may have been in part fuelled by the social dislocation caused by the decline of traditional trades in the thirteenth and fourteenth century and the related ascendancy of service trades that orientated around the university. Although for a time a middling town in economic terms, during the post-medieval period Oxford enjoyed renewed growth from the late sixteenth century, a brief resurgence in status as Royalist capital during the Civil War, and has remained a favoured location for architectural patronage and innovation because of its ties to money and power. The presence of the university further distorted Oxford's development as an industrial centre with disproportionally large numbers of people, in national terms, working in the domestic service sector into the early twentieth century. Whilst pockets of industrial activity developed close to the historic core, for example breweries and the first Morris car garage, these employers were ultimately forced to relocate to the suburbs in order to expand and become more central to Oxford's twentieth-century economy. These processes, only partially documented, have all left archaeological traces worthy of study.[5]

TO DIG OR NOT TO DIG?

Archaeologists have excavated and therefore removed a significant amount of archaeology in Oxford since the advent of Planning Policy Guidance Note 16 (PPG16) in 1990.[6] This is a both a cause for celebration and a suitable moment to pause and reflect on the trajectory of investigation in the coming years. Over the last decade there have been sizeable developments in the central area involving new basements, and therefore full removal of archaeological deposits

[3] For the regional character and background of the medieval university intake and the early ambivalence of the aristocracy to this new institution see L.W.B. Brockliss *The University of Oxford: A History* (2016), pp. 34–7.

[4] The examination of coroners' rolls from fourteenth-century Oxford and London has resulted in estimates in the order of 25 to 110 homicides per 100,000 inhabitants, while estimates for other areas of England typically vary between 8 and 25 homicides per 100,000: M. Eisner, 'Long-Term Historical Trends in Violent Crime', *Crime and Justice*, 30 (2003), p. 100.

[5] For example, the original Morris Garage workshop on Holywell Street was investigated in 2017 (OA forthcoming) and the eighteenth- to nineteenth-century Swan Brewery site on Paradise Street in 2003 and 2018 (D. Hart, 'An Archaeological Excavation at Telecom House Paradise Street Oxford' (2005), unpublished JMHS report, and A. Simmonds et al., 'Former Cooper Callas Building, 15 Paradise Street, Oxford Post-Excavation Assessment', unpublished OA report (2019)).

[6] Planning Policy Guidance Note 16 introduced archaeology formally into the planning process and required developers to fund archaeological investigations.

at the Radcliffe Observatory Quarter, the Westgate Shopping Centre car parks, The Queen's College library, Lincoln College Garden Building and Magdalen College library. This is in addition to a multiplicity of schemes involving localised piling, strip foundation or stanchion grid impacts where remains may have been partially preserved below. At the time of writing consented schemes were in the pipeline for new basements at Corpus Christi and Oriel College and more are being considered in pre-application discussions.

To understand the significance of this development trajectory one must appreciate that a great deal of the archaeology of the Anglo-Saxon and medieval town was fortuitously preserved by the laying out of College quads, gardens and kitchen yards across central Oxford from the thirteenth century onwards and within other institutional gardens and precincts. This process has created an exceptional resource, but one that is perhaps fated not to remain fossilised in perpetuity. This is because the same historical processes that led to this degree of preservation have also left a legacy of financially independent, self-governing colleges. In a parallel and ideal world, the below ground physical archive of Oxford would perhaps be preserved until archaeologists have had a chance to refine their investigation techniques and sharpen their research questions. The twenty-first century reality, with thirty-eight colleges and an expanding university, is that the heritage 'interest' and 'values' of these below ground assets must periodically go head to head with competing concepts and values such as 'public benefit' and 'architectural innovation' as institutions in constrained locations seek to update facilities and compete within dynamic local and international educational markets. If one considers that retaining a significant proportion of the town's below ground heritage is intrinsic to Oxford's 'sense of place' then this poses a significant heritage management challenge over the coming decades.

Furthermore, the desire by all tiers of government to grow the local economy, with Oxford voted by one investment firm as the eighth most dynamic city in Europe in 2018,[7] continues to place considerable pressure on the concept of 'sustainable development' as set out in the current National Planning Policy Framework. Archaeologists have long made the point that archaeological remains are 'finite and non-renewable' and the principle that excavation only ever provides a partial record of the complex relationships preserved within such remains is well established. In a hundred years the techniques available to us to retrieve data will certainly be more advanced. Thus, there is a precarious balance, and a necessary tension, between on the one hand producing new data to stimulate public interest in archaeology and advance our knowledge of the past, and on the other 'sustaining significance' through preservation in-situ. One cannot look at the long list of sites excavated over the last few decades balanced against those which were redesigned to secure preservation in-situ without the sense that we are perhaps expending Oxford's archaeological assets more rapidly than is prudent. It is with this caveat in mind that I discuss some of the fascinating and frustrating questions that further archaeological work in the town might help us resolve.

MAKING SENSE OF THE VOLUME OF DATA

A number of important syntheses of the town's late-Anglo-Saxon to post-medieval archaeology have been produced since the 1950s.[8] In terms of the late Anglo-Saxon and Norman periods, the publication of the 2003 Oxford Archaeology monograph *Oxford Before the University*

[7] Savills Investment Management Dynamic Cities index 2018; http://www.oxfordmail.co.uk/news/16316787.oxford-ranked-europes-eighth-most-dynamic-city/ (accessed Sept. 2018).

[8] E.M. Jope, 'Saxon Oxford and Its Region', in D.B. Harden (ed.) *Dark Age Britain* (1956), pp. 234–58; T. Hassall, 'Archaeology of Oxford City', in G. Briggs et al. (eds.) *The Archaeology of the Oxford Region* (1986), pp. 115–34; J. Blair, *Anglo-Saxon Oxfordshire* (1994). The contribution that archaeology can make to our understanding of the medieval and post-medieval periods has also been previously been discussed by J. Steane, 'Medieval Oxfordshire 1100–1540 (The Tom Hassall Lecture for 2000)', *Oxoniensia,* 66 (2001), pp. 1–12, and J. Munby, 'Post-Medieval Oxfordshire, 1540–2000 (The Tom Hassall Lecture for 2001)', *Oxoniensia,* 68 (2003), pp. 1–15.

has provided a substantive collation of the key archaeological evidence. The collation of a similar volume for the medieval university town and later periods remains only an aspiration given existing publication commitments and funding opportunities, although a substantial new monograph on the castle was published in 2019, and another on the Franciscan friary is forthcoming.[9] In addition, the East Oxford Community Archaeology project has produced a monograph covering field work at Littlemore priory and Bartlemas leper hospital, and a forthcoming Historic Towns Atlas will present period-based reviews of current data.[10]

At a national level, outside of the specialist interest groups looking at certain artefact types such as pottery, animal bones, and metalwork finds, the wider synthesis of the large amounts of data recovered from towns in England since the advent of PPG16 (and before) has proved a challenging prospect for archaeologists, perhaps explaining why published overviews of the archaeology of post-Conquest English towns seem to have peaked in the early 1990s. In the place of a national synthesis of urban archaeology or a national medieval research agenda we have seen the development of period-based thematic regional syntheses and agenda that encompass late Anglo-Saxon, medieval and post-medieval urban themes, for example the 2014 Solent-Thames Resource Assessment and Research Agenda. For Oxford another tier has been added to this process with the production of the Oxford Archaeological Plan in 2013 and the related period based thematic resource assessments and research agendas.[11] Whilst these provide an important framework that allows for periodic review of the 'value' of material being excavated and also accountability for money spent it can be noted that the scope of the current city and regional frameworks do not always encourage perspectives or studies that necessarily transcend city and regional boundaries. For the medieval period, processes that would require a broader focus would include, for example, the impact of cloth production or the development of service trades in relation to patterns of urban growth. Another example would be studies of the material culture and architecture of academic halls and secular and monastic colleges. A full consideration of the potential for Oxford to contribute to the wide range of research themes now emerging in medieval and post-medieval studies is beyond the scope of this article; instead I will highlight some selected themes.[12]

THE INFLUENCE OF THE PREHISTORIC LANDSCAPE

From the middle Neolithic through to the early Bronze Age an extensive ritual and funerary landscape of enclosures, barrows, avenues, satellite burials, flat graves, enigmatic linear features and at least one sizeable henge monument was established on the Summertown-Radley or second gravel terrace encompassing central and north Oxford. In the absence of any visible surviving earthworks in the modern townscape it is easy to forget that this busy landscape of earthworks, only partially denuded by later Iron-Age and Roman fields and droveways, was inherited by post-Roman communities.[13]

[9] Munby, *Oxford Castle*; B.M. Ford et al., *The Oxford Greyfriars – Excavations at the Westgate Oxford Shopping Centre 2007–2016: Late Saxon, Medieval and Post-Medieval Suburban Development at the End of the Oxford Promontory*, Thames Valley Landscapes Monograph, in preparation.

[10] D. Griffiths and J. Harrison (eds.), *The Archaeology of East Oxford: Archeox, the Story of a Community* (2020); A. Crossley (ed.), *British Historic Towns Atlas, Volume VII: Oxford*, forthcoming.

[11] https://www.oxford.gov.uk/info/20200/archaeology/740/oxford_archaeological_plan (accessed April 2019).

[12] In 2001 John Steane highlighted four long standing trajectories of investigations into medieval archaeology in the town: 1) the origins of the medieval city; 2) the plan and date of its defences and streets; 3) the layout and nature of its domestic buildings; 4) the examination of more specialised buildings (Steane, 'Medieval Oxfordshire', p. 1).

[13] Due to space constraints, the rural Iron-Age and Roman landscapes that underlie the town are not addressed here.

The importance of understanding how the pre-urban geography of a place might influence its later urban development is an established theme in urban archaeology.[14] For Oxford the influence of the large prehistoric earthworks established on the second gravel terrace on the evolution of the later urban landscape remains speculative, but after the discovery of a large Neolithic henge at St John's College in 2008 we should consider the possibility that the morphology of the town was influenced by the presence of these earthworks to a greater degree than previously thought. The henge was evidently a major physical presence in the landscape in the late Anglo-Saxon period as demonstrated by the use of the extant ditch as the location of a mass grave at this time. Here the bodies of at least thirty-five brutally killed young men were carted, stripped and dumped into an open ditch before rigor mortis set in.[15] The diversion of the line of the Banbury Road–St Giles' Street and Parks Road routes around this earthwork gives weight to the idea that these are routes of considerable antiquity. The town's primary north–south axis following St Giles' Street–Cornmarket–St Aldate's has long been thought to be at least Roman in origin and aligns with a middle Anglo-Saxon, and perhaps prehistoric, crossing point over the Thames at Folly Bridge.[16] The date of Parks Road is less certain but the discovery of the henge revives John Blair's suggestion that a parallel route of considerable antiquity ran along the approximate line of Schools Street and Oriel Street down to an undated ford over the Thames in Christ Church meadow, traces of which were encountered in the nineteenth century.[17] Together these parallel routes could conceivably have provided a framework around which the later town was laid out.

The presence of prehistoric monuments in the late-Anglo-Saxon landscape is hinted at in various medieval documents and place-names, for example the twelfth-century reference to the 'Croft of the Three Barrows' on Woodstock Road and the references to 'Beautiful mounds' captured in the names Beaumont Field and Beaumont Street (now Parks Road).[18] Furthermore, whilst other hypotheses for the curve in the eastern end of the High Street have been proposed the evidence for a significant prehistoric earthwork at Logic Lane, that may have provided an obstacle for the early track to negotiate, is another theory to be tested.[19] Elsewhere the recent identification of a possible prehistoric earthwork at St Ebbe's Church and the previous recovery of an antler pick from the highpoint of the second gravel terrace at Cornmarket should alert us to the potential for further discoveries that might potentially have a bearing on later urban geography.[20] In this volume a large 'V'-shaped ditch is reported north of the Canterbury Quadrangle of St John's College following the line of a medieval parish boundary. The ditch produced Neolithic optically stimulated luminescence (OSL) dates from the sediment in its basal fill but twelfth-century pottery from a later recut. Like the henge to the north, this feature appears to have been visible and re-utilised in the early medieval landscape, yet another

14 For example: B. Ayers, 'Norwich Before Norwich: An Exploration of the Pre-Urban Landscape of the Medieval City', in S. Ashley and A. Marsden (eds.) *Landscapes and Artefacts: Studies in East Anglian Archaeology Presented to Andrew Rogerson* (2014), pp. 129–37.

15 C. Falys, 'The Human Bone', in S. Wallis, *The Oxford Henge and Late Saxon Massacre; with Excavations of Medieval and Post-Medieval Occupation at St John's College, Oxford*, TVAS Monograph, 17 (2014), pp. 41–2.

16 Dodd, *Oxford*, pp. 12–13.

17 J. Blair, 'St Frideswide's Monastery: Problems and Possibilities', *Oxoniensia*, 53 (1988), fig. 90 and pp. 223–4.

18 The settlement of 'Buricroft' in the vicinity of the current the Radcliffe Observatory Quarter was first recorded between 1154 and 1163: Salter, *Oseney*, vol. 2, p. 195. Beaumont Street, now Parks Road, was recorded c.1250: A. Clarke (ed.), *The English Register of Godstow Nunnery*, 3 vols., EETS, 129–30, 142 (1905–11), vol. 2, pp. 493–4. Land east of the Banbury road was called 'Beaumont field' c.1260: S.R. Wigram (ed.), *The Cartulary of the Monastery of St Frideswide at Oxford*, 2 vols., OHS, 28, 31 (1895–6), vol. 1, p. 426.

19 The character of these earthworks is discussed by F. Radcliffe, 'Excavations at Logic Lane, Oxford. The Prehistoric and Early Medieval Finds', *Oxoniensia*, 26–27 (1961–2), pp. 39–40.

20 'St Ebbe's Church, Oxford, Archaeological Investigation Report', unpublished OA report (2018). For the Cornmarket antler pick: H. Case and J.R. Kirk, 'Archaeological Notes: A. Prehistoric, Roman and Anglo-Saxon', *Oxoniensia*, 19 (1954), p. 118.

indicator that the full extent of the prehistoric influence on Oxford's later urban morphology remains to be discovered.[21]

ENCLOSED MINSTER AND TRADING SETTLEMENT OR POLYFOCAL HUB?

John Blair has recently emphasised that outside of the three major seventh- to eighth-century emporia (London, Ipswich, and Southampton) the available evidence suggests that the development of fully formed urbanism in England did not take place until after *c.*950 other than in the sense of symbolic and hierarchical distinctions between minsters and other settlements.[22] He suggests that in the late ninth- and early tenth-century proto-urban settlements may have been more commonly polyfocal in character comprising linked clusters of specialised activity and with only a few exceptional locations displaying classic centralised urban settlement characteristics before the urban 'take off' of the mid tenth century. Such a pattern of development for Oxford remains possible but not yet proven. We now have slight evidence for four or more potentially distinctive activity areas on the gravel terrace that could predate the creation of a centralised street grid within the *burh*.

Firstly, we have evidence of dumped domestic waste, leather footwear, flax-retting and a putative middle-Anglo-Saxon causeway at Nos. 79–80 St Aldate's and adjacent Linacre College. These remains can reasonably be adduced to have been deposited or constructed by the ninth century from the exceptionally long and well dated stratigraphic sequence excavated here.[23] Further north along St Aldate's, on the second gravel terrace, the recovery of a seventh-century radiocarbon date from a burial located within Christ Church Cathedral Garden, alongside an eighth- or ninth-century burial from Corpus Christi College,[24] and other broadly ninth- to tenth-century burials from Christ Church and around St Aldate's church, provide a distinctive cluster of middle to late Anglo-Saxon burials close to the site of the putative middle to late Anglo-Saxon minster of St Frideswide's.[25] Further north again, closer to the central part of the rectilinear street grid of the later *burh*, we have slight traces of domestic activity, a probable hearth and three shallow postholes, sealed by a street surface of 'primary' character at No. 8 Queen Street and a stake-hole and sunken floor dated to a seventh- to late ninth-century range from Nos. 114–119 St Aldate's and Nos. 4–5 Queen Street.[26] Collectively these finds hint at an early religious centre and settlement predating the street grid, perhaps a minster with nearby domestic, trading and manufacturing activity, close to the then more pronounced gravel scarp overlooking the Thames crossing with settlement activity extending along the north–south track that later formed the St Aldate's/Cornmarket axis.

Secondly, we have a small amount of eighth-century Ipswich ware, usually seen as indicative of long distance trading networks, from the Sackler Library and the Ashmolean Museum, which together with the recovery of contemporary tweezers from the latter site and a coin of Offa from near the Martyrs' Memorial on St Giles' Street hint at distinctive area of activity located

[21] Chapter 10, below. It remains an open question whether this ditch forms part of a more extensive linear prehistoric earthwork and indeed whether a defensive line was established in the same location during the resumption of Viking attacks in the early eleventh century: D. Sturdy, *Historic Oxford* (2003), pp. 28–9.

[22] J. Blair, *Building Anglo-Saxon England* (2018), pp. 164, 246–7, 269, 275–6.

[23] Dodd, *Oxford*, pp. 16, 425; B. Durham, 'Archaeological Investigations in St Aldate's, Oxford', *Oxoniensia*, 42 (1977), pp. 179–81.

[24] R. Bashford and A. Dodd, 'Medieval and Post-Medieval Remains from Excavations on the Site of the New Auditorium, Corpus Christi College, Oxford, 2008', *Oxoniensia*, 79 (2014), p. 178.

[25] T.G. Hassall 'Excavations at Oxford, 1972: Fifth Interim Report', *Oxoniensia*, 38 (1973), p. 271; Dodd, *Oxford*, pp. 18–19. For discussions about the origins of St Frideswide's minster: H.E. Salter, *Medieval Oxford*, OHS, 100 (1936), p. 5; Blair, 'St Frideswide's Monastery', pp. 226–8.

[26] Dodd, *Oxford*, pp. 14, 248; chapter 4, below.

to the north of the late Anglo-Saxon defences.[27] The potential of these fragmentary discoveries to represent a meaningful and distinctive activity zone is currently supported by the results of modern archaeological excavations around the town that have failed to identify the presence of Ipswich ware pottery elsewhere.

Thirdly, a possible clue to another activity centre, or perhaps a misdirection, is the large 3 m-wide north–south ditch found underneath the 'primary' street metalling along Church Street which the excavator suggested would likely have had an associated bank located to the west, thus hinting at a defended enclosure preceding the street grid towards the west end of the later town.[28] The possibility that St George's Tower, located to the west within the Norman castle complex, predates the Conquest and therefore could be part of an elite complex or gate-church in the area of the later castle, leaves open the question of a pre-existing defended compound in this part of the town, though there is no evidence to suggest that the tower itself preceded the Conquest by more than a decade or so.[29] Excavations at Oxford Castle in 2003–5 also recovered a middle Anglo-Saxon finger ring and the remains of a possibly pre-Alfredian building.[30] Elsewhere within the area enclosed by the late Anglo-Saxon defences observations of large ditches that might potentially predate the late Anglo-Saxon ramparts have been made at Exeter College, Brasenose College and Corpus Christi College although none of these sightings are closely dated or well-understood. We must therefore remain open to the possibility that earlier boundary or enclosure patterns may yet be identified.[31]

To the east, in a part of the town long thought of as being a later extension to a primary central *burh*, we have the surprising recovery of four scientific dates from two separate locations at New College raising the possibility that the late Anglo-Saxon bank or rampart in this location originated in the eighth century.[32] We should be cautious because we are dealing with three OSL dates and one broader radiocarbon date here. Nevertheless, these currently provide the most robust dating evidence retrieved from any investigations of the base of the Anglo-Saxon rampart, the age of which has historically proved difficult to establish because of the absence of datable contemporary pottery. Whether the New College bank was simply a remnant agricultural feature, an enclosure around a second minster at St Peter-in-the-East or indeed a finished or unfinished Mercian defensive earthwork remains unclear. It may be significant that for both the New College rampart and the rampart excavated at St Michael's Street in 1985, the latter located in the area of the proposed primary late Anglo-Saxon defences, there is a suggestion that clay from the floodplain may have been brought to reinforce the earthwork.[33] Perhaps we will have to rethink our understanding of the development of the late-Anglo-Saxon defences at more fundamental level.

These disparate finds and observations could perhaps represent different polyfocal zones of activity across the gravel terrace; a market or zone of exchange in St Giles' Street, perhaps two minsters at St Frideswide's and St Peter-in-the-East,[34] a cloth-producing trading settlement

[27] Chapter 11, below.

[28] Hassall, 'St Ebbe's, Part I', pp. 106–8.

[29] For a discussion of the importance of the Anglo-Saxon western approach to Oxford: A. Crossley, 'The Western Approach to Anglo-Saxon Oxford', *Oxoniensia*, 83 (2018), pp. 1–22.

[30] Munby, *Oxford Castle*, pp. 25, 261.

[31] D. Sturdy notes a large ditch north of Exeter College chapel seen in 1856 that is too far south to be the town ditch and another ditch at Brasenose College: *Historic Oxford* (2004), pp. 27, 28. At Corpus Christi a 4-metre deep ditch was noted in Front Quad in 1972: T. Hassall 'Excavations at Oxford 1972, Fifth Interim Report', *Oxoniensia*, 38 (1973), p. 274 and fig. 3. An east–west ditch or channel at Corpus Christi bastion is another unexplained feature: R. Bashford and A. Dodd, 'Medieval and Post-Medieval Remains from Excavations on the Site of the New Auditorium, Corpus Christi College, Oxford, 2008', *Oxoniensia*, 79 (2014), pp. 179–80.

[32] I am grateful to Ben M. Ford for access to these dates in advance of publication.

[33] R. Bashford and S. Teague, 'New College, Oxford, Kitchen and Wine Cellar Link, Post-Excavation Assessment', unpublished OA report (2018), p. 25; M. Robinson, 'Environmental Evidence from 24A St Michael's Street', in Dodd, *Oxford*, pp. 387–8.

[34] J. Haslam, 'The Two Anglo-Saxon *Burhs* of Oxford', *Oxoniensia*, 25 (2010), pp. 15–35.

located above the river crossing at St Aldate's, and a possible defended enclosure to the west? One or more of these zones may have been protected by a large rampart of eighth-century date running east–west across the second gravel terrace which need not fully follow the line of the later-medieval walls to the south and east. Conversely, the picture could shift with the discovery of more Ipswich ware elsewhere in the town, the closer dating of the 'primary' rampart, the discovery of primary east or west defensive lines or the reinterpretation of the Church Street ditch. Making sense of this disparate activity and clarifying how and where the middle-Anglo-Saxon settlement developed is perhaps one of the more challenging questions to be addressed by further investigation.

THE EARLY DEFENDED AREA AND STREET GRID

Careful assessment of the available evidence has previously led Anne Dodd to point to the likely foundation of a sub-rectilinear settlement, defended by a 'primary' rampart and ditch and with a central rectilinear metalled street grid, in the late ninth or early tenth century.[35] The recent recovery of ninth-century scientific dates from pits along the High Street and Queen Street perhaps suggest that the main axial routes of the town focused on Carfax were in place by this time.[36] Given the absence of conclusive evidence for eighth- or early to mid ninth-century occupation orientated on or respecting the street grid, so far as such activity can be identified given the difficulty of closely dating occasional finds of grass-tempered pottery from across the town, an act of concerted planning under Alfred, or his son Edward the Elder or daughter Æthelflæd, remains the most likely scenario for the laying out of the grid. The uniformity of the primary street surfaces and the recovery of a coin of Edward the Elder from the primary street surface in New Inn Hall Street provide the best evidence to-date for such a foundation.[37]

The 1899 excavations at the Clarendon Quadrangle identified a southward running wall with traces of rampart behind, providing evidence for a possible eastern boundary for a smaller primary rectilinear or sub-rectilinear *burh*.[38] However, physical evidence to confirm the presence of such a foundation has proved elusive. The results of the 2003–5 castle excavation and small scale works at Oriel College in 2017 combine to suggest that if a smaller primary *burh* was constructed in the late ninth or early tenth century it had a less rectilinear shape than previously thought.[39] We must also be open to the possibility that the 1899 wall was perhaps part of a gate structure rather than a returning wall.[40] Thus, the character of any primary defences on the west, south and eastern sides of the *burh* remain unclear and at present it is not possible to say conclusively whether the tenth-century activity areas recorded at The Queen's College and the Castle Quarter are intra or extramural in character.

35 Dodd, *Oxford*, pp. 21–3.

36 At Nos. 6–7 High Street a radiocarbon date from a grain of barley recovered from a pit gave a date of cal. AD 771–898 (91.2 per cent probability): J. Boothroyd and S. Leech, '6–7 High Street, Oxford, Archaeological Excavation Report', unpublished OA report (2014), https://library.thehumanjourney.net/998/. At Nos. 114–119 St Aldate's and Nos. 4–5 Queen Street, features have produced charred plan remains with late eighth- to ninth-century calibrated dates (chapter 4, below).

37 Dodd, *Oxford*, p. 406, GAZ 72.

38 J. Munby, 'Excavations on the Line of the City Wall in the Clarendon Quadrangle 1899', in Dodd, *Oxford*, pp. 172–83.

39 The 2003–5 castle excavations located a western rampart that may be of two phases: the upper part contained late tenth- to early eleventh-century pottery, but it was not possible to closely date the lower layers: Munby, *Oxford Castle*. At Oriel College an east–west close borehole transect failed to identify any 'primary' north–south defensive ditch near the projected line of the wall observed in the Clarendon Quadrangle in 1899 (if taken to be following a straight trajectory): B.M. Ford et al., 'Oriel College, Oxford Kitchen Project Geophysical Survey, Archaeological Borehole and Watching Brief Report', unpublished OA report (2017).

40 Personal communication from Ben M. Ford.

Within the central street grid there is some fragmentary evidence for possible functional zoning within the late Anglo-Saxon town. A Bayesian date of cal AD 890–1030 for wooden structures overlain by burnt grain at All Saints Church along with further charred grain noted at nearby Lincoln College kitchen may suggest an area used for grain storage, malting or baking.[41] Elsewhere, distinctive primary cobbled surfaces well-worn with use have been observed south of the properties at the eastern end of Queen Street, some extending southwards from the Queen Street frontage by eight metres, suggesting either a much wider street in late Anglo-Saxon times or perhaps a market or martialling area near to Carfax area that had been built over by the eleventh century at the latest.[42] These are perhaps traces of a lost geography beneath the more uniformly developed street grid and housing that had emerged by the twelfth century.

THE CREATION OF TENEMENTS

The date and extent of regularised town planning in the late Anglo-Saxon period, encompassing street systems, tenement boundaries and defensive lines, remain live research questions in British archaeology. Unfortunately, the principal street frontages in Oxford are generally too built-up, cellared, or of a character that is unlikely to see large open area investigation, meaning that any new insights will likely need to be pieced together from small-scale observations. Our working model for the layout of Anglo-Saxon plots within the central part of the walled town relies heavily on the 1954–7 excavations at the Clarendon Hotel on Cornmarket and the work by Martin Biddle in Winchester in the 1960s. The model postulates that initially large late ninth-century, or perhaps more likely early tenth-century, plots were defined by gridded streets and lanes. Within these plots 'urban manors' belonging to the Anglo-Saxon elite may have developed, perhaps initially as versions of their rural counterparts or hybrids with spacious and unstructured arrangements of residential, craft and religious buildings set back from the main street frontages.[43] Over time the front strips of these plots were utilised for stalls or shops and related storage pits, giving their owners access to the emerging urban market.

Anne Dodd has suggested a three-phase model of plot evolution in Oxford based on investigations at All Saints Church on the High Street: 1) In the late ninth to early tenth century fenced plots with ephemeral post, mud or clay walled buildings, 2) In the late tenth century more substantial buildings set on timber posts, 3) In the early eleventh century plank lined cellars with substantial above ground structures.[44] There is currently little evidence for more intensified use of urban plots until the second quarter of the eleventh century when urban cellar pits or cellared houses become more prevalent. It should be noted that our information rests mostly on early and partial archaeological investigations and that it remains possible that popular building forms predating the emergence of structures with 'cellar pits' have left little trace. At Winchester the subdivision of large plots into narrower 10–15 m wide strips by the late ninth or early tenth century has been suggested by targeted scientific dating and Bayesian analysis at Tower Street and Staple Gardens.[45] However, this dating is not accepted by Blair, who argues for later subdivision as more consistent with wider patterns of urban development post-950.[46]

41 Dodd, *Oxford*, p. 210; Z. Kamash et al., 'Late Saxon and Medieval Occupation: Evidence from Excavations at Lincoln College, Oxford', *Oxoniensia*, 67 (2002), pp. 203–5, 261–5.

42 Dodd, *Oxford*, pp. 27, 408, GAZ 84.

43 M. Biddle (ed.), *Winchester in the Early Middle Ages: An Edition and Discussion of the Winton Domesday*, Winchester Studies, 1 (1976), pp. 341, 452–4.

44 Personal communication from Anne Dodd.

45 B.M. Ford and S. Teague, *Winchester A City in the Making, Archaeological Excavations between 2002 and 2007 on the Former Sites of Northgate House, Staple Gardens and the Former Winchester Library, Jewry St.* (2011), pp. 76–9, 189, 190–3, 232–6.

46 Blair, *Building Anglo-Saxon England*, p. 275 n., 276.

The more regimented pattern of some of Winchester's late Anglo-Saxon buildings, with gable ends fronting onto the street, is not yet known to be paralleled by the limited Oxford evidence. At the Clarendon Hotel site, the evidence pointed to more irregular arrangements of buildings within expansive plots. Given the potential influence of remnant Roman structures on Winchester traditions it may be that the Wessex and Mercian towns followed different trajectories. In Oxford the frontages of the larger plots would eventually have been subdivided by their owners to facilitate commercial activity along the main frontages, perhaps with larger plots retained to the rear where principal houses were located.

Attempts to understand the character of suburban activity in the late Anglo-Saxon period remain frustrated by the lack of clarity over where the eastern and western defences lay and whether settlement activity in these areas was extra or intra mural, and therefore potentially shaped by political and economic factors related to tolls and legal jurisdictions. For the other later suburban zones of Osney Island, St Giles, Holywell and St Clements we are still largely relying on hints in documentary sources for the presence of pre-Conquest properties. Only to the south along the main route to the river crossing is there firm archaeological evidence for tenth-century settlement that is demonstrably extramural and suburban.

THE WESTERN APPROACH, MILLS, AND WATERWAYS

To the west of Oxford significant questions remain regarding the location and relative importance of any western approach to the town prior to the ascendency of the north–south route across the floodplain in the Norman period.[47] The reworking and canalisation of Thames floodplain palaeo-channels close to the town in the late Anglo-Saxon and or Norman period is another process that requires further investigation. The distinctive oval channel pattern around Osney Island remains to be adequately explained and the suggestion of late Anglo-Saxon canalisation in this area made by Rhodes and Blair also needs further investigation.[48] The results of the 2018 excavation at the former Cooper Callas warehouse site on Paradise Street suggest a post-Conquest date for the backstream (the Wareham Stream) in St Thomas' suburb.[49] Neither this site nor a previous excavation to the north of St Thomas' Street have produced any evidence that the Castle Mill Stream, itself located on the line of a prehistoric palaeo-channel or channels, was reworked or canalised prior to the Conquest, although such evidence may be preserved further east or could conceivably have been removed by later channel works.[50] Elsewhere the extensive evaluation undertaken in 2017 in advance of the proposed Oxford Flood Alleviation Scheme presented a rare opportunity to further understand the evolution of the Thames Floodplain and its palaeo-channels in prehistory.[51] By contrast, the major transformation of these channels that must have accompanied the development of multiple mills along the Thames in the late Anglo-Saxon and Norman periods remains poorly understood.

ANGLO-SAXON POTTERY AND ANIMAL BONE

The need to recover further well stratified and well dated late Anglo-Saxon pottery assemblages, both from Oxford and neighbouring *burhs*, in order to help us refine chronologies and place the ceramic traditions of Oxford in a regional context, has been previously identified by Maureen

47 Crossley, 'The Western Approach to Anglo-Saxon Oxford'.
48 J. Blair (ed.) *Waterways and Canal-Building in Medieval England* (2007), pp. 133–52, 254–94.
49 Simmonds et al., 'Former Cooper Callas Building, 15 Paradise Street'.
50 Ibid.; A. Norton 'Excavations at 67–69 St Thomas' Street, Oxford', *Oxoniensia*, 71 (2006), pp. 347–92.
51 T. Black et al., 'Oxford Flood Alleviation Scheme Archaeological Evaluation Report', unpublished OA report (2018).

Mellor.[52] Luckily, the post-excavation analysis of late Anglo-Saxon and medieval pottery in Oxford has enjoyed considerable consistency over a sustained period through the skills and energies of Maureen Mellor, John Cotter and Paul Blinkhorn, and significant advances continue to be made, for example the large and well-preserved late Anglo-Saxon pottery assemblage from the Castle Quarter excavation which produced rare examples of red painted early Stamford ware.[53] Thus, for every site where the assemblage is described as 'typical for Oxford' there is another, such as Lincoln College Garden Building in this volume, where 'in all phases there are individual items which extend known typologies of these wares or add to the interpretation of site function and status'.[54]

Models to explain patterning in the distribution of certain pottery forms and late Anglo-Saxon pottery wares such as St Neots ware and local shelly ware products have been discussed previously by Maureen Mellor, who suggests that these may, in part, reflect the cultural preferences of indigenous and newly arrived communities.[55] Mellor has suggested various processes that may be tracked by use patterns in the town and suburbs, including the potential for incoming migrants with a greater affinity for wheel-thrown pottery from territory under greater Scandinavian influence to first settle peripheral plots and subsequently, perhaps post the ascendancy of King Cnut, to occupy more central locations. The gradual popularisation of St Neots ware requires explanation, this potentially being the result of gradual cultural assimilation or the failure of the local industry to meet the demands of growth and adapt to wheel technology. It should be noted that an alternative theory has been proposed by Paul Blinkhorn who sees the differences in the pottery forms used in areas of Danelaw and Anglo-Saxon England as more indicative of residual historic rivalries between Wessex and Mercia.[56]

General patterns of consumption and form use, both over time and spatially, also warrant further investigation, bearing in mind the suggestion by Mellor that industrial or commercial zoning or perhaps the implementation of tolls on bounded areas may be influencing pottery use patterns. The quest for additional well preserved late Anglo-Saxon faunal assemblages also continues as they might enable us to further test the model of domestic refuse deposition proposed in 2003 by Bob Wilson and more clearly understand changes in eating habits and the animal husbandry economy from the earliest establishment of the settlement at Oxford through to the later economic success of the Anglo-Saxon town.[57]

NORMAN AND LATER GROWTH

John Blair has recently suggested that at a national level greater emphasis on growth and continuity in the eleventh century may be warranted rather than over-reading the dislocation caused by the Conquest.[58] However, for Oxford, how exactly the following processes can be reconciled and explained requires further investigation: 1) evidence for early eleventh-century urban intensification, 2) subsequent dislocation caused by the creation of the Norman castle, 3) the documentation of extensive properties as 'waste' in the Domesday survey, then 4) substantial investment in late eleventh-century building projects and evidence for economic growth.

[52] M. Mellor, 'Late Saxon Pottery at Oxford: Conclusions', in Dodd, *Oxford*, p. 345; R. Beckley and D. Radford, 'Oxford Archaeological Research Agenda – Anglo-Saxon and Scandinavian Period' (2012), accessed online June 2019.

[53] P. Blinkhorn, 'The Pottery from the Castle Excavations', in Munby, *Oxford Castle*, pp. 233–4.

[54] J. Cotter, 'Lincoln College Garden Building Post Excavation Assessment' (2015), unpublished OA report, p. 40.

[55] Mellor, 'Synthesis', p. 60.

[56] Blinkhorn, 'The Pottery from the Castle Excavations'.

[57] B. Wilson, 'Mapping the Household Activity of Early Oxford the Spread of Domestic and other Bone Refuse', in Dodd, *Oxford*, pp. 362–4.

[58] Blair, *Building Anglo-Saxon England*, pp. 383–4.

Archaeology may be able to contribute to this discussion by clarifying patterns of trade and consumption prior to the decisive expansion in the range and quality of domestic pottery assemblages that can be seen in the twelfth century. For example Paul Blinkhorn has noted how the pottery assemblage from the 2003–5 excavations at Oxford Castle indicate that the establishment of a Norman power base here is not reflected in any obvious distinctive cultural preferences in terms of pottery use.[59] Furthermore, a forthcoming study of tenth- through to thirteenth-century diets in Oxford combines work on organic residue analysis, isotope analysis of human and animal bones and human tooth dentine and palaeopathological analysis of human skeletal remains. It suggests that dietary changes documented among elites were gradually adopted by lower-status town dwellers as a process of urban intensification and marketisation took place. This again suggests that the Conquest caused less disruption to this process than documentary sources may imply.[60]

There is fragmentary documentary and limited archaeological evidence for suburban activity on all four sides of the town *c.*1086. The suburbs appear to dramatically expand in the twelfth century along St Aldate's, St Giles' Street, St Thomas' Street, and perhaps elsewhere. By the thirteenth century we see the densely packed town so wonderfully captured by H.E. Salter's *Survey of Oxford* compiled from the available documents.[61] The subdivision of early urban plots into more familiar narrow tenements or burgage plots and the filling out of the street network appears to have been largely completed by the end of the twelfth century, but we have yet to understand the full complexity and patterning of this process.

We have a great deal of documentary data from the late thirteenth century onwards on trade and university-related activities in different geographical areas, for example the locations of cordwainers, butchers, brewers, copyists, harp-makers and goldsmiths, and the spread of academic halls. Yet we are still far from a detailed understanding of functional zoning within the medieval town. Over the last ten years, excavations have produced a wide range of evidence for manufacturing and processing activities, for example dyeing, tanning and brewing (the latter perhaps not surprisingly from Brewer Street), and widespread evidence for the processing of horn cores from a surprising array of intramural and suburban sites.[62] Evidence for dyeing in the form of madder dye on pottery comes from Nos. 7 and 8 Brewer Street, Cornmarket (The Clarendon Centre), Pembroke Street (The Story Museum) and the High Street (Lincoln College), for the working of precious metals at Queen Street and Lincoln College sites and for craft and vellum production from the Cornmarket/Shoe Lane area (The Clarendon Centre), demonstrating the potential to reconstruct more detailed patterns of production and commerce around the town from archaeological insights.[63]

To date investigations have recovered environmental evidence for at least two likely medieval herb or physic gardens, one at the Blackfriars but the other from a tenement in the suburb of St Thomas indicating that these were not necessarily associated with colleges or religious precincts. The remains of opium poppies, hops and cannabis recovered from No. 4A Merton Street may be evidence of another such site, perhaps associated with Merton College.[64] Elsewhere

59 Blinkhorn, 'The Pottery from the Castle Excavations', p. 1.

60 E. Craig-Atkins et al., 'The Dietary Impact of the Norman Conquest: A Multiproxy Archaeological Investigation of Oxford, UK', *PLOS ONE*, 15 (2020), https://doi.org/10.1371/journal.pone.0235005.

61 Salter, *Survey of Oxford*.

62 For horn cores from both sides of St Giles' Street and also High Street and Merton Street: below, chapters 8 and 11; B.M. Ford, 'New Library Extension, Magdalen College, Oxford, Post-Excavation Assessment and Updated Project Design', unpublished OA report (2019).

63 S. Teague and B.M. Ford, 'Excavations in Oxford's South Suburb at Brewer Street, Littlegate Street and Rose Place', unpublished OA report (2019); A. Douglas et al., *Medieval Craft-Working in Oxford: Excavations at 15–17 Clarendon Centre* (2015); R. Bashford, 'The Story Museum, Pembroke, Street, Oxford Archaeological Evaluation Report', unpublished OA report (2018); chapter 7, below.

64 M. Robinson, 'Plant and Invertebrate Remains from the Priory Drains', in G. Lambrick, 'Further Excavations on the Site of the Dominican Priory, Oxford', *Oxoniensia*, 50 (1985), pp. 196–201; M. Robinson, 'Macroscopic

an unusual assemblage of early fourteenth-century distilling equipment covered in untested residues was recovered from the garderobe of a building located under Peckwater Quad and may be linked to early alchemical experimentation.[65] Such finds point to the potential for further discoveries related to scientific experimentation or the production of medicines, even in mundane locations. They also provide a tangible connection to the active application of academic knowledge rather than its simple documentation and reproduction and complement the more ubiquitous finds of book clasps, parchment prickers, styli and so on that might be found associated with many ecclesiastical and urban centres associated with book work.[66] Another distinctive local recovery pattern, perhaps linked to Oxford's role as an educational centre, is the extensive distribution of shelled lamps from the Brill and Boarstall potteries that can perhaps be associated with evening reading.[67]

In terms of understanding domestic structures, we have seen well-preserved floor levels from gradually amalgamated medieval house plots excavated at Magdalen College New Library and the exceptional remnants of fourteenth-century halls that once lined King Edward Street, exposed in Peckwater Quad in 2005, complete with several courses of stonework, entrance steps, and surviving internal plaster.[68] The potential for lost architectural details to be recovered from archaeological excavations has been well demonstrated by the reused building timbers and stone tracery recovered from the thirteenth-century floodplain reclamation levels at the Westgate Centre site and elsewhere by the stone window tympanum from a likely twelfth-century house located outside the Northgate and similar window fragment from the 2018 Cooper Callas excavations on Paradise Street.[69] It remains to be demonstrated whether the latter two finds are indicators of a pattern of twelfth-century suburban stone house construction that is otherwise unrecorded.

Medieval Oxford was the location of the county court and prison. It saw the foundation and re-foundation of abbeys and priories in the twelfth century and attracted the bulk of the mendicant orders in the thirteenth century. The ongoing investigation of Oxford's buildings with specialised functions such as the castle, parish churches, hospitals and religious houses is a research theme highlighted by John Steane in an article in *Oxoniensia* and it is worth noting how many specialised buildings have come under development pressure since this was published in 2001. A number of religious institutions have been subject to substantive investigation in recent years, including the Hospital of St John the Baptist, Littlemore priory, the Franciscan friary, and St Bartholomew's leper hospital, and smaller investigations have taken place at the

Plant Remains', in A. Hardy, 'Archaeological Excavations at 54–55 St Thomas's Street, Oxford', *Oxoniensia*, 61 (1996), pp. 263–7; Poore, 'No. 4A Merton St.', p. 229.

65 A.M. Chadwick et al. (eds.), "… *Quadrangles Where Wisdom Honours Herself" – Archaeological Investigations at Christ Church, Oxford*, JMHS Monograph, 1 (2012), pp. 249–54.

66 For example, the thirteenth- to fourteenth-century book clasps from the Franciscan friary: S. Teague, 'Westgate Centre, Oxford Post-Excavation Assessment and Updated Project Design, Volume 2: Appendices and Bibliography', unpublished OA report (2019), p. 17. For post-medieval examples: below, chapters 6, 10, 11.

67 With reference to the large volume of Brill made lamp fragments found at St Giles' Street (chapter 11, below) it may be relevant that Brockliss notes that in the thirteenth century some students would have taken rooms in town houses or as a group renting whole properties, and that 'many students congregated outside the north gate'. Such arrangements were gradually replaced by the development of academic halls in the thirteenth and fourteenth century largely concentrated either side of High Street and to the west of Fish Street (now St Aldate's) and by endowed colleges founded in the eastern part of the walled town and north of the walls and that eventually came to dominate. In 1410 scholars were banned from living with private citizens. See Brockliss *The University of Oxford*, p. 40. For a more cautious view of the implication of these lamp assemblages: below, chapter 3.

68 Chadwick, et al. "… *Quadrangles Where Wisdom Honours Herself*", pp. 42–9.

69 S. Teague et al., 'Westgate Centre, Oxford, Post-Excavation Assessment and Updated Project Design Volume 1', unpublished OA report (2019) pp. 49, 51; chapter 11, below; Simmonds et al., 'Former Cooper Callas Building'. For twelfth-century stone houses in the city and suburbs: J. Munby, 'Stone Houses in Oxford', in Poore, 'No. 4A Merton St.', pp. 305, 340–1.

Austin friary, the Dominican friary and Osney abbey.[70] The work undertaken on churches has been more limited. Nevertheless, it should be noted that many specialised institutions remain poorly defined and understood. For the larger religious institutions, the comparative study of different orders and between high and lower-status institutions (including those of the same religious order, for example the Benedictine convents at Godstow and Littlemore), and also the retrieval of basic data on functional layout, material culture, adaptation of landscapes and post-Dissolution use, all offer fertile ground for further study.

MEDIEVAL CERAMICS

The study of pottery continues to be central to developing our understanding of the town, providing increasingly detailed insights into wealth and consumption patterns, from the expansion of the number of pottery forms in use in the twelfth century through to the town's long relationship with the Brill and Boarstall pottery industry. Bespoke college orders for dedicated designs are well attested to in the post-medieval period but may yet be traced back to the beginnings of the Brill industry as suggested by the thirteenth-century sherd marked 'rton' recovered from a Merton College property pointing to the otherwise unrecorded bulk orders of specially made products.[71] We continue to map the non-uniform use of both common local wares and imported wares, examine residues for evidence of dyes or diets, consider sooting patterns, identify evidence for storage or industrial functions, and bear in mind the potential for pottery assemblages to provide cultural identity 'kits' for minority populations. Along with mapping the expansion of drinking wares (the tripod pitcher) and the use of specially made leisure wares (the puzzle jug) and evidence for the emergence of mass catering in the colleges (dripping dishes) these studies all have potential to further our understanding of the town's changing cultural complexity. Similar patterns may be gleaned from the developing body of information on roof and floor tile use and also specialised ceramics such as stove tiles.[72]

ANIMAL BONE, DIET AND FOOD SUPPLY

There remains a considerable amount of potential to learn more about medieval diets and related themes of consumption patterns, comparative economic status and cultural changes and influences that may vary between institutions and streets across the town. For some colleges, where medieval kitchens either remain in service or at least fossilised below, there is exceptional potential. For example, unique waste assemblages have been recovered from Lincoln College, The Queen's College, Merton College, and New College.[73] Already there seem to be patterns of consumption with some colleges clearly enjoying higher-status food than others in particular

[70] Ford, 'New Library Extension, Magdalen College'; Griffiths and Harrison (eds.), *The Archaeology of East Oxford*; B.M. Ford et al., *The Oxford Greyfriars*; R. Bashford, 'Undergraduate Centre and Access Centre, Wadham College, Oxford, Archaeological Evaluation Report', unpublished OA report (2017), https://library.oxfordarchaeology.com/3536/; S. Porter, 'Lucy Faithfull House, Oxford Report on Archaeological Evaluation', unpublished MOLA report (2018); T. Black, 'Gibbs Crescent, Osney, Oxford, Archaeological Evaluation Report', unpublished OA report (2019); L. Spark and S. Teague, 'Osney Power Station, 17 Russell Street, Oxford, Archaeological Evaluation Report', unpublished OA report (2019).

[71] P. Blinkhorn, 'Pottery', in Poore, 'No. 4A Merton St.', pp. 275–8.

[72] For stove tiles: chapter 10, below. For the production of stabbed Wessex tiles at Boarstall: M. Farley with B. Hurman 'The Production of Medieval Decorated Floor-Tiles at Boarstall, with a Note on Boarstall's Late Medieval Map', *Records of Buckinghamshire*, 57 (2017), p. 123.

[73] It should be noted that similar remains have been excavated at Trinity College, Cambridge: R. Newman, 'Trinity College Kitchens, Cambridge: An Archaeological Excavation and Watching Brief', unpublished Cambridge Archaeological Unit report (2011).

periods.[74] The further study of college records may also prove fruitful in establishing college dietary patterns over time and emerging patterns can be linked to pottery and glass assemblages that show shifts towards communal catering and elite dining. The value of targeted intensive sampling strategies can be seen at New College kitchen where the excavation of parts of the kitchen floor and associated external waste pits has produced an exceptional medieval fish bone assemblage offering fresh insights into the local fish trade and consumption patterns.[75]

Further institutional variation can be seen at elite sites such as the castle and at religious institutions (for example, kitchen related waste from recent excavations at Littlemore priory and the Greyfriars complex), building up an increasingly impressive corpus of data on diet and food supply. It should also be noted that excellent work has been done by Oxford's Jewish Heritage Committee collating and popularising the rich documentary evidence of the twelfth- and thirteenth-century Jewish community in Oxford. The identification of likely kosher food remains from a thirteenth-century waste pit within a Jewish-owned property on St Aldate's discussed in this volume (chapter 4) highlights the potential for hard archaeological data to start fleshing out and populating this historical framework.

The potential for studies in the hinterland of Oxford, both in the now urbanised villages of the local authority area and beyond, to further our understanding of changing patterns of mixed farming, woodland management and economic expansion and contraction remains underexplored. Sites reported in this volume have provided insights into changing patterns of oak and beech use. A few small excavations, such as those undertaken in 2012 and 2013 by TVAS in New Marston, have illustrated how the expansion and contraction of village cores might be better understood.[76] Elsewhere we have fragmentary evidence for isolated craft production in the form of antler working debris from St Anne's College on the Woodstock Road and evidence for dispersed settlement at Littlemore that suggests there is some way to go in terms of understanding local patterns of nucleation.[77]

It is perhaps instructive that the most detailed study of a hinterland village was undertaken by Martin Biddle as long ago as 1958–9 at the deserted settlement of Seacourt, where a highpoint in the extent of the open-field landscape was suggested in the thirteenth century.[78] Around Oxford potentially complex patterns of limited early enclosure, for example that known from documents to have been carried out by the abbess of Godstow,[79] have not been tied together with any systematic archaeological work on boundaries. Fragments of ridge and furrow survive around the city and experimental work on dating the ridges has been undertaken by the Oxford University Research Laboratory for Archaeology and the History of Art; but, generally, the dates and phasing of the open fields are poorly understood.

[74] Documents show that in the thirteenth and fourteenth century Merton and New College enjoyed wealthy endowments, Queen's was moderately wealthy, and University, Balliol, Exeter and Oriel were less well off: Brockliss, *The University of Oxford*, p. 69.

[75] R. Nicholson, 'Fish Bone', in Bashford and Teague, 'New College Oxford: Kitchen and Wine Cellar Link Tunnel Projects'.

[76] J. Lewis et al., *Medieval Occupation in Marston, Oxford*, TVAS Occasional Paper, 4 (2014).

[77] At St Anne's College on Woodstock Road two rubbish pits containing sixteenth-century pottery were found. One contained a sawn deer antler, indicative of small-scale antler working: S. Teague, 'New Kitchen, St Anne's College, Oxford, Archaeological, Evaluation and Watching Brief', unpublished OA report (2011), https://library.oxfordarchaeology.com/1815/. At Littlemore, outside the historic core of the village, postholes and pits associated with eleventh- to thirteenth-century pottery were recorded at the Oxford Science Park, the density of which suggested settlement in the Saxo-Norman period, perhaps relating to an outlying farm: I. Grundon, 'Phases 2 and 3 of An Archaeological Evaluation at the Oxford Science Park, Littlemore, Oxford', unpublished AOC Ltd report (1999).

[78] M. Biddle, 'The Deserted Medieval Village of Seacourt, Berkshire', *Oxoniensia*, 26–27 (1961–2), p. 118.

[79] Salter, *Medieval Oxford*, p. 146.

LIFE AND DEATH

The last ten years have seen the accumulation of a significant body of data on human remains from Oxford that constitutes a major resource for future study, encompassing the late Anglo-Saxon massacre victims from the St John's College henge, the sizeable burial assemblage from Magdalen College Longwall Quad likely associated with the medieval hospital of St John the Baptist and the predominantly female assemblage from the medieval cemetery of Littlemore priory.[80] These can be added to previous assemblages recorded at Christ Church Cathedral, the Franciscan and Dominican friaries and the more fragmentary and problematic remains recovered from the church of All Saints Church on the High Street.[81] The potential for aDNA, osteological and isotopic studies to produce important information about diet, health, medical care, age and gender distinctions is clear.[82] There remains excellent further potential for isotopic analysis of human remains to contribute towards our understanding of population movement and consumption patterns as highlighted by the studies on the Oxford Castle, St John's College, Corpus Christi and Littlemore assemblages.[83]

LATE-MEDIEVAL URBAN DECLINE – MAPPING THE WINNERS AND LOSERS

The apparent reduction in pottery use in the fifteenth-century town conforms to the established view of urban decline in England during this period. Local economic decline from the fourteenth century onwards has been linked with a range of factors including the impact of the Black Death and fluctuations in the wool and cloth trades exacerbated by changes in patterns of long distance trade.[84] The assemblages recovered in Oxford over recent years from a variety of intra- and extramural, institutional and residential sites appears to confirm a contraction in the quantity of pottery in use in the late fourteenth and fifteenth century.[85] However, this broad pattern is likely to be influenced by other factors such as changing patterns of waste disposal and the increasing use of metal vessels.

Recent debates in medieval archaeology have stressed the need to move beyond the post-Black Death decline or continuity paradigm and recognise that economic outcomes continued to vary within urban communities.[86] In Oxford the available documentary evidence suggests that in the fourteenth century a shift took place from merchant dominance towards a service-based economy facilitating the seasonal needs of the university. Thus, whilst there may be evidence of peripheral urban decay and plots becoming affordable enough to be bought up by endowed

80 That can be compared with the extensive cemetery of St John's Hospital in Cambridge excavated in 2012–14.

81 R. Beckley and D. Radford, 'Oxford Archaeological Resource Assessment: Saxon and Viking Oxford (410–1066)' (2012), pp. 37–9 and 'Oxford Archaeological Resource Assessment: The Medieval Period (1205–1540)' (2012), pp. 50–9, accessed online Oct. 2019.

82 For an overview of current investigative techniques: C.A. Roberts, *Human Remains in Archaeology: A Handbook* (2009).

83 A.M. Pollard and P. Ditchfield, 'Stable Isotope Analysis of the Human Bones from Oxford Castle', unpublished RLAHA, University of Oxford report (2010), https://library.oxfordarchaeology.com/4679/; A.M. Pollard et al., '"Sprouting Like Cockle Amongst the Wheat": The St Brice's Day Massacre and the Isotopic Analysis of Human Bones from St John's College, Oxford', *Oxford Journal of Archaeology*, 31:1 (2012), pp. 83–102; A.M. Pollard and P. Ditchfield, 'Stable Isotope Analysis of the Human Bones from Corpus Christi College', RLAHA, University of Oxford, unpublished report (n.d.); C. Scull, 'Diet and Lifestyle at Littlemore Nunnery, Preliminary Carbon and Nitrogen Stable Isotope Analysis', unpublished University of Reading report (2016).

84 D. Perring, *Town & Country in England: Frameworks for Archaeological Research*, CBA Research Report, 134 (2002), pp. 29–30; *VCH Oxon*. 4, pp. 40–1.

85 Based on a rapid assessment of post-excavation assessment finds reports from Brewer Street, Queen Street, Lincoln College, the Castle, and New College kitchen.

86 B. Jervis, 'Decline or Transformation? Archaeology and the Late Medieval "Urban Decline" in Southern England', *Archaeological Journal*, 174:1 (2017), pp. 211–43.

colleges in the late fourteenth and fifteenth century the same period saw the intensification of house building along the principal street frontages of the central crossroads that hosted the bi-weekly market. The first documented three- to four-storey town houses along these streets were recorded in the mid fourteenth century.[87] In the fifteenth century the range of foodstuffs and ceramic table wares available for wealthy townsfolk was expanding, even if periodic stresses can be seen in the varying quality of products from the nearby Brill and Boarstall pottery industry, products that nevertheless found a market.[88] The increasing range and quality of foodstuffs available to residents from the fifteenth century onwards is demonstrated by the rich assortment of fruits enjoyed by some of the residents of St Giles' Street at this time.[89]

The town's apparent mercantile decline in the fourteenth and fifteenth century is likely to have been offset in sections of the local economy by the dynamism of construction work around the colleges. The fifteenth century saw the foundation of Lincoln, All Souls and Magdalen Colleges and numerous major building projects besides, constituting what Geoffrey Tyack describes as the century when the colleges made their 'decisive impact on the urban fabric of Oxford'. Exactly how this variation in economic outcomes between different employment sectors and different parts of the town is reflected, whether in patterns of domestic debris or features preserved in remnant structures, requires further mapping and study. One example of this is the quality of building work at New College that has been demonstrated by the recording work undertaken by Roland Harris during the renovation of the fourteenth-century kitchen in 2013–2014. Here the craftsmanship of master carpenter Hugh Herland was revealed in greater detail and careful recording also showed that attic rooms had been added to the kitchen and hall range soon after its completion in the 1380s. A similar process of rapid subdivision can be seen in the fifteenth century west range of the Great Quad at Magdalen College where recording work by MOLA in 2017 showed that a large room built as an open hall had been quickly subdivided by the addition of attic rooms.[90] Both projects show the capacity of archaeology to provide fresh insights into changing patterns of use within these institutions. Another notable dimension of Oxford's relationship with national elites and changing fashions is the early appearance of new high-status items and foodstuffs in the archaeological record, for example the appearance of hops and fine glass table ware in the fourteenth century and in the sixteenth to seventeenth century the consumption of turkey and then coffee.[91]

THE TUDOR PERIOD, CIVIL WAR AND POST-RESTORATION REVIVAL

After the trauma of the Dissolution the stability of the reign of Elizabeth I saw the town population and university numbers grow significantly. Colleges grew physically upwards with

[87] G. Tyack, *Oxford: An Architectural Guide* (1998), p. 47.

[88] M. Mellor, *Pots and People that have Shaped the Heritage of Medieval and Later England* (1997).

[89] Chapter 11, below.

[90] Personal communication from R. Harris; G. Laban and A. Nicola, 'Fellows' Common Room and the Old Picture Store, Magdalen College, High Street, Oxford, Archaeological Standing Building Recording Report', unpublished MOLA report (2018).

[91] The remains of hops and fragments of a decorated high-lead emerald green beaker have been found in a thirteenth- or early fourteenth-century garderobe at No. 4A Merton Street: R. Tyson, 'Glass', in Poore, 'No. 4A Merton St.', p. 292. For other examples of similar high-status glassware: R. Tyson, 'Glass', in Chadwick, et al., *Quadrangles Where Wisdom Honours Herself*; I. Scott, 'Glass', in 'The Buttery and Kitchen and Buttery, University College, High Street, Oxford, Phase 3 Excavation and Watching Brief', unpublished OA report (2008). Turkey was introduced via the New World in the sixteenth century and appears in Oxford in the seventeenth century, for example at the Ashmolean: chapter 11, below. Coffee is anecdotally referred to at Balliol College in 1637 and Oxford claims the first coffee shop in England in 1650: B. Cowan, *The Social Life of Coffee: The Emergence of the British Coffeehouse* (2005). Stoneware coffee pots of eighteenth-century date have been recovered from Radcliffe Square, representing the initial floruit of coffee consumption in the town: Mellor, *Pots and People*, p. 45.

the addition of attic storeys or 'cock lofts' in the later sixteenth century.[92] The era of coach travel after 1550 saw the growth of coaching inns, and the drinking establishments flourished.[93] The wider town saw infilling, subdivision and large-scale rebuilding with taller town houses ornamented and enhanced with pargetting, bargeboards and carved brackets.

The growth of the town can be appreciated by comparing the maps of Agas (1578), Hollar (1643),[94] and Loggan (1675). The potential for above-ground structures to provide new insights into this period of growth has been demonstrated by a steady pattern of building recording projects, for example the early seventeenth-century Kettle Hall on Broad Street and No. 7 Brewer Street, the latter illustrating 'the transition from traditional carpentry techniques to a cheaper and less refined method of building when external appearance (smooth rendered surfaces and showy dormers) were more important than craftsmanship'.[95] Another insightful investigation by the OBR examined the 1630s rear wing of No. 84 St Aldate's which appeared to be used for a mixture of domestic accommodation and storage and the owner of which, the manciple of Corpus Christi College, provided accommodation to servants of the royal court during the Civil War.[96]

Recent projects that have examined below ground post-medieval building remains include the investigation of well-preserved post-medieval rear wings of houses that once fronted onto Bridge Street at Magdalen College Longwall Quad.[97] Another significant below-ground discovery was the uncovering in 2010 of a forgotten and intact eighteenth-century barrel-vaulted cellar below a flower bed to the north of No. 34 High Street which has subsequently been adapted by The Queen's College as an occasional music room.[98] This surprise discovery should remind us that the historic robbing and re-use of building stone in the town was not always extensive and comprehensive, perhaps because of the proximity and abundance of local quarries, also that the scope for significant architectural discoveries remains high. This is further borne out by the discovery of previously unknown wall paintings in several college buildings over the last ten years and the exciting results of a variety of other dendrochronology and building recording projects around the town.[99]

In about 1644 Bernard de Gomme, then a low-ranking Royalist soldier, produced a map showing perhaps both existing and intended lines of defences designed to protect the town during its brief period as the Royalist capital. Whilst some of the defences remained extant into the nineteenth century, only a small 'L'-shaped sequence of ramparts now survives above-ground between Rhodes House and the University Club on Mansfield Road. The precise line, character and phasing of the defences and associated infrastructure have yet to be fully established. Over recent years there have been a number of small excavations that have examined the now buried ditches of the inner and outer line and also investigated now buried parts of the rampart at Savile House and Manor Place. These have produced new information on the composition of different parts of the rampart, for example the rampart at Savile House is comprised of redeposited tips loam and gravel whilst at Manor Place only gravel was used, deposited in distinctive lenses

92 G. Tyack, *Oxford*, p. 85.

93 See the tavern waste from the Mermaid Inn, below, chapter 4.

94 Hollar's map is generally unreliable in terms of its detail but provides a general impression of the level of development.

95 J. Steane and J. Ayres, *Traditional Buildings in the Oxford Region c.1300–1840* (2013), pp. 148–56; D.R. Clark, 'Nos. 7–8 Brewer Street, Oxford', unpublished OBR report, 134 (2011).

96 D.R. Clark, '84 St Aldate's, Oxford', unpublished OBR report, 147 (2012).

97 Observed by author; Ford, 'New Library Extension, Magdalen College'.

98 S. Teague and A. Norton, 'Late Saxon, Medieval and Post-Medieval Archaeology at the Nun's Garden, The Queen's College, Oxford', *Oxoniensia*, 80 (2015), p. 152.

99 'Brasenose College The Stocker Room and Staircase 3 Wall Paintings, Wall Painting Condition Survey', unpublished Perry Lithgow Partnership report (2016); A. Kelly et al., 'Building Recording and Test Pits at Brasenose College, Oxford', *Oxoniensia*, 81 (2016), pp. 247–52; D.W.H. Miles, 'The Tree-Ring Dating of the Old Picture Store, Magdalen College, Oxford', unpublished Oxford Dendrochronology Laboratory report, 2015/19 (2015); R. Harris and D.W.H. Miles, 'New College Kitchen'.

against a possible gabion.[100] Elsewhere, evidence for the re-cutting of the inner defensive ditch has been recovered from Mansfield College.[101] In Christ Church Meadow a consolidated rubble platform was encountered on the projected line of the defences, perhaps part of a firing platform and at the Tinbergen Building site on Parks Road an arrangement of steep sided pits may be defensive 'mantraps' or 'pitfalls'.[102] Another surprise find was the burial of a young woman in a garden near St Giles' Street, a possible 'recusant' (a Catholic objector to Church of England practices) who may have died during the siege.[103] The mystery of the young woman's identity featured in a 'Live Friday' event at the Ashmolean Museum and it is hoped that the remains will be subject to pathogen DNA analysis to investigate whether if a siege-related illness was responsible for her death. Such investigations point to the potential for further discoveries to provide insights into how local people experienced the siege and to further clarify the character and extent of the geography of the Civil War town.

After the Restoration, the university saw numbers drop and notable local industries, such as glove and cutlery making, went into decline. Documents indicate that university numbers halved between 1650 and 1750,[104] and the economy at this time remained inward-looking and service-based. A notable feature of the post-Civil War university was a brief floruit in scientific experimentation. Significant new infrastructure was constructed during the seventeenth century; the Bodleian Library and Schools Quadrangle, the Botanic Garden, the University Press at the Clarendon Building and the Old Ashmolean Museum. Mellor describes Oxford as 'the scientific centre of the nation' at this time, whilst Brockliss is more sanguine pointing to the poor quality of experimental facilities in comparison with other comparable European institutions and noting little willingness by the university to relate to Enlightenment advances in science except for a brief window after the Civil War and a short second wave after the construction of the Old Ashmolean.[105] Nevertheless, a distinctive aspect of the town's archaeological record is the occasional recovery of artefacts that may be related to this phenomenon, the clearest example being the seventeenth-century anatomical and alchemical assemblage recovered from the basement of the Old Ashmolean in 1999.[106] That Broad Street was a natural focus for such activity is also suggested by the recovery of a ceramic distillation vessel from this area including eight mid to late seventeenth-century wheel-thrown red earthenware distillation vessels recovered from the site of the New Bodleian.[107] These finds were recorded not far from where the 'Oxford Philosophical Club' of post-Civil War scientific enthusiasts held their meetings in the Warden's Lodgings at Wadham College.[108] A little further south a domed red ware alembic of similar date, along with glass phials and drug pots from an apothecary's shop or similar, have been recovered from Catte Street, close to where contemporary leases show the occupiers as practisers of 'physic'.[109]

100 R. Bashford, 'Savile House, Music Practice Rooms, New College, Oxford, Evaluation Report', unpublished OA report (2014); P.A. Harding and A.D. Crockett, 'Land at Manor Place, Oxford Archaeological Evaluation Report', unpublished Wessex Archaeology report (2012).

101 Below, chapter 13.

102 G. Keevill, 'Christ Church, Oxford: The Thatched Barn, Archaeological Evaluation Report', unpublished Keevill Heritage Ltd report (2014); chapter 13, below.

103 Below, chapter 12.

104 Brockliss, *The University of Oxford*, p. 159.

105 Ibid. pp. 312–14.

106 An archaeological evaluation and subsequent watching brief in 1998–2000 uncovered a range of human and animal anatomical specimens and chemical ceramics and glassware dating from the late seventeenth to the early eighteenth century to the rear of the Old Ashmolean Building. Chemical analysis of residues associated with the ceramic crucibles revealed traces of mercury, sulphur, zinc, lead glass, manganese and antimony, suggesting possible alchemical use: M. Martinón-Torres, 'Inside Solomon's House: An Archaeological Study of the Old Ashmolean Chymical Laboratory in Oxford', *Ambix*, 59:1 (2012), pp. 46–7.

107 Mellor, *Pots and People*, p. 39.

108 Brockliss, *The University of Oxford*, p. 313.

109 Mellor, *Pots and People*, pp. 38, 39, 41.

As student numbers declined the colleges expanded to accommodate changing expectations regarding comfort and privacy. The spending of money on architecture and leisure pursuits in post-Restoration Oxford continued apace, with extensive college building and the adoption of formal gardens as detailed by the seventeenth-century maps of Wenceslaus Hollar and David Loggan. This was a period during which social differentiation was becoming more marked, a trend also reflected in pottery use with a greater variety of pottery types catering to domestic households, communal eating houses, new industrial uses and also developing leisure activities, for example gardening.[110] Recent archaeological insights into the development of college structures of this period include small projects revealing hidden fabric at Christ Church and Brasenose College.[111] As yet, garden archaeology has only produced fragments of earlier formal schemes; nevertheless, significant potential remains across numerous sites.[112]

THE EIGHTEENTH AND NINETEENTH CENTURIES

It is worth noting at this juncture that the endowed college was an invention of twelfth-century Paris and a tradition that was extinguished in France by the Revolution of 1789. Thus, whilst the endowed college system flourished elsewhere in Europe during the Middle Ages, only in Oxford and Cambridge have such medieval foundations survived into the present day. Thus, from the late eighteenth century onwards they became exceptional features of these two towns.[113]

Oxford in the eighteenth century saw notable civic improvements and building projects in the form of new bridges and roads, a rebuilt county prison, new workhouses, the construction of the Radcliffe Infirmary and indoor market. These institutions have seen varying degrees of archaeological investigation, with the prison, redeveloped in 2003, being subject to extensive excavation and becoming one of Oxford's most evocative heritage attractions.[114] Perhaps the most impressive archaeological results come from investigations into post-medieval burial assemblages including the gruesome assemblage from the castle ditch at Oxford prison dating to the sixteenth to eighteenth century incorporating executions and evidence for anatomisation. Important remains have also been recovered from the late eighteenth- and nineteenth-century Radcliffe Infirmary burial ground, representing the second largest assemblage of its kind from England and containing a wealth of data pertaining to demography and pathology, including evidence for surgery.[115] Other notable burial sites include the seventeenth-century burial from St Cross College on St Giles' Street and the small late nineteenth-century assemblage from Littlemore Baptist Chapel.[116]

110 Ibid. p. 44.

111 G. Keevill and C. Underwood, 'Christ Church Oxford: Report of Fire Safety and Refurbishment Works on the Upper Floors of Killcanon', unpublished Keevill Heritage Ltd report (2012); Kelly et al., 'Building Recording and Test Pits at Brasenose College'.

112 For example, remnant garden paths and a large stone- and clay-lined water feature at Trinity College and the reworked Civil War mound at New College: L. Sparks and B. Ford, New Teaching and Residential Building, Trinity College, Oxford', unpublished OA report (2018); C. Bell, 'New College Mound, Oxford: An Archaeological Investigation', unpublished OAU report (1993), https://library.oxfordarchaeology.com/3280/.

113 Brockliss, *The University of Oxford*, pp. 63–4. For the distinction between Oxford and Cambridge and other 'college' foundations: C. Burgess and M. Heale (eds.), *The Late Medieval English College and its Context* (2008), p. 12. See also A.B. Cobban, 'The Role of Colleges in the Medieval Universities of Northern Europe, with Special Reference to England and France', *Bulletin of the John Rylands Library* 71:1 (1989), pp. 49–70.

114 Munby, *Oxford Castle*; N. Jefferies et al., 'Development of the former Radcliffe Infirmary, Oxford, 1770–1900', *Post-Medieval Archaeology*, 49:2 (2015), pp. 238–68; 'Excavations in Rewley House Gardens', unpublished OAU report (1994).

115 Munby, *Oxford Castle*; L. Loe et al., 'Radcliffe Infirmary Burial Ground, Oxford, Post Excavation Assessment', unpublished OA report (2014).

116 Below, chapter 12; R. McCarthy et al., 'The Baptist Chapel Burial Ground, Littlemore, Oxford', *Post-Medieval Archaeology*, 46:2 (2012), pp. 281–90.

Only in the nineteenth century did the population growth resume on a significant scale with employment still goods and service-based. Workers were employed as college servants, in the University Press, gasworks and breweries. The seasonal unemployment caused by the university holidays continued to have a significant impact on the local economy. By the mid nineteenth century the only industries of note were the railways, Lucy's iron works, the breweries and two clothing factories. Oxford's first major industrial breakthrough was the production of William Morris's first car on Holywell Street in 1912. He transferred his works to Cowley the following year, with related works coming to dominate this side of the town.

Our understanding of the archaeology of post-medieval to modern manufacturing in the town remains piecemeal, for example we have fragmentary evidence for post-Dissolution horn-working waste from the large former Dominican friary precinct at Luther Court and Lucy Faithfull House, but no coherent overview of the post-Dissolution re-use of friary precincts nor of the character or extent of post-medieval industrial processes across the city.[117] There have also been a small number of investigations of early modern industrial sites, for example the site of the nineteenth-century Swan Brewery site in the suburb of St Thomas, and the first Morris car garage workshop in Holywell Street.[118]

Investigations into demolished nineteenth-century domestic buildings have been undertaken in St Ebbe's and recording work on standing structures of this date include the kitchen of No. 10 Walton Street and the modest softwood timber structure to the rear of No. 24 Holywell Street.[119] Such investigations can be combined with the recovery of targeted early nineteenth-century waste assemblages, for example those recovered from recent excavations at the Westgate Centre and in Walton Street.[120] Such assemblages predate the advent of municipal waste removal and allow us to glimpse the advent of mass production in the domestic detritus of poor and middle-class households, building on the ground-breaking work on post-medieval assemblages undertaken at St Ebbe's in the 1970s. This is an area of study where sampling strategies require careful consideration given the volume of material potentially remaining in the ground.

THE FUTURE

This chapter has given a rapid and selective tour of research themes that further investigations in the town may illuminate. It would be remiss of me to conclude without mentioning some of the heritage management challenges that the production of such data will entail. Firstly, there is the question of securing adequate curated storage for excavated artefacts, an outcome that is reliant on the two collecting museums for the city, the County Council Museum Store and the Ashmolean Museum, having capacity to take the volume of material being excavated. Secondly, there is the matter of how the information is signposted and disseminated. With regards to storage capacity the only observation I would make is that in the age of government austerity the future looks uncertain. In terms of data storage, the city now has an integrated Historic Environment Record and Urban Archaeological Database which is in part accessible online through the Heritage Gateway and functions well for development control purposes. The unified database

117 C. Pickard, 'Luther Court, Thames Street, Oxford, Archaeological Evaluation Report, Phase 1', unpublished OA report (2014), https://library.oxfordarchaeology.com/2946/; S. Porter, 'Lucy Faithfull House, 8 Speedwell Street Oxford, Report on an Archaeological Excavation', unpublished MOLA report (2018). For the research interest of post-Dissolution friary precincts: D. O'Sullivan, *In the Company of the Preachers: The Archaeology of Medieval Friaries in England and Wales*, Leicester Archaeology Monograph, 23 (2013), pp. 25–6.

118 OA reports, in preparation.

119 Forthcoming OA report; B. Davis, 'Harris Manchester College, 24 Holywell Street, Oxford, Historic Building Recording', unpublished Wessex Archaeology report (2013).

120 Ford et al., *The Oxford Greyfriars*; R. Bashford, 'Phase 1 Area: Somerville College, Walton Street, Oxford, Archaeological Evaluation Report', unpublished OA report (2017), https://library.oxfordarchaeology.com/4555/.

nevertheless currently poses ongoing management challenges because of the inherited data structures and related issues of search functionality and accessibility.

It is also the case that in terms of the dissemination and presentation of archaeological information the full potential of 3D modelling and social media platforms largely remains to be explored. In terms of the publication of archaeological excavations in journals and monographs Oxford has a strong record and the publication backlog remains modest, though understandably frustrations can arise as the post-excavation process, which necessarily involves the input of hard-pressed specialists whose numbers are dwindling, can take several years to complete.

A 2017 report by the British Academy highlighted the distinctive capacity of archaeology as a subject to provide a bridge between science and the humanities.[121] This relationship is likely to remain important for the future of archaeological investigation and engagement as we move into the twenty-first century, both in terms of how we store and communicate information electronically and how we extract new insights from archaeological remains, for example through scientific dating or aDNA analysis. The merging of medieval science, art, technology and popular archaeology in the Westgate Archaeology Trail neatly captures this science–humanities overlap as well as highlighting a distinctive strand of the town's unique below-ground heritage.

In recent years the potential for the archaeology of Oxford to engage the imaginations of residents and visitors has been demonstrated by the enthusiastic participation in the East Oxford Community Archaeology Project (Archeox) and also the volunteer-supported pop-up museums and well attended open days resulting from the 2015–16 Westgate excavation. The challenge we face is to grow and facilitate greater public involvement and engagement, building on the dynamic of recent successes, in order to make Oxford's exceptional archaeological resource an inspiration for the next generation.

121 The British Academy, *Reflections on Archaeology* (2017), available online.

2.

Fifty Years of Excavations in Oxford, 1968–2018

T.G. HASSALL

SUMMARY

This chapter is a historiography of the practice of archaeology in Oxford over the last fifty years. It does not attempt to describe the many outstanding discoveries which have been made during the same period. Instead it traces how the dominant role of the Ashmolean Museum in the city's archaeology was eventually superseded by the appointment of an archaeologist by Oxford City Council so that archaeology became fully integrated into the city's planning system. Excavations were originally conducted by staff drawn from the university who were assisted by volunteers, many of whom were recruited from the Oxford University Archaeological Society. Today, archaeology in the city is conducted by a variety of professional contracting organisations led by Oxford Archaeology, a charity and limited company which grew out of the local authority and university initiatives of the 1960s and 1970s. Changes in excavation and post-excavation techniques and publication are summarised, together with an account of the ways in which archaeologists have tried to explain their discoveries to the public by means of outreach initiatives, often involving the local media and the arts. The attempts to establish a permanent museum of Oxford's archaeology are outlined. Throughout the review tribute is paid to the many personalities who have played a part in this story.

On Thursday 2 May 1968 HM the Queen visited the archaeological excavations in Church Street, St Ebbe's at the invitation of the city council.[1] These excavations were being conducted in advance of the building of the Westgate Centre. Eight years later, in March 1976, HM the Queen returned, this time accompanied by the Duke of Edinburgh, to view the completed shopping centre. The royal party was shown plans of the development and a display of some of the archaeological objects which had been excavated (Fig. 2.1). On seeing this material, the Duke asked the city architect, the designer of the new complex, and the author of this chapter, who was then the director of the Oxford Archaeological Excavation Committee (OAEC), when they thought the new shopping centre would be demolished and its remains would be excavated. The members of the civic party laughed dutifully. However, in February, 2018, only a few metres away from where the royal party had been standing, a wall-mounted display of medieval floor tiles excavated from the cloister walk of the Oxford Greyfriars was unveiled (Fig. 2.2). These tiles were discovered during a second Westgate excavation campaign which was undertaken by Oxford Archaeology (OA) in 2015–16. This excavation took place as a result of the northern end of the original centre being refurbished, its southern end, together with its original multi-storey

[1] This chapter derives from the Tom Hassall lecture presented to the OAHS on 12 February 2019.

Fig. 2.1 The Queen and the Duke of Edinburgh inspect a model of the Westgate Centre 5 March 1976, with (from left) the Lady Mayoress; Douglas Murray, the city architect and planning officer; Tom Hassall, director of the Oxfordshire Archaeological Unit; and Bill Fagg, the Lord Mayor. Photograph: Oxford Mail.

Fig. 2.2 Unveiling the tiled pavement from Greyfriars cloister excavated during the second Westgate excavations, February 2018: Ben M. Ford, Oxford Archaeology's project manager (centre); Councillor Colin Cook, Oxford City Council's heritage champion (second from right); Duncan Wilson, one-time member of Oxford University Archaeological Society and since 2015 chief executive of Historic England (right). Photograph: Oxford Mail.

Fig. 2.3 The original Westgate excavators meet their twenty-first-century counterparts in September 2015. Tom Hassall, director of the first Westgate excavations, standing (centre) behind a cake baked in the shape of the reconstructed Greyfriars church; Ben M. Ford, Oxford Archaeology's Westgate project manager, sitting cross-legged (centre). Photograph: Brian Durham.

car park, being demolished, and a massive extension and new 1,000-space underground car park being built.

The second Westgate excavation campaign provided an excuse for a reunion of the original Westgate excavators in September 2015. On that occasion the veteran archaeologists were taken on a tour of the excavations by OA's project manager, Ben M. Ford. After the site visit the twentieth-century excavators took tea with their twenty-first century counterparts followed by the ceremonial cutting of a cake baked in the shape of a reconstruction of the Greyfriars church (Fig. 2.3). This reunion was more than just a social occasion: it provided an opportunity for the archaeologists to compare and contrast the two Westgate excavation campaigns and to reflect on the changes in approaches to Oxford's archaeology which have taken place in the fifty years that separated them.

This chapter and the lecture on which it is based were inspired by that reunion. It is very much a personal memoir: a basis for what the author might be able to report to Her Majesty if she ever visited an Oxford excavation again. In looking back, the author feels rather like a cross between the Ancient Mariner and the central character of Brian Aldiss' novel *Greybeard*.[2] The novel was written in the early 1960s when Aldiss was living in Paradise Square in St Ebbe's just at the time when the major demolition of the nineteenth-century suburb was getting under way to make way for the first Westgate Centre and its associated infrastructure. *Greybeard* opens prophetically in the 'dusty year' of 2018 in a dystopian Oxford occupied by a childless and ageing population. Some years later, in an essay entitled *An Exile on Planet Earth*, Aldiss described his time in St Ebbe's, mourned the destruction of its community, and railed against the arrival of 'The days of the supermarket and the credit card'.[3]

2 B.W. Aldiss, *Greybeard* (1964).
3 B. Aldiss, 'Paradise Square', in *An Exile on Planet Earth, Articles and Reflections* (2012), pp. 13–23.

The chapter will consider the ways in which the practice of archaeology in Oxford has changed radically over the last half century. No attempt will be made to summarise the actual results of the excavations that have taken place. Readers who wish to learn about these are referred to David Radford's chapter in this volume and, for more detail, also to the *Oxford Archaeological Resource Assessment and Research Agenda 2012* which can be found on Oxford City Council's website.[4] Our knowledge of the city's archaeology is comprehensively summarised in the *Resource Assessment*, which contains nine detailed period-based reviews which are fully referenced to both published and unpublished work. Details of excavations undertaken since 2012 can also be found in the same website in the form of work summaries which are produced three times a year.

The most obvious first point to make is that the organisation of Oxford's archaeology has evolved dramatically since the 1960s. At the outset Oxford University's Ashmolean Museum was the main focus for archaeological activity in the city and the county. This was of course not the museum's prime purpose at the time which was to provide a teaching resource for the university. So far as the city's archaeology was concerned, the key member of the museum's staff was David Sturdy. He was steeped in Oxford's long and distinguished tradition of professional and amateur archaeological research. He had been a pupil at Magdalen College School, and was then an undergraduate at Christ Church. As an undergraduate he was much involved with the Oxford University Archaeological Society (OUAS) and took part in the salvage excavations on the Clarendon Hotel.[5] As a postgraduate he had researched the topography of medieval Oxford. He became an assistant keeper at the Ashmolean in 1958 and held that post until 1966.

David Sturdy's early career was mirrored by that of other aspiring Oxford archaeologists at the time. There was no school of Archaeology within the university, although the Institute of Archaeology, founded in 1962, provided for postgraduate studies. Undergraduates with an interest in archaeology were only catered for by the flourishing OUAS which had been founded in 1919. A steady stream of archaeologists started their careers through membership of the society.

Alongside the Ashmolean Museum and the OUAS the other institution directly involved in the city's archaeology was the Oxfordshire Architectural and Historical Society (OAHS). At times in the past the OAHS and its members had taken an active role in excavations such as the Clarendon Quadrangle in 1899.[6] By the 1960s the society's chief role was in disseminating excavation results via its lecture programme and above all through the publication of *Oxoniensia*. From 1936 this journal was the main vehicle for local excavation reports. In the 1960s the society also played a role in stimulating the interest of young people in archaeology through its junior branch, The Ashmole Club. Club members could take part in small research excavations in the city directed by David Sturdy whose charismatic personality inspired a generation of future archaeologists.

Research excavations have always been rare in the city and most opportunities for what would come to be called rescue and salvage excavations were provided by university, college and commercial developments. Oxford had avoided bomb damage during World War Two so that unlike many other historic cities opportunities for excavation were relatively few; nevertheless, the size of commercial developments began to change dramatically from the late 1950s as major 'high street' stores began to develop sites in Cornmarket Street and Queen Street. In 1959 Oxford archaeologists met this challenge in the way which was commonplace at that time by establishing a local excavation committee, the Oxford Excavation Committee (OEC). The committee's purpose was to bring together all interested parties in order to raise money

4 R. Beckley with D. Radford, 'Oxford Archaeological Resource Assessment and Agenda', Oxford City Council (2011): https://www.oxford.gov.uk/downloads/download/445/oxford_archaeological_resource_assessment.

5 E.M. Jope, 'The Clarendon Hotel, Oxford, Part 1, The Site', *Oxoniensia*, 23 (1958), pp. 1–29.

6 F.H. Penny, *Buried Oxford Unearthed* (1899).

from national and local sources and to employ temporary excavation staff, as had previously happened in Oxford in the 1890s.

OEC carried out a number of major rescue excavation over its six-year life, but it came to an end in its original form because of major changes in the local organisational framework and the city's impending comprehensive redevelopment proposals.[7] In 1964 the Oxford City and County Museum (OCCM) was established jointly by the two local authorities. The first chairman of the new museum's joint committee was a county councillor, Jack Peers, whose father had been the first chief inspector of ancient monuments. OCCM was based at Woodstock. It was energetically directed by Jean Cook who was assisted by the museum's first field officer, Don Benson. The Ashmolean Museum immediately relinquished its lead role for archaeological activity in the region and for a while even ceased to add local material to its collections.

Two years after OCCM was established, the city council published the *City of Oxford Development Plan Review 1966–1981, Written Analysis*. This development plan identified the nineteenth-century south-western suburb of St Ebbe's as the future focus for major commercial development which was to be serviced by associated roads and car parks. In response to this impending threat to the city's archaeology Jean Cook and Don Benson wrote *City of Oxford Redevelopment, Archaeological Implications*, which was published in 1966. This report was to become a model for similar urban archaeological implication reports which were subsequently published in a number of other UK cities and towns. The Oxford report not only identified the potential scale of damage to the city's archaeology, but also realised that an appropriate archaeological response would be beyond the resources of either the museum or the OEC. Jean Cook and Don Benson recognised that the answer to this archaeological challenge was to remodel OEC as a full-time organisation, the Oxford Archaeological Excavation Committee (OAEC), a registered charity with public benefit at the heart of its purpose.

OAEC was formally established in 1967. The author was appointed as director of excavations, initially for five years. This appointment was one of the first, if not the first, appointment of a full-time rescue archaeologist anywhere in the country. The city provided administrative services and office accommodation in various condemned houses, first in Bulwarks Lane and later in Cambridge Terrace. The county provided financial services. Both local authorities provided core funding as did the Ministry of Public Buildings and Works. As a charity OAEC was also able to access funds which would not have been available to OCCM. Financial support came from Oxford Colleges and various grant giving organisations, notably The Oxford Preservation Trust. Not all fund-raising efforts were successful. At one fundraising event at the Town Hall the bishop of Oxford was invited to speak. The bishop rose to his feet, quoted *Luke 16:3* ('I cannot dig; to beg I am ashamed') and then sat down again, leaving the audience rather nonplussed. For a short time at the outset of the excavations unstratified sherds of medieval pottery were even sold to visitors on site as souvenirs to raise funds, a not uncommon practice at the time. Help in kind also came from local businesses who loaned site equipment. The British Motor Corporation loaned a Mini Moke. This loan was arranged by Ken Revis, the corporation's press officer, who had lost his eyesight in World War II while defusing mines on Brighton's West Pier (Fig. 2.4).

The results of the OAEC's St Ebbe's excavations cumulatively transformed our knowledge of Oxford's medieval South-West Ward. H.E. Salter's *Map of Mediaeval Oxford* and *Survey of Oxford* had provided the context for the excavations, but away from the central streets and tenements the documentary information on the history of the ward was fairly sparse.[8] The excavations provided extensive information on the dating of the streets, the line and nature of the city wall, the eastern defences of the castle, and the layouts of the Greyfriars and the Blackfriars

7 D. Sturdy and J. Munby, 'Early Domestic Sites in Oxford: Excavations in Cornmarket Street and Queen Street', *Oxoniensia*, 50 (1985), pp. 47–94.

8 H.E. Salter, *Map of Mediaeval Oxford* (1934), map 4; Salter, *Survey*, vol. 2, pp. 63–79, 120–32.

Fig. 2.4 Ken Revis, press officer of The British Motor Corporation (right) loaning a Mini Moke to the Oxford Archaeological Excavation Committee, January 1968, accompanied by: J.N.L. Myres, Bodley's Librarian (left); the Lord Mayor, Alderman Frank Pickstock (centre left); and Tom Hassall, director of excavations (centre right). Photograph: Oxford Mail.

churches, and cast much light on the daily lives of the townspeople.[9] This excavated evidence was combined with documentary research by Hilary Turner and John Wood who were able to add to Salter's work by examining the later documentary evidence. This documentary research was not published with the excavation reports, but it was later to be a useful component of the second Westgate excavations.

Two external factors combined to contribute to OAEC's success. The first factor was that the majority of the excavated sites were owned by the city council itself and councillors of all parties were fully supportive of the work. This political support was essential given that archaeology at that time had no status in the planning system: access to sites and time for excavation had to be negotiated with the city officials. There were three key city councillors: Peter Spokes, Frank Pickstock, and Michael Maclagan. Alderman Peter Spokes, a conservative, with a background in recording historic buildings and cataloguing local collections in the Bodleian Library, was the first chairman of OAEC. Frank Pickstock was the Labour Lord Mayor during OAEC's first crucial year of operations (see Fig. 2.4). He was at the time the deputy director of the Oxford University Delegacy for Extra-Mural Studies, now the Department of Continuing Education. He had a great enthusiasm for local archaeology and history. It was Frank Pickstock who had invited the Queen to visit the excavations in Church Street in 1968. The third key councillor, Michael Maclagan, was the last independent university councillor. He was a fellow of Trinity College and Richmond Herald, and he succeeded Frank Pickstock as Lord Mayor.

9 G. Lambrick and H. Woods, 'Excavations on the Second Site of the Dominican Priory, Oxford', *Oxoniensia*, 41 (1976), pp. 168–231; T.G. Hassall, 'Excavations at Oxford Castle, 1965–73', *Oxoniensia*, 41 (1976), pp. 232–308; Hassall, 'St Ebbe's, Part I'; Hassall, 'St Ebbe's, Part II'.

The second factor which contributed to OAEC's success was that the councillors' support was matched by wide-spread popular interest in the progress of the excavations. The citizens of Oxford were fascinated to witness the city's pre-university history uncovered, followed by the uncovering of east Oxford's Roman industrial past at the Churchill Hospital, all of which contributed to a sense of civic pride. Local interest was in part fostered by the extensive coverage of the excavations in the local media. From the outset *The Oxford Mail*, edited by Mark Barrington Ward from 1961–79, was very supportive of the work. The paper regularly printed articles by its local history correspondent, John Owen, and by one of its feature writers, Don Chapman (under his pseudonym, 'Anthony Wood').

When BBC Radio Oxford began broadcasting in October 1970 one of its presenters, Andy Wright, also realised the potential for using Oxford's archaeology to engage local listeners. One memorable weekly series looked at the archaeology and history of the city wall. The series was broadcast on Radio Oxford's early morning programme and when it concluded Andy Wright invited listeners to take a guided tour of the walls. According to local radio legend the Radio Oxford switchboard was then inundated with calls for several days. This incident apparently allowed the station to assess the size of its listening public for the first time. There was no local television then, but archaeological evaluation in the basement of Sainsbury's original store in the High Street featured in an episode of Blue Peter, BBC One's children's programme.

OAEC, like OEC before it, had only a six-year life before Oxford's archaeology underwent another structural change. In 1973 OAEC became federated with the newly formed Oxfordshire Archaeological Committee (OAC) which brought together all archaeological interests in the county in anticipation of local government reorganisation the following year. OAC was very much based on the model of OAEC.[10] Professor Barry Cunliffe of the Oxford University Institute of Archaeology and Trevor Rowley of the Oxford University Department of Continuing Education were leading forces behind this development. Like OAEC, OAC was established as a registered charity. The county treasurer continued to provide financial services. When this support came to an end in 1983 OAC added to its charitable status by becoming a limited liability company to protect individual members of the committee from any financial claims that might be made against them.

OAEC at first remained as a distinct entity within the larger Oxfordshire structure in order to retain funds specifically granted to Oxford's archaeology. However, in 1978 the city council ceased providing core funding and secretarial support to OAEC, so that the following year the committee then became fully integrated into the OAC structure. Although OAEC no longer existed, an Oxford Advisory Committee of OAC continued to oversee archaeological work in the city.

The OAC's executive arm was at first called the Oxfordshire Archaeological Unit (OAU) which became known as the Oxford Archaeological Unit in 1982 and then Oxford Archaeology (OA) from 2001. At the outset the unit, like OAEC before it, depended on political support from county and district councillors, notably from the chairman of the county council, Robert (Bob) Weir. It was symbolic that when the Queen and the Duke of Edinburgh visited the new county in 1976 Bob Weir presented the Duke with a copy of *Historic Towns in Oxfordshire*, edited by Kirsty Rodwell which had been published by OAU the previous year to commemorate European Architectural Heritage Year.[11] This publication included a section on Oxford's archaeology and buildings by the author of this chapter and John Ashdown, the recently appointed city council conservation officer.

Like OAEC before it, the OAU was accommodated in buildings in the city which were destined for demolition, first, a row of houses in Luther Terrace and then at No. 46 Hythe

10 B.W. Cunliffe et al., 'The Oxfordshire Archaeological Unit', *Antiquity*, 47 (1974), pp. 93–8; D. Miles, 'Oxford Archaeological Unit: The First Twenty-Five Years', *Oxoniensia*, 63 (1998), pp. 1–9.

11 K. Rodwell (ed.), *Historic Towns in Oxfordshire: A Survey of the New County* (1975).

Bridge Street, which had been built originally as the Running Horses public house. A carved stone relief of the unit's logo, based on the design of a Roman brooch from Dorchester depicting the Roman god Janus, was placed above the front entrance. The carver was David Brown, at that time an assistant keeper at the Ashmolean. The unit and the Janus relief were to move in 1996 to the appropriately named Janus House at Osney Mead. The original somewhat scruffy offices in Hythe Bridge Street have avoided demolition and have recently been converted into the luxurious Swailes Suites.

Funding of excavations remained an ongoing concern for OAU, since central and local government ceased giving core grants. The Department of the Environment and its successor body, English Heritage, switched instead to giving annual grants related to specific excavation and post-excavation projects. In Oxford at least it was still possible to continue to raise funds from the colleges and the Oxford Preservation Trust, whose secretary was Frank Pickstock from 1978–82, for unspecified excavations. Shortfalls in funding were increasingly made good by employing staff drawn from various job creation schemes funded by the Manpower Services Commission (MSC). Some of the MSC recruits, such as Alan Hardy, became full-time archaeologists. OAU also had a contract with OUDCE, organised by Trevor Rowley, to provide teaching services to the Department and to make student placements available to the highly successful professional in-service training scheme. Some of the trainees, such as Claire Halpin, Michael Wilcox and John Wood, made important contributions to the post-excavation programme, while Leigh Allen became a full-time member of the OAU staff.

When the OAU was first set up the staffing structure consisted of a director and a number of subject based field officers. The author was appointed the first director, while Brian Durham was appointed as the field officer responsible for excavations in the city (Fig. 2.5). Brian had first been involved in the city's archaeology during the final phases of the excavation of the choir of the Greyfriars church in the winter of 1969; he had subsequently gone on to direct the excavations of key sites including Nos. 79–80 St Aldate's and All Saints church; and had been appointed OAEC's Deputy Director.[12]

Commercial and university-related developments began to replace the city's comprehensive development of its own sites.[13] As a result, it became necessary constantly to monitor planning applications. The OAU director would meet on a fortnightly basis with John Steane who had succeeded Don Benson in 1975 as county archaeologist at OCCM; together they would go through the weekly planning lists for the city and the other newly created districts and discuss what archaeological response might be appropriate. This process required a combination of personal knowledge and consultation of the developing Sites and Monuments Record (SMR).[14] The crucial work of updating the Oxford section of the SMR was carried out by Elizabeth Leggatt, a volunteer at the OCCM.

Where a planning application was considered to require an archaeological response, the city planning authority was alerted. However, since the planning regulations of the time did not consider archaeology as a 'material consideration', the applicant was under no compulsion to make any provision of either money or time for excavation. Because of this situation some sites which should ideally have been examined in detail were not. For example, Nos. 11–18 Queen Street was a key site redeveloped by Marks & Spencer. The street frontage, although heavily disturbed by cellars, could have produced evidence comparable to the major sites previously excavated in Cornmarket Street. However, it was only possible to negotiate access to the vacant rear of the site where the remains of Hinxey Hall were examined. The Queen Street frontage

12 B. Durham, 'Archaeological Investigations in St Aldate's, Oxford', *Oxoniensia*, 42 (1977), pp. 83–203; Dodd, *Oxford*, pp. 204–42.

13 T. Hassall, 'Oxford: An Urban Case Study', in T. Rowley and M. Breakell (eds.), *Planning and the Historic Environment* (1975), pp. 64–5.

14 D. Benson, 'A Sites and Monuments Record for the Oxford Region', *Oxoniensia*, 37 (1972), pp. 226–37.

Fig. 2.5 Brian Durham, Oxford Archaeological Unit's Oxford field officer, standing beside the High Street surface water drain, work in progress in 1981. Looking east along the High Street with All Saints Church in the centre. Photograph: Oxford Archaeology.

was only recorded cursorily because of the combination of the dangerous condition of the site and the lack of time for excavation.[15]

Archaeology's status within the planning system changed dramatically in November 1990 when the government published *Planning Policy Guidance 16, Archaeology and Planning (PPG 16)*. Archaeology was henceforward put on a firm footing by the application of the 'polluter pays' principle. At a stroke the funding basis for archaeology was transformed. Resources became available not only to excavate threatened sites, but also to write up and publish the results. The implementation of this policy in Oxford owed much to John Ashdown, the city conservation officer, and his colleagues in the planning department who pushed for the application of *PPG16* in a way which was going to be acceptable to the council.

In order for the new system to work the former ad hoc arrangement of advice to the planners provided by OCCM and OAU had to be replaced by archaeological expertise within the planning department itself. At first the city was reluctant to establish and to fund such a post itself. An arrangement was therefore arrived at between the city and OAU that Brian Durham should provide an Oxford Archaeological Advisory Service (OAAS) with half his salary paid for by English Heritage. A potential problem with this arrangement was that commercial developers, who were free to employ whatever archaeological contracting organisation they wished, might

15 C. Halpin, 'Late Saxon Evidence and Excavation of Hinxey Hall, Oxford', *Oxoniensia*, 48 (1983), pp. 41–70.

have considered OAU at a competitive advantage when tendering for such work. To eliminate this obvious conflict of interest, English Heritage insisted that a 'Chinese wall' should be created within OAU, which separated Brian Durham from his contracting colleagues within the unit in respect of developments within the city.

The OAAS remained in place until 2000 when English Heritage ended its contract with Oxford Archaeology (OA), as OAU had then become known. From that time onwards, the city took over full responsibility for providing in-house archaeological capacity within the planning office. Brian Durham was appointed as the city's first archaeologist and he left OA. In this role he not only continued to deal with the archaeological requirements of planning applications, but he also oversaw the compilation of Oxford's Urban Archaeology Database (UAD) which was created as part of English Heritage's Urban Archaeology Strategy Programme. The UAD was a parallel system to the original SMR by then renamed the Historic Environment Record (HER) and it was compiled by OA. In 2014 the county council transferred the management of Oxford's HER data to the city council. The city council now maintains a unified HER/UAD database for Oxford using the Historic Buildings, Sites and Monuments Record system. The monument data for the Oxford HER is available online via the Heritage Gateway website.

In 2008 Brian Durham retired and his place as Oxford City Council's archaeologist was taken by David Radford. Two years later, English Heritage grant-aided the city to produce *Oxford Archaeological Action Plan 2013–18*, which comprised an archaeological strategy, period research assessments and agendas and the completion of a programme of historic urban and landscape characterisation. The assessment was compiled by David Radford with Ruth Beckley, who was employed on an English Heritage grant by the council.

In 2012 *PPG16* was replaced by the *National Planning Policy Framework*, which was itself revised in 2018. These administrative changes did not alter the status of archaeology which remained firmly embedded within the planning process. Today prospective developers can find on the city's website a clear explanation of what is required of them and the procedures which have to be followed when archaeology is likely to be impacted by their proposals.

Although archaeology has a recognised status in the planning system the support of those councillors, who recognise the broad benefit of archaeology, is still extremely valuable and indeed essential. This support is particularly necessary in cases where archaeological requirements are challenged by a developer. On these occasions, councillors can provide vital support to the planning staff. During the second Westgate excavations David Radford was keen to engage as many councillors and planning officials as possible in the unfolding excavation of the Greyfriars claustral area. Councillors were invited to wine-receptions with 'roof-top tours' to view the archaeology being uncovered below. The councillor who has been most supportive of the city's archaeology in recent years is Colin Cook, the heritage champion of Oxford. Councillor Cook was nominated by the council to fulfil this role as one in a network of heritage champions established by English Heritage in 2004 to promote the interests of the historic environment within local authorities (Fig. 2.6). It was in his champion's role that Councillor Cook accompanied Ben M. Ford and staff of OA to a ceremony in London when the second Westgate excavations received the British Archaeological Award for the Best Archaeological Project in 2016. He then arranged for a special meeting with the then Lord Mayor who formally congratulated Ben M. Ford and his supervisory team. In 2018 Councillor Cook became Lord Mayor himself and during his year in office took an active role in the discussions which were taking place at that time about the redisplay of the City Museum.

From 1967 to 1990 there was a tacit presumption that OAEC or OAU would carry out all rescue excavations in the city, although at no time did either organisation have an actual monopoly. As a result, both organisations built up a formidable knowledge of the city's archaeology. However, the new planning regime after 1990 was founded on the principles of the market economy. It was assumed that from that time onwards developers would be free to employ whatever archaeological organisation they chose regardless of its staff's knowledge of the city's archaeology in general or of a particular site. Often price was, and remains, a deciding factor,

Fig. 2.6 Councillor Colin Cook, Lord Mayor and Oxford's heritage champion, photographed during the dismantling of the reconstructed Churchill Hospital Roman pottery kiln in the former Museum of Oxford in the town hall basement, January 2019. Photograph: Tom Hassall.

but at least the city council's archaeologist ensures a level playing field between contractors by providing a transparent 'brief' which specifies what archaeological mitigation is required.

Although OA has the largest in-house expertise and experience in examining and interpreting Oxford's past, there are now many other archaeological contractors who work in the city. By way of example within the six months preceding the writing of this chapter, in addition to OA, the following archaeological contractors were excavating in the city: Cotswold Archaeology, Foundations Archaeology, JMHS, Keevil Heritage Ltd, and TVAS; building recording was carried out by Asset Heritage Management. OA itself also operates outside its original core area and has grown to become one of the largest archaeological consultancies and contracting organisation in the country.

However, OA is still the dominant contractor in Oxford and it is unsurprising that it won the contract for the second series of Westgate excavations. The developers, Westgate Oxford Alliance (a partnership between Land Securities and the Crown Estate), were assisted in their negotiations with the planning authority, the choice of an archaeological contractor and the oversight of the actual excavations by a consultant, Myk Flitcroft of CgMs Heritage (now part of the RPS Group). Such archaeological consultancies arose in the post *PPG16* era when larger developers required guiding through the planning process. In the case of Westgate, the city's archaeologist also established a one-off Westgate Archaeological Advisory Panel to assist in the academic oversight of the project.

Ben M. Ford was appointed OA's project director for the second Westgate excavations. Most of the excavations and watching briefs targeted the large areas of the development where the full archaeological sequence was to be completely removed, for example: the massive basement car park; the culvert that diverted the Trill Mill Stream; and the large storm water attenuation tank.

On the main excavation area, where the majority of the Greyfriars complex was expected, Ben M. Ford took a different approach. In this area, the full archaeological sequence was to be impacted by a large number of foundation piles, but there was no basement. The shallower depths to which the pile mat (the construction working surface), the ground floor slab, and the pile caps (the large concrete blocks that link groups of individual piles) extended was going to leave the deeper archaeological deposits undisturbed. The positions of the piles themselves reflected the design of the building and were spread relatively evenly across the site; naturally they did not relate to the underlying archaeology. Excavation of the exact pile positions would therefore have resulted in multiple small excavations which would have been difficult to interpret and might even have been located in areas where the archaeology had already been badly disturbed by the foundations of the former multi-storey car park. Since such an approach would potentially not have contributed to the understanding of the site, Ben M. Ford proposed that rather than targeting the exact impact areas of the piles, an area of 400 sq m should be reserved for deeper excavation. This approach was endorsed by the city's archaeologist. During the excavation process the chosen area was split into a number of smaller areas whose positions and shapes were designed to answer some of the specific academic research questions set out in the site's Written Scheme of Investigation (WSI). A benefit from such an approach was that the cost to the developer was the same, but the understanding and potential research value was greatly increased, while some stratified deposits remain preserved.

By taking this approach, Ben M. Ford was able, for example, to gain information on the pre-friary activity in areas where this evidence was relatively un-truncated by later activity, the different phases and levels of construction between the friary buildings, and the Greyfriars' diet (from a number of waste pits associated with the friary kitchens). The conventional approach of only examining direct impact areas would not have contributed comparable information. However, such an approach does raise the philosophical and ethical questions as to whether in similar, future circumstances the potential academic gain outweighs the potential loss of threatened evidence and the possibility of preserving intact stratification for future examination.

The OAHS only occasionally becomes involved in the planning process where archaeology is involved, but when it does so it is advised by one of its sub-committees, The Oxford City and County Archaeological Forum (OCCAF). The OAHS established OCCAF in the post *PPG16* era when it became clear that OA's focus was no longer on the city and county, but there remained a need for local archaeologists to monitor what was happening. OCCAF receives six-monthly reports prepared by both the city and county archaeologists and discusses both academic and practical issues. On rare occasions OCCAF has recommended that the society comments on specific planning applications. One such occasion was the second Westgate planning application. OAHS, as one of the consultees, duly commented on the *Environmental Impact Statement (Archaeology)*, based on a draft provided by OCCAF. Occasionally OCCAF has also advised on other potentially controversial issues such as the collecting policies of the Ashmolean and Oxfordshire County Museum Service where sites in the city are concerned.

The major organisational changes in Oxford's archaeology over the last fifty years have been mirrored by the steady growth in the number of professional archaeologists involved. In 1967 OAEC's director was appointed on an initial five-year contract. He was assisted at first by some paid temporary supervisors and labourers, but the bulk of the excavations were dug by volunteers who were sometimes given a subsistence allowance (Fig. 2.7). Most volunteers were either at school or university and were therefore usually only available during their holidays. Some of the paid supervisors, such as Grenville Smyth, Hugo Blake, Ken Sheridan, and Jeremy Haslam, came from outside Oxford, but most lived and studied locally. Of particular significance was the strategic partnership formed between OAEC and the OUAS. Building on an already established tradition the undergraduate society was the obvious source of project directors, supervisors and volunteers. A succession of OUAS members accordingly played a key role in the city's

Fig. 2.7 Nos. 31–34 Church Street, St. Ebbe's, 1968. Volunteer diggers and Oxford University Archaeological Society site supervisors. John Huntriss, standing with site notebook and ranging rods (left) and Christopher Young, sitting cross-legged with site notebook (right). Photograph: Graham Baker.

archaeology, including such names as Tim Allen, Jerome Bertram, John Blair, David Ganz, John Huntriss, Philip Kenrick, George Lambrick (who started excavating in Oxford during his 'gap year'), Elizabeth Leedham-Green, Nicholas Palmer, Mark Robinson, Ian Sanders, Duncan Wilson, and Christopher Young, most of whom went onto have distinguished archaeological or academic careers. Local students from schools such as Cheney School, Magdalen College School, Oxford High School and St Edward's also took part, some taking a weekday afternoon off school when they might otherwise have been playing games or training in the cadet corps. Names in this group included Roger Ainslie, Mark Horton, and Julian Munby. During the summers of 1968 and 1969 volunteers from outside Oxford were recruited via the Council for British Archaeology's *Calendar of Excavations*. In 1968 accommodation and meals were provided in Christ Church Cathedral Choir School and the following year in the Balliol Boys' Club in St Ebbe's. However, the demands of the bulk excavation of the Westgate basement in the winter of 1969 and most subsequent city rescue sites required full time staff working all the year round and not just at weekends and holidays. The process of professionalization gathered pace in the 1970s and was universal by the time *PPG16* was introduced. Today for instance OA employs well over 300 staff across its three UK offices at Oxford, Lancaster, and Cambridge.

The professionalization of archaeology has meant that the opportunities for both undergraduates and school children to take part in Oxford's archaeology have dwindled. The OUAS became a pale shadow of its former self. This process accelerated after 1992 when the university introduced a bachelor's degree in anthropology and archaeology and the new School of Archaeology became the focal point for undergraduate and post-graduate studies. From 2017 it looked as if OUAS might disappear altogether, but, at the time of writing, moves are afoot to resurrect it.

Fig. 2.8 Tim Allen (top left) and fellow members of the Oxford University Archaeological Society examining the relationship of the south wall of the choir of the Greyfriars church and the cloisters, 1976. Photograph: Oxford Archaeology.

The OAHS's own Ashmole Club did not survive into the 1970s. The Club's role was taken over by the national Young Archaeologists Club (YAC). YAC was present in the county for a while based on OCCM and later on the Pitt Rivers Museum, but no meetings have been held since 2015. However, between 2011 and 2015 there was a brief opportunity for Oxford's school children to be actively involved in the city's archaeology thanks to the East Oxford Archaeology and History Project (Archaeox).[16] This project was directed by David Griffiths and Jane Harrison of the Oxford University Department for Continuing Education. The project was funded by the Heritage Lottery Fund and the John Fell Fund and endorsed eloquently by the then East Oxford MP, Andrew Smith. The project was a model of community involvement and was a worthy recipient of Oxford University's first ever Public Engagement with Research Award in 2016. There currently appear to be no opportunities for young people to take a direct part in the city's archaeology, thus ending a tradition which goes back to the boyhood of T.E. Lawrence.

Part of the explanation for the demise of the involvement of amateurs in archaeology is due to the increasing burdens of insurance, coupled with the application of health and safety legislation. It became increasingly difficult to insure young volunteers whose parents were expected to waive any claims that might be made against the excavation organisers. Sites were also positively dangerous. For instance, a dumper truck driven by the director of OAEC fell 12 feet into the Nos. 31–34 Church Street site, narrowly missing one of the supervisors, Christopher Young, who mercifully jumped clear. Photographs of the recording of the Westgate basement during the bulk excavation and piling show W.A. Pantin, resplendent in Carnaby Street flared trousers, and the director of OAEC, with no sign of hard hats, goggles, fluorescent

[16] D. Griffiths and J. Harrison (eds.), *The Archaeology of East Oxford: Archeox, the Story of a Community* (2020).

Fig. 2.9 Members of Oxford Archaeology's professional team of excavators, wearing full personal protective equipment, working on the Greyfriars cloisters in 2016. Photograph: Oxford Archaeology.

vests, or protective boots. Another photograph shows Tim Allen and fellow members of the OUAS in 1976 wearing shorts and little else excavating the north-east corner of the Greyfriars cloister (Fig. 2.8). Shoring of trenches was minimal and excavators tended to put their faith on the concept of the 45-degree angle of repose. Today, excavators are required to wear full personal protective clothing, including helmets, boots, gloves, goggles and ear defenders, and trenches are appropriately stepped or shored (Fig. 2.9).

There have been similar major changes in excavation tools, techniques and recording. The Nos. 31–34 Church Street site, the first Westgate site, was cleared by a JCB with a hydraulic back actor. This type of equipment was just coming into use at the time, but much of the Greyfriars church was exposed by a drag-line excavator which was hardly a precision tool. A JCB or similar, preferably with 360 degrees action, and a toothless bucket is now the machine of choice for site clearing and this type of machine was used throughout the second Westgate excavations. The army surplus galvanised fire buckets which were used in the first St Ebbe's excavations were happily exchanged for lighter black plastic ones. It sometimes seems that the WHS drop forge pointing trowel is the only tool that has been employed by archaeologists throughout the period of this review.

In the 1960s the classic method of excavation made popular by Sir Mortimer Wheeler (1890–1976), particularly on Roman sites, employed a grid of trenches with recording by layers and features and their positions fixed in imperial measurements by triangulation from the corners of the trenches. At first sight the published plan of the Clarendon Hotel excavations appears to show such a system in use, but in truth that layout was dictated by the foundation design of the Woolworths building (now remodelled as the Clarendon Centre).[17] However, in the

[17] E.M. Jope and W.A. Pantin, 'The Clarendon Hotel, Oxford', *Oxoniensia*, 23 (1958), fig. 1, p. 5.

Fig. 2.10 Nos. 31–34 Church Street, St. Ebbe's under excavation in 1968: the 1 metre site grid is marked out with unprotected steel spikes. James Spriggs is sighting the dumpy level; Roger Ainslie is holding the staff; and Tom Hassall is holding the site notebook. Photograph: Graham Baker.

1960s Martin Biddle at Winchester was pioneering the technique of open area excavation with recording by metric coordination. This was a clearly a more appropriate way of examining Oxford's late Anglo-Saxon and medieval structures than trench excavation would have been. These methods were accordingly adopted at Nos. 31–34 Church Street (Fig. 2.10).[18] The 1m site grid was physically set out on the site with metal spikes. The tops of the spikes were unprotected, but luckily no-one did themselves an injury. Wire mesh 1 m by 1 m frames were used for planning. The system worked well in the relatively horizontal stratification at the highest levels of the site, but because lower down the site was honeycombed with deep intercutting pits John Huntriss had to modify the system. However, where conditions allow open area excavation has been ubiquitous in Oxford ever since.

In 1967 all site records were paper based. Features and layers were recorded in hard backed green notebooks; plans and sections were still drawn on paper, but, again techniques employed at Winchester were adopted at Oxford. Plastic film (permatrace) quickly replaced paper. Note books with their features and layers were eventually abandoned to give way to context sheets. The subsequent analysis of the relationships between contexts was achieved by John Huntriss by means of hand drawn flow diagrams which in the form of the Harris-Winchester matrix were to become universal.[19]

By the time of the second Westgate excavations the application of information technology had transformed recording. Context sheets, although still compiled by hand, were digitised. Matrices were used on site rather than being created retrospectively. They too were hand drawn,

18 'St Ebbe's, Part I', pp. 83–7.
19 E.C. Harris, *Principles of Archaeological Stratigraphy* (1979).

Fig. 2.11 Oxford Archaeology's site surveyors on the Greyfriars cloisters site in 2016 using a total station theodolite (left) and a global positioning system (right). Photograph: Oxford Archaeology.

but were then put into Excel which meant that they could be manipulated flexibly and shared with specialists. The site grid was virtual and depended on GPS which offered great flexibility in that local grids could be established where required and then be linked together using GIS or CAD (Fig. 2.11). Site plans were still hand drawn, but then translated into GIS output by the site surveyor which was then transferred to OA's graphics department.

On-site photography on the first Westgate excavations depended at first either on volunteers, such as Graham Baker and Philip Kenrick, or on professional photographers such David Carpenter, who owned the appropriate high-quality equipment which OAEC itself could not at first afford. Black and white record photography was in medium 2¼ inch square format. Thirty-five-millimetre film was reserved at first for colour slides which were just seen as 'snaps', but of course were essential for popular talks and lectures. Some slides were still being mounted between glass. Today photographic prints and transparencies are still used and these media have not been entirely supplanted by digital photography, because of issues surrounding the long-term curation of digital archives.

In the early excavations high-level photographs of the excavations could only be taken from vantage points on neighbouring buildings, precarious scaffolding towers or, *in extremis*, from the terrifying perspective of the city fire brigade's 120-foot escape turntable ladder (Fig. 2.12). Most famously Brian Durham's ingenious device for hauling aloft a camera up to the ceiling of All Saints Church produced superb vertical photographs of that spectacular excavation.[20] This mechanism was affectionately known as Skylab after the US photographic satellite then circling the globe. Today digitised low-level photography can be taken with a pole cam, and higher level photography by a drone (Fig. 2.13). The recent photography of the Westgate shows how the resultant photographs can be 'rubber sheeted' and geo referenced and three-dimensional models generated through a combination of standard archaeological survey techniques combined with photogrammetry.

[20] Dodd, *Oxford*, plate 5.6, p. 223.

Fig. 2.12 Composite view of the first Westgate excavations in 1969 from the top of Oxford City Fire Brigade's 120-foot high turntable ladder, looking north. The Greyfriars church (bottom) with the standing stone wall (right) marking the line of the north wall of the choir. The former Church Street (centre) crosses the site westwards from St Ebbe's church with excavated domestic tenements (centre left). Photograph: Ken Sheridan; reformatted by Oxford Archaeology.

Fig. 2.13 Drone view of the second Westgate excavations showing the Greyfriars claustral area looking north, with Trill Mill Stream (bottom), precinct wall (left), kitchen (top centre), and cloister (top right). The excavators are grouped in the centre. Photograph: Oxford Archaeology.

Excavation directors have always been anxious to engage Oxonians with the excavations while they are in progress. In the case of OAEC and OAC this was necessary to fulfil their commitment to public benefit enshrined in their charitable constitutions. During the first Westgate excavations this aspiration was relatively straightforward to achieve since the public could easily view the excavations of medieval tenements and the Greyfriars church on both sides of Church Street. Simple typed notices explained what was happening and what had been discovered and passers-by could lean over the fence and actually talk to the excavators themselves. Later, at All Saints Church the western gallery provided a ready-made viewing platform. A different approach was tried during the excavations at the Churchill Hospital which were not so publicly accessible. Here a specific public open day was arranged. Open days have since become the usual way of allowing the public to visit sites where there is the appropriate access. This was the approach taken by the East Oxford Project, and during the second Westgate excavations where elaborate arrangements had to be put in place to comply with health and safety requirements. The second Westgate open days were supplemented by a number of 'pop up' museums, talks and local media coverage, all of which contributed to OA receiving their British Archaeological Award in 2016.

However, open days are not feasible at most urban rescue excavation sites. To compensate for the fact that sites are now largely hidden behind solid hoardings with only the occasional peep hole, information boards with high-quality graphics are now a normal requirement of planning permission. Information on the second Westgate excavations was also made available on line. In the case of the recent excavations of the Swan Brewery and medieval tenement remains at the site of the new Marriot Hotel site opposite St George's Tower, David Radford has pioneered an innovative approach by putting a short video on Facebook and YouTube in which he describes the investigations. This video has received thousands of views.

The way in which the conduct of excavations has changed from amateur to professional and the impact of information technology has been mirrored in the post-excavation process. In 1967 there was a tacit assumption that the director of OAEC would be responsible for the greater part of the final St Ebbe's reports, including drawing the published plans and compiling the pottery reports. In the first interim report this was the approach taken.[21] However, as the scale of the operation became clearer it was obvious that there would be a need for a dedicated post-excavation team if the results were ever to be published in full.

The first obvious sign of this change from amateur to professional was in the case of drawings for publication. A drawing office was established by Hugh Richmond. A house style was designed for published plans and sections which employed the classic Times New Roman font. This style meant that a number of different draughtspeople could be employed, but the drawings looked generically similar. Subsequently, after the creation of OAU, the font was changed to the more 'modern' font of Helvetica. Initially, pottery drawing was also entrusted to volunteers. Philip Kenrick, then a first-year undergraduate at Balliol College, compiled a photocopied manual entitled *The Drawing of Pottery* to guide OAEC volunteer draughts people. One such was Eleanor Beard, a trained architect, who was later to become a valued draughtsperson on the paid staff.

Pottery analysis went through the same process of professionalization. The first interim report on the St Ebbe's excavations included a discussion of a single group of pottery from one pit written by OAEC's director. Soon, as the scale of the quantity of material from the excavations became clearer, it was necessary to appoint full-time ceramic specialists. Regina Haldon and then Maureen Mellor took on the formidable task of analysing the late Anglo-Saxon and medieval pottery from Oxford, building on the earlier research of Martyn Jope and Rupert Bruce-Mitford. The excavation of well stratified sites such as Nos. 79–80 St Aldate's and The Hamel were crucial to refining the ceramic typology and Maureen Mellor's studies

21 T.G. Hassall, 'Excavations at Oxford, 1968, First Interim Report', *Oxoniensia*, 34 (1969), pp. 5–20.

were subsequently extended throughout the region.[22] For earlier and later periods Christopher Young, later assisted by Sarah Green, established a fabric series for the Oxford Roman pottery industry;[23] while Josephine de Goris initiated the analysis of the pottery for the post-medieval period which was then taken forward to publication by Maureen Mellor and Gwynne Oakley.[24]

After the pottery the biggest post-excavation challenge which faced the first Westgate excavation in terms of sheer bulk of excavated material was the animal bone. As with all the other elements of the post-excavation process the initial approach was to rely on unpaid help, in this case from a retired professor of zoology, Brian Marples, whose work was then carried forward by Bob Wilson on the fulltime staff of OA.[25]

There were many other specialisms involved and many of the experts were not on OA's payroll. For example, the report on the ironwork was compiled by Ian Goodall and formed part of his doctoral thesis.[26] Environmental archaeology was another area of post-excavation research which was in its infancy in the late 1960s, but which was to become increasingly significant in the latter work of OA. Andrew Brown and Mark Robinson of the OUAS were to blaze a trail in this area. Mark Robinson has recently applied the skills that he originally learnt excavating the cesspits of St Ebbe's to Pompeii and Herculaneum.[27]

In the final St Ebbe's publications there were reports from seventeen specialists, only a few of whom had been employed full-time. By the time of the second Westgate excavations the impacts of post-excavation professionalization and of information technology was fully felt. Information on every feature on the site was linked to a database containing all the information about it, including its description, a photograph, dating evidence and finds. Final CAD and GIS drawings may look less elegant than their 1970s counterparts, but the information itself is clear. The finds themselves are to be analysed by an in-house team of specialists. At the time of the original tender by OA for the Westgate work seventeen internal specialists were named. Amongst these specialists Liz Stafford, the geoarchaeologist should perhaps be singled out. This discipline was hardly considered in the first Westgate excavations, but was to become increasingly significant following Mark Robinson's and George Lambrick's work on the Thames floodplain.[28]

Dating methods have also developed. When the original Westgate was dug dating usually depended on dating by association with the pottery, occasionally assisted by coins dated by Michael Metcalfe and Nicholas Mayhew of the Heberden Coin Room at the Ashmolean. However, thanks to the proximity of the Atomic Energy Establishment at Harwell and the Oxford University Research Laboratory it was sometimes possible to obtain radiocarbon and thermoluminescence dates. Such techniques are now commonplace, particularly radiocarbon dating which has been used to good effect on a number of sites. This technique is carried out for OA by the Scottish Universities Environmental Research Centre on a commercial basis. In the second Westgate excavations dendrochronology conducted by Dan Miles has also played a part, although the results on the many reused waterlogged timbers which were used for underpinning the Greyfriars precinct wall bordering the Trill Mill Stream have been more limited than had been anticipated.

The study of human skeletal remains has seen some of the most profound changes to approach both scientifically and philosophically. The first St Ebbe's excavations produced two groups of skeletal material from the sites of the Greyfriars and Blackfriars churches which were later supplemented with those from All Saints. This material was the subject of research

22 Mellor, 'Synthesis'.

23 C. Young, 'The Roman Pottery Industry of the Oxford Region', *British Archaeological Reports*, 43 (1977).

24 M. Mellor and G. Oakley, 'A Summary of the Key Assemblages…', in 'St Ebbe's, Part II', pp. 181–219.

25 B. Wilson et al., 'Medieval Animal Bones and Marine Shells', in 'St Ebbe's, Part I', pp. 258–68.

26 I.H. Goodall, 'Iron Objects', in 'St Ebbe's, Part I', pp. 227–31.

27 A.P. Brown and M.A. Robinson, 'A Summary of Plant and Insect Remains from the Post-Medieval Pits at Church Street (Site A)', in 'St Ebbe's, Part II', pp. 268–9.

28 M. Robinson and G. Lambrick, 'Holocene Alluviation and Hydrology in the Upper Thames Basin', *Nature* (1984), pp. 308, 809–14.

by Eric Edwards and Mary Harman who were able to identify age, sex, mortality profiles, and pathology.[29] It was always assumed that the material would be retained in perpetuity so that as scientific techniques developed further analysis could be undertaken. New techniques have indeed been developed, such as the stable isotope analysis conducted by the Oxford University Laboratory for Archaeology and the History of Art which can trace a skeleton's geographical origins.

Attitudes towards human remains were a little more cavalier in the 1970s than today. This fact is exemplified by the 'Femur of the Unknown Freeman'. During the bulk excavation of the Westgate site this human bone was smuggled out by one of the contractors. The bone then became the trophy presented to the highest scoring freeman in the annual Aunt Sally match between the freemen of Oxford and the Sheriff of Oxford's team which takes place after the sheriff's annual inspection of Port Meadow. In contrast to this disrespectful approach, the present Dominicans in Oxford have asked to have their medieval brethren returned to them for reburial. This request has echoes of the recent return of human remains to Maori and Australian Aboriginal communities from the Pitt Rivers Museum and the Oxford University Museum of Natural History. Such an approach, while respectful of the feelings of indigenous communities, could prevent scientific re-examination of this material.

When OAEC was established, the committee's focus was on the below ground impact of the city's redevelopment; the need to record the city's buildings was hardly taken into consideration, even though Oxford had a distinguished record in this area of research. The OAHS had established its sub-committee for old houses in 1912 which continues to this day as the society's listed buildings sub-committee. W.A. Pantin, an active member of OAEC, virtually invented the discipline of 'above ground archaeology' when he recorded the buildings in Broad Street which were demolished to make way for the New Bodleian, now the Weston, Library.[30] Pantin later recorded the Clarendon Hotel before its demolition. Peter Spokes, OAEC's chairman, had also recorded buildings photographically for the National Buildings Record during the Second World War. He had then surveyed Oxford's first list of buildings of special architectural or historical interest when this protection regime was established in the Town and Country Planning Acts of 1944 and 1947.

The continuing need to protect or to record systematically the city's historic buildings was brought into sharp focus in May 1972 at No. 126 High Street.[31] Planning permission had been granted for the demolition and rebuilding of the rear of this building, but no thought had been given to its recording. An eighteen-year-old Julian Munby passed by the site and saw fragments of sixteenth-century timbers being removed. He was already steeped in Oxford's archaeology and history. He had left Magdalen College School, before going to read archaeology at the Institute of Archaeology, London. In the interim he was working as a volunteer at the Bodleian Library for W.O. Hassall, the assistant keeper of Western Manuscripts (such volunteers were nicknamed 'Hassall's Vassals') studying the library's Oxford topographical drawings collection. Munby undertook a survey of the surviving structures of No. 126 High Street and also studied its documentary history. This incident inspired David Sturdy to publish a satirical pamphlet entitled *How to Pull a Town Down* in which he lampooned 'Aldermen, Chairman of Planning Committees and other tireless workers' – the latter included urban archaeologists.[32] Munby himself was to go on to record many other buildings in Oxford and elsewhere and became head of buildings archaeology at OA in 1990.

Fortuitously, the week that No. 126 High Street hit the headlines John Ashdown took up his appointment as the city council's first conservation officer. Thanks to John Ashdown and his successors, the city's historic building stock has been much better protected and there have

[29] E. Edwards and M. Harman, 'Human Remains from Greyfriars (Site B)', in 'St Ebbe's, Part I', pp. 255–68.
[30] W.A. Pantin, 'The Recently Demolished Houses in Broad Street, Oxford', *Oxoniensia*, 2 (1937), pp. 171–200.
[31] J. Munby, '126 High Street, The Archaeology of an Oxford House', *Oxoniensia*, 40 (1975), pp. 254–308.
[32] D. Sturdy, *How to Pull a Town Down* (1972).

been some notable building recording projects by John Blair, David Clark with the Oxfordshire Buildings Record, Roland Harris, and Julian Munby.

It is still possible for an historic building to slip through the net. A case in point is No. 29A Castle Street. This is a building in obvious need of repair. It was spot listed in 1977 thanks to the Oxford Civic Society. In the list description the building is described as 'probably C18 but may be late C17'. In reality John Blair discovered in 1976 that the original structure is actually late medieval. It must therefore be one of the two buildings shown on Agas' map of 1578 which had been built on the castle moat south of the main castle bridge. This building is thus the only building ever to have stood on the site and it is worthy of restoration.

For most of the earlier years under review both above and below ground Oxford archaeological projects concentrated on the city's medieval and immediate post-medieval past with comparatively little attention paid to more recent times. For instance, when the suburb of St Ebbe's was demolished and the first Westgate excavations took place there was neither the money or the inclination to record nineteenth- and twentieth-century buildings or recover contemporary artefacts, although some groups of material were retrieved from nineteenth-century cesspits. Potentially the most significant discovery was the footings of the former 1893 City Technical School. This building was to become the City of Oxford School of Technology, Art, and Commerce in 1934, with John Henry Brookes as its principal. The site was therefore in the first home of what was later to become Oxford Brookes University.[33]

In recent years Oxford's nineteenth-century history and industrial archaeology has begun to receive the recognition it deserves. OA was able to properly excavate two small areas of nineteenth-century St Ebbe's tenements, as part of the second Westgate excavations. The most significant project, however, has been the recording of the former 1851 L&NWR, subsequently LMS, Rewley Road railway station.[34] The structure of the building followed the design of the Great Exhibition's Crystal Palace. English Heritage's decision to allow the dismantling and re-erection of this listed innovative structure at the Buckinghamshire Railway Centre is still the cause of unease amongst Oxford archaeologists. At least the associated scheduled swing bridge over the Sheepwash Channel has remained in situ with its original mechanism designed by Robert Stephenson still in working order. The Oxford Preservation Trust hopes to conserve this special structure. The wider context of these structures and the physical remains of Oxford's industrial past have been the subject of publications by Liz Woolley.[35]

Oxford's excavators have a good publication record. All the major medieval sites excavated by the OEC, OAEC and OA and others except the most recent have been published, usually in *Oxoniensia*. The reports' authors have been assisted by a distinguished succession of editors including David Hinton, John Blair, and Stephen Mileson. The size of many of the reports has often given the editors a cause of concern since they have quite properly recognised that members of the OAHS expect to see a balance of archaeological, architectural and historical articles. The issue of archaeological publication nationally was addressed by the Department of the Environment in 1975 in its working party report *Principles of Publication in Rescue Archaeology*, popularly known as the 'Frere Report', after its Chairman, Professor Sheppard Frere and again in 1982 by the Council for British Archaeology and the Department for the Environment in their Working Party report *The Publication of Archaeological Excavations*, popularly known as the 'Cunliffe Report', after its Chairman, Professor Barry Cunliffe. The most visible result of the policy recommendations of these reports was that, between 1980 and 1989, most of the larger archaeological reports published in *Oxoniensia* made extensive use of microfiche. In part this approach was assisted by the developing technology which allowed the production of 'camera ready copy'. For this purpose, in 1980 OA was loaned a 'golf ball'

33 B. Brown, *John Henry Brookes, The Man who Inspired a University* (2015).

34 J. Munby et al., *From Studium to Station, Rewley Abbey and Rewley Road Station, Oxford*, Oxford Archaeology Occasional Paper, 16 (2007), pp. 64–105.

35 Notably, L. Woolley, 'Industrial Architecture in Oxford, 1870–1914', *Oxoniensia*, 75 (2010), pp. 67–96.

typewriter for producing copy by St Cross College with whom the unit had a special relationship between 1973 and 1985. In 1982 OA acquired its first computer (a RML 380Z) which was capable of word processing. The use of microfiche was never popular, since microfiche readers were mainly found in libraries and the fiche themselves were not easy to use. During the programme to make *Oxoniensia* fully available on line these original fiches have been digitised and as a result are now readily available to researchers.

With the abandonment of microfiche some excavation reports have been considered too long for *Oxoniensia*, since the OAHS traditionally did not wish to publish volumes devoted solely to a group of sites or a single large site. As a result, some Oxford excavations have been published in monographs, particularly by OA. For instance, OA's publication *Oxford Before the University* contains a series of key site reports, while the reports on Beaumont Palace, the Whitefriars, Rewley Abbey, and the Rewley Road Station were published as single reports.[36] Some smaller sites have only been 'published' as 'grey literature'. Such sites are sometimes difficult to access, but many are held by the Archaeology Data Service and in the case of OA these reports can be found in its online Digital Library. In this context the present volume represents a new departure for the OAHS.

Apart from the publication of final reports, annual notes and news on excavations in the city and county have also witnessed changing approaches. It was the usual practice for *Oxoniensia* to contain such regular summaries, but from 1971 the decision was taken not to publish in the journal but instead to publish in *Council British Archaeology Group 9 Newsletter*, retitled *South Midlands Archaeology* in 1983. The earlier decision was subsequently reversed and from 2010 summaries of work carried out in the city and county have again been published in *Oxoniensia*, alongside (from 2011) notes on finds reported to the Portable Antiquities Scheme.

In addition to academic publication, there have been a number of popular publications on Oxford's archaeology following the examples first set in 1899 by the OAHS with its booklet *Buried Oxford Unearthed*.[37] In 1972, to mark OAEC's first five years, a booklet was published entitled *Oxford: The City Beneath Your Feet*; this was followed up fifteen years later by *Oxford, The Buried City*, edited by Jean Cook and Ian Burrow and superbly designed by John Rhodes.[38] In 2004 David Sturdy published *Historic Oxford*, which contains useful information both on the author's ideas on the early topography of Oxford and on his own excavations in the 1960s, but this work is less helpful on subsequent research.[39] Finally in 2018 David Radford published *The Archaeology of Oxford in 20 Digs*.[40] This is a profusely illustrated book which includes a helpful commentary on nearly all of the key excavations of the last fifty years.

Already by the 1960s it was clear that there was going to be a problem of storage of the vast bulk of pottery, bone and 'small finds' from excavations. The Ashmolean basement, which now houses the museum café and shop, was already bursting at the seams. Further collections were held by individual excavators. For the Ashmolean the situation was at least temporarily solved by a decision to opt out of local collecting following the formation of OCCM. For the latter museum the impending avalanche of material was held at bay in the interim, because OAEC and subsequently OAU retained the material for study at least until up to the time of publication. For OAEC the temporary solution was to store the material in various condemned buildings in St Ebbe's, but these were both short lived and unsuited to the task. Other solutions had to be found. One such was the World War Two American military hospital at Wheatley where OCC made available one of the large, abandoned huts. Another more bizarre solution was to be found in the shape of the city's former nuclear bunker at No. 270 Woodstock Road to which the Council and senior staff were to retreat in the event of a Soviet nuclear attack. It was never

36 Dodd, *Oxford*, pp. 65–391; Poore, *Beaumont*; Munby et al., *From Studium to Station*, pp. 64–105.

37 F.H. Penny, *Buried Oxford Unearthed* (1899).

38 T.G. Hassall, *Oxford, The City Beneath Your Feet* (1972); T. Hassall, *Oxford, The Buried City* (1987).

39 D. Sturdy, *Historic Oxford* (2004).

40 D. Radford, *The Archaeology of Oxford in 20 Digs* (2018).

made clear how all the racking and artefacts were to be removed in the event of a four-minute warning being given.

OA now keeps its own security copies of archive off-site and has its own dedicated finds warehouse. Finds from Oxford destined for final curation by the County are housed in the magnificent Oxfordshire County Council Museum Resource Centre at Standlake. This store has had to be extended and in future finds may have to be stored in the former USAAF base at Upper Heyford.

Some finds have required conservation. The first St Ebbe's excavations and their successors presented OCCM with a major challenge because of the sheer quantity of material coming out of the ground. The conservation laboratory at Woodstock was managed first by Brian Arthur and then by Ahmed Shistawi. Conservation students who were studying conservation at the Institute of Archaeology in London worked on material during their vacations. It was Ahmed Shishtawi who organised one of the largest conservation projects – the lifting of two Roman pottery kilns from the Churchill Hospital excavations. Today, in the case of OA, finds are stabilised in-house and are then transferred to an external conservation laboratory before they are deposited in the appropriate receiving museum.

As long ago as 1858 the OAHS had been calling for a permanent museum of Oxford's antiquities. In 1939 W.A. Pantin repeated the call for 'a special museum to house the relics and illustrate the history of Oxford and its neighbourhood'.[41] He went on to write 'I suppose Oxford is one of the few great historic cities of the civilized world which lacks a museum specifically devoted to its own local antiquities'. Subsequently the Ashmolean devoted some gallery space to fulfilling this function. David Hinton, when he was an assistant keeper, redisplayed the medieval gallery and gave prominence to finds from Oxford. Some Oxford finds also feature in the Museum's more recent redisplays. However, the Ashmolean's purpose is not to tell the story of Oxford through its antiquities. This fact was recognised by Thomas Sharp in his 1948 book *Oxford Replanned*. Accordingly, he made provision for a city and county museum on the site of the prison within the castle site.[42] When the OCCM was finally established Jean Cook enthusiastically took up the idea of a dedicated city museum. Richard Foster who succeeded Jean in 1970 was equally supportive.

In order to explore what might be achieved the material excavated from the Churchill Hospital and the first St Ebbe's excavations was brought together in a large temporary exhibition entitled 'How Old is Oxford?' which was held in Old County Hall in 1972. Three years later, thanks to the work of Crispin Paine, Jon Hall and Martyn Heighton, the Museum of Oxford was opened in the former Library and basement of the Town Hall. The museum told the history of Oxford and its university through its archaeology, architecture and environment. Archaeology took centre stage in the first galleries: one of the pottery kilns excavated at the Churchill Hospital formed a focal point, while there were excellent displays of Anglo-Saxon and medieval material from the St Ebbe's excavations. The museum was exactly what the OAHS envisaged.

The Museum of Oxford was a credit to the city, but budget cuts in the late 1990s nearly caused its closure which was again contemplated in 2009. It looked for a while as if the museum might go the same way as The Oxford Story which had presented the history of the university in Broad Street for nearly twenty years before it closed in 2007. A financial compromise was finally reached. The main museum was closed and a much-reduced gallery was opened in 2012 in the town hall with Heritage Lottery Fund (HLF) support, staffed by volunteers and backed by a friends group. A few archaeological objects were displayed or could be viewed in a chest of drawers.

A successful HLF bid for £3.2 million in 2018 means that a new museum, entitled Oxford's Hidden Histories, will now re open in 2020 in the original space. Unfortunately, the museum

41 W.A. Pantin, 'The Oxford Architectural and Historical Society, 1839–1939', *Oxoniensia*, 4 (1939), p. 190.

42 T. Sharp, *Oxford Replanned* (1948), pp. 138, 141–2.

Fig. 2.14 David Radford, Oxford City Council archaeologist (left), and Brian Durham, his predecessor (right), dismantling the reconstructed Roman pottery kiln from the Churchill Hospital in the former Museum of Oxford in the basement of the Town Hall in January 2019. Photograph: Tom Hassall.

project team did not engage with local archaeologists about the new displays. Archaeology has inevitably been downgraded. Symbolically the Churchill pottery kiln was dismantled in 2019 as part of the museum refurbishment (Figs. 2.6 and 2.14). Following an outcry, OA has now been appointed to advise the museum project on its archaeological content. However, it seems probable that the actual new museum will hardly fulfil the OAHS's original objectives and the Society may once again have to campaign for an appropriate museum of Oxford's archaeology, possibly at the castle as originally envisaged. In the meantime, it would appear that the only museum dedicated to the display of Oxford's archaeology is to be found in the parallel universe imagined by the author Philip Pullman in *Lyra's Oxford*.[43]

Oxford has a long-standing tradition of marking sites of archaeological interest by plaques and other signs. For instance, following the OAHS excavations of the city wall in the Clarendon Quadrangle in 1899 the diagonal course taken by the wall at this point was marked out in the paving. In 1917 Friar Roger Bacon and the site of the Greyfriars was commemorated by a plaque in King's Terrace, St Ebbe's. This plaque was relocated when the first Westgate shopping centre was built close to where the surviving pier bases from the Greyfriars church were preserved in the basement of Sainsbury's supermarket. The line of the north wall of the choir of the church and the line of the city wall were also preserved in the southern wall alignments of the new shopping centre. Another plaque was erected in Littlegate Street to commemorate the

43 P. Pullman, *Lyra's Oxford*, 3rd edn (2017), pp. 32–3.

eponymous gate and its excavation in 1971. When the Westgate was rebuilt the deliberate siting of its original south wall on the line of the city wall was abandoned. However, one of the new pile caps was rotated to preserve the last fragment of un-mortared stone wall footings which probably belong to the late Anglo-Saxon defences. The Roger Bacon plaque itself was relocated in Greyfriars Place and a well-preserved fragment of medieval tile pavement from the Greyfriars cloister walk has been wall mounted in the South Arcade (see Fig. 2.2). OA have also designed a number of information panels which have been attached to or positioned adjacent to the new building at strategic positions. The panels are supplemented by an archaeological trail pamphlet which guides visitors around the site.

There are other examples of archaeology being incorporated into new buildings, for instance at the castle and the Saïd Business School. At the castle, a section of the late Anglo-Saxon defences has been displayed accompanied by a series of information plaques which were set up around the site when the 'Oxford Castle Quarter' and the heritage attraction Oxford Unlocked, now Oxford Castle and Prison, were established in 2005. At the Saïd Business School the north-east corner of the new building was built at an angle to the north wall of the new building to reflect the alignment of the excavated cloisters of Rewley Abbey. According to Brian Durham, this misalignment with the main building also conforms to the Muslim principle that no building should be perfect in honour of the religion of its benefactor. An information board about the abbey was placed in Rewley Road, while a metal plaque in the pavement outside the School commemorates the later Rewley Road L&NWR station and its removal to the Buckinghamshire Railway Centre.

Oxford's archaeology has also found its way into various arts initiatives. When the St Ebbe's demolitions were taking place for the first Westgate Centre Elizabeth Mitchell, an artist from Woodstock used to visit the site to pick up found objects which she turned into collages which commemorated the vanishing suburb. The first excavations themselves inspired the Oxford poet Maida Stanier to write an evocative poem about the lost lives which were being discovered.[44] By the time of the second Westgate excavations art was a requirement of the planning permission. The developers funded an ambitious programme of temporary and permanent works of art curated by Modus Operandi. Rachel Barbaresi undertook a project entitled 'urbansuburban' which used the history of St Ebbe's as an inspiration for an art project entitled 'Future Knowledge' which was displayed at Modern Art Oxford in 2017. Rachel Barbaresi also designed a temporary walk through sculpture based on the 'golf ball' control room of the original multi-storey car park. Within the new Westgate Centre David Batchelor was commissioned to design a permanent free-standing sculpture based on the armillary sphere held by Roger Bacon in the sculpture of him by Henry Hope Pinker in the court of Oxford University Museum of Natural History. In Greyfriars Place William Cobbing sculpted a series of enigmatic quarried stone boulder forms, each inlaid with a ceramic tile depicting plants from medieval woodcuts and inspired by the environmental remains which were found in Ben M. Ford's excavations of the friary.

One final aspect of Oxford's archaeology over the last fifty years is worth emphasizing and that is the relationships that have developed between those who have taken part. Oxford has been fortunate in the calibre of all those involved, some of whose names have been mentioned in the preceding paragraphs. Their involvement has not only created a network of academic colleagues, but also friendships and indeed in some cases marriages. Their eighteenth-century predecessors, according to the Oxford antiquary Thomas Hearne, used to meet in a tavern in Hythe Bridge Street, named Antiquity Hall after its clientele.[45] A satirical engraving of this tavern appears in Joseph Skelton's *Oxonia Antiqua Restaurata*, published in 1823. For a while Antiquity Hall's spiritual successor was The Nag's Head pub which stood opposite the former OA offices. For a period, this pub was even renamed Antiquity Hall in honour of its illustrious predecessor,

44 M. Stanier, 'St Ebbe's', *The New Oxford Spy*, 2nd edn (1969), pp. 79–80.
45 T.W. Squires, *In West Oxford* (1928), p. 158.

Fig. 2.15 Members of 'The Wednesday Lunch' meeting to discuss Oxford's heritage at The Golden Cross (Pizza Express), Christmas 2018. Photograph: Tom Hassall.

although it is now called The Oxford Retreat. Oxford's modern antiquaries no longer meet at that pub, but since 1983 an informal group of them has met every Wednesday lunchtime. According to the group's founder, John Ashdown, the idea was for the members to exchange information on the heritage of Oxford and to discuss responses to planning applications affecting the city's historic environment. The group, now known as The Wednesday Lunch, first met in The Jolly Farmers in Paradise Street, but has gathered in various venues since. Currently the group meet at The Red Lion in Gloucester Street and enjoy a regular pre-Christmas lunch in the Pizza Express restaurant in the 1535 wing of The Golden Cross with its surviving wall paintings (Fig. 2.15). The Wednesday Lunch provides a regular and congenial opportunity for old colleagues and friends to discuss all aspects of Oxford's heritage very much in the spirit of their eighteenth-century predecessors.

In conclusion, James Bond and Trevor Rowley in their account of archaeology in Oxfordshire between 1965 and 1980 described that time as the 'Golden Age'.[46] If that epithet is correct, then the period from 1980 up to the introduction of PPG 16 must have been the Silver Age. We are now presumably in the Bronze Age. It remains to be seen how research into the city's archaeology will develop in the forthcoming ages of Heroes and of Iron. Given the development of archaeology in the city over the last fifty years, the message to Her Majesty, were she to return to Oxford to visit another excavation, is that, while the city's archaeologists clearly face challenges, there is every reason to be optimistic.

[46] J. Bond and T. Rowley, 'The "Golden Age" of Oxfordshire Archaeology, 1965–1980', *Oxoniensia*, 80 (2015), pp. 75–96.

ACKNOWLEDGEMENTS

I wish to thank all my friends and colleagues with whom I have discussed the archaeology of Oxford over the last fifty years. I am particularly grateful to John Ashdown, Brian Durham, Ben M. Ford, John Huntriss, Julian Munby, David Radford, and John Steane who have helped me compile this review and corrected many of my misrememberings and provided useful suggestions and comments.

3.
Overview of the Excavation Results

ANNE DODD

SUMMARY

This chapter summarises the key findings of the excavations presented in the volume, paying particular attention to the way in which they add to knowledge gained from previous archaeological work in the city. The discussion is arranged chronologically, working from the Anglo-Saxon period to the seventeenth-century. In conclusion, it is suggested that the volume of archaeological data from Oxford is now sufficient to form a basis for creating an independent picture of everyday life in the city over the longue durée which can augment and, where necessary, contest well-known historical narratives.

Since its foundation in 1973, Oxford Archaeology (OA) has had a close involvement with the archaeology of its home city. The legacy of this work includes more than fifty articles in *Oxoniensia*, the journal of the OAHS, and the synthetic monograph *Oxford Before the University*.[1] In addition, a large number of the client reports generated by OA's fieldwork in the city have now been made freely available online via the OA Library. This volume presents the results of eleven recent OA excavations within the historic walled city and in the extramural areas just to its north.[2] The eleven sites are a characteristic cross-section of archaeological evidence from the city, and each in its own way offers new data and insights that touch on many different periods of the city's past. A notable feature of these sites is the wealth of information that can be recovered from humble back yard pits, where we find so much of the essential evidence for diet, economy, culture and the environment. This overview highlights the key discoveries and how they contribute to the evolving interpretations discussed by David Radford (above), and it emphasises in particular the importance of seeing the archaeological evidence in its historical context: Oxford's status as the first English university city ensures that the archaeological evidence is strongly supported by a rich documentary and cartographic record which sheds essential light on topography and property history. Indeed, the quantity of documentation is rivalled by only a handful of comparable towns, including Winchester and Cambridge.

While the work presented in this volume specifically relates to the historic city centre, the northern suburb and the north-eastern Civil War defences, it is complemented by other major OA excavations elsewhere in Oxford. The castle has been discussed in detail in a recent monograph,[3] while the Greyfriars site and the southern suburb will be examined in the forthcoming publication of the Westgate and Brewer Street excavations, and the eastern suburb in the publication of the Magdalen College Library site. In the discussion below, sites named in italics are those reported on in this volume (Fig. 3.1).

1 Dodd, *Oxford*.
2 Two of the sites, at Mansfield College and the Tinbergen Building, are combined in a single report.
3 Munby, *Oxford Castle*.

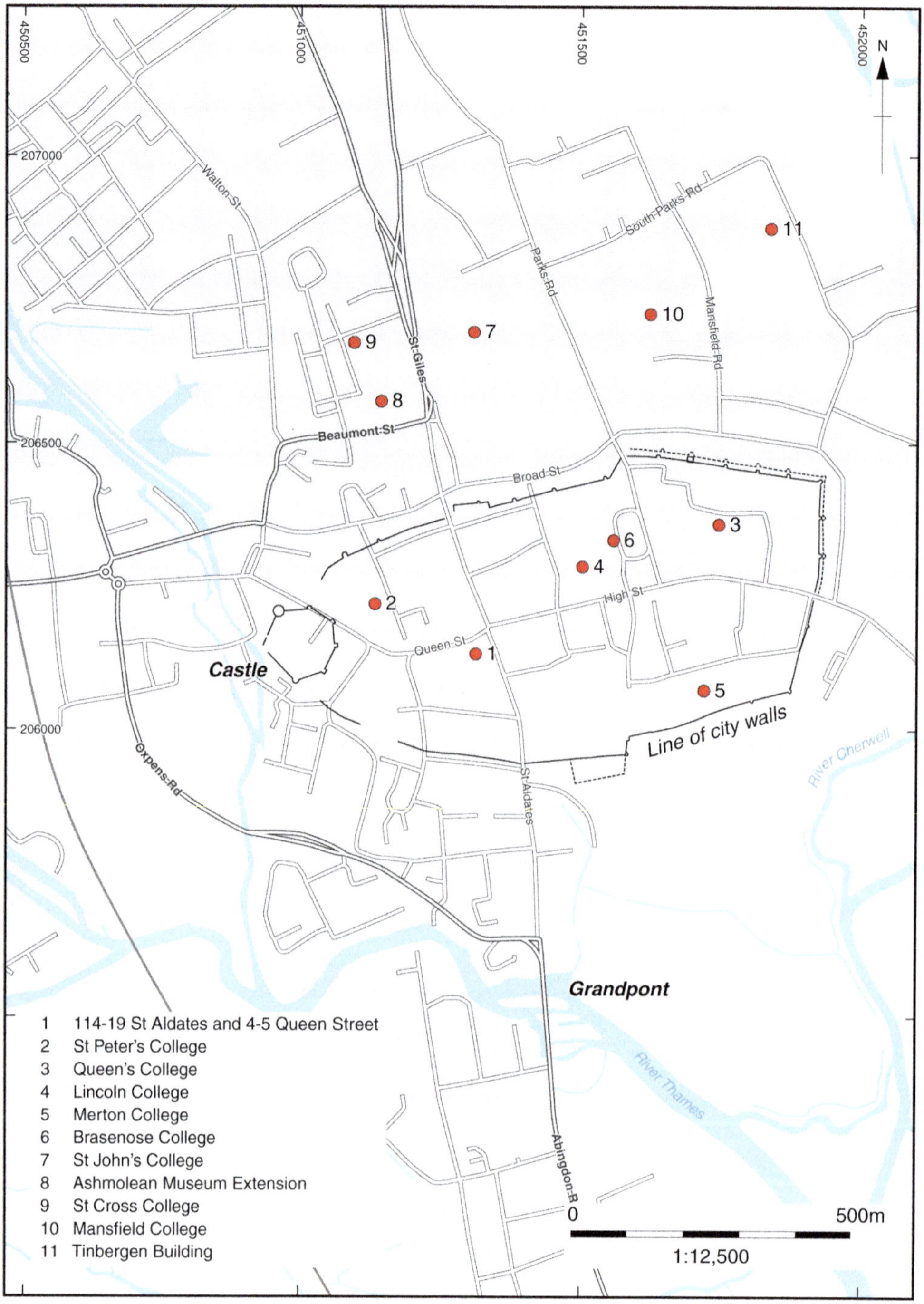

Fig. 3.1 Site locations.

BEFORE THE ANGLO-SAXON *BURH*

The ditch investigated at *St John's College* continues to be the subject of much speculation. It was suggested by David Sturdy that it may have originated as a defensive line of the eleventh century, later to become the boundary between St Mary Magdalen and St Giles parishes, and the boundary of the Northgate hundred.[4] No evidence to support an eleventh-century origin was found in the recent excavations; an OSL date obtained from the basal fill of the ditch is broadly late Neolithic. While the purpose of the ditch is unclear, it may have formed part of the complex of late-Neolithic to early Bronze-Age ritual monuments that extended across the north Oxford gravel ridge. The ditch was recut in the twelfth century and again in the late-medieval period (or around the time of the foundation of the college); if it was indeed late-Neolithic in origin it had clearly (like the henge just to the north) remained a visible feature in the landscape for a very long time.

David Radford draws attention to the many questions that remain about occupation at Oxford before the creation of the *burh* (or defensive enclosure) during the Viking wars of the late ninth and early tenth centuries. The excavation at *Mansfield College* has located further features belonging to the Roman settlement known to have existed in the Science Area. This latest excavation seems to have been located towards the edge of the settlement area and probably lay in fields and paddocks that formed part of the wider enclosed landscape to the north. First established in the later first century AD, the settlement appears to have shrunk or been relocated in the middle Roman period, but was re-established on a different alignment during the fourth century. No evidence for early Anglo-Saxon occupation was seen here, and only a few sherds of characteristic early to middle Anglo-Saxon handmade pottery have come from the sites reported in this volume. Evidence for early Anglo-Saxon occupation thus remains very slight. The single largest assemblage of early pottery from the city centre remains the twenty-three sherds found at Oxford Castle.[5] By comparison, around 1,000 sherds have now been recovered at Littlemore, where the buildings of an Anglo-Saxon settlement are being discovered over a substantial area.[6] The contrast points to the conclusion that there was no significant early Anglo-Saxon presence in the area of the medieval town, and the discovery of a sunken-featured building during excavations at the former Radcliffe Infirmary,[7] together with evidence for early Anglo-Saxon burials in north Oxford, suggests that settlement remains are likely to lie further north and west.

However, a significant discovery of middle Anglo-Saxon Ipswich Ware was made at the *Ashmolean Museum Extension* site. Ipswich Ware is datable to the period *c.*725–850; common in East Anglia and middle Anglo-Saxon London, it is generally rare elsewhere and taken as an indicator of places integrated into contemporary trading networks, places that may often have been associated with high-status occupation. The only other Ipswich Ware so far known in Oxford has come from the immediately adjacent excavations at the Sackler Library.[8] A contemporary coin of Offa, king of Mercia, was reputedly found in 1841 in the foundations of the Martyrs' Memorial nearby, but otherwise finds of this period are sparse, and the local context of the Ipswich Ware remains unclear. These finds raise the intriguing possibility that Henry I's palace of Beaumont, built here in the early 1130s, reoccupied an earlier high-status site. David Radford notes that some of the best evidence of middle Anglo-Saxon occupation at Oxford has generally come from the south end of St Aldate's where there is evidence for a crossing of the Thames formed by alluvial islands in the floodplain. Timbers interpreted as piles from a bridge here were

4 D. Sturdy, *Historic Oxford* (2004), p. 28, fig. 11. The parish of St Giles included a main street of the same name (St Giles', or St Giles' Street).

5 Munby, *Oxford Castle*.

6 J. Moore, 'Excavations at Oxford Science Park, Littlemore, Oxford', *Oxoniensia*, 66 (2001), pp. 189–97; A. Mudd et al., 'Anglo-Saxon and Prehistoric Remains at Oxford Academy, Littlemore, Oxford: Excavations in 2009', *Oxoniensia*, 78 (2013), pp. 184–5.

7 'Radcliffe Infirmary Site, Oxford. Post-Excavation Assessment Report', unpublished MOLA report (2011).

8 Poore, *Beaumont*, pp. 43–4.

radiocarbon dated to the middle to late Anglo-Saxon period;[9] immediately to the east is the reputed site of St Frideswide's minster, where numerous burials radiocarbon dated to the middle and middle to late Anglo-Saxon period have been found.[10] No Ipswich Ware has been found in this area, but late eighth- and early ninth-century imported continental wheel-thrown grey and black wares were identified at Nos. 79–80 St Aldate's, in layers of flood-deposited silts that also contained flax seeds, shoes, and domestic debris.[11] An agricultural landscape at the west end of the later town is implied by results from the excavations at Oxford Castle, which found evidence for grazed pasture and middle to late Anglo-Saxon cereal grain; substantial quantities of wheat and barley grains were found here in association with a possible granary or storage building.[12]

The excavations reported in this volume add to the growing evidence for early occupation at sites close to the central crossroads of Oxford, at Carfax. Part of a possible cellar pit was seen in a test pit excavation at Nos. 6–7 High Street; evidence for a possible wooden floor was recorded, along with a posthole, and a barley grain from the layer above the floor gave a late eighth- to late ninth-century radiocarbon date.[13] Similar radiocarbon dates have been obtained from charred grains sampled from postholes within early structures at *Nos. 114–119 St Aldate's/ Nos. 4–5 Queen Street*, reported in this volume. Previously, postholes and a hearth predating the earliest street surface of the late Anglo-Saxon town were found nearby at No. 8 Queen Street.[14] At the two sigma confidence level these date ranges span the period from the seventh to the tenth centuries, but at one sigma there is a notable clustering in the late eighth to late ninth century range. These dates are consistent with features roughly contemporary with the foundation and earliest years of the *burh*, but could perhaps also be indicating an undocumented expansion of activity at Oxford during the preceding century.

THE ANGLO-SAXON *BURH*

As David Radford notes, the date and form of the *burh* founded at Oxford in the late ninth or early tenth century is still a topic of debate. It has been suggested that the original fortification (the 'primary *burh*') was smaller than the full extent of the walled late Anglo-Saxon and medieval town; the length of the defences of Oxford implied by the Burghal Hidage, and the form of the contemporary fortifications at Wallingford and Cricklade, created an expectation that Oxford too would originally have been laid out as a rectilinear fort arguably inspired by Roman military planning. This theory sees the more irregular west and east ends of the medieval town as later additions, possibly datable to the second Viking wars of the early eleventh century when Oxford itself was under attack.[15] A sequence of discoveries during the 1970s and 80s led to the suggestion of a primary western defensive line parallel to New Inn Hall Street and St Ebbe's Street, later superseded by the theory that the primary western defences had run roughly along the line of the later castle defences, which had destroyed them, and would have extended at least as far

[9] GU-5333, cal AD 660–900 at 95 per cent confidence, cal AD 680–810 at 68 per cent confidence: Dodd, *Oxford*, p. 420, table A2.2.

[10] Dates from Christ Church and St Aldate's Church are reported in Dodd, *Oxford*, pp. 421–4, table A2.3, fig. A2.2; for Corpus Christi, an elderly adult (probably female) burial just beyond the later boundary of St Frideswide's Priory was dated to the period cal AD 776–880 at 95 per cent confidence (NZA34675), in R. Bashford et al., 'Medieval and Post-Medieval Remains from Excavations on the Site of the New Auditorium, Corpus Christi College, Oxford, 2008', *Oxoniensia*, 79 (2014), p. 201.

[11] R. Haldon, 'Late Saxon and Medieval Pottery', in B. Durham, 'Archaeological Investigations in St Aldate's, Oxford', *Oxoniensia*, 42 (1977), pp. 111–132; M. Mellor, 'The Saxon and Medieval Ceramic Finds from the Town Sites', in Dodd, *Oxford*, table 6.8.

[12] Munby, *Oxford Castle*.

[13] '6–7 High St., Oxford. Archaeological Excavation Report', unpublished OA report (2014), https://library.thehumanjourney.net/998/.

[14] For No. 8 Queen Street: Dodd, *Oxford*, p. 248.

[15] The theory of the primary *burh* and its extensions is discussed in detail in ibid. pp. 21–6, fig. 2.4.

south-westwards as the west end of Church Street (or approximately to the position of the town's medieval West Gate).[16] The recent investigations in *Chavasse Quad, St Peter's College* have found variations in the depth of gravel that suggest the possibility of a deep negative feature such as a defensive ditch on the original proposed line, parallel to New Inn Hall Street, although this could also be explained as natural undulations in the gravel surface. Nevertheless, the discovery that the late Anglo-Saxon rampart extended as far west as St George's Tower suggests that the defensive perimeter was taken right down to the western edge of the gravel terrace from an early point, if not from the outset,[17] which would mean that the erratic gravel levels at St Peter's College have another explanation.

On the east side of the town the excavations at *Queen's College Provost's Garden* have produced evidence for a primary layout of the area on a completely different axis from that prevailing in the late Anglo-Saxon town to the west. The excavated area was crossed by a north-west to south-east aligned metalled road or trackway that may have been in use before, or by, the earliest years of the *burh* at Oxford, lasting until the twelfth century. If projected beyond the limits of the excavated area the road would appear to run from the site of medieval Smith Gate in the north-west to the medieval East Gate in the south-east, and thus towards the Cherwell crossing. Theories based on projected lines have often turned out to be wrong, and so must be treated with great caution, but the fact that the adjacent late Anglo-Saxon building plot follows the alignment of the road suggests that this was indeed more than a localised surface, and does represent an early organising principle in this area. This plot, to the north-east of the road, was marked out by fences and later by ditches; two timber-lined pits were constructed, roughly 2.5 m square in plan and less than 1 m deep, suggesting that they were not true cellars, but possibly supported above-ground structures. A radiocarbon date of the late ninth to late tenth century was obtained from animal bone in one of the posthole fills, but the pottery from the pits indicates that they were backfilled in a relatively short space of time during the third quarter of the eleventh century, and the site seems to have been used only for quarrying and rubbish disposal from the start of the twelfth century. The backfills of the pits contained smithing debris, furnace lining, a sherd from a Stamford ware crucible, and two hones or whetstones, as well as small quantities of smelting slag; the origin of the smelting slag is not clear. A small number of neonatal sheep/goat bones suggest that animals were grazing nearby, which might imply a considerable amount of open space. Although a regular grid of streets is a feature of late Anglo-Saxon towns, it was by no means universal, and at both Wallingford and Cricklade it has been suggested that areas within the defences were purposely left as open ground to support a range of functions such as mustering of troops, accommodation of large numbers of people in times of trouble, and the grazing of animals.[18]

Whether the site lay inside or outside the *burh* defences remains unclear; interim results from recent excavations of the eastern rampart at New College have been considered above by David Radford but remain inconclusive. Two previous excavations within Queen's College have revealed a small number of late Anglo-Saxon pits, but these shed no further light on the early topography of the area. A key, if poorly understood, influence in the eastern part of the early town was the wealthy church of St Peter-in-the-East; its extensive parish implies it was originally a church of minster status. Small-scale excavations carried out inside the church by David Sturdy have never been fully reported, but would seem to suggest that a timber (or timber and stone) church was constructed over an area of earlier domestic buildings, and was itself replaced by a stone church in the late tenth or early eleventh century. St Peter's is close

16 The developing theories relating to the western defences of the proposed primary *burh* are set out most clearly in the concluding discussion of the St Ebbe's excavations: Hassall, 'St Ebbe's, Part I', pp. 268–72.

17 Munby, *Oxford Castle*.

18 N. Christie and O. Creighton, with M. Edgeworth and H. Hamerow, *Transforming Townscapes: From Burh to Borough: The Archaeology of Wallingford, AD 800–1400*, Society for Medieval Archaeology Monograph, 35 (2013) pp. 394–6; J. Haslam, 'Excavations at Cricklade, Wiltshire, 1975', *Internet Archaeology*, 14 (2003).

to the west-south-west to east-north-east alignment of the churches along the central axis of Oxford, though the southwards curve of the High Street disguises this relationship; this could reflect origins in the early stages of planning of the *burh*.[19] For the present, little more can be said with any certainty about the way in which this important church may have influenced the surrounding area; an interesting comparison (though beyond the scope of the present discussion) would be the evidence for activity in the vicinity of the contemporary minster of St Frideswide, on the southern edge of the town.

The excavations reported here from *Nos. 114–119 St Aldate's/Nos. 4–5 Queen Street* were centrally located in the late Anglo-Saxon town, next to the main crossroads where there may have been an early market place lost to encroachment in the early eleventh century. It is possible, as discussed above, that the first structures seen here date from before, or around, the foundation of the *burh*; Structure 1.1, probably to the rear of Queen Street, was represented by a series of floor layers with an associated posthole and scorching from a nearby hearth, very similar to the earliest evidence recovered from the neighbouring site at No. 8 Queen Street. Structure 1.2 (probably to the rear of St Aldate's) appears to have been a wattle-lined pit, too shallow to have been a true cellar. It has been suggested that small pits of this kind might have served as storage space within larger structures.[20] The very early associated radiocarbon dates raise the question whether tents or temporary buildings from the early years of the *burh* might have had such pits dug inside them to store food and valuables. It would certainly seem too far back from the street frontage to have been a market stall. Structure 1.2 was replaced by a larger sunken structure, 2.1, which was much deeper (at 1.84 m) and had good evidence for a substantial timber lining; as such, it appears entirely typical of the kind of cellared buildings that appear on Oxford urban plots in the later tenth and early eleventh century.

The overwhelming dominance of Oxford shelly ware pottery in the backfill of cellar 2.1, and the virtual absence of St Neots-type ware, is of considerable interest. Shelly ware is generally considered the earliest of the late Anglo-Saxon and Saxo-Norman ceramic traditions in the town, and may have come into use by the late eighth century. It is usually the principal pottery type on tenth-century sites in St Aldate's, although elsewhere in the town St Neots-type ware becomes more common as the tenth century progresses. By the early eleventh century St Neots-type ware has become the dominant pottery type across the town, and shelly ware seems to be replaced by Cotswold-type ware. The pottery assemblage in this cellar backfill is unusual, and has a distinctly 'St Aldate's' aspect; the presence of the imported Beauvais-ware wine jug adds to this impression, with imported pottery consistently present in late Anglo-Saxon assemblages from St Aldate's. It is unclear whether the explanation is chronological here, whether it reflects cultural preferences, or whether it represents differences between this part of the town and others. Whatever the reason, this assemblage will make an important contribution to this ongoing debate.[21] A lead pan weight from a Phase 1 dump layer is an interesting find from a site close to a potential market place.

THE MEDIEVAL TOWN

According to Domesday Book, there was a very large amount of waste (that is, vacant/derelict property that yielded no tax) in Oxford in the years after the Norman Conquest, and it seems unlikely that this could all be accounted for by houses lost to the building of the castle. A number of previously excavated sites share a pattern of abandonment of late Anglo-Saxon buildings in

[19] D.A.M. Sturdy, 'Excavations in St Peter-in-the-East Church, Oxford', *Oxoniensia*, 37 (1972), p. 245; Sturdy, *Historic Oxford*, p. 52; personal communication from Ben M. Ford.

[20] D. Sturdy and J. Munby, 'Early Domestic Sites in Oxford: Excavations in Cornmarket and Queen Street, 1959–62', *Oxoniensia*, 50 (1985), p. 93.

[21] For discussions of pottery distributions in late Anglo-Saxon Oxford: M. Mellor, 'Discussion: The Pottery Used at the Town Sites', in Dodd, *Oxford*, pp. 340–5, and P. Blinkhorn, 'The Pottery from the Castle Excavations', in Munby, *Oxford Castle*, pp. 229–44.

the later eleventh century, followed by up to a century in which the land appears to lie empty, used only for quarrying and rubbish disposal.[22] This seems also to have happened at the *Queen's College Provost's Garden* site, where pottery dates the backfilling of the two sunken structures to the late eleventh century, and in the twelfth century the only activity at the site appears to have been the digging of quarry and rubbish pits. After the Conquest, the important church of St Peter-in-the-East passed to the d'Oilly family, the castellans of Oxford, whose patronage is likely to have been directed principally at their own foundations of St George's in Oxford Castle, and subsequently Osney abbey. Might this be reflected in the decline of the area around St Peter's in these years? By contrast, at *Nos. 114–119 St Aldate's/Nos. 4–5 Queen Street* the street frontages in this prime site continued to be occupied, and there is a clear signature here for metal working, also previously identified at the adjacent site at Nos. 7–8 Queen Street, where a post-Conquest workshop with iron slag, lead waste and copper alloy waste was found.[23] At the new site, fragments of lead waste occurred in the backfill of cellar 2.1, and fragments from some seven crucibles were recovered from late eleventh- and twelfth-century pits. Paul Blinkhorn comments that the crucibles show no sign of heating to very high temperatures, and so had either not been used, or had been used at temperatures below 900°C; the metals that would melt at or below this temperature are lead, tin, and (marginally) silver, and a link with the lead waste in the cellar backfill seems a possibility.

It is clear that Oxford developed rapidly and substantially during the twelfth century, with much of its prosperity founded on wool and cloth. The sites reported in the present volume add to the growing body of archaeological data. The earliest evidence is for flax processing by the river south of the town, from perhaps as early as the ninth century.[24] Here, flax was retted in wattle-lined gullies; a small number of flax seeds found at the *Queen's College Provost's Garden* site may attest to flax processing in pits waterproofed with clay. Spindle whorls are often found in small numbers at sites throughout the town, and would have been used for women's domestic spinning of yarn, though this may increasingly have been piece work for payment rather than for the domestic production of cloth. A potsherd reworked as a spindle whorl was found in a pit at *Queen's College Provost's Garden*. Two fine ceramic spindle whorls and a bone example came from the site at *Nos. 114–119 St Aldate's/Nos. 4–5 Queen Street*; three stone spindle whorls (two of chalk) and a further ceramic example were recovered in the earlier excavations at Nos. 7–8 Queen Street.[25] Dyeing of yarn is attested at Oxford by finds of potsherds stained on the inside with a red/purple pigment which has been identified as madder. This is thought to result from the boiling of madder root in domestic cooking pots, in which hanks of yarn could be dyed. A possible madder-stained sherd was identified at *Queen's College Provost's Garden*. The largest assemblage in Oxford comes from excavations at Brewer Street, where forty-five stained sherds were recovered; the site at Brewer Street has substantial evidence for tanks, drains and pits probably associated with dyeing and fulling during the twelfth century. Together with the previously published excavations at Church Street and St Ebbe's, this represents some of the best evidence known from Oxford to date for the location of this key industry.[26] Numerous sherds of pottery sooted on the outside and containing an internal purple residue were found in excavations at the Clarendon Centre, and interpreted as evidence of small-scale preparation of dyes for colouring textiles or possibly the manufacture of coloured inks. This was not positively identified as madder, and it is suggested that large quantities of elderberry seeds from thirteenth- and fourteenth-century contexts could have been used for making wine, ink or dye, as they are unlikely to have been palatable as food.[27]

22 Discussed in Dodd, *Oxford*, pp. 51–3.
23 Ibid. p. 258.
24 Ibid. p. 34.
25 Ibid. pp. 322–4.
26 S. Teague and B.M. Ford, 'Excavations in Oxford's South Suburb at Brewer St., Littlegate St., and Rose Place', unpublished OA excavation report (2019); Hassall, 'St Ebbe's, Part I'.
27 A. Douglas, *Medieval Craft-Working in Oxford: Excavations at 15–17 Clarendon Centre* (2015).

Another sign of Oxford's increased importance is the presence of a Jewish community by 1141.[28] The excavation at *Nos. 114–119 St Aldate's/Nos. 4–5 Queen Street* has recovered some remarkable evidence for Jewish occupation at what may have been part of the documented property of Jacob's Hall. The assemblage of food remains and pottery vessels from a late twelfth- or early thirteenth-century latrine and associated levelling layers over earlier occupation is entirely consistent with Jewish dietary requirements, unlike earlier and later groups at the site. There is a complete absence of pork, pork fats, shellfish and eel, and a high proportion of domesticated bird bones (with goose more common even than cattle), and meat and dairy fats had not been mixed. While this cannot prove that the remains are from a Jewish household they are certainly consistent with a Jewish presence, and provide a rare and encouraging insight into a distinctive community of medieval Oxford.

This period also sees the expansion of Oxford's medieval suburbs, although the evidence suggests that this did not happen on any scale until the late twelfth century. The recutting of the early ditch seen at *St John's College* is perhaps the first sign of suburban change from the sites reported in the present volume. Whatever its earlier function, in the medieval period the ditch marked the boundary between the parishes of St Giles to the north and St Mary Magdalen to the south. The church of St Giles was founded by *c.*1132/3 and soon became a parish church, with the tithes of Walton. The formal marking of the new parish boundary would seem likely to have occurred around this time. A radiocarbon date from animal bone in the recut ditch would suggest that it was filling up during the mid to late twelfth century.

The excavations reported here at the *Ashmolean Museum Extension* are important for the evidence they have revealed about the origins, development and character of Oxford's northern suburb. This is the fourth site in the area to have been excavated in recent times, providing an insight into the development of seven adjacent medieval tenements.[29] These long, thin suburban plots lay between the boundary of Beaumont Palace to the west, and the main northern approach to the town on the east. On the basis of pottery and tile dating, the suburb seems to have developed from the late twelfth century. Oxford's western suburb of St Thomas's, and southern suburb of Grandpont, have similar evidence suggesting development (or re-development) at this time.[30] Building must have begun almost immediately and the evidence suggests that the houses here were substantial. Stone architectural fragments from a backfilled well included a piece from a window tympanum with round arches that is of twelfth-century date. The same backfill contained part of a stone window frame with the remains of corroded metal bars, from a lower status building, but one that suggests the inhabitants had cause to be concerned for security. It is likely that these came from stone houses on or near the site itself, and they add to the growing evidence for the construction of these buildings in late twelfth-century Oxford. Similar evidence from earlier excavations at No. 4A Merton Street shows a stone house quite clearly in the possession of a middle ranking burgess family, and such houses may therefore have been much more widespread than was previously thought.[31] Buildings at the *Ashmolean Museum Extension* site were roofed with stone or clay tiles, with at least one chimney, and there may have been floors of plain green- and brown-glazed tiles. By the middle of the thirteenth century the property was occupied by Master Ralph of Swalcliffe, one of the earliest medical doctors known by name at the university; he was actively buying out his neighbours to expand his holding here at the time, and he (or his landlords, the Templars) may have been responsible

[28] Roth, *Jews*, pp. 2–3.

[29] Previously, P. Andrews and L. Mepham, 'Medieval and Post-Medieval Extramural Settlement on the Site of the Ashmolean Museum Forecourt, Beaumont Street, Oxford', *Oxoniensia*, 62 (1997), pp. 179–223; Poore, *Beaumont*; A. Norton and G. Cockin, 'Excavations at the Classics Centre, 65–67 St Giles', Oxford', *Oxoniensia*, 73 (2008), pp. 161–94.

[30] For excavations in St Thomas's, J. Munby, 'The Archaeology and History of Oxford's West Suburb', *Oxoniensia*, 71 (2006), pp. 343–6, and for St Aldate's, Dodd, *Oxford*, p. 56.

[31] Poore, 'No. 4A Merton St.', pp. 229–34.

for an updating project that consigned the twelfth-century windows to a decommissioned well. The same well contained a notable quantity of ceramic lamps, suggesting the need for reading and working beyond the hours of daylight.

A number of the sites reported in this volume reflect the development of the medieval university. The university took root gradually within the existing urban framework. Students and masters lodged in town houses; some lodged with townspeople until the practice was banned in 1410, but increasingly over the course of the thirteenth and fourteenth centuries many students took lodgings in academic halls.[32] These were essentially town houses leased by licensed masters, accommodating between ten and thirty students, who were usually studying the same subject and might often be from the same part of the country; two to four students would share a room, and they ate in a common hall. Over time an increasing amount of teaching and both pastoral and academic supervision was provided within halls, in addition to board and lodging. Some 123 academic halls of the early fourteenth century are mapped and listed by Catto, although numbers had halved by the middle of the fifteenth century as a result of amalgamations and declining student numbers. A typical academic hall was a building with a narrow frontage to the street and a long two-storey range behind, in which the communal dining hall was located. It is estimated that by the fifteenth century some three quarters of students lived in academic halls. The remainder were either student monks and friars who lived and were taught within the houses of their orders,[33] or students at the relatively small colleges. The colleges were foundations with endowments of money and income from land that enabled them to provide free board and lodging for poor students, but often with an intake restricted to the kin of the founder, particular areas of the country or (in the case of New College) the feeder school of the founder at Winchester.[34]

The substantial numbers of pottery lamps found during the excavations at the *Ashmolean Museum Extension* and the adjacent site at the Classics Centre may be a sign that students were lodging at the properties by the mid to late thirteenth century, although there are no records of any academic halls here, most being located within the eastern part of the town. The only academic hall known for certain on St Giles' Street was the fourteenth century Batayl Hall, the north edge of which was seen in the Ashmolean Forecourt investigations, immediately south of the *Ashmolean Museum Extension* site. Here, a substantial stone structure, probably a hall and service wing behind a street frontage building, was constructed sometime after the middle of the fourteenth century.[35] Batayl Hall ceased to be an academic hall after the fourteenth century and there are no halls on St Giles' Street in Rous's 1444 list. Another academic hall has been investigated at *St Peter's College*, which occupies the site of the former New Inn Hall, one of Oxford's longest-lasting academic halls. This may have originated as the mid fourteenth-century Trillock's Inn, a substantial private house held by the brothers John and Thomas Trillek, respectively bishop of Hereford and bishop of Rochester. Briefly used as a temporary base by Cistercian monks in the early fifteenth century, it occurs in John Rous's 1444 list of academic halls, and continued to function until its closure in 1887. The medieval buildings were demolished in 1832 and 1900, but appear on early maps of Oxford, and were engraved by Loggan, although

32 This brief account is based on L.W.B. Brockliss, *The University of Oxford: A History* (2016). For more detail: J.I. Catto (ed.), *The History of the University of Oxford Volume I: The Early Oxford Schools* (1984); J.I. Catto and T.A.R. Evans (eds.), *The History of the University of Oxford, Volume II: Late Medieval Oxford* (1992).

33 Gloucester, Durham and Canterbury colleges for Benedictines, Rewley abbey and St Bernard's for Cistercians, Frewin Hall for Augustinian canons; for the friars, the Dominican, Franciscan, Carmelite and Austin friaries.

34 The first such colleges, University College, Balliol and Merton, date from the mid to late thirteenth century; the fourteenth century saw the foundation of Exeter, Oriel, Queen's and New College, followed in the fifteenth century by Lincoln, Magdalen and All Souls. Brasenose and Corpus Christi were founded in the early sixteenth century, with Cardinal Wolsey's incomplete Cardinal College (later Christ Church) the last of the pre-Reformation foundations. St John's was founded on the site of the former Cistercian St Bernard's College, following the Dissolution, and Jesus College on the site of a former academic hall in 1571.

35 Andrews and Mepham, 'Ashmolean Museum Forecourt'.

he only shows the street frontage range. The excavations reported in this volume located what appears to have been part of a western range of a quadrangle, perhaps the location of the kitchen and buttery, suggesting a much more developed plan than the earlier modified town houses, and this may represent part of the documented fifteenth-century rebuildings of the hall.

Limited excavations are reported here from *Merton College*, the earliest of the colleges represented in the present volume. The excavations found pits of twelfth- to early thirteenth-century date that predated the foundation of the college; the pits were sealed by later medieval garden soils and a yard surface. The excavations at *Queen's College Provost's Garden* similarly span the period before and after the foundation of the college, in an area of former tenements absorbed into the college by 1355 and thereafter kept as a garden and used for gravel quarrying and rubbish disposal. There is no clear horizon in the pit assemblages marking the change of ownership, but some of the large quarry pits might have been dug for gravel in connection with college building. A number of interesting items appear among the finds from fourteenth to fifteenth-century pits, and provide insights into early college life. Perhaps the most notable is a curved fragment of bone with an internal groove, which is likely to be a fragment from the rim of a bone spectacle frame. Spectacles were invented in Italy at the end of the thirteenth century and were being imported into England from Italy in large numbers during the fifteenth century. Also probably from the early college are a group of jetons that would have been used for mechanical calculation on a counting table or abacus, perhaps for drawing up the college's accounts of income and expenditure. A similar group was discovered in excavations at No. 4A Merton Street, and Merton College bursar's accounts for 1291 make several references to purchases for making a *mensa computer*, or counting table.[36] Increasing numbers of objects associated with books and writing also appear in late medieval and early post-medieval contexts. A small writing lead was found in the fill of a late twelfth-century ditch at the *Ashmolean Museum Extension*, but most examples come from late-medieval and early post-medieval university contexts, including styli of lead and bone from *Queen's College Provost's Garden*; groups of styli were also found at No. 4A Merton Street and in excavations at Christ Church. These sites also produced numerous pieces from book mounts and from book clasps, which were attached to leather straps on book covers and hooked over a catch plate on the opposite cover to keep books closed.[37]

Fragments from a number of ceramic 'double-shell' lamps were found at *Queen's College Provost's Garden*, and are considered to be a characteristic component of Oxford ceramic assemblages from sites associated with the university (see above). They largely date from the mid thirteenth to late fourteenth centuries, and are thought to have been used to provide individual lights for close work such as study. Sizeable groups have also been found at No. 4A Merton Street, contemporary with the college, and recently at Jesus College, where they are likely to derive from Great White Hall, a medieval academic hall for lawyers that was incorporated into the new foundation of Jesus College in 1571.[38] However, lamps are also found at sites with no known medieval academic connections, for example at the *Ashmolean Museum Extension* site discussed above, at Brewer Street, where some sixteen examples have been identified, and at Magdalen College, where ninety-six sherds representing some forty to sixty lamps were recovered, clearly predating the establishment of the college. It thus seems likely that lamps were used in a domestic and craft-work setting, as well as by students; while they may signal the presence of student lodgings they do not necessarily do so.[39]

[36] Poore, 'No. 4A Merton St'.

[37] A.M. Chadwick et al. (eds.), *'Quadrangles where Wisdom Honours Herself': Archaeological Investigations at Tom Quad, Peckwater Quad and Blue Boar Quad, Christ Church, Oxford*, JMHS Monograph, 1 (2012).

[38] A. Simmonds et al., 'A Further Sequence of Medieval and Early Post-Medieval Deposits at Jesus College', *Oxoniensia*, forthcoming.

[39] For discussions of lamps in Oxford: P. Blinkhorn, 'Pottery', in Poore, 'No. 4A Merton St', pp. 258–78, and J. Cotter, 'Pottery', in 'Rainwater Harvesting Tank, Jesus College, Oxford: Archaeological Watching Brief report', unpublished OA report (2019), appendix A.1.

The excavations at *Lincoln College* reported in this volume have provided an unusually well-dated insight into activity in the heart of the fourteenth-century town. Over a period stretching from the fourteenth century into the early fifteenth century a small building here was used for metalworking and baking. The earliest evidence may be from a phase of bronze or pewter working. Subsequently the building seems to have been used as a kitchen, with significant amounts of charred cultivated legumes; the presence of large parts of dripping pan, usually associated with mass catering, suggests the possibility that this could have been cooking for sale rather than domestic consumption. The hearth was replaced by a circular bread oven, which contained large amounts of charred bread/rivet wheat grains, but exceptionally also a significant quantity of unprocessed rye. This is most unusual in Oxford and is discussed further below. There was a further change of use in the excavated building in the late fourteenth century, when it reverted to use as a metal workshop. A substantial number of crucibles were found here in association with hearths and hearth debris; analysis of crucible sherds found traces of silver and gold. This may be connected with the documentary evidence for a Nicholas Goldsmith who held the neighbouring house on Turl Street in 1388 and 1393. The area, in the heart of the medieval town, was the location of the spicery and the goldsmiths' quarter.

The quantity of rye here is very notable; both late Anglo-Saxon and medieval charred cereal assemblages in Oxford are almost invariably dominated by bread wheat, and rye is present, if at all, in very small quantities. The presence of whole plants, instead of the more usual cleaned and processed grain, suggests that rural-type processing was taking place in the town at this time. Although this cannot be closely dated, the fourteenth century was a period when agriculture would have been more than usually subject to periodic disruption, through poor weather and harvest failure, disease, labour shortages and civil conflict, and the rye at *Lincoln College* may be a product of exceptional circumstances. Another sample dominated by rye came from a less well-dated context of the fourteenth to sixteenth centuries at Jesus College; the presence of whole plants here was thought to mean that the rye had been brought in for thatching. However, the sample came from an area that is likely to have been within the kitchen of Great White Hall.[40] This suggests that a useful research aim for future work in Oxford would be sampling from late-medieval deposits to see if the appearance of rye is part of a general shift in consumption, or an exceptional event. Rye was used, often in mixtures with wheat, to make cheap bread. Evidence for the better type of bread comes from *Nos. 114–119 St Aldate's/Nos. 4–5 Queen Street*, possibly associated with one of the nearby inns (see below), where John Giorgi notes that very fragmented cereal bran from a thirteenth- or fourteenth-century occupation layer is an indication of the well-sieved flour used for the best wheat bread. Two successive bread ovens of fourteenth- and possibly fifteenth-century date were found at the Ashmolean Forecourt. Samples here were much more typical for Oxford, and were dominated by bread wheat, with a little barley, a trace of rye and no positively identified oats. The presence of burnt fish bone suggested the ovens might also have been used for drying fish.[41]

Archaeology has also revealed change in the supply of fuel wood to the medieval town. Early assemblages are always dominated by oak and a variety of brushwood of the type that could have been collected from hedgerows. From the later medieval period, however, there is a very marked shift to a dominance of beech, and this can be seen at a number of the sites reported in the present volume, and is discussed in detail by Sheila Boardman in the report on *Lincoln College*. This may represent a change from local sourcing to dependence on the highly organised Chiltern industry trading on the Thames from Henley that produced much of London's fuel.[42]

40 R. Bashford and B.M. Ford, 'Eleventh-Century, Later-Medieval and Early Post-Medieval Evidence from Investigations at Jesus College and Market Street, Oxford', *Oxoniensia*, 79 (2014), pp. 233–4.

41 Andrews and Mepham, 'Ashmolean Museum Forecourt'.

42 J.A. Galloway et al., 'Fuelling the City: Production and Distribution of Firewood and Fuel in London's Region, 1290–1400', *Economic History Review*, ns 49:3 (1996), pp. 447–72.

INNS AND TAVERNS

Two of the excavations reported in this volume recovered evidence that can be associated with inns and taverns.[43] The late medieval period saw a marked growth in the numbers of public drinking places, and places offering accommodation. These were generally of three kinds. Medieval alehouses, as the name suggests, sold ale (and later beer), increasingly only for consumption on the premises. They catered, on the whole, for the working people and were to become important centres of communal life and recreation. Taverns sold wine, and their proprietors were often vintners or vintners' agents. Wine doubled in price during the late medieval period, as the Hundred Years' War (1337–1453) and the loss of Gascony (in 1451–3) interrupted supplies, which meant that taverns and wine-drinking were largely beyond the reach of the ordinary working people. Most customers were therefore from the upper and middling ranks of society. Although some taverns acquired a bad reputation for gambling and prostitution, many were prestigious and respectable, and Oxford taverns were used by the mayor and aldermen of the fourteenth century to entertain important guests, or to buy wine. Many of Oxford's taverns were simply vaulted cellars set half-underground. Inns provided accommodation and stabling as well as food and drink, which could be quite elaborate. Inns appear regularly in Oxford records from the mid fourteenth century, and Munby suggests that they seem to be a genuine innovation at this time; several had previously been owned by individuals known to have been connected with the wine trade. It is suggested that the growing numbers of inns reflect a decline in traditional sources of hospitality (typically that of religious foundations) at a time when there may have been increasing numbers of travellers needing accommodation. By the start of the fifteenth century there were twenty-one inns trading in Oxford, which suggests a considerable level of demand; they were concentrated outside North Gate, and along Cornmarket, St Aldate's and the High Street.

The excavations at *Nos. 114–119 St Aldate's/Nos. 4–5 Queen Street* were located in the back yards of some of Oxford's best-known medieval hostelries. To the east, fronting onto St Aldate's, were Battes Inn, mentioned in 1338/9, and the Red Lion, mentioned in 1384, while on the corner of Carfax was the notorious Swindlestock Tavern, present already as a tavern by 1279. Here, an argument on 10 February 1355, between the tavern keeper and two students over the quality of the drink, sparked off the most serious of the town and gown riots, which left many dead on both sides. Battes was one of the more popular inns in Oxford during the medieval period, and entertained distinguished guests; in 1368/9 the king's justice and the sheriff took fruit and wine there.[44] A good inn could offer a range of comforts and facilities, including stabling for numerous horses (which would be fed on hay, horse-bread and oats). 'House' wine would be available, or a wider range could be fetched in from a tavern; food could be home cooked or brought in from a cook shop, and a wide choice of meat, cheese and fruit was on offer. Some of this is reflected in an environmental sample from a thirteenth- to fourteenth-century layer at *Nos. 114–119 St Aldate's/Nos. 4–5 Queen Street*, which may be from Battes or the Red Lion. It was dominated by the remains of damson/greengage type fruits, sloe/blackthorn, cherry, grape, wild strawberry, blackberry, apple and apple/pear, with occasional evidence for mulberry, rowan and hazelnuts. Coriander and fennel, and *Brassica/Sinapis* remains (from cabbages, turnips or mustards) were also present. The same sample also contained residues of stabling material. A notable ceramic find was a fragment of early Malagan or Valencian lustreware, of fourteenth-century date, undoubtedly a prestigious piece of display or table ware. A dump of fifteenth- to mid sixteenth-century drinking pottery may also be from Battes Inn, and comprised pieces from Raeren stoneware drinking jugs and Cistercian ware cups or tygs (see below). Drinking

[43] The following brief account is based on J. Munby, 'Zacharias's: A 14th Century Oxford New Inn and the Origins of the Medieval Urban Inn', *Oxoniensia*, 57 (1992), pp. 245–309 and P. Clark, *The English Alehouse: A Social History 1200–1830* (1983).

[44] Munby, 'Zacharias's', p. 303.

pottery is again conspicuous in the late sixteenth to early seventeenth century, with Frechen/Cologne stoneware. Clay tobacco pipes and wine bottles are present from the early to mid seventeenth century, one with the seal of the landlord of the Mermaid Tavern, which succeeded the Swindlestock, and the other from the Crown Inn, a tavern on Cornmarket.

THE LATER MEDIEVAL AND EARLY POST-MEDIEVAL TOWN

Like many old towns whose prosperity had been built on wool and cloth, Oxford seems to have been in decline as a mercantile and manufacturing centre in the later medieval period. The university became increasingly central to the economy of the town, with many townspeople now employed in supplying goods and services. The food, drink and distributive trades were predominant, although leather workers and tailors were still numerous, presumably also supplying university needs as well as those of the market and townspeople. However, there is also clear evidence of specialised trades. One of these appears to have been musical instrument making, for what was clearly a good local market. Two bone tuning pegs, one for an open-framed instrument such as a harp, lyre, lute or fiddle, and the other for a closed-box instrument such as a psaltery, were found in late fifteenth- to sixteenth-century contexts at *Queen's College Provost's Garden*. Tuning pegs have also been found in late-medieval and early post-medieval contexts at the Clarendon Centre, and at Jesus College.[45] A late-medieval instrument maker's workshop was identified in excavations at *Nos. 79–80 St Aldate's*, where tuning pegs suitable for a psaltery, and others for a lyre or fiddle, were found with abundant working waste.[46]

Oxford's town and university populations were considerably reduced in the later medieval period, and the picture of the town given by Ralph Agas' bird's-eye view of 1578 is of a place with much open space. While some of this could represent decay and abandonment, it is by no means the case that open space (or at least, enclosed and private open space) was not appreciated, and it is striking how consistently colleges created gardens within their new precincts; in 1600, for example, *St John's* acquired four acres of the common fields north of their original site, to be enclosed within their Grove (this volume, below). The excavations at *Queen's College* and *Lincoln College* reported in this volume were both situated in open ground, although whether these were gardens or just open space at this date is not clear. Ornamental and orchard trees were identified in a remarkable medieval waterlogged sample from No. 4A Merton Street, which may date either from the early years of Merton College's ownership, or the preceding period when the property was occupied by the Edrich family, who were middle ranking burgesses. A number of trees including lime, field maple, birch, beech and willow suggest ornamental planting in an urban context, and remains of grape, plum, damson-type fruits, cherry and walnut suggest orchard planting on the site or nearby. Blackberry, raspberry and hazelnuts could have been grown in a garden or imported from the wild. The same site produced evidence for possible medicinal planting, with crushed cannabis seeds, opium poppy and hops.[47] Garden plants are rarely identified in Oxford assemblages, and so the seeds of violet found in a seventeenth-century pit at the Clarendon Centre are worth noting; these could be from an ornamental garden plant, or could have been cultivated for culinary or medicinal purposes.[48]

Classic signs of reduced urban populations and declining civic prosperity in the late Middle Ages include the closure and amalgamation of parish churches for lack of parishioners, and shrinking suburbs. The presence of the university at Oxford, however, complicates the picture. Vacant plots inside the walls in the eastern half of the town were taken up by colleges, notably New College in the late fourteenth century, and a number of parish churches were appropriated

45 Douglas, *Medieval Craft-Working in Oxford*; Bashford and Ford, 'Jesus College'.
46 Durham, 'Archaeological Investigations in St Aldate's', p. 165.
47 Poore, 'No. 4A Merton St.'.
48 Douglas, *Medieval Craft-Working in Oxford*.

by colleges, or suppressed. The process by which *Lincoln College* gradually acquired its site in the fifteenth and sixteenth centuries is instructive, and can be followed in this volume, below; at its foundation the old church of St Mildred was suppressed and absorbed into the college, and its parish was amalgamated with St Michael at the North Gate. A number of the properties acquired by the college were academic halls, and others are later described as vacant, or as gardens. The transfer of so much land inside the walls to colleges during the late medieval period may be linked to the fortunes of the suburbs in quite subtle ways. The availability of suitable property in the suburbs would have reduced pressure for land in the town, thus leaving it available for colleges; at the same time, once intramural land was absorbed into colleges it would no longer be available to anyone else, and this may in time have contributed to the survival of the suburbs and to the overcrowding that is evident from the late sixteenth century (see below). Certainly, the western suburb of St Thomas's, which had a particularly industrial character, was notably prosperous in the late medieval period. The evidence from the *Ashmolean Museum Extension* site is consistent with continuing occupation but at a less intensive level; a garden soil built up in the northern part of the area, and was to persist until the nineteenth century. Far fewer pits were datable to this period, which may be a sign that the central property was not always occupied, but could equally reflect a change in the way people disposed of rubbish. The adjacent property at the Classics Centre site to the north appeared to have been abandoned.[49] On the opposite side of St Giles' Street, St Bernard's and its successor *St John's College* were separated from the open fields by the parish boundary ditch, discussed above. This appears to have been used as a rubbish dump during the medieval period, and its excavated stretch contained the remains of at least three dead dogs, and meat bones, possibly butchers' waste, that had been gnawed by dogs and rodents.

The population decline of the late medieval period also had more positive effects, however. In broad terms, from the 1370s (after the Black Death), the price of staple cereals fell, while labour shortages meant that labourers' wage rates rose and the conditions of many agricultural workers improved. Thus, it is generally accepted that people in the middle ranks of society will have experienced a much improved standard of living; this allowed them much more discretionary spending than previously, and the opportunity of more leisure time.[50] The increased purchasing power of ordinary people is reflected in a number of areas that should be visible to us archaeologically: a better diet, with less dependence on basic cereals, and more consumption of dairy produce and younger animals; better housing, more furniture and greater domestic comfort, better quality clothes and more personal possessions, and perhaps also the increasing popularity of alehouses. The main difficulty is isolating and dating late-medieval activity, particularly in the fifteenth century, as pottery assemblages are often very small, with only limited numbers of vessel and fabric types that are exclusively fifteenth-century in date. It is thought that this reflects a decline in pottery use and an increase in the use of metal vessels, and also a decline in the practice of disposing of rubbish in back yard pits; there is clearly a need to find better ways of dating and identifying late-medieval archaeology.

Largely for these reasons, not much evidence from the sites reported in the present volume can be attributed exclusively to the fifteenth century, but what is clear here, as in other Oxford assemblages, is that many people had attained a new level of prosperity and had access to a much wider range of commodities by the seventeenth century. The *Ashmolean Museum Extension* is perhaps the most informative site, and also the most likely to reflect the lives of townspeople rather than of members of the university. Here, an increase in juvenile cattle bone during the early post-medieval period is interpreted as a sign of increased dairy production in the region, as demand for milk, cheese and butter rose. Another indicator of improving standards of living and perhaps also of social change is the evidence that foods such as swan, hare, venison and rabbit,

49 Norton and Cockin, 'Excavations at the Classics Centre'.

50 See, for example, C. Dyer, 'A Golden Age Rediscovered: Labourers' Wages in the Fifteenth Century', in M. Allen and D. Coffman (eds.), *Money, Prices and Wages: Essays in Honour of Professor Nicholas Mayhew* (2015), pp. 180–95.

which were once exclusive to the higher ranks of society, were becoming much more widely available. The late-medieval and early post-medieval inhabitants of the *Ashmolean Museum Extension* site ate swan, venison, rabbit and peafowl as well as a wide range of river fish, and fruit, comprising fig, wild strawberry, apple, blackberry, elderberry, grape, possible pear, and quince. Similar food assemblages occur in the medieval period, for example at Merton College and at the town centre inns at *Nos. 114–119 St Aldate's/Nos. 4–5 Queen Street* (see above), but the key difference may be the social status of the consumers.

In terms of improving standards of building and domestic comfort, this period sees the much more widespread appearance of window glass, which occurs on all the sites reported in this volume. An unusual insight into domestic comfort comes from *St John's College*, where pieces from a tiled stove had been discarded in the early to mid seventeenth century. The stove itself was probably made in Germany and installed in the college not long after its foundation. It is thought that tiled stoves were used for steam baths in England, although they were also used for central heating on the continent. Many were discarded in the early seventeenth century when the government placed restrictions on the use of wood for domestic heating. Floor tile that was thoroughly medieval in style was being laid in Queen's College chapel in 1519, one of those found in the *Queen's College Provost's Garden* excavations depicting the rebus of the college's benefactor Robert Langton, but a slightly later group of tiles (*c*.1575–1625) were newly fashionable and highly prestigious imported polychrome tin-glazed wall tiles, with floral designs of blue petalled flowers with yellow centres and turquoise leaves. These were perhaps from a fireplace surround. Sixteenth- and seventeenth-century bricks with grey vitrified surfaces may have been used for diaper work in walling, but could also have been used for the installation of an oven, fireplace or chimney. An almost complete candle snuffer or wick cutter was found in a pit at *St John's College*; this would have been used to trim candle wicks to prevent guttering, and represents the general shift from oil lamps to candles in the late-medieval and early post-medieval periods. There were also a number of small hooks that would have been used for wall hangings or tapestries; a drape ring found at the *Ashmolean Museum Extension* site would have had the same function.

The same period saw increasing refinement in dining habits, with much greater emphasis on functional specialisation of vessels and utensils, and greater emphasis on forms for personal rather than communal use; this was supported by a range of technological and commercial developments in both ceramics and glass production.[51] One of the most marked changes in Oxford assemblages is the much readier availability of glass. In the Middle Ages glass drinking vessels were rare and valuable, and the sherd from a late thirteenth- or fourteenth-century goblet, probably of French make, from *St John's College* is therefore a very notable find. It predates not only the college but also its predecessor, the Cistercian college of St Bernard, and therefore presumably derives from earlier secular occupation at the site.[52] Glass drinking vessels become much more common in Oxford from the late sixteenth century onwards in the form of drinking beakers and goblets, and examples are noted in most of the reports in this volume. Glass drinking vessels were imported from Venice at this time, but glass in Venetian style (*façon de Venise*) was also being made by Venetian migrants in many European cities, including London, where the most notable London maker, Jacopo Verzelini, was working from 1573. Other contemporary glassware is represented by a shallow glass dish from *Lincoln College*, part of a glass storage jar decorated with an optic-blown mesh design from the *Ashmolean Museum Extension*, and part of the rim and neck of a sandglass from the same site.

[51] For ceramics: D. Gaimster, 'English Households in Transition *c*.1450–1550: The Ceramic Evidence', in D. Gaimster and P. Stamper (eds.), *The Age of Transition: The Archaeology of English Culture 1400–1600* (1997), pp. 171–95. For glass: R. Tyson, *Medieval Glass Vessels Found in England c.AD1200–1500* (2000) and H. Wilmott, *Early Post-Medieval Vessel Glass in England c.1500–1670* (2002).

[52] Pieces of three German glass vessels, a goblet, a bowl and a beaker of the same date range were found at Christ Church, and may have been the possessions of the wealthy owners of Vine Hall: R. Tyson, 'Glass', in Chadwick et al., *Christ Church.*

Metal spoons first appear in significant numbers in this period, although wooden spoons had been in use since at least the Anglo-Saxon period. Two spoons of copper alloy and a spoon bowl of lead were found in seventeenth-century pits at *Queen's College*. More unusual are the two forks from mid sixteenth- to mid seventeenth-century pits at *St John's College*; although forks were known in the west during the Middle Ages they were considered to be an unnecessary affectation and were not commonly used in England until the late seventeenth century.

A range of new vessel types also appear in late-medieval and early post-medieval ceramics. The period from the mid fourteenth to the mid fifteenth centuries saw a contraction of the native ceramic industries, with the disappearance of the highly decorated pottery of the high medieval period, to be replaced by a much plainer range of kitchenware.[53] For decorative, high-quality ceramic tablewares the urban mercantile and artisan classes turned increasingly to foreign imports, notable the technologically superior Rhenish stonewares, mass-produced on an industrial scale in a range of cups, mugs, beakers and drinking jugs for wine and beer. The Rhenish industries were adept at imitating more exclusive metal and glass tableware, notably with the introduction of applied surface ornament from the beginning of the sixteenth century, and David Gaimster comments that they captured a 'niche' market in fashionable pottery for the socially aspirant townspeople. English manufacturers copied and diversified, with the most notable industries ('Tudor green' from the Surrey/Hampshire borders, and 'Cistercian ware' from Yorkshire and the North Midlands) producing a much wider range of specialised vessels from the late fifteenth century. These vessel types occur on all the sites reported in this volume. Over 900 sherds of Frechen stoneware were recovered from the site at *Brasenose College*, which is probably the single largest group known from Oxford to date. The most prestigious pottery, designed undoubtedly for display or even devotional purposes, is represented by the imported tin-glazed earthenwares, Spanish lustreware and Italian and Netherlandish maiolica.

The period also sees the adoption of entirely new introductions. An apricot stone was found in an early to mid seventeenth-century pit at *St John's College*; apricots were introduced into England in the sixteenth century and became popular plants for sunny walls. Turkey bones were found in a late sixteenth- to mid seventeenth-century pit at the *Ashmolean Museum Extension*; the first British record of turkey dates from 1541, and it has occurred in the late sixteenth century at Jesus College, and in the seventeenth century at the former Greyfriars site and at Corpus Christi College. Another New World import was tobacco, and clay tobacco pipes become ubiquitous in Oxford during the seventeenth century. The earliest record from the sites reported in the present volume comes from *St John's College*, where two pipes of the period *c.*1580–1610 were found. These are among the earliest recognisable tobacco pipes in England. At this time pipe bowls were small as tobacco remained very expensive, being imported from the New World or grown in small quantities in gardens. Smoking appears to have been very much the preserve of the well-to-do. Most of the pipe assemblages reported in this volume date to the seventeenth century, with particularly closely dated groups from 1630–70. At the *Ashmolean Museum Extension* there was evidence for pipes that had been coloured red, which may have been a common practice in the Oxford region; the coloured pipes probably date from the late seventeenth century. It is clear that there were numerous pipemakers in Oxford, and pipe making debris of late seventeenth- to early eighteenth-century date has been found at George Street.[54]

A little evidence can be linked with the tumultuous years of the Reformation. Late-medieval window glass, including painted grisaille glass, found in late sixteenth- to mid seventeenth-century pits at the *Ashmolean Museum Extension* site is likely to have come from the demolished buildings of the dissolved Carmelite friary that occupied the site of Beaumont Palace during

53 The following is based on Gaimster, 'English Households in Transition'.

54 '33–35 George Street, Oxford: Archaeological Watching Brief Report', unpublished OA report (2012), https://library.oxfordarchaeology.com/1015/. In addition, pipe-making waste of late eighteenth- to early nineteenth-century date has recently been found at Paradise Street: 'Former Cooper Callas Building, 15 Paradise Street, Oxford. Post-Excavation Assessment and Updated Project Design', unpublished OA report (2019).

the later Middle Ages. On the opposite side of St Giles' Street, *St John's College* was founded by Sir Thomas White in 1555, on the site of the recently dissolved Cistercian St Bernard's College, with the aim of providing educated Roman Catholic priests to support the counter-reformation under Mary Tudor. Two small copper alloy badges or buttons stamped with the motif of Christ on the cross flanked with the letters I and C were found in mid sixteenth- to mid seventeenth-century pits here; these are typical of the kinds of tokens and medallions with religious scenes and saints that are commonly found in the Catholic world.

THE CIVIL WAR AND AFTER

A number of recent excavations have shed light on aspects of Oxford during the Civil War.[55] The university (with few exceptions) strongly supported the king's cause when the Civil War broke out in 1642. The townspeople, much less enthusiastic, seem to have adopted an essentially pragmatic approach. The king's army entered Oxford on 29 October 1642, following the Battle of Edgehill, and as it became clear he would not be able to retake London, he chose instead to make Oxford his capital. For the next four years Oxford was the king's headquarters, the base for his court and government, a garrison for royal troops and a refuge for Royalists displaced from elsewhere in the country. Academic life came to a virtual standstill, with many students leaving Oxford or staying away, while others enlisted. The king and his sons were accommodated at Christ Church and the queen at Merton; college rooms and rooms in large town houses were taken over by the wealthy and well placed, while the common soldiers were packed into lodgings in requisitioned houses. Although numbers fluctuated, at times there were thousands of troops in the city. College and university buildings, and workshops and mills of the town, were taken over to make, store and repair arms and Magdalen Grove became a park for artillery. A group of thirteen musket balls and a powder holder cover found in garden soils during the *Ashmolean Museum Extension* excavations are likely to date from the Civil War period, perhaps belonging to a soldier billeted at the house or nearby, or even to the householder. A garrison of some 600–700 academics and townsmen was raised in the city and presumably had access to arms, but equally the ever-present threat of theft and disorder may have prompted citizens to take their own measures.

Work on the defences began immediately and all males aged between 16 and 60 were supposed to contribute one day's labour a week; some 3,320 men from the city parishes had to provide four days' labour, and some 1,500 from the university two days. The academics seem to have been enthusiastic, at least initially, but the service was widely evaded by the townsmen. The Civil War defences have been investigated in a number of recent excavations, and are discussed in detail in the report on *Mansfield College* and the *Tinbergen Building*. The excavation at *Mansfield College* has helped to clarify the sequence of construction of the inner line of defences to the north of the city. A short-lived defence here of the summer of 1642 appears to have been re-established and strengthened once the king had adopted Oxford as his capital, and probably remained the primary defensive line here for some while. A more substantial outer line was constructed under the direction of the engineer Bernard de Gomme, but was only 'newly completed' in May 1646, a month before the city surrendered to the Parliamentary army. The outer defences incorporated an external ditch up to 11 m wide and 2.4 m deep, and the *Tinbergen Building* excavation identified an area of mantraps (pitfalls) placed in front of the ditch. These traps could have been up to *c*.2 m deep and may have had iron or wooden stakes set within them.

55 This brief summary of Oxford during the Civil War draws on I. Roy and D. Reinhart, 'Oxford and the Civil Wars', in N. Tyacke (ed.), *The History of the University of Oxford, Volume IV* (1997), pp. 687–731; and I. Roy, 'The City of Oxford 1640–1660', in R.C. Richardson (ed.), *Town and Countryside in the English Revolution* (1992), pp. 130–68. For a detailed account of the experience of one parish: R. Kelly, 'A City Parish in the English Civil War: St Aldate's, Oxford, 1642–6', *Oxoniensia*, 76 (2011), pp. 39–53.

The defences were slighted by Parliament, but the excavations at Mansfield College suggest that the inner line was left to decay; within a few decades it had reverted to grazed pasture.

As the war progressed conditions in Oxford seem sometimes to have become truly appalling. Although the influx of people created a huge market for goods and services, many debts were never paid and the city was burdened with continual demands from the king for loans and contributions amounting to thousands of pounds for the construction of the defences and the maintenance of troops. The overcrowding created very insanitary conditions in parts of the city; the river channels were heavily polluted with dung and dead animals, and a serious fire in October 1644 destroyed large numbers of houses, bakehouses, breweries, malthouses and grain and fuel stores on the west side of the city. There was a severe outbreak of typhus in 1643, and it is estimated that over a thousand townspeople died at this time. Further outbreaks of disease, including the plague, smallpox and typhus, came in the following years, and it is probable that at least a thousand more townspeople died before the surrender of the city in June 1646. Excavations at *St Cross College* recovered the grave of a young woman who had been buried in a tenement garden here sometime during or after 1640. While there may be a number of different explanations for this unusual discovery, it remains a strong possibility that she was a victim of one of these epidemics and may have been buried here when the local parish burial ground was overwhelmed by the number of deaths.

Relatively little later post-medieval evidence was recovered in the excavations reported in this volume, but some themes emerge. Wine bottles are common finds from post-medieval contexts and occur in quantity from the excavations reported in this volume. Nevertheless, wine itself was not a cheap and readily available commodity; wine prices rose consistently from the fourteenth to the eighteenth century, as supplies were disrupted by war and the government imposed heavy import duties. As Peter Clark notes,[56] this put wine drinking beyond the means of all but the well-to-do; poorer people would drink water, beer or cider, or (increasingly from the middle of the seventeenth century) spirits such as gin. Wine bottles would therefore seem to be an indicator of privileged consumers. At the opposite end of the social scale, the increasing numbers of poor and vagrants in the city were causing alarm amongst the city authorities well before the Civil War, and both the city centre and the suburbs were filling up with cottages and 'squabs'. David Loggan's bird's-eye view of 1675 shows a very different city from that depicted by Agas a century earlier. Rows of cottages stretch back into the tenements behind the street frontage houses and shops. The excavations at *Lincoln College* recorded some evidence for the area of cottages known as Rotten Row that stood here between the college's Chapel Quad and the lane around All Saints churchyard. Perhaps surprisingly, the excavations found carefully and even decoratively laid out cobbled courtyards and pathways here, and this is a rare insight into the standard and appearance of housing of this kind. The excavated area at the *Ashmolean Museum Extension* appeared to have been subdivided in the seventeenth century, with evidence for buildings extending far into the back yard. Nevertheless, the property seems to have had rather fashionable eighteenth-century occupants who cleared out their old pottery, perhaps to make way for new tablewares in lead crystal glass, with pieces being recovered from a lead crystal wine glass, a decanter and jelly glasses. Lead crystal glass was first manufactured on an industrial scale by George Ravenscroft in the 1670s, and by the eighteenth century English lead crystal was popular throughout Europe. A fragment from a bevelled-edge mirror from the same site would also have been a luxury item at this time.

How to summarise these various findings? A key point is that after almost a century of sustained investigation and reporting of Oxford's archaeology, the quantum of archaeological data can now be seen to be telling its own story of daily life in the city, that can amplify and if necessary, challenge the familiar historical accounts. This volume once more shows that the cost and effort of recovering this story has been and will remain a worthwhile enterprise.

56 Clark, *The English Alehouse*, p. 8.

PART 2

Life and Learning within the Town Walls

4.

Anglo-Saxon to Post-Medieval Occupation and Evidence for the Medieval Jewry at Nos. 114–119 St Aldate's and Nos. 4–5 Queen Street

STEVEN TEAGUE, EDWARD BIDDULPH and CARL CHAMPNESS

with contributions by LEIGH ALLEN, ENID ALLISON, PAUL BLINKHORN, LEE G. BRODERICK, GERALDINE CRANN, JULIE DUNNE, RICHARD P. EVERSHED, JOHN GIORGI, DAVID A. HIGGINS, REBECCA NICHOLSON, CYNTHIA POOLE, IAN R. SCOTT and RUTH SHAFFREY

SUMMARY

Excavations at Nos. 114–119 St Aldate's and Nos. 4–5 Queen Street shed light on some of the oldest and grandest parts of the medieval town. The earliest evidence comprised sunken floors and pits that date to the middle/late Anglo-Saxon period. Those features, relating to wooden buildings, appear to predate the Anglo-Saxon *burh*, which was founded by the early tenth century. A series of later rubbish pits dating to the late Anglo-Saxon and early Norman period was cut through this horizon. The pits contained pottery and bone fragments, representing general rubbish, as well as faecal material and the raked-out fuel waste from ovens, fires and hearths. A stone-lined latrine cut through the rubbish pits. The latrine contained a rich assemblage of twelfth- or early thirteenth-century pottery, animal bone and other domestic material. The well-constructed nature of the feature suggests that it was associated with a house of a wealthy individual. It is known that during this period part of the site was in Jewish ownership, and this is supported by the faunal remains and organic residues on pottery, which are consistent with Jewish dietary laws. A stone-built structure, part of a cellar, lay to the east of the latrine. The later fills of the cellar contained a small assemblage of fifteenth- or sixteenth-century pottery, which almost exclusively comprised drinking vessels that are likely to have derived from Battes Inn (by then known as the Fleur de Luce) on St Aldate's. Another latrine, of seventeenth- and eighteenth-century date, contained an assemblage of pottery, vessel glass, clay pipes, and fruit remains that indicate wealthy inhabitants here during this time. Subsequent levels were poorly preserved owing to modern truncation.

Oxford Archaeology (OA) was commissioned by Gilbert-Ash on behalf of Reef Estates and the British Airways Pension Trust, with consultation by Will Bedford of Orion Heritage, to undertake an archaeological investigation at Nos. 114–119 St Aldate's and Nos. 4–5 Queen Street

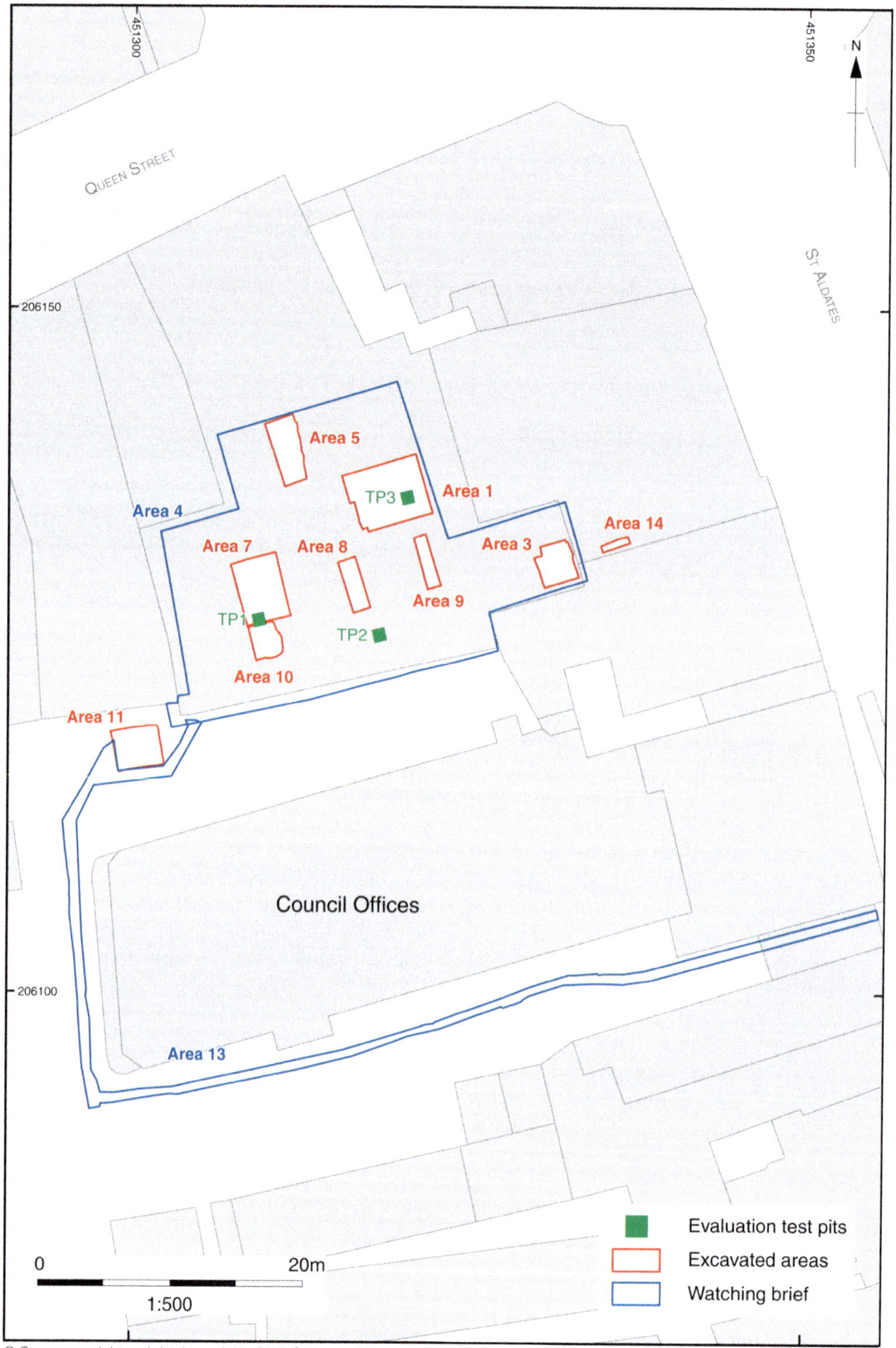

Fig. 4.1 Site location.

Table 4.1 Excavation areas and methods of excavation.

Area	Method	Notes
Area 1	Full excavation to natural	Crane base
Area 3	Full excavation to natural	
Area 4	Plan of exposed archaeological horizon only. Limited excavation along the southern edge of the slab. Watching brief	Removal of existing basement slab
Area 5	Machine assisted excavation to natural	
Area 7	Limited machine-assisted excavation to formation level. Watching brief	Pile cap/groundbeam
Area 8	Limited machine-assisted excavation to formation level. Watching brief	Pile cap/groundbeam
Area 9	Limited machine-assisted excavation to formation level. Watching brief	Pile cap/groundbeam
Area 10	Full excavation to natural	
Area 11	Machine excavation to latest archaeological levels only	
Area 13	Limited machine-assisted excavation to formation level. Watching brief	Service run
Area 14	Limited machine-assisted excavation to formation level	Service run

ahead of redevelopment (Fig. 4.1). An evaluation by OA in 2015 identified extensive remains of undisturbed late Anglo-Saxon to early medieval horizons preserved underneath the basement levels at the site.[1] Where possible, the proposed development was designed to minimise the impact on the archaeological remains. A programme of archaeological excavation and watching brief was devised where impacts could not be avoided, and was carried out in 2016–17. A post-excavation assessment presented the preliminary findings of the fieldwork and identified the potential of the results to address research questions.[2]

The area of development, located at grid reference SP 51320 06130, encompasses 0.135 hectares. The north end of the site lies at about 64.7 m above Ordnance Datum (OD), with a gentle slope to the south. Terraces were created on this slope in order to accommodate the construction of the buildings on the site. The natural fall of the slope is visible along St Aldate's. The first river terrace lies approximately 250 m to the south at around 58.5 m OD, and the River Thames lies 45 m to the south. The archaeological mitigation strategy involved the combination of excavation by hand and machine, and a watching brief on service trenches. A summary of the areas excavated and how they were approached is provided in Table 4.1, and their locations shown on Figure 4.1.

This report summarises the key results of the investigations. Full versions of specialist reports are available to download from the OA Library.[3] The archive will be deposited with Oxfordshire County Museum Service under accession number 2015.150.

1 '114–119 St Aldate's and 4–5 Queen Street, Oxford: Archaeological Evaluation Report', unpublished OA report (2015), https://library.oxfordarchaeology.com/4887/.

2 '114–119 St Aldate's and 4–5 Queen Street, Oxford: Post-Excavation Assessment', unpublished OA report (2017).

3 https://library.oxfordarchaeology.com/4449/.

ARCHAEOLOGICAL AND HISTORICAL BACKGROUND

The site lies in the heart of the Anglo-Saxon town, at the central crossroads where the north–south and east–west street axes met. To the south, Grandpont was one of the principal crossing points over the River Thames. The south gate of the town was located at the southern end of St Aldate's. Queen Street was also laid out in the Anglo-Saxon period, and parts of the late Anglo-Saxon street frontage have been recorded in various interventions along Queen Street, including at Nos. 4, 7–8 and 11–12.[4]

The twelfth and thirteenth centuries saw the development of Oxford's Jewish quarter around St Aldate's, following William the Conqueror's invitation to Jews from France to settle in England and establish a network of credit and trading functions. The earliest documentary evidence for the Jewry at Oxford dates to 1142 when Matilda was besieged at Oxford Castle. Two of the four properties partly exposed by the area of excavation have been identified as being in Jewish ownership. Both fronted onto St Aldate's (formerly Fish Street), with one, Jacob's Hall, being one of the most substantial private houses in Oxford. The other two properties were held by the bishop of Lichfield and fronted onto Queen Street (formerly Butcher Row/Great Bailey). The Jewry came to an end in 1290 when the Jews were expelled from England by Edward I. By the fourteenth century, all properties were in Christian ownership. Several drinking establishments existed around Carfax, Queen Street and the northern end of St Aldate's, with two in the investigation area being recorded as the site of Battes Inn and the Red Lion Inn.[5] Battes Inn was apparently favoured by royal justices and other dignitaries. By 1514 it was known as the Fleur de Luce, and it had closed down before 1804.[6] Extensive cellars belonging to the Swindlestock Tavern, which was established on the south-west corner of Carfax in the thirteenth century and pulled down in the early eighteenth century (by which time the tavern was known as the Mermaid), were used as wine cellars in the eighteenth and nineteenth centuries.[7]

Excavations at Carfax, the Post Office on St Aldate's, and Nos. 117–18 St Aldate's have uncovered the remains of medieval plots, rubbish pits and other evidence for occupation, with traces of the probable contemporary road surface buried some 4 m below the modern ground level. Loggan's map shows that the medieval plots along St Aldate's had been subdivided by the seventeenth century, and the 1876 Ordnance Survey map shows that site was occupied by up to six buildings on St Aldate's and two on Queen Street. By the mid twentieth century, the properties had been amalgamated into two main blocks, and remained in this form to the time of excavation.

DISCUSSION

Anglo-Saxon

Apart from two sherds of residual pottery that suggest Roman-period activity in the vicinity of the site, the earliest activity dates to the middle/late Anglo-Saxon period. Evidence for two structures was uncovered. Structure 1.1 in Area 5 comprised a series of floor layers and an associated posthole. Structure 1.2 in Area 3 was represented by a sunken floor. A stakehole against the side of the floor and filled with organic matter is likely to be a remnant of a wattle lining. Potentially, both structures are contemporary. A radiocarbon date obtained from charred grain from Structure 1.1 spanned the late eighth to late tenth century cal. AD, while a determination from Structure 1.2 ranged from the late seventh to late ninth century cal. AD (Table 4.2). At

4 Dodd, *Oxford*, chapter 5.

5 Roth, *Jews*; P. Manix, 'Oxford: Mapping the Jews', in A. Haverkamp (ed.), *The Jews of Europe in the Middle Ages (Tenth to Fifteenth Centuries): Proceedings of the International Symposium held at Speyer, 20–25 October 2002* (2004), pp. 405–20.

6 *VCH Oxon.* 4, p. 438.

7 Ibid.; Salter, *Survey*, vol. 2, pp. 101–10, SW 131–138.

Table 4.2. Summary of radiocarbon dates. All calibrated age ranges in this volume were determined using the University of Oxford Radiocarbon Accelerator Unit calibration program OxCal v4 and the IntCal13 curve.

Laboratory no.	Context	Feature	Material	$\delta^{13}C$ (‰)	Radiocarbon age (BP)	Calibrated date (95.4% confidence)
SUERC-78793	1071	Structure 3.1	Sheep/goat radius	−21.6	930 ± 35	Cal AD 1023–1184
SUERC-78794	3088	Posthole 3084	Charred grain (*Triticum*)	−22.9	1213 ± 35	Cal AD 689–751 (18.2%) Cal AD 760–893 (77.2%)
SUERC-78795	5034	Posthole 5033	Charred grain (*Triticum*)	−23.4	1173 ± 35	Cal AD 769–969
SUERC-80171	1050		Pig mandible	−21.5	1025 ± 29	Cal AD 904–918 (1.5%) Cal AD 966–1044 (92.4%) Cal AD 1105–19 (1.5%)

a 68.2 per cent confidence level, however, both results match each other more closely, sitting within the late eighth to late ninth century. Pits dug in Area 1, presumably an open area at this time, received domestic waste, possibly belonging to the occupants of Structure 1.1. Pottery from the features indicate that these continued to fill up to the late tenth or early eleventh century.

Structure 1.2 was replaced by another structure (2.1) with a sunken floor or cellar by the late tenth or early eleventh century, based on pottery recovered from the gravel floor of the later structure. Postholes suggest that the structure had a timber revetment around the sides. Pottery from backfill deposits and the fills of a pit cut into the infilled cellar suggests that the structure had been abandoned by the end of the eleventh century. An area of pits in Area 10 may be contemporary with Structure 2.1, though the ceramic dating is equivocal.

The evidence from Phase 1 is limited, but critical, providing as it does tentative evidence for settlement in St Aldate's predating the Anglo-Saxon *burh*, which had been founded by the early tenth century.[8] The occupation lay along a routeway that passes close to the reputed site of St Frideswide's minster, believed to have been founded in the early eighth century, and led to the middle Anglo-Saxon river crossing, established by the end of the seventh century.[9] Evidence of contemporary occupation at other nearby sites is sparse, but tantalising. A feature recorded as a cellar pit with the remains of a timber lining at Nos. 6–8 High Street, some 100 m to the north-east of the current site, may have been contemporary with Structure 1.2. Charred grain from the degraded remnants of its floor surface was radiocarbon dated to the late eighth or ninth century cal. AD.[10] While the level of the floor was higher than that of Structure 1.2 at *c.*61.4 m OD, compared with *c.*60.3 m OD, this corresponds to the difference in topography at the two sites, rather than the height of occupation levels.[11] Together, the structures suggest that occupation before the *burh* extended to either side of Carfax.

Phase 2 Structure 2.1 belongs more certainly to the occupation that developed after the *burh* had been established. Postholes and a hearth below street surfacing associated with the *burh* have been recorded at No. 8 Queen Street,[12] while evidence for late Anglo-Saxon occupation nearby

8 Dodd, *Oxford*, pp. 31–2.

9 Ibid. pp. 17–19.

10 SUERC-43616, cal. AD 771–898 (91.2 per cent probability); '6–7 High Street, Oxford: Archaeological Excavation Report', unpublished OA report (2012), https://library.thehumanjourney.net/998/.

11 '6–7 High Street, Oxford', fig. 4, section 1001.

12 Ibid. p. 17.

includes cellars associated with street surfaces and pits at No. 4 Queen Street and Nos. 7–8 Queen Street.[13] A posthole within the cellar in the former site, which must have been close to the structures reported here, may relate to a pit lining,[14] similar to those seen in Structures 1.2 and 2.1 and the cellar pit from the High Street. A late Anglo-Saxon bun-shaped loomweight found beneath No. 121 St Aldate's during building work in 1931[15] joins the evidence for domestic craft activity at the current site.

Artefactual and ecofactual evidence paints a similar picture of life in this part of Anglo-Saxon Oxford in both Phases 1 and 2. Meals were prepared in jars over a fired clay hearth or in an oven. Charred plant remains comprised mainly grain, dominated by free-threshing wheat and hulled barley, which would have been made into pottages, porridges and bread. Smaller quantities of oats and rye were recorded, the former providing fodder for livestock; sheep-breeding or keeping is attested in Phase 2. Beef (including the marrow), mutton and pork was consumed. Butchery marks on cattle vertebrae suggest that the emphasis was on good-sized portions, rather than the quality or attractiveness of the cut. Chickens were kept for eggs, and oysters and freshwater fish were occasionally eaten. Spinning and bone-working, the latter utilising deer bones as well as (probably) waste from domesticated species, were among the craft or domestic activities carried out within the properties represented here or nearby. No germinated grain, potential evidence of malting and brewing, was identified. There was, however, some indication of change. The locally produced late Anglo-Saxon Oxford shelly ware, in which all the pottery from the site's pre-*burh* phase was found, had been replaced after the establishment of the *burh* entirely by St Neots shelly ware from Cambridgeshire. Exotica in the form of a jar or pitcher in Beauvais ware from France, possibly used for transporting wine, was also found. This reason for this difference is unclear – late Anglo-Saxon Oxford shelly ware is found in *burh*-phase deposits elsewhere in Oxford – but it is possible that the area around this part of Queen Street and St Aldate's was settled after the establishment of the *burh* by a different social group with high-status connections or wider trade links.

Medieval Period

During the late eleventh and twelfth centuries (Phase 3), the site is likely to have become an open area or yard. Excavation revealed pitting across the site, which received household waste presumably from nearby properties. Stone-built Structure 3.1 is identified as a latrine and was located outside the building it served. Postholes in Area 3 relate to a fence or other timber structure, while Structure 3.2 belonged to a wall that divided two buildings, one extending to the north, the other to the south (and beyond the area of investigation). Rectangular holes and stone projections seen on the north face of the wall marked the position of a wooden floor.

Phase 3 corresponds with the earlier part of the date range ascribed to Oxford's Jewish quarter, which developed around Carfax and along St Aldate's and is conventionally dated to the twelfth to late thirteenth century.[16] The site is situated within two properties mapped as being in Jewish ownership: Jacob's Hall and a property owned by Elias or Elekin.[17] Structure 3.1 appears to be within the boundary of Jacob's Hall, and it is in this structure that archaeological evidence consistent with Jewish occupation was found. An obvious means by which an archaeological 'signature' of Jewish occupation might be detected is through a comparison of the animal bone assemblage with Jewish dietary law or *kashrut*. A Jewish assemblage would not be expected to contain any wild animals (including birds), pig bones, horse bones, bones showing disease, or bones from the hind-quarters of cattle. Shellfish and fish without fins or scales (for instance eels) would also be absent. What is remarkable about the assemblage from Structure 3.1 is that

13 Dodd, *Oxford*, p. 408.

14 Ibid.

15 Oxford Urban Archaeological Database, 682.

16 Manix, 'Oxford: Mapping the Jews'.

17 Ibid.

pig specimens are completely absent, while domestic fowl specimens (mainly goose) dominate, being even more common than cattle bones. Fish bones from the feature included herring, but no eel. Of the eighty-nine fragments of marine shell recovered from Phase 3 deposits, just one came from Structure 3.1. The animal bone assemblage stands in sharp contrast to that of Phase 2, in which pig bones were present in quantity and bird bones barely present. As the animal bone analysis was targeted on selected groups, no Phase 4 groups were analysed, but assessment data showed that pig was present in thirteenth- to fourteenth-century contexts.[18] The pattern also contrasts with the assemblage recovered from Phase 3 pits within Area 1, again recorded, but not subject to detailed analysis. Notably, these features contained pig bones, marine shell and eel bones, and it is probable that the pits predate the latrine and relate to a period in the earlier part of the phase before the property was transferred to Jewish ownership. This is supported by the ceramic data. Pottery from the pits was characterised by medieval Oxford ware, with a date range commencing in the late eleventh century, and Cotswold-type ware, which dates from the late tenth century. The pottery assemblage from Structure 3.1, however, contained early Brill/Boarstall ware dating after *c*.1200 (technically belonging to the earliest part of Phase 4).

Evidence supporting the findings of the animal bone analysis was obtained by organic residue analysis (ORA). Samples from 10 vessels, mainly jar rims but including some body sherds, from Phase 3 and 4 contexts were analysed by gas chromatography and carbon isotope analysis. The samples were compared to 10 contemporaneous samples from Queen's College (chapter 6, below), and results of ORA on samples from Phases 1 and 2 of St Aldate's from an earlier study were also considered. The analysis showed in Phase 3 and 4 samples an absence of non-ruminant fats (that is, porcine) and presence in all but one of the samples of ruminant fats (cattle and sheep). In contrast, two samples from Phase 1 and 2 were mixed, with both ruminant and non-ruminant fats represented. While seven of the Queen's College samples showed ruminant fats only, the remainder fell within the ruminant/non-ruminant part of the spectrum, demonstrating mixed use. In summary, the Phase 3 and 4 samples show that the pottery was not used to process or cook pork and suggest that, as with the animal bone assemblage from Structure 3.1, pork was absent from the pottery users' diet. In contrast, pottery was used in the processing of pork in the middle/late Anglo-Saxon phases of St Aldate's and at early medieval Queen's College, at least some of the time.

One other interesting observation is that the pottery in Phases 1 and 2 and Queen's College show mixed fats; in other words, the same pottery vessels were used to cook beef or mutton and pork. Dairy fats were occasionally recorded – such fats were identified in one sample from Phase 1/2 and one from Phase 4 at St Aldate's – but in those vessels, no other fats were seen. This suggests that dairy processing, such as the production of cheese or butter, was rarely undertaken at a domestic level in Oxford whatever the period – possibly such products were acquired ready-made from sellers – but when it was undertaken, it was done so in jars dedicated to the task. This aspect is consistent with Jewish occupation, as according to the principles of *kashrut*, it was important to keep meat and dairy separate, although on current evidence, a similar separation is apparent in pre-Jewish phases.

It should be noted that none of the Phase 3 ORA samples came from Structure 3.1, but instead were taken from vessels recovered from Area 1 pits. However, their respective contexts were in the upper part of the sequence of filling and contained no pig bones, eel bones or marine shell, and may belong to episodes of levelling related to the construction of the property (Jacob's Hall?) represented by the Structure 3.1. While the combined evidence of ORA and the animal bone does not conclusively identify Jewish habitation at St Aldate's, it nevertheless points very strongly to it. As such, this is the first (very likely) medieval Jewish signature in British zooarchaeology. Given the stratigraphy and the dating evidence from Area 1, a case can be made for dating this

[18] L. Broderick, 'Animal Bone', in '114–119 St Aldate's and 4–5 Queen Street, Oxford: Archaeological Evaluation Report', appendix C.1.

Jewish phase from the later part of the twelfth to the early thirteenth century, certainly after the period of pit-digging, and perhaps spanning a single generation of residents. This is some decades before the expulsion of the Jews from England in 1290 and suggests that the property had been taken relatively abruptly out of Jewish ownership, possibly having been confiscated, rather than being allowed to pass to heirs.

The finds and environmental evidence from the areas of excavation reveal interesting aspects about daily life in and around the site during the late eleventh and twelfth centuries. A leather shoe from a pit in evaluation test pit 1 and broadly contemporary with Structure 3.1 may have been worn by the Jewish residents. Ceramic building material suggests that buildings had tiled roofs with chimneys and (at least partially) tiled floors. This is consistent with the stone walls of Structures 3.1 and 3.2, which denote wealthy buildings (contrasting with the wooden buildings of earlier phases). The pottery was generally of a domestic character, but included ceramic crucibles that point to small-scale metalworking. Craft or industrial activity is also suggested by a whetstone, while a possible hoe among the metal objects suggests garden-related or horticultural work. Apart from abstinence from pork, shellfish and eel in the Jewish phase, diet consisted of bread and grain-based pottages, the latter including beef or mutton, at least occasionally. Goose was consumed by Jewish residents. Fish was presumably purchased from stalls from the north end of St Aldate's (formerly Fish Street) and included freshwater species, such as pike, burbot and (before the Jewish phase) eels, and marine species, among them herring, haddock and plaice, which arrived in barrels preserved in salt or brine.

During the fourteenth and fifteenth centuries (Phase 4), all properties represented at the site reverted to Christian ownership, indicated not least by the recovery of oyster shell, pig bones and eel bones from deposits associated with this phase. Structures assigned to this phase comprise walls (Structures 4.2, 4.3, 4.4 and 4.5) that correspond to property boundaries mapped by H.E. Salter as belonging to Battes Inn and the Red Lion Inn.[19] Part of a cellared structure (4.1) was also recorded that could potentially have belonged to the Red Lion.

The contents of pits and layers dated to this phase reveal something of the diet, activities, and status of the people who lived here at the time. Grain continued to be used mainly for bread (albeit made with refined flour) and pottages. (Cats, attested in this phase, had been kept at least since the eleventh century at the site to prevent mice reaching stores of grain.) Small quantities of barley might have been used for malting and brewing ale, though no definitive evidence for such activities was found. Beef, mutton and to a lesser extent pork were consumed, as well as the occasional hare and freshwater and cured marine fish. A relatively large quantity of fruits, among them sloe, cherry, damson-type fruit, grape, fig, wild strawberries and pear or apple, were recovered from a layer of domestic and faecal waste (10013), with coriander and fennel also recorded. Meals were cooked and served in a fairly standard range of domestic pottery, but a fragment of early Malagan or Valencian lustreware points to the presence of rare and exotic household items. The roofs of the buildings here or nearby were tiled, but floors were generally plainer – timber boards or trampled-earth floor were more usual than tiles – and part of the properties provided accommodation for animals, as indicated by the recovery of stabling waste in layer 10013. Window glass was recorded, and light was also provided by an oil lamp. The overall impression of the Phase 4 material is of high-status households, perhaps those of merchants with connections with coastal trade.

The late-medieval period (Phase 5: fifteenth to mid sixteenth century) saw the construction of several new structures (Structures 5.1 and 5.2 and drainage group 13004) relating to cellars and the division of properties. The composition of the pottery assemblage was noticeably different to that of Phase 4, comprising almost exclusively drinking vessels (cups, mugs and jugs), rather than the jars and bowls of a more domestic character seen in the previous phase. The mercantile

19 H.E. Salter, *Map of Mediaeval Oxford* (1934). These were properties of Merton College, but no early plans survive.

households, it seems, had been replaced by the commercial activity of an inn, probably Battes Inn, within whose boundary Structures 5.1 and 5.2 lay. An alternative possibility is that the assemblage may derive from labourers involved in some form of industrial or building activity.

Post-Medieval Period

Part of the site became open between the mid sixteenth and mid seventeenth centuries (Phase 6), as the drains in Area 11 were removed and the immediate area levelled, while in other areas rubbish pits were dug. It is uncertain whether this relates to activity associated with inns, as the pottery recovered is of a domestic character. However, evidence of Phase 7 (mid seventeenth to early eighteenth century) can be linked to activity related to drinking establishments more readily. In Area 1, a thirteenth-/fourteenth-century building associated with Structure 4.1 is likely to have been demolished. A stone-lined latrine (Structure 7.1) was inserted against what has been mapped as the southern wall of Battes Inn,[20] its function as a latrine revealed by the presence of faecal matter and traces of sedge collected from the riverbank or the floor of stables to dampen aromas. While its use by the patrons of the inn cannot be confirmed, the latrine was certainly filled with some evidence of drinking-related activity; the glass assemblage included fragments of 'globe and shaft' bottles carrying the seals of two other establishments, the Mermaid and the Crown, the latter being located at No. 3 Cornmarket. A large group of clay tobacco pipes was also recovered from the feature; twenty or so complete or near-complete examples could be reconstructed from the fragments. Among the ecofactual evidence from the feature were the remains of fig, blackberry, raspberry, grape, strawberry, elder and apple. Such fruit was also recorded at Corpus Christi College and Merton College and points to a high-status diet.[21] The animal bone assemblage, comprising domestic mammals and fowl, was typical of an urban pattern of consumption.

Given their quantity and nature of deposition, the pipes are likely to relate to a level of use beyond that of a normal household. The glass bottle seals point to the supply of wine from a variety of local drinking establishments, while the fruit represents the consumption of relatively exotic foodstuffs. Taken together, the contents of the latrine are likely to represent the dumping of waste deriving from a source of some affluence, perhaps accommodation or an establishment favoured by wealthy individuals from a mercantile or collegiate background.

Evidence belonging to Phase 8 (early eighteenth to nineteenth century) was restricted to the remains of at least two buildings that fronted a passage leading off St Aldate's adjacent to the New Inn. A cobbled surface also uncovered is likely to have been a modern repair of an earlier surface associated with this passage. A possible bone stylus or quill-holder attests to literacy in this area, possibly relating to commercial activity.

ARCHAEOLOGICAL DESCRIPTION

Phases 1–2: Middle to Late Anglo-Saxon (Fig. 4.2)

Structure 1.1 Within Area 5, there was a laminated sequence of compacted clay/gravel floors and charcoal-rich occupation deposits suggesting the presence of a structure (Structure 1.1; Figs. 4.2 and 4.3). These sealed a posthole (5033) that may have been associated with an early phase of the structure. A charred grain from the posthole produced a radiocarbon date of cal. AD 769–969 (SUERC-78795: Table 4.2). Part of one floor showed evidence of scorching, suggesting the presence of a nearby hearth. The earliest floor produced a sherd of medieval

20 Salter, *Map of Mediaeval Oxford*.

21 W. Smith, 'Charred and Waterlogged Plant Remains', in R. Bashford et al., 'Medieval and Post-Medieval Remains from Excavations on the Site of the New Auditorium, Corpus Christi College, Oxford, 2008', *Oxoniensia*, 79 (2014), p. 206; for Merton College, chapter 8, below.

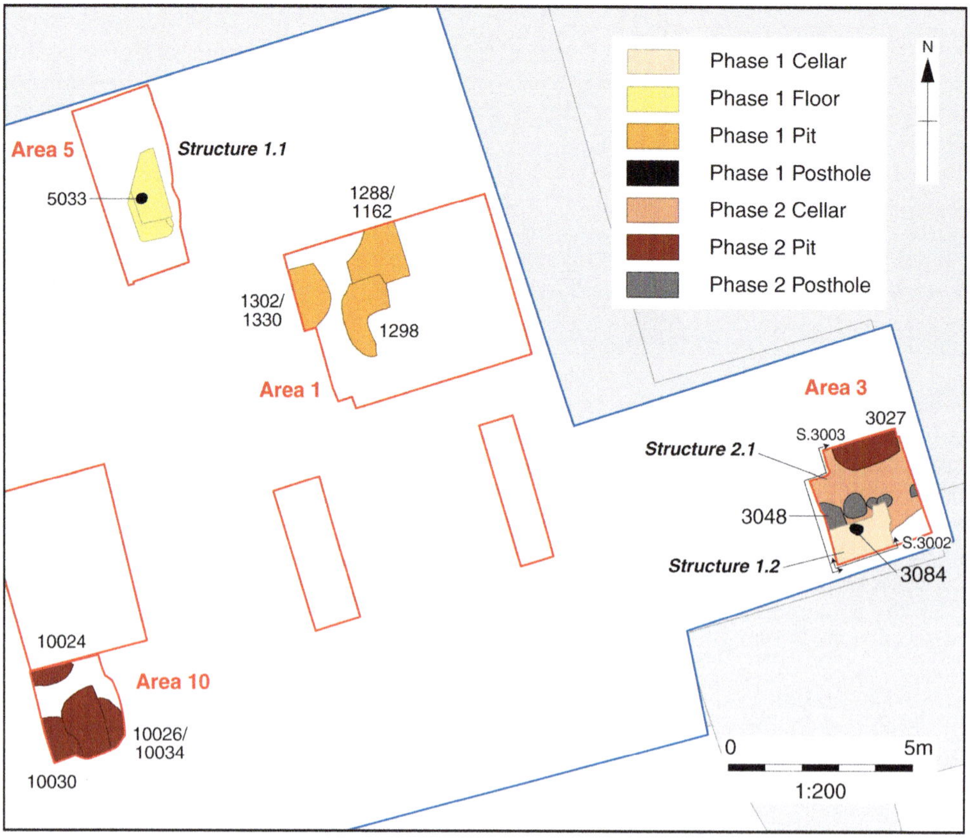

Fig. 4.2 Phases 1–2: late Anglo-Saxon.

Oxford ware dating from the late eleventh century, although it is likely to be intrusive from the pits that subsequently cut these levels during Phase 3.

Structure 1.2 Within Area 3 was a sunken timber-built structure (Structure 1.2) that probably represented a precursor to cellared Structure 2.1. Only part of its eastern edge was visible, having been largely truncated by the later structure, but it measured at least 1.48 x 1.20 m and survived to a depth of 0.95 m. At its base, close to its eastern edge, was a shallow posthole (3084), 0.36 m in diameter, that may have held timber shuttering that once lined its sides. A 'stakehole' (3091) filled with decayed organic material that was revealed in section (Fig. 4.4, Section 3002) against its eastern edge may have marked the position of one such shutter or an earlier lining of wattle. No evidence for internal floors was found and the structure appears to have been deliberately dismantled and levelled with material containing sherds of late Anglo-Saxon Oxford shelly ware. A radiocarbon date of cal. AD 689–893 was obtained from a grain recovered from within the infilled posthole (SUERC-78794: Table 4.2).

Structure 2.1 Structure 1.2 was replaced by a second probable timber-lined cellar pit (Structure 2.1) during Phase 2. Its extents, apart from its southern side, lay beyond the trench edges, but must have measured over 2.7 x 2.6 m and was *c.*1.84 m deep. A line of five postholes cut into the base of the pit probably formed part of a post and plank revetment along its southern side. At least one of the posts (3048) seems to have rotted in situ after the cellar was backfilled (Fig. 4.4, Section 3003). It had a 'floor' of concreted and laminated gravel on which large sherds of late Anglo-Saxon Oxford

Fig. 4.3 Floors of Structure 1.1 with north wall of Structure 5.1 behind figures. View towards the north.

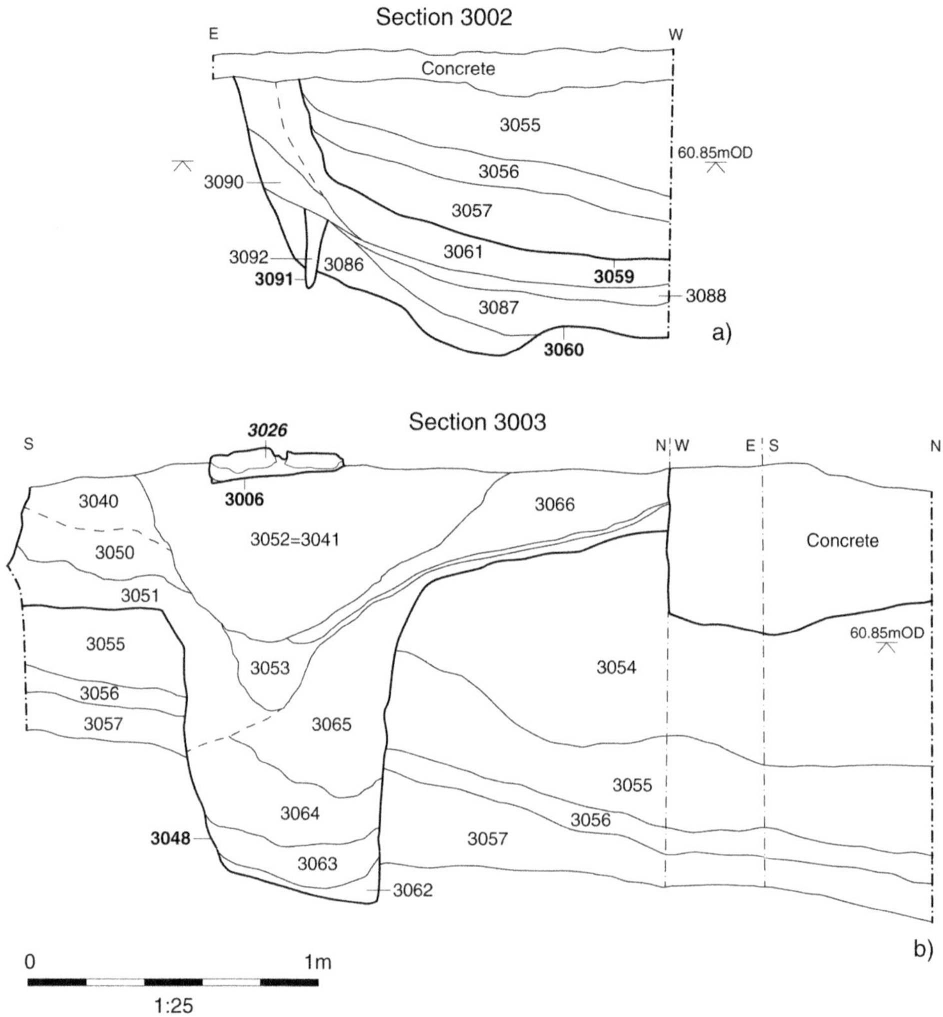

Fig. 4.4 a) Section 3002; b) Section 3003.

shelly ware were recovered, together with Cotswold-type ware, suggesting a late tenth- or early eleventh-century date. Overlying the floor were silt spreads that were rich in charcoal and charred cereal grain, including free-threshing wheat, and also produced a ceramic spindle whorl of late Anglo-Saxon/early medieval type. The cellar pit was backfilled by the end of the eleventh century, after which pit 3027 was cut through its fills. This pit also contained eleventh-century pottery. It is possible that the cellar extended eastwards into Area 14 where the fill (1485) of a large early feature that encompassed the whole trench was recorded. However, no dating evidence was recovered.

Pits Area 1 contained several pits that were probably used for the disposal of rubbish, possibly from the occupants of Structure 1.1. The earliest of these (1288, recut as 1162) was rectangular and 0.70 m in depth and was filled with succession of dumps containing appreciable quantities of pottery and animal bone. The pottery comprised solely late Anglo-Saxon Oxford shelly ware, apart from a single sherd of red-painted Beauvais-type ware, suggesting a ninth- or tenth-century date. In contrast, later pits 1298 and 1302, both circular, each contained a single sherd of St Neots ware and must date after the mid ninth century. Pit 1302 was 0.90 m deep and was later recut during Phase 2 as pit 1330. It contained further sherds of St Neots ware, together with large sherds of Cotswold-type ware and Flemish/Rhenish greyware, suggesting a late tenth- or early eleventh-century date for deposition.

Several inter-cutting rubbish pits (10024, 10026, 10030, and 10034) were found within Area 10. The phasing of these pits is tentative, given the lack of excavation and dating evidence obtained from them. Pit 10026 (= 10034), which post-dated pit 10030, contained Cotswold-type ware, suggesting a late tenth- or eleventh-century date for deposition.

Phase 3: Late Eleventh to Twelfth Century (Fig. 4.5)

This phase saw an increase in the degree of pitting within Area 1 and for the first time pitting within Area 5, presumably after Structure 1.1 had been demolished. Further pits were recorded in Area 10, implying that much of the site was external during this time. Two postholes found within Area 3 suggest the presence of a timber structure or fence. This phase saw the construction of the first stone-built structures (Structures 3.1 and 3.2).

Structure 3.1 This rectangular structure, probably a latrine, comprised a rectangular shaft measuring 1.7 x 1.3 m and about 1.1 m deep, lined with roughly squared limestone blocks bonded by a firm reddish brown sandy/gravel mortar (Figs. 4.5–4.7). There was a pair of opposing putlog holes on its east and west walls near to its excavated depth, presumably to hold temporary supports

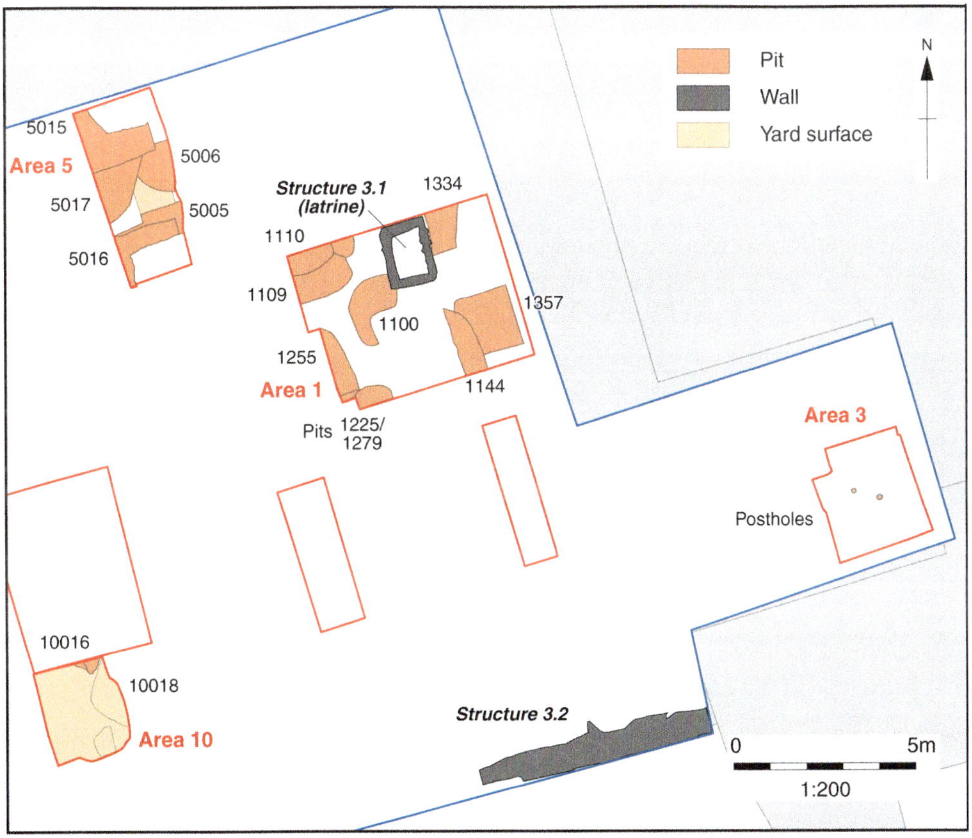

Fig. 4.5 Phase 3: late eleventh to twelfth centuries.

Fig. 4.6 Area 1 under excavation, showing latrine Structure 3.1 with cellared Structure 4.1 in foreground. View towards south-west.

Fig. 4.7 Detail of latrine Structure 3.1, after removal of south wall. View towards north. Scales: 1 m and 0.3 m.

during its construction. Its internal wall faces were rendered with a thin whitish mortar wash. Its basal fill (1101) comprised a thin greenish silty sand with lenses of charcoal that contained small amounts of mineralized concretions, potentially faecal waste. The shaft was subsequently infilled with a considerable quantity of domestic waste, suggesting that it later served as a rubbish pit. The animal bone assemblage was notable for its predominance of bird bones and a complete absence of pig bones. The pottery from its earliest fill comprised a large number of early Brill ware sherds datable from the early thirteenth century. A sheep or goat bone from a later fill was radiocarbon dated to cal. AD 1023–1184 and is likely to be residual (SUERC-78793: Table 4.2).

Structure 3.2 This structure represented the earliest evidence for stone-built buildings on the site and extended along the southern side of Area 4. It terminated and possibly returned towards the south at its western extent, suggesting that it formed the north wall of a building that lay to the south outside the excavated area. It appears to have been demolished and robbed during this phase as it was overlain by a sequence of dumps containing medieval Oxford ware.

Pits It is likely that most of the pits recorded in Areas 1 and 5 were used for the disposal of rubbish, though their intercutting nature also suggests that some may have originally served as gravel quarries. In contrast to latrine Structure 3.1, the pottery from them was dominated by medieval Oxford ware and Cotswold-type ware, suggesting a date prior to the late twelfth century. A pig mandible from pit 1051 returned a radiocarbon date of cal. AD 904–1119 with high probability that it dates before the Norman conquest, suggesting residuality (SUERC-80171: Table 4.2). Within Area 1 the animal assemblage, in contrast to that recovered from the latrine, included a wide range of meat-bearing domesticated mammals, including pig and appreciable quantities of shellfish, largely oyster. The upper fill (1214) of pit 1225 contained an exceptionally rich charred wheat assemblage, whilst pit 1279 (a recut of 1225) contained probable charred hay, either stabling or floor covering waste (fill 1129).

Within Area 10 pit 10018 was notable for containing possible faecal waste and uncharred fruit seeds (fill 10019). This part of the site appears to have formed part of a yard since the pit cut a compacted gravel surface which was replaced after the pit was filled.

Phase 4: Thirteenth to Fourteenth Century (Fig. 4.8)

This phase probably saw the construction of a series of structures that ran alongside the southern edge of Areas 3 and 4 (Structures 4.2, 4.3, 4.4 and 4.5) and along the east side of Area 1 (Structure 4.1), the last probably the rear extent of a substantial building. Structures in Areas 3 and 4 may have marked the division between two properties. Owing to the truncation by the modern basement, evidence for structures on the north side of the basement in Area 4 did not survive. Any associated structure to the south side lay largely outside the area of the excavation. Probable garden soils were revealed immediately below the modern basement slab across Area 4 and within Areas 7–9. A small area along the southern side of Area 4 was investigated. Here, the soil was found to contain Brill/Boarstall ware. Similar pottery was recovered from the garden soils recorded in Areas 7 and 8. The only pit assigned to Phase 4 was possible cesspit 4087 that contained Brill/Boarstall ware.

Structure 4.1 Straddling the east side of Area 1, this structure formed the south-west corner of a cellared building that apparently abutted a limestone wall foundation (1048) that corresponds to the rear extent of Salter's property SW 133, known later in the medieval period as the Red Lion. The interior of the structure could not be investigated, though a small sondage suggested that the cellar was at least 1.4 m in depth. The structure was constructed with randomly coursed limestone blocks that had been roughly squared to form its interior sides, bonded by a yellowish mortar. Unfortunately, no dating evidence was recovered, though the nature of its construction suggests a medieval date. It cut Phase 3 pits 1334 and 1357 that contained medieval Oxford ware. Overlying the pits to its west were trampled spreads of silt and charcoal, over which was a trampled dump of mortar-like gravel reminiscent of the walls of Structure 4.1, suggesting

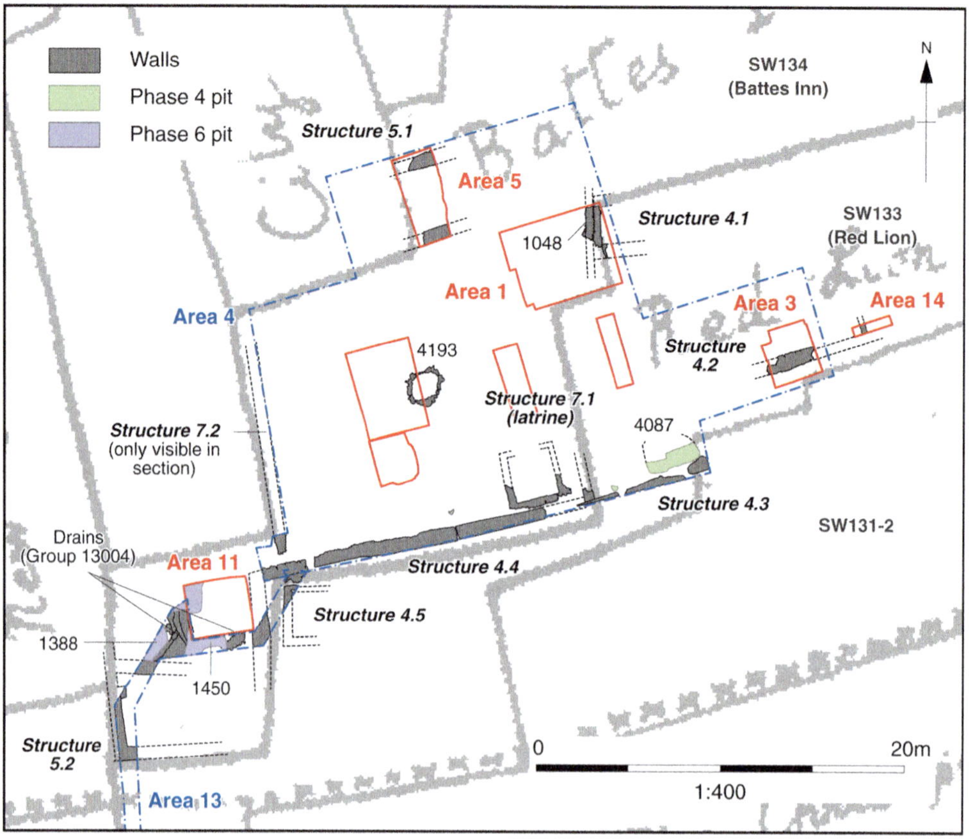

Fig. 4.8 Phases 4–7: thirteenth to early eighteenth century, plotted on H.E. Salter's reconstruction of medieval property boundaries in his Survey of Oxford.

construction debris. The underlying silt contained Minety-type ware datable from the early thirteenth century.

Structure 4.2 This undated, but possibly medieval, limestone wall within Area 3 was 0.85 m wide, sufficiently substantial to support a two-storey building (Fig. 4.9). A second but much narrower wall, bonded by yellowish mortar, ran perpendicular to its north side within Area 14 to the east. It is feasible that this wall was contemporary and formed an internal wall of this structure.

Structure 4.3 This was formed by an east–west wall foundation that replaced the earlier boundary wall of Phase 3 (Structure 3.2). It may have formed the wall of a building that extended to the north, since a contemporary wall projected northward from it. Alternatively, the north–south wall could have represented a subsequent boundary, as it corresponds with the rear of Salter's Property SW 133 (the Red Lion). Both walls comprised limestone rubble foundation bonded with a firm brownish yellow silty sand. Sherds of Brill/Boarstall ware were recovered from their foundation trenches and from an earlier garden soil that survived the basement truncation, along the southern edge of Area 4.

Structure 4.4 This limestone wall foundation may have been the westwards extension of Structure 4.3, although at this point it corresponds with the southern boundary of Salter's property SW 134 (Battes Inn) that doglegs behind the rear of the Red Lion. A probable southwards

Fig. 4.9 South side of Area 4 with basement slab in situ, showing Structure 4.4 with latrine Structure 7.1 in background. View towards east.

return was recorded during the watching brief in Area 13, which would also correspond to Salter's eastern boundary of this property.

Structure 4.5 Located within the internal angle of boundary Structure 4.4 (within Property SW134) was a probable stone-lined cesspit that remained largely unexcavated. Though no dating evidence was recovered, a garden soil that accumulated against it and Structure 4.4 contained Brill/Boarstall ware.

Phase 5: Fifteenth to Mid Sixteenth Century

Several new structures have tentatively been assigned to the late medieval period (Fig. 4.8), though given the paucity of the dating evidence and the lack of excavation (within Area 14) a later date is feasible for some of these structures. The cellared building (Structure 4.1) in Area 1 was infilled with rubble containing fresh sherds of late medieval Brill/Boarstall ware and Raeren stoneware, suggesting a late fifteenth- or sixteenth-century date.

Structure 5.1 Two east–west aligned limestone wall foundations were revealed in Area 5, though it is uncertain whether they pertained to the same building. The more substantial, north wall was built on relieving arches (Fig. 4.3), which presumably carried it over underlying soft ground resulting from earlier pitting, suggesting that it was load-bearing and formed part of a building. Pottery from an earlier pit, likely to represent its foundation trench, produced appreciable quantities of Brill/Boarstall ware. No surfaces were found that were contemporary with the walls, although a garden soil containing Frechen stoneware and clay pipe fragments dating to the seventeenth century apparently abutted the south wall, suggesting that this area was external by this time.

Structure 5.2 Evidence for a building was revealed in Area 13 and positioned, according to Salter, within a parcel of land located to the rear of Battes Inn. Parts of its north, south and west walls were exposed, which showed that the structure measured 5.3 m across (north–south) and that its west wall had an internal buttress that was added later (Fig. 4.10). Its walls were fairly substantial at 0.70–0.75 m thick, constructed with limestone rubble bonded by yellowish grey clay mortar. Late medieval Brill/Boarstall ware, dating to the fifteenth to early seventeenth centuries, was recovered from its north wall and its walls cut into a pre-existing garden soil.

Group 13004 A system of stone-built drains, some with capping stones still surviving, were located immediately to the north of Structure 5.2 and appear to have predated the building. As with Structure 5.2, they were constructed over a pre-existing garden soil. A small sherd of Cistercian ware of late fifteenth- or sixteenth-century date was recovered from the fabric of a drain wall.

Phase 6: Mid Sixteenth to Mid Seventeenth Century

The drains within Area 11 appeared to have been robbed during this phase and the area levelled. Subsequently, rubbish pits 1388 and 1450 were dug (Fig. 4.8). Pit 1388 was cut up to and possibly encroached on the north wall of Structure 5.2. Pit 1450 contained mid seventeenth-century clay pipe fragments and pottery spanning the mid sixteenth to mid seventeenth century, whilst a sherd of Frechen stoneware recovered from the top fill of pit 1388 suggests a similar or possibly slightly earlier date. Pit 1388 also contained medieval roof tile fragments together with a late medieval ridge tile and glazed brick fragment of fifteenth- to seventeenth-century date. Within Area 4, stone-lined well 4193, a late feature within the unexcavated levels of Area 4, is probably post-medieval in date.

Phase 7: Mid Seventeenth to Early Eighteenth Century

There was little evidence for activity during this phase. The building to which cellared Structure 4.1 may have belonged in Area 1 was probably demolished by this time (Fig. 4.8).

Fig. 4.10 The south part of Structure 5.2 within Area 13. View towards the south.

Structure 7.1 A stone-lined latrine (4073) was built against the boundary wall that extended alongside the southern side of Area 4. It measured 2.3 m across (east–west) and probably no more than 2.1 m (north–south), though its walls here did not survive the basement truncation. It was constructed with roughly hewn limestone blocks that had been roughly faced on their internal sides, bonded by reddish brown sandy mortar. It survived to ten courses deep or about 1.2 m in depth. Its fill was rich in cess-like deposits, one of which (4061) contained an abundance of mineralised fruit remains, largely grape, fig, blackberry/raspberry and elderberry seeds. A large assemblage of clay pipes, tightly dated to *c.*1650–70, was recovered from the feature. The pottery included a near-complete chamber pot and other pottery of seventeenth-century date. Also recovered were number of wine bottle fragments, some bearing the seal of Mermaid Tavern and the initials of Anthony Hall, the licensee of the tavern until his death in 1675. Another seal has the letters 'W.M.A.' above a crown, this coming from the Crown Inn at No. 3 Cornmarket and identifying William Morrell, who died in 1679, and his widow Anne, who continued as licensee until 1696.

Structure 7.2 Traces of a north–south substantial limestone wall foundation, probably a boundary wall, were revealed in section after the removal of the western wall of the basement. Deposits adhering to its north side though were either remnants of earlier stratigraphy or fills of its construction trench. Although pottery predominantly of thirteenth- or fourteenth century date was retrieved, several mid seventeenth-century clay pipe stems were recovered from the lower levels of these deposits. A fragment of the same wall was revealed in plan immediately to the south-west of basement and seventeenth-century glass was recovered from its foundation trench.

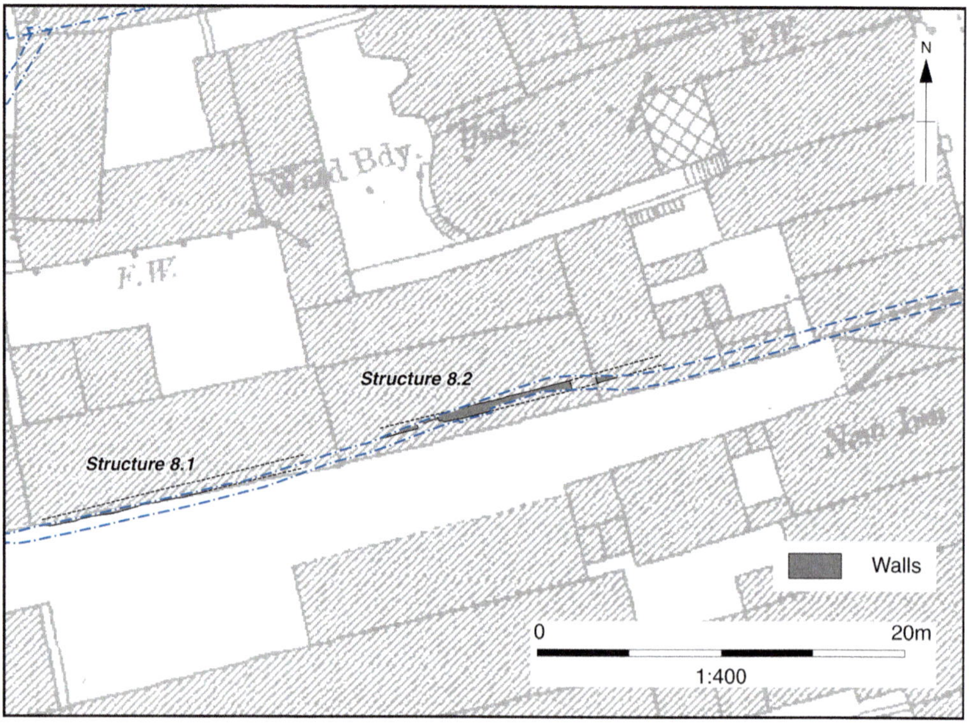

Fig. 4.11 Phase 8: early eighteenth to nineteenth century.

Phase 8: Eighteenth to Nineteenth Century

The bulk of the evidence was recorded during the watching brief in Area 13 and comprised parts of at least two buildings revealed within its southern arm, probably buildings fronting a passage leading off St Aldate's adjacent to the New Inn (Fig. 4.11). A cobbled surface of granite within bluestone repairs that directly underlay the existing slab was observed throughout the length of the southern arm of Area 13. The bluestone cobbles were probably a modern repair of the surface of the nineteenth-century phase of this passage.

Structure 8.1 This length of wall was composed of brick and limestone and corresponds to a building depicted on the Ordnance Survey map of 1876, but is not present on Taylor's map of 1750.

Structure 8.2 This substantial wall was composed of limestone blocks and had a stone-built threshold presumably leading out on to the lane. A large sherd of post-medieval redware obtained from the wall would support a late seventeenth- or eighteenth-century date for the construction of this building. It had been demolished prior to the construction of the cobbled surface.

POTTERY by PAUL BLINKHORN

The pottery assemblage comprised 2,028 sherds with a total weight of 38,767 g. The estimated vessel equivalent (EVE), by summation of surviving rim sherd circumference, was 24.57. It was recorded using the conventions of the Oxfordshire county type-series,[22] as follows.

OXAC Cotswold-type ware, AD 975–1350. 268 sherds, 4861 g, EVE = 2.78.
OXAG Abingdon ware, late eleventh–fourteenth century. 3 sherds, 94 g, EVE = 0.19.
OXAM Brill/Boarstall ware, AD 1200–1600. 225 sherds, 3717 g, EVE = 1.88.
OXAW Early Brill coarseware, AD 1180–1250. 83 sherds, 2371 g, EVE = 1.71.
OXB Late Anglo-Saxon Oxford shelly ware, late eighth–early eleventh century. 121 sherds, 2381 g, EVE = 1.09.
OXBB Minety-type ware, early thirteenth–sixteenth century. 4 sherds, 95 g, EVE = 0.05.
OXBF North-East Wiltshire ware, AD 1050–1400. 34 sherds, 798 g, EVE = 0.19.
OXBK Medieval shelly coarseware, AD 1100–1350. 5 sherds, 79 g, EVE = 0.
OXBN Tudor green ware, late fourteenth–sixteenth century. 2 sherds, 6 g, EVE = 0.
OXBS Beauvais-type ware, ninth–eleventh century. 6 sherds, 186 g, EVE = 0.
OXBX Late medieval Brill/Boarstall ware, fifteenth–early seventeenth century. 29 sherds, 947 g, EVE = 1.00.
OXCL Cistercian ware, AD 1470–1600. 10 sherds, 84 g, EVE = 0.07.
OXR St Neots ware, AD 850–1200. 43 sherds, 571 g, EVE = 0.68.
OXY Medieval Oxford ware, AD 1075–1350. 1065 sherds, 17138 g, EVE = 12.57.
OXZ Stamford ware, AD 850–1150. 7 sherds, 55 g, EVE = 0.30.

The post-medieval wares were recorded using the conventions of the Museum of London Type-Series,[23] as follows:

BORDB Brown-glazed Border ware, 1600–1700. 2 sherds, 6 g.
BORDG Green-glazed Border ware, 1550–1700. 3 sherds, 44 g.
BORDY Yellow-glazed Border ware, 1550–1700. 55 sherds, 557 g.
CREA Creamware, 1740–1830. 1 sherd, 6 g.
DERBS Derby stoneware, 1700–1900. 10 sherds, 17 g.
FREC Frechen stoneware, 1550–1750. 13 sherds, 553 g.
LONS London stoneware. 1680 +. 6 sherds, 118 g.
METS Metropolitan-type slipware, 1480–1900. 2 sherds, 34 g.
MLOJ Montelupo oil jar, 1750–1900. 1 sherd, 246 g.
PMBL Post-medieval black-glazed redware, late sixteenth–seventeenth century. 1 sherd, 14 g.
PMR Post-medieval redware, 1550+. 28 sherds, 1852 g.
RAER Raeren stoneware, 1480–1600. 8 sherds, 992 g, EVE = 1.82.
REFW Refined whiteware, 1800–1900. 21 sherds, 219 g.
STSL Staffordshire slipware, 1650–1800. 1 sherd, 4 g.
SWSG Staffordshire white salt-glazed stoneware, 1720–1800. 1 sherd, 2 g.
TGW English tin-glazed ware, 1600–1800. 3 sherds, 23 g.

The following, not included in the Oxford type-series, were also noted:

22 Mellor, 'Synthesis'.
23 A.G. Vince, 'The Saxon and Medieval Pottery of London: A Review', *Medieval Archaeology*, 29 (1985), pp. 25–93.

F1	Early/middle Anglo-Saxon organic-tempered ware, 1 sherd, 15 g, EVE = 0.
F102	Thetford-type ware.[24] 2 sherds, 48 g, EVE = 0.06.
F104	Flemish/Rhenish greyware, eleventh–twelfth century. 5 sherds, 138 g, EVE = 0.
F401	Spanish tin-glazed ware, late fourteenth–sixteenth century. 1 sherd, 15 g, EVE = 0.11.
F1001	Romano-British. 5 sherds, 96 g.
F1002	Iron Age. 4 sherds, 159 g, EVE = 0.07.

The general range of pottery types is fairly typical of sites in Oxford, albeit with some exotica in the form of late Anglo-Saxon, medieval and post-medieval imports. This is a pattern that has been noted in the past at other excavations in the St Aldate's area. The excavations in the late 1960s and early 1970s, centred around 79–87 St Aldate's, produced an assemblage similar to this one.[25] There, the middle–late Anglo-Saxon assemblage was dominated by OXB, with St Neots ware (OXR) a relatively minor ware, and a number of mainly Saxo-Norman continental imported types, such as Andenne, North French and Rhenish/Flemish greywares,[26] also present. Here, pottery from France (Beauvais ware) and the Low Countries/Germany (Flemish/Rhenish greyware) is present. Such pottery is not common in Oxford, but similar types were also noted at nearby excavations in St Aldate's,[27] Queen Street and All Saints Church.[28] In most cases, OXB was also the dominant middle-late Anglo-Saxon pottery type. The sherds of Beauvais ware do not refit, but appear to be mostly, if not entirely from the same vessel, a red-painted, fairly large jar or pitcher, a typical product of the tradition. The inner surface is somewhat degraded, which is typical of pottery that was used to store slightly acidic liquids,[29] so the vessel may have been used for transporting wine.

The single sherd of early/middle Anglo-Saxon hand-built pottery is a rare find in the city, although one of the very few relatively large assemblages from Oxford occurred at nearby Nos. 31–4 Church Street.[30] Thetford ware, represented here by two sherds from pitchers or storage jars, is also an uncommon occurrence in Oxford, although some sites have produced one or two sherds, such as Lincoln College.[31] It is likely that these pots were arriving as containers for traded goods, rather than as desirable goods in their own right.

Surprisingly, given the amount of well-documented late Anglo-Saxon activity within the immediate vicinity of these excavations, stratified late Anglo-Saxon pottery is very scarce, with just eight sherds noted, although it is possible that some of the groups which only contained OXB date to this time. As noted above, OXR is rare in this area of the town, with OXB seeming to have continued to be the dominant ware in the late Anglo-Saxon period, possibly reflecting the ethnic identities of populations of differing backgrounds living in the town at that time.[32] Thus, some of the contexts which produced only OXB and are dated to ceramic phase (CP) MSAX (Table 4.3), may be of late Anglo-Saxon (LSAX) date.

24 A. Rogerson and C. Dallas, *Excavations in Thetford 1948–59 and 1973–80*, East Anglian Archaeology, 22 (1984).

25 R. Haldon, 'Late Saxon and Medieval Pottery', in B. Durham, 'Archaeological Investigations in St Aldate's, Oxford', *Oxoniensia*, 42 (1977), pp. 111–39.

26 Ibid. table 1.

27 Ibid. table 1.

28 Dodd, *Oxford*, table 6.7.

29 G. Perry, 'Beer, Butter and Burial', *Medieval Ceramics*, 32 (2011), pp. 9–22.

30 M. Mellor, 'Pottery', in Hassall, 'St Ebbe's, Part I', p. 198.

31 P. Blinkhorn, 'The Pottery', in Z. Kamash et al., 'Late Saxon and Medieval Occupation: Evidence from Excavations at Lincoln College, Oxford 1997–2000', *Oxoniensia*, 67 (2002), p. 232.

32 P. Blinkhorn, 'No Pots Please, We're Vikings: Pottery in the Southern Danelaw, 850–1000', in D. Hadley and L. Ten Harkel (eds.), *Everyday Life in Viking Towns: Social Approaches to Towns in England and Ireland c.800–1000* (2013), pp. 157–71.

Table 4.3. Ceramic phase chronology, occurrence and defining wares.

Phase	Defining wares	Date	No. sherds	Weight (g)	Mean sherd weight (g)	EVE
RB	All Roman	1st–4th C	2	39	19.5	0
MSAX	OXB	E8th–9th C	31	741	23.9	0.14
LSAX	OXBS, OXR, OXZ	10th–early 11th C	8	60	7.5	0
SN	OXAC, OXBF	E–L 11thC	80	1844	23.1	1.08
M1	OXY	L 11th–12th C	837	12,924	15.4	9.64
M2	OXAM	13th–14th C	823	15,415	18.7	8.9
M3	OXBX, OXBN	E–L 15th C	24	851	35.5	1.24
M4	OXCL, RAER	L 15th–M 16thC	45	1760	39.9	3.16
PM1	PMR, FREC, BORDY, BORDG	M–L 16th C	35	1502	42.9	0
PM2	TGW, WEST, PMBL	E–M 17th C	31	1659	53.5	0
PM3	TGW	M–L 17th C	0	0	0	0
PM4	LONS	L17th–E18thC	7	500	71.4	0
PM5	DERBS, MLOJ, SWSG	18th C	13	270	20.7	0
MOD	WHEW	19th C	92	1202	13.1	0
Total			2028	38,767		

The bulk of the Saxo-Norman (CP SN) material consists of OXB (55.4 per cent of the CP assemblage by weight) (Table 4.4). It is possible that it could all be residual, and that there was considerable disturbance of late Anglo-Saxon strata during CP SN, but many of the OXB sherds are large and fresh, suggesting that this was not the case. Another possibility is that OXB may have carried on in use for a little longer than its traditional dating suggests, or, alternatively, that some of the OXAC from the site is earlier than is usual for sites in Oxford, and that contexts containing just OXB and OXAC are late Anglo-Saxon rather than Saxo-Norman. While OXAC is not normally found in quantity in Oxford before the eleventh century, earlier groups are known; for example, a vessel was found in a secure early tenth-century context at Trill Mill.[33]

The Saxo-Norman and medieval pottery is much more typical of other sites of the period in the town, being dominated first by OXAC, then OXY, and finally with Brill/Boarstall wares (OXAW, OXAM and OXBX) common from the thirteenth century onwards. The largest assemblages, as is often the case in Oxford, date to the late eleventh to fourteenth century, with deposition dropping off quite sharply after that time. The late-medieval and post-medieval assemblages mostly comprise small groups of mainly residual material with a few large fragments of well-represented contemporary pottery.

Much of the earlier medieval material is the product of secondary deposition, as is often the case, with the pottery presumably having been first deposited in domestic middens or the like before being utilized as back-fill for earth-cut features such as pits, etc. The CP M1 material is largely typical of domestic assemblages of the period in the town, other than the fact that there are a relatively large number of crucible fragments present, with such vessels making up 8.4 per cent of the rim assemblage (five examples) and body sherds from another two noted, suggesting

33 Mellor, 'Synthesis', p. 51.

Table 4.4. Pottery occurrence per ceramic phase by fabric type, expressed as a percentage of the total weight (g) per phase, major fabrics only. Shaded cells: residual material.

Fabric	MSAX	LSAX	SN	M1	M2	M3	M4	PM1	PM2	PM4	PM5	MOD
OXB	100%	0	55.7%	3.4%	0.9%	0	0	0	0	0	0	2.3%
OXR	–	90.0%	5.4%	2.0%	1.0%	1.3%	0	0	0	0	0	0
OXZ	–	0	0.5%	0.2%	0.1%	0	0	0	0	0	0	0.4%
OXBS	–	10.0%	8.4%	0.2%	0	0	0	0	0	0	0	0
OXAC	–	–	22.4%	22.9%	8.3%	11.2%	0	4.5%	0.4%	0	0	1.4%
OXBF	–	–	2.6%	1.1%	2.2%	0	0	17.3%	0	0	0	0
OXY	–	–	–	67.1%	52.0%	18.7%	6.8%	0.9%	0.9%	8.0%	0	7.1%
OXAW	–	–	–	–	15.5%	0	0	0	0	0	0	0
OXAM	–	–	–	–	17.9%	37.4%	5.9%	1.5%	0	10.8%	0.4%	29.7%
OXBX	–	–	–	–	–	31.1%	29.4%	4.4%	1.7%	0	0	5.8%
OXCL	–	–	–	–	–	–	1.6%	2.4%	1.2%	0	0	0
RAER	–	–	–	–	–	–	56.3%	0	0	0	0	0
PMR	–	–	–	–	–	–	–	58.2%	20.8%	80.6%	0	19.1%
FREC	–	–	–	–	–	–	–	7.0%	25.0%	0	0	2.7%
BORDY	–	–	–	–	–	–	–	3.5%	43.8%	0	0	0
BORDG	–	–	–	–	–	–	–	0	2.6%	0	0	0
TGW	–	–	–	–	–	–	–	–	0.8%	0	0	0.7%
PMBL	–	–	–	–	–	–	–	–	0.8%	0	0	0
LONS	–	–	–	–	–	–	–	–	–	0.6%	0	9.6%
DERBS	–	–	–	–	–	–	–	–	–	–	6.3%	0
MLOJ	–	–	–	–	–	–	–	–	–	–	91.1%	0
WHEW	–	–	–	–	–	–	–	–	–	–	–	18.2%
Total weight (g)	741	60	1844	12,924	15,415	851	1757	1502	1659	500	270	1202

Table 4.5. Vessel occurrence per ceramic phase by EVE, expressed as a percentage of the total per phase.

Vessel	MSAX	LSAX	SN	M1	M2	M3	M4
Jar	100%	0	85.2%	83.1%	62.8%	15.3%	1.9%
Bowl	0	0	14.8%	3.4%	5.3%	84.7%	0
Jug	0	0	0	3.9%	30.6%	0	31.6%
Lamp	0	0	0	1.1%	0	0	0
Crucible	0	0	0	8.4%	1.3%	0	0
Lid	0	0	0	0	0	0	6.6%
Cup/mug	0	0	0	0	0	0	59.8%
Total EVE	0.14	0	1.08	9.64	8.90	1.24	3.16
Dripping dish	0	0	0	0	0	0	1

that metalworking or the like was taking place at the site. However, the crucible assemblage all appears to have not been subjected to intense heat for prolonged periods. One or two of them show very slight vitrification on the outer surface, and others appear to have oxidized, but none of them had any visible residues on either surface, and either they were not used, or they were used in relatively low temperature environments, probably below 900 degrees centigrade, the temperature at which earthenware begins to vitrify.[34] All the crucible fragments except one came from Area 1, with the other occurring in Area 4. It is perhaps significant that the lamp rim also came from this area of the site. Recent work has suggested that lamps were often used as illumination in relation to craftwork in some areas of the country, particularly to the west of Oxford.[35] Relatively large groups of crucible fragments are not common from Oxford sites of this date. Industrial activity dating to the late eleventh to mid twelfth century was noted at Nos. 79–80 St Aldate's,[36] but crucibles were not among the finds from there,[37] although a number were noted at Nos. 31–4 Church Street, probably of late eleventh- to twelfth-century date.[38] One or two fragments of crucibles were also noted in the Saxo-Norman levels at All Saints Church.[39]

The CP M2 (thirteenth- to fourteenth-century) assemblage is large and entirely typical of the period in Oxford, and appears to be of a domestic nature, with vessels associated with eating, drinking, cooking and lighting noted (Table 4.5). A single crucible rim was noted, but it is of Stamford type, and thus very likely to be residual, and presumably contemporary with those noted in the previous phase. One rarity is a fragment of a rim sherd in Spanish tin-glazed ware. Such pottery is a very rare find in Oxford and, assuming it is not intrusive, it is likely to be a fragment of early Malagan or Valencian lustreware.[40] Such pottery has become reasonably well-recognised in England in the past couple of decades, and while it occurs at high-status 'magnate' residences, it is also found at urban sites away from the coast.[41] Its presence here may be an indication that people of greater than normal wealth and/or status lived at the site in the

34 P.M. Rice, *Pottery Analysis: A Sourcebook* (1987), p. 5.

35 P. Blinkhorn et al., 'Fiat Lux: Functional Analysis of Three Saxo-Norman Pottery Lamps from Berkeley, Gloucestershire', *Medieval Archaeology*, 61 (2017), pp. 104–16.

36 Durham, 'Archaeological Investigations in St Aldate's', p. 100.

37 Haldon, 'Late Saxon and Medieval Pottery', p. 132.

38 Mellor, 'Pottery', pp. 201, fig. 45, no. 4.

39 Dodd, *Oxford*, p. 338.

40 A. Gutierrez, 'Cheapish and Spanish: Meaning and Design on Imported Spanish Pottery', *Medieval Ceramics*, 21 (1997), pp. 73–82.

41 Ibid. fig. 3.

fourteenth century or thereabouts,[42] so the site may have been the residence of a merchant at this time.

Pottery deposition at the site drops off very rapidly after this time. The pottery assemblages dating to the fifteenth century and late fifteenth to mid sixteenth century (CP M3 and M4) weighed just *c.*2.5 kg in total, much of which was residual, with most of the rest made up of a handful of well-represented vessels. Previous excavations in St Aldate's have shown a similar picture, with relatively little fifteenth- to sixteenth-century pottery occurring.[43] The fact that the CP M4 assemblage is made up almost entirely of drinking vessels does however correspond with the presence of drinking establishments in the area.

The entire post-medieval and modern assemblages totalled around 6 kg of pottery, with the CP assemblages showing a similar pattern to those of the late medieval period, being groups of small and mostly residual sherds along with a few large fragments of individual vessels, such as the near-complete BORDY chamber-pot from CP PM2. Perhaps the most notable was the large sherd from an eighteenth-century context of a Montelupo oil-jar. Such pots, used for transporting Italian olive oil, were extremely large, with a capacity of around 20 gallons not unusual, and are known from many eighteenth- to nineteenth-century sites in Britain, Europe and North America, and once empty, were often used as shop signs or garden ornaments.[44] The oil-jar aside, the post-medieval material appears entirely of a domestic nature.

Overall, the assemblage has many parallels with material from previous excavations in the St Aldate's area of Oxford. In the Saxo-Norman and earlier medieval periods in particular, the area was a thriving centre, with the presence of imported pottery and crucibles showing that there was industrial activity and trade, and suggesting that this was an area of economic importance in the town. By the thirteenth to fourteenth century, the pottery assemblages have a much more domestic nature with a sharp drop-off in pottery deposition from the fifteenth century onwards.

Catalogue of Illustrated Pottery (Fig. 4.12):

1. Fabric OXY. Full profile of a jar. Uniform light grey fabric, outer surface is evenly sooted below the neck, patches of burning on the inner surface of the body and base. Ctx 1167, pit 1334, Phase 3.
2. Fabric OXAW. Near-complete miniature jar. Orange-pink fabric with grey surfaces. Patch of glaze on interior surface of base. Ctx 1090, pit 1058 (latrine 3.1), Phase 3.
3. Fabric OXAM. Complete small bowl. Buff fabric with partially unvitrified green glaze on the inner surface. Ctx 10011, Phase 5.
4. Fabric OXBX. Base and lower body of jug. Dark red fabric with dark grey surfaces, patchy dark green glaze on the outer surface, inner fairly extensively lime-scaled. Ctx 10011, Phase 5.
5. Fabric RAER. Full profile of mug. Uniform grey fabric with patches of brown iron-wash on the outer surface under a clear salt-glaze. Inner surface unglazed pale brown. Large fragment of kiln waste stuck to the outside of the base. Ctx 1069, Phase 5.
6. Fabric BORDY. Near-complete chamber-pot. White fabric with pale grey surfaces, even yellow glaze on the inner surface. Ctx 4067 and 4102, Structure 7.1, Phase 7.

42 Ibid. p. 79.

43 Haldon, 'Late Saxon and Medieval Pottery', pp. 135, 137.

44 J. Ashdown, 'Oil Jars', *International Journal of Nautical Archaeology*, 1:1 (1972), pp. 147–53.

Fig. 4.12 Pottery.

ORGANIC RESIDUE ANALYSIS OF POTTERY by JULIE DUNNE and RICHARD P. EVERSHED

Selected pottery vessels from Phases 3 (four samples) and 4 (six samples) were examined to determine whether organic residues were preserved and, if so, which commodities were processed in the vessels and whether a 'Jewish' signal could be identified. For the purposes of comparison, organic residue analysis was additionally carried out on a contemporaneous assemblage (ten samples) from Queen's College, Oxford.[45] The Queen's College material derived from domestic and industrial deposits that were away from the Jewry and predated the college and therefore should not correlate to restricted or high-status diets. Furthermore, comparison was also made to pottery samples from Phase 1 and 2 of the St Aldate's site (eight samples) and Phase 3 and 4 (two samples) previously analysed by Lucy Cramp and Helen Whelton from the University of Bristol.[46]

There is extensive regulation and detail regarding animal consumption within the Jewish faith, but, in brief, in terms of the mammal species allowed, they need to have both cloven hooves and chew their cud (that is, be ruminants). Animals that only meet one characteristic (such as pig) are not permitted. Aquatic species with both fins and scales are allowed as are certain bird species, including chicken, geese and duck.[47] The results, determined from high-temperature gas chromatography (GC), gas chromatography-mass spectrometry (GC-MS) and carbon isotope analyses (GC-C-IRMS), demonstrate that six of the eight lipid residues from the earlier non-Jewish phases (1 and 2) at St Aldate's were predominantly from processing ruminant products (cattle, sheep or goat), but with the addition of some non-ruminant products (pig). Two vessels were used to process dairy products (milk, butter or cheese). In these phases, animal bones comprised 40 per cent domestic cattle, 40 per cent caprine and 20 per cent pig. The presence of unsaturated fatty acids $C_{20:1}$, $C_{22:1}$ and $C_{24:1}$ suggests that seed oil from *Brassica* species may have been used in the cooking of the ruminant carcass products in two vessels.

In contrast, nine of the twelve pottery samples from St Aldate's Phase 3 and 4 vessels were used solely to process ruminant carcass products, with a very minor amount of mixing of animal products in a further two potsherds. This could originate from non-ruminant products (pig) or possibly from birds, such as chicken, geese or duck. These data strongly suggest vessel specialisation, in that they were only used to process ruminant products, confirming a possible Jewish origin. One vessel was used solely to process dairy products, which is consistent with the known Jewish prohibition against the mixing of meat and milk.

Lipid residue results from the contemporaneous site at Queen's College show that four vessels were used to process solely ruminant carcass products with the remainder being used to process both ruminant and non-ruminant products, whether contemporaneously or over the lifetime of use of the vessel.

In summary, this data provides strong evidence that, at both the earlier St Aldate's Phases 1 and 2, and the contemporaneous site of Queen's College, vessels were being used to process both ruminant and non-ruminant (porcine) products. In contrast, during the 'Jewish' phase, it seems that non-ruminant (pig) processing was either very minor, or, effectively, non-existent.

A further question raised by this study is the near absence of dairy products found in the vessels. This is in contrast to lipid residue studies of prehistoric pottery in Britain[48] and late

45 Chapter 6, below.

46 H. Whelton and L. Cramp, 'Summary of the Organic Residue Analyses of Norman pottery from Southern England', unpublished University of Bristol report (2017).

47 S. Valenzuela-Lamas et al., 'Shechita and Kashrut: Identifying Jewish Populations through Zooarchaeology and Taphonomy. Two Examples from Medieval Catalonia (North-Eastern Spain)', *Quaternary International*, 330 (2014), pp. 109–17.

48 M.S Copley et al., 'Dairying in Antiquity. I. Evidence from Absorbed Lipid Residues Dating to the British Iron Age', *Journal of Archaeological Science*, 32.4 (2005), pp. 485–503.

Anglo-Saxon to early medieval pottery from West Cotton, Northamptonshire,[49] where dairy products are shown to play a significant part in local subsistence strategies. This absence may be because dairy products were processed in different types of vessels (e.g. wooden bowls) or were perhaps not produced in individual households but rather purchased ready-made from sellers of butter and cheese. Certainly, dairy products, sometimes referred to as 'white meats' of the poor, are thought to have been mainstays of the medieval peasant's diet.[50]

FIRED CLAY ARTEFACTS by CYNTHIA POOLE

Two spindle whorls, one complete and a broken half made in fine sandy clay, were found in occupation layers 3071 and 1010 respectively. The former context was phased to the eleventh century and its spindle whorl is likely to be broadly contemporary in date. The broken whorl must be residual in layer 1010, which is phased to the eighteenth to nineteenth century. Both spindle whorls are typical of Anglo-Saxon or early medieval forms, though they are notably heavier than the average weight of 20–30 g quoted by Wild[51] and are similar to disc-shaped examples from Mucking.[52] Examples of spindle whorls with concentric incised decoration have been found at Blue Boar Lane in York in features dating to the ninth century.[53] Hemispherical and disc-shaped fired clay spindle whorls were found at Barrow Hills, Radley, in the back fills of sunken-featured buildings.[54] A ceramic spindle whorl was found in previous excavations at St Aldate's, but stone spindle whorls were more common including two with incised concentric circles.[55] The ceramic spindle whorls would have been personal items and provide evidence for the primary phases of cloth production.

BUILDING MATERIALS

Structural Fired Clay by Cynthia Poole

The structural fired clay comprised 70 fragments (874 g), much of which was indeterminate and either entirely amorphous in character or with a single moulded, usually flat, surface. One piece may have been shaped into a ball, but this could be the accidental effect of breakage and wear. Shaped pieces included several fragments with wattle impressions, some of which had a roughly moulded curving surface with finger marks typical of oven walls. The wattle impressions included interwoven examples based on their angles to one another, or lying flat and parallel. The wattles ranged in size from 10–20 mm in diameter. The fabrics consisted of a fairly coarse sandy clay matrix, which sometimes contained limestone grit, and at least one was heavily micaceous. Organic or grass inclusions were present in a few pieces. Most were fired to varying shades of red, pink and brown, with occasional black or grey reduced areas or mottles.

The structural fired clay derives from oven or hearth structures and occurs predominantly in Anglo-Saxon or early medieval deposits of Phases 1–3. Though the fragments are not intrinsically datable, fired clay started to be replaced by brick and tile in the later medieval

49 S.N. Dudd and R.P. Evershed, 'Direct Demonstration of Milk as an Element of Archaeological Economies', *Science*, 282.5393 (1998), pp. 1478–81.

50 M.W. Adamson, *Food in Medieval Times* (2004).

51 J.P. Wild, *Textiles in Archaeology* (1988), p. 55.

52 H. Hamerow, *Excavations at Mucking Volume 2: The Anglo-Saxon Settlement*, English Heritage Archaeological Report, 2 (1993), p. 65.

53 C. Spall and S. Ashby, 'Craft and Industries: Textile Working', in C. Spall and N. Toop (eds.), *Blue Bridge Lane and Fishergate House, York: Report on Excavations; July 2000 to July 2002* (2005).

54 R. Chambers and E. McAdam, *Excavations at Barrow Hills, Radley, Oxfordshire, 1983–5. Volume 2: The Romano-British Cemetery and Anglo-Saxon Settlement*, Oxford Archaeology Thames Valley Landscapes Monograph, 25 (2007), pp. 254–5.

55 Durham, 'Archaeological Investigations in St Aldate's', pp. 152–3.

period for structures such as ovens and hearths that required fireproof materials. The assemblage probably reflects activities of a domestic character related to cooking or food preparation or artisan activities undertaken on the site during the earlier phases of its use.

One fragment (context 11023) had a rough exterior surface and two wide flat impressions of laths or split poles each over 30 mm wide. These were separated by a narrow ridge of clay 7 mm wide. The fragment was 22–36 mm wide and is possibly the daub render of a wattle and daub wall panel.

Plaster and Mortar by Cynthia Poole

There are 28 fragments (1,475 g) of mortar, wall plaster, cement and concrete. This included coarse sandy cream or brown lime mortar, frequently with coarse grits used as wall render. The fragments ranged from 6–30 mm thick, though most were under 20 mm thick. Some of the plaster or render had lath impressions ranging in size from 17–27 mm wide and 6–16 mm deep. Some fragments of plaster are painted in white or where coloured mostly dull shades of green, but also brown and anil. Most of this mortar and plaster comes from Phases 6–9; where it occurs in earlier deposits it is in several cases associated with intrusive nineteenth-century material.

Ceramic Building Material by Cynthia Poole

The assemblage (1,262 fragments, 120 kg) is dominated by roof tile, which includes some unusual pieces, among them a peg tile with a single central peg hole and a ridge tile with a peg hole, two varieties not previously noted in Oxford. A possible chimney pot is also a rare find, though one, dated to 1150–75, had previously been found at St Aldate's and another is known from the Hamel, where it is dated to the early thirteenth century.[56] Ceramic building material was used on the site predominantly for roofing during Phases 3 and 4, which are dated to the late eleventh to fourteenth centuries, though it is unlikely that tile came into use before the late twelfth century towards the end of Phase 3.

The medieval buildings standing on the site were roofed with glazed and unglazed peg tile surmounted by plain glazed ridge tile without crests as is typical of many buildings in Oxford at this period. The roof tile in Phase 3 deposits of late eleventh- to twelfth-century date was concentrated in Area 1. Flat roof tiles of plain rectangular form are referred to in documentary evidence and roof tile has been found in later twelfth-century contexts in several English towns and cities, including London, and at Eynsham Abbey, Oxfordshire.[57] An assemblage of roof tile very similar in character and of similar date to the St Aldate's assemblage was recently found at Merton College relating to buildings of twelfth- to thirteenth-century date, preceding the college foundation.[58] Nearly all the roof tile deposited during Phase 4 was recovered from Area 4, much of it coming from the garden soil layers. About a dozen fragments of medieval roof tile had burnt edges, indicating that they had been used (or reused) set on edge in the floors of hearths or ovens.

The very small quantity of plain floor tile suggests that this was restricted to small areas of flooring and that in general other materials such as timber boards, stone paving or trampled earthen floors were the norm. Previous excavations at St Aldate's produced similarly small quantities of floor tile, though this included two decorated 'stabbed-Wessex' type floor tiles.[59]

56 Haldon, 'Late Saxon and Medieval Pottery', fig. 19, no. 16; M. Mellor, 'Pottery', in N. Palmer, 'A Beaker Burial and Medieval Tenements in the Hamel, Oxford', *Oxoniensia*, 45 (1980), fig. 9, no. 18.

57 T.P. Smith, 'London's Earliest Medieval Roofing Tiles: A Comparative Study', *Medieval Ceramics*, 22–23 (1998–9), pp. 66–71; N. Mitchell, 'The Floor and Roof Tile', in A. Hardy et al., *Aelfric's Abbey: Excavations at Eynsham Abbey, Oxfordshire, 1989–92*, Thames Valley Landscapes Monograph, 16 (2003), p. 214.

58 Chapter 8, below.

59 Durham, 'Archaeological Investigations in St Aldate's, Oxford', p. 140.

Structural Stone by Ruth Shaffrey
Structural stone includes blocks of oolitic limestone ashlar from Phase 3 pit fill 10019 and Phase 7 Structure 7.1, and a piece of dwarf column, probably originally octagonal, also from Structure 7.1. The last is made from a spar prominent oolitic limestone, possibly from the Windrush valley. This presumably originated in the higher-status buildings known to have been on the site.

A relatively small quantity of stone roofing was also recovered, perhaps reflecting a preference for ceramic roofing. It includes six fragments (2.1 kg) with diagnostic perforations and 54 non-diagnostic fragments (4.9 kg), probably but not certainly, used as roofing. These are of the shelly limestone (Pusey Flags) and calcareous sandstone (Stonesfield Slate type) so typical of Oxford roofing.

Window Glass by Ian R. Scott
Fourteen fragments of window glass were recovered, occurring in contexts from Phase 3 onwards. A small weathered and devitrified sherd of window glass from layer 1029 was possibly medieval, and a small piece of window glass from context 1390 (Structure 4.5) with opaque weathering might be medieval or post-medieval in date. The remainder of the material is post-medieval or undated.

VESSEL GLASS by IAN R. SCOTT

The vessel glass assemblage is quite small (89 fragments) but it is clearly dominated by bottles, particularly wine bottles of seventeenth- to nineteenth-century date, and also contains a small number of sherds from drinking vessels.

Phase 6 context 11021 produced two pieces of post-medieval vessel glass, one a body sherd with optic blown ribs, the other a pedestal base. Although there is no refit, it is possible that the sherds are from the same pedestal beaker. The form dates to the second half of the sixteenth or first half of the seventeenth century.

The vessel glass from Phase 7 context 4056 comprises a distinctive baluster from a stemmed vessel of early seventeenth century date and possibly of Venetian manufacture, but more likely to be English in the *façon de Venise*.

The most interesting wine bottles were two seventeenth-century 'globe and shaft' bottles from Phase 7 context 4014, both which have datable bottle seals. One seal shows a mermaid, with the waves of the sea in the background, holding a mirror and apparently brushing her hair (Fig. 4.13). The letters 'A.H.' to the right are the initials of Anthony Hall senior, who was licensee of the 'Mermaid' on the southwest corner of Carfax from *c.*1660–75 and mayor of Oxford in 1673–4.[60] His son, also Anthony Hall, was licensee from 1675–91. The second seal has the letters 'W.$^{M.}$A.' above a crown. The letters form the cipher of William and Anne Morrell, who were licensees of the 'Crown' from 1660–79. William Morrell died in 1679 and his widow Anne continued as licensee until 1696.[61] The Crown was located at what is now No. 3 Cornmarket and is not to be confused with the present Crown Inn at No. 59A Cornmarket.[62]

60 E.T. Leeds, 'Oxford Tradesmen's Tokens, 355–453', in H.E. Salter (ed.), *Surveys and Tokens*, OHS, 75 (1923), pp. 405–7; E.T. Leeds, '17th and 18th Century Wine-Bottles of Oxford Taverns', *Oxoniensia*, 4 (1941), pp. 46–7, plate ix, no. 5. See also F. Banks, *Wine Drinking in Oxford 1640–1850: A Story Revealed by Tavern, Inn and Other Bottles; with a Catalogue of Bottles and Seals from the Collection in the Ashmolean Museum*, BAR, 257 (1997).

61 Leeds, '17th and 18th Century Wine-Bottles', pp. 47–8, plate ix, no. 9.

62 Ibid. p. 46.

Fig. 4.13 Seal of the Mermaid Tavern, from 'globe and shaft' bottle. Ctx 4014, Structure 7.1, Phase 7.

CLAY TOBACCO PIPES by DAVID A. HIGGINS

The excavations produced 160 fragments of pipe (50 bowl, 104 stem and 6 mouthpiece fragments) weighing a total of 1,614 g. The pipes were recovered from 22 different contexts in five of the excavated areas (1, 4, 5, 10 and 11). The pipe assemblage as a whole is in very good condition with many large stem fragments and most of the bowls comprising complete examples. Almost all the pipes recovered belong to a very narrow time band; almost all of the stems are of general seventeenth-century types while the more closely datable bowls range from *c.*1640–80, with the majority dating from *c.*1650–70. The only notable exceptions are two stems of late eighteenth century or later date from context 1376. From the pipe evidence, it would appear that there was a brief but intense period of activity resulting in the deposition of archaeological material across this site during the third quarter of the seventeenth century.

The majority of the pipes were recovered from the fills of postholes or pits, the most notable of which was Phase 7 stone-lined cesspit 4073. This feature produced by far the largest number of pipes from the site (82 per cent of all the pipes recovered) and is discussed in detail below. None of the pipes from the excavations are marked and the only decorated examples come from latrine fill 4073. A context summary of all the pipes has been provided for the site archive but just the large pit group is discussed here.

Latrine Group 4073

There were nine pipe-bearing contexts (4005, 4006, 4013, 4014, 4044, 4058, 4061, 4066 and 4067) associated with this cesspit, which produced a total of 131 pipe fragments (43 bowl, 82 stem and 6 mouthpieces). There were numerous cross joins between these fragments showing that the pit was filled as a single event. It was also possible to reconstruct around twenty substantially complete pipes and three fully complete pipes, all of which date from *c.*1650–70. Complete pipes are rarely recovered and only around thirty seventeenth-century examples were recorded during a study in the 1980s to which another twenty or so have since come to light.[63] These are the first examples of any date from Oxfordshire or its surrounding counties and the recovery of three together makes this group of national significance. The pit was located behind the site of the Red Lion Inn and the fill included sealed bottles made for Anthony Hall, who was licensee of the Mermaid Tavern until his death in 1675. Numerous fig and grape seeds were also found in the pit, suggesting an affluent establishment/clientele. The pipe group can, therefore, be interpreted as having been discarded at one point in time from a prosperous tavern, most likely sometime around 1660.

A number of other closely datable mid seventeenth-century pipe groups have recently been recovered from Oxford,[64] but this is the only one to have produced fitting fragments that now allows a number of substantially complete pipes to be compared and contrasted. The other sites do, however, provide useful reference points for the bowl forms and manufacturing techniques. Where more than one bowl occurs in any of the contexts from this pit it has been allocated an additional suffix (A, B, C, etc.) to act as a unique identifier so that it can be individually referred to, the relevant letter having been pencilled inside the bowl.

At least 43 pipes were discarded in the pit, 40 of which fit well as a contemporary group. There was one bowl from the wall of the pit itself that seems unusually large for the group, and must represent an early introduction of a form that would otherwise be dated *c.*1660–80 (Fig. 4.14, no. 8). The other two slightly later looking forms also date from *c.*1660–80, but came from 4014, one of the upper fills of the pit, where they could be intrusive or have been introduced from elsewhere when the pit was being filled. Unlike most of the other pieces, neither has any surviving stem and they are so similar that they were probably made in the same mould (Fig. 4.14, no. 9). They also stand out as being the only two bowls from the pit made of a fine sandy fabric from Shotover Hill.[65] The author has noted that this sandy fabric declined in use during the Commonwealth and does not appear to have been used at all during the 1660s, with a resurgence towards the end of the century.[66] The material from 4073 supports this observation and shows that imported clays were almost exclusively used for pipemaking in Oxford when the pit was filled.

One bowl was missing its base, but the others comprise 36 spur forms and six heel forms. One or two of the pipes had stem bores of either $^{6}/_{64}$" or $^{9}/_{64}$" but the rest were all of either $^{7}/_{64}$" (16 examples) or $^{8}/_{64}$" (23 examples). Only four of the heel forms had complete heels and all of these were round or oval in plan (e.g. Fig. 4.14, nos. 3–4); none had the pointed tail sometimes found on early to mid seventeenth-century pipes in Oxford. Spur forms appear to have been regarded as the more prestigious style of the two and this is reflected by the fact that 34 of these had burnished bowls (94 per cent), whereas none of the heel bowls were burnished (cf. Fig. 4.14). Furthermore, 29 of the spur bowls (81 per cent) had a good or fine quality burnish (in other words, better than average) and 27 of 31 examples with surviving stem also had this burnish as well (87 per cent). The quality of the stem burnish was often a little less good than that of the bowls but the overall pattern is clear – spur pipes almost all had burnished bowls and most of them had burnished stems too, while the heel forms were completely unburnished. Reconstruction of around 20 substantially complete pipes has also allowed the length of the stem burnishing to be assessed for the first time. There were 16 spur pipes where this could be measured, showing that burnishing extended to between 130 mm and 205 mm from the bowl junction (the length of the longest strokes measured), invariably ending with strokes of irregular length so as to fade into the unburnished section running up to the mouthpiece. Most of the examples had between 150 mm and 185 mm of burnished stem (12 examples, representing 75 per cent of the sample).

63 D.A. Higgins, 'The Interpretation and Regional Study of Clay Tobacco Pipes: A Case Study of the Broseley District', University of Liverpool Ph.D. thesis (1987): https://www.academia.edu/34528546/Higgins_1987_-_The_Interpretation_and_Regional_Study_of_Clay_Tobacco_Pipes.

64 D.A. Higgins, 'Clay Tobacco Pipes', chapters 6 and 10, below.

65 See Higgins, 'Clay Tobacco Pipes', chapter 6, below, for a discussion of this fabric.

66 Higgins, 'Clay Tobacco Pipes', chapter 10, below.

There was less distinction with regard to the amount of rim milling between the two forms, with both styles exhibiting both fully milled and unmilled examples (four of six heel forms were fully milled and eight of 36 spur types; one of six heel types were unmilled and twelve of the 36 spur types). Although these two extremes (either completely milled or completely unmilled) were the most numerous types, there were also various intermediate levels of milling for both styles. This general pattern accords with a group of *c.*1650–70 from the Queen's College, where more variable levels of milling were found to have replaced the almost consistently fully milled pipes from earlier groups.[67] Milling is generally taken as an indicator of the quality of a seventeenth-century pipe, the more complete the milling the better the quality. In mid seventeenth-century Oxford, however, this does not seem to follow, with the burnished spur forms being just as variable as the cheaper heel types. Figure 4.15, no. 11, with its ornately decorated stem and finely burnished bowl, must have been a more expensive pipe and yet it has no rim milling at all.

Maker's marks are not very common on Oxford pipes and none was recovered from the excavation. Likewise, decoration at this period was rare and only two decorated pipes were present. One just has a single band of milling 20 mm from the bowl where the stem has been repaired during manufacture (Fig. 4.15, no. 10). The pipe had broken again at this point showing where the broken ends had been pushed back together and there are irregularities flanking the milling where the stem has been smoothed. Repairs of this type, usually disguised with milled bands, are not infrequent finds across the country. In contrast, the other decorated piece has an ornately decorated stem that starts 60 mm from the bowl and extends for a further 127 mm along the stem (Fig. 4.15, no. 11). The central section comprises chevron decoration that has been created by scraping a toothed implement, perhaps a milling tool, at alternate angles across the stem. This created slight facets to the stem, 12 or 13 in total, with one small strip that has been missed or left plain deliberately on each side. The chevron decoration is flanked at each end by a series of stem borders that have been created by impressing a toothed blade into the clay at a slight angle to form each band – eight on the bowl side and nine towards the mouthpiece end. This technique of using a decorated blade in an opposing manner to form paired bands is a technique that appears to be peculiar to Oxford region, where it was used from the mid seventeenth century to the early eighteenth century.

The bowl forms all suggest local production for the pipes from this pit. The high level of finish on the spur forms makes it impossible to carry out reliable mould identification using surface flaws, but subtle differences in profile and overall shape show that several (perhaps many) different moulds must be represented. Apart from the three larger types mentioned above (Fig. 4.14, nos. 8–9) the spur bowls are all a very uniform style, showing that the Oxford makers were working to a common standard of shape and finish (Fig. 4.14, nos. 5–7 and 10–11). The principal variation is simply that of overall size, which varies slightly, probably reflecting the gradual evolution towards larger size that was a characteristic of the seventeenth century (cf. Fig. 4.14, nos. 5 and 7). The heel forms are almost as uniform, with just two slightly smaller and more variable pieces (Fig. 4.14, nos. 1 and 2), but the other four being very similar in size and shape (e.g. Fig. 4.14, nos. 3 and 4).

The most important outcome of this study is the reconstruction of three complete pipes from this group. Only six mouthpieces were available and, had more been recovered, there is no doubt that many other pipes could have been reconstructed. A study of the evolution of stem length has shown that stems got longer during the course of the seventeenth century, but that different lengths also existed at any one time, being related to the style and quality of pipe.[68] The three pipes reassembled from this pit are all spur types (Fig. 4.15, nos. 5–7). The shortest has a relatively small bowl form and thin stem, with a stem length of 289 mm (11⅜"; Fig. 4.15,

[67] Higgins, 'Clay Tobacco Pipes', chapter 6, below.

[68] Higgins, 'The Interpretation and Regional Study of Clay Tobacco Pipes'.

no. 5). The other two pieces both have slightly larger bowls and chunkier stems, with lengths of 293 mm (11½"; Fig. 4.15, no. 6) and 304 mm (12"; Fig. 4.15, no. 7). These two are so similar in bowl form that it is likely that they come from the same mould, the difference in length being accounted for by the stretching/compression of the clay during manufacture, the point at which the stem was cut off to form a mouthpiece, and shrinkage during firing. Similar differences between pipes made in the same mould has been noted previously,[69] and so some variation is not unexpected. In broad terms, however, these spur pipes had stem lengths that ranged from around 11½" to 12". No complete heel pipes were recovered, but two almost identical examples each had surviving stems of around 245 mm (for example, Fig. 4.15, no. 4) and their stem taper suggests that they would have been of a comparable length.

The complete pipes are of a similar length to the mid-range of other known examples of this period.[70] Without more complete examples to compare, it is not known whether longer or shorter examples were also current in Oxford at this time (perhaps with identical bowl forms) or whether this was the standard length for all pipes produced at this particular centre. The former is more likely, since various prices/lengths are recorded in many other parts of the country. Of particular significance in relation to these new finds is the 1710 mould size agreement implemented by the Bristol pipemakers to standardise their products. This listed six different styles of pipe with stem lengths ranging from 8" to 16", including 'Penned Heels' and 'Gauntletts' of 11½" each.[71] These two styles almost certainly equate, respectively, to the spur and heel forms found at Oxford, showing that these forms already existed with comparable stem lengths some half a century before the mould size agreement was drawn up.

List of Illustrations (Figs. 4.14 and 4.15):
A representative range of bowl forms, together with the decorated pieces from pit 4073, are shown at life-size in Figure 4.14, with reduced illustrations showing the overall form of some of the more complete pieces in Figure 4.15. All these pieces come from contexts associated with pit 4073 of *c.*1650–70 (Phase 7), although bowl 9 is a slightly later style of *c.*1660–80 from one of the upper fills of the pit, and so could be intrusive.

1. Three quarters milled; stem bore 7/64". Ctx 4067.
2. Fully milled; stem bore just over 8/64". Ctx 4014.
3. Fully milled; stem bore just over 7/64". Ctx 4067.
4. Fully milled; stem bore 8/64". Ctx 4066.
5. Three quarters milled; good burnish on bowl and poor burnish on the rather thin and waney stem; stem bore 7/64". Stem is 289 mm (11⅜") long with 175 mm burnished. Ctx 4067.
6. Fully milled; good burnish on bowl and stem; stem bore 9/64". Stem is 293 mm (11½") long with 207 mm burnished. Stem bends slightly to the right, but much straighter than no. 5. Possibly made in the same mould as no. 7. Ctx 4014.
7. Three quarters milled; good burnish on bowl and stem; stem bore 8/64". Stem is 304 mm (12") long with 180 mm burnished; good straight stem. Possibly made in the same mould as no. 6. Ctx 4067 and 4058.
8. One quarter milled; stem bore just over 8/64". Ctx 4005.
9. Half milled; stem bore just over 8/64". A near identical example from the same context (4014 (L)) was probably made in the same mould. Ctx 4014.
10. Fully milled; stem bore 7/64". The stem was broken and repaired during manufacture, the mend being partially disguised with a band of milling 20 mm from the bowl. The stem is burnished up to 155 mm from the bowl. Ctx 4006.

[69] Ibid. pp. 56–60.
[70] Ibid. p. 64.
[71] R. Jackson and R. Price, *Bristol Clay Pipes: A Study of Makers and Their Marks*, Bristol City Museum Research Monograph, 1 (1974), p. 85.

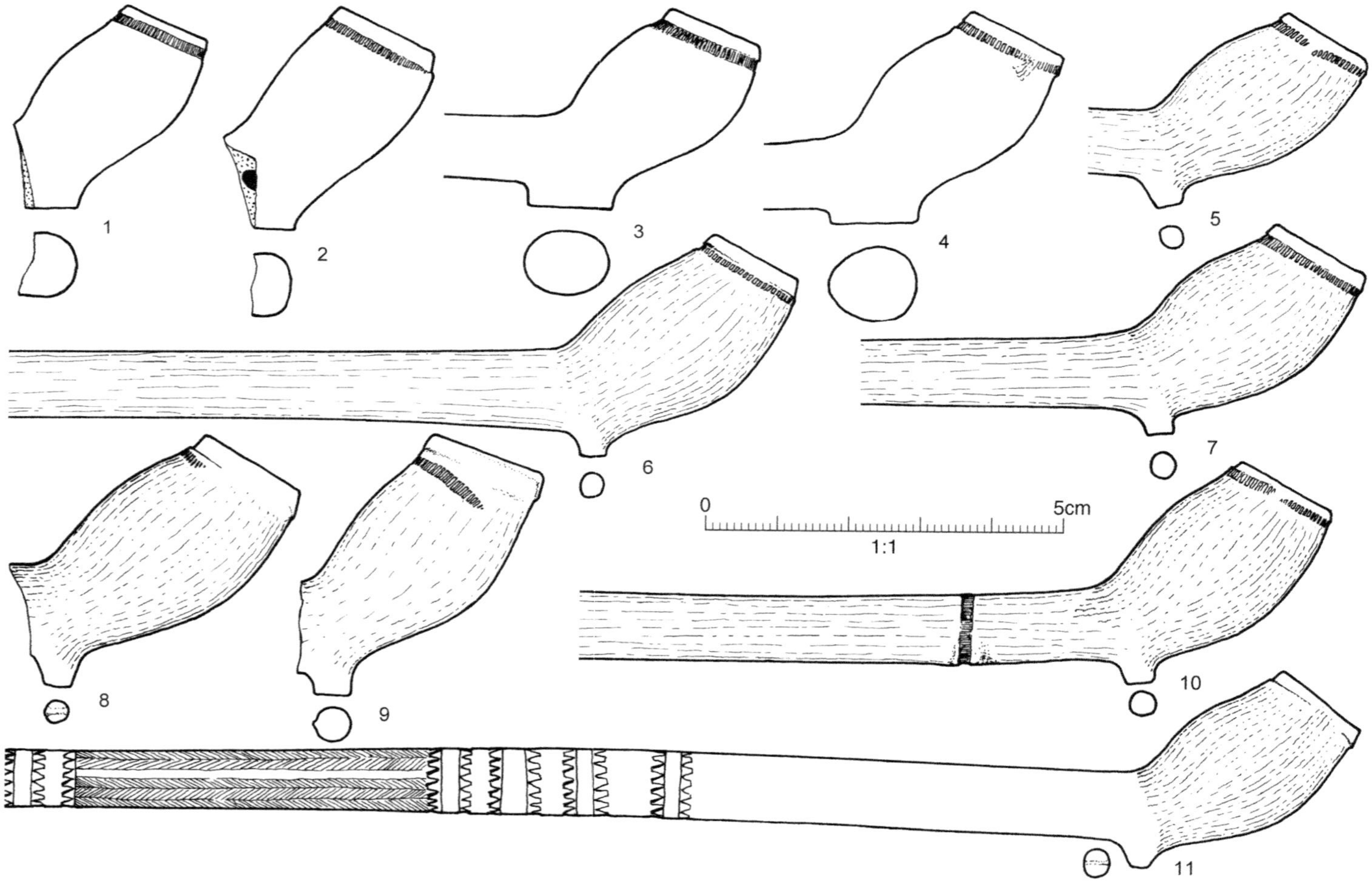

Fig. 4.14 Clay tobacco pipe bowl forms from pit group 4073 of c.1650–70. Drawings by David A. Higgins.

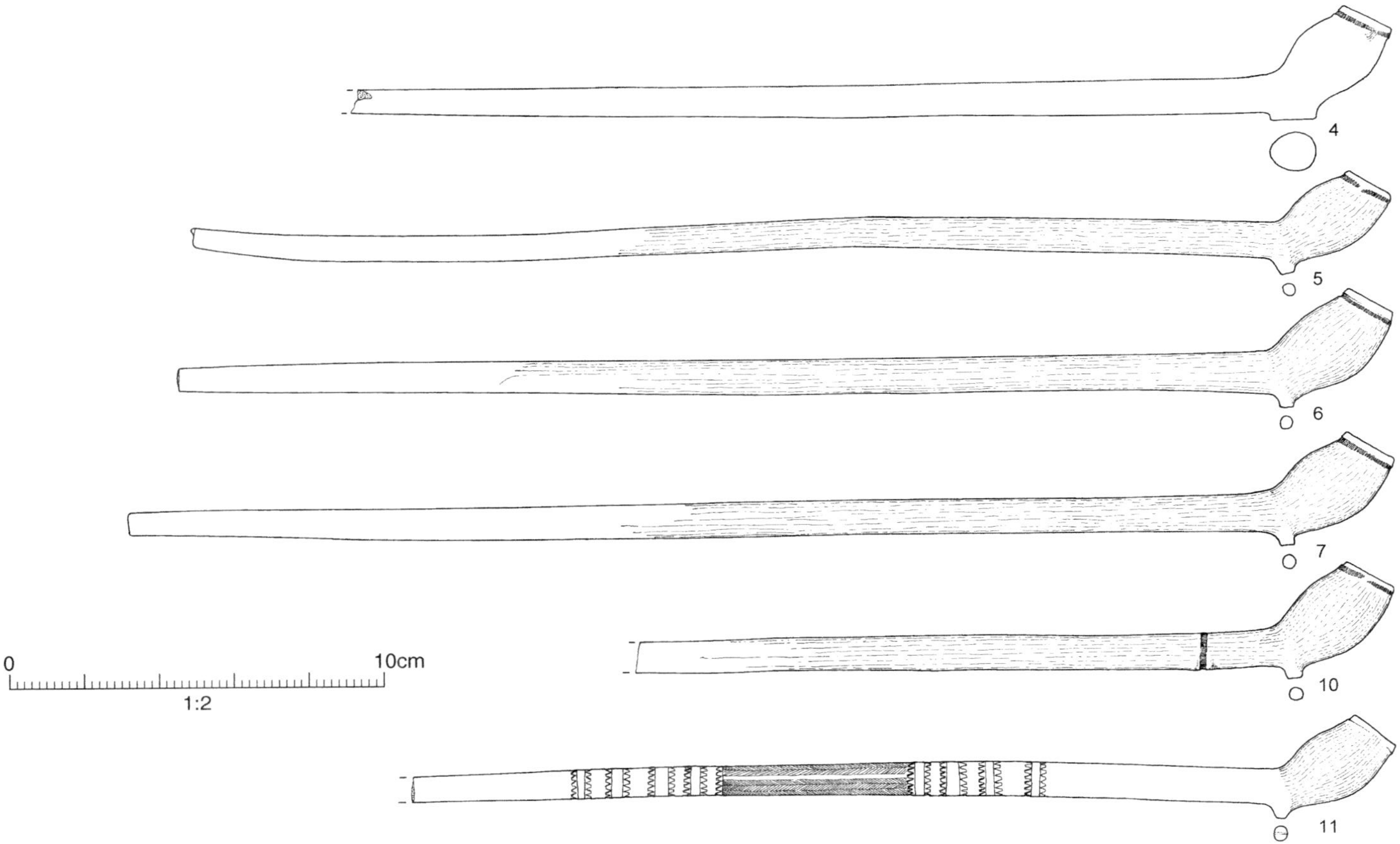

Fig. 4.15 Clay tobacco pipes from pit group 4073 of c.1650–70, showing stem form and finish. Drawings by David A. Higgins.

11. No rim milling; stem bore 7/64″. This pipe has an elaborate scheme of stem decoration forming a band 127 mm long (starting 60 mm from the bowl and ending 187 mm from it). Ctx 4044 and 4014.

METALWORK AND WORKED BONE by LEIGH ALLEN

A single metal artefact, a cylindrical lead pan (lay) weight with a slightly domed top was recovered from a Phase 1 dump layer in Area 3. The object weighs 6¼ ounces (178 g). These weights are for setting in the pans of scales rather than for suspension from the arms of a steelyard and would have been used in shops, markets and fairs to check on the weight of goods.

Phase 2 contexts produced mainly fragments of lead waste from occupation and dump layers within timber lined cellar pit 3059. A hemispherical worked bone spindle whorl fashioned from the head of a bovine femur was also recovered from this feature. Femur head spindle whorls first appear in the Iron Age and continue in use sporadically into the Norman period when they enjoyed a renewed burst of popularity.[72]

Phase 3 contexts produced four items of horse gear, a knife, a socketed implement, and a staple. The tips from two horseshoes and two horseshoe nails came from dump layers in Area 1. The shoe fragments both have two circular nail holes set in rectangular countersinkings and are from a form of shoe that predominated throughout the twelfth century.[73] The horseshoe nails are of two different forms. One is a 'fiddle key' nail designed for use with the type of shoe mentioned above, while the other, with its rectangular, tapering head, is generally used on later shoes. The knife and the socketed implement came from the fills of cesspit 1058, in Area 1. The knife is complete and has a centrally placed whittle tang and a long, triangular blade. Knives of this simple form date from the tenth century and continued in use into the late medieval period.[74] The socketed implement has two prongs or arms and could be an incomplete hoe used in gardening for weeding and breaking up the soil.[75] The double-spiked 'U'-shaped staple was recovered from the fill of pit 4113 in Area 4. It would have been used to secure chains and hasps on doors and gates and to support tethering rings and various types of handle.[76] Numerous nails (32) were recovered from this phase mainly from the fills of latrine 1058 (Structure 3.1).

The majority of the copper alloy objects came from Phase 4 contexts and include dress accessories, lock furniture, domestic items and fixtures and fittings recovered from garden soil and occupation layers in Area 4 and an additional dress accessory from a dump layer in Area 10. The dress accessories comprise a hooked tag, a moulded pin from a buckle, a solid spherical button with an integral attachment loop and a tongue-shaped strap-end with a forked spacer. Hooked tags were used to secure light clothing or hose. Buttons probably first came into common use in Britain in the early thirteenth century, when the new close fittings fashions of the day demanded a fastener at the collar and on the sleeves.[77] Composite strap-ends with forked spacers were introduced in the late thirteenth or early fourteenth century.[78]

[72] A. MacGregor, *Bone, Antler, Ivory and Horn. The Technology of Skeletal Materials Since the Roman Period* (1985), p. 187.

[73] J. Clarke, *Medieval Finds from Excavations in London: The Medieval Horse and Its Equipment c.1150–c.1450* (1995), p. 96.

[74] I.H. Goodall, 'Knives', in M. Biddle, *Object and Economy in Medieval Winchester*, Winchester Studies, 7:2 (1991), p. 838.

[75] I.H. Goodall, *Ironwork in Medieval Britain: An Archaeological Study* (2011), pp. 79–80.

[76] Ibid. p. 162.

[77] G. Egan and F. Pritchard, *Medieval Finds from Excavations in London: 3. Dress Accessories c.1150–c.1450* (1991), p. 272.

[78] Ibid. pp. 145–6.

Fig. 4.16 Shallow-lipped dish, possibly a pan from a cresset oil lamp. Ctx 4008, Phase 4.

A small incomplete copper alloy key (the bit is missing) was recovered from context 4047 (an occupation layer). Only the ring bow and part of the stem survives and there is a moulding at the junction of the bow and the stem. Small keys such as this could have been used on caskets, cupboards or padlocks.

The domestic items were recovered from garden soil in Area 4 (4008) and comprise a long needle with a damaged eye and a small circular, shallow lipped dish (diameter 67 mm), which could be a pan from a 'cresset' oil lamp (Fig. 4.16). Lamps such as these would have been filled with oil with a wick floating in it. The pan has a small hole in the base indicating that it was probably mounted on a stand or bracket. Four lengths of chain were also recovered from Area 4 garden soil (4001). They are made up of 'S'-shaped links, each link measuring *c.*12 mm in length. Chains have a variety of uses, both ornamental and practical.

Structural objects recovered from this phase include a 'U'-shaped staple from context 1027 and a wall hook from context 4047 with a tapering shank for driving into wood or masonry joints. A small number of nails (13) were recovered from the fill of pit 4048.

The only identifiable objects recovered from Phases 5–7 are nails. In Phase 5 they come exclusively from contexts associated with decayed timbers within context 1069. In Phase 7 they are all from demolition layers and cesspit fills (4004).

A possible stylus fashioned from a goose radius with an obliquely cut end was recovered from context 1007, a trample layer in Area 1 (Fig. 4.17). The function of these objects is a subject of

Fig. 4.17 Possible stylus fashioned from a goose radius. Ctx 1007, Phase 8.

debate.[79] They could have functioned as rudimentary pens, although they lack the cleft point which would have given the necessary flexibility for writing. However, they may have been better employed for line drawing. It has also been suggested that they could have been used for holding broken quills.[80] These objects first appear in the thirteenth or fourteenth century.

WORKED STONE ARTEFACTS by RUTH SHAFFREY

A small fragment of Mayen lava is almost certainly from a rotary quern but was an unstratified find (36 g). A rectilinear-sectioned whetstone demonstrating significant use across all its faces was found in Phase 3 pit fill 1063. It is made of a very fine-grained sandstone. Such finds are generally typical of medieval Oxford, representing domestic, or in the case of the whetstone, possibly light industrial activity.

LEATHER SHOE by GERALDINE CRANN

The remains of a leather boot upper and a boot lace fragment were recovered from the fill (101) of pit 102, uncovered in evaluation Test Pit 1 (Fig. 4.18). Based on the associated pottery and ceramic building material, the shoe is likely to date to the thirteenth or fourteenth century.

ANIMAL BONE by LEE G. BRODERICK

In all, 5,072 animal bone specimens were recovered from the site, mostly through hand-collection although environmental samples were taken and sieved at 10 mm, 4 mm and 2 mm fractions (Table 4.6). This material was assessed according to current guidelines,[81] and a subset was selected for full recording on the basis of that assessment and the project research aims. The final selection of material for study targeted the Anglo-Saxon layers of the site (Phases 1 and 2) as well as cesspits from Phases 3 and 7. This selected assemblage consists of 798 specimens, including 131 recovered through environmental sampling. It was recorded using a diagnostic zone system,[82] and the reference collection kept by OA. Material from the environmental samples that could not be identified using the diagnostic zones was not recorded, except for vertebrae and rib fragments, which were recorded as large, medium or small mammal or bird.

79 MacGregor, *Bone, Antler, Ivory and Horn*, pp. 125–6.

80 M. Henig, 'Objects of Bone, Antler and Shell', in Durham 'Archaeological Investigations in St Aldate's', pp. 160–3.

81 P. Baker and F.L. Worley, *Animal Bones and Archaeology: Guidelines for Best Practice* (2014).

82 A. Cohen and D. Serjeantson, *A Manual for the Identification of Bird Bones from Archaeological Sites* (1996); D. Serjeantson, 'Animal Bone', in S. Needham and T. Spence, *Runnymede Bridge Research Excavations, Volume 2: Refuse and Disposal at Area 16 East, Runnymede* (1996), pp. 194–223.

Fig. 4.18 Possible thirteenth- or fourteenth-century leather shoe recovered from pit 102.

Table 4.6. Animal bones: NISP (Number of Identified SPecimens) and NSP (Number of SPecimens) figures for the hand collected and sieved components of the assemblage.

	Phase						
	1	**2**	**3**	**7**	**2 (sieved)**	**3 (sieved)**	**7 (sieved)**
Domestic cattle	26	72	12	11		1	2
Domestic cattle?	2	3	1	1			
Caprine	20	41	21	18	6	1	2
Caprine?		1	1	1			
Sheep	2	7	2	3			
Pig	12	29		3			1
Pig?	2	2					
Horse	1	1					
Cat			1		1		
Red deer		1					
Roe deer		1					
Small rodent					1		
Black rat							2
Small mammal			4			2	
Medium mammal	14		43	4	5	18	
Large mammal	39	102	34	15	5	1	
Total mammal	118	260	119	56	18	23	7
Bird			3		1	39	
Greylag/domestic goose		1	12	1		2	1
Domestic duck/mallard						1	1
Domestic fowl	1		43	2	1	34	
Domestic fowl?		3					
Domestic fowl/pheasant		1					
Woodcock						2	
Total bird	1	5	58	3	2	78	2
Frog/toad			1		1		
Total amphibian			1		1		
Total NISP	119	265	178	59	21	101	9
Total NSP	128	283	192	64	21	101	9

Phases 1 and 2: Middle–Late Anglo-Saxon

The Anglo-Saxon assemblage was dominated by the three principal domesticates – domestic cattle (*Bos taurus taurus*), caprine (sheep *Ovis aries* and/or goat *Capra hircus*) and pig (*Sus ferus domesticus*). Of these, domestic cattle was the most common species by NISP (Number of Identified SPecimens). No obvious bias to any particular body part was observed among these specimens, with head, limb and torso elements all being present. Butchery consisted exclusively of chopmarks; of nine specimens observed with chopmarks, eight were axial chops. Four of these specimens with axial chops were humeri and the ninth specimen was also a humerus, with an oblique chop through the proximal end and possible signs of helical fracture. Two other specimens showed signs of helical fracture as well and, taken together with the axial chops through bones it suggests that, whether due to taste or necessity, marrow fat formed a regular part of the diet of the site's inhabitants.

Cutmarks were observed on five large mammal ribs from this phase, whilst six vertebrae had been chopped through, three obliquely and three axially, suggesting that more concern was paid to meat portion size than to anatomy. Although horse (*Equus caballus*) was observed in the assemblage, it was rare, with just one specimen each in Phases 1 and 2. As such it is very probable that the large mammal specimens are also domestic cattle.

Unfortunately, the sample size was too small to offer meaningful insight into the age profile of any of the animals in the site, although it is possible to state that both young and old individuals were present.

All these statements – about sample size, ageing and butchery – could equally be written about the caprine specimens from the site, among which it was possible to identify sheep but not goat. There were more oblique chopmarks among the caprine bones (four of seven specimens) but axial chopmarks (two) and a cutmark were also present, as were helical fractures. It was also possible to identify a foetal/neonatal metacarpal, suggesting that breeding (or, at least, housing) of stock was taking place on or near the site.

Butchery marks were rarer on the pig bones but these were far more likely to be unfused epiphyseally, suggesting a mainly young population. Since pigs have little economic use other than their meat, and reach slaughter weight before being skeletally mature, this is not surprising.

Poultry (domestic fowl *Gallus gallus* and goose *Anser anser*) were present in small numbers, and although wild species are represented in the assemblage by both red deer (*Cervus elaphus*) and roe deer (*Capreolus capreolus*) it is far from clear that these represent food waste. The red deer specimen is a shed antler with a chop through the base of the first spine. As such, this almost certainly represents craft activity. The roe deer specimen is more equivocal in its possible interpretation, however, being a metatarsal, which could potentially have been left attached to a hide. This specimen also had an exostosis on the anterior of the midshaft. Unfortunately, it is not possible to suggest a cause of the pathology.

Phase 3: Late Eleventh–Twelfth Century

All the material analysed from Phase 3 came from a single feature – Structure 3.1 – which was a latrine conjectured to be associated with Jacob's Hall within Oxford's Jewry. Jewish laws contain specific proscriptions on the types of animals and the parts thereof that can be eaten. This is in contrast to Roman Catholic Christianity, which adopts a far more laissez-faire attitude to what food its followers consume outside fasting periods. This is of importance for the zooarchaeological investigation of the site, since the potential for differentiating between these two religious groups might be possible if their refuse disposal on the site was intensive. Specifically, according to the ways that rabbinic law was interpreted in medieval Northern Europe, we would not expect to find any of the following in deposits associated with Jewish sites: any wild animal, including birds; pig bones; horse bones; bones showing pathologies, particularly any which might be linked with TB or other lung diseases; and bones from the hind-quarters of cattle.

Interpreting the assemblage in this light, two factors leap out – the complete absence of any pig specimens and the dominance of domestic fowl specimens (with goose specimens also more common than those of domestic cattle). Material recovered through environmental samples suggests that this pattern may be even more dramatic than might appear from the hand-recovered assemblage. The high proportion of bird bones recovered from the site, in particular, is exceptional and demands comparison not only with other British sites, including those from Oxford, of this period but also with sites in Europe where zooarchaeological investigations into medieval Jewries have been carried out.[83]

Lesions consistent with osteochondrosis were present on some of the domestic cattle bones, but this is a relatively benign condition which would not have caused the animal any discomfort in life and so people would be unlikely to suspect the condition.[84] Among the twenty-one caprine specimens recovered from this feature were five foetal or neonatal specimens recovered from context 1071. These may represent an ABG (Associated Bone Group) and include left and right, hind- and fore-limbs. Being small it is reasonable to suspect that other bones of the individual may have been missed. It is not clear how such an individual would end up in this feature were it simply stillborn and it may be that it represents a delicacy.

Eight of the domestic fowl bones were also from juvenile individuals and one adult specimen came from a male individual. It is possible that the juvenile specimens also come from males, since they would not be able to lay eggs and it is not needed to keep male and female fowl in a fifty/fifty ratio for a viable flock.

Phase 7: Mid-Seventeenth–Early Eighteenth Century

Another latrine was identified in Phase 7 (Structure 7.1) and the assemblage derived from it stands in stark contrast to that from Phase 3, both in terms of size and in terms of composition. With regards to species proportions, it is far closer to the Anglo-Saxon assemblage than to that other latrine and, indeed, resembles a typical British urban medieval or post-medieval assemblage, containing domestic animals, principally domestic cattle and caprines, but also domestic fowl, geese and pig. The exception to the domestic mammals is the presence of black rat (*Rattus rattus*), which would have been a pest in early modern Oxford.

Conclusions

The material recovered from the Anglo-Saxon phases on the site adds to our developing understanding of this phase of Oxford's history and is consistent with other sites studied to date. Of particular interest, though, is the latrine associated with Jacob's Hall. This is the first time that a Jewish signature has been identified in British zooarchaeology, and just the third time in medieval Europe.

FISH REMAINS by REBECCA NICHOLSON

A single clupeid (probably herring) vertebra came from the flot of sample 3007, from dump or occupation layer 3088 in Phase 1 Structure 1.2. Dating to Phase 2, a single eel vertebra came from occupation layer 3071 in Structure 1.2 and a large salmonid caudal vertebra, probably salmon, came from occupation layer or dumped deposit 3068 in Structure 2.1.

All the fish remains from Phase 3 deposits came from Areas 1 and 10, mostly from pits containing domestic refuse and/or latrine waste. The identified remains include marine fish

[83] L. Daróczi-Szabó, 'Animal Bones as Indicators of Kosher Food Refuse from 14th Century Buda, Hungary', in S. Jones O'Day et al. (eds.), *Behaviour Behind Bones: The Zooarchaeology of Ritual, Religion, Status and Identity* (2004), pp. 252–61; Valenzuela-Lamas et al., 'Shechita and Kashrut'.

[84] L. Sewell, 'Osteochondrosis in Sheep and Cattle: Differential Diagnosis and Estimating Prevalence', unpublished University of York report (2010).

(herring, gadids including haddock and whiting, and plaice, flounder or dab). The herrings are likely to have been cured by salting and packing in barrels with salt or brine. It is also likely that the gadids and flatfish were preserved by salting and/or drying, but a whiting articular from dump deposit 1188 shows that fish were purchased with their heads on.

Freshwater fish are fairly common and are likely to have been caught locally in the Thames or Cherwell and eaten fresh. The remains include small pike (generally *c.*300–350 mm in total length based on visual comparison with modern specimens), small cyprinid and probable immature burbot (total length of *c.*180 mm based on comparison with a modern fish), the only freshwater gadid. Burbot are now probably extinct in British waters, but other examples of this nocturnal fish have been reported from late Anglo-Saxon and medieval sites in Oxford,[85] and it seems likely from the small size of the bones that they were captured locally; it has previously been suggested that burbot may have once been found in the Thames.[86] Burbot are bottom-living fish that frequent the river edge and can be caught on eel lines set overnight.[87] Eels are one of the most common fish identified in Anglo-Saxon fish assemblages and in Domesday records and are likely to have been locally abundant, particularly around the mill leats.

As a fish without fins and scales, eels should have been avoided by any Jewish inhabitants (kosher fish including only those with fins and scales, following Leviticus 11:9), and so evidence of eel in pit fills 1129, 1188, 1214 and 10019 suggests that these deposits predated the Jewish occupation.

The only other context from this phase that produced fish remains was cesspit fill 1080, from Structure 3.1, and the sample from that fill included only a single herring vertebra and indeterminate fin rays. Since pig bones were also absent from the fills of this structure, it may be directly associated with the Jewish occupation and so it can perhaps be tentatively suggested that the Jewish occupants ate little fish. However, this supposition has to be qualified because of the small number of soil samples that were processed and, in particular, from deposits dating to the later part of the twelfth century.

Phase 4 comprised 17 bones identified from six processed soil samples, most of them from occupation layer 10013. Apart from herring, unidentified gadid and flatfish, all the remains come from freshwater fish or eel. Bones from eel were identified in contexts 10013 and 5034. A large salmonid (probably salmon) caudal vertebra from pit fill 1333 probably came from a cured fish since barrelled salmon was widely traded.[88]

Phase 5 bones were limited to a single fragment of a ling parasphenoid, comparable in size to a fish of a total length of 780 mm, from levelling deposit 1122 and a cleithrum fragment from a fairly large flatfish came from pit fill 10011. Both bones were hand recovered on site.

The most notable feature of the Phase 7 assemblage is the presence of at least three cleithra (minimum two fish) and other bones from the back of the head and posterior part of the spine of extremely large ling that were recovered by hand from cesspit fill 4067 in Structure 7.1. The exclusive presence of these elements, together with cut marks to a ling post-temporal (oblique knife cut at the base of the articular facet, medial aspect and the inferior process has been chopped through) and to a ling supracleithrum (two cuts to the caudal aspect) suggests these were dried fish. A large cod supracleithrum from fill 4061 from the same latrine is also likely to come from a stored fish. When large gadids are preserved by air drying (stockfish) sometimes accompanied by salting (klippfish), most of the head elements are typically removed at the production site and only a few appendicular elements (those from the back of the head

85 R.A. Nicholson, 'Fish Bones', in A. Norton and J. Mumford, 'Anglo-Saxon Pits and a Medieval Kitchen at The Queen's College, Oxford', *Oxoniensia*, 75 (2010), pp. 210–14.

86 B.J. Muus and P. Dahlstrøm, *The Freshwater Fishes of Britain and Europe* (1971), pp. 154–5.

87 Ibid.; R. Philipps and M. Rix, *Freshwater Fish of Britain, Ireland and Europe* (1985), p. 118.

88 A. Locker, 'The Role of Stored Fish in England 900–1750 AD: The Evidence from Historical and Archaeological Data', University of Southampton Ph.D. thesis (2000), pp. 50, 74–83.

including the cleithra, post-temporals and supracleithra) and some of the vertebrae, especially those closest to the caudal fin, are left in the fish to provide support to the fillet.

The ling would have been substantial fish. Very much larger than any of the available reference material, these fish are likely to have been at least 1.4 m long (total length). Jennings *et al.* report that a fish of this length would weight about 16.5 kg.[89] Ling is found throughout the north-east Atlantic; along with other whitefish, dried ling was a significant export from Shetland in the sixteenth and seventeenth centuries.[90] Other fish from this phase include herring, eel and perch.

Discussion

The small fish assemblage from medieval contexts includes fish acquired from both coastal and freshwater fisheries. Much of the sea-fish, and probably also the salmon, is likely to have been preserved by pickling or salting, since transporting fresh fish to Oxford rapidly enough to avoid spoiling would have been expensive. Fish was, however, readily available, since their remains regularly feature in samples from the late Anglo-Saxon period onwards in the city. In the early fourteenth century, fishmongers' stalls were located in Fish Street (now St Aldate's), with permanent shops grouped in a side street known as Winchelsea Row, and by 1360 fishboards had been erected against properties near the town hall. In 1360, the fishmongers' stalls in St Aldate's comprised eighteen stalls for 'Winchelsea fish', and others for stockfish and herrings. To what extent the inhabitants of Jacob's Hall and surrounding properties enjoyed the fish is unclear, since the recovered assemblage is small for an urban site in Oxford, although this may simply be a reflection of the relatively small volume of sieved soil from rubbish deposits and cesspits. Likewise, the possibility of identifying a Jewish signature by the absence of eel is intriguing, but would require a greater sample size and securely dated deposits to be conclusive.

Cured fish were widely traded throughout the medieval period. By the sixteenth century North Sea, Icelandic and Newfoundland fisheries for cod and other large gadids were at their peak and purchase of stored fish, including 'stockfisshe', was a regular part of household expenditure.[91] The ling and cod bones in latrine Structure 7.1 evidence the consumption of this popular stored product, which requires soaking for several days before cooking.

AVIAN EGGSHELL by REBECCA NICHOLSON

A small quantity of avian eggshell (4 g) was recovered from cesspit 1058 and pit 1225, both belonging to Phase 3. It is very likely that these are the remains of domestic fowl (chicken) eggs.

MARINE SHELL by REBECCA NICHOLSON

A total of 273 fragments of marine shell, weighing 3034 g, were recovered by hand from the excavations, with an additional 73 g of shell extracted from sieved soil sample residues. The material was rapidly scanned and appears to comprise exclusively valves of European flat oyster (*Ostrea edulis*) in variable condition and size, although lacking very large examples. Oyster shells are a common find in medieval and post-medieval assemblages, and the assemblage from St Aldate's confirms that they must have been regularly eaten, although not in large amounts in the properties relating to this site. Only three fragments come from deposits provisionally phased as late Anglo-Saxon (Phase 1) and ten contexts phased as eleventh century (Phase 2).

89 S. Jennings et al., 'Weak Cross-Species Relationships Between Body Size and Trophic Level Belie Powerful Size-Based Trophic Structuring in Fish Communities', *Journal of Animal Ecology*, 70.6 (2001), table 3.

90 H. Smith, *Shetland Life and Trade 1550–1914* (1984).

91 J. Wubs-Mrozewicz, 'Fish Stock and Barrel. Changes in the Stockfish Trade in Northern Europe *c.*1360–1560', in L. Sicking and D. Abreu Ferreira (eds.), *Beyond the Catch. Fisheries of the North Atlantic, the North Sea and the Baltic 900–1850* (2009), pp. 187–209; Locker, 'The Role of Stored Fish'.

PLANT REMAINS by JOHN GIORGI

Following assessment, twenty-two samples were selected for analysis; four from middle/late Anglo-Saxon deposits (Phase 1), sixteen from medieval contexts (Phases 2 to 4), and two from post-medieval fills (Phase 7). Variable amounts of charred plant remains were recovered from all the samples, with the bulk of this material being from the middle to late Anglo-Saxon and early medieval deposits. The charred remains consisted of almost equal amounts of cereal grains (52 per cent) and other plant/weed seeds (48 per cent), with only traces of cereal chaff (<1 per cent). The cereal grains were poorly preserved and many were unidentifiable with variable but sometimes large amounts of uncounted small cereal grain fragments in all the samples. There was a rich 'waterlogged' plant assemblage in a Phase 4 layer, while two fills of a Phase 7 stone-lined latrine contained good amounts of both mineralized and 'waterlogged' botanical remains. There were occasional and small numbers of uncharred seeds in most of the other samples, but it is difficult to establish whether or not these are contemporary with the sampled features; *Sambucus* (elder) seeds were the most common, these being fairly robust seeds which may survive for long periods in the soil.

Phase 1: Middle to Late Anglo-Saxon

Four samples from this phase contained charred plant remains; one from the fill of a possible pit/cellar in Area 3, and three from Area 5, two from a sequence of compacted gravel floors and charcoal-rich deposits, and one from a posthole fill.

The four samples contained broadly similar charred plant assemblages consisting largely of cereal grains. The two main cereals represented in these samples were (six-row) hulled barley (*Hordeum vulgare*), particularly in layer 5027, and free-threshing wheat (*Triticum aestivum/ turgidum*), the main cereal in fill 3088; a rachis fragment in layer 5027 showed the presence of hexaploid bread wheat (*Triticum aestivum*). The samples contained only a few grains of oat (*Avena*) and rye (*Secale cereale*). These grains may have become accidentally burnt while being dried before milling and/or storage or as a result of cooking accidents.

These assemblages represent virtually fully processed cereals, grains making up 96 per cent and 86 per cent of the quantified remains in the two richest assemblages from fill 3088 and layer 5027 respectively. The samples contained few chaff fragments or potential arable weed seeds, the latter including *Agrostemma githago* (corn cockle), *Fallopia convolvulus* (black bindweed) and *Bromus* (brome), all large weed seeds difficult to separate from the grain other than by hand-sorting and often found in cereal storage deposits. An *Anthemis cotula* (stinking chamomile) seed in one sample may point to the cultivation of calcareous soils while a few *Eleocharis* (spike-rush) and *Carex* (sedge) seeds suggest that this included damper areas of ground. All four samples also contained a few charred hazelnut fragments (*Corylus avellana*), probably food waste from the collection and consumption of this wild food resource.

The two main cereals in these samples, free-threshing wheat and hulled barley, along with a little evidence for rye and oats, are the main grains found in the late Anglo-Saxon period in southern England,[92] free-threshing wheat and hulled barley being the dominant grains from other sites of this period in Oxford, for example, in mid to late Anglo-Saxon deposits close-by at Nos. 11–12 Queen Street,[93] while other late Anglo-Saxon deposits included a large assemblage of free-threshing wheat at All Saints Church,[94] and another of barley and wheat on the north side of Lincoln College.[95]

92 J. Greig, 'The British Isles', in W. van Zeist et al. (eds.), *Progress in Old World Palaeoethnobotany* (1991), p. 315.

93 M. Robinson, 'Waterlogged Plant and Invertebrate Evidence', in C. Halpin (ed.), 'Late Saxon Evidence and Excavation of Hinxey Hall, Queen Street, Oxford', *Oxoniensia*, 48 (1980), p. 69.

94 M. Robinson, 'Environmental Evidence from All Saints Church', in Dodd, *Oxford*, p. 389.

95 Z. Kamash et al., 'Late Saxon and Medieval Occupation: Evidence from Excavations at Lincoln College, Oxford, 1997–2000', *Oxoniensia*, 67 (2002), pp. 199–286.

Cereals during the Anglo-Saxon period may have been used for gruel or porridge, which probably made up a significant part of the diet,[96] although the main use of the wheat grains would have been for bread, a staple food at the time with a preference for white leavened wheat bread.[97] Other uses of barley were for ale – although there were no germinated grains to suggest such a use – and animal fodder.

Phases 2 to 4: Eleventh to Fourteenth Century

There is a similar range of cereals in all three medieval phases (eleventh to fourteenth century) of the site with free-threshing (including bread) wheat (*Triticum aestivum*) and hulled barley (*Hordeum vulgare*) being the main grains together with smaller amounts of oats (*Avena*) and traces of rye (*Secale cereale*), similar to the results from the middle to late Anglo-Saxon phase. This is the usual range of cereals for the medieval period in southern Britain,[98] with similar dated (eleventh- to thirteenth-century) finds from other medieval sites in Oxford, free-threshing (including bread) wheat often being the main cereal; for example, from Corpus Christi College,[99] Jesus College (along with hulled barley),[100] the Nun's Garden, Queens College[101] and Merton College.[102] Closer to the site, free-threshing (including bread) wheat, hulled barley and oats were the main grains in eleventh- to thirteenth-century deposits from excavations at Queen Street.[103] The only other evidence for arable crops in the medieval samples were a few possible peas (cf. *Pisum sativum*) and perhaps some of the larger legume fragments which may be from cultivated pulses.

Wheat made the best and therefore most sought after and expensive bread in the medieval period,[104] particularly wheat bread using the finest and well sieved flour to remove as much bran as possible; the very fragmented cereal bran in Phase 4 occupation layer 10013 also suggests well-sieved flour. Barley was used for bread and ale, but there was no evidence except a few loose cereal coleoptiles to suggest brewing activities on site. All the cereals may have added to pottage,[105] while barley and oats were used as fodder.

Historical records from around 1300 suggest that the catchment area for cereal production and supply to the Oxford extended to a radius of no more than twelve miles,[106] with the virtually clean grain assemblages in the samples suggesting that they were being imported into the town as processed cereals.

There are similar weed seed assemblages in the different medieval phases of the site with a number of weeds, including stinking chamomile (*Anthemis cotula*) and corn gromwell (*Lithospermum arvense*) and thorow-wax (*Bupleurum rotundifolium*), suggesting the cultivation of calcareous loams. A similar range of weeds has been found on other medieval sites in Oxford

96 A. Hagen, *A Handbook of Anglo-Saxon Food. Processing and Consumption* (1994), p. 60.

97 Ibid. p. 125.

98 Greig, *Progress in Old World Palaeoethnobotany*, p. 321.

99 Smith, 'Charred and Waterlogged Plant Remains', in Bashford et al., 'Medieval and Post-Medieval Remains from Excavations on the Site of the New Auditorium, Corpus Christi College', p. 207.

100 W. Smith, 'Charred and Mineralised Plant Remains', in R. Bashford and B.M. Ford, 'Eleventh-Century, Later Medieval and Early Post-Medieval Evidence from Investigations at Jesus College and Market Street, Oxford', *Oxoniensia*, 79 (2014), pp. 231–4.

101 J. Giorgi, 'Plant Remains', in S Teague et al., 'Late Saxon, Medieval and Post-Medieval Archaeology at the Nun's Garden, The Queen's College, Oxford', *Oxoniensia*, 80 (2015), pp. 179–85.

102 J. Giorgi, in chapter 6, below.

103 J. Giorgi, 'The Plant Remains from Queen Street, St Ebbe's, Oxford (OXCMS97)', unpublished OA report (1999).

104 P.W. Hammond, *Food and Feast in Medieval England* (1995), p. 2.

105 C.A. Wilson, *Food and Drink in Britain* (1991), p. 199.

106 B.M.S. Campbell et al., *A Medieval Capital and its Grain Supply. Agrarian Production and Distribution in the London Region c.1300*, Historical Geography Research Series, 30 (1993), p. 173.

including the Nun's Garden, Queen's College,[107] and Queen Street.[108] Several other species, however, for example corn cockle (*Agrostemma githago*) and knotgrass (*Polygonum aviculare*), may tentatively suggest that sandy loams were also used for growing crops, while sedge (*Carex*) and *Eleocharis* seeds in the medieval grain assemblages suggest that areas of cultivation may have included damper areas of ground probably closer to the river.

There is tentative evidence from the weed seeds for both the spring-sowing of cereals, for example black bindweed (*Fallopia convolvulus*), and autumn-sowing, for instance thorow-wax and cleaver (*Galium aparin*). Of the two main cereals in the samples, bread wheat would have usually been winter-sown, while barley may have been sown in both winter and spring.[109] The presence of relatively short weeds, including stinking chamomile and thorow-wax, suggests that the cereals were reaped fairly low on the straw.

'Waterlogged' Plant Assemblage from Layer 10013 (Phase 4) This layer produced a plant assemblage dominated by large amounts of fruit remains. Large numbers of *Prunus* fruit stones included plum/bullace-type, probably *P. domestica* spp. *insititia* (bullace/damson/greengage) on the basis of the size and morphology of the better preserved stones. Both cultivated and wild plum stones, however, were identified in a thirteenth-century pit fill at No. 4A Merton Street.[110] There were also fruit stones of *Prunus spinosa* (sloe/blackthorn), cherry and possibly *Prunus cereasus* (sour/dwarf/Morello cherry). Other fruits were represented by large numbers of grape (*Vitis vinfera*), fig (*Ficus carica* L.), wild strawberry and *Rubus glandulosus* (blackberry) seeds, smaller numbers of apple (*Malus*) and pear/apple (*Pyrus/Malus*) seeds and occasional records for *Morus nigra* (mulberry) and *Sorbus* fruits including possibly rowan (cf. *Sorbus aucuparia*). There was also a small amount of fragmented hazelnut shell in this sample.

The fruits represented in this layer have been found on other medieval sites in Oxford, for example in eleventh- to thirteenth-century deposits from No. 4A Merton Street.[111] Grapes and figs may have been imported as dried fruits, while grapes may have also been locally grown at this time during the early medieval warm period (950–1250). Some of these fruits may have been cultivated in kitchen gardens and in orchards while the wild fruits and nuts (blackberry, hazelnuts, sloe/blackthorn, possible rowan and dog rose) may have been gathered from hedgerows and woodlands outside the town.

Other food plants included evidence for culinary herbs, represented by a few finds of coriander (*Coriandrum sativum*), fennel (*Foeniculum vulgare*) and possibly some of the mineralized Apiaceae seeds in this sample. Coriander and fennel were both common flavourings at the time according to the archaeobotanical evidence.[112] There were also large amounts of fragmented cereal bran, some of which was identified as wheat and/or rye, both cereals also being represented by small numbers of charred grains in this sample. These fine bran fragments (mainly smaller than 1 mm) may indicate finely milled or well-sieved wholemeal flour. There were also large amounts of very fragmented corn cockle seed in the sample, such fragments frequently found together with cereal bran because these large weed seeds were difficult to remove other than by hand-sorting and therefore were often milled together with the grain.

Occasional hemp (*Cannabis sativa*) seeds were also identified in this sample. This plant was mainly grown for its fibres, although the oil from the seeds may have been used for cooking

[107] Giorgi, 'Plant Remains', in Teague et al., 'Late Saxon, Medieval and Post-Medieval Archaeology at the Nun's Garden', pp. 179–85.

[108] Giorgi, 'The Plant Remains from Queen Street, St Ebbe's'.

[109] L. Moffet, 'The Archaeology of Medieval Plant Foods', in C.M. Woolgar et al. (eds.), *Food in Medieval England: Diet and Nutrition* (2006), p. 48.

[110] R. Pelling, 'Charred and Waterlogged Plant Remains', in Poore, 'No. 4A Merton St', p. 335.

[111] Ibid. pp. 326 and 335.

[112] J. Greig, 'Archaeobotanical and Historical Records Compared – A New Look at the Taphonomy of Edible and other Useful Plants from the 11th to the 18th centuries AD', *Circea: The Journal of the Association for Environmental Archaeology*, 12:2 (1996 for 1995), p. 217.

and lighting and as animal feed.[113] Cannabis was also identified in a thirteenth-century pit fill from No. 4A Merton Street.[114] The *Brassica/Sinapis* (cabbages, turnips, mustards) seeds in this layer may also be food remains.

The sample also contained evidence for a small range of potential cereal weeds, by-products from the final stages of crop-cleaning, together with evidence for the residues of hay fodder represented by *Ranunculus acris/repens/bulbosus*, *Leontodon* (hawkbit), *Prunella vulgaris* and good number of *Carex* seeds. The sedges may also be from flooring materials, possibly collected from the margins of the river along with several other wetland plants, *Eleocharis* and *Oenanthe* (water dropwort) identified in the sample and possibly incidentally collected at the same time. Indeterminate stem fragments may also be from flooring materials. Seed remains of *Rosa canina* (dog-rose) and *Cornus sanguinea* (dogwood) along with the *Rubus* (brambles) seeds may be evidence for hedgerows close-by.

The botanical remains in this sample represent general food waste as well as probably faecal remains given the presence of cereal bran, small-seeded fruits and large amounts of fly puparia. There is also evidence for the residues of hay and flooring (including possibly stabling) materials.

The plant remains from this layer provide a partial insight into the diet of the inhabitants in this area at the time although it is not possible to establish whether this deposit is associated with Jewish or post-Jewish occupation of the site because the context was dated to the thirteenth to fourteenth century therefore covering the period prior to and post-dating the expulsion of the Jews from the town. In any event, it is not possible to distinguish a Jewish diet on the basis of the plant remains alone; suffice to say, however, that the range of foodstuffs represented in this sample suggest a high-status diet.

Phase 7: Mid-Seventeenth to Early Eighteenth Century

Two samples from the fills of a stone-lined latrine (4073) produced rich and similar botanical assemblages. Both contained a few charred grains, including wheat and oat, but the bulk of the plant remains consisted of 'waterlogged' and mineralized fruit remains, including large numbers of fig, blackberry and raspberry (*Rubus idaeus*) seeds, smaller numbers of grape pips and occasional wild strawberry, elder and apple (*Malus domestica*) seeds. There were also a few plum/bullace fruit stones in fill 4014 and a charred hazelnut shell fragment in fill (4061). These remains, particularly the small fruit seeds, may be indicative of faecal waste, which is also suggested by large amounts of mineralized concretions and mineralized fly puparia in both fill samples.

Other post-medieval deposits from sites in Oxford have produced similar ranges of fruit; for example, in sixteenth- to eighteenth-century fills from two stone-lined cesspits at Corpus Christi College[115] and in the fills of an eighteenth-century well at Merton College.[116]

There was also a good number of *Carex* seeds in both samples, which may be the residues of discarded flooring materials dumped in the pit to dampen down the smells; the presence of several wetland plants in the samples, including *Ranunculus sceleratus* (celery-leaved crowfoot), *Alisma* (water plantain), *Juncus* (rush) and *Eleocharis*, may suggest that the sedges were collected from the river bank; mineralized ribbed stem fragments in both samples may be from flooring/stabling materials.

113 J. Greig, 'Plant Resources', in G. Astill and A. Grant (eds.), *The Countryside of Medieval England* (1988), p. 122.

114 Pelling, 'Charred and Waterlogged Plant Remains', p. 335.

115 Smith, 'Charred and Waterlogged Plant Remains', in Bashford et al., 'Medieval and Post-Medieval Remains from Excavations on the Site of the New Auditorium, Corpus Christi College', p. 207.

116 Chapter 6, below.

INSECTS by ENID ALLISON

One sub-sample from a waterlogged occupation deposit (10013) assigned to the thirteenth to fourteenth century (Phase 4) was submitted for examination of insect remains. The proportions of various ecological groups of insects in the assemblage are shown in Table 4.7; a complete list of insects and other invertebrates is provided in the full report available from the OA Library.

The deposit had clearly contained a significant amount of cess. The most numerous insect remains were fly (Diptera) puparia, the dominant species being *Thoracochaeta zosterae*, which is particularly characteristic of medieval cess deposits, even though its natural habitat appears to be in wet decaying seaweed.[117] The species appears to be indicative of cesspits containing foul matter graduating from saturated to damp through to drier conditions.[118] Spiracles of rat-tailed maggots (the larvae of a hoverfly (Syrphidae), probably *Eristalis tenax*) were common, these being characteristic of foul standing liquids.

Beetles were well-represented (a minimum of 214 individuals of 47 taxa, a concentration of >100 individuals per litre), and a large proportion (75 per cent) were synanthropes. The rove beetle *Creophilus maxillosus* is a predator typically found in carrion but it would probably also exploit other habitats rich in fly larvae.[119] Several *Bruchus ?rufimanus* are likely to have arrived directly in faeces, adding to evidence for diet. The larvae develop within medium and large legume seeds, especially in field beans[120] and they were frequently consumed within infested pulses. The beetles survive passage through the gut well, and in archaeological contexts the presence of their remains is generally characteristic of faeces. No pulses were noted among the plant remains from this sample, but this is not unusual in waterlogged deposits since legume seeds that are neither charred nor mineralised do not preserve well.[121]

Almost half of the beetles (47 per cent) consisted of taxa that are characteristic of litter from ancient houses or other buildings.[122] Such material appears to have been used in many cess-containing features, perhaps to reduce odours. It is also possible that some taxa within this group lived in the drier parts of cess deposits or in associated structures. The group was dominated by *Epauloecus unicolor* (formerly *Tipnus unicolor*), found in damp mouldy debris,[123] on its own accounting for a fifth of the whole beetle assemblage. Archaeological evidence suggests that this spider beetle is particularly characteristic of long-lived high-quality buildings, with the proportion increasing with general cleanliness.[124] Other members of the building fauna

117 R.D. Belshaw, 'A Note on the Recovery of *Thoracochaeta zosterae* (Haliday) (Diptera: Sphaeroceridae) from Archaeological Deposits', *Circaea*, 6:1 (1989), pp. 39–41; S.C. Webb et al., 'The Seaweed Fly *Thoracochaeta zosterae* (Hal.) (Diptera: Sphaeroceridae) in Inland Archaeological Contexts: δ13C and δ15N Solves the Puzzle', *Journal of Archaeological Science*, 25 (1998) pp. 1253–7.

118 D.N. Smith, 'Defining an Indicator Package to Allow Identification of "Cesspits" in the Archaeological Record', *Journal of Archaeological Science*, 40 (2013), pp. 526–43.

119 D.A. Lott and R. Anderson, 'The Staphylinidae (Rove Beetles) of Britian and Ireland Parts 7 & 8: Oxyporinae, Steninae, Euaesthetinae, Pseudopsinae, Paederinae, Staphylininae', *Handbooks for the Identification of British Insects*, 12, Part 7 (2011), p. 252.

120 A. Hoffman, 'Coléoptères Bruchides et Anthribides', *Faune de France*, 44 (1945), p. 43.

121 E.P. Allison and A.R. Hall, 'The Plant and Invertebrate Remains', in M. Hicks and A. Hicks, *St Gregory's Priory, Northgate, Canterbury: Excavations 1988–89*, The Archaeology of Canterbury, New Series Volume II (2001), pp. 334–8; W. Carruthers and E. Allison, 'Plant and Insect Remains from Medieval Features at 70 Stour Street, Canterbury, Kent (Site Code SSC(70).EX13)', unpublished Canterbury Archaeological Trust report 2015/79 (2015).

122 A.R. Hall and H.K. Kenward, 'Environmental Evidence from the Colonia: General Accident and Rougier Street', *Archaeology of York*, 14:6 (1990), pp. 289–434; H.K. Kenward and A.R. Hall, 'Biological Evidence from 16–22 Coppergate', *The Archaeology of York*, 14:7 (1995), pp. 435–797; J. Carrott and H. Kenward, 'Species Associations among Insect Remains from Urban Archaeological Deposits and Their Significance in Reconstructing the Past Human Environment', *Journal of Archaeological Science*, 28 (2001), pp. 887–905.

123 A.F. O'Farrell and P.M. Butler, 'Insects and Mites Associated with the Storage and Manufacture of Foodstuffs in Northern Ireland', *Economic Proceedings of the Royal Dublin Society*, 3 (1948), pp. 343–407.

124 H. Kenward, *Invertebrates in Archaeology in the North of England, Northern Regional Review of Environmental Archaeology*, Research Department Report Series, 12 (2009), p. 309.

Table 4.7. Proportions of beetles from different ecological groups.

Total individual adult beetles	**214**
% Dry decomposers	41
% Foul decomposers	<1
% Eurytopic decomposers	32
% Total decomposers	73
% Aquatics	0
% Damp ground taxa	1
% Plant-associated taxa	1
% Outdoor taxa	2
% Grain pests	4
% Wood/timber taxa	3
% House/building fauna	47
% Strong synanthropes	38
% Typical synanthropes	15
% Facultative synanthropes	21
% Total synanthropes	75

included *Ptinus ?fur*, *Tenebrio obscurus*, *Blaps*, *Xylodromus concinnus*, *Latridius minutus* group, *Cryptophagus* spp., *Atomaria* spp., *Aglenus brunneus* and *Mycetaea subterranea*. Modern records of *Mycetaea subterranea* are mainly from decaying straw and wood in dry cellars, barns and stables and in association with the dry rot fungus *Merulius lacrymans*.[125] Woodworm (*Anobium punctatum*) and death watch (*Xestobium rufovillosum*) beetles were probably also associated with the building fauna. Death watch beetle primarily infests oak timbers that have been subject to microbial attack following exposure to damp.

Distinguishing the types of buildings that litter might have come from is often not possible, since from a beetle's point of view human dwellings with floors strewn with cut vegetation or other organic litter, would have included many of the same habitats as stables. Here, ectoparasites provided a hint that at least some of the litter was from human habitation; human louse (*Pediculus humanus*) can exist only in close proximity to man, although human flea (*Pulex irritans*), while primarily associated with human dwellings, can sometimes be found in buildings occupied by domestic animals.[126]

Stable waste can often be identified if several characteristic groups of insects are present, namely a fauna from within buildings, grain pests, insects either collected with hay or exploiting it in storage, and decomposers living in foul, open-textured nutrient-rich material.[127] Two species of grain pests were recorded (*Sitophilus granarius, Oryzaephilus surinamensis*; 4 per cent of the assemblage) and the numbers are probably not high enough to indicate the dumping of

[125] H.E. Hinton, 'The Ptinidae of Economic Importance', *Bulletin of Entomological Research*, 31 (1941), pp. 331–81; T. Palm, 'Die Holz- und Rinden-Käfer der süd- und mittelschwedischen Laubbäume', *Opuscula Entomologica Supplementum*, 16 (1959).

[126] F.G.A.M. Smit, *Siphonaptera, Handbooks for the Identification of British Insects*, 1:16 (1957); R.S. George, in P. Harding (ed.), *Atlas of the Fleas (Siphonaptera) of Britain and Ireland* (2008), p. 14.

[127] H. Kenward and A. Hall, 'Enhancing Bioarchaeological Interpretation Using Indicator Groups: Stable Manure as a Paradigm', *Journal of Archaeological Science*, 24 (1997), pp. 663–73.

spoiled cereals. In deposits interpreted as dumps of spoiled grain, the pest species often make up over 50 per cent of the insect fauna.[128] While an origin in human faeces is possible, is probably unlikely in this case since the cereal bran is indicative of finely milled flour and the beetles are largely represented by complete undamaged sclerites. It may therefore be more likely that the grain pests arrived with stable litter or straw containing a residue of grain. The saw-toothed grain beetle (*O. surinamensis*) is particularly found in damp, mouldy cereals, and poor-quality grain is more likely to have been used for animal feed rather than for human consumption. The plant remains have provided convincing evidence for the presence of a residue from hay in this deposit, and the beetles *Typhaea stercorea* and *Omonadus floralis* or *O. formicarius* are suggestive of mouldering hay. *Sitona* and an ?apionid weevil, the only two plant-feeding taxa in the assemblage, are both common in grassland habitats and are often found with other insects where hay is suggested.[129] Decomposers associated with foul matter, typically dung, were very poorly represented, however (a single specimen of *Platystethus arenarius*; <1 per cent of the assemblage), but it is possible that this might simply reflect the rapid and regular clearance of manure from stables, perhaps on a daily basis, leaving insufficient time for substantial populations of foul decomposers to develop.

There was little unequivocal evidence for an outdoor component in the beetle assemblage (that is, taxa not usually found within buildings or in accumulations of decomposing organic material), although *Lesteva longoelytrata* and Dryops may suggest damp ground and wet muddy conditions. The general lack of outdoor taxa suggests that the material making up the deposit had accumulated under closed conditions.

ACKNOWLEDGEMENTS

The authors gratefully acknowledge Gilbert-Ash, with consultation by Orion Heritage, for commissioning the excavation and post-excavation projects on behalf of Reef Estates and the British Airways Pension Trust. The authors would like to thank Will Bedford of Orion Heritage and David Radford, Oxford City Council archaeologist, for their support throughout the archaeological programme. The fieldwork was managed by Carl Champness and directed on site by Vix Hughes and Ben Attfield, supported by Robin Bashford, Isobel Bentley, Tom Black, Sophie Bojadziev, Anne-Laure Bollen, John Boothroyd, Thomas Brook, John Carne, Rachael Daniel, Maria Diaz Tena, Mark Dodd, Adam Fellingham, Raul Gonzalez, James Green, Victoria Green, Camille Guezennec, Gareth Hatt, Neil Holbrook, Elizabeth Kennard, Lisa Kennard, Martin Locker, Javier Martinez-Jimenez, Robert McIntosh, Michael McLean, Jeremy Mordue, Conan Parsons, Emma Powell, Bernadetta Rzadek, Mike Sims, Lee Sparks, Ashley Strutt, Peter Vellett and Georgia Wood. Edward Biddulph managed the post-excavation project. Thanks are also due to the staff that processed the finds under the management of Leigh Allen, processed the environmental samples under the management of Rebecca Nicholson, and prepared the archive under the management of Nicola Scott.

[128] D. Smith and H. Kenward, '"Well, Sextus, What Can We Do With This?" The Disposal and Use of Insect-Infested Grain in Roman Britain', *Environmental Archaeology*, 17:2 (2012), pp. 141–50.

[129] Kenward, *Invertebrates in Archaeology*, p. 289.

5.

Evidence for the Anglo-Saxon *Burh* Defences, Medieval Tenements and New Inn Hall: Investigations at Linton and Chavasse Quads, St Peter's College

ANDREW SIMMONDS, ROBIN BASHFORD, LEE GRANA, MIKE SIMS and GERRY THACKER

with contributions by JOHN COTTER and PAUL BLINKHORN

SUMMARY

Investigations in Linton Quad and Chavasse Quad at St Peter's College included small-scale excavations, a watching brief and a borehole survey. An augur hole and borehole recorded evidence for a large negative feature that lies on one possible projected alignment of the western defences of the Anglo-Saxon *burh*, though the interpretation of this feature remains uncertain. Evidence was also found for medieval tenements that occupied this part of New Inn Hall Street before the eponymous academic hall was built, and the western range of the medieval hall itself was exposed.

A programme of archaeological investigations was carried out at St Peter's College between 2014 and 2016 as a part of the Perrodo Project, a scheme to improve the college's public spaces. The college lies towards the western edge of the historic core of Oxford, *c.*250 m west of Carfax and *c.*100 m inside the line of the medieval town walls. It is centred on NGR SP 511 062 and fronts onto the west side of New Inn Hall Street, with Bulwarks Lane forming the rear, western boundary. New Inn Hall Street (formerly Little Bailey) formed part of the original street system and part of the earliest cobbled road surface found outside Nos. 22 and 24 produced a coin of Edward the Elder.[1] The land on the west side of the street was occupied by a number of tenements by at least the late thirteenth century. Linton Quad lies within a property identified by Salter as Rose Hall, which is likely to have originated as one of the many academic halls that were the precursors to the university colleges, while the southern part of the area now occupied by the college formerly comprised Trillock's Inn, an academic hall that possibly originated as the private house of the brothers John Trillek (bishop of Hereford 1344–60) and Thomas Trillek (bishop of Rochester 1364–72), who obtained a licence for a private oratory there in 1340 and 1348. It passed in 1361 to William of Wykeham, bishop of Winchester, and thence to New College in 1392, who maintained it as an academic hall, with most of the buildings being replaced during

[1] Dodd, *Oxford*, p. 28.

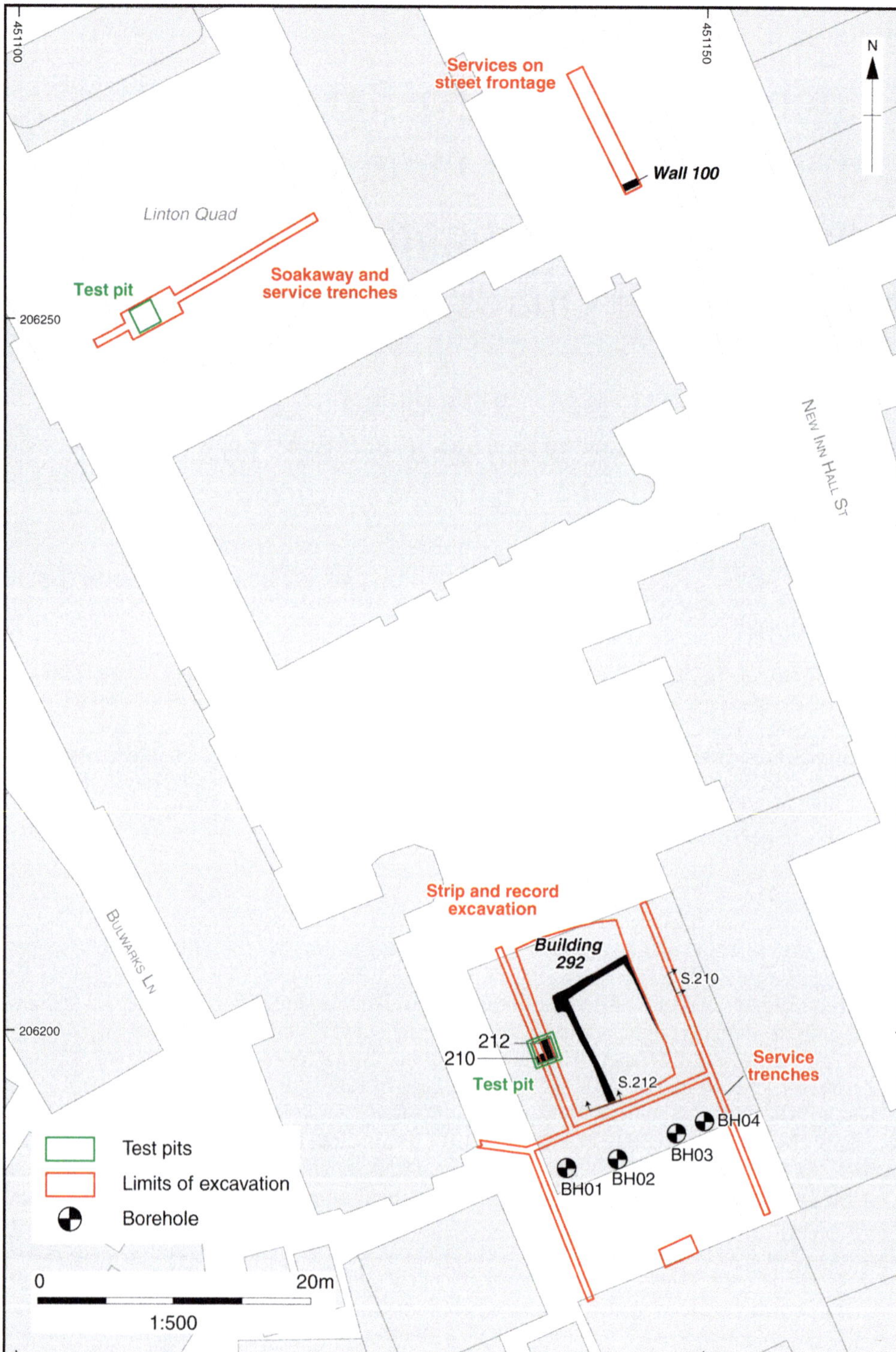

Fig. 5.1 Site location.

the nineteenth century.[2] In 1887 the hall was merged with Balliol College and closed. Most of the site was purchased by the city council for construction of the Central Girls' School (1901), and St Peter's College was established (originally as St Peter's Hall) on the northern part in 1928, subsequently expanding southward to encompass the school.[3]

The investigations were located within Linton Quad, which lies within the northern part of the college grounds, and Chavasse Quad, situated to the south (Fig. 5.1). The investigations within Linton Quad comprised the digging of a test pit at the proposed location of a soakaway pit followed by a watching brief that monitored the groundworks, including the reduction of the existing quad surface by *c*.0.50 m, the excavation of a soakaway and associated drainage trenches, and drainage works adjacent to the New Inn Hall Street frontage. In Chavasse Quad, a test pit was dug and a borehole survey carried out, after which a strip and record excavation was undertaken on the footprint of a proposed attenuation tank and a watching brief on the excavation of ground beams and services, as well as a test pit to investigate the foundation design of the existing New Road Baptist Church, which forms the southern side of the quad.

This report summarises the key results of the investigations. The full report is available from the OA Library.[4] The archive will be deposited with Oxfordshire County Museum Service under accession number 2014.183.

DISCUSSION

The investigation, although limited in extent, uncovered evidence for activity spanning the occupation of Oxford. The most significant discoveries are a large negative feature that may represent part of the original western boundary of the late Anglo-Saxon *burh*, evidence for medieval tenements that occupied this part of New Inn Hall Street before the academic hall was founded, and the western range of the medieval hall.

Possible Primary Burh *Defences*

The Pleistocene strata that underlay the site were recorded at 60.93 m OD by hand-auguring within the test pit in Linton Quad and 59.62–60.15 m OD in boreholes BH2–4 in Chavasse Quad, the difference between the two areas reflecting the topography of the site, which slopes down toward the River Thames to the south. They were buried beneath a considerable thickness of build-up, which amounted to 4.1 m in Linton Quad and 4.15–4.68 m in the boreholes. There were, however, two locations where the gravel was significantly deeper; in Chavasse Quad, auguring in the test pit extended to 6.1 m below ground level (58.00 m OD) and Borehole BH1 reached 59.23 m OD without encountering gravel. This may be a product of the undulating profile of the gravel, but could alternatively indicate the presence of negative features that truncated the gravel at these locations. There is insufficient evidence to establish the character of any such features, but it is worth noting that the site lies on one possible projected alignment of the western defences of Oxford's original *burh*.[5]

The line of the defences on this side of the town is highly problematic, but it has long been suggested that a sub-square primary *burh* enclosing an area centred on Carfax, constructed around the turn of the tenth century, was subsequently extended to the east and west to form the circuit that was later followed by the line of the medieval town wall.[6] Until recently, the only potential evidence for the western side of the putative primary *burh* was from an excavation

2 Salter, *Survey*, vol. 2, pp. 178–9, NW 90–98.
3 *VCH Oxon*. 3, pp. 336–8.
4 https://library.oxfordarchaeology.com/4852/.
5 Dodd, *Oxford*, fig. 2.4.
6 Ibid. pp. 21–5; J. Haslam, 'The Two Anglo-Saxon *Burhs* of Oxford', *Oxoniensia*, 75 (2010), pp. 15–34.

at 40 George Street in 1977–8 that found evidence for a very large ditch aligned north–south.[7] The ditch was at least 12 m wide, suggesting proportions appropriate to a defensive feature, and pottery from the fill indicated that it was filled in during the early thirteenth century, not long before the town wall was constructed over the top. If the ditch was indeed part of the *burh* defences, the projected alignment parallel to New Inn Hall Street would encompass the negative features in Chavasse Quad, an interpretation that is consistent with the single sherd of pottery dating from 1050–1300 from the lowest layer (243) in borehole BH1. However, more recent excavation has revealed a late Anglo-Saxon rampart running along the south-western side of Oxford Castle, extending as far west as St George's Tower.[8] This suggests that the defensive perimeter was taken right down to the western edge of the gravel terrace from an early point, if not from the outset, casting doubt on the putative George Street/New Inn Hall Street alignment.[9] The interpretation of the negative feature in borehole BH1 must therefore remain open to question.

Medieval and Later Tenements

Stone wall 212, which was recorded in the test pit in Chavasse Quad, produced a sherd of Minety-type ware probably dating to the thirteenth or fourteenth century and was associated with a soil layer (208) that contained a joining sherd, as well as others of similar date. These deposits are therefore likely to be associated with either Trillock's Inn, which was the precursor of New Inn Hall, or earlier domestic tenements fronting onto New Inn Hall Street. Within the limited exposure provided by the test pit, it was not possible to ascertain whether the wall represented part of a building or a tenement boundary, possibly dividing tenements fronting onto New Inn Hall Street from those to the west associated with Bulwarks Lane. The poor condition of the charred plant remains recovered from a soil sample from layer 208 would be consistent with an occupation layer close to a kitchen area, and the sample also produced remains from both freshwater and saltwater fish, the former probably caught locally in the Thames and Cherwell but the latter indicating that the diet of the occupants was supplemented by fish imported from the coast.

A wall (100) and cellar uncovered during the drainage works on the New Inn Hall Street frontage at Linton Quad represent the remains of a building that fronted onto the street. No dating evidence was recovered and the building may therefore be of either medieval or post-medieval date. This area was occupied by Rose Hall during the medieval period, but Agas' 1578 map of Oxford shows it as a vacant plot, suggesting that it experienced a period of abandonment during the sixteenth century before construction of the large properties shown on Loggan's map. It is therefore surprising that pit 15 in the Linton Quad test pit dated from precisely this period, producing pottery dated *c.*1550–1625.

New Inn Hall

Building 292 corresponds with the west range of the former New Inn Hall, as depicted on Agas' 1578 map (Fig. 5.2) and subsequent historic maps. Identification of the structure as a medieval building is somewhat at odds with the dating evidence from the excavation, since soil layers into which the foundations were cut produced pottery and clay tobacco pipes dating from the late seventeenth century, but this might indicate no more than that the layers continued to be reworked (and artefactual material incorporated into them) during this period. Nothing of the range survives above ground, since the hall was largely demolished during the nineteenth and twentieth centuries, and the layout of the hall is mainly known from a study by Pantin, which was based on cartographic depictions, specifically a 1675 view of the front of the hall by Loggan

7 B. Durham et al., 'Oxford's Northern Defences: Archaeological Studies 1971–1982', *Oxoniensia*, 48 (1983), pp. 18–19.

8 Munby, *Oxford Castle*.

9 See also chapter 6, below, for further discussion of the putative primary *burh* defences.

Fig. 5.2 Detail of New Inn Hall on Agas' 1578 map of Oxford (north to bottom).

in *Oxonia Illustrata*, William Williams' 1733 plan in *Oxonia Depicta* and King's 1848 plan of the hall.[10] The hall appears to have originally been a private house that was converted to use as an academic hall (originally Trillock's Inn) during the fourteenth century, and Pantin reconstructed it as comprising a main range that extended along the road frontage, separated from the rear, western range by a small quadrangle. The part that was exposed by the excavation comprised the north end of the western range. It is uncertain whether the structure revealed in the excavation was part of the original house or a fifteenth-century construction. The New College accounts show that when they took possession of the hall in 1392 it had a hall, solar, chapel, and various chambers, which Pantin places on the street frontage.[11] Whether the western range existed at this time is unknown, but there was certainly significant building work in 1420–1 and 1476–9. Wood suggested that the hall was entirely rebuilt during this time, and that it was for this reason

10 W.A. Pantin, 'The Halls and Schools of Medieval Oxford: An Attempt at Reconstruction', in A.B. Emden (ed.), *Oxford Studies Presented to Daniel Callus*, OHS, ns 16 (1964), pp. 31–100.

11 Ibid. p. 74.

that it gained the name 'New Inn', and it is possible that the western range was added then.[12] Its recorded width of 5.5 m corresponds well with Pantin's estimated dimension of 20 feet (6 m) wide.[13] His reconstruction of the hall indicates that the part of the western range that was exposed within the excavation comprised a kitchen and buttery, with chambers to the south.[14]

Demolition layer 291 yielded two large, fresh end-pieces of 'Tudor' red brick and a large fragment from a thirteenth- or fourteenth-century crested ridge tile, which provide some indication of the appearance of the building. A decorated floor tile bearing a white slip design, including fleur-de-lys and fabulous beasts (Fig. 5.6), may also have adorned the hall, although its date of *c.*1330–1400 may indicate that it originated from the buildings of Trillock's Inn. The yard between the western range and the buildings on the road frontage had a cobbled surface (271), although it is uncertain whether the underlying layer (274) represented a make-up layer for the surface or an earlier soil layer. To the rear of the western range, garden soil 290 corresponds with the gardens and orchards depicted here by Agas and Loggan. The immediately adjacent part of the layer was overlain by a sequence of deposits built up against the wall of the range, which may represent surfaces and occupation soils. Pit 210, dated by pottery to *c.*1660–1725, was also situated here.

The finds assemblages associated with the hall were modest in size. The most interesting element of the pottery assemblage was part of a Bellarmine bottle or jug with an applied medallion depicting an anchor and the monogram 'PVA' for Pieter van den Ancker, a Dutch merchant who settled in London in the mid seventeenth century (Fig. 5.5). This is only the second example of this monogram to be found in Oxford.

The latest depiction of the western range appears on Faden's map of 1789, and it is absent from King's 1848 plan of the hall. This suggests that the most likely context for the demolition of the building is the programme of rebuilding undertaken by principal John Cramer (1831–47), during which the building now known as Hannington Hall was constructed.[15] When New Inn Hall was handed to Balliol College in 1887, the principal's lodging (the older part of the hall) was sold to the city and demolished, and its site used to build the Central Girls' School (Building 295).

EXCAVATION RESULTS

Linton Quad

Test Pit The earliest deposits encountered in the test pit were only seen along the northern edge, as they had been truncated elsewhere by a later pit (15). These layers produced no artefactual material and comprised a fairly homogeneous silty clay deposit (22), a fairly compacted, *c.*0.2 m-thick mixed layer of limestone rubble and a 0.28 m-thick silty clay deposit (17). Pit 15, which occupied most of the test pit, was excavated by hand to a depth of 0.68 m. Hand-auguring penetrated for a further 1.88 m before reaching an obstruction, possibly the natural gravel, at *c.*4.1 m below ground level (60.93 m OD). It is not possible to be certain whether this represents the base of the pit or that of some earlier feature beneath the pit. The hand-excavated part of the pit produced sixteenth- to seventeenth-century pottery and animal bone. The pit was overlain by a garden soil (12), a series of deposits (11, 10, 9, 8, 5, 4) which probably represent phases of landscaping, and compacted layers 2 and 3, which may have formed a rudimentary surface predating the deposition of the existing topsoil of the Linton Quad lawn.

12 A. Wood, *The History and Antiquities of the Colleges and Halls in the University of Oxford* (Oxford, 1786), p. 676.
13 Pantin, 'The Halls and Schools of Medieval Oxford', p. 75.
14 Ibid. figs. 10 and 11.
15 *VCH Oxon.* 3, p. 338.

The Soakaway and Service Trenches The soakaway excavation measured 4.2 x 3.1 m (Fig. 5.1) and was excavated to a depth of 1.5 m below the grass surface. It uncovered a similar sequence of deposits to the upper part of the test pit, none of which were likely to predate the nineteenth century.

Service Trench on the New Inn Hall Street Frontage A service trench was excavated parallel and adjacent to New Inn Hall Street, in the grassed area adjacent to the college entrance (Fig. 5.1). The trench measured 16 m long and up to 2.2 m wide and was *c.*0.4 m deep, with a narrow deeper central section reduced to a maximum depth of 1.85m. At the southern limit of the trench was a wall (100) constructed of limestone bonded in a sandy mortar. The wall, which was orientated broadly west-south-west to east-north-east, was perpendicular to the line of New Inn Hall Street and measured 0.6 m wide. The stones that formed the wall did not appear to have been laid in courses, and averaged 250 mm on a side. The revealed section of the wall measured 1.1 m in height, and a length of *c.*1.9 m was present within the excavated area. To the south of the wall a void allowed a glimpse into a cellar (106), which would have been contemporary with the wall. The roof of the cellar was only briefly observed, but was constructed of slightly smaller limestone blocks than the wall and was bonded with what appeared to be the same mortar. Only around 0.50 m of the cellar was observed, the remainder appearing to have been backfilled with rubble. Following a site visit and advice from David Radford, the Oxford city archaeologist, the cellar void was infilled with fine gravel, and not further impacted upon. The wall and cellar were overlain by deposit 105, which appeared to relate to the demolition phase of the building, and was composed of *c.*30 per cent limestone rubble. This was sealed by a thin peaty layer and the topsoil and turf.

Chavasse Quad

Test Pit An auger hole in the base of the test pit recorded a roughly uniform deposit of grey sandy clay (214) at a depth of between 3.25 m and 6.10 m below ground level. Overlying this was a 0.3 m-thick deposit of rounded gravel and flints within a mid to dark brownish grey sandy clay matrix (215). Above layer 215 was a 0.8 m-thick layer of dull yellow-brown clayey silt (208), which was observed both within the auger hole and the base of the hand-excavated part of the test pit. This deposit produced charcoal flecking together with fragments of pottery and tile dating from 1250–1400. An environmental sample contained cereal grains including barley, wheat and oats, in addition to charcoal and fish and mammal bones.

Cut into the surface of layer 208 was a vertical-sided foundation trench (213) containing the footings of a stone wall (212), which measured 0.7 m wide and 0.25 m deep and was orientated north–south. The wall was built using local ragstone and bonded with an orange-yellow lime mortar. A sherd of pottery recovered from the wall dated from AD 1250–1400. A possible occupation layer comprising a dark grey-brown clay silt (211) butted up to the eastern edge of wall 212, and a sherd of pottery recovered from this dated from AD 1225–1450. Sealing both layer 208 and wall 212 was a 0.42 m-thick layer of grey-brown clayey silt (207) which produced charcoal, pottery and fragments of clay pipe dating from 1660–1725.

In the south-west corner of the test pit, the edge of a roughly circular feature *c.*1.8 m in diameter (210) was observed cutting layer 207, interpreted as a cesspit or rubbish pit. The pit appeared to be vertical-sided and contained numerous medium to large sized irregular limestone blocks. Pottery recovered from the fill dated from AD 1660–1725. An environmental sample contained cereal grains, nut shells and the bones of fish and mammals.

Overlying the pit was a sequence of layers that produced pottery and clay pipe dating from the eighteenth century onwards.

Boreholes The natural Pleistocene strata of the Summertown-Radley terrace were identified at the base of three of the boreholes (BH2, BH3 and BH4) between 4.15 m and 4.68 m below ground level. The contact between the Pleistocene strata and overlying deposits was very sharp, suggesting some truncation has occurred and no weathered land-surface was identified. The overlying sequences can be characterised by a series of variable and mixed dump/disturbed deposits of medieval date; no natural silting deposits were encountered that would suggest the primary natural silting of a large feature. Borehole BH1, at the western end of the transect, extended to 59.23 m OD but did not reach Pleistocene strata. Whether this represents the fill of a discrete or linear feature is unclear.

Strip and Record Excavation and Service Trenches Exposed in the base of the strip and record excavation and in the service trench to the east were two layers of very dark grey clayey silt with lenses of demolition material and burnt material, which contained pottery and fragments of clay pipe dating to the late seventeenth century. Cut into the surface of these layers was the foundation for a rectangular building (292) measuring 5.5 m wide and at least 9 m long north–south (Figs. 5.3 and 5.4). The foundation was constructed using local ragstone and a yellowish

Fig. 5.3 The western wing of New Inn Hall exposed during the watching brief, facing north. Scale: 1 m.

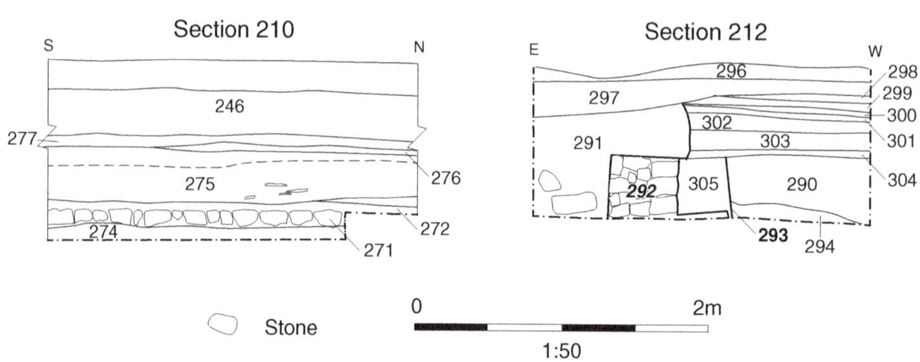

Fig. 5.4 Sections of New Inn Hall.

orange lime mortar. Observed within a service trench east of the building was a cobbled surface (271). This appears to be associated with the building and may represent an external courtyard or path surface.

Along the western, exterior side of the building, a sequence of deposits had built up against the wall that comprised alternating floor surfaces and charcoal-rich soil layers. The only dating evidence for this sequence was provided by four seventeenth-century pipe stems. Demolition of the building was represented by a vertical-sided robber trench (306) that cut through these layers. At the southern and north-eastern edges of the trench this robbing had left three courses of stone in situ, but elsewhere the robbing had reduced the wall down to one course. The remnants of the wall were overlaid by a deep deposit of demolition material, consisting of stone fragments, including stone roof tile, brick and clay tiles, which was also seen in the services trenches. Cobbled surface 271 was overlain by a layer of loose yellow-brown silty sand with fragments of stone, which may be a continuation of the demolition debris 291.

These deposits were cut by the concrete foundations supporting the brick walls of the rectangular building of the Central Girls' School (Building 295), built in 1900.

POTTERY by JOHN COTTER and PAUL BLINKHORN

Pottery was recovered from all four stages of the investigation, although the Linton Quad watching brief produced only a single sherd. The assemblage amounted to 229 sherds (1,708 g). Most of this is of post-medieval date with a smaller component of a dozen medieval sherds. Ordinary domestic pottery types are represented and all typical of the wares commonly found in Oxford.

The three earliest pieces are small and worn and all residual and include a cooking pot sherd in late Saxon Oxford shelly ware (*c*.775–1050), a sherd of St Neots-type ware (*c*.900–1100) and a sherd of Kennet Valley A ware (*c*.900–1250). There were also three sherds of Cotswold-type ware (normally dating *c*.1050–1250 in Oxford, but can be as early as *c*.875) and a few sherds of medieval Oxford ware (*c*.1075–1300), including a cooking pot rim. As usual in Oxford, the dominant medieval type comprises sherds of glazed Brill/Boarstall ware jugs (*c*.1225–1625) including decorated pieces typical of the thirteenth to fourteenth centuries. A fairly fresh sherd from the body of a jug in Olney Hyde-type shelly ware (*c*.1150–1400), from north Buckinghamshire or Northamptonshire, is one of the rarer medieval fabrics from the city, and joining sherds probably from a large storage jar in Minety-type ware represent a regional import

Fig. 5.5 Medallion from a stoneware bottle or jug bearing the monogram of Dutch merchant Pieter van den Ancker. Chavasse Quad test pit.

Fig. 5.6 Penn/Chiltern decorated floor tile. Chavasse Quad, Ctx 290.

from north-west Wiltshire and is a relatively uncommon type from Oxford sites. A particularly interesting item is a sherd of decorated Frechen stoneware from the test pit in Chavasse Quad. This has the upper part of an applied medallion from the front of a Bellarmine bottle or jug bearing the monogram 'PVA' for Pieter van den Ancker – a Dutch merchant who settled in London in the mid seventeenth century (Fig. 5.5). Pieter traded in French and German wine and also imported stoneware bottles from Frechen – some of them marked with his monogram (showing an anchor in the lower half of the medallion). The mark is closely datable to *c*.1655–65. Several examples of this mark are known from London but this is only the second example identified from Oxford.[16]

CERAMIC BUILDING MATERIAL by JOHN COTTER

An assemblage of 47 pieces of ceramic building material weighing 7.7 kg was recovered, mostly fragments of plain flat roof tile (peg tile). Of more interest was a complete medieval decorated floor tile belonging to the Penn/Chiltern tradition (*c*.1330–1400) and two corner fragments from separate tiles, all from post-medieval levels in Chavasse Quad. The white slip design on the complete tile shows it to have been one quadrant (quarter) of a four-part design with a large roundel extending over four adjacent tiles – all symmetrical in most details. Within the roundel is a frieze of poorly impressed decorative motifs including fleur-de-lys and fabulous beasts (Fig. 5.6). The design is paralleled in Oxford at Brewer Street.[17]

[16] D. Gaimster, *German Stoneware, 1200–1900* (1997), cat. no. 70.

[17] J. Cotter, 'Ceramic Building Material', in S. Teague and B.M. Ford, 'Excavations in Oxford's South Suburb at Brewer Street, Littlegate Street and Rose Place', unpublished OA report (2019).

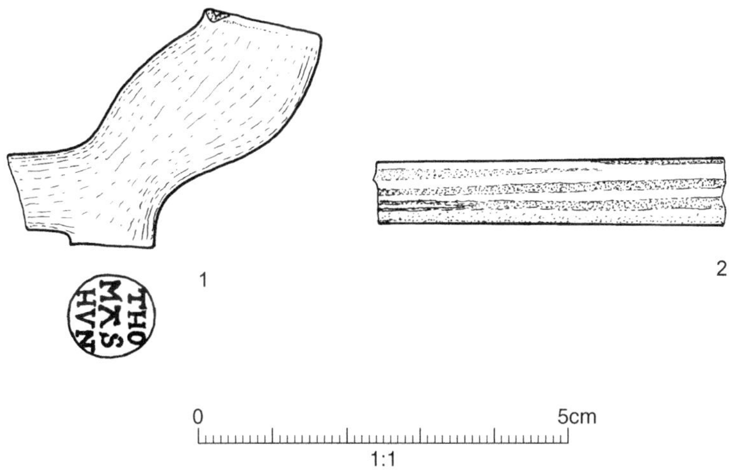

Fig. 5.7 Clay tobacco pipes from Chavasse Quad. 1: Bowl with stamp for Thomas Hunt of Marlborough, unstratified; 2: Stem decorated with lines of red ochre, Ctx 270. Drawings by David A. Higgins.

OTHER FINDS

The clay tobacco pipe assemblage (258 fragments) belongs mostly to the late seventeenth to early eighteenth century. The only marked piece is a bowl of *c.*1660–90 with the incuse stamp THO/MAS/HVNT, for one of the Thomas Hunts of Marlborough, Wiltshire (Fig. 5.7, no. 1). One stem associated with bowls of *c.*1660–90 is decorated with lines of red ochre (Fig. 5.7, no. 2). This is a rare form of decoration but various other instances have been recorded from Oxford (cf. eight examples from the Ashmolean Museum site, chapter 11), suggesting that this was a distinctive local trait. Small quantities of bottle glass, window glass, structural stone, metal, oyster shells and animal and fish bones were also recovered, but no pieces of any significance were found.

ACKNOWLEDGEMENTS

The fieldwork, post-excavation programme and publication were funded by St Peter's College, Oxford. The authors are grateful to Waterman Project Management for commissioning the archaeological work. The authors are also grateful to David Radford, Oxford County Council archaeologist, for his advice and guidance. The fieldwork was managed for OA by Gerry Thacker. The different stages of fieldwork were variously supervised by Robin Bashford, Lee Grana, Vix Hughes and Mike Sims, with the assistance of Kate Brady, Matthew Fenn and Rowan Kendrick. The post-excavation analysis was managed by Andrew Simmonds. The clay tobacco pipes were analysed by John Cotter and David A. Higgins, the metalwork and glass by Ian R. Scott, the stone by Ruth Shaffrey, the animal bone by Lee Broderick and Lena Strid, the fish remains and marine shell by Rebecca Nicholson and the environmental samples by Sharon Cook. Thanks are also due to the staff that processed the finds under the management of Leigh Allen, processed the environmental samples under the management of Rebecca Nicholson, and prepared the archive under the management of Nicola Scott.

6. Anglo-Saxon to Post-Medieval Occupation at the Provost's Garden, The Queen's College

STEVEN TEAGUE and RICHARD BROWN

with contributions by LEIGH ALLEN, PAUL BLINKHORN, SHEILA BOARDMAN, LEE G. BRODERICK, JULIE DUNNE, RICHARD P. EVERSHED, DAVID A. HIGGINS, LYNNE KEYS, REBECCA NICHOLSON, CYNTHIA POOLE, IAN R. SCOTT and RUTH SHAFFREY

SUMMARY

Excavations within the Provost's Garden, The Queen's College, revealed a north-west to south-east aligned and heavily rutted metalled thoroughfare, possibly dating from the late ninth century. Its alignment could suggest that it predates the postulated eastern extension of the late Anglo-Saxon burh. Occupation to its north included a well-defined plot that contained two timber-lined sunken structures dating to the tenth century together with fence lines and pits. The structures were probably filled during the second half of the eleventh century when the road ceased to be used. The pits contained evidence for flax retting, iron smithing and possibly smelting. During the medieval period and after its acquisition by The Queen's College in 1355, the site appears to have been waste ground, used for quarrying and for the disposal of rubbish. The fills of the earlier pits produced smithing debris together with horn-working evidence, whilst the later pits contained material related to the college, such as book clasps, styli for writing on wax tablets, and Venetian glass goblets. Two of the latest pits, of mid seventeenth-century date, each contained large assemblages of clay tobacco pipes that may have been deposited during the Commonwealth and Protectorate. In the late seventeenth century, a small building was constructed, possibly a workshop associated with the rebuilding of the college at this time.

Construction of a new underground library in the Provost's Garden at The Queen's College[1] necessitated an archaeological investigation of the development site during 2015. The college is located centrally within the historic core of Oxford, to the north of the High Street and within the north-east corner of the former medieval defences. The new library occupies the greater part of the footprint of the Provost's Garden, bounded by the pre-existing library to the east and the Grade 2 listed boundary wall (built 1485) alongside Queen's Lane to the north (NGR SP 5174 0636; Fig. 6.1). The topography of the site was generally flat, at *c.*62 m OD. The archaeological investigations began with a watching brief and building recording during

1 For the sake of brevity, hereafter simply 'Queen's College'.

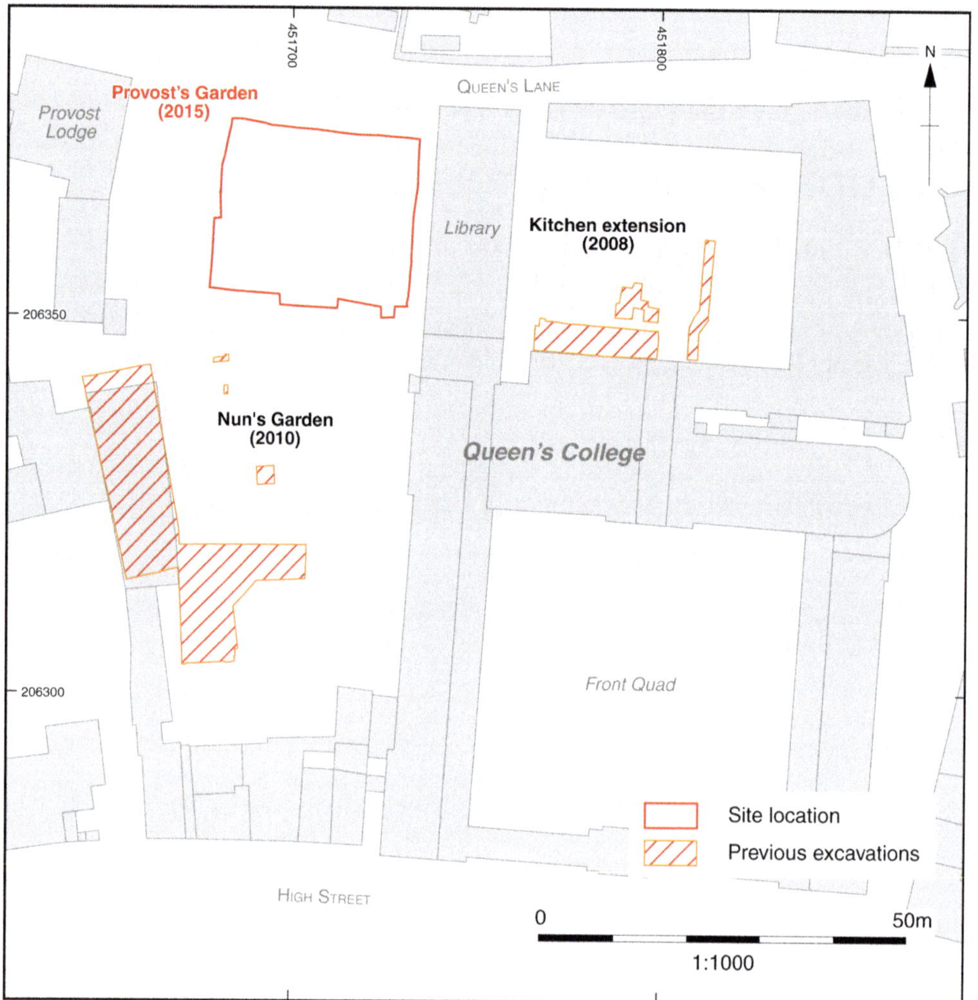

Fig. 6.1 Site location.

development enabling works in January 2015, including the dismantling of the north-west corner of the northern boundary wall to allow site access. Full excavation of the footprint of the new building, comprising *c.*786 sq m, followed during March to May 2015, after which a watching brief was carried out until December 2015.

This report includes summaries of the analyses of the artefacts and environmental evidence. The full specialist reports and accompanying data can be accessed via the OA Library.[2] The archive will be deposited with Oxfordshire County Museum Service under the accession number 2015.30.

2 https://library.oxfordarchaeology.com/5768/.

ARCHAEOLOGICAL AND HISTORICAL BACKGROUND

Queen's College lies within the eastern part of the late Anglo-Saxon *burh* of Oxford. It is still unclear whether this area was part of the *burh* in its earliest late ninth- to tenth-century form, or whether it was subsequently incorporated into an eastern extension.[3] Observations of the primary street surfaces of the *burh* have been made along the High Street as far east as the Examination Schools, along with numerous records of late Anglo-Saxon occupation. A previous archaeological evaluation within the area of the present site revealed a gravel surface and a large pit containing slag, provisionally dated to the tenth century.[4] Domestic occupation in the form of six late Anglo-Saxon pits was found during excavations in 2008 for the college's kitchen extension; one of the pits also contained a halfpenny of Æthelred II that was probably in circulation from 997–1003.[5] Excavations within the college at the Nun's Garden, to the south of the present site, in 2010 revealed a late Anglo-Saxon pit together with a small assemblage of St Neots ware pottery of tenth- or eleventh-century date.[6]

The site lay within the medieval walled town on land situated immediately to the north of tenements that fronted the High Street. Queen's Lane extends along the eastern and northern boundaries of the college, and was until 1772 known as St Edmund Hall Lane (eastern side of college) and Torald Street (northern side). Torald Street may have originally continued past the parish church of St Peter's towards the eastern town wall. Little is known concerning the early development of Torald Street as most properties were probably incorporated into Queen's College and New College after their foundations in 1341 and 1379 respectively. Salter places the Provost's Garden within part of a large plot (NE 207) that may have belonged to St Frideswide's in *c.*1200, but was given to Osney abbey in 1248 when it is referred to as being 'once of William of St John'. Later rentals refer to it as the 'house of Giles of Stockwell'; the Stockwells also appear to have had an interest in the adjacent property to the east (NE 208), corresponding to the present Back Quad of Queen's College. The plot was granted to University College in 1311 by Thomas de Sowy when it was described as 'two messuages'. It was probably still inhabited as it was described as a 'tenement' when Robert de Eglesfield acquired it in 1340 for the foundation of Queen's College, before it was transferred to the college in 1355, when it became a garden.[7]

Views drawn by Agas (1577/88) and Loggan (1675, Fig. 6.2), along with Loggan's more detailed view of the east front (1675), depict the medieval college buildings prior to their rebuilding between 1693 and the 1730s. They show the area of the present site as orchards and gardens. Later maps of Taylor (1750) and Faden (1789) both depict the site as occupying part of a large bowling green.

DISCUSSION

The Late Anglo-Saxon Burh *(Figs. 6.3–6.8)*

The earliest evidence for activity on the site is a heavily rutted metalled surface that is almost certainly of late Anglo-Saxon date. It ran approximately north-west to south-east at an obtuse angle to Queen's Lane, implying that it predated the setting out of this medieval street. It was

3 For a summary of the evidence: Dodd, *Oxford*, pp. 24–5; and for a recent re-evaluation, J. Haslam, 'The Two Anglo-Saxon *Burhs* of Oxford', *Oxoniensia*, 75 (2010), pp. 15–34.

4 'Provost's Garden, Queen's College, Oxford. Archaeological Evaluation Report', unpublished OA report (1998), https://library.oxfordarchaeology.com/1742/.

5 A. Norton and J. Mumford, 'Anglo-Saxon Pits and a Medieval Kitchen at The Queen's College, Oxford', *Oxoniensia*, 75 (2010), pp. 178, 202.

6 S. Teague et al., 'Late Saxon, Medieval and Post-Medieval Archaeology at the Nun's Garden, Queen's College, Oxford (Nos. 33–38 High Street)', *Oxoniensia*, 80 (2015), pp. 143–85.

7 Salter, *Survey*, vol. 1, pp. 151–3, NE 207–8; H.E. Salter, 'Appendix C', in J.R. Magrath, *The Queen's College*, vol. 1 (1921), pp. 326–31.

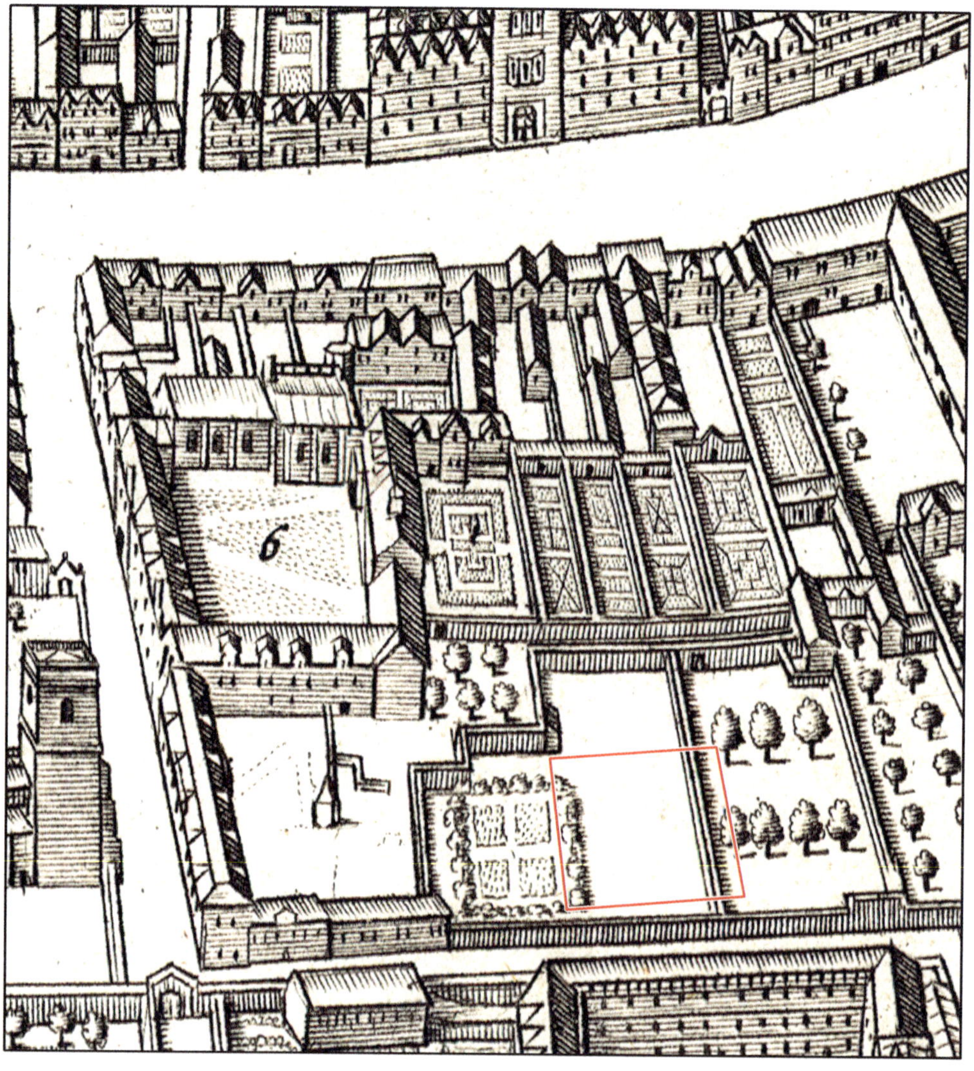

Fig. 6.2 Detail from Loggan's map of Oxford (1675).

carefully constructed with a surface of rounded pebbles on a bed of sand pushed into the remains of a subsoil that appears to have been largely removed. As such it compares well with the primary late Anglo-Saxon street surfaces found at Castle Street and Church Street.[8] Two radiocarbon dates were obtained from animal bones that had been pressed into the surface of the street at Queen's College (Table 6.1), The results suggest that the street was potentially in use as early as the late ninth century, a date contemporary with or possibly predating the formation of the *burh* in the late ninth/early tenth century. However, unlike the other aforementioned streets, it appears not to have been maintained or resurfaced and may have ceased to be used by the eleventh or twelfth centuries, perhaps suggesting some reorganisation of the area by that time.

[8] Dodd, *Oxford*, pp. 26–9.

Table 6.1. Summary of radiocarbon dates.

Laboratory no.	Context	Feature	Material	$\delta^{13}C$ (‰)	Radiocarbon age (BP)	Calibrated date (95.4% confidence)
SUERC-68393	1480	–	Sheep/goat tibia	-22.1	1076 ± 34	cal AD 893–1020
SUERC-68394	1521	1520	Cattle tibia	-21.9	1142 ± 34	cal AD 776–794 (6.6%); cal AD 800–980 (88.8%)
SUERC-77178	1480	–	Sheep/goat femur	-21.7	1173 ± 18	cal AD 774–895 (92.1%); cal AD 929–939 (3.3%)

Its alignment is of some interest; if projected south-eastwards it would meet the site of the medieval East Gate of the town, presumably leading to the crossing point over the River Cherwell. Conversely, if projected north-westwards it would correspond closely with the junction of Catte Street with Smith Gate, the medieval postern gate that is suggested to have marked the north-east corner of the primary *burh* defences (Fig. 6.3). Although these projections are speculative, together they could suggest an extramural 'bypass' route leading from the Cherwell and perhaps joining the north end of Catte Street at a point where it meets Parks Road, a thoroughfare dating from at least the medieval period.[9] Observations suggest that Catte Street itself is of late Anglo-Saxon origin, as its primary surface was constructed with tightly packed pebbles, comparable to the earliest street surfaces found within the primary *burh*,[10] and its route runs immediately alongside (outside) the postulated primary *burh* defences. However, recent work appears to contradict the hypothesis of the eastern *burh* 'extension'. At New College a radiocarbon date of cal AD 775–968 implies that the defensive bank found here dates from the foundation of the *burh*, although it also provided an OSL date of AD 596–786, suggesting an even earlier date.[11] The absence of pottery and other evidence below the bank dating to the Anglo-Saxon period on this site and at earlier excavations located immediately to the west on Holywell Street[12] suggests that the bank predates significant nearby settlement activity. A recent geophysical survey and geoarchaeological transect across the central quad at Oriel College, over the predicted line of the proposed primary *burh* eastern defences, found no evidence for such an earthwork, though it feasibly could have been located further east.[13] If the radiocarbon date for the New College earthwork is accepted then it would have enclosed the early tenth-century occupation predating the proposed late tenth-century timber/stone predecessor to the church of St Peter-in-the-East,[14] and presumably also the street found at Queen's College.

It has been speculated that the church of St Peter-in-the-East originated as an Anglo-Saxon minster, possibly one of a series of such establishments on the peripheries of Mercian centres created by Alfred's daughter Æthelflæd prior to AD 918, and that the bank found at New College may have formed part of its precinct. This minster could in turn have influenced the street layout in this area, resulting in their non-rectangular arrangement,[15] though it has been noted

9 Ibid. fig. 2.9.
10 Ibid. fig. A1.1, gaz. 16 and p. 42.
11 'New College, Oxford: Kitchen and Wine Cellar Link Tunnel Projects. Post-Excavation Assessment', unpublished OA report (2018).
12 Dodd, *Oxford*, pp. 183–8.
13 'Oriel College, Oxford. Kitchen Project: Geophysical Survey, Borehole and Watching Brief Report', unpublished OA report (2018).
14 D. Sturdy, 'Excavations in St Peter-in-the-East Church, Oxford', *Oxoniensia*, 37 (1972), p. 245.
15 J. Blair, 'Oxford Before Queen's: The Archaeology of the New Library and Oxford's Eastern Extension', unpublished paper (2017).

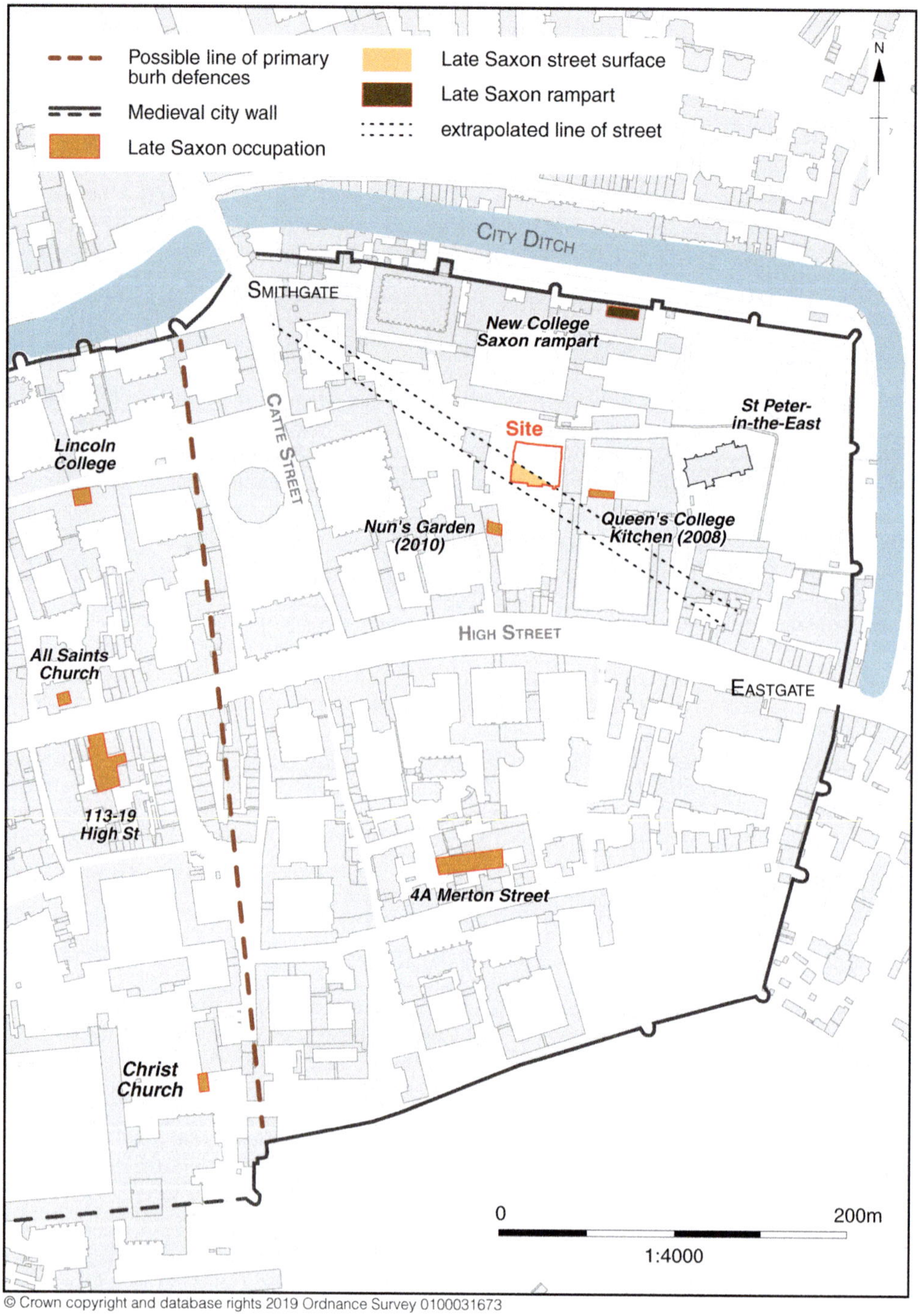

Fig. 6.3 The late Anglo-Saxon road in relation to the burh and the medieval town defences.

at Wallingford that the grid arrangement of streets is confined within only one quarter of the *burh*.[16] However, the fact that the medieval town wall followed the line of the New College Anglo-Saxon earthwork suggests that, as with town defences elsewhere, the area was under the auspices of the king. The sharp southwards turn of the Anglo-Saxon bank revetment wall found at the Clarendon Quadrangle during excavations in 1899 is often cited as the principal evidence for the eastern extent of the 'primary' *burh*.[17] An alternative explanation could be that the inward turn reflects the site of an earlier gateway through the *burh* defences. Here the bank, in contrast to that at New College, was provided with a retaining wall in order to protect its eastern terminus, though a corresponding western terminus has yet to be identified. This may go some way to reconcile the contradictory nature of the present evidence regarding the configuration of the *burh*. The issue could be resolved by further targeted excavation, particularly within the postulated eastern extension of the *burh*.

The north side of the Queen's College thoroughfare saw a fairly intensive period of occupation, possibly dating from the tenth century, largely confined between two possible plot boundaries represented by ditches 2500 and 2501 (Fig. 6.4), suggesting some degree of organisation. Within the plot were at least two sunken timber structures similar in nature to the 'cellar pits' that have been excavated elsewhere within the 'primary' *burh*, as at the Clarendon Hotel site (Cornmarket Street), Queen Street, All Saints Church (High Street) and recently at 114–119 St Aldate's.[18] A radiocarbon date of cal AD 776–980 (SUERC-68394; Table 6.1) was obtained from a posthole from one of the Queen's College cellars, suggesting occupation here commenced well before the end of the tenth century. The Queen's College 'cellar' pits are the first to be firmly identified to the east of the 'primary' *burh* and suggest similar activities to those found within the 'primary' *burh* occurred from an early date. The square pits measured *c*.2.5–2.7 m across and survived to depths of up to 0.80 m. Their size and the location mirror those found at the Clarendon Hotel, where nine cellars were positioned alongside the street frontage, probably within separate plots or tenements. Those at the Clarendon Hotel differed in that they were considerably deeper at *c*.1.8 m, so could be seen as true cellars.[19] This raises the possibility that the shallower pits at Queen's College supported above-ground structures, especially given the substantial nature of the postholes that surrounded the base of pit 1527. As with those at the Clarendon Hotel, no apparent evidence was found to support the possibility that they were contained within buildings, unless some of the postholes to the east of pit 1527 and fence 2503 pertained to such a structure. A cesspit (1718), perhaps with an overlying timber structure, was located to the north-east, downwind from these structures. As with the cellar pits found elsewhere in Oxford, they appear to have been backfilled during the second half of the eleventh century.

The pits around the structures, probably originally gravel/sand quarries, as well the backfills of the cellar pits and boundary ditches, contained debris associated with iron smithing and possibly smelting. Although the quantities are small and possibly related to resurfacing of nearby streets, it does suggest that such activity was being undertaken near to the site during the tenth or eleventh centuries. To date there is relatively little evidence for contemporary smithing elsewhere in Oxford, apart from a few sites on High Street and Cornmarket Street.[20] Sherds of Stamford ware crucibles could indicate non-ferrous metalworking in the vicinity. Flax seeds possibly indicating retting were found only in the late Anglo-Saxon pit fills though their numbers were small. Such activity is normally confined to near rivers where there is a plentiful

[16] N. Christie et al., *Transforming Townscapes. From Burh to Borough: The Archaeology of Wallingford, AD 800–1400* (2013).

[17] Dodd, *Oxford*, pp. 172–83.

[18] Dodd, *Oxford*, pp. 35–41; chapter 4, above.

[19] E.M. Jope, 'The Clarendon Hotel, Oxford, Part 1, The Site', *Oxoniensia*, 23 (1958), pp. 9–10.

[20] Dodd, *Oxford*, pp. 42–3.

supply of water, as at 89–91 St Aldate's.[21] It is possible that an early clay-lined pit (2064), that seems to have held liquid, may have been used for such activity.

The animal bone assemblage, though modest, compares well to that of other late Anglo-Saxon sites such as Church Street and similarly reflects a predominance of cattle, sheep and pig meat.[22] Likewise there is evidence for table waste from meat-bearing joints of beef where the joint was prepared at the table. The presence of red deer suggests that the inhabitants were either hunting locally or wealthy enough to purchase more expensive meats. This possible enhanced social status could be supported by the finds of a barrel padlock case and key, the former from sunken structure 1527, implying the need to protect valuable possessions. The presence of neonatal sheep/goat bones implies the rearing of such animals on site. Unlike pigs, these would require a sizeable area to graze, suggesting a fairly open or large plot. Although there is nothing conclusive to suggest that butchery was being undertaken on any scale there seems to be some evidence, from the presence of horncores and phalanges chopped from sheep and cattle, for waste from craft activity such as horn working. Of interest is the fish and marine shell assemblage that included a large number of small and tiny fish such as gudgeon, roach and minnow together with a number of oyster shells. This suggests that locally caught fish were either consumed or used as bait for fishing in the nearby Thames or Cherwell. The shell clearly demonstrates that as elsewhere within the *burh*, such as at Nos. 79–80 St Aldate's, the inhabitants had sufficient resources to access imported foodstuffs from the coastal regions.[23]

Medieval Activity Before the Acquisition of the Site by Queen's College (Fig. 6.9)

From the start of the twelfth century the site was used for quarrying and rubbish disposal. This continued unabated even after the site was acquired by Queen's College in 1355. Pits cut across the line of the metalled street (Phase 2a), possibly to extract the cobbling, suggesting that it had ceased to be used by this time or perhaps its course had moved south beyond the limits of the excavation. The lack of early Brill coarseware from these pits suggests that the street had ceased to be used prior to the late twelfth century. Similarly, other pits cut across the earlier postulated plot boundaries and there is no convincing evidence that the site was contained within more than one property after the mid to late twelfth century. Indeed, the alignment of the late Anglo-Saxon plot boundaries and street bears little relationship to the later layout of the area. This could imply a reorganisation of the street system within this part of the Anglo-Norman town, perhaps influenced by the rebuilding of the wealthy parish church of St Peter-in-the-East, located some 70 m east of the site. Such early rearrangements are known elsewhere, as at Cornmarket Street and Queen Street/Castle Street, and encroachments by All Saints Church onto Turl Street deflected its line to the west.[24] Perhaps this rearrangement was made easier by the dislocation following the Norman Conquest which probably resulted in the merging of some of the smaller Anglo-Saxon holdings into larger, perhaps unoccupied plots, or waste ground.[25]

The finds and environmental assemblages can give some insight into the pre-college activities, though the provenance of such material is uncertain for the reason given above. Several pits from each of the twelfth- to fourteenth-century phases (Phases 2a and 2b) contained small amounts of iron smelting slag, although the almost total lack of hammerscale from floor sweepings suggests that smithies were not located immediately nearby. Perhaps the horseshoe fragments and associated nails found during this phase imply the presence of a farrier. During the twelfth century (Phase 2a) there is a noticeable increase in the evidence for other craftworking activities, particularly horn working, as attested by the number of caprine and sheep horncores from adjacent pits 1397 and 1659. A possible madder-stained pottery sherd from a thirteenth- to

[21] Ibid. p. 46.
[22] Ibid. pp. 44–5.
[23] Ibid. p. 45.
[24] Ibid. p. 59.
[25] Ibid. pp. 51–3.

fourteenth-century context hints at dyeing in the vicinity. The animal bone suggests that the meat consumed was from less than prime animals and possibly included horsemeat, and indeed there was much less evidence for gnawing by dogs implying that most of the meat had been removed prior to disposal. This could suggest that waste was dumped from less affluent households implying a reduction of status compared to the pre-Conquest period.

Queen's College (1355 Onwards) (Fig. 6.9)

The acquisition of the site by Queen's College in 1355 did not result in any significant changes in the use of the site, and indeed the intensity of the pitting increased during the fourteenth to the sixteenth century and continued unabated up to the seventeenth century. The increase in the size of the pits would have provided significant quantities of gravel for the construction of the new college buildings as well as material for paths and courtyards. Recent excavations at St John's College revealed a similar intense period of gravel extraction from the mid sixteenth century, the time of the foundation of that college.[26] Regardless of their original function the pits would have ultimately been used for the disposal of the large quantities of waste that the college would have undoubtedly generated.

Although no medieval structures were built on the site the quantities of ceramic and stone building material in the pits do show a marked increase from the time of the college (Phase 2b and later). Although the roofing material includes peg tiles and both plain and decorated ridge tiles, common to many ordinary buildings in Oxford, fragments of Penn floor tiles and painted window glass do point to structures of some pretension. Distinctive late-medieval roof tiles similar to those found during excavations within the college kitchens[27] together with Anglo-Dutch wall tiles of early post-medieval date testify to the continuous refurbishment of the college buildings.

The pits produced a large assemblage of other finds that give insights into the inhabitants of the college. The late-medieval material included a fragment from early spectacles, a small but significant assemblage of book clasps and related material together with a number of styli for writing on wax tablets, undoubtedly used by the college. One such item, a highly decorated strap end, is of identical design to an example recently found at the site of the Greyfriars and may derive either from the same maker or perhaps from the same set of books. A number of pairs of shears, possibly used for the cutting of hair, together with increasing quantities of dress accessories attest to the attire of the college members. The consumption of fish and shellfish showed a greater variety compared to the pre-college phases and included large sea bream and salmon, expensive food eaten by the better off. Further evidence for this increased prosperity in the late medieval and early post-medieval periods included the use of imported Venetian glass goblets, together with Spanish and Italian ceramics, undoubtedly intended to impress at the dining table.

Two seventeenth-century pits (1475 and 1085) each contained an exceptionally large assemblage of clay tobacco pipes that appear to have been deposited during two single events, probably between *c*.1630–45 and *c*.1650–70 respectively. One of the stems from pit 1085 had a farthing token issued by the vintner Humphry Bodicott attached to it. Another seventeenth-century pit contained a wine bottle fragment with Bodicott's seal. Humphry Bodicott was the licensee of the Three Tuns between 1639 and 1660, located on the High Street opposite the college. He was a senior bailiff between 1636–44, and briefly mayor in 1647, but was excluded by parliament later that year. A Royalist during the Civil War, in 1646 he lent £20 towards the payment of the soldiers of the garrison.[28] Pit 1085 also contained two 'slip' spoons, items

[26] Chapter 10, below.

[27] J. Cotter, 'The Ceramic Building Material', in Norton and Mumford, 'Anglo-Saxon Pits and a Medieval Kitchen', pp. 196–8.

[28] Oxford History: Mayors and Lord Mayors (http://www.oxfordhistory.org.uk/mayors/1603_1714/boddicott_humphrey_1647.html), accessed 18/07/2018.

listed in a grant of college plate to the king in 1642–3 to help fund the fortification of Oxford. It is tempting to assign these assemblages to the time of the Commonwealth, and perhaps pit 1085 dates to the time of the Protectorate during 1653–9. Possibly Bodicott had a role in the successful compromises that the college made during negotiations with Parliament,[29] perhaps also accommodating the visitors in his tavern.

The site continued to be used for rubbish disposal well into the mid seventeenth century, after which a stone building was constructed along the southern side of the site. The maps of Hollar (1643) and Loggan (1675) do not show any corresponding structure but depict an open plot of land immediately to the west of an orchard on the site of the present library (built 1693–6). Adjacent cesspits were probably in use at the same time as they contained clay tobacco pipes dated to *c.*1690–1730. Perhaps the building served as a temporary workshop during the rebuilding of the college at the turn of the eighteenth century. Taylor's map shows the site as a bowling green in 1750, by which time pit digging had ceased.

STRATIGRAPHIC SUMMARY

Phase 1: Late Ninth to Eleventh Centuries (Figs. 6.4–6.8)

The Road and Associated Features Two areas of metalled surfaces (1480 and 1959) formed a west-north-west to east-south-east-aligned roadway measuring at least 4.3 m wide (Figs. 6.4–6.6). The surface was formed from small to medium rounded pebbles on a bedding of light orange silty sand. It had been heavily rutted with the density of the wheel ruts clearly indicating that the surface had been heavily used. A sheep tibia partially pushed in below and partially within surface 1480 produced a radiocarbon date of cal AD 893–1020. A second bone fragment from the same surface, a sheep/goat femur, returned a radiocarbon date of cal AD 774–939 (SUERC-68393; SUERC-77178; Table 6.1). Additionally, a sherd of late Anglo-Saxon Stamford ware was recovered from surface 1480. Overlying the surface was a 0.10–0.20 m thick deposit of loose greenish grey silt (1478; Fig. 6.5), probably laid down when the road went out of use or had ceased to be maintained. It contained predominantly late Anglo-Saxon St Neots ware, though the presence of Cotswold-type ware and medieval Oxford ware implies that the silt continued to accumulate into the late eleventh century or later. Overlying the silt was a thin deposit of redeposited natural sand/gravel with patches of burnt sand (1477) that may have represented the remnants of a second surface that had largely been worn away. It supported a 0.17-m thick accumulation of greenish/grey sandy silt (1476) containing frequent small rounded pebbles, that probably derived from the otherwise worn underlying surface. No dating evidence was recovered from these later levels though they were cut by twelfth-century pit 1281.

The northern edge of the road was demarcated by a line of small shallow postholes (Group 2503) that followed the alignment of the road and wheel ruts. They probably represented part of a fence but did not extend to the north-west unless pit 1765, that follows the alignment, formed part of it.

Flat-bottomed ditch 2502 survived for a length of 15 m and predated ditches 2500 and 2501 that formed part of subsequent possible plot apportionments. It measured up to 1.0 m in width and 0.24–0.46 m in depth and contained up to four silty fills, suggesting that it filled up over a significant period of time. It may have survived further west as shallow 'pit' 2018 that predated ditch 2500. Pottery obtained from it was predominantly St Neots ware with lesser quantities of Cotswold-type ware suggesting it was filling from the early eleventh century. The presence of a few sherds of Kennet Valley ware could imply that it continued to fill up to the mid eleventh century. Its relationship with the road is uncertain; it may have represented a roadside drainage ditch though its skewed alignment with it would seemingly preclude this.

[29] *VCH Oxon.* 3, pp. 132–43.

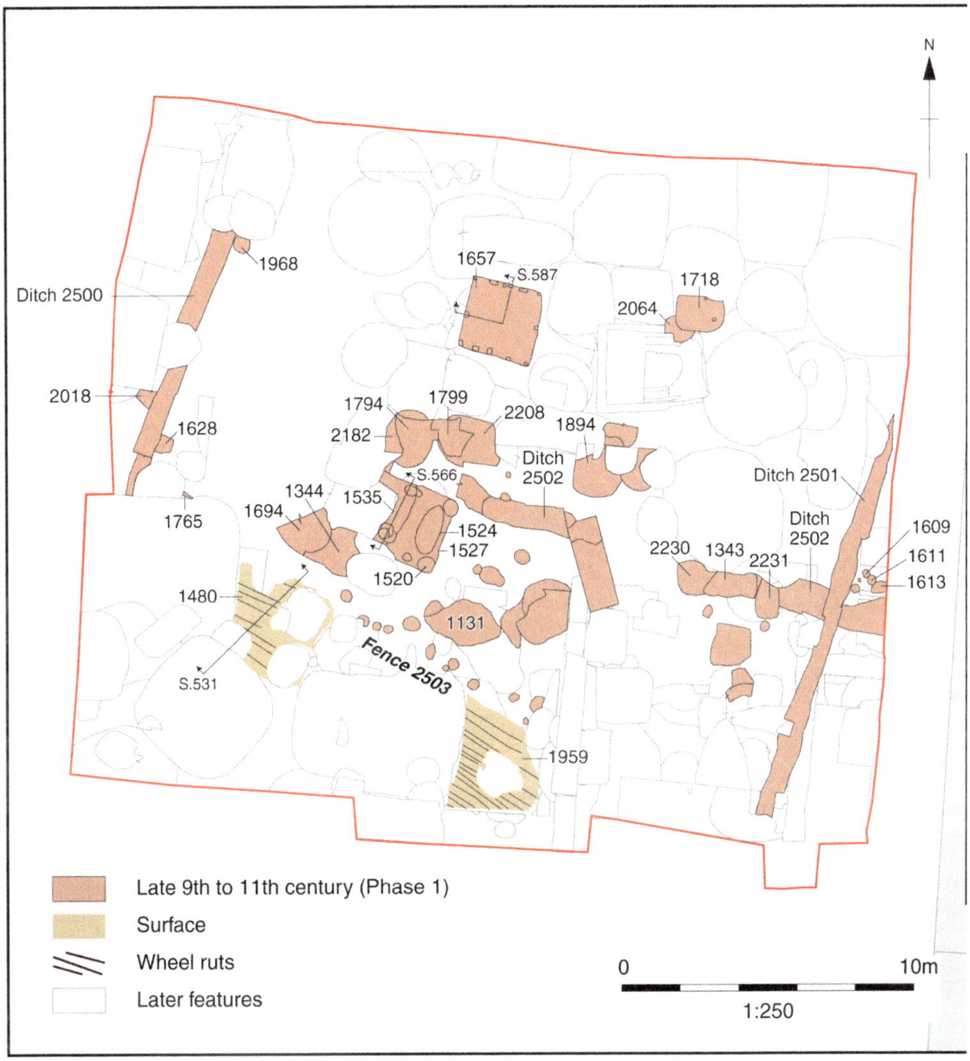

Fig. 6.4 Phase 1: late ninth to eleventh century.

Plot Boundaries Parallel ditches 2500 and 2501 ran perpendicular to the north side of the road and seemingly respected it. They were probably contemporary and are likely to represent boundary ditches of a plot or property abutting the road. It is possible that they had replaced earlier fences given the proximity of postholes 1628 and 1968, both of which predated ditch 2500. Similarly, a cluster of postholes (for example, 1609, 1611 and 1613) located adjacent to ditch 2501 could have formed part of an earlier fence or an adjacent structure. Both ditches were similar in size, measuring 0.7–0.8 m in width with steep edges and flat bases and surviving to 0.20–0.33 m in depth. They both contained single fills of reddish brown clayey silt suggesting that they had been deliberately infilled. The ditches contained predominantly Cotswold-type ware with small quantities of St Neots ware. A small quantity of medieval Oxford ware was also present which, if not intrusive, would imply that the ditches were filled early during the currency of the pottery, perhaps during the late eleventh or early twelfth centuries.

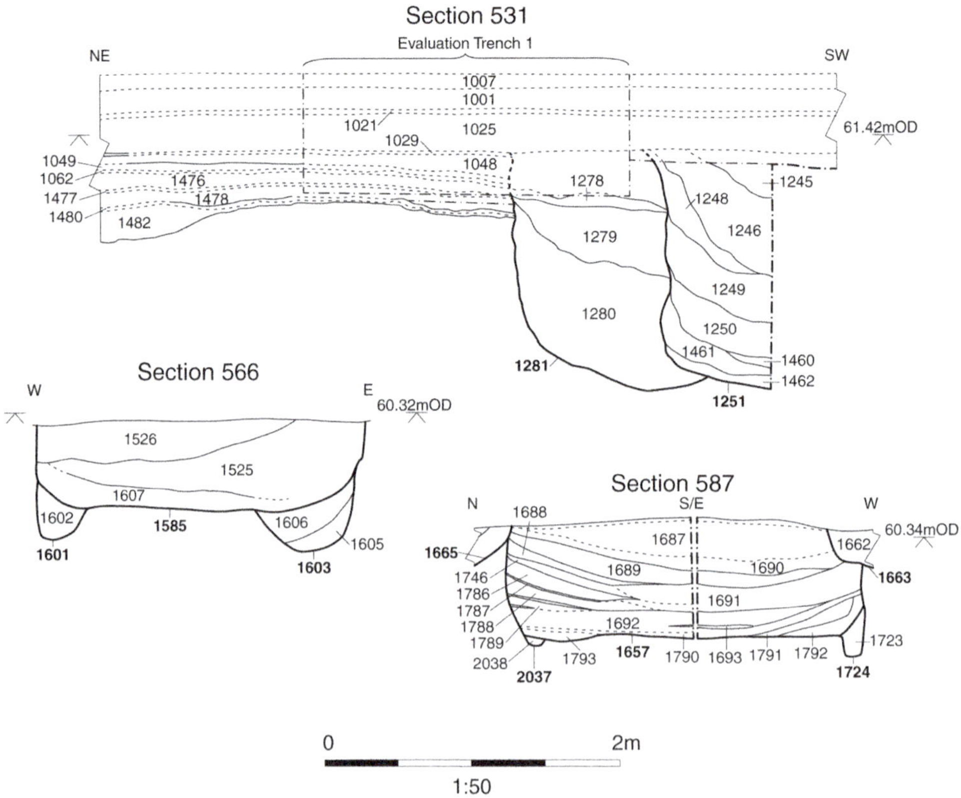

Fig. 6.5 Sections of Phase 1 features.

Fig. 6.6 Road surface 1480, looking east. Scales: 1 m and 2 m.

Timber-Lined Structures Located to the north of the road and confined to the area between ditches 2500 and 2501 were a number of pits, four of which (1524, 1535, 1657 and 1718) showed evidence for being lined with timber and were probably small cellars or sunken-floored structures. The southernmost pit (1524) was located *c.*2.0 m north of the road and was also aligned with it suggesting the two were contemporary. It was rectangular, measuring 2.6 m (north–south) by 1.5 m (east–west) and *c.*0.35 m in depth (Fig. 6.7). Its relationship with early ditch 2502 is uncertain but it seemed to respect its southern side, suggesting that this possible boundary was still extant. The north-eastern and south-eastern corners of pit 1524 each contained large postholes cut into the base of the pit, both measuring *c.*0.55 m in diameter and 0.34–0.45 m in depth. Their substantial nature could imply that they supported an above-ground structure as well as serving as the primary supports for the horizontal planking that presumably lined the edges of the pit. Less substantial postholes 1522 and 1523 located along its northern and southern sides probably held in place horizontal timber planking placed against the sides of the pit as they were set back slightly from its edges. A shallow oval pit (1527) was aligned within the eastern side of the structure and seems to have been associated with its use, possibly a robbed structural installation. The possible extension to pit 1524 (1535) was slightly narrower in width but extended it by at least 1.2 m further west. The base of the structure was significantly deeper at *c.*0.60 m and contained fairly substantial postholes on its eastern corners with diameters of 0.32–0.35 m (Fig. 6.5). The southern posthole showed evidence that it replaced earlier installations though it is not certain whether they pertained to the original structure. The postholes from both structures were all removed before both pits were apparently infilled simultaneously. A radiocarbon determination obtained from a cattle tibia from posthole 1520 from the earlier structure returned a date range of cal AD 776–980 (SUERC-68394; Table 6.1). The pottery from backfills of the structures and pit 1527 was predominantly St Neots ware and Cotswold-type ware with lesser quantities of Kennet Valley ware. If the tiny amount of medieval Oxford ware that was also present is intrusive then a date during the early to mid eleventh century at the latest is likely for the filling of the two structures. The backfill of pit 1524/1535 also contained iron working debris including a smithing hearth bottom, tap slag, furnace slag and lining. A sandstone hone was recovered from pit 1535.

Fig. 6.7 Cellar pit 1524, looking south-east. Scales: 1 m and 2 m.

Fig. 6.8 Cellar pit 1657, looking north-west. Scale: 1 m.

The second timber-lined pit (1657) was located *c*.5 m to the north-west (Figs. 6.4, 6.5 and 6.8). It was square and measured 2.5 m across and *c*.0.8 m deep and had steep straight sides and a flat base. A number of small square or oval postholes, none more than 0.25 m across and deep, were arranged symmetrically around the sides and on each corner of the pit. They presumably marked the positions of timber uprights and were all placed tight against the sides of the pit. Given their size, it is likely that they formed part of a wattle lining of the pit rather than more substantial timber planking. No evidence for flooring or trampled surfaces was found at the base of the pit. After the postholes had been removed the pit was systematically but rapidly backfilled with soil, redeposited natural and rubbish (Fig. 6.5). Pottery dating suggests a process of rapid backfilling in the period *c*.1050–75. Also recovered was smithing debris similar to that found in pit 1524/1535.

The northernmost pit (1718) had been heavily truncated by later activity though was probably smaller, measuring *c*.1.8 m by at least 1.2 m, and survived to a depth of 0.40 m. Two small postholes cut into its base, though in contrast to the other pits they were not positioned against its edges. Additionally, the pit was backfilled with material containing small amounts of mineralised seed fragments and a few pupae of probable seaweed fly (sample 22). This could indicate that the pit was a latrine, perhaps with an associated structure built above it. The pottery suggests that it was backfilled at the very beginning of the eleventh century at the latest, and possibly during the tenth century.

Other Pits Largely confined to the southern part of the site and clearly respecting fence-line 2503 to the south were a number of irregularly shaped pits, many of which exceeded 1 m in depth. They formed several clusters of intercutting pits which could imply that they were originally utilised as quarries for the underlying sand and gravel. Their relationship with the extant timber-lined pits is uncertain, though Structure 1535 seemingly cut the southern side of one such cluster that included pits 1794 and 2182. A second cluster (pits 1343, 2230 and 2231) cut along the line of ditch 2502, implying quarrying along the edges of an open and visible feature. Most of the pits contained an appreciable quantity of pottery and bone suggesting that, ultimately, they were utilised for the disposal of rubbish. The pottery assemblages were similar to those found in the timber-lined pits though there is some suggestion that the northern pit cluster, that includes pit 1894, may be the latest; this was the only example that contained small quantities of medieval Oxford ware.

Pit 2064 predated timber-lined pit 1718. It was circular with a diameter of 1.0 m and a depth of 0.90 m. It had been lined throughout with a thick deposit of yellowish clay, presumably to retain a liquid of some sort. It contained finely laminated sandy silts that were probably deposited from the standing liquid. No finds were recovered from the pit.

Most of the pits – especially 1131, 1694, 1799 and 2208 – contained evidence for iron smithing and smelting including furnace lining fragments, tap and furnace slag and smithing hearth bottoms.

Phase 2a: Twelfth to Thirteenth Century

This phase saw an apparent reorganisation of the area, and an increase in the density of pitting, largely confined to the southern half of the site (Fig. 6.9). Some of the pits (for example, 1281, 1499

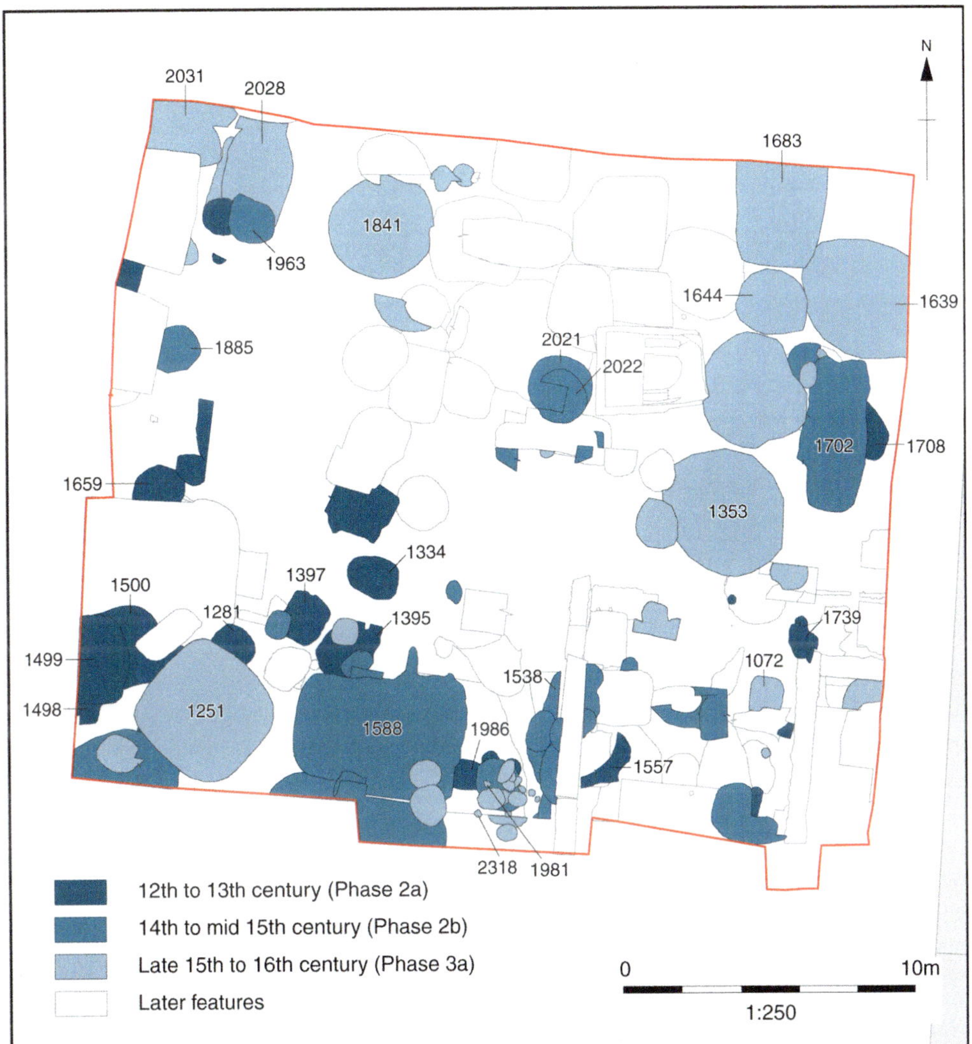

Fig. 6.9 Phases 2a–3a: twelfth to sixteenth century.

and 1557) cut through the metalling of the late Anglo-Saxon road implying that it had ceased to be used as a thoroughfare. Similarly, some pits cut across the two possible plot boundary ditches (such as 1659, 1708, 1739), again implying that they were no longer in use. It is probable that the larger and intercutting pits (for example, 1498/1499/1500 and 1557/1558) were primarily used as sand and gravel quarries. Shallow pits such as 1395 and 1986 that cut through the former road could have been purposely dug to remove the stone metalling for use elsewhere. Pits 1281, 1334, 1397 and 1659 may have been dug for the disposal of rubbish given the quantities of pottery and bone recovered from them. Pit 1334 was notable for containing several lamp fragments, and an appreciable quantity of slag was recovered from pit 1659.

The dominant pottery from the pits was medieval Oxford and Cotswold-type ware, with only small quantities of early Brill coarseware present in some of the pits suggesting that they date towards the end of the twelfth century. Early Brill coarseware was notably absent in pits 1986 and 1397 which cut into the former road, suggesting that they could date earlier within the twelfth century.

Phase 2b: Fourteenth to Mid Fifteenth Century

The site remained open and was used for pits, which as previously were largely distributed within the southern half of the site. It is possible that smaller and shallower pits and other features may have been removed by the intensive pitting that occurred within the northern part of the site during the post-medieval period. As before the larger rectangular pits were probably quarries, particularly as they occupied those parts of the site that had largely been free of earlier pitting. The quarry pits were larger than those of the previous periods, two of them (1588 and 1702) measuring more than 5 m across and 1.2 m deep, suggesting a need for gravel on a more substantial scale. These pits, particularly 1588, had irregular and undercutting sides as may be expected if gravel was being extracted. Ultimately such large pits served as useful receptacles for the deposition of rubbish, once they had ceased to be used as quarries. The smaller circular pits (such as 1885, 1963 and 2021/2022) are likely to have served as rubbish pits given their regular and straight edges. None exceeded 1.1 m in depth, which would preclude their use as wells.

Both sets of features contained a reasonable amount of rubbish, the contemporary pottery largely comprising Brill/Boarstall ware dating from the thirteenth century. Lesser amounts of its later variant (late-medieval Brill/Boarstall ware) together with small quantities of Tudor green wares suggest that deposition continued into the fifteenth century. Notable pottery included a sherd of Andalusian lustreware found in pit 2021, a rare find in Oxford and associated with high-status sites outside London. French jetons of late fourteenth- or fifteenth-century date were found in pits 1538 and 2105.

Phase 3a: Late Fifteenth to Sixteenth Century

The site continued to be largely utilised for quarrying and rubbish disposal on much the same scale as previously. In contrast to the earlier phases the larger pits, probably quarries, were largely confined to the northern half of the site, an area that had been previously free of such activity. The south-eastern part of the site contained several small pits that probably represented *ad hoc* disposal of rubbish. A concentration of small postholes located near the southern edge of the site (for example, 1981 and 2318) and isolated posthole 1864 suggest some form of structure, though too little survived to suggest any form or function. The contemporary pottery is dominated by late-medieval Brill/Boarstall ware together with introduction of imported wares such as Raeren and Frechen stonewares from the late fifteenth century. The pottery from quarry 1251 and rubbish pit 1072 also includes later local glazed red earthenware and Border ware, introduced from the mid sixteenth century. A Nuremberg jeton of sixteenth-century date was recovered from the near the top of pit 1353.

Phase 3b and 4a: Seventeenth to Mid Eighteenth Century

This phase saw the construction of a stone-founded building (Building 1) in the south-eastern part of the site, located *c.*2 m west of the existing library (constructed during 1693–6). The area to its north and west continued to be open and used for pit digging (Fig. 6.10).

The building comprised at least one room measuring 7.1 m across, defined to the east by wall 1012 and to the west by wall 1031. The room may have been subdivided at some stage as there were traces of a possible shallow robber trench (1830 and 1922) running east–west within the room. A gravelled passage, 2.0 m in width, seems to have led into its north side from the east delimited by wall 1030 to the south and by a narrow kerb (1172) to the north. Two wall fragments to the north (1094 and 1385) may have formed further elements of the building, though too

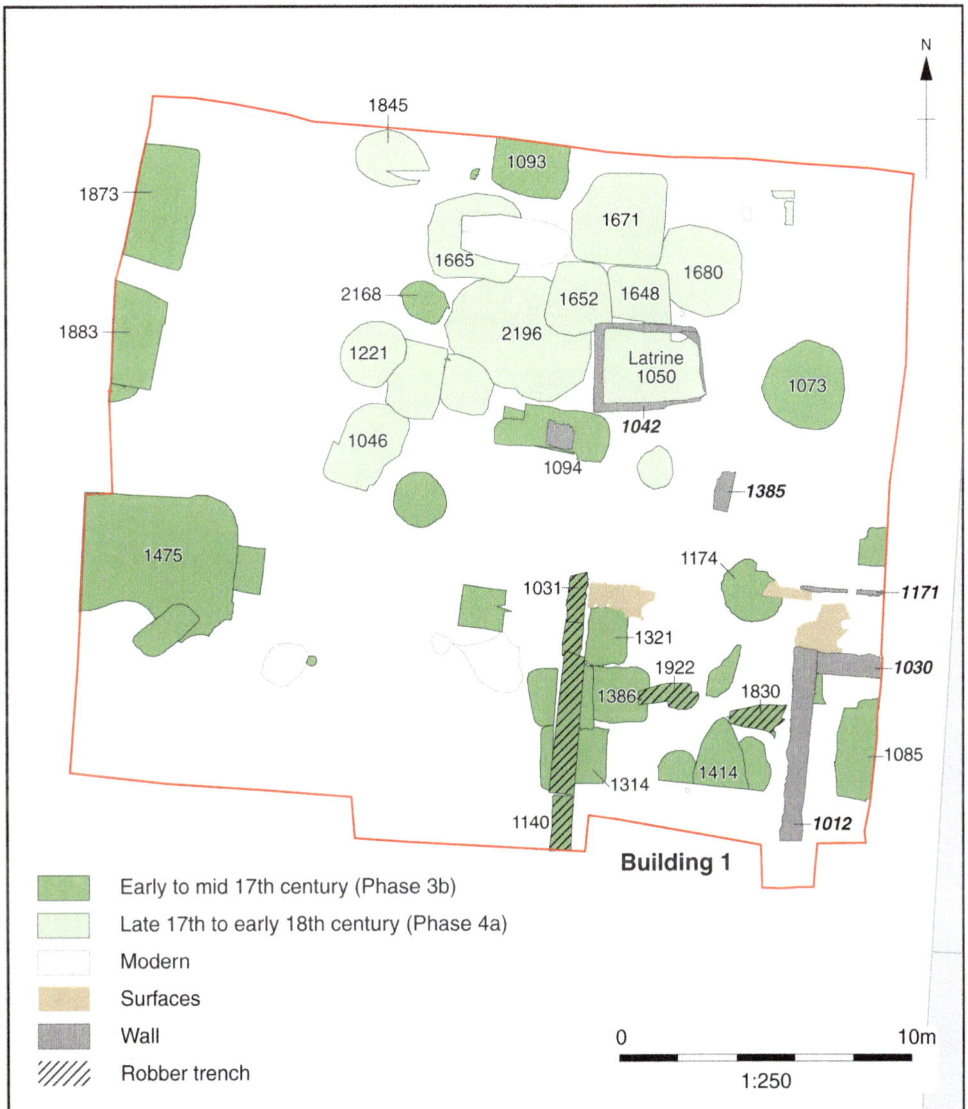

Fig. 6.10 Phases 3b–4a: seventeenth to early eighteenth century.

little survived to establish any coherent arrangement. The walls of the building were fairly substantial, measuring 0.50 m in width and 0.52 m deep, and survived as limestone/sandstone rubble foundations (walls 1012 and 1030) or were robbed (1031 and 1140).

The structure cannot date to before the mid to late sixteenth century as a sixpence of Elizabeth I, dated to 1569, was recovered from wall fabric 1012. It is however likely that the structure was not built before the seventeenth century. Its west wall cut earlier pits 1314, 1321 and 1386, two of which had been deliberately emptied and refilled with clay and stone. A sherd of tin-glazed earthenware was recovered from pit 1386 and dates to the seventeenth century or later, while pit 1314 contained a tobacco clay pipe bowl dated to 1670–1700.

Most of the pits formed a cluster located to the north of the building, and given their size they were probably gravel extraction pits later used for the disposal of domestic rubbish and building rubble. They represented a systematic extension of the Phase 3a quarries. Similarly, isolated rectangular pits (1475 and 1873) located to the west represented continuation of quarrying from the earlier phase in this part of the site. Few pits can be identified as having been used for other purposes, exceptions including stone-lined latrine 1050 that post-dated the quarrying in this area. This was aligned with the west wall of Building 1 and therefore was probably associated with its use. It was at least 1.0 m in depth, and its earliest fill was a thick cess-like deposit which contained a large number of clay tobacco pipes dated to *c.*1690–1730 and a wine bottle seal bearing the date 1707. This material is likely to have been deposited after the pit ceased to be used. A second unlined cesspit (1046), also late in the sequence, again contained a large assemblage of clay pipes of similar date together with early eighteenth-century glass bottle and flask fragments.

POTTERY by PAUL BLINKHORN

The pottery assemblage comprised 4,462 sherds with a total weight of 67,858 g. The estimated vessel equivalent (EVE) by summation of surviving rim sherd circumference was 20.46 for the late Anglo-Saxon and medieval vessels. It was recorded using the conventions of the Oxfordshire County type-series, as follows (the alphanumeric codes prefixed with 'F' are those used in the database):[30]

OXAC	Cotswold-type ware, AD 975–1350. 821 sherds, 8,742 g, EVE = 2.16.
OXAM	Brill/Boarstall ware, AD 1200–1600. 651 sherds, 7,667 g, EVE = 1.26.
OXAW	Early Brill coarseware, AD 1180–1250. 54 sherds, 713 g, EVE = 0.57.
OXB	Oxford shelly ware, late eighth–early eleventh century. 45 sherds, 442 g, EVE = 0.20.
OXBB	Minety-type ware, early thirteenth–sixteenth century. One sherd, 14 g, EVE = 0.
OXBC	Brill/Boarstall 'Tudor green ware', 1475–1600. One sherd, 2 g, EVE = 0.
OXBEW	Staffordshire manganese-glazed ware, late seventeenth–mid eighteenth century. 24 sherds, 1,082 g.
OXBEWSL	Staffordshire-type slip-trailed earthenware, 1650–1750. Two sherds, 102 g.
OXBF	Kennet Valley ware, AD 1050–1400. 238 sherds, 3,244 g, EVE = 1.73.
OXBG	Surrey whiteware, mid thirteenth–mid fifteenth century. Eight sherds, 112 g, EVE = 0.24.
OXBN	Tudor green ware, late fourteenth–sixteenth century. 37 sherds, 209 g, EVE = 0.39.
OXBX	Late Brill/Boarstall ware, fifteenth–seventeenth century. 407 sherds, 10,743 g, EVE = 2.07.

30 M. Mellor and G. Oakley, 'A Summary of the Key Assemblages …', in 'St Ebbe's, Part II', pp. 181–219; Mellor, 'Synthesis'.

OXCE	Tin-glazed earthenware, 1600–1800. 108 sherds, 1,852 g.
OXCL	Cistercian ware, 1450–1700. 21 sherds, 292 g, EVE = 1.60.
OXDR	Glazed red earthenwares, 1550+. 197 sherds, 6,956 g.
OXEAH	Midland blackware, mid sixteenth–seventeenth century. 28 sherds, 327 g.
OXEST	London stoneware. 1680 +. Six sherds, 571 g.
OXFH	Border wares, 1550–1700. 153 sherds, 2,837 g.
OXFH	Brown-glazed Border ware, 1620–1700. 16 sherds, 153 g.
OXFI	Chinese porcelain, 1650+. Two sherds, 11 g.
OXK	Michelmersh ware, early tenth–mid eleventh century. 17 sherds, 162 g, EVE = 0.08.
OXR	St Neots ware, AD 850–1200. 633 sherds, 5,539 g, EVE = 5.59.
OXST	Frechen stoneware, AD 1480–1700. 270 sherds, 6797 g.
OXST	Raeren stoneware, 1450–1600. 31 sherds, 1,082 g, EVE = 0.46.
OXST	Westerwald stoneware, 1600–1800. Four sherds, 76 g.
OXST	Langerwehe stoneware, fifteenth century. One sherd, 107 g.
OXST	Siegburg stoneware, mid fourteenth–fifteenth century. One sherd, 32 g.
OXY	Medieval Oxford ware, AD 1070–1350. 632 sherds, 7,114 g, EVE = 3.82.
OXZ	Stamford ware, AD 850–1150. 31 sherds, 214 g, EVE = 0.14.
WHEW	Mass-produced white earthenwares, nineteenth–twentieth century. 2 sherds, 159 g.

In addition, five residual sherds (69 g) of Romano-British pottery were noted. The following, not covered by the Oxfordshire type-series, were also present:

F401	Spanish lustreware, fifteenth century.[31] Three sherds, 185 g, EVE = 0.05.
F407	Midland purple ware, fifteenth–seventeenth century.[32] Four sherds, 37 g, EVE = 0.10.
F408	Low Countries redware, fifteenth–seventeenth century.[33] Six sherds, 199 g, EVE = 0.
F409	Portuguese redware, fourteenth–seventeenth century.[34] One sherd, 6 g, EVE = 0.
F415	Ligurian majolica, 1550–1600.[35] One sherd, 9 g.

The bulk of the pottery consists of material which is well known in the Oxford region, although there are a small number of sherds of types which are rarely noted in the city, in the form of Michelmersh ware and an unusually wide range of imported medieval and early post-medieval pottery types, particularly the Spanish and Italian tin-glazed wares (F401 and F415) and the European redwares (F408 and F409). Michelmersh ware was noted at All Saints and St Aldate's, and Spanish tin-glazed wares occurred at St Ebbe's.[36]

It is worthy of comment that usually fairly common early to mid eighteenth-century pottery types such as Staffordshire white-glazed stoneware (Oxford fabric OXFM) and creamware (OXCRW) are entirely absent, suggesting pottery deposition at the site had ceased by the time these wares were in circulation.

[31] J.G. Hurst et al., *Pottery Produced and Traded in North-West Europe 1350–1650*, Rotterdam Papers, 6 (1986), p. 42.

[32] M.R. McCarthy and C.M. Brooks, *Medieval Pottery in Britain AD 900–1600* (1988), p. 42.

[33] Hurst et al., *Pottery Produced and Traded in North-West Europe*, p. 130.

[34] Ibid. p. 69.

[35] Ibid. p. 26.

[36] Dodd, *Oxford*, table 6.8; Mellor and Oakley, 'A Summary of Key Assemblages', p. 201.

Table 6.2. Ceramic phase chronology, occurrence and defining wares. * Raeren stoneware; **Brown-glazed Border ware; *** Typological evidence.

Phase	Defining wares	Date	Sherds	Weight (g)	Mean Sherd Weight (g)
MSAX	OXB	8th–9th C	3	54	18.0
LSAX	OXR, OXZ	10th C	117	1701	14.5
SN	OXAC, OXBF	11th C	321	3426	10.7
M1	OXY	Late 11th–12th C	579	5337	9.2
M2	OXAM	13th–14th C	1012	11,750	11.6
M3	OXBX, OXBN	15th C	248	3643	14.7
M4	OXCL, OXST*	Late 15th–mid 16th C	108	1968	18.2
PM1	OXDR, OXST, OXFH	Mid-late 16th C	950	14,284	15.0
PM2	OXCE, OXST, OXFH**	Early-mid 17th C	199	5187	26.1
PM3	OXCE***, OXBEWSL	Mid-late 17th C	356	5334	15.0
PM4	OXBEW, OXEST	Late 17th–18th C	567	15,015	42.2
MOD	WHEW	19th C	2	159	79.5
Total			4462	67,858	

Chronology
Each stratified, context-specific pottery assemblage was given a ceramic phase date ('CP') based on the range of ware and vessel types present. The veracity of each date was checked against the stratigraphic record and adjusted where necessary. The chronology, defining wares and the amount of pottery per phase is shown in Table 6.2. The occurrence of the major fabrics per ceramic phase is shown in Table 6.3, a fairly typical pattern of pottery consumption for sites in Oxford. In some cases, residuality is very high, notably in CP M1, with 30 per cent (by weight) of residual St Neots ware suggesting extensive disturbance of earlier strata. The low mean sherd weight for the CP reflects this. This appears to be due to the fact that large amounts of earlier pottery were incorporated into the backfill of the late Anglo-Saxon cellared buildings, a pattern of site clearance which has been noted elsewhere in the city.[37]

The Ceramic Phased Assemblages

Ceramic Phase LSAX, Tenth Century. 117 sherds, 1,701 g, EVE = 1.74 The late Anglo-Saxon assemblage is dominated by St Neots ware, with small quantities of OXB and OXZ. All the sherds of the latter are unglazed. Most of the seven rim sherds in St Neots ware are quite small, with a rim diameter less than 160 mm, which is typical of the earlier, tenth-century, products of the tradition.

Most of the groups of this date were quite small, with just two features, pits 1367 and 1694, producing more than twenty sherds. Some of the vessels (for example, Fig. 6.11, no. 2) were extensively sooted. Given the good condition of the assemblage, it seems likely they were taken directly with material from domestic middens or the like and used as backfill material. One of the cellar pits, 1718, may date from this period, although it produced very little pottery.

Ceramic Phase SN, Early/Mid–Late Eleventh Century. 321 sherds, 3,426 g, EVE = 2.40 This ceramic phase sees the introduction of OXAC and OXBF, while most of the St Neots ware jar rims were

37 Dodd, *Oxford*, pp. 51–2.

Table 6.3. Pottery occurrence per ceramic phase by fabric type, expressed as a percentage of the total weight per phase, major fabrics only. Shaded cells: residual material; * Raeren stoneware; ** Frechen/Cologne stoneware.

Fabric	LSAX	SN	M1	M2	M3	M4	PM1	PM2	PM3	PM4
OXB	7.8%	2.1%	1.6%	0.7%	0	0.7%	0	0	0	0
OXR	85.8%	35.5%	28.4%	6.2%	2.0%	4.0%	2.1%	0	1.2%	0.7%
OXZ	6.3%	0.8%	1.0%	0.2%	0.2%	0	0	0	0	0
OXAC	–	39.5%	32.3%	23.1%	8.3%	4.0%	14.1%	3.8%	1.4%	1.9%
OXBF	–	17.2%	15.9%	7.3%	4.8%	8.3%	2.3%	1.4%	1.2%	1.0%
OXY	–	–	20.7%	34.5%	4.4%	6.1%	6.6%	3.5%	4.5%	2.1%
OXAM	–	–	–	22.2%	13.6%	13.8%	14.6%	7.6%	19.8%	0.5%
OXAW	–	–	–	5.9%	0	0	0	0.4%	0	0
OXBX	–	–	–	–	59.7%	45.7%	22.5%	19.4%	8.6%	19.9%
OXBN	–	–	–	–	3.9%	0	0.3%	0.2%	0.2%	0
OXST*	–	–	–	–	–	3.0%	3.0%	2.8%	0	2.9%
OXCL	–	–	–	–	–	6.4%	0.4%	0.3%	0.1%	0.6%
OXST**	–	–	–	–	–	–	17.4%	29.7%	20.0%	11.3%
OXDR	–	–	–	–	–	–	11.0%	21.0%	7.1%	26.1%
OXFH	–	–	–	–	–	–	3.7%	2.8%	17.5%	8.1%
OXEAH	–	–	–	–	–	–	0.1%	1.8%	1.7%	0.9%
OXCE	–	–	–	–	–	–	–	3.4%	14.6%	6.0%
OXBEW	–	–	–	–	–	–	–	–	–	7.2%
OXEST	–	–	–	–	–	–	–	–	–	3.8%
Total weight (g)	1701	3426	5337	11,750	3643	1968	14,284	5187	5334	15,015

larger than those in CP LSAX deposits, and thus later. St Neots ware fell fairly rapidly from use in Oxford around the middle of the eleventh century.[38] Most of the groups of pottery of this date are very small, and there seems to have been very little disturbance of strata and features of this date in the medieval period. Some of the cellared buildings appear to have been occupied at this time. The sherds of Michelmersh ware (OXK) all appear to be from a single vessel which has an applied collar and stamped applied strips on the body (Fig. 6.11, no. 3). It is very similar to a pitcher from the kiln site in Hampshire.[39] Most of the fragments came from context 2205, a deposit in pit 2182.

Ceramic Phase M1, Late Eleventh to Twelfth Century. 579 sherds, 5,337 g, EVE = 3.36 This phase saw a fairly major reorganization of the site, including the backfilling of the remaining cellared buildings, and the pottery assemblage reflects this. Residuality is very high and the material is very fragmented. The major ware is OXAC, although some of this is likely to be residual SN material. The Stamford ware (including a small crucible fragment), OXB and a single Romano-British sherd are also residual.

38 Mellor, 'Synthesis', p. 57.
39 McCarthy and Brooks, *Medieval Pottery*.

Of the contemporary material, 24 jar rims in OXAC, OXBF and OXY were present. Two, one in OXY and the other in OXAC, had thumbed "piecrust" rims which are typical of the period.[40] In the case of the bowls, two were in fabric OXAC and the other was OXBF, one in each fabric (Figs. 6.11, nos. 4–5) surviving to a full profile. Oxford ware tripod pitchers were represented by three glazed sherds, although no rims, spouts or handles were present. A short tubular spout from a pitcher in OXBF was noted. Such vessels are rare but not unknown in Oxford.[41]

Ceramic Phase M2, Thirteenth to Fourteenth Century. 1,012 sherds, 11,750 g, EVE = 7.42 This is by far the largest medieval ceramic phase assemblage, but it is also the longest, representing around two centuries of activity. The material is generally in fairly good condition, with lower residuality. Despite this, the assemblage is largely fragmented and scattered, with near-complete or reconstructable vessels largely absent, indicating that most of the pottery is the product of secondary deposition.

The period sees a large increase in the proportion of glazed wares, mainly in the form of OXAM, which represents nearly a quarter (23.8 per cent) of the non-residual pottery. The major ware is OXY, including 52 glazed fragments of pitchers and jugs. A single unglazed sherd from context 1196 has what appears to be madder staining on the inner surface. Fabric OXAC still makes up around a quarter of the assemblage and OXBF, along with OXAW, are significant minor wares. The only other contemporary pottery present was a single small sherd of Surrey whiteware. This often occurs in small quantities at sites in Oxford.[42]

The rim assemblage is dominated by jars and jugs. Bowls are very scarce, but rims from other vessel types are also present in the form of double-shell lamps, small skillets, a lid and a stamped and glazed vessel (see below) which defies categorization, all in Brill/Boarstall ware (OXAM). Non-rim fragments from a further four lamps were noted, as was a sherd of OXAC which has a post-firing drilled hole and appears to have been reworked as a spindlewhorl.

Many of the glazed jugs were highly decorated, as was often the case at this time, with applied strips, stamping and coloured slips all used. Particularly notable is an OXAM vessel which has decoration reminiscent of French jugs of the period, specifically Rouen types (Fig. 6.11, no. 6). Other British potters were making such copies at this time, such as in London, where Rouen-style jugs are usually dated to the late twelfth–mid/late thirteenth century.[43] The double shell lamps are a common find, albeit in small numbers, at sites in the Oxford region.[44] The same comments apply to the small skillet fragments.

The most intriguing vessel is a stamped and glazed OXAM item represented by two non-joining sherds, a rim sherd and a handle (Fig. 6.11, nos. 7–8). The profile of the former suggests it has a rounded, closed form, and it also has what appears to be the beginning of the terminal of a handle or lug on the rim-top. It has no obvious parallels amongst the corpus of OXAM from Oxford.[45] The handle could be from an aquamanile, and an example with similar decoration is known from Oxford,[46] but the fragment of the rim is very unlikely to be from such a pot. One possibility is that it may be part of a lantern or fuming-pot,[47] but the complete

40 Mellor, 'Synthesis', fig. 18.

41 Ibid. fig. 14, no. 2.

42 P. Blinkhorn, 'Pottery', in A.M. Chadwick et al. (eds.), "... *Quadrangles Where Wisdom Honours Herself". Archaeological Investigations at Tom Quad, Peckwater Quad and Blue Boar Quad, Christ Church, Oxford* (2012), pp. 112–41.

43 J.E. Pearce et al., *A Dated Type-Series of London Medieval Pottery. Part 2: London-Type Ware*, London and Middlesex Archaeology Society Special Paper, 6 (1985), fig. 9.

44 Mellor, 'Synthesis', fig. 54.

45 Mellor and Oakley, 'A Summary of the Key Assemblages'.

46 Ibid. fig. 51, no. 24.

47 *A Guide to the Classification of Medieval Ceramic Forms*, Medieval Pottery Research Group Occasional Paper, 1 (1998), forms 8.3 and 8.7.

lack of internal sooting would suggest otherwise. A more convincing possibility is that they are fragments of a side-handle urinal,[48] but these are otherwise unknown in Brill/Boarstall ware.

Ceramic Phase M3, Early–Mid Fifteenth Century. 248 Sherds, 3,643 g, EVE = 2.17 The assemblage from this ceramic phase is considerably smaller, but it is only around fifty years long, indicating that the rate of pottery deposition remains largely unchanged despite the social and political upheavals of the fourteenth century.

Much of the stratified material is in very good condition, although only a few large fragments of OXBX jugs were reconstructable. The illustrated example is typical of the tradition at this time, with sparse glazing other than a 'bib' at the front below the pouring lip.[49]

Brill/Boarstall products are by far the major ware, mainly in the form of OXBX (74.3 per cent of the non-residual pottery by weight), and OXAM (17.0 per cent), although it is likely that a fair proportion of the latter is residual. Surrey/Hampshire 'Tudor green' wares (fabric OXBN) are a significant minor ware, making up 4.9 per cent, with the rest of the contemporary material comprising three sherds of Surrey whiteware along with single sherds of Andalusian lustreware (fabric F401), Midland purple ware and Low Countries redware.

The stratified rim sherd assemblage was dominated by OXBX jugs, with smaller quantities of bowls. This is not unusual for later medieval assemblages, as metal had largely replaced pottery for cooking vessels by this time.[50] The other vessel rims present were a skillet and a lugged costrel, both in OXBX, and three fragments of Surrey/Hampshire 'Tudor green' lobed cups. The costrel is quite an unusual vessel type, although a few other Brill/Boarstall examples have occurred in Oxford.[51]

Two non-rim fragments of OXAM puzzle jugs were also noted. One of them is a hollow tubular handle, while the other is the terminal of either a similar handle or a false spout (Fig. 6.11, no. 9). Puzzle jugs are rare finds in Oxford, although a near-complete, highly decorated vessel is known from excavations at Oxford Town Hall and dated to the late thirteenth century.[52]

As noted above, the sherd of Andalusian lustreware is a rare find in Oxford, with such pottery generally not common at inland sites in England, other than those of high status.[53] However, this fabric and Low Countries redware are reasonably common finds in the port of London.[54] This is the most likely source for the vessels occurring at this site, given that other pottery from the London region such as Surrey whitewares and Border wares are present. The sherd of lustreware (Fig. 6.11, no. 10) is probably from an albarello, a waisted jar which was a common product of the tradition, and often imported containing luxury foodstuffs such as spices, honey, marmalade or syrup. A near-complete Valencian lustreware example occurred at Eynsham Abbey,[55] and a sherd from another Spanish vessel, from Seville, was also noted there.[56] The Low Countries sherd is from the rim of a plate or dish.

Ceramic Phase M4, Late Fifteenth–Mid Sixteenth Century. 108 sherds, 1,968 g, EVE = 0.93 This assemblage is fairly small given the length of the ceramic phase and suggests a period during which there was a relatively low level of activity. The non-residual component of the assemblage is once again dominated by Brill/Boarstall products, with OXBX nearly 60 per cent of the

48 Ibid. form 10.28.2.

49 Mellor, 'Synthesis', p. 132.

50 McCarthy and Brooks, *Medieval Pottery*, p. 101.

51 Mellor, 'Synthesis', fig. 67, no. 8.

52 Ibid. fig. 57, no. 1.

53 A. Gutiérrez, 'Cheapish and Spanish. Meaning and Design on Imported Spanish Pottery', *Medieval Ceramics*, 21 (1997), pp. 73–82.

54 A.G. Vince, 'The Saxon and Medieval Pottery of London: A Review', *Medieval Archaeology*, 29 (1985), figs. 22, 32 and 33.

55 A. Gutiérrez, 'The Spanish Jar', in A. Hardy et al., *Aelfric's Abbey. Excavations at Eynsham Abbey, Oxfordshire, 1989–92* (2003), pp. 199–200.

56 P. Blinkhorn, 'The Pottery', in ibid. p. 186.

assemblage by weight, and OXAM 17.9 per cent. Some of the OXAM is very likely to be residual. Cistercian ware is well-represented (8.3 per cent). The only other pottery types present were six sherds of Raeren stoneware and one each of OXBC, Langerwehe stoneware, Minety-type ware and a Surrey whiteware jar, of coarse Border ware type. It had a bifid rim-form, a common early–mid fifteenth-century product of the tradition.[57]

Ceramic Phase PM1, Mid–Late Sixteenth Century. 950 sherds, 14,284 g This is the second-largest ceramic phase assemblage from the site. Residuality is quite high, however, with less than half the assemblage (420 sherds) being contemporary pottery, dominated by late Brill/Boarstall ware fabric OXBX. Imported Frechen/Cologne stonewares also make up a significant proportion of the contemporary material (29.0 per cent), as do glazed red earthenwares (OXDR; 18.3 per cent). Other regional and continental imports in the form of Border ware (OXFH) and Raeren stoneware are significant minor wares, with Cistercian ware (OXCL) comprising just 0.6 per cent. A wide range of other wares were represented by small numbers of sherds. English wares were present in the form of Surrey/Hampshire 'Tudor green' ware, Midland purple ware and Midland blackware, but an unusually wide range of imported wares were also present: Low Countries redware, Andalusian lustreware, Siegburg stoneware, and Ligurian majolica.

Most of the assemblages have a similar character, comprising less than thirty sherds, with a few large fragments of contemporary wares in most. This indicates that there was certainly a primary element to the deposition of some of the pottery. The German stonewares are all vessels associated with the storage and consumption of drink, mainly bottles and drinking jugs. Red earthenwares and Border wares are a largely utilitarian mixture of cooking and tablewares, with the OXBX assemblage mostly bowls, although the base of a chafing dish (a portable stove) was also noted (Fig. 6.12, no. 11), as was the handle from another puzzle jug. The Low Countries redware assemblage includes a small rim sherd from a plate or shallow dish similar to that from CP M3, and may be residual, but a large fragment of a rim, probably from a *grape*, a specialist cooking vessel,[58] was also present. The sherd of Ligurian tin-glaze is from the rim of a shallow dish or plate with an even coating of mid-blue glaze, and with a dark blue painted design on the rim-flange. It is very similar to a shallow dish from Alkmaar in the Netherlands, albeit with the decoration in mirror image.[59] The Andalusian sherd is also from the rim of a plate or dish and has a badly degraded glaze with no sign of any decoration other than thin concentric cordons of lustre on the lower surface of the rim-flange. It is probably residual.

The range of imported wares is worthy of comment, as, the German stonewares aside, it is unusual for sites in Oxford. The pottery assemblage from the Nun's Garden, Queen's College,[60] did not produce any of the exotic tin-glazed or Low Countries wares seen here.

Frechen/Cologne stonewares, usually in the form of bottles, mugs or drinking jugs, are well-known at sites in Oxford, and, indeed, most of the world with contacts to Europe at that time, but the quantity occurring here is unusually large. For example, such pottery made up just under 10 per cent of the material from the sixteenth- to eighteenth-century groups from No. 4A Merton Street.[61] The only comparable assemblages are those from Tom Quad at Christ Church, where between a quarter and a third of the pottery from the early post-medieval assemblages were German stonewares of this type, and from the Old Cloisters, Brasenose College.[62] In the case of Tom Quad, the period saw two visits from Elizabeth I and her entire court, and, later, Charles I and his parliament on at least two occasions, not to mention the Royalist army, meaning large amounts of drinking pottery would have been required.

57 J. Pearce, *Border Wares* (1988), p. 85.
58 Hurst et al., *Pottery Produced and Traded in North-West Europe*, for example fig. 59.
59 Ibid. fig. 11, no. 20.
60 J. Cotter, 'Post-Roman Pottery', in Teague et al., 'Nun's Garden', pp. 159–67.
61 P. Blinkhorn, 'Pottery', in Poore, 'No. 4A Merton St.', pp. 258–78.
62 Blinkhorn, in Chadwick et al., "... *Quadrangles Where Wisdom Honours Herself*", pp. 112–41; chapter 9, below.

Ceramic Phase PM2, Early to Mid Seventeenth Century. 199 sherds, 5,187 g Most of the pottery groups comprised less than 20 sherds, but also usually with one or two very large fragments, showing some of the material was the product of primary deposition.

Frechen/Cologne stoneware is the major ware, making up 36.9 per cent of the non-residual assemblage by weight, which is a remarkably high proportion for a site in Oxford. Glazed red earthenwares (OXDR) and Brill earthenwares (OXBX) each form roughly a quarter of the assemblage. A fairly wide range of minor wares present comprise small quantities of tin-glazed earthenware, Border ware (including brown-glazed sherds), Midland blackware and Cistercian ware. Also present were three sherds of Westerwald/Cologne stoneware, the only sherd of Portuguese redware from the site (a small body sherd from a closed form) and a single sherd of Low Countries redware. The last two aside, this is a fairly common range of fabric types at this time in Oxford.

The Frechen/Cologne stonewares are mainly bottles and jugs, some with *Bartmann* face-masks and armorial moulded prunts on the belly. One of these survived to a full profile (Fig. 6.12, no. 12). A fragment of another vessel has the rather unusual moulded design of a rampant lion, the arms of Scotland. It cannot be said with certainty that this is what it represents, but the arms of many other countries including England are known from stoneware bottles of this type.[63] The stonewares aside, the rest of the assemblage consists largely of utilitarian earthenwares, mainly jars, bowls and jugs, with one OXBX bowl surviving to a full profile, although small numbers of fragments of finer tablewares in the form of painted OXCE dishes, plates and bowls were also noted.

Ceramic Phase PM3, Mid–Late Seventeenth Century. 356 sherds, 5,334 g Frechen/Cologne stoneware once again dominates the contemporary assemblage, at nearly 28 per cent, but there are also relatively large amounts of Border ware (26.0 per cent) and tin-glazed earthenware (20.5 per cent). Glazed red earthenwares are relatively scarce at roughly 10 per cent, as is OXBX (12.1 per cent) and small quantities of Midland blackware are also present (2.4 per cent). Single sherds of Westerwald/Cologne stoneware and Chinese porcelain were also noted.

Large quantities of drinking pottery are present. All the German stoneware is again bottles, jugs and mugs, and tin-glazed earthenware (OXCE) is fragments of mugs with purple manganese decoration on the exterior. Such vessels were a staple product of the London tin-glazed industry in and around the third quarter of the seventeenth century.[64] They are mainly represented here by rims and bases, and are all from different vessels. One of the sherds (Fig. 6.12, no. 13) has a post-firing graffito on the base which appears to be the Union flag but may be a maker's or owner's mark. A fragment of a costrel in brown-glazed Border ware also occurred. These appear to have been a largely seventeenth-century product of the industry.[65] The Chinese porcelain is the complete foot-ring of a tea-bowl.

The rest of the assemblage consists of more utilitarian wares, but some of the OXCE is of extremely high quality, such as a painted bowl from context 1153, which has parallels with a pot from a dump of manufacturing waste at Mark Brown's Wharf in London.[66] Another fragment of this bowl occurred in a CP M4 feature (1143). Both sherds are illustrated here (Fig. 6.12, no. 14). The decoration is Orton's 'Group A' style, and typical of the first half of the seventeenth century.[67]

Ceramic Phase PM4, Late Seventeenth–Eighteenth Century. 567 sherds, 15,015 g This is the largest ceramic phase group from the site, and also has the largest general mean sherd weight at 42.2 g. Residuality is fairly high during this phase, and some of the apparently redeposited

63 Ibid. p. 213.

64 C. Orton, 'Post-Roman Pottery', in P. Hinton (ed.), *Excavations in Southwark 1973–76 and Lambeth 1973–79*, MoLAS and DGLA Joint Publication, 3 (1988), p. 321.

65 Pearce, *Border Wares*, p. 31.

66 Orton, 'Post-Roman Pottery'.

67 Ibid. p. 321.

material is in very good condition and near-complete, suggesting that some of it had been curated for some time. It includes at least two partially complete Raeren mugs which are very unlikely to date to any later than 1550, and a large fragment of a Spanish lustreware shallow dish, which is most likely to be Valencian and to date from the fifteenth century.

The stratified material is dominated by glazed red earthenwares, including Brill/Boarstall types, and mainly in the form of bowls. Frechen/Cologne stonewares are still very common, with significant minor wares being Border ware (10.2 per cent) and Staffordshire manganese ware (8.5 per cent). Tin-glazed earthenwares also make up a significant proportion of the assemblage, 7.1 per cent, including a number with Chinese-style decoration which are typical of the last quarter of the seventeenth century.[68] English stoneware is rare, comprising 4.5 per cent of the group, and Midland blackware 1.0 per cent. The only other contemporary pottery present is a partially complete posset cup in Staffordshire slipware (OXBEWSL).

A large, near-complete OXBEW tankard from context 1672 has a stamped "AR" ale-mark of Queen Anne on the body, thought to date from the early part of her reign (Fig. 6.12, no. 15).[69] A small tankard in the same fabric was also well-represented, and a near-complete English stoneware (OXEST) mug or 'tavern gorge' also occurred, but neither was stamped. The complete lack of white salt-glazed stoneware (OXFM) from the site suggests that pottery deposition at the site ended sometime between *c.*1705 and 1730, which corresponds with a period of intense rebuilding at the college, including the nearby library, and would indicate that the area of the site covered by these investigations was given over to the Provost's Garden after that time.

It is also striking that a considerable proportion of the assemblage consists of drinking pottery. All the Frechen/Cologne stoneware, along with the OXEST, OXBEW, OXBEWSL and OXEAH, nearly 21 per cent of the pottery in total, is cups, mugs, tankards or bottles. Some of the earthenwares are also drinking pottery, such as a bottle in OXBX. This is almost certainly due to the fact that the area appears to have functioned as a 'builder's yard' during this phase. Large quantities of drinking pottery are a feature of sites which featured heavy physical work in both the medieval and post-medieval periods.[70]

As well as the drinking pottery, there was a large collection of utilitarian tableware, particularly in the form of Border ware. Two unusual vessels were noted. One is a piece of a lobed dish, virtually identical to a mid to late seventeenth-century example from London,[71] and the other is a globular vessel with a pedestal foot which does not have a parallel in Pearce's corpus, but may be a baby-feeder (Fig. 6.12, no. 16). Full profiles of other vessels in this fabric were present, such as a shallow flanged dish and a skillet. The former has a lot of wear and scratches towards the centre of the upper face, suggesting it was well used by the time of disposal. Such vessels were staples of the tradition and made and used throughout most of its life. The tin-glazed earthenwares also fall into this category, with most vessels being bowls or dishes, although a few fragments of chamber-pots were also present.

Catalogue of Illustrated Pottery (Figs. 6.11–6.12):

1. Fabric F202. Rim and body from a jar. Thick sooting on outer surface, heavy lime-scaling on the lower interior. Ctx 1688, 2091 and 2223.
2. Fabric OXR. Jar rim and upper body. Grey fabric with grey-brown surfaces. Outer surface heavily sooted, lime-scaling on the inner. Ctx 1695.
3. Fabric OXK. Rim from a decorated ?pitcher. Grey fabric with reddish brown surfaces. Ctx 2205.

68 Orton, 'Post-Roman Pottery', p. 327.

69 M. Bimson, 'The Significance of "Ale-Measure" Marks', *Post-Medieval Archaeology*, 4 (1970), p. 166.

70 For example, P. Blinkhorn, 'The Pottery', in P. Blinkhorn and G. Pugh, *Excavation of the Medieval Waterfront at King Stable Street, Eton, Berkshire* (2000), pp. 19–24.

71 Pearce, *Border Wares*, fig. 18.

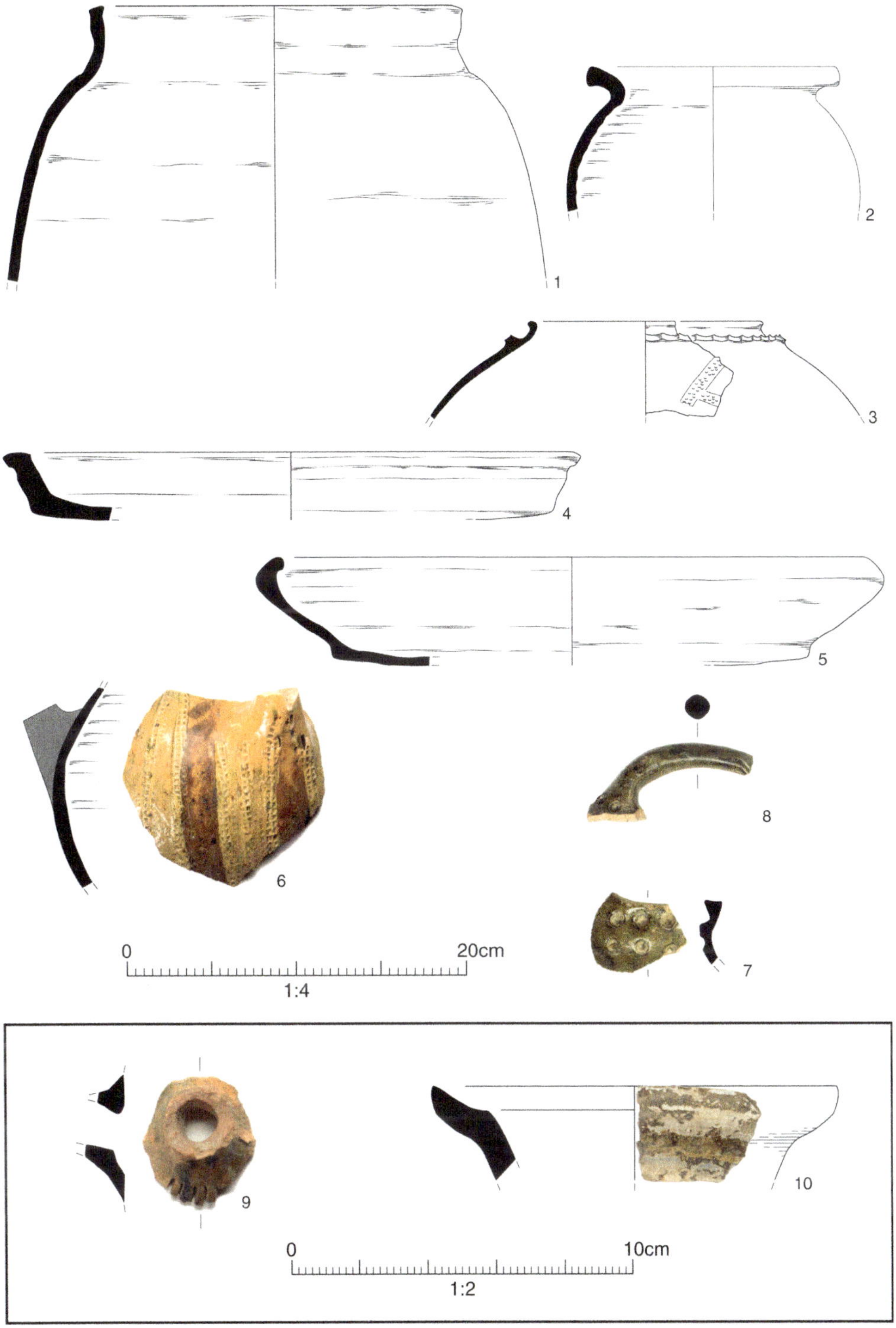

Fig. 6.11 Pottery, nos. 1–10.

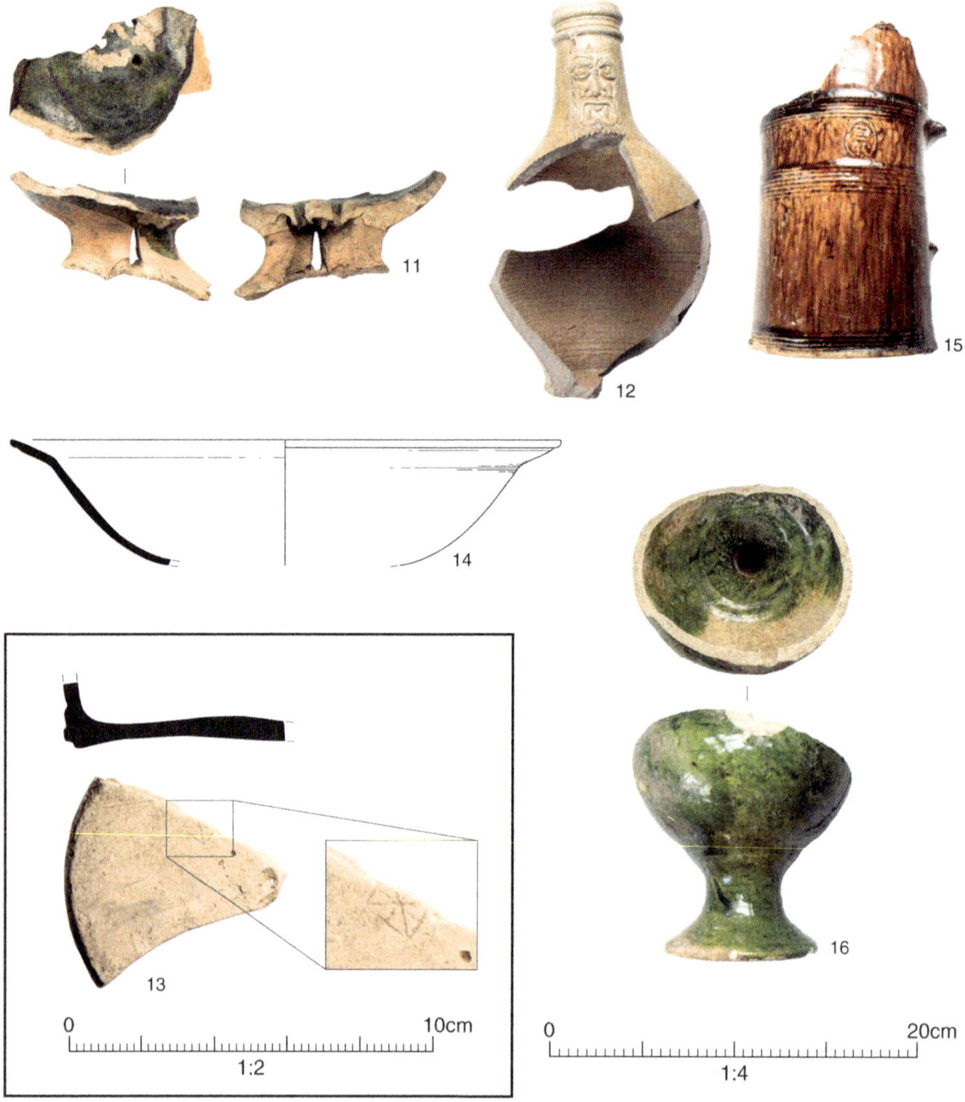

Fig. 6.12 Pottery, nos. 11–16.

4. Fabric OXAC. Full profile of bowl. Grey-brown fabric with darker surfaces. Sooting on exterior. Ctx 1899.
5. Fabric OXBF. Full profile of bowl. Dark grey fabric with variegated dark brown and dark grey surfaces. Ctx 1510.
6. Fabric OXAM. Body sherd from highly decorated jug. Pale orange fabric with light grey inner surface. Outer has alternate vertical bands of red slip and rouletted strips in the body-clay, all over glaze appearing yellow over the latter. Ctx 1497.
7. Fabric OXAM. Rim from a ?urinal. Pale orange fabric with buff inner surface, rich, glossy, apple-green glaze on the outer surface. Ctx 1996.
8. Fabric OXAM. Handle from same vessel as no. 7. Same colour and glaze. Ctx 1512.

9. Fabric OXAM. Hollow handle/false spout terminal from a puzzle jug. Orange-pink fabric with a variegated yellow and green glaze. Ctx 2336.
10. Fabric F401. Rim sherd from an ?albarello. Uniform white fabric. Degraded tin glaze with horizontal bands of gold lustre and blue paint. Ctx 2068.
11. Fabric OXBX. Fragment of the body and base of a chafing dish. Buff fabric with orange-pink surfaces, rich glossy green glaze on the inner surface of the dish, some areas of burning. Ctx 1032.
12. Frechen/Cologne stoneware. Full profile of a *Bartmann* jug. Grey fabric with a pinkish-brown inner surface, brown speckled outer. Ctx 1667.
13. Fabric OXCE. Mug base. Pinkish-buff fabric with white glaze and purple sponged decoration on the outer body, plain white glaze on the interior. "Union Flag" graffito on the unglazed base. Ctx 1188.
14. Fabric OXCE. Polychrome bowl. White fabric with lead glaze on the outer, white tin-glaze on the interior with blue, green and ochre decoration, and a clear lead glaze over all. Ctx 1143 and 1153.
15. Fabric OXBEW. Near full profile of a tankard with an "AR" ale-mark. Buff fabric with brown, manganese streaked glaze all over except the outer base-pad. Ctx 1672.
16. Fabric OXFH. Lower part of ?baby-feeder. White fabric with glossy green glaze on the outer surface, patchy on the inner. Ctx 1646.

ORGANIC RESIDUE ANALYSIS OF POTTERY by JULIE DUNNE and RICHARD P. EVERSHED

Selected pottery vessels were analysed to determine whether organic residues were preserved, to provide a comparison with the material from the site at Nos. 114–119 St Aldate's, in the medieval Jewish quarter. The selected samples comprised one Cotswold-type ware vessel from Phase 1, and a total of nine vessels in Cotswold-type ware and medieval Oxford ware from Phase 2. The methods used were high-temperature gas chromatography (GC), gas chromatography-mass spectrometry (GC-MS) and carbon isotope analyses (GC-C-IRMS). The results show that four vessels were used to process solely ruminant carcass products with the remainder being used to process both ruminant and non-ruminant products, whether contemporaneously or over the lifetime of use of the vessel. Further discussion can be found in chapter 4, above.

FIRED CLAY AND CERAMIC BUILDING MATERIAL by CYNTHIA POOLE

A large quantity of building material was recovered from the excavation, amounting to about 1700 fragments weighing in the order of 100 kg. The majority of this was ceramic building material (CBM) of which roughly half was fully processed and recorded, with the remainder scanned for significant pieces. Six fragments of Roman tile were present, including a tegula.

Fired Clay

The fired clay came predominantly from Saxo-Norman and early medieval deposits. Material recovered from the Saxo-Norman levels (Phase 1) was of indeterminate form, probably from ovens, except for a fragment of vitrified furnace or smithing-hearth lining from the fill of pit 1367. Two further fragments of vitrified furnace lining were recovered from Phase 2a pit 1659. Analysis of the slag (see below) shows that both smelting and smithing of iron was taking place during the Saxo-Norman and early medieval phases. Fired clay from Phase 2a was recovered from pits and the cellar pit. Five fragments had a roughly moulded exterior surface and interwoven wattle impressions on the interior that probably derive from ovens, possibly supporting a suspended floor in a two-chamber structure, rather than forming the oven walls. An additional three fragments with wattle impressions were found in late-medieval (2b) and later post-medieval (4a) phases. Fragments from a possible metalworking mould were found in an earlier post-medieval pit (1353).

Roof Tile

Roof tile (1,153 fragments, 52,833 g) formed the bulk of the assemblage. Over half were plain flat fragments, including a proportion of glazed pieces that could derive from either peg tile or ridge tile. The typical medieval roof tile (mainly thirteenth to fifteenth century) was produced in a limited range of fabrics, the most common being an orange-red sandy fabric (Fabric IIIB). The tile recovered from Phase 2a was dominated by slightly earlier group VII fabrics (thirteenth to fourteenth century). These are primarily the cream VIIA, pink VIIB and VIIBB with a reddish surface and grey core, all characterised by small chalk inclusions or leached voids in a moderately sandy clay matrix. These were probably produced somewhere in north-east Oxfordshire and are generally dated to the early to mid thirteenth century. A fairly small proportion of the roof tile (59 fragments, 4,075 g) was formed by the distinctive late-medieval peg tile recognised by Cotter from the earlier excavations in the area of the medieval kitchen.[72] They were made in the same fine red fabric with a thick grey core, as noted by Cotter akin to some late-medieval/early post-medieval redware pottery fabrics. The medieval roof tile is generally recognisable by its fairly rough finish and irregular manufacture, and variations in tile thickness and the form of peg holes are discussed in the full report. Four pieces of roof tile had been burnt along one edge, a characteristic that is usually indicative of it having been used in the pitched floor surface of a hearth or oven.

Ridge tile (125 fragments, 9,227 g) was identified in a variety of fabrics and forms ranging from late twelfth to fifteenth century in date. The earliest were 11 fragments (1,085 g) in cream-buff oolitic limestone gritted fabric IB, which dates to the late twelfth to early thirteenth century. This type is thought to have come from north-west Oxfordshire.[73] It was used for glazed crested ridge tile, and over half the fragments had evidence of cut triangular spurs, often with thumb prints at the base from attaching the crest. They were quite crudely made and thinly glazed with amber or green bands alongside the crest deteriorating to splashes towards the edges. Later ridge tile in fabric groups III and VII was probably plain glazed with a rounded or angular apex and without a crest. Amber and brown glaze occurs most frequently, with olive green slightly less common. The character of tile fabric IIIA is similar to the Brill/Boarstall pottery fabric (OXAM) and is generally dated to the fourteenth century.

Floor Tile

Floor tile (99 fragments, 15,681 g) was recovered from late-medieval to modern deposits, but 70 per cent was found in post-medieval deposits of Phase 3b (seventeenth century) suggesting this was a major period of refurbishment. Both decorated and plain medieval and late-medieval to early post-medieval tiles were present. Reference to floor tile designs are prefixed LH and refer to numbering used in the catalogue of Oxfordshire floor tiles produced by Haberly.[74]

The earliest type was a corner fragment of 'stabbed Wessex' tile probably made between 1270 and 1330, in a fabric consistent with the Brill/Boarstall production site, with one of the most commonly found designs (LH.XXIV/XXV).[75]

A number of decorated and plain tiles in fabric IIIB may be from a more local source. These include examples with a crude finish, thin inlay or stamping, an absence of keying and a sandy

[72] J. Cotter, 'Pottery', in Norton and Mumford, 'Anglo-Saxon Pits and a Medieval Kitchen', p. 196.

[73] Ibid.

[74] L. Haberly, *Mediaeval English Paving Tiles* (1937).

[75] M. Farley, 'The Production of Medieval Decorated Floor-Tiles at Boarstall, with a Note on Boarstall's Late Medieval Map', *Records of Buckinghamshire*, 57 (2017), p. 123.

clay fabric similar to that used for fired clay. Evidence of floor tile production in the form of wasters has been noted at Bagley Wood, located between Oxford and Abingdon.[76]

Floor tiles with stamped decoration (15 fragments, 3,018 g) from the Penn/Chiltern tileries were found in pit fills and other deposits dating to Phases 3a and 3b, apart from one in a late medieval (Phase 2b) pit (2368). The possible decorative designs on a number of these are discussed in the full report. One of the most interesting is the single example of tile LH.CCLIX from layer 1313, which depicts the rebus of Robert Langton, who endowed Queen's College to build the chapel in 1519. Designs LH.CCLIX and LH.CCLV are both linked to the chapel and can be dated to 1519.[77]

A small number of plain tiles with a dark green-black or amber-olive green glaze may have been used in conjunction with the decorated tiles to form plain borders around blocks of decorated tile, though differences in size could indicate some were used as plain paved areas.

Brick

Bricks were concentrated in pit fills and layers of Phases 3a to 4a. They were made in fabrics similar to those used for earlier tiles and included a red-orange coarse sandy fabric akin to IIIB, lighter orange or pink laminated fine sandy clay that appears to continue the group IV fabrics and fine sandy orange-red fabric that is typical of post-medieval brick. The bricks are of sixteenth- to seventeenth-century type measuring 42–60 mm thick and 100–118 mm wide. Some fragments which were very crudely finished could be late medieval in date, though much of the brick had a fairly rough finish. Grey vitrified surfaces were common, which may indicate their use for diaper work in walling. However, it could be a secondary effect as many had extensive burning and sooting especially along the edges with one brick worn to a width of only 80 mm as a result of heat damage. It is probable that much of the brick had been used in the construction of an oven, fireplace or chimney.

Wall Tiles

A group of early post-medieval Anglo-Netherlands tin-glazed wall tiles (eight fragments, 254 g) were recovered from a Phase 3b pit (1085). These were made in cream and pink fine sandy fabrics that are Flemish in origin. They had smooth flat or cut bevelled edges and measured from 14–17 mm thick. They were glazed in a decorative design in blue, green/turquoise and ochre on a white ground. Two pieces had a possible foliate or floriate design. Five fragments had a floral design with fleurs-de-lys in the corners and blue petalled flowers with yellow centres and turquoise leaves. A frame of concentric circles enclosed a scene of a possible building on one tile. This style of tile dates to *c.*1575–1625.

STRUCTURAL STONE by RUTH SHAFFREY

A total of seventeen fragments of stone roofing (5 kg) are made from a mixture of non-shelly and shelly limestone, grey sandstone and slate. The earliest phase from which these were recovered is Phase 2b (late medieval) suggesting that some stone roofing was in use on the earliest college buildings, as do those recovered from Phase 3a (early post-medieval) features (six fragments, 2.6 kg). Fragments found in Phase 4a (later post-medieval) features (five fragments, 1.2 kg) probably relate to the eighteenth-century demolition of earlier buildings and the rebuilding of the college. There is no chronological pattern to the use of different materials. Limestone and sandstone were the roofing materials of choice in Oxford and these stones come from the Stonesfield slate, Pusey flags, Forest Marble and Collyweston slate. Such roofing is a regular occurrence in archaeological assemblages and was certainly in use from the thirteenth century

76 Mellor, 'Synthesis'.

77 Haberly, *Mediaeval English Paving Tiles*, designs CCLIX and CCLVIII.

in Oxford, although Arkell only found documentary evidence for the use of stone roofing from the fourteenth century.[78]

WINDOW GLASS by IAN R. SCOTT

A total of 118 fragments of window glass were recovered. Eight pieces of partly de-vitrified window glass were recovered from pits of Phase 2b, dating from the fourteenth to the mid fifteenth century. These include a fragment of colourless glass with a painted fleur-de-lys from pit 1538 (context 2337) and one sherd with two lines of red-brown paint from layer 1095. Eleven sherds of undiagnostic window glass came from Phase 3a contexts, increasing to 55 sherds from Phase 3b (seventeenth century). However, most of this is unremarkable, with the only pieces of note being four refitting fragments from pit 1873 which are painted with natural-looking stems. The glass is de-vitrified and opaque, suggesting it may be redeposited medieval material.

VESSEL GLASS by IAN R. SCOTT

Some 193 sherds of vessel glass were recovered. The earliest glass comprised a single tiny sphere from phase 1 pit 1657 and two probable vessel bases from pits of Phase 2b; these are partly de-vitrified and their form and date are unclear. Glass from a number of goblets and beakers occurs in contexts of Phase 3a, including sherds from late sixteenth- or early seventeenth-century beaker bases with rigaree decoration, and sherds from Venetian or *façon de Venise* goblets. The vessel glass from the seventeenth century (Phase 3b) includes more beaker sherds and sherds from a small bottle or phial, along with an early wine bottle neck and three examples of wine bottle seals. One of these shows tennis players (Fig. 6.13, no. 1), similar to those of Thomas Wood, licensee of the Salutation, who operated the tennis court behind the tavern.[79] Another, slightly later, shows a plain shield with chevron and fleur-de-lys (Fig. 6.13, no. 2). The third shows a vintner's bush with the initials H.B. above three tuns (Fig. 6.13, no. 3). Humphry Bodicott was the licensee of the Three Tuns between 1639 and 1660.[80] In general, the Phase 4a (early to mid eighteenth-century) glass assemblage is dominated by wine bottles but has fragments from cylindrical phials or pharmaceutical bottles of eighteenth-century date, and some pieces of other flasks or bottles. There is only a little other vessel glass, although there is the upper portion of a sand glass of late-medieval or early post-medieval date, from context 1138. Two wine bottle seals show three tuns with the date 1707, and a bell flanked by the initials E.H. (Fig. 6.13, no. 4), which be for Edward Haynes of the Bell in Magdalen Street, dating from the later seventeenth century.[81]

Catalogue of Illustrated Glass (Fig. 6.13):

1. Wine bottle seal. Tennis players. Missing upper portion with licensee's initials. Dark green glass with opaque weathering. Almost certainly T.W. for Thomas Wood of The Salutation, 1647–63. D: 47 mm. Fill 1013, pit 1085, phase 3b.
2. Wine bottle seal. Plain shield with chevron, single very small fleur-de-lys to each side and above the shield. Dark green glass. D of seal: 40 mm x 37 mm. Fill 1074, pit 1073, SF 11, Phase 3b.

[78] W.J. Arkell, *Oxford Stone* (1947), pp. 129–30.

[79] E.T. Leeds, '17th- and 18th-Century Wine Bottles of Oxford Taverns', *Oxoniensia*, 6 (1941), p. 45, plate ix, 1. See also F. Banks, *Wine Drinking in Oxford 1640–1850*, BAR BS, 257 (1997).

[80] Leeds, '17th- and 18th-Century Wine Bottles', p. 48, plate x, 23.

[81] E.T. Leeds, 'Glass Vessels of the XVI Century and Later from the Site of the Bodleian Extension in Broad Street, Oxford', *Oxoniensia*, 3 (1938), p. 155, plate xii, D 8.

Fig. 6.13 Wine bottle seals.

3. Wine bottle seal. Vintner's bush flanked by initial H.B. above three tuns. Green glass. Licensee Humphry Bodicott, at the Three Tuns, 1639–60. D: 34 mm x 33 mm. Fill 1074, pit 1073, SF 14, Phase 3b.
4. Wine bottle, with squat body form and long tapered neck with cracked off a slightly tooled rim, and horizontal string rim. Seal: bell flanked by initials E.H. Green glass. Possibly for The Bell in Magdalen Street; the licensee may be Edward Haynes. Later seventeenth century? Ht extant: 160 mm. Fill 1036, pit 1050, Phase 4a.

CLAY TOBACCO PIPES by DAVID A. HIGGINS

The excavations produced 978 fragments of pipe, comprising 190 bowl, 752 stem and 36 mouthpiece fragments from 71 different contexts. Most date from the seventeenth to mid eighteenth century, with late eighteenth- and nineteenth-century material being completely absent. Two large pit groups produced nearly half of all the pipes from these excavations. One (from pit 1475) dates from *c.*1630–45 and is probably the best assemblage of this date to have been recovered from anywhere in Oxford (and good groups of this date are rare nationally). The other (from pit 1085) dates from soon after, around 1650–70 and, taken together, they provide a regionally significant benchmark for pipe assemblages of *c.*1630–70 from this region. These two groups are presented in detail in the author's full report on this assemblage, which can be accessed in the OA Library. In addition, selected other pieces from the excavations, such as the marked pipes, are described there.

Smoking was introduced to England towards the end of the sixteenth century but was initially confined to the wealthy because of the very high cost of tobacco at this date. Students at the Oxford colleges would have come from the right social background to be indulging in this new habit but, at the same time, may have been constrained by college rules and the well-known loathing of smoking expressed by James I. None of the very earliest pipes (*c.*1580–1610) were found on these excavations, although these are always very rare and dependant on deposits of the right nature and date surviving.

There are, however, pipes of *c.*1610–40 from the site, including good quality examples. This not only shows that smoking was becoming established in the colleges but also that well-made pipes would have been in demand. This would have encouraged pipemakers to set up business in the town and, by the 1630s, large numbers of pipes were being consumed on this site, as evidenced by what is only a partial sample from pit 1475. The majority of these appear to have been locally made, with the marked pipes of the well-connected pipemaker Miles Higges making up a significant proportion of them. Alongside the local products are high-quality pipes imported from the West Country, showing that the market was sufficiently developed and nuanced for this to happen. The quantity of pipes present also suggests that the students were regularly smoking, whatever the social constraints on this may have been.

Plot specifically mentions the manufacture of tobacco pipes in Oxford using local clays during the 1640s,[82] and so presumably demand was maintained despite the disruption to normal life caused by the Civil War. Pit 1085 produced another large assemblage of pipes, this time straddling the Commonwealth and Restoration periods. Smoking seems to have remained as popular as ever in Oxford throughout this period, despite the rapidly changing and diametrically opposed social values that were sweeping the country.

Smoking had clearly become a well-established part of college life by the end of the seventeenth century, as is shown by a story relating to Henry Aldrich (1648–1710), dean of Christ Church. One undergraduate wagered a friend that he would find the dean smoking at ten o'clock in the morning, but lost his bet because the dean was only filling his pipe at the time.[83] This shows that it was not only the students, but also the tutors that had embraced this habit, thus sustaining the demand for pipes and their acceptance as a part of college life.

The pipes produced in Oxford are generally well made and finished and broadly follow London fashions. Pipemakers in the town appear to have been particularly well-connected and able to accumulate significant wealth, which is unusual. They also seem to have engaged with civic affairs and played a more active role within the town's administration than is typical (pipemakers were more normally relegated to the poorer margins of towns and to have been towards the bottom of the social scale).

82 R. Plot, *The Natural History of Oxfordshire* (Oxford, 1677), pp. 65–6.
83 E.F.A. Suttle, 'Henry Aldrich, Dean of Christ Church', *Oxoniensia*, 5 (1940), p. 135.

One of the most significant findings of this study, however, has been the identification of different fabric types that can be recognised using a hand lens. These are not only related to the changing clay sources used by the local pipemakers but also to the different origins of traded goods, as represented by the imported pipes. Most pipe production centres do not have this diversity of recognisable fabric types, while the information provided by Plot indicates two likely sources that can now be tested against the archaeological evidence. The seventeenth-century pipes from Oxford provide an unparalleled opportunity for an analytical scientific study to examine the exploitation and movement of pipe clays during this period.

Illustrations (Figs. 6.14–6.16):
The illustrated fragments are shown at 1:1 with the die details of the stamped marks shown at twice life size. All the marks are in relief. The die numbers given for the stamped marks relate to the as yet unpublished national catalogue that is being compiled by the author. Burnished surfaces are indicated with light broken lines.

1. Pipe bowl of *c.*1610–30 with a bottered and milled rim and a very diminutive spur. The surface has a fine burnish and the stem bore measures $^{8}/_{64}$". A very early spur form made of a fine fabric but with one large rounded inclusion of white quartz (*c.*0.75 mm) in the broken section. The broken sections have a grey core, suggesting reducing conditions in the kiln during firing – a characteristic often noted on other early pipes, including another early spur form from Oxford Castle.[84] Ctx 2019.
2. Spur bowl with a bottered and half milled rim. The surface is not burnished, and the finishing is quite poor, with a lop-sided bowl form and heavy-handed trimming. Stem bore $^{8}/_{64}$". Ctx 1002.

Items 3–14 are all from deposits within Pit 1475, which was filled *c.*1630–45.

3. Neatly formed and finished spur bowl with a bottered and fully milled rim. Not burnished; stem bore $^{8}/_{64}$". Same basic mould type as Item 4. Ctx 1153.
4. Spur bowl of the same type as Item 3, but with the spur trimmed short and at an unusual angle. Otherwise neat bowl form and finish. Bottered and fully milled rim; stem bore $^{8}/_{64}$". Ctx 1474.
5. Spur bowl with a bottered and fully milled rim. The back of the bowl has a pronounced hump in it and the surface has a fine burnish. Stem bore $^{9}/_{64}$". Context 1151.
6. Spur bowl with a very similar form to Item 3, except that it has a distinctive forward pointing spur. Bottered and fully milled rim. Stem bore unusually large at just over $^{10}/_{64}$". Ctx 1151.
7. Spur bowl with a bottered and fully milled rim; quite a heavy-handed finish. Stem bore $^{9}/_{64}$". Ctx 1143.
8. Heel bowl with a bottered rim but no milling and a finely burnished surface. The style is typically 'West Country' and the fabric is extremely fine without any obvious sandy inclusions, even under a 10x lens. This fabric is in contrast with that used for other bowl forms from the pit and supports this being an imported pipe, most likely from Wiltshire. Stem bore just over $^{7}/_{64}$". Ctx 1151.
9. Heel bowl with a bottered and fully milled rim. Heel trimmed at a slanting angle from side to side. Stem bore $^{9}/_{64}$". Ctx 1143.
10. Heel bowl with a bottered and fully milled rim. Joining stem giving 126 mm surviving. The fabric is very hard fired and so this pipe may have shrunk a little more than others in the group. Stem bore $^{9}/_{64}$". Ctx 1153.

[84] D.A. Higgins, 'Clay Tobacco Pipes from Excavations at Oxford Castle', in Munby, *Oxford Castle*, fig. 7.34, no. 1.

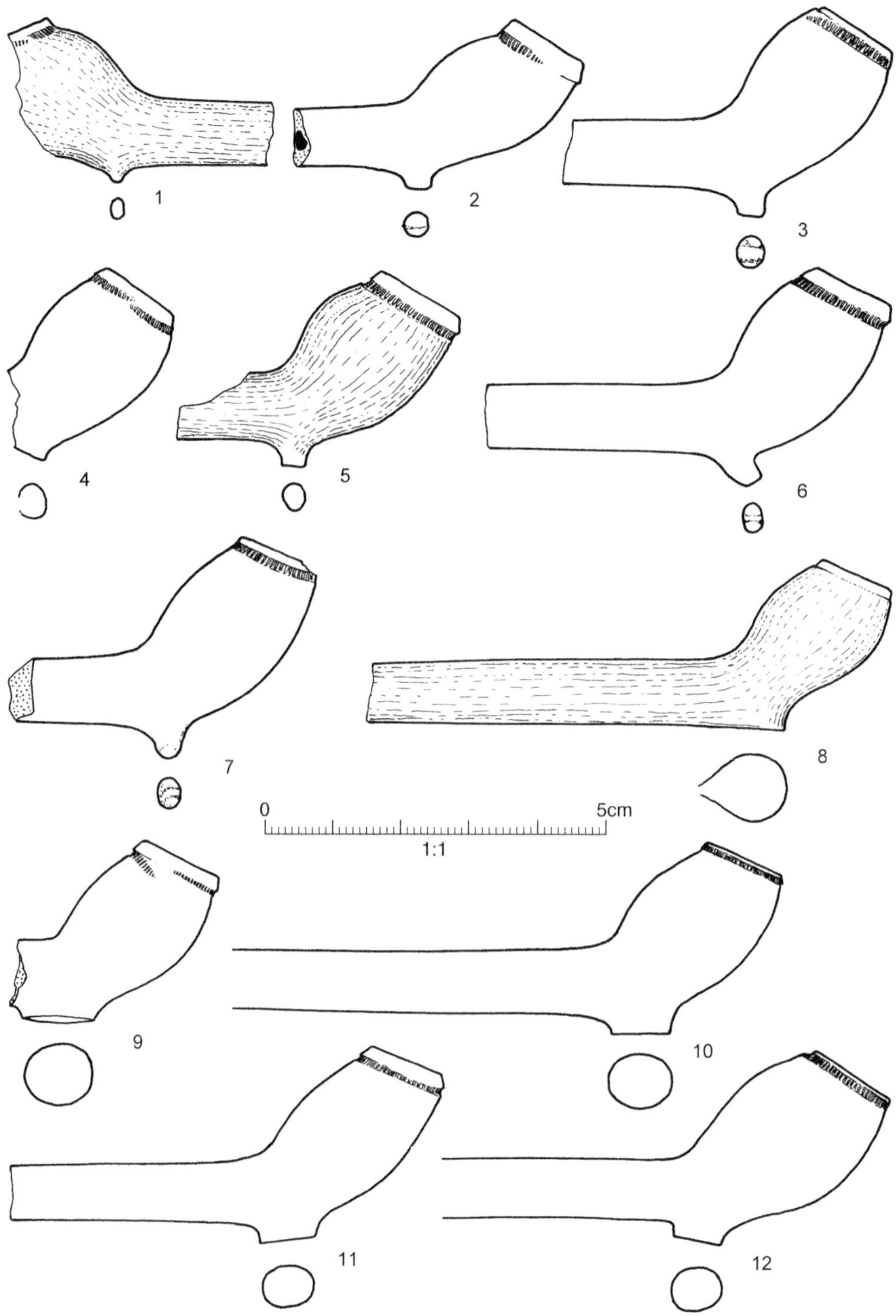

Fig. 6.14 Clay tobacco pipes, nos. 1–12.

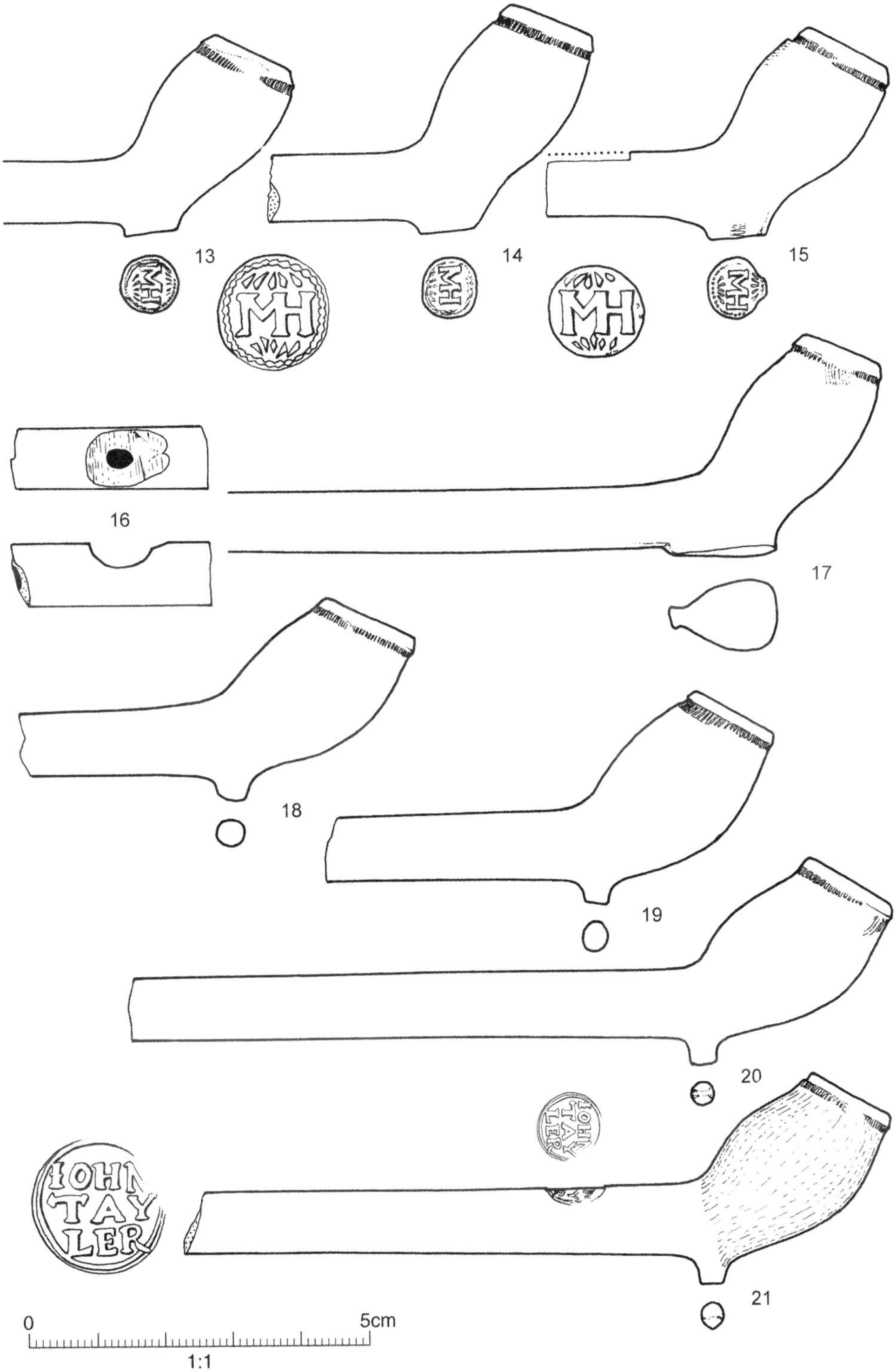

Fig. 6.15 Clay tobacco pipes, nos. 13–21.

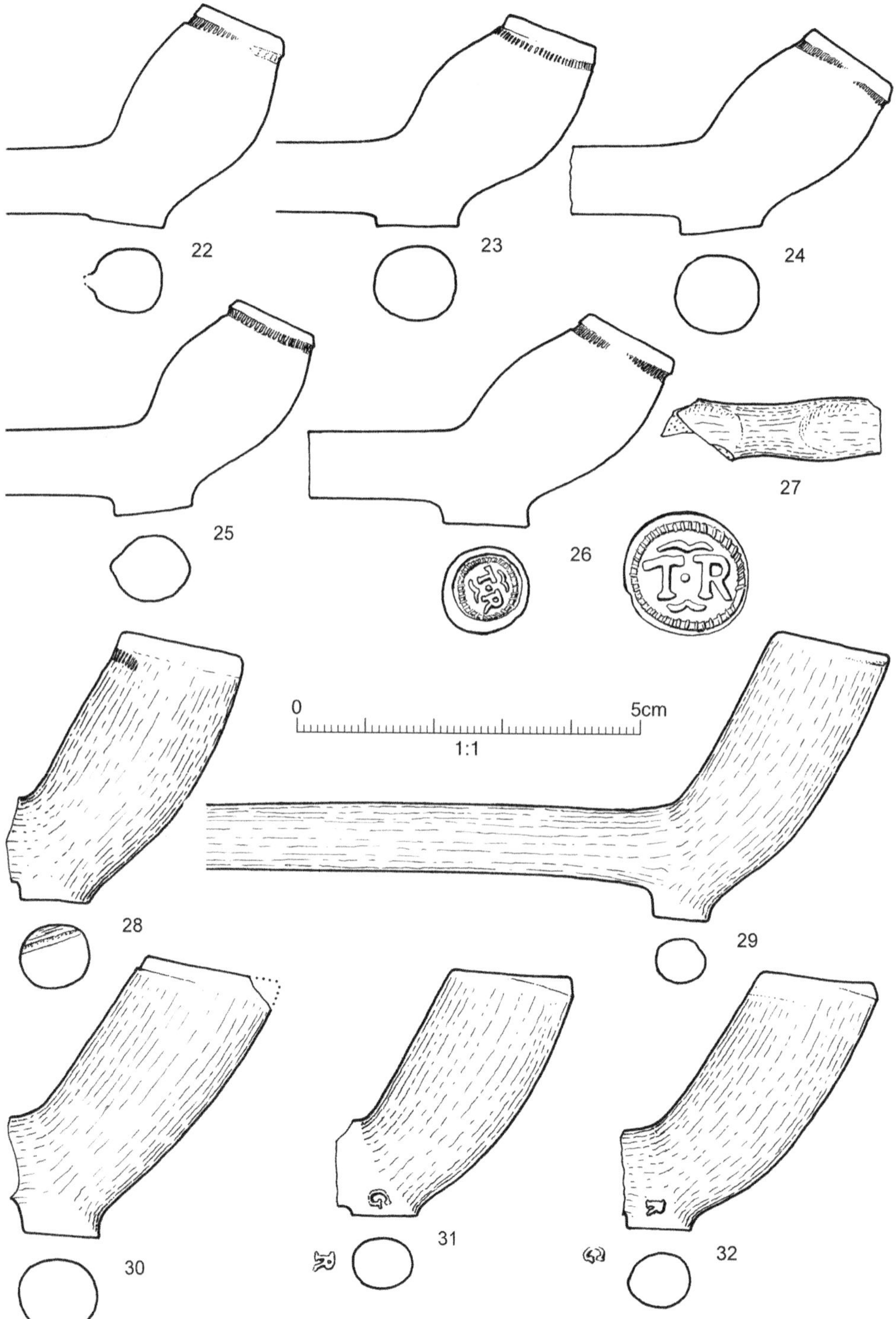

Fig. 6.16 Clay tobacco pipes, nos. 22–32.

11. Heel bowl with a bottered and fully milled rim; quite a slender form. Stem bore $\frac{7}{64}$". Ctx 1143.
12. Heel bowl with a bottered and fully milled rim. Unexpectedly large form for the period, but the bowl quite narrow when viewed 'end on'. Stem bore $\frac{8}{64}$". Ctx 1151.
13 Heel bowl with a bottered and fully milled rim. Heel stamped with a ligatured MH mark (Die 1120) for Miles Higges of Oxford (married 1630; d. 1643). See also Item 15. Stem bore $\frac{9}{64}$". Ctx 1151.
14. Heel bowl with a bottered and fully milled rim. Heel stamped with a ligatured MH mark (Die 339) for Miles Higges. Fabric has a granular fracture and contains very fine sand grains, visible under a 10x lens. Stem bore $\frac{9}{64}$". Ctx 1151.
15. Heel bowl of *c.*1630–50 with a bottered and fully milled rim. Heel stamped with a ligatured MH mark (Die 339) for Miles Higges. A poorly designed heel with clear mould flaws on its right-hand side show that this pipe was made in a different mould to that used for Item 13, despite the similar profile. Stem bore just over $\frac{8}{64}$". Ctx 1044.
16. A stem fragment from a deposit of *c.*1640–60 with a neatly scraped cut into the stem bore made after firing, perhaps to make the pipe into a whistle. Both ends of this fragment are broken and it has a stem bore of just over $\frac{8}{64}$". Ctx 1067.
17. Heel bowl of *c.*1660–80 with a heart-shaped heel, which has been trimmed at a slanting angle when the pipe is viewed end on. The rim is bottered and fully milled. There is 86 mm of surviving stem (freshly broken), with a bore $\frac{8}{64}$". Ctx 1197.

Items 18–27 are all from deposits within pit 1085, which was filled *c.*1650–70.

18. Spur bowl with a bottered and three-quarters milled rim. Stem bore $\frac{8}{64}$". Ctx 1013.
19. Spur bowl with a bottered and fully milled rim. Stem bore $\frac{8}{64}$". Ctx 1013.
20. Spur bowl with a bottered and fully milled rim. Stem bore $\frac{7}{64}$". Ctx 1013.
21. Spur bowl with a bottered and three-quarters milled rim. The bowl has a fine burnish, but the stem is unburnished. There is a previously unrecorded variant of a relief IOHN/TAY/LER stamp for John Tayler of Oxford (d. 1684) across the top of the stem. Stem bore $\frac{8}{64}$". Ctx 1013.
22. Heel bowl with a bottered and fully milled rim. Stem bore just over $\frac{8}{64}$". Ctx 1084.
23. Heel bowl with a bottered and fully milled rim. Stem bore $\frac{8}{64}$". Ctx 1013.
24. Heel bowl with a bottered and fully milled rim. Stem bore $\frac{7}{64}$". Ctx 1013.
25. Heel bowl with a bottered and fully milled rim. There is an accidental cut into one side of the stem surface (pre-firing) at about 62 mm form the bowl, where the stem has later broken. Stem bore just under $\frac{8}{64}$". Ctx 1084.
26. Heel bowl with a bottered and fully milled rim. The pipe has a reduced grey core, just being oxidised on the very outer surface, and it has a good, well-made form with a previously unrecorded TR stamp (Die 2227) on the heel. The mark is boldly cut and can be attributed to Thomas Reeve of Oxford, who is recorded as a pipemaker from at least 1667–1700. Stem bore $\frac{8}{64}$". Ctx 1084.
27. A stem fragment that has been alternately pinched by the pipemaker while still in a plastic state to create a 'barley twist' effect. The stem has also been given an average-quality burnish. The stem bore is distorted from squeezing but would have been about $\frac{8}{64}$". Ctx 1013.
28. Heel bowl of *c.*1680–1720 with a bottered and one-quarter milled rim. The surface has a good-quality burnish; there is no internal bowl cross. The fabric has fine sandy inclusions, visible with a lens. Stem bore $\frac{7}{64}$". Ctx 1044.
29. Heel bowl of *c.*1690–1730 with an internally trimmed and bottered rim but no milling. The surface has a poor-quality burnish; there is no internal bowl cross. The stem survives to 102 mm in length and warps slightly to the smoker's right. The fabric has fine sandy inclusions, visible with a lens. Stem bore just over $\frac{7}{64}$". Ctx 1036.

30. Heel bowl of *c.*1690–1730 with an internally trimmed and bottered rim but no milling. The has a good-quality burnish; there is no internal bowl cross. The fabric has very fine sandy inclusions, visible with a lens. Stem bore just over 6/64". Ctx 1272.
31. Heel bowl of *c.*1690–1750 with an internally trimmed and bottered rim but no milling. The surface has a fine-quality burnish; there is no internal bowl cross. There are a few very fine sandy inclusions in the fabric, visible with a lens. The maker's initials RG for one of the Robert Gadneys of Oxford are relief moulded on the sides of the heel. Stem bore just over 6/64". Ctx 1664.
32. Heel bowl of *c.*1690–1750 with an internally trimmed and bottered rim but no milling. The surface has a fine quality burnish; there is no internal bowl cross. The pipe has fine sandy inclusions in the fabric, visible with a lens. The maker's initials GR are relief moulded on the sides of the heel, probably having been cut the wrong way round from usual for one of the Robert Gadneys. Stem bore just over 6/64". Ctx 1672.

METALWORK by LEIGH ALLEN

A total of 1,315 identifiable metal objects were recovered, comprising 389 copper alloy objects, 911 iron objects and 15 lead objects. Items from the following functional categories have been identified: dress accessories (including 110 pins and 188 lace tags), objects associated with books and writing, household items, horse gear, lock furniture, tools, fixtures and fittings and structural objects (including 816 nails). The notable finds are discussed below by phase.

The earliest metal finds from the site, from Phase 1, include the corroded remains of an iron key for a mounted lock, the fin from a barrel padlock case, the arm of a horseshoe, a small number of knives and a strap-hinge fragment from a door or shutter. Finds from Phase 2a consist of fragments from two horseshoes and a horseshoe nail, a lock bolt from a barrel padlock, and the corroded remains of a possible knife. A large assemblage of metalwork (347 objects) was recovered from later medieval contexts of Phase 2b, although this is mostly due to an increased number of iron nails (195) and dress accessories (including 65 lace tags and 16 pins). Horse gear, lock furniture, knives and fixtures and fittings are again present in this phase, with most of the metalwork coming from pits 1538, 1772, 1920 and 2105. There is a well-preserved handle of a scale tang knife with decorative copper alloy cap and rivets (Fig. 6.17, no. 5); this type of knife dates from the late fourteenth century onwards.[85]

Phase 3a contexts (late fifteenth to sixteenth century) produced the greatest number of metalwork finds from the site (385 objects) and a greater variety of objects compared to previous phases. Book clasps and items associated with writing appear for the first time, there are more items associated with horse harness amongst the horse gear and the tools include a notable number of shears as well as a large number of knives. The numbers of lace tags, pins and nails are also greatly increased. The assemblage from pit 1353 is one of the most interesting, producing two book clasps and a lead writing stylus, buckles, a rowel spur (Fig. 6.17, no. 1) and a number of knife fragments. Fixtures and fittings including chain links and a hooked plate and numerous fragments of lead window came were also recovered from the fills of the pit. The lead writing stylus has a circular section and a rounded point and would have been used for writing on wax tablets. Notable among the knives is a very corroded folding pocket knife and a blade tip fragment. The two large and highly decorated hooked clasps (Fig. 6.18, nos. 6–7) are complete and have an upper hooked plate and a lower rectangular back plate attached by rivets. Hooked clasps would have been attached to leather straps on the covers of books and would have hooked over a catch plate on the opposite cover to keep the book closed. It is possible that the two clasps come from the same book cover.

85 J. Cowgill et al., *Knives and Scabbards*, Excavations in London, 1 (1987), pp. 86–100, fig. 63.

A folded strap-end from context 1022 (Phase 3b) has the same decoration on the upper face and a hooked clasp with identical decoration was recovered from the recent excavations at the Westgate Centre, Oxford.[86] We are perhaps seeing the hand of a local metalworker producing items with a trademark decoration. Book clasps have a wide distribution on both secular and ecclesiastical sites and are found throughout the late-medieval and post-medieval periods. Further examples from the present site came from pit 1053, pit 1319, layer 1032 and layer 1171 (Fig. 6.18, no. 8).

The large assemblage of metalwork (276 objects) from Phase 3b contexts is again dominated by iron nails, pins and lace tags. The remaining identifiable objects comprise book clasps, dress accessories (including an ornate hooked tag decorated with roses), fixtures and fittings, horse gear and knives as seen in previous phases, but in addition there were three slip spoons recovered. The majority of the material came from pits, including a nearly complete spur of sixteenth- and seventeenth-century type from pit 1069 (Fig. 6.17, no. 2), and two further book clasps (Fig. 6.18, nos. 9–10). An unusual find was a length of copper alloy wire mesh from pit 1069, which is made of fine wire that has been looped, coiled and twisted to form a foliage pattern; it is very light and could have been used to decorate head dress, clothing (such as a decorative braid) or possibly a book cover.[87]

Pit 1085 produced two spoons (Fig. 6.17, nos. 3–4) with simple slip top ends to the handles and fig-shaped bowls. The longer handled spoon has a maker's mark 'iI' on the back. Slip top spoons are listed in a grant of college plate to the king in 1642–3 to help fund the fortification of Oxford. The college parted with '36 tankers, 14 two-eared potts, 3 white large bowles, 20 lesser bowles, many saltes, large and small tunnes, guilt bowles, goblets and spoons apostle, slip and guilt'.[88] A third spoon came from pit 1386, which also produced a second lead stylus; this is pointed at one end and flattened at the other. The pointed end was for writing and the flattened possibly for marking out lines or erasing mistakes.[89]

Other than nails, lace tags and pins there are only eighteen identifiable objects from Phase 4a (early to mid eighteenth century), comprising two further book clasps, dress accessories, fixtures and fittings, horse gear, lock furniture and household items. These included the base from a candlestick, decorative tacks from upholstery or furniture, part of a bell, and two thimbles.

Catalogue of Illustrated Metalwork (Figs. 6.17–6.18):

1. Rowel spur, iron, incomplete, L: 120 mm. SF 121, Ctx 1377, Phase 3a.
2. Rowel spur, iron, near complete, L: 95 mm. SF 9, Ctx 1067, Phase 3b.
3. Spoon, copper alloy, incomplete, L: 115 mm. SF 27, Ctx 1083, Phase 3b.
4. Spoon, copper alloy, complete, L: 175 mm. SF 26, Ctx 1084, Phase 3b.
5. Scale tang knife, iron and copper alloy, incomplete, L: 152 mm. SF 199, Ctx 2063, Phase 2b.
6. Decorated book clasp, copper alloy, complete, L: 46 mm. SF 111, Ctx 1365, Phase 3a.
7. Decorated book clasp, copper alloy, complete, L: 40 mm. SF 116, Ctx 1385, Phase 3a.
8. Decorated book clasp, copper alloy, incomplete, L: 56 mm. SF 24, Ctx 1171, Phase 3a.
9. Decorated, hinged book clasp, copper alloy, complete, L: 35 mm. SF 25, Ctx 1151, Phase 3b.
10. Decorated strap-end, copper alloy, complete, L: 31 mm. SF 3, Ctx 1022, Phase 3b.

86 'Westgate Centre, Oxford. Post-Excavation Assessment', unpublished OA report (2019).

87 Egan and Pritchard, *Dress Accessories c.1150–c.1450*, p. 294.

88 J.R. Magrath, *The Queen's College*, vol. 1 (1921), p. 260.

89 M. Biddle, *Artefacts from Medieval Winchester: Part 2, Object and Economy in Medieval Winchester* (1990), pp. 735–8.

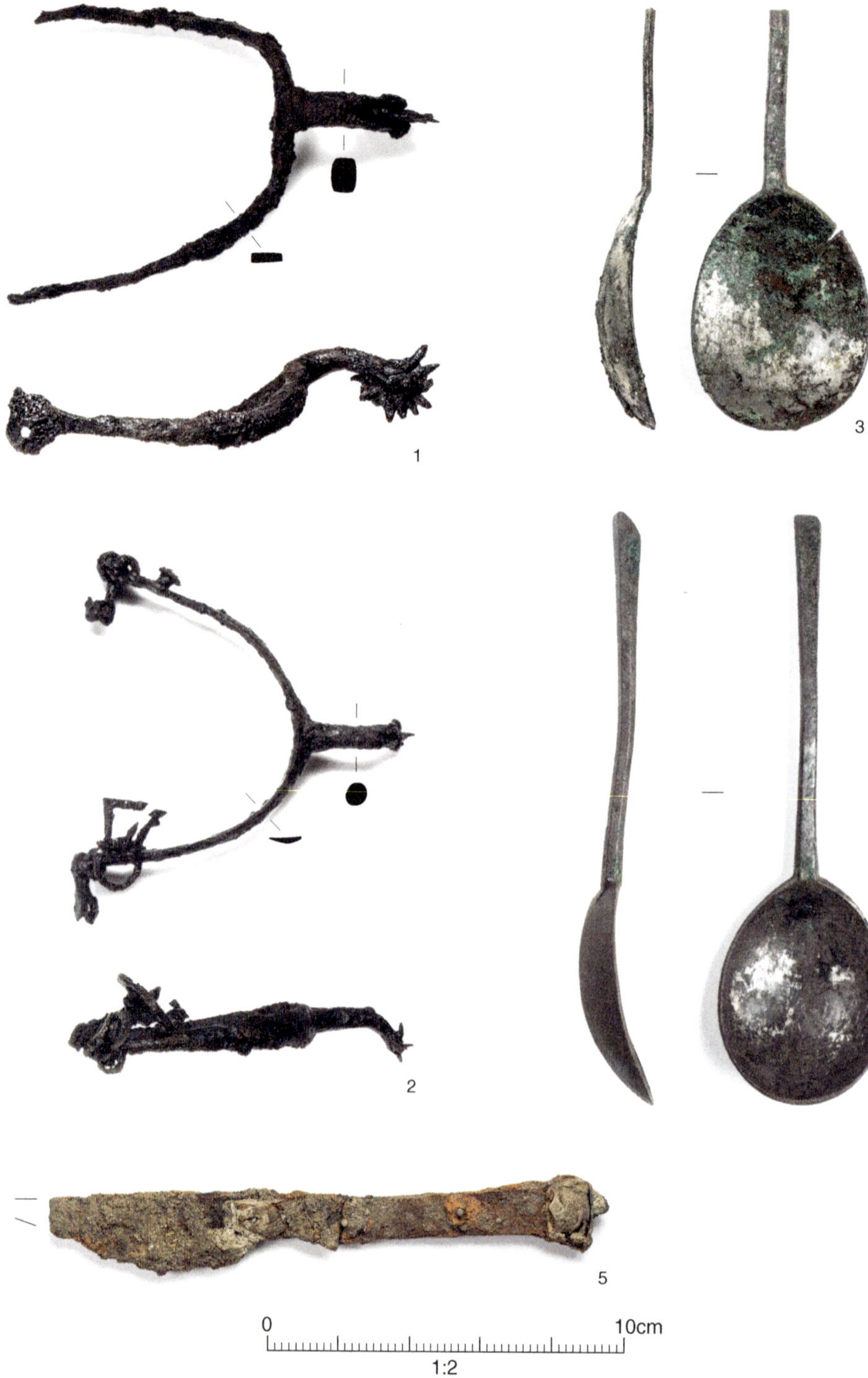

Fig. 6.17 Metalwork, nos. 1–5.

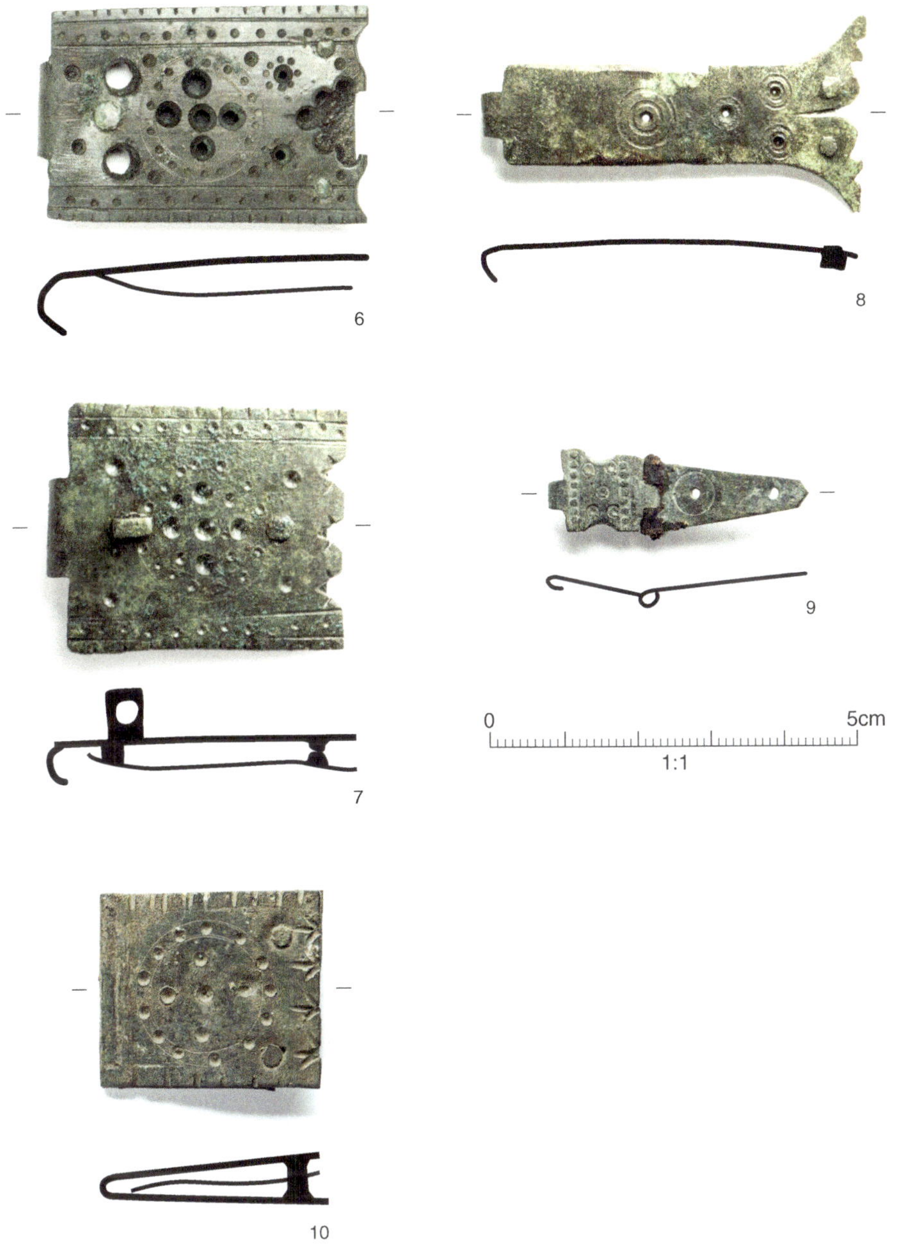

Fig. 6.18 Metalwork, nos. 6–10.

WORKED BONE OBJECTS by LEIGH ALLEN

Sixteen worked bone or antler objects were recovered. The assemblage comprises personal objects, domestic items, components from musical instruments, handles from knives and a writing implement. A number of off-cuts of both bone and antler were also recovered and indicate possible small-scale bone working on the site.

The earliest finds (Phase 1, late ninth to eleventh century) comprise a fragment of bone comb, an awl made from deer antler (used for making holes in soft material such as leather), and three fragments of worked bone and antler. Phase 2b contexts (fourteenth to mid fifteenth century) produced two pieces from scale tang knife handles, but also one of the most interesting objects from the whole site, a curved fragment with an internal groove, possibly a fragment from the rim of a bone spectacle frame. The groove would have held the lens in place. A more complete set of spectacle frames was recovered from Trig Lane, London, dated to the mid fifteenth century.[90] Eight bone items were recovered from Phase 3a contexts (late fifteenth to sixteenth century), comprising a stylus, two musical instrument pegs, two whittle tang handles, a needle and two miscellaneous fragments. The neatly turned bone stylus (Fig. 6.19, no. 3) has a spherical head and a sharp pointed tip. The object has been broken in antiquity and resharpened. It would originally have terminated in a rounded end with a metal point in it. These objects are common finds on scholastic and ecclesiastical sites and were used for writing on wax tablets.

The tuning pegs are of two different forms. The first (Fig. 6.19, no. 2) has a square head, a cylindrical shaft and a perforation for the string at the end of the shaft indicating that this a type of peg was used on an open-framed instrument such as a harp, lyre, lute or fiddle. The second peg (Fig. 6.19, no. 1) also has a square head and cylindrical shaft but the perforation for the string is just below the head indicating that it is from a closed box-like instrument such as a psaltery (a member of the zither family). Large numbers of instrument pegs were recovered from excavations at 79–80 St Aldate's, where it is believed there was a small production site in the fourteenth and fifteenth century.[91]

Two whittle-tang handles and three miscellaneous fragments of worked bone were recovered from Phase 3b contexts (seventeenth century). The most interesting of these is a thin fragment of bone inlay incised with the faint outline of a face. The face has prominent nose and lips and bouffant curled hair reminiscent of the hair styles and wigs of the seventeenth to eighteenth century. An apple corer, a needle case and a miscellaneous worked fragment were recovered from Phase 4a contexts. A highly ornate cosmetic implement combining a tooth-pick or nail-cleaner and an ear scoop was recovered from an unstratified context (Fig. 6.19, no. 4). The object might have been modelled on a hand-thrown harpoon and line with its elongated leaf-shaped point and twisted cable decoration carved into the shank. Cosmetic tools are generally made from metal or wire; bone examples are less common. This example probably dates to the nineteenth century.

Catalogue of Illustrated Bone Objects (Fig. 6.19):

1. Tuning peg, complete, L: 43 mm. SF 51, Ctx 1246, pit 1251, Phase 3a.
2. Tuning peg, complete, L: 49 mm. SF 152, Ctx 1032, Phase 3a.
3. Stylus, complete/modified, L: 61 mm. SF 182, Ctx 1907, pit 1905, Phase 3a.
4. Nail cleaner/scoop, complete, L: 97 mm. Unstratified.

[90] A. MacGregor, *Bone, Antler, Ivory and Horn. The Technology of Skeletal Materials since the Roman Period* (1985), p. 122, fig. 65.

[91] Durham, 'Archaeological Investigations in St Aldate's, Oxford', pp. 163–6, fig. 39.

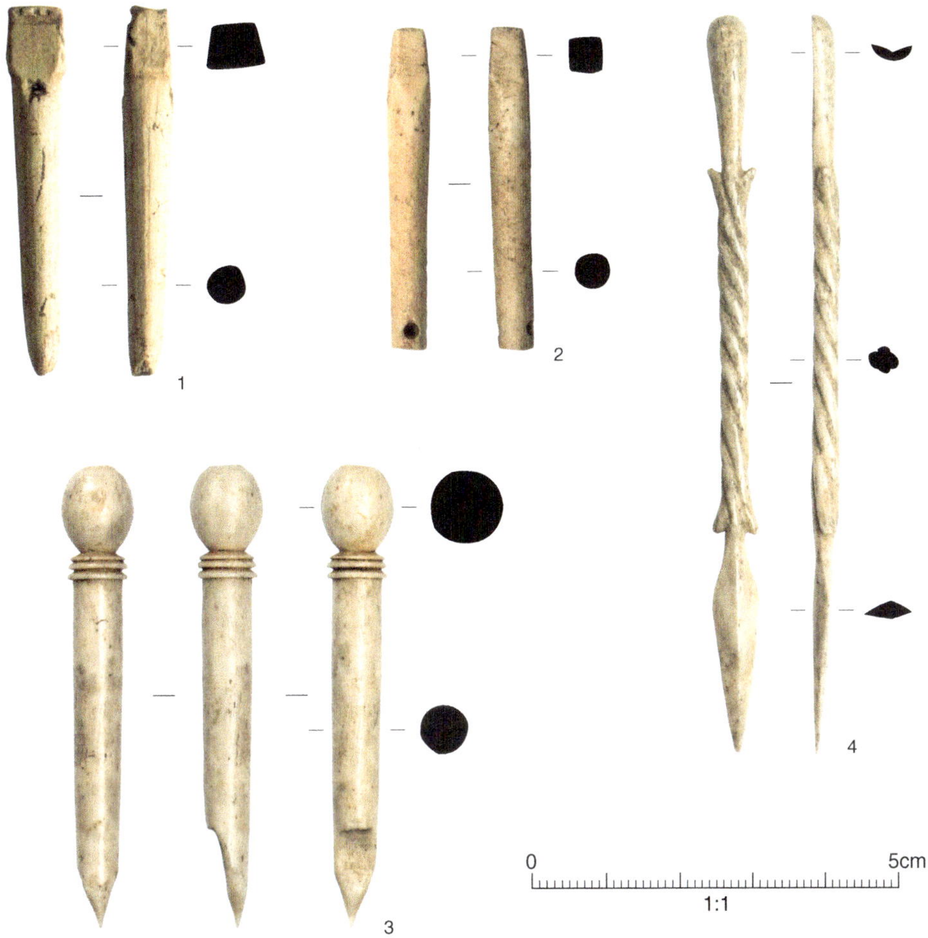

Fig. 6.19 Worked bone.

COINS, TOKENS AND JETONS by IAN R. SCOTT

A total of twenty-four coins, tokens and jetons were recovered during the excavations, and a full catalogue is available from the OA Library. The coins are a (redeposited) Irish farthing of Edward I from the Dublin mint, 1282–5, a counterfeit of an Edward VI base shilling, a sixpence of Elizabeth I (Fig. 6.20, no. 3), a counterfeit farthing of James I, and two farthings of Charles I (including Fig. 6.20, no. 6). The two tokens (Fig. 6.20, nos. 8 and 10) are from Oxford traders. A total of 21 recognisable jetons include an English medieval jeton of Edward I, five late-medieval French or Tournai jetons (including Fig. 6.20, nos. 10 and 14), and seven sixteenth-century Nuremberg 'rose and orb' jetons (including Fig. 6.20, no. 21).

Catalogue of Illustrated Coins, Tokens and Jetons (Fig. 6.20):

3. Sixpence, Elizabeth I, dated 1569. Silver. Bust facing L with rose behind. Bust very worn. Legend: ELIZABETH:D:G ANG:FR:ET:HIB:REGINA // Shield with Royal Arms on cross fourchée, date 1569 above. Legend: POSVI:DEV:ADIVTOREM:MEV. Mint mark worn, possibly crown. D: 26mm. Ctx 1012, wall cut 1388, SF 233, Phase 3a.

Fig. 6.20 Coins and jetons.

6. Farthing, Charles I, Rose type 3. Cu alloy. Crossed sceptres through double arched crown; Legend: CAROLVS D.G. MAG BRI, mullet mint mark after BRI // Double arched crown over Rose; Legend: FRAN:ET:HIB:REX, mint mark mullet after REX. 1637–44. D: 14 x 13 mm. Ctx 1182, pit 2196, SF 38, Phase 3b.
7. Farthing token issued by Thomas Dennis, mercer. Cu alloy. Legend: (mullet) THOMAS. DENNIS.AT.THE around three kings standing facing. // Legend: (mullet) .3.KINGS. IN.OXON.1652, around cable twist inner circle containing .D. over T (rosette) A. Thomas Dennis (*c*.1602–*c*.1663) served as mayor of Oxford in 1642–3 and again in 1657–8. D: 15mm. Ctx 1188, pit 1187, SF 32, Phase 4a.
8. Farthing token issued by Humphry Bodicott, vintner. Concreted to pipe stem (see clay tobacco pipe report). Cu alloy. Legend: HVMPHRY.BODICOTT. around a vintner's bush // Legend: VINTENER.IN.OXON. around a cable twist circle containing three tuns. It is uncertain whether the token has mullet or anchor privy marks. The tokens issued by Bodicott are undated but were probably issued from *c*.1652 onwards, when it seems that the city council agreed to issue farthing tokens, and could have circulated as late as 1672.[92] D: 15 mm; Ctx 1013, pit 1085, Phase 3b.
10. Jeton, probably made in Tournai. Later fourteenth century or fifteenth century. Cu alloy. Shield with beaded edge and three lis within a beaded circle; Legend: TOVRNAI TOVRNAI TOVRN . . // Triple strand cross fleury with lis in the quarters within a crudely executed quatrilobe. Letters A and V in alternate spandrels. D: 28 mm. Ctx 1242, pit 1386, SF 49, Phase 3b.
14. Tournai 'Moor's head' jeton, *c*.1350 to sixteenth century. Cu alloy. Bare head facing right. Legend: + AVE MARIA:GRACIA:PL[E? Double crosslet stops. // Bowed cross fleury with lis in centre. Lettering not legible, badly corroded. D: 21 mm. Ctx 1003, SF 52, Phase 3b.
21. Nuremberg 'rose and orb' jeton, Hans Schultes. Late sixteenth century. Cu alloy. Three crowns and lis around a rosette, with groups of three annulets between lis. Legend: HANS[SCH] VLTES.NOR. Triangle stop. // Orb with a trilobe, pellets in spandrels. The orb has been partly overstamped with an R. Illiterate legend: A V O B A V O . . B O V . A O L B. D: 25.5 mm. Ctx 1078, SF 10, Phase 3a.

IRON SLAG AND RELATED HIGH-TEMPERATURE DEBRIS by LYNNE KEYS

Almost 13.6 kg of slag and related debris was recovered by hand during excavation and from soil samples. For this report the assemblage was examined by eye and categorised on the basis of morphology and magnetic properties. Tables giving full quantifications, and statistical data for the smithing hearth bottoms, are available from the OA Library. Smelting slag – in small quantities – is present in deposits (mainly in pits) from Phase 1 into the medieval period, as is a small amount of smithing slag. The smelting slag is that produced by tapping slag from the furnace to enable easier extraction of the rough bloom of iron. The largest groups of material came from Phase 1 pits 1131 and 1657. Pit 1131 contained 1.02 kg of slag, most of this weight from one smithing hearth bottom. Although the slag group may be the product of smithing, containing as it does some very occasional smithing flakes, there is one fragment of tap slag (from smelting) and some vitrified hearth lining. Deposits in cellar pit 1657 (1.03 kg) consist of undiagnostic slag and small amounts of tap slag and slag dribbles. One smithing hearth bottom (representing smithing) was recovered, along with hammerscale flake and large spheres.

The assemblage is significant because it indicates both smelting and smithing took place in this part of Oxford in the late Anglo-Saxon/early Saxo-Norman period (Phase 1). The same can

[92] E.T. Leeds, 'Oxford Tradesmen's Tokens', in H.E. Salter (ed.), *Surveys and Tokens*, OHS, 75 (1923), p. 359.

be said of Phase 2a (the early medieval period) and possibly 2b. This activity, however, does not seem to have taken place on the site.

WORKED STONE OBJECTS by RUTH SHAFFREY

Four objects can be classified as hones or whetstones. One of these, a sandstone chunk with sharpening grooves and a worn face, is from a Anglo-Saxon context (1607, fill of cellar pit 1535). A second example is an irregular fragment of an elongate slate whetstone, perhaps a broken sliver from an originally much larger example. This was found in a Phase 1 fill of ditch 1851 (1854). These tools are likely to represent domestic activity. One hone was found in a post-medieval context: Phase 3a fill of pit 1065 (1066). This example is an unmodified quartzite pebble with some use wear. The fourth example is a neat small perforated slate whetstone that has broken lengthwise (Fig. 6.21, no. 2). This is from a Phase 2b context (1116) but is of a type that is likely to have been a personal belonging.

A fifth piece of worked stone is a slate with three cut edges (SF 59). This was found in the post-medieval (Phase 4a) fill of pit 1087 (1088). The shape of the edges is reminiscent of writing slates, but the third edge is cut at an angle and it seems more likely that this was intended as a piece of inlay. It has subsequently been used as a drawing slate and has a lightly incised pattern on both sides; the pattern on one side is smaller and simpler than that on the other side but otherwise very similar. The pattern fills an approximately square area and has a continuous cruciform pattern overlain by a square with heart-shaped projections in each corner (Fig. 6.21, no. 1). The pattern seems likely to have been a doodle and is reminiscent of the patterns seen on medieval floor tiles. An exact match could not be found on the Ashmolean database (of 2,848 examples), but it has similarities to a tile pattern found at Great Bedwyn (Wiltshire), which also has a four-part overlapping line but angled to the corners. The central part of this design (the part seen inside the square on our tile) does appear, however, on a number of tiles from Oxford: at Queen's College (at the site of the antechapel), in the cathedral, at Osney and at Rewley (Ashmolean reference numbers O063, O016, O168 and O170 respectively). The doodle on this tile may therefore be a copy of patterns seen on local floor tiles. Inscribed slates are uncommon and no parallel for this pattern could be found on slate, but other graffiti items show that the ability to recognise slate as an easy material to draw on had been recognised long before this piece was deposited in Oxford. A piece inscribed with a cobweb design, for example, was found at the Coventry free school in a context dated to 1545–58.[93]

Fragments from two stone mortars suggest kitchen activity in the form of food preparation. One of these is a piece of a heavy-bottomed Purbeck marble mortar (SF 46, unstratified). The other is a piece of a heavily smoothed vertical-sided mortar of Purbeck limestone (pit fill 2996). The surviving fragment retains one simple rib with spout set into the rim. The surviving circumference suggests that this mortar had two ribs (rather than four). Mortars are not common finds in medieval or post-medieval Oxford. This example dates to 1650–1700 (Phase 3b), during which it was discarded, so that its use can be related to earlier periods. Other examples from Oxford are of comparable date and lithologies.[94] However, Purbeck marble mortars tend to be of medieval date (thirteenth to fourteenth centuries), as at Southampton and Winchester,[95] and it is therefore likely that these are residual.

93 C. Woodfield, 'Finds from the Free Grammar School at the Whitefriars, Coventry, *c.*1545–*c.*1557/58', *Post-Medieval Archaeology*, 15 (1981), p. 106.

94 M. Mellow and P. Powell, 'Stone Objects', in C. Halpin, 'Late Saxon Evidence and Excavations of Hinxey Hall, Queen Street, Oxford', *Oxoniensia*, 48 (1983), p. 67; R. Shaffrey, 'Worked Stone', in K. Moon and R. Bashford, 'St Cross College Western Quad, Oxford: Archaeological Evaluation Report', unpublished OA report (2016), https://library.oxfordarchaeology.com/3091/.

95 M. Biddle and D. Smith, 'Mortars', in Biddle, *Object and Economy in Medieval Winchester*, pp. 890–908; R. Shaffrey and C. Allum, 'Worked Stone', in R. Brown and A. Hardy, *Trade and Prosperity, War and Poverty.*

Fig. 6.21 Worked stone objects.

Catalogue of Illustrated Stone Objects (Fig. 6.21):

1. Incised decorated slate. Slate. Palette with three cut edges; all are straight rather than bevelled or chamfered. Fine scratch marks on both faces and incised patterns on both faces of a rolling cruciform shape. The fourth edge is broken. Surviving fragment 95 x 64 mm high x 5 mm. 35 g. SF 59. Ctx 1088, pit 1087, Phase 4a.
2. Half whetstone. Slate or similar. Broken lengthwise with biconical perforation of 3 mm at narrowest point. 53 x 8 mm thick x >6 mm wide. 5 g. Ctx 1116, Phase 2b.

MAMMAL AND BIRD BONE by LEE G. BRODERICK

The medieval zooarchaeology of Oxford is relatively well studied in comparison with other British cities but the Anglo-Saxon and early post-Conquest periods are less well known.[96] As such, this assemblage is of considerable local importance. This study has focused on the animal bone from the pre-college deposits of the Anglo-Saxon and earlier medieval periods (Phases 1–2a; Table 6.4), and the full report is available from the OA Library. The material from Phases 2b–4 has been studied by Thomas Fowler as part of a post-graduate research project at the University of Nottingham, and will be published separately.

Phase 1 Cellar Pits (Late Ninth to Eleventh Century)

The greater part of this assemblage derived from three different cellar pits, which were deliberately backfilled. By far the most common species, by NISP (Number of Identified SPecimens), was caprine (sheep *Ovis aries* and/or goat *Capra hircus*). Among 260 caprine specimens it was possible to identify thirty-seven as being sheep, with no goat specimens identified (Table 6.4). Around half as many domestic cattle (*Bos taurus taurus*) specimens were present compared with caprine, and a little more than half as many pig (*Sus scrofa domesticus*) as domestic cattle. Domestic fowl (*Gallus gallus*) also made a substantial contribution to the assemblage. A small amount of Anglo-Saxon material has been found in previous excavations at Queen's College and the interpretations made then are compatible with this larger dataset.[97]

Three foetal/neonatal caprine bones and one pig were identified amongst this material. The former is important, as it demonstrates that caprines were being kept and bred on the site. The pig specimen demonstrates the same fact but is less significant as it is known that the keeping of pigs in urban areas continued through the medieval period.

Although not present in the cellar-pit assemblage, dogs (*Canis familiaris*) were present on the site at the time, with a total of 144 specimens having been gnawed by canids. At over 10 per cent of NSP, this proportion is in keeping with the generally high proportion of canid gnawing of specimens on medieval urban sites. The canid gnawed bones included specimens of the three domestic mammals already mentioned as well as horse (*Equus caballus*) and goose (*Anser anser*). There were also two specimens from this period – a caprine femur and a domestic fowl coracoid – gnawed by rodents and one – a domestic fowl tibiotarsus – gnawed by a felid, suggesting that domestic cats (*Felis cattus*) were also present.

The frequency of observed butchery marks in the assemblage was even greater than for gnawing, with 147 specimens from this phase having butchery marks, although notably there were no butchery marks among the fourteen horse specimens. Hippophagy was the subject of a papal edict

An Archaeological and Historical Investigation into Southampton's French Quarter, OA Monograph, 15 (2011), pp. 207–14.

[96] e.g. B. Wilson, 'Mortality Patterns, Animal Husbandry and Marketing in and Around Medieval and Post-Medieval Oxford', in A.R. Hall and H.K. Kenward, *Urban-Rural Connexions: Perspectives from Environmental Archaeology* (Oxford, 1994), pp. 103–16.

[97] L. Strid, 'Animal Bone', in Norton and Mumford, 'Anglo-Saxon Pits and a Medieval Kitchen at The Queen's College, Oxford', pp. 203–10.

in Anglo-Saxon Britain and so began a taboo that continues to this day.[98] Limited evidence for possible industrial activity comes from cutmarks on cattle and sheep horncores and phalanges.

In total, five specimens of house sparrow were present in the environmental sample from this pit, as well as bones from two other commensal species, the European robin (*Erithacus rubelcula*) and the house mouse (*Mus musculus*). Bones from the common frog (*Rana temporaria*) in this sample and of the common toad (*Bufo bufo*) from cellar pit 1657 probably reflect the damp environment present in these features. Finally, a woodcock (*Scolopax rusticola*) bone from pit 1657, like the two red deer (*Cervus elaphus*) specimens from cellar pit 1527, demonstrate that the inhabitants had access to wild game, either through hunting or through trade. Previous excavations at Queen's College have also found roe deer (*Capreolus capreolus*) specimens from this period.[99]

Other Phase 1 Features (Late Ninth to Eleventh Century)

Aside from the cellar pits, the Phase 1 assemblage was derived from pits unassociated with other features, as is common at medieval urban edge sites.[100] Species proportions were broadly similar to those recovered from the cellar pits, however. A small assemblage from late Saxo-Norman Queen's College has been studied previously and this data is not inconsistent, although that assemblage has a more equal distribution of domestic cattle and caprine specimens.[101] In all, twenty-seven specimens showed evidence of having been gnawed by canids. Of the chopmarks recorded, two were through the base of caprine horncores, adding to the evidence for possible horn-working in the vicinity.

Phase 2a (Twelfth to Thirteenth Century)

The majority of the zooarchaeological assemblage derives from pits, as in the previous phase. The number of specimens studied from this phase was similar to that from the cellar pits and the proportions of species were again broadly similar. Pathologies on cattle bones suggest a long life of use as traction animals and indicate that some of the meat consumed on the site was from less than prime animals. Lesions present on ten caprine specimens are the result of infection.[102] Two horse specimens from pit 1397 had extensive pathological damage and the horse (or horses) must have been lame for some time. In all, two of the seventeen horse specimens from this phase had been gnawed by canids and five had been butchered (one specimen suffering both taphonomic processes). The butchery marks, chops and cuts, are all likely to have been caused during primary butchery. Cutmarks on a cattle metatarsal are consistent with skinning and suggest processing for leather. Four caprine metapodials had the same marks, and nine sheep horncores had been chopped through at the base; together with two goat horncores from this phase, this provides increased evidence for hornworking in the area.

The incidence of gnawing in the assemblage from this phase was greatly reduced, with just forty-nine specimens showing this type of damage. Of these, two domestic fowl specimens had been gnawed by a cat and a rodent. The remaining forty-seven specimens had all been gnawed by canids and included domestic cattle, caprine, pig and horse.

The environmental samples from this period demonstrated that house mouse was still present on the site and another commensal species – European starling (cf. *Sturnus vulgaris*) – was also present.

98 K. Poole, 'Horses for Courses? Religious Change and Dietary Shifts In Anglo-Saxon England', *Oxford Journal of Archaeology*, 32 (2013), pp. 319–33.

99 L. Strid, in Norton and Mumford, 'Anglo-Saxon Pits and a Medieval Kitchen at The Queen's College, Oxford', pp. 203–10.

100 L.G. Broderick, 'Social Taphonomy: Agency, Biography and Chaîne Opératoire of Cattle Bones in a Mediaeval European City', York University Ph.D. thesis (2017).

101 A. Bates, 'Animal Bone', in Teague et al., 'Nun's Garden', pp. 177–8.

102 Bartosiewicz and Gál, *Shuffling Nags, Lame Ducks.*

Table 6.4. NISP (Number of Identified SPecimens) and NSP (Number of SPecimens) figures for the hand collected and sieved components of the faunal assemblage.

	Phase			
	1	**2a**	**1 (sieved)**	**2a (sieved)**
Domestic cattle	185	179	1	
Domestic cattle?	5	3		
Caprine	339	240	13	
Caprine?	4	2		
Sheep	54	46		
Goat		2		
Pig	103	62	10	
Pig?			1	
Horse	25	17	1	
Dog	1	2		
Dog?		1		
Cat	3	2	2	
Red deer	1	1		
Red deer?	1			
Small rodent			3	
Mouse			1	2
House mouse			1	3
Micro mammal				1
Small mammal	3	5	4	15
Medium mammal	429	280	13	6
Large mammal	534	471	10	
Total mammal	1687	1313	60	27
Bird	2	26	14	5
Swan?		1		
Greylag/domestic goose	8	25		2
Domestic duck/mallard		4		
Domestic fowl	50	35	3	2
Domestic fowl?	1			
Pigeon?		1		
Woodcock	1	2		
Small passerine			1	
European starling?		1		
Starling/thrush				1
European robin			1	
House sparrow			4	
House sparrow?			1	
Total bird	62	95	24	10

	Phase			
	1	2a	1 (sieved)	2a (sieved)
Amphibian			16	
Frog/toad			5	
Common frog			3	
Common toad	1			
Total amphibian	1		24	
Total NISP	1750	1408	108	37
Total NSP	2085	1679	108	37

FISH BONE by REBECCA NICHOLSON

Fish remains were recovered from each of the main phases, dating from the late Anglo-Saxon period (Phase 1) to the modern period, but for this study only those bones dated from Phase 1 to 3a inclusive have been recorded, since later features generally contained large amounts of residual material. The richest assemblages came from deposits dated to the period of college construction and early use (Phase 2b), particularly from samples taken from the fills of pits 1558 and 1772 which seem to contain waste from college kitchens.

The Assemblage

Table 6.5 provides a summary of the numbers of identified specimens present (NISP) for each species in each of the phases. From the identified bones and scales, at least thirty-six species of fish taxa were recorded, twenty-two marine/estuarine, two migratory and twelve freshwater species. Of the marine fish the most common were cod, whiting, haddock, herring, plaice, gurnards, sea bream(s) and thornback ray. Species identified from a small number of bones include pollack, hake, torsk, ling, conger eel, flounder, sole and john dory. The migratory taxa include eel and salmon. Exclusively freshwater fish include pike, perch and several cyprinids including roach, rudd, chub, dace, tench, gudgeon and minnow as well as nine-spined stickleback and, probably, barbel.

Phase 1 (Late Ninth to Eleventh Century) The majority of fish remains came from samples taken from the fills of cellar pits 1657 and 1718. Typically for deposits of this date in Oxford,[103] the assemblage comprised bones from herring and eel as well as smaller flatfish including plaice and small and tiny cyprinids. As an oily fish, the herrings would have been preserved by salting, while both the eels and the cyprinids would have been available in the Rivers Thames and Cherwell, although it is possible that the eels were also imported as salted fish, which would extend their palatability. The plaice (only identified from pit fill 2182) may also have been preserved: only caudal vertebrae, a cleithrum and an anal pterygiophore were present.

Sample 22 from fill 1717 (cellar pit 1718) included over 100 tiny and fragile bones of small and tiny cyprinids such as gudgeon, roach and minnow. Although these fish are not now considered edible, they seem to have been widely eaten in the past (see below). The excellent condition of these bones makes it extremely unlikely that they derive from latrine waste, fish guts or bird pellets and as the site was not likely to have been inundated by river flooding this source of small fish can also be excluded. The tiny fish may, however, have been discarded as unsuitable

[103] For example, R. Nicholson, 'Fish Remains from Excavations at Oxford Castle', in Munby, *Oxford Castle*, pp. 391–4.

Table 6.5. Fish bone identifications: number of identified bones (excludes most ribs, rays and scales).

		Phase				
Taxa		**1**	**2a**	**2b**	**3a**	**Total**
Elasmobranchii	Elasmobranch			1		1
Pleurotremata	Sharks		1			1
Rajidae	Rays			3	2	5
Raja clavata	Thornback ray		4	1	12	17
Anguilla anguilla	Eel	10	27	303	520	890
Conger conger	Conger eel		3	33	2	38
Clupeidae	Herring family		12	135	1	148
Clupea harengus	Herring family	31	372	436	229	1068
Sardina pilchardus	Pilchard		1			1
Salmonidae	Salmon family		1	22	2	25
Salmo salar	Salmon family			4		4
Salmo trutta	Trout			1		1
Esox lucius	Pike	2	7	185	20	214
Cyprinidae	Cyprinid (carp family)	127	12	303	150	592
Rutilus rutilus	Roach		1	7	4	12
Scardinius erythrophthalmus	Rudd			3		3
Squalius cephalus	Chub			10		10
Leuciscus leuciscus	Dace			1		1
Squalius/Leuciscus sp.		1				1
Phoxinus phoxinus	Minnow			1		1
Gobio gobio	Gudgeon		1			1
Tinca tinca	Tench			2	2	4
?*Barbus barbus*	Barbel			8		8
Gadidae	Gadid (Cod family)		112	210	37	359
Gadus morhua	Cod		11	63	26	100
Gadus/Pollachius			1	2		3
Pollachius pollachius	Pollack		3	2		5
Pollachius sp.	Pollack/saithe		1			1
Merlangius merlangus	Whiting		22	315	66	403
Merlangius/Gadus morhua					1	1
Melanogrammus aeglefinus	Haddock		4	205	18	227
Molva molva	Ling			4	2	6
Brosme brosme	Torsk		1			1
Merluccius merluccius	Hake		2	19	2	23
Zeus faber	John dory			11		11
Gasterostidae	Sticklebacks			2		2
Pungitius pungitius	3-spined stickleback		1			1

Taxa		Phase 1	Phase 2a	Phase 2b	Phase 3a	Total
Triglidae	Gurnards		27	83	37	147
Eutrigla gurnardus	Grey gurnard		1	9	4	14
Aspitrigla gurnardus	Red gurnard		1	3		4
Trigla lucerna	Tub gurnard			50	7	57
Trigla sp.				5	25	30
Percidae	Perch family			1		1
Perca fluviatilis	Perch	1	2	53	5	61
Dicentrarchas labrax	Bass			3		3
Sparidae	Sea breams		2	9	1	12
Pagellus bogaraveo	Red sea bream		3	13		16
Pagellus/Sparus sp.				21		21
Scomber scombrus	Mackerel		1	13		14
Scomber sp.				1		1
flatfish indet			1	20	3	24
Scopthalmidae	Turbot/brill/megrim			1		1
Scopthalmidae/Bothidae	Left-eyed flatfish			2		2
Pleuronectidae	Right-eyed flatfish		1	373	20	394
Platychthys flesus	Flounder			9		9
Pleuronectes platessa	Plaice	3	1	27	1	32
Pleuronectes/Plathychthys				53		53
Solea solea	Sole			38	1	39
Unidentified		2	2	49	7	60
Total		177	643	3129	1207	5156

for consumption, perhaps after cleaning out material accidentally caught in nets or traps, or collected for use as bait.

Phase 2a (Twelfth to Thirteenth Century) The only fish remains from deposits securely dated to the early medieval period came from pit fill 1335 in pit 1334. Clupeids dominate the assemblage by number of bones, notably herring but including at least one vertebra from sardine, but smaller gadids including haddock and whiting, eel and gurnard are also common. Several bones from mature cod and plaice and small pike were also identified as well as a tiny spine from nine-spined stickleback and a gudgeon pharyngeal. It is likely that the herring and gadids and probably also the plaice were sold as preserved fish while the juvenile pike (picarel), gudgeon and stickleback would have been caught locally, the last probably as an unintended by-product of a freshwater fishery, caught in a fine net. Also present were a single fragment of mackerel vertebra, and a thornback ray dermal denticle. Mackerel were typically sold fresh, but as an oily fish they spoil rapidly so it is possible that this fish was salted.

Phase 2b (Fourteenth to Mid Fifteenth Century) The majority of fish remains came from samples taken of pit fills likely to represent waste from the college kitchens and these are compositionally fairly similar, including a diverse assemblage numerically dominated by herring, smaller gadids (especially whiting and haddock), flatfish (particularly plaice), gurnards, small cyprinids and eel. Augmenting these fish were smaller quantities of sea bream, salmon and/or trout, skates/rays, perch, larger cyprinids, pike, mackerel, sea bass and john dory. Large red sea bream would have been an expensive fish; this species has been identified in several samples and together with large conger eel and john dory is an indicator of affluence relating to the early years of Queen's College. The salmon would also have been a luxury purchase. Freshwater fish include pike, perch and cyprinid, none of them especially large and some of the cyprinid bones including roach come from small individuals.

Gadids and related species include occasional hake, pollack and torsk as well as cod and whiting. The presence of several cranial bones from large cod indicates that not all large gadids were sold as dried stockfish or similar product, since the head would have been removed during the preparation of these widely traded fish. Of the small and medium-sized gadids, mainly whiting, both cranial and post-cranial bones were present again indicating the procurement of entire and probably fresh fish. Of the two hake bones, both caudal vertebrae, one was chopped through in a manner seen today when hake is cut into steaks. Torsk is a fish found in northern waters and is likely to have been dried. A large conger eel dentary also demonstrates that whole fish were purchased. Gurnards were common and included both grey gurnard, red gurnard and tub gurnard; again, both cranial and post-cranial bones indicate entire fish. Herring, eel and small flatfish bones were present but were not abundant.

Phase 3a (Late Fifteenth to Sixteenth Century) The fish identified from the early post-medieval period are generally of similar types to those from the preceding phase but some of the more expensive fish such as sea bream and salmon are absent or infrequent. Whether this is a true reflection of a change in circumstance is, however, uncertain since the total number of identified fish bones is significantly less. Eel are more frequent than in the preceding phases, but while this could indicate the consumption of cheaper fish, sourced locally, eel have large numbers of vertebrae so the presence of a relatively small number of additional fish could skew the pattern in favour of this species and in fact the majority of eel bones come from a single sample from pit fill 1374. There are also occasional bones from more expensive fish[104] such as large salmonid (salmon or sea trout), as well as fairly large pike and cyprinids and conger eel in addition to the herrings, gadids, smaller flatfish, rays and gurnards.

Discussion

The fish remains reflect the development of the site from extra-mural settlement to college. The preponderance of eel, herring, flatfishes and small cyprinids in Phase 1 is typical of contemporary sites in Oxford[105] and indicates the consumption of preserved fish supplemented with small-scale fishing in the Thames and the Cherwell or their tributaries. The collection of tiny bones in pit 1718 is interesting and indicates that even tiny fish were brought home either intentionally (as food) or unintentionally (caught in the fine nets or traps and later removed when the nets were cleaned). Even tiny fish such as minnows were eaten: the term minnow – probably used for a variety of tiny freshwater fish – occurs relatively frequently in household accounts or records of banquets.[106] They could have been fried or made into a fritter or soup. The consumption of small freshwater fish clearly continued in the medieval period (Phase 2a). The identification of a sardine suggests some trade with the south-west where these fish formed an important fishery.

[104] For the relative cost of different types of fish: C. Dyer, 'The Consumption of Fresh-Water Fish in Medieval England', in M. Aston (ed.), *Medieval Fish, Fisheries and Fishponds in England*, BAR BS, 182 (1988), pp. 27–38.

[105] R.A. Nicholson, 'Fish Bones', in Norton and Mumford, 'Anglo-Saxon Pits and a Medieval Kitchen at The Queen's College, Oxford', pp. 210–14; C. Ingrem, 'Bird, Fish and Small Mammals', in Z. Kamash et al., 'Late Saxon and Medieval Occupation: Evidence from Excavations at Lincoln College, Oxford 1997–2000', *Oxoniensia*, 67 (2002), pp. 252–5; Dodd (ed.), *Oxford Before the University*, pp. 347–58, 361–2.

[106] R. Phillips and M. Rix, *Freshwater Fish of Britain, Ireland and Europe* (1985), p. 46; M.W. Adamson, *Food in Medieval Times* (2004), p. 105.

A much greater range of fish were evidently purchased and consumed in the fourteenth–fifteenth centuries and it is very likely that this relates to early college dining. Both stored fish (especially dried stockfish and salted herrings) were bought but the relative frequency of gurnards, sea bream and occasional larger salmon, conger eel, john dory and pike suggest meals for wealthy individuals, although the assemblage lacks the sturgeon identified from earlier excavations at Queen's College[107] and from the Dominican Priory.[108] A variety of marine and freshwater seafood was a major component of the diet of fellows and scholars of fifteenth-century King's College, Cambridge[109] and the fish assemblage has many similarities to those recovered from other high and late-medieval college deposits,[110] although the material from Queen's is more diverse. Records held by Magdalen College provide a useful indication of the kinds of fish regularly purchased by an aristocratic household in the fifteenth century, in this case the family of John Moulton,[111] and it would appear that a similar diet was followed at least for college dignitaries and fellows. According to a rare Magdalen College account from 1537 (Magdalen College Archives MS 946), both river fish and salt fish were purchased for college meals.[112]

While it is likely that much of the fish was purchased from suppliers in London, hake and conger eel are more likely to have come from Southampton or Bristol and it may be significant that Queen's College held estates in and around Southampton from the time of Edward III.[113] Both torsk and ling are found in more northerly waters and are likely to have been traded as dried fish from Orkney, Shetland or Norway, perhaps together with cod. The rapid transport of fresh fish from the coastal ports as far inland as Oxford is attested by the consistent presence of seafish such as sea bream as well as shellfish which would almost certainly not have been salted. By around 1360 fishmongers in St Aldate's were selling herrings, stockfish and 'Winchelsea fish' from over 18 stalls,[114] so clearly fish was a fairly widely available food for those who could afford it.

AVIAN EGGSHELL by REBECCA NICHOLSON

Avian eggshell weighing *c.*130 g was recovered from twenty-nine bulk samples. Almost all came from the fills of Phase 2b pits 1538 and 1772, with small quantities coming from Phase 3a contexts. Most of the shell is likely to be from domestic chicken eggs.

MARINE SHELL by REBECCA NICHOLSON

This report provides a summary of the securely phased and washed hand-collected shell, and shell recovered from sieved flotation samples, from secure late Anglo-Saxon or medieval deposits (Phases 1–2b). A full report detailing constraints and methodology can be accessed

107 Nicholson, 'Fish Bones', in Norton and Mumford, 'Anglo-Saxon Pits and a Medieval Kitchen at The Queen's College, Oxford', pp. 210–14.

108 M.R. Wilkinson, 'The Fish Remains', in G. Lambrick, 'Further Investigations on the Second Site of the Dominican Priory, Oxford', *Oxoniensia*, 50 (1985), pp. 192–3.

109 F. Soyer, 'Dining at King's in the Fifteenth Century' (2006) http://webcms.kings.cam.ac.uk/sites/default/files/archives/dining-fifteenth-century.

110 As at Queen's College, Merton College and New College in Oxford: R.A Nicholson, 'Fish Remains', in D. Poore, 'No. 4A Merton St.', pp. 306–11; Nicholson, 'Fish Bones', in Norton and Mumford, 'Anglo-Saxon Pits and a Medieval Kitchen at The Queen's College, Oxford'; R.A. Nicholson, 'Fish Bone', in 'New College, Oxford: Kitchen and Wine Cellar Link Tunnel Projects'.

111 C.M. Woolgar, 'The Development of Accounts for Private Households to *c.*1500 AD', Durham University Ph.D. thesis (1986), citing Magdalen College, Oxford Estate Paper 85/2 (household accounts of John Moulton).

112 U. Aylmer, *Oxford Food: An Anthology* (2005).

113 http://www.queens.ox.ac.uk/history.

114 *VCH Oxon*. 4, pp. 305–12.

from the OA Library, and detailed records of the recorded assemblage will be available as an Excel spreadsheet in the archive.

Apart from a single small fragment of cockle (*Cerastoderma* sp.) from cellar pit fill 1687, all of the thirteen shells identified from late Anglo-Saxon deposits (Phase 1) were oyster. These included small and large examples as well as shells with chalky deposits, chambering and opening notches as described by Winder.[115] The recorded shellfish from Phase 2b came mainly from pits 1538 and 1772. Oysters were especially common in the fills of pit 1538 and were of very variable size and shape, consistent with collection from wild beds where some crowding was occurring. The evidence for growing conditions is discussed further in the full report. Whelks, cockles and mussels were present in several samples

The presence of small quantities of marine shell in later Anglo-Saxon deposits is significant in that it demonstrates the rapid movement of a perishable product inland from the coast to the late Anglo-Saxon *burh*. Small numbers of oysters as well as periwinkle and possible scallop were identified in late Anglo-Saxon deposits at the castle[116] and in both cases it seems unlikely that the shellfish had been preserved since that would render the transport of shells unnecessary.

Mussels become common in samples dating to the fourteenth–fifteenth centuries (Phase 2b) post-dating the college foundation and in fact the majority of all the shellfish come from the fills of large rubbish or quarry pits which seem likely to have been used to dispose of waste from the college kitchens. Since the composition of each fill within pit cut 1772 varied in terms of faunal composition it is possible that they represent kitchen waste from short-lived events, perhaps large meals.

Considered together, it is clear that a variety of shellfish was enjoyed during the earlier centuries of college occupation, including not only the ubiquitous oysters, likely to have been served in the shell, but also mussels, whelks and cockles. Mussels are likely to have been collected from rocks at low tide, but whelks are found in the lower intertidal zone and deeper water. Whelks are usually harvested using baited traps hauled in from boats, but baited lines have also been used in east coast estuaries by 'trotting', where lines are laid across the tide for about six hours and then hauled in.[117]

The oysters are likely to have been harvested from natural beds, as evidenced by the irregular shapes and sizes of shells as well as occasional examples of adhering spat or shells attached to each other. Although the shellfish could have been harvested by hand, from rocks in the intertidal zone, the presence of juvenile oysters and whelks as well as inedible saddle oysters (*Anomiidae*) in some samples probably indicates the dredging of inshore shallow waters as well as fairly unselective hand collection. It also suggests the bulk purchase of unsorted shellfish.

There is no good evidence to indicate where, geographically, the shellfish were collected from, but the presence of chalky deposits and chambers within a fairly high proportion of the oysters may indicate collection from shallower, estuarine waters or creeks with changing salinity.[118] Given the need to transport the perishable shellfish inland to Oxford, a source along the south coast, perhaps in the Solent, or along the Thames estuary seems likely. The shellfish would have been packed in sacks or barrels and transported probably by barge up the Thames (which was probably not navigable above Henley in the fourteenth century due to the number of fishweirs),[119] and by road, using waggons and specialist carriers known as ripiers.

Notches cut into the edges of some oysters suggest that they were opened and eaten fresh, although oysters can be opened more easily when heated and occasional blackened examples may attest to this method.

115 Ibid.

116 R.N. Nicholson, 'Marine Shells from Excavations at Oxford Castle', in Munby, *Oxford Castle*, pp. 394–5.

117 J.M. Winder, 'Oysters and Other Marine Shells', in M. Atkinson and S.J. Preston, 'Heybridge: A Late Iron Age and Roman Settlement, Excavations at Elms Farm 1993–5', *Internet Archaeology*, 40 (2015).

118 Ibid.

119 R.H.C. Davis, 'The Ford, the River and the City', *Oxoniensia*, 38 (1973), p. 264.

Shellfish have not previously been reported from excavations at Queen's College, but shellfish, particularly oyster and mussel but also occasionally periwinkles (*Littorina litorea*) were fairly abundant in predominantly late fourteenth- and fifteenth-century pit fills at New College[120] and oysters and mussels were also recovered in deposits associated with the kitchens at Greyfriars.[121] The more mixed shellfish assemblage from the Provost's Garden may indicate a wealthier consumer, able to afford a more diverse range of foodstuffs. This would be consistent with college dining, since even scholars are likely to have been used to fine dining as indicated by the fifteenth-century records from King's College, Cambridge which document the purchase of fish and shellfish, the latter particularly oysters but also mussels and whelks.[122]

WOOD CHARCOAL AND CHARRED PLANT REMAINS by SHEILA BOARDMAN

Sixty-six soil samples (0.5–40 litres in volume) from early Saxo-Norman through to later post-medieval deposits were previously assessed for wood charcoal and charred and mineralised plant remains.[123] Of these, twenty-one samples were selected for wood charcoal analysis and eight for the analysis of charred plant remains (and any mineralised material present). The wood charcoal samples all came from pit or cellar pit fills and the study was undertaken in order to ascertain the preferred fuels in the various phases, to provide evidence for how different features were used and for the supply of fuelwood to this part of the town. Six samples investigated for charred plant remains came from different Phase 1 cellar pit fills. One sample came from a Phase 1 ditch fill and one was from a Phase 2a pit fill. None of the samples was rich in charred material, so the main aims were to identify the range of crops and other species present, and the evidence, if any, these provide for the use(s) of the features and areas.

Wood Charcoal

Phase 1 (Late Ninth to Eleventh Century) All three samples were dominated by oak charcoal. In samples 22 and 24, there was a fairly even mix of oak heartwood and sapwood, while oak heartwood dominated sample 63. In contrast to most samples from the later phases, there was little or no beech charcoal. Additional taxa present in the Phase 1 samples include hazel (*Corylus avellana*), Pomoideae, blackthorn/cherry (*Prunus*), willow/poplar (*Salix/Populus*), field maple (*Acer campestre*), elm (*Ulmus*) and birch (*Betula*). Many of these were represented by roundwood fragments with 3–10 growth rings.

Phases 2a (Twelfth to Thirteenth Century) and 2b (Fourteenth to Mid Fifteenth Century) One Phase 2a sample (10, context 1335) was dominated by oak with very little beech. The other sample (35, context 1777) produced about 100 beech fragments. By Phase 2b, all the samples were dominated or co-dominated by beech. Sample 41 (context 1927) had similar quantities of oak, elm and beech, with the oak dominated by heartwood. The other taxa present in the Phase 2a samples were blackthorn/plum (*Prunus spinosa/domestica*), ash, hazel, elm and field maple. The full range of charcoal taxa from this site are present in the Phase 2b samples (including beech, oak, elm, Pomoideae, ash, hazel, blackthorn/plum, birch and holly).

120 R.N. Nicholson, 'Marine Shell', in 'New College, Oxford: Kitchen and Wine Cellar Link Tunnel Projects. Post-Excavation Assessment', unpublished OA report (2018).

121 R.N. Nicholson, 'Marine Shell', in 'Westgate Centre, Oxford. Post-Excavation Assessment', unpublished OA report (2019).

122 F. Soyer, 'Dining at King's in the Fifteenth Century' (2006), http://www.medievalists.net/2012/10/dining-at-kings-college-in-the-15th-century/.

123 S. Boardman, 'Appendix 26: Charred and Mineralised Plant Remains'; and 'Appendix 27: Wood Charcoal', in R. Brown, 'Provost's Garden, The Queen's College Oxford, Post-Excavation Assessment and Updated Project Design', unpublished OA report (2016), pp. 106–12.

Phase 3a (Late Fifteenth to Sixteenth Century) Four samples were dominated by beech, and one by oak. Two other samples had more equal proportions of both taxa. The full range of charcoal taxa from the site were again present, and there were many roundwood fragments, particularly of Pomoideae, elm, field maple and ash (with 3 to 15 growth rings).

Phase 4a (Early to Mid Eighteenth Century) The single Phase 4a sample (2) was beech dominated, with more moderate amounts of beech roundwood as compared to the Phase 2 and 3 samples. The other taxa were oak, birch, Pomoideae, field maple and ash. Other than in the smaller proportion of beech roundwood, this sample was very similar to the samples from Phases 2 and 3.

Standardisation in Fuel Wood Supplies

The shift from oak to beech as the main fuel wood utilised has been recorded at a number of sites in Oxford,[124] and farther afield. From the samples here, this would seem to have taken place sometime during the period covered by Phase 2a (see above). By Phase 2b, all the samples were dominated or (or co-dominated) by beech. Where measurable, the age of roundwood in both phases suggests collection from underwood rather than managed woodlands. In contrast, for Phase 3a, two peaks in the growth rings are indicated, at 7–11 rings and, to a lesser extent, 14–16 growth rings. This suggests that at least two different gauges of roundwood were in use by this time.

Previous work at Lincoln College put the transition from oak to beech as the main fuel wood at the fifteenth/sixteenth century boundary,[125] and it was suggested that beech roundwood or rods here were cut on long coppice cycles of 18–20 years. More recent work at Lincoln College[126] has indicated increased beech utilisation from the early to mid thirteenth century onwards. The results from the current site appear to be broadly consistent with this picture, with increased beech occurring somewhere from the late twelfth to the early to mid fourteenth century onwards. Late-medieval beech roundwood stems recovered from kitchens and related deposits have also been investigated at Queen's College.[127] From a study of roundwood growth ring patterns and season(s) of harvest, as well as the numbers of rings and roundwood sizes, it was concluded that some of the beech firewood was supplied from coppiced woodland, and this was harvested on fifteen- to twenty-year rotational cycles. Other gauges of roundwood were also present.[128] The growth ring data for the charcoal from the Provost's Garden does not appear as consistent as this.

Charred Plant Remains

The eight samples analysed all had moderate quantities of charred plant remains and much of these were poorly preserved. Cereal grains were the most common material. The majority were identified as wheat (*Triticum* sp.) or oats (*Avena* sp.). The wheat grains were of the broad, rounded free-threshing type. A few wheat rachis internodes were recovered from the Phase 2a sample 10 (context 1335), two of which were from hexaploid wheat (*Triticum aestivum/compactum*). The other rachis fragments in this sample and a fragment from the Phase 1 sample 51 (context 1745) were too poorly preserved for identification. Two types of free-threshing wheat

[124] D. Challinor, 'The Wood Charcoal', in Kamash et al., 'Excavations at Lincoln College, Oxford 1997–2000', pp. 271–4; Boardman, 'Wood Charcoal', in S. Teague and B. Ford, 'Medieval and Post-Medieval Tenements at Lincoln College, Turl Street, Oxford', unpublished OA report (2017), https://library.oxfordarchaeology.com/3261/; D. Druce, 'Merton College: Charcoal Assessment', unpublished OA report (2006); D. Challinor, 'The Wood Charcoal', in Norton and Mumford, 'Anglo-Saxon Pits and a Medieval Kitchen at The Queen's College, Oxford', pp. 214–16; D. Druce, 'Charred Plant Remains and Charcoal', in 'New College, Oxford: Kitchen and Wine Cellar Link Tunnel Projects'.

[125] Challinor, 'The Wood Charcoal', in Kamash et al., 'Excavations at Lincoln College'.

[126] Chapter 7, below.

[127] Challinor, 'The Wood Charcoal', in Norton and Mumford, 'Anglo-Saxon Pits and a Medieval Kitchen at The Queen's College, Oxford'.

[128] Ibid.

have been identified at other Anglo-Saxon and medieval sites in Oxford.[129] The main hexaploid wheat and, economically, the most important crop in these periods was bread wheat (*Triticum aestivum*).[130] Tetraploid wheat (*T. turgidum/durum*) is sometimes present in small quantities, for example at Lincoln College.[131] This is all probable rivet wheat (*T. turgidum*), which was used for bread (with a different texture) and the straw was used for thatching. In recent years this has become more widely found in medieval deposits across central England and the Midlands.[132]

Oats are represented by grains only. The presence of large and small grains may indicate that both cultivated oats (*Avena sativa*) and wild species (for example, *Avena fatua*) were present. Hulled barley (*Hordeum vulgare*) grains were found throughout the samples. This was the second most important crop grown in these periods.[133] The presence of some asymmetric barley grains indicates the six-row variety, but there were no rachis internodes to confirm this or other barley varieties. Small quantities of rye (*Secale cereale*) grains were present in four samples (22, 24, 56, 10) from Phases 1–2a, and a few fragments of rye chaff were recovered from sample 10, from the Phase 2a pit fill (context 1335). Rye straw was also valued as a thatching material in the past.[134]

Other frequent finds were large legume seeds and fragments, identified as bean/vetch/pea/wild vetch (*Vicia/Pisum/Lathyrus*). These probably include additional crops such as pea (*Pisum sativum*) or broad/horse beans (*Vicia faba*), plus possibly larger seeded, wild legume species. Four Phase 1 samples had one or two seeds or fragments of flax (*Linum usitatissimum*) or possible flax. Flax seeds in low numbers have been recovered from many Anglo-Saxon and medieval sites in Oxford, and flax retting seems to have taken place in the St Aldate's area.[135] The scattered seeds in these deposits may have had a largely culinary use.

Hazelnut (*Corylus avellana*) shell fragments were present in all but sample 10 (context 1335) from Phase 2a. A single possible hawthorn (cf. *Crataegus* sp.) fruit stone was tentatively identified in sample 19 (context 1687) from a Phase 1 deposit. There were fewer remains of wild and cultivated fruit and nuts, vegetables, culinary plants and/or forage crops compared to other contemporary sites in Oxford, suggesting that the excavated areas here in Phases 1 and 2a were not strongly associated with either crop processing or food preparation.

The cereal grains were accompanied by smaller seeds and fruits of wild species. including probable weeds of cultivation. These were not present in large numbers and many were in poor condition. Corncockle (*Agrostemma githago*), stinking mayweed (*Anthemis cotula*) and cleavers (*Galium aparine*) all have large seeds or seed heads, so have to be removed from crops by handpicking. These are reasonably common on urban sites. All three are also associated with autumn-sown crops. Stinking mayweed and cleavers are typical weeds of the heavier calcareous clays around Oxford, which are suited to bread wheat production. Some of the other species may have grown on disturbed, nitrogen-rich ground around the town, in gardens or with spring-sown crops. These include black bindweed (*Fallopia convolvulus*), docks (*Rumex* spp.), goosefoots/oraches (*Chenopodium/Atriplex*) and some mallows (*Malva* spp.). Plants which are more typical of grasslands include grasses (Poaceae), sedges (*Carex* spp.), plantain (*Plantago* sp.) and small-seeded legumes (*Vicia/Lathyrus*, Fabaceae).

129 Chapter 7, below.

130 P.W. Hammond, *Food and Feast in Medieval England* (1995).

131 Chapter 7, below.

132 J. Greig, 'The British Isles', in W. van Zeist et al. (eds.), *Progress in Old World Palaeoethnobotany* (1991), p. 229–334; J. Greig, 'Archaeobotanical and Historical Records Compared – A New Look at the Taphonomy of Edible and Other Useful Plants from the 11th to the 18th centuries AD', *Circaea*, 12 (1996), pp. 211–47; L. Moffett, 'The Archaeology of Medieval Plant Food', in C.M. Woolgar et al. (eds.), *Food in Medieval England. Diet and Nutrition* (2006), pp. 41–55.

133 Hammond, *Food and Feast*.

134 J.B. Letts, *Smoke Blackened Thatch. A Unique Source of Late Medieval Plant Remains from Southern England* (1999).

135 Dodd, *Oxford*, pp. 65–134, 388–9.

ACKNOWLEDGEMENTS

OA would like to thank David Goddard and Amanda Saville of The Queen's College, who project managed the works, and Knowles and Son for overseeing the excavation. The archaeological programme of work was managed for Oxford Archaeology by Richard Brown; on-site archaeological direction was provided by Vix Hughes, with a team including Ben Attfield, Robin Bashford, Sophie Bojadziev, Kate Brady, Adam Fellingham, Matthew Fenn, Rose Grant, Victoria Green, Camille Guezennec, Trevor Jose, Charles Rousseaux, Mike Sims, Caroline Souday, Lee Sparks, Jeremy Stone and Andrzej Zanko. Thanks are also due to the staff that processed the finds under the management of Leigh Allen, processed the environmental samples under the management of Rebecca Nicholson, and prepared the archive under the management of Nicola Scott.

7.

Medieval and Post-Medieval Tenements at the Garden Building, Lincoln College

STEVEN TEAGUE and BEN M. FORD

with contributions by LEIGH ALLEN, SHEILA BOARDMAN, JOHN COTTER, DAVID A. HIGGINS, REBECCA NICHOLSON, CYNTHIA POOLE, IAN R. SCOTT, RUTH SHAFFREY and LENA STRID

SUMMARY

Proposals for a new arts centre at Lincoln College led to excavations and a watching brief within the gardens that occupy the south-east part of the college. The earliest evidence comprised pits dating from the late eleventh to the mid thirteenth centuries that were probably located to the rear of one or more of the substantial medieval tenements in the area, fronting onto Turl Street and All Saints churchyard. The pits probably served a variety of purposes including as quarries and were later used for the disposal of rubbish. From the late thirteenth century one or more masonry buildings were constructed that subsequently extended northwards over most of the excavated area. Possibly originally domestic in character, the buildings appear to have been used for baking and metalworking during the fourteenth and early fifteenth centuries, with several phases of stone-built ovens and hearths. Notable remains include unusual quantities of rye, and crucible fragments with precious metal residues. The building was reconstructed by the early seventeenth century, with a fireplace built into its north wall associated with a flue or drain that contained furnace or mould fragments, though it may later have taken on a more domestic function with the addition of a well-house. By the early eighteenth century the area to the south and south-east of the college was occupied by cottages known as Rotten Row, and remains of some associated walls and courtyards were uncovered in the excavation. Following the extension of Lincoln College's precinct in the late eighteenth century the cottages were demolished and the area was incorporated into the Rector's and Fellows' Gardens from 1808.

Proposals by Lincoln College to create a new arts centre with seminar and lecture facilities led to a programme of archaeological work undertaken between October 2012 and August 2013. The archaeological excavation was focused on the footprint of the new building which replaced the former 1906 lecture room and was to be provided with a basement. A watching brief was maintained during groundwork and the installation of services associated with the new building. A historic building survey of the existing listed Garden Building, whose renovation was included in these works, was also undertaken.[1] The archaeological work was preceded by a desk-based assessment detailing the historical background, and a test-pit evaluation.[2]

1 J. Gill, 'The Garden Building, Lincoln College: Historic Building Investigation and Recording', unpublished OA report (2013), https://library.oxfordarchaeology.com/3290/.

2 G. Coppack, 'The Garden Building, Lincoln College, Oxford', pre-application desk-based assessment (2010); 'Lincoln College Garden Building: Archaeological Evaluation', unpublished TVAS report (2010).

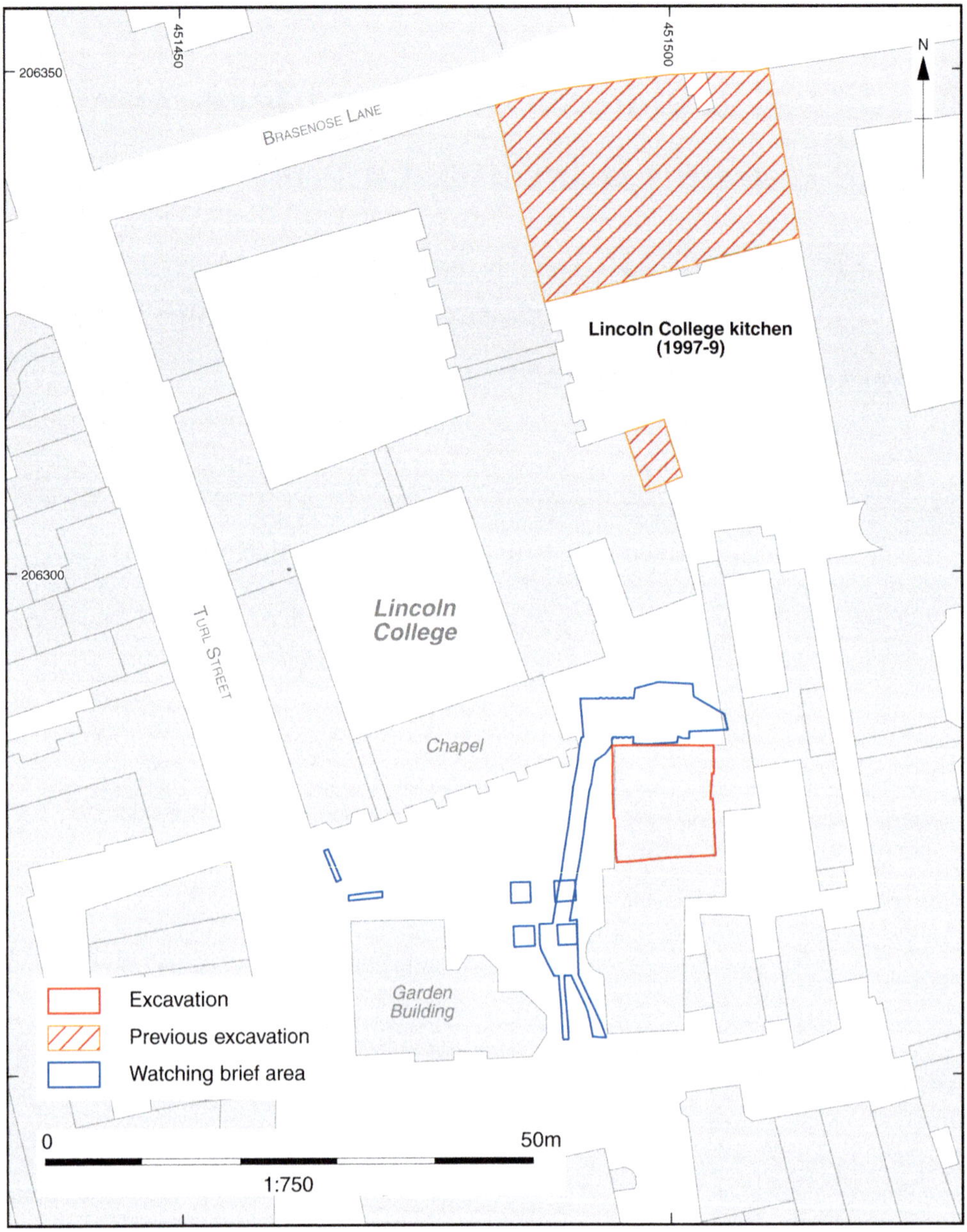

Fig. 7.1 Site location.

The site (centred on NGR SP 5149 0628) now lies within the confines of Lincoln College (Fig. 7.1). It is located immediately to the south-east of the Chapel Quadrangle and to the north of All Saints Church (now the college library).

This report includes summaries of the key findings of the specialist analyses. The full reports along with their tabulated data and detailed illustration catalogues can be found via the OA Library.[3] The archive will be deposited with Oxfordshire Museum Service under the accession number 2012.11.

FIELDWORK METHODOLOGY

Archaeological excavations took place in the footprint of the basement of the new building according to the methodology set out in the written scheme of investigation.[4] This area (measuring 12 m x 10.5 m) was to be reduced to a level of 62.1 m OD (*c.*2.1 m below ground level). The new building was to be constructed on piled foundations with contiguous piles around the sides of the new basement. The depth of the proposed works and the impact of the piled foundations necessitated full excavation of all archaeological deposits in this area to the level of the natural substrate or a depth of 61.5 m OD. Prior to construction, excavation to a maximum safe depth was made possible by the battering of the four sides of the excavation. During construction, following the installation of the contiguous piling, excavation proceeded down to the natural. Any further excavation was confined to the remaining deeper pits. Where necessary, these were excavated to a maximum depth of *c.*60 m OD. As such the basal levels of these deepest features were preserved in situ.

A watching brief was maintained on all groundwork associated with the new development. This included relatively shallow ground drainage and service trenches (maximum 1.2 m in depth) that did not impact on significant archaeological levels. However, four small trenches measuring 2 m x 2 m, pads for the construction of a crane base, were each dug to a level of 62.00 m OD (*c.*2.2 m below ground level).

ARCHAEOLOGICAL AND HISTORICAL BACKGROUND

Lincoln College was founded in 1427 by Richard Fleming, Bishop of Lincoln, absorbing the suppressed church of St Mildred and its graveyard and rector's house, at the corner of Turl Street and Brasenose Lane, and gradually acquiring and building over the surrounding tenements over the course of the next two centuries.

The college was located in the heart of the walled medieval town. Previous excavations at the college kitchen and at All Saints Church recovered important evidence for occupation from the late Anglo-Saxon period onwards, the quality of late Anglo-Saxon buildings and the presence of imported pottery suggesting a prosperous pre-Conquest mercantile quarter.[5] All Saints Church appears from excavated evidence to have been founded during the second half of the eleventh century; St Mildred's, only a short distance to the north, was in existence by *c.*1122 but its date of origin is not known.

The area remained a desirable location in the medieval period, with the shops of the Spicery located eastwards along the High Street from All Saints churchyard, and goldsmiths to the west, while Brasenose Lane (then known as St Mildred's Lane) led directly into Schools Street and the heart of the medieval university. Several of the tenements surrounding St Mildred's

3 https://library.oxfordarchaeology.com/3261/.

4 'Lincoln College, Garden Building, Oxford: Written Scheme of Investigation for an Excavation and Historic Building Recording', unpublished report (2012).

5 Z. Kamash et al., 'Late Saxon and Medieval Occupation from Excavations at Lincoln College, Oxford 1997–2000', *Oxoniensia*, 67 (2002), pp. 199–286; Dodd, *Oxford*, pp. 204–42.

Fig. 7.2 H.E. Salter's reconstruction of medieval property boundaries, from his Survey of Oxford, showing the approximate position of the excavated building.

were academic halls by the fourteenth century although those to the south appear to have had a more domestic and commercial bias. The medieval documentary evidence is summarised in Salter's *Survey of Oxford*,[6] and his accompanying map is reproduced here as Figure 7.2. There is considerable uncertainty about the position of tenements in this area, particularly towards the south and east, and Salter's own notes in his *Survey* suggest he was not satisfied with the initial conclusions he had reached. It is therefore not possible to suggest a direct correlation between the excavated remains and documented tenements and tenants, although the character of the area can be reviewed at a more general level.

It is clear that there was a lane around the north and east sides of All Saints churchyard in the medieval period, serving a series of small tenements, many of which passed via the Bicester family to their Chantry of St Anne at All Saints; the block of land immediately north of the churchyard (NE59) had been acquired for Lincoln College by the 1480s, along with other

6 Salter, *Survey*, vol. 1; the complicated evidence was also reviewed by J. Munby, in Dodd, *Oxford*, pp. 208–9, and by G. Coppack in the unpublished desk-based assessment.

endowments of the chantry. To the north and east of this, Salter places a large tenement (NE60) that is notable for its unusually full early documentation, and for its repeated association with bakers and millers. It may first appear described as land with a mill held by Godric in the churchyard of All Saints, probably around 1180.[7] In *c.*1210 Stephen Molendinarius (miller) held a capital messuage (chief dwelling house) here fronting onto Turl Street, with a second house, an oven, a mill, a brewhouse and cottages that were let for rent behind, on what appears to have been a separate, but apparently contiguous, property. Among the witnesses to Stephen's deed was a Roger Molendinarius, who held the neighbouring property to the north.[8] Stephen's property passed to his daughter Juliana and son-in-law Walter of Osney, baker and miller, and following Walter's death Juliana granted both properties to the Hospital of St John in 1237/8. The hospital then leased the whole to Adam Crust, describing it as a messuage and another messuage behind, with an oven and horse mill; also included in the lease is what appears to be an adjacent tenement, held by Gervase the Baker, which he is to hold of Adam Crust. Gervase's tenement may have been part of the block NE59, and was described as a messuage with an oven, in the corner next to the cemetery of All Saints Church when it was sold to Robert of Bicester (also a baker) in 1257/8.[9] Later references are much less informative, although in 1388 and 1393 the hospital property is recorded as being held by Nicholas Goldsmith.[10] The Aurifabers (Goldsmiths) were a leading family in Oxford in the thirteenth and fourteenth centuries, and held much property, including some on the west side of Turl Street. The surname may have endured whether or not individual members of the family continued in the trade, but the coincidence of this record with the excavated evidence is notable (see below).

Salter appears to have been less confident about the identity of the property immediately to the east (NE154?), known as Bate's tenement, and much less information is available about it. In the late fourteenth century, it was held by Thomas Baldwin, skinner, and then passed to Thomas Warwick, barber, who was followed by his son John, and grandson William. William sold to Walter Bate, clerk, in 1463, who subsequently left the property to Lincoln College on his death in 1479.[11]

It seems likely that the area of the present excavations lay within one or both of these properties, and may not have passed completely into the college's control until the end of the eighteenth century. Its changing character can be understood further from a brief review of the evidence for the gradual expansion of the college. The North, or Front, Quadrangle of Lincoln College was built in stages between the foundation and the early 1480s, as the college acquired neighbouring properties extending from Oliphant Hall on the east to Sekyll Hall on the south, and additional endowments to finance expansion (Fig. 7.2). With the addition of a kitchen east of the north range, and a house for the Rector to the south of the hall, this was to remain the extent of the college's main site for the next century and a half. The single quadrangle appears on the 1578 Oxford view of Ralph Agas, with college-held land to the east and south apparently largely open (Fig. 7.3a). The small building Agas shows on the southern boundary of the college's property may well correspond to structures found in the present excavations, since the area of excavation lay immediately south-east of the college chapel. The South, or Chapel, Quadrangle was added between 1608 and 1631, extending to the southern limit of the college's property, with the chapel forming its southern range. The extended college with its two quadrangles can be seen on Loggan's view of 1675 (Fig. 7.3b). The area of garden shown by Loggan east of the college

7 S.R. Wigram (ed.), *Cartulary of the Monastery of St Frideswide's at Oxford*, 2 vols., OHS, 28, 31 (1895–6), vol. 1, p. 15.

8 For the property of Stephen Molendinarius and the subsequent grants to Walter and Juliana, to the Hospital of St John, to Adam Crust and later tenants: H.E. Salter (ed.), *A Cartulary of the Hospital of St John the Baptist*, 3 vols., OHS, 66, 68–9 (1914–17), vol. 2, pp. 14–30.

9 Salter, *Survey*, vol. 1, pp. 49, 116, NE 59/153.

10 Ibid. p. 50.

11 Ibid. pp. 116–17.

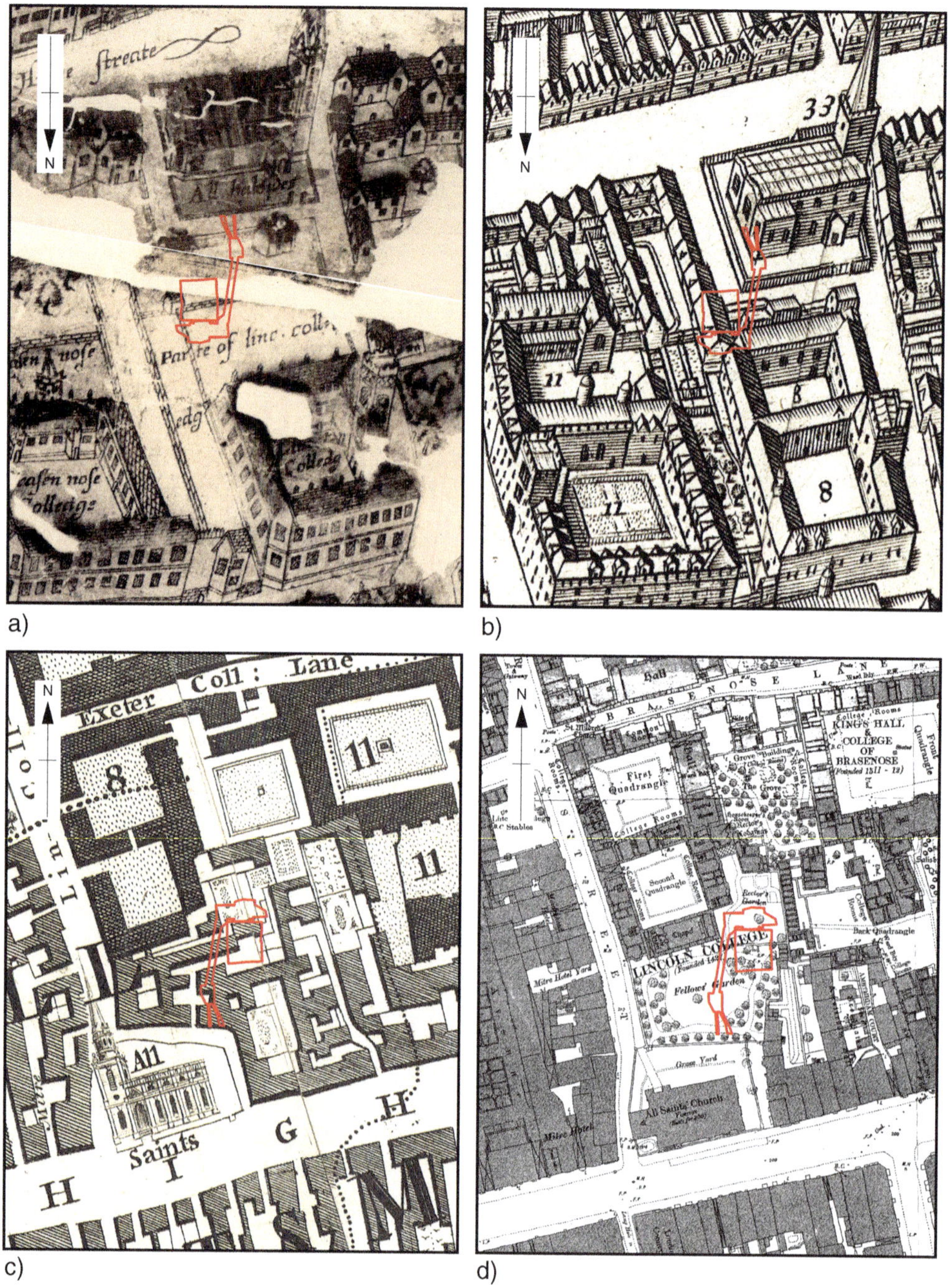

Fig. 7.3 The excavation area on historic maps: a) Agas' map of 1578 (south to the top); b) Loggan's map of 1675 (south to the top); c) Faden's map of 1789; d) Ordnance Survey map of 1876.

was laid out as a formal garden known as the Grove by the end of the century. To the south of the college Loggan clearly shows the lane around All Saints churchyard, with a row of cottages (or shops) on the east side, and a rather foreshortened view of a jumble of cottages immediately south of the Chapel Quadrangle. This area of cottages, known as Rotten Row, persisted into the late eighteenth century and can be seen more clearly on Faden's map of 1789 (Fig. 7.3c). In 1772 the college completed its acquisition of the whole block of land with the purchase of the remainder of the former property of the Hospital of St John (Salter NE60) from Magdalen College. With funds from a further bequest the college was able to demolish Rotten Row in 1808 (which consisted by then of eleven houses with a rental value of £50); a new wall was built along the Turl Street frontage, and the land east and south of the Chapel Quadrangle was laid out to form the Rector's and the Fellows' Gardens. The resulting change in the character of the area can be seen on the 1876 Ordnance Survey map (Fig. 7.3d).

In 1905–6 the New Library was built on the east side of the Fellows' Garden, with the single-storey Lecture Room attached on its north side. The library moved into the redundant All Saints Church in 1974 and the 1906 building was modified to form the Garden Building, providing a room for concerts and lectures, and teaching space. The present archaeological excavations arise from a new redevelopment of the Garden Building, with the main area of excavation located over the footprint of the demolished 1905–6 Lecture Room, and extending some 2 m northwards into the Rector's Garden. The 1808 wall between the gardens, which can be seen on Figure 7.3d, had been built into the north wall of the Lecture Room and was removed as part of the demolition works.

DISCUSSION

Phases 1 and 2: The Site Before the Fourteenth Century

In contrast to the adjacent excavations at the college kitchen to the north and at All Saints Church,[12] no features predating the late eleventh century could be identified. At the former site, late Anglo-Saxon occupation was fairly intensive and comprised early to mid eleventh-century timber buildings that had been prone to fire, together with evidence for associated metalworking and grain storage. The present excavation identified a scatter of largely undated postholes that could have formed part of a structure or a fence-line from this period (Fig. 7.4), though equally they may have been contemporary with or even later than the late eleventh- to thirteenth-century pits (see below). Indeed, one posthole (2259) cut one of the pits and produced late eleventh- to thirteenth-century pottery. Only twelve sherds of St Neots-type ware pottery and no other exclusively late Anglo-Saxon wares were found on the site. The only other Anglo-Saxon find was a copper-alloy hooked tag, used to secure light clothing. At the college kitchen, an excavation of a similar size produced 755 sherds of St Neots-type ware, much of which was found in later contexts.[13] This stark contrast between the two areas suggests that any late Anglo-Saxon occupation on the present site was not intensive or had been removed by later pits.

The excavations have shown that before the late thirteenth century the area of the new basement was open ground used for the digging of pits, probably for the extraction of gravel and for the disposal of rubbish. The larger gravel pits tended to be earlier and were probably dug to obtain material for the construction of nearby buildings, yards and lanes. In many ways such activity is typical of that found towards the rear area of many early medieval tenements in Oxford, before such space was subsequently set aside for construction of buildings and workshops.[14] Indeed the excavations at Lincoln College kitchen revealed that the area was

12 Kamash et al., 'Lincoln College, Oxford 1997–2000'; Dodd, *Oxford*, pp. 233–6.

13 P. Blinkhorn, 'The Pottery', in Kamash et al., 'Lincoln College, Oxford 1997–2000', pp. 232–40.

14 For example, P. Andrews and L. Mepham, 'Medieval and Post-Medieval Extra-Mural Settlement on the Site of the Ashmolean Museum Forecourt, Beaumont Street, Oxford', *Oxoniensia*, 62 (1997), pp. 179–223; A. Norton

similarly used throughout the twelfth to fourteenth centuries.[15] There is a possibility that one of the pits was timber lined as it contained a posthole in one of its corners (context 2582), suggestive of a small cellar or lined latrine. Although too little of it was investigated to be characterised further, it could represent one of the late Anglo-Saxon and Norman features increasingly being recognised within the town.[16]

The finds and environmental evidence from the pits provide little to match the rich picture of the area in the documentary sources. Indeed, with only 47 sherds of contemporary pottery recovered in the excavations, the houses, ovens, mills, brewhouse and cottages described in the thirteenth-century deeds must have been located elsewhere, presumably closer to the frontages of Turl Street and All Saints churchyard. A Stamford ware water-sprinkler (Fig. 7.10, no. 1) is a rare find in Oxford and suggests a well-to-do household in the vicinity during the eleventh or twelfth century. The animal bone assemblage is too small to draw firm conclusions from, but the greatest variety of game occurred in these early pits. The charred plant remains were not particularly abundant and were dominated by free-threshing bread or rivet wheat grains, with some oats and barley, and occasional rye. A small quantity showed evidence for germination that could suggest malting or alternatively parching to prevent further germination prior to milling. Though most of the wood charcoal probably represents fuel debris, there is tentative evidence that some of the hazel roundwood came from wattle hurdle elements – perhaps used for walling or pit lining – that were subsequently burnt.

Phases 3 and 4: The Fourteenth and Fifteenth Centuries

A masonry building occupied the southern part of the excavation area probably from the late thirteenth century onwards (Fig. 7.5). It was subsequently enlarged northwards in the early part of the fourteenth century. This enlarged building would remain more or less on the same footprint, albeit with modifications, until the land was acquired by Lincoln College for the establishment of the Fellows' and Rector's Gardens in 1808. The long-lasting west wall of this building, which remained on the same alignment until it was demolished in the early nineteenth century, could suggest that this was the line of a property boundary, but the location of early tenements in this area is so unclear that this cannot be considered certain. Some support for this idea comes from Agas' map of 1578, which shows a small isolated structure at the southern boundary of Lincoln College's land, the approximate position of the excavated building (see above and Fig. 7.3a); conceivably the west wall of the structure depicted by Agas is on the same line as the east wall of the Front Quadrangle and the garden wall that runs south from it. Two larger houses are shown by Agas fronting the northern arm of the lane that ran around All Saints churchyard. These may represent early elements of what was to become Rotten Row; no evidence for these structures was found in the southern part of the watching brief, since levels of this date were not revealed. By the time of Loggan's map of 1675, the east and north frontages of the lane are shown as being densely built-up. It is likely that the east–west-aligned wall found in the crane pits belonged to one of these buildings.

It is possible that the earliest function of the medieval building was domestic and that it was relatively high status, as considerable care had been taken in the construction of its north wall, which employed well-built relieving arches to compensate for the underlying soft ground previously utilised for rubbish pits. A stone-lined latrine was built against the exterior side of the wall and contained an impressive assemblage of pottery jugs and cooking pots of late thirteenth to mid fourteenth-century date, including a highly decorated Brill 'tripledecker' strip jug (Fig. 7.10, no. 5), an item probably used by a middle-ranking household. Furthermore, a

and G. Cockin, 'Excavations at the Classics Centre, 65–67 St Giles', Oxford', *Oxoniensia*, 73 (2008), pp. 161–94; S. Teague et al., 'Late Saxon, Medieval and Post-Medieval Archaeology at the Nun's Garden, Queen's College, Oxford', *Oxoniensia*, 80 (2015), pp. 143–85.

15 Kamash et al., 'Lincoln College, Oxford 1997–2000', pp. 209–14.

16 Dodd, *Oxford*, pp. 35–41.

Table 7.1. Summary of radiocarbon dates.

Laboratory no.	Context	Feature	Material	δ¹³C (‰)	Radiocarbon age (BP)	Calibrated date range (95.4% confidence)
SUERC-54895 (GU34826)	2397	2398	Charcoal, beech (*Fagus sylvatica*) roundwood	−28.3	549±36	Cal AD 1307–1385
SUERC-54896 (GU34827)	2296	–	Charcoal, beech (*Fagus sylvatica*) roundwood	−25.6	567±36	Cal AD 1300–1381
SUERC-55475 (GU35156)	2635	–	Charcoal, beech (*Fagus sylvatica*) roundwood	−24.6	592±30	Cal AD 1299–1380
SUERC-55476 (GU35157)	2429	2412	Charcoal, *Prunus* sp. roundwood	−27.1	668±30	Cal AD 1275–1350

fragment from a glass urinal was also found in the latrine, a class of item usually affordable only to wealthier households.

After the building was enlarged northwards, probably during the early part of the fourteenth century, it developed a more industrial character, at least within the area of it that was exposed during excavation. An early hearth (2285) contained highly vitrified furnace fragments, suggesting a process requiring high heat, indicative of an industrial rather than a domestic function. Portable x-ray fluorescence (pXRF) analysis of one fragment obtained from the fill of the hearth showed high levels of copper with significant traces of tin and lead, which could suggest either bronze or pewter working. A fragment of a possible unfired crucible from a levelling layer covering this hearth was the earliest direct evidence for such industrial processes. However, the north wall of the enlarged building cut a charcoal dump that contained possible mould fragments suggesting that the manufacture of objects occurred prior to the remodelling. This deposit provided a radiocarbon date of cal. AD 1299–1412 (SUERC-55475; Table 7.1). The north room of the enlarged building was later remodelled and given a replacement hearth (2412). It was associated with significant amounts of charred cultivated legumes and a chain that could have been used to suspend a cooking vessel over a fire, with no industrial material. This could suggest that this part of the building functioned as a kitchen at that time. Charcoal from the hearth was radiocarbon dated to cal. AD 1275–1392 (SUERC-55476; Table 7.1). A cesspit (2572/2575) located to the north of the enlarged building contained large parts of dripping pan and six plain jugs, possibly of later fourteenth-century date, items that may have originated from this kitchen.

A large circular oven (2398), which replaced hearth 2412 (Fig. 7.7), contained large amounts of charred bread wheat/rivet wheat grains together with a significant quantity of rye, strongly suggesting that it was used to bake bread. Medieval bread ovens were typically domed structures measuring around 2 m or more in diameter and 1 m in height.[17] Such structures would have been beyond the reach of many single families for private use as it would require great expense to fire up for a daily loaf, so a commercial user (or a wealthy individual) would have utilised such structures.[18] The medieval documentary evidence for the site suggests a very strong link with milling and baking at the site in the late twelfth and early to mid thirteenth century. However,

17 P.B. Newman, *Daily Life in the Middle Ages* (2001), p. 15.
18 Ibid.

oven 2398 is unlikely to have been built before the fourteenth century and a radiocarbon date of cal. AD 1307–1437 (SUERC-54895; Table 7.1) was obtained from fuel sampled from its final firing. The documentary evidence does not identify any bakers here at this time, but the archaeological results suggest that the property remained attractive for commercial use by both metalworkers and bakers.

By the late fourteenth century, baking in the building seems to have ceased and it may have gone into decline or have been used only intermittently as a workshop. Two small hearths found adjacent to the former bread oven were associated with crucible fragments, suggesting small-scale industrial activity, presumably for the production of non-ferrous objects, though it is possible that any hearths/furnaces to the east could have been removed by modern truncation. The southern part of the building seems to have been used for the dumping of material associated with this activity or perhaps from elsewhere. Analysis of one of these dumped crucible fragments (context 2248) revealed traces of silver. A crucible fragment found residually in the same area within an early post-medieval consolidation deposit produced a high gold reading (context 2220). It is notable that NE60 is recorded as being held by one Nicholas Goldsmith in 1388 and 1393, and his dates would correspond with the late Brill ware pottery and a near-complete decorated Penn/Chiltern floor tile found in these dumps. Furthermore, a radiocarbon sample taken from one deposit produced a date of cal. AD 1300–1430 (SUERC-54896; Table 7.1).

The Post-Medieval Period

Probably by the later sixteenth or early seventeenth century the building was partially reconstructed and a large stone hearth (2051) added to its north-west corner (Figs. 7.7 and 7.8). A stone-lined channel (2351) with a capped roof appears to be associated with the use of the hearth, perhaps as a flue, as it had an opening on its west end, close to the hearth. It seems, at least initially, to have continued as a workshop, possibly for the production of pewter objects. A slightly curved fragment of pewter found in a robber trench may have been manufacturing waste from a large vessel. A clay mould, possibly for the production of a candlestick or decorative handle, was found in a pit located immediately to the north of the building and further mould fragments were found within the flue. Pewter candlesticks were common in the seventeenth century, prior to the introduction of brass in the eighteenth century.[19] To the south were several small bowl 'hearths' that perhaps held moulds associated with the manufacturing of these objects. The wood charcoal analysis from these (and the earlier) industrial hearths was dominated by beech charcoal with 10–75 per cent roundwood (used to increase temperatures rapidly), though it was not possible to determine whether the original fuels were wood or wood charcoal. However, it was noted that the earlier medieval domestic hearth and bread ovens utilised diverse taxa from timber rather than roundwood. There was still a hint of a well-to-do household in the pottery assemblage as it included a South Netherlands polychrome maiolica flower vase and a Beauvais sgraffito ware dish, both expensive sixteenth-century continental imports (Fig. 7.12, nos. 16–17).

Later during the seventeenth century the building appears to have taken on a more domestic function, or at least it ceased to be utilised for metalworking, although it is unclear whether it continued to be permanently occupied. A well-house with a carefully constructed cobbled floor was added to the north side of the building in an area previously utilised for pit digging (Fig. 7.8), though it is possible that this was added during the use of hearth 2051. The southern part of the building appears not to have been occupied, as its internal walls were robbed and a large rubbish pit dug within it. There is evidence for post-built structures within the building, although they may have been posts for temporary scaffolding for internal repairs or perhaps formed the base of a staircase. However, it is likely that at this time the building was in a rather decrepit state and would have fitted the contemporary description by Lincoln College accounts which describe

[19] G. Campbell (ed.), *The Grove Encyclopaedia of Decorative Arts, Volume 1* (2006), p. 209.

the properties between the churchyard and its southern quad as 'Rotten Row', land it was keen to acquire.[20] Some attempt was made to refurbish the area in the late seventeenth or eighteenth century since alterations were made to the building and the area to its north and south-west, which were given well-built cobbled floors. New buildings with a possible cellar and a well were constructed to the north, possibly forming a separate tenancy. However, the buildings were later demolished and garden soils developed over the area, corresponding to the formation of the Rector's and Fellows' Gardens in 1808.

STRATIGRAPHIC SUMMARY

Phase 1: Late Eleventh to Early Thirteenth Century (Fig. 7.4)

Natural gravel occurred at 61.37–61.50 m OD across the basement excavation area, approximately 2.5–2.6 m below the existing ground level. The earliest features within the basement excavation comprised a number of large pits, none of which can be dated to before the late eleventh century. The largest (2548, 2569, 2602/2617 and 2636) were probably gravel quarries. They were confined to the western and northern sides of the area and represented the earliest in the sequence of pits in these areas. They tended to be sub-rectangular in shape. The largest (2602) measured over 5.5 m across with rather irregular edges, and all were at least 1.1 m deep, with pit 2602/2617 being more than 1.6 m deep. The earliest exposed fills of pit 2602/2617 comprised dumps of largely sterile redeposited gravel and sand. These fills contained perhaps the earliest pottery on the site, notably fresh sherds of Cotswold ware and part of a Stamford ware water-sprinkler suggesting a date of *c.*1070–1150 (Fig. 7.10, no. 1). The upper fills of the possible quarries contained noticeably more refuse, suggesting that they subsequently served as rubbish pits.

The remaining pits were largely circular and the shallowest examples (2434, 2445 and 2486) were probably dug as rubbish pits given that they were 0.27–0.60 m in depth. The largest (2477) measured 2.5 m in depth and could have served as a well or possibly a deep cesspit, though no waterlogged or mineralised remains were present in soil samples, the fills apparently comprising deliberate backfill and rubbish dumping. The pit produced predominantly early medieval pottery including a large and fresh sherd of Cotswold ware, together with East Wiltshire ware and medieval Oxford ware, suggesting a date between *c.*1150 and 1225, given the lack of the ubiquitous Brill/Boarstall ware in the assemblage. A copper-alloy hooked tag was also recovered though this seems to be residual as they are normally dated to the middle or late Anglo-Saxon period. The pit was notable for containing worn sherds of St Neots and South-West Oxfordshire ware, suggesting that the material had derived from disturbed late Anglo-Saxon deposits. The animal bone was predominantly of cattle and sheep but also included roe deer and cat. The adjacent pit (2486) produced relatively little rubbish apart from a few fresh sherds from a medieval Oxford ware cooking pot, broadly datable to *c.*1075–1300. The remaining pits produced similar pottery and moderate amounts of animal bone, including duck, goose and fowl from pit 2612 and goose/fowl from pit 2434.

The only other pit of note is a possibly rectangular pit (2582) that seems to have had a slight step or ledge at a depth of 1.2 m through which a posthole had been cut, after which the base of the pit was at least 0.55 m deeper. Owing to the extent exposed, the interpretation of this feature is difficult, though some form of timber-lined pit seems likely, possibly a cellar or latrine.

A number of postholes were also revealed, of which four (2239, 2452, 2460 and 2462) and possibly a fifth (2259) may have formed a north-east–south-west alignment, suggesting a structure or a fence. It is not certain whether the postholes were contemporary or otherwise with the above pit sequences though posthole 2239 predated pit 2237, whereas possible posthole

20 Coppack, 'The Garden Building, Lincoln College, Oxford'.

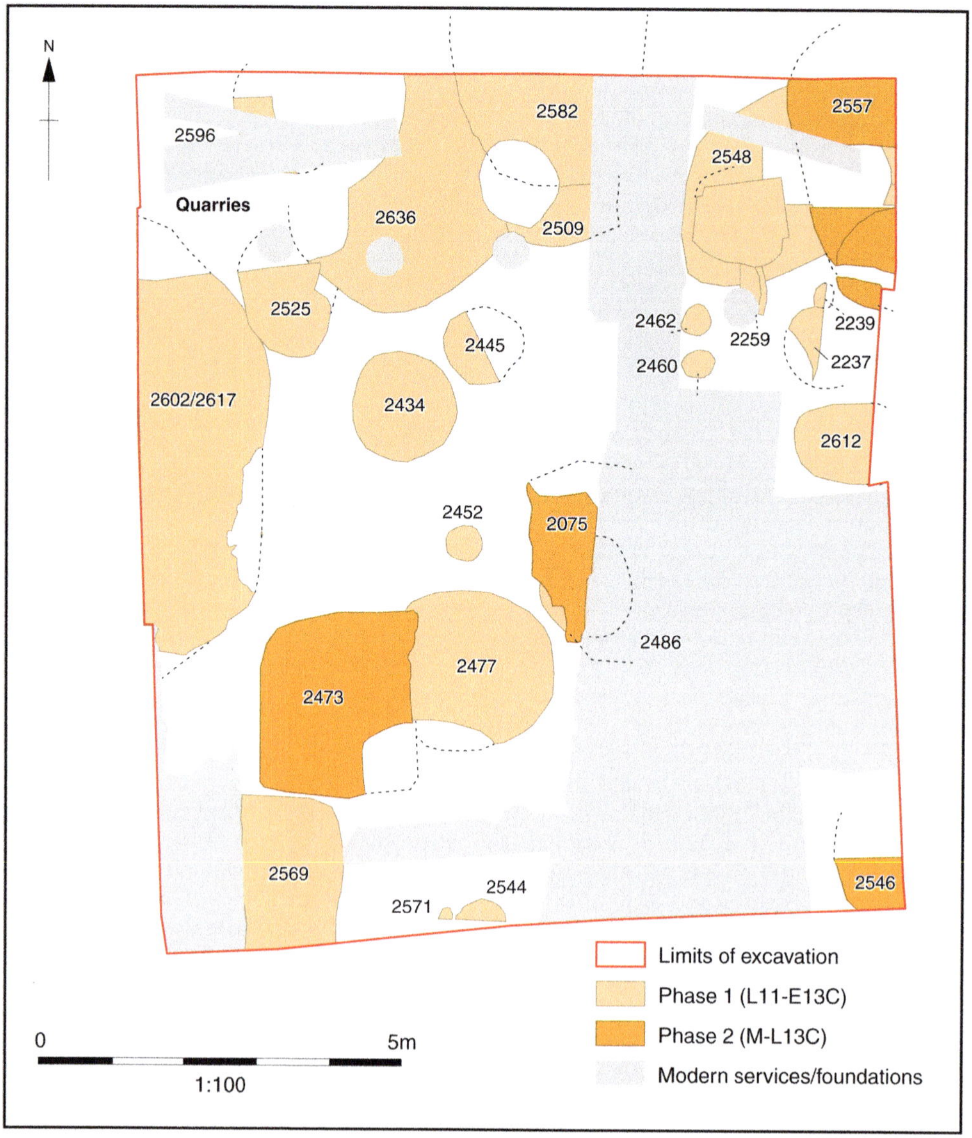

Fig. 7.4 Phases 1–2: late eleventh to late thirteenth century.

2259 cut the possible quarry pit 2548. The latter posthole produced the only dating evidence: a fresh sherd of medieval Oxford ware (*c*.1075–1300).

Phase 2: Mid to Late Thirteenth Century (Fig. 7.4)

The area continued to be utilised for pitting into the latter part of the thirteenth century, prior to the construction of a building during the fourteenth century. These pits (2075, 2473, 2546 and 2557) were dated by the introduction of Brill/Boarstall ware in their fills. The most notable pit (2075), which predated Phase 3 wall 2471 and hearth 2285, contained sherds from a decorated biconical jug in Brill/Boarstall ware dated to *c*.1275–1350.

Phase 3: Early to Mid Fourteenth Century (Fig. 7.5)

This phase saw the construction of one (or more) masonry buildings within the southern half of the excavation area over the external area that was formerly set aside for pit digging. Later rebuilding during Phase 5 and further disturbances rendered the earliest phases of these structures difficult to reconstruct. The western extent of the building may have been delimited by wall 2527, the earliest in a sequence of walls retained and rebuilt during the later phases of the site, possibly representing a tenement boundary. Wall 2459 may have been the external north wall of the earliest phase of this building, before its subsequent enlargement northwards.

Wall 2459 was constructed on two piers that supported a relieving arch that spanned the earlier Phase 1 pit 2477. In order to construct the arch, the upper soft fills of the pit were emptied to a

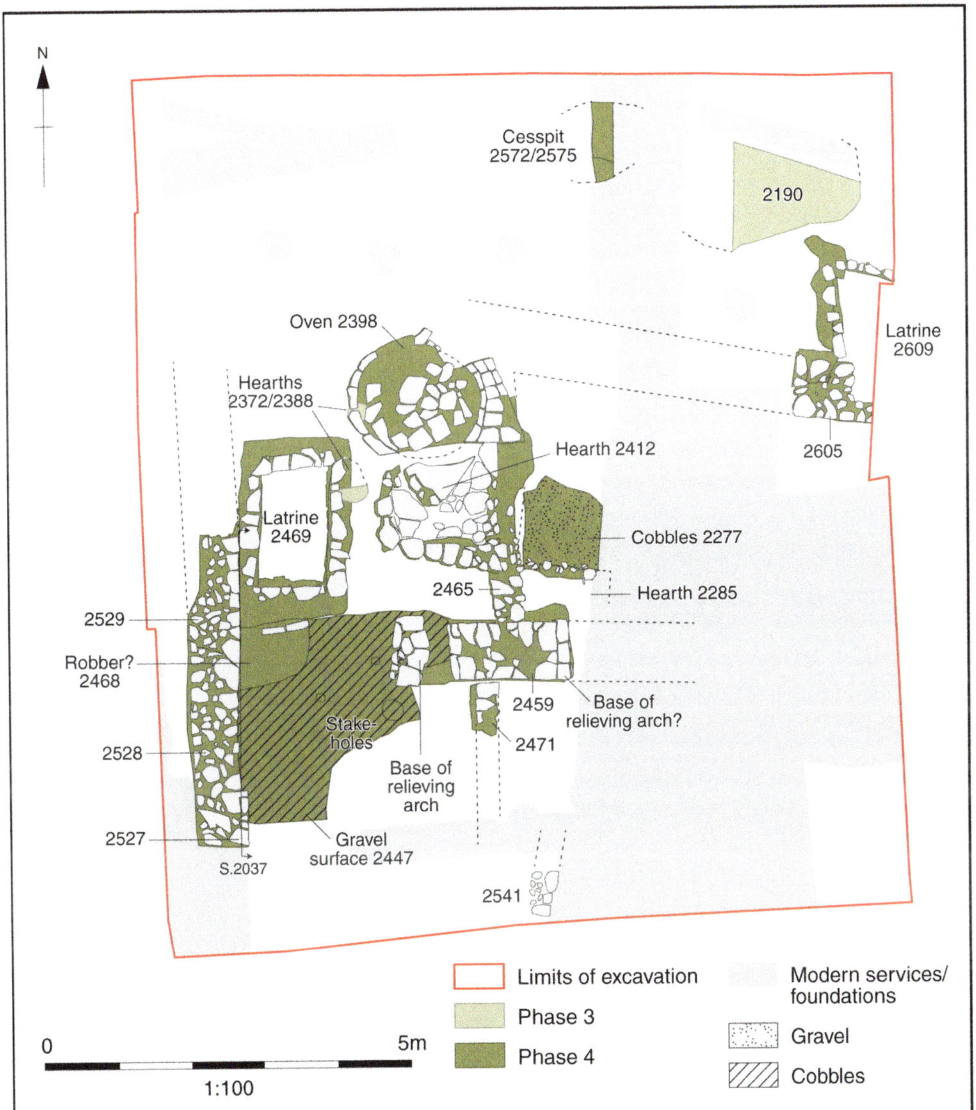

Fig. 7.5 Phases 3–4: early fourteenth to early sixteenth century.

depth of *c*.0.90 m within the footprint of the wall and replaced with sand and gravel as the wall was built. The arch was well constructed with upright and large rectangular limestone slabs with occasional roof tile bonded by a concreted, very pale matrix of sand and gravel. The arch supported a foundation of roughly hewn limestone blocks in a soft mid clay grey/brown silt. The backfill of the construction trench contained pottery dated to 1225–1300, though a small, probably intrusive sherd of possible Tudor green ware (*c*.1380–1550) was also found. The wall did not survive beyond the extent of the earlier pit, having been removed by modern disturbance to the east and by later robbing to the west. However, pit 2468 contained upright stones along its northern edge and may have been the remains of a wall foundation on the line of wall 2459. As pit 2468 did not extend up to the wall, it is possible that there was an opening or doorway at this point. The west wall of the structure had two phases of construction. The earliest element comprised a short length of wall (2527) that might have formed the south-west corner of a separate and earlier structure (Fig. 7.6). It seems to have been extended northwards by wall 2528 to a point corresponding with the projected line of the north wall (2459). The earlier wall was built of roughly hewn rectangular limestone blocks on a slightly offset foundation that extended from the north and east sides. Possible shallow wall foundation 2471 may have formed an internal division within the building, though its relationship with wall 2459 was not established with any certainty.

The internal area of the building was floored with gravel that only survived as a slumped deposit over Phase 2 pit 2473 and extended through the postulated door in wall 2459. It is not clear whether this deposit acted as a floor or levelling deposit put down during the construction of the building to counteract the soft underlying pits. It produced the smashed remains of a highly decorated baluster strip jug datable to *c*.1225–1350. Later shallow scoop 2455, probably also slumping, contained charcoal-rich silt that 'over-spilled' towards the door and probably represents debris from occupation within the structure. It contained sherds from a thick-walled vessel in Brill/Boarstall ware, possibly dating to the fourteenth century.

The area directly to the north of the building initially seems to have remained external, as a large stone-lined pit (2469), probably a latrine, was placed immediately to the north of the building. It predated the expansion of the building as the west wall of the extension was built over its western edge. Its position, directly in front of the possible door, is somewhat problematic, though a later robber trench in this area could imply that the door was blocked at this stage. Its internal shaft measured 1.55 m x 0.90 m and was excavated to a depth of 0.81 m, though augering revealed it to be 1.61 m deep. It was constructed with irregular courses of angular limestone blocks with no mortar apparent. Its earliest excavated fill was a 0.56-m thick deposit made up of several lenses of alternating greenish cessy silts and gravel, the latter possibly representing capping in between usages. However, no mineralised remains were found in an

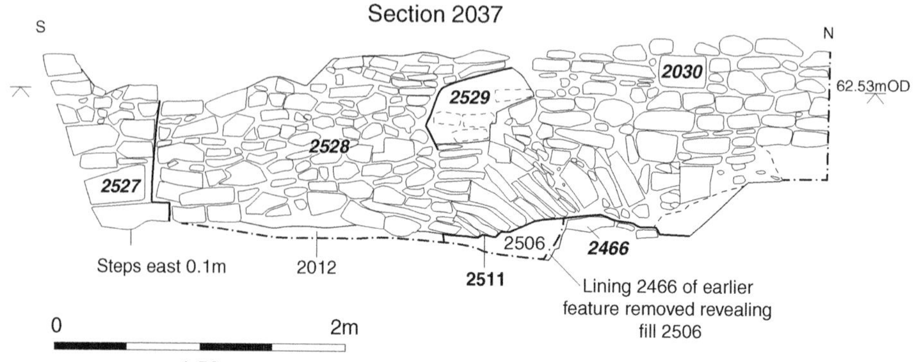

Fig. 7.6 Section 2037.

assessment of a sample taken from this deposit, though a small amount of animal bone and roof tile of thirteenth- or fourteenth-century date was recovered. The mainly rubble backfill of the pit contained an exceptional assemblage of pottery including large parts and profiles from at least seven jugs in highly decorated Brill/Boarstall ware and near-complete parts of several cooking pots. The collection can be dated to *c.*1275–1350. Also recovered from the same fill was a sherd from a glass vessel, possibly a urinal.

The structure was subsequently enlarged northwards with the insertion of ovens into one or more of the created rooms. The western side of the enlarged structure was delimited by wall 2529 which overlay the west wall of latrine 2469, presumably after it had gone out of use. It is not clear how far north this wall originally extended as it was subsequently rebuilt (see Phase 5). It may have extended as far north as the east–west-aligned wall fragment (2605) that predated stone-lined pit 2609, but otherwise modern disturbance and the Phase 5 building appear to have removed further evidence. The walls were constructed with roughly hewn limestone blocks with wall 2529 showing evidence for a relieving arch, similar to wall 2459 from the earlier phase of the building. Wall 2605 overlay a charcoal lens (2635) that had slumped into an underlying pit (2642). A radiocarbon date of cal. AD 1299–1412 (SUERC-55475; Table 7.1) was obtained from a charred beech roundwood fragment recovered from the lens. The upper fill of 2642 also contained fourteenth-century pottery and fragments from one or more moulds.

The earliest hearth (2285) survived in a rather fragmentary state and was probably built against the north side of wall 2459. It survived as a rectangular area of burnt clay delimited to the north by a narrow kerb wall of stones, the remains of the hearth surround. To its north was a contemporary cobbled surface (2277) from which a sherd of pottery dated to 1300–1425 was recovered. Remnants of highly fired, vitrified hearth lining were found within it, suggesting an industrial furnace that required a high temperature. A fragment from a crucible (possibly unused) was recovered from a levelling deposit post-dating its use together with a second jug sherd in early Brill ware (1175–1400) that may have also been utilised as a crucible or similar vessel.

After hearth 2285 went out use, the room in which it stood was partitioned with the construction of shallow limestone wall foundation 2465, comprising a single course of limestone rubble bonded by yellow-brown sandy clay. Built up against the western side of this partition wall was a second rectangular hearth 2412. The northern side had been removed by later oven 2398; otherwise its limestone surround survived to a height of 0.18 m. It was floored with limestone flagstones and cobbles bonded with the same material as the hearth surround: orange-brown sandy clay. The hearth was filled with charcoal, with relatively low counts of charred cereal grains in which rye predominated, but it also contained a significant quantity of cultivated legumes, suggesting that the hearth was used for cooking. A piece of wood charcoal produced a radiocarbon date of cal. AD 1275–1392 (SUERC-55476; Table 7.1), which agrees with the fourteenth-century date of the pottery recovered from the feature. A compacted gravel surface to the south of the hearth and partially overlying levelled latrine 2469 probably represented the contemporary floor surface. It was overlain by an extensive charcoal spread that probably related to the use of hearth 2412. It contained a similar assemblage of charred plant remains and also had a high concentration of cultivated legumes. A short length of copper-alloy chain recovered from this deposit could have supported a cooking vessel over a hearth.

Hearth 2412 was replaced by circular oven 2398 (Fig. 7.7). This may have been built up against the north wall of the building, which did not otherwise survive. It was constructed within a shallow pit about 0.25 m deep, walled with roughly squared limestone blocks and floored with irregular limestone slabs, all bonded by a light-coloured mortar. The internal diameter of the oven measured about 1.60 m and intense heating had heavily scorched its base. The oven contained a thick deposit of charcoal and ash. A fragment of roundwood from this deposit produced a radiocarbon date of cal. AD 1307–1437 (SUERC-54895; Table 7.1), with a slightly higher probability for a date within the later part of the range. The deposit was very rich in cereal grain with high concentrations of bread wheat, rye and barley suggesting the baking of bread.

Fig. 7.7 Top: oven 2398 and hearth 2412, facing south; bottom: hearth 2051, facing north. Scales: 1 m.

The area to the north of the enlarged building appears to have remained external, as indicated by the presence of two cesspits. Pit 2609 was lined with limestone blocks and appears to have been subsequently built against the north wall of the building (2605), possibly as a replacement for earlier latrine 2469. It was *c.*1.0 m in depth and contained rubble with no evidence for any primary fills, which had perhaps been cleaned out prior to demolition. The backfill of the pit contained a few sherds of fifteenth- and sixteenth-century pottery and fragments of late-medieval peg tile. The second pit (2572/2575) had been largely truncated, but contained greenish silt at its base, recorded at a depth of 1.6 m. A sample from the fill was rich in mineralised fruit stones and seeds including sloe/cherry, apple/pear, strawberry and grape, as well as textile fibres, the latter possibly utilised as 'toilet paper'. The fill also contained parts of several jugs and part of a dripping pan, which together can be dated to *c.*1350–1425.

Phase 4: Late Fourteenth to Early Sixteenth Century (Fig. 7.5)

During the late fourteenth or early fifteenth century, the building appears to have declined in use with little further modification apparent from the surviving evidence. Oven 2398 was demolished and levelled with dumps of rubble that spread throughout the area of the north-west room, filling areas that had slumped into earlier latrine 2466. They contained pottery dated to *c.*1350–1500, including sherds from a conical jug that was possibly used as a urinal. Within the north-west room, the levelling deposits were cut by two small pits which seem to have served as hearths, possibly associated with metalworking. Hearth 2388, though partially removed by a later feature, was probably oval and measured *c.*0.64 m across and 0.04 m in depth. It was filled with heavily scorched and compacted lenses of burnt clay and ash. To its north a second smaller circular hearth (2372), measuring 0.23 m in diameter and 0.09 m in depth, also contained burnt material with evidence for scorching in its immediate surrounds. Hearth 2388 contained fragments from two crucibles, and fragments of vitrified hearth lining were recovered from hearth 2372. Dumps of ash and rubble adjacent to the hearths also contained several crucible fragments.

Within the southern room were deposits of sandy silts, ash and charcoal, which appear to have formed deliberate dumps, probably consolidating soft ground over earlier pits (not illustrated). Wall 2471 appears to have been replaced by shallow foundation 2541, although too little survived to be more certain. The deposits were notable for containing a number of crucible fragments, which were obtained from several separate contexts within these dumps. A radiocarbon date of cal. AD 1300–1430 (SUERC-54896; Table 7.1) was obtained from beech roundwood from one of these dumps. Found in association with the crucibles was a near-complete decorated Penn/Chiltern floor tile dating to *c.*1330–1400 and sherds of late-medieval Brill ware (*c.*1400–1650).

To the north of the building were the truncated remains of a large pit (2190) that contained fragments from at least two ceramic moneyboxes and jugs in late Brill ware (*c.*1425–1625). The moneyboxes showed evidence for intensive heating and were covered with a cindering deposit, having perhaps been reused as crucibles. A rim sherd from a vessel in Minety ware (*c.*1225–1525) had also been intensely scorched and may have been similarly used as an industrial vessel.

Phase 5: Mid Sixteenth to Early Seventeenth Century (Fig. 7.8)

At some point during the early post-medieval period, the building underwent substantial modification or was partially rebuilt (Building 2230). Its north wall was reconstructed on an obtuse alignment with the west wall and the latter wall was also partially rebuilt at its northern end. The dividing wall of the north room seems to have been retained, as its robber trench (2262) is stratigraphically later, but it was presumably at least partially rebuilt and extended up to the new north wall of the building. Indeed, the base of the robber trench on its north end was deeper, suggesting the presence of a separate or deeper foundation. Similarly, the south wall of the north room was robbed at a late point (robber trench 2243) during this phase suggesting that this wall was also retained in the remodelled building. A second robber trench (2144) ran immediately adjacent to trench 2243, suggesting the presence of a separate structure to the south or perhaps a later remodelling.

The new north wall (2031) was constructed with limestone rubble bonded with an orange-brown sandy clay matrix. It was keyed-in and bonded with the partially rebuilt west wall (2030), which was of a similar build. Both walls were well faced with limestone blocks on each side. The north wall cut several large pits (2057, 2068, 2072) which may have been contemporary and respected the earlier phase of building, though it is possible some pits could relate to the construction of the new wall. The pits all contained a reasonable quantity of pottery dating to

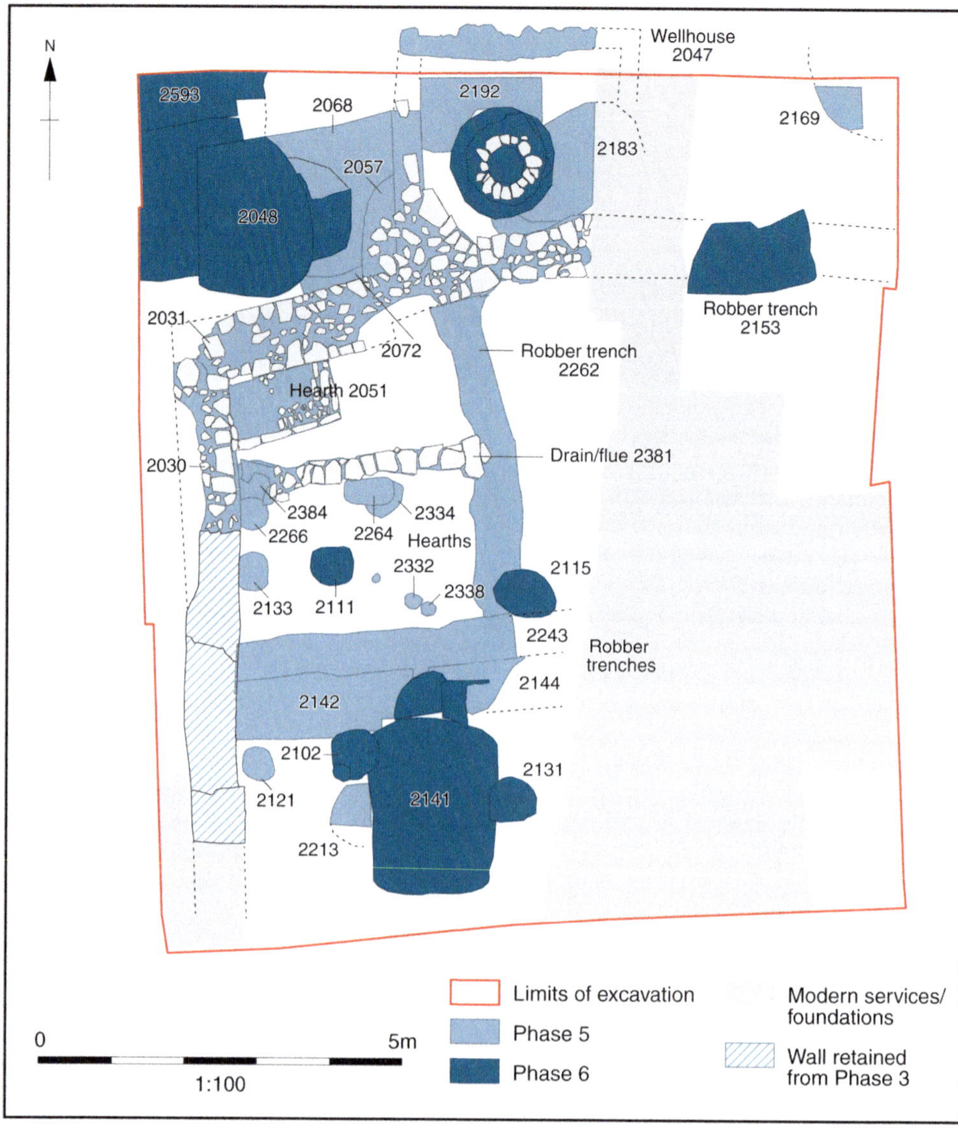

Fig. 7.8 Phases 5–6: mid sixteenth to early seventeenth century.

*c.*1550–1625, including large body sherds in early post-medieval ware jars and large fragments from fifteenth- to sixteenth-century roof tiles. The latest pit (2057) contained much animal bone and rubble, the latter perhaps derived from the construction of the wall.

Within the north-west corner of the remodelled building was a rectangular stone-built hearth (2051; Fig. 7.7), bonded into and contemporary with the construction of the new walls. Limestone blocks formed the surround on its east and south sides and had been heavily scorched and cracked as the result of intense heat. The floor of the hearth was constructed with roughly shaped upright triangular blocks (probably limestone) arranged point-downwards on a bed of clay so that their upper surfaces were flat. The floor was overlain by fire-reddened clay and ash, likely to represent the final firing of the hearth. A rudimentary gravel surface that covered much of the north-east room and abutted the hearth probably represented the original floor of the remodelled building. Extensive spreads of charcoal and ash with episodic floor repairs or patching are likely to have been associated with the use of the hearth. These deposits contained sherds of pottery datable to *c.*1550–1625 and vitrified hearth or oven lining fragments. One deposit also contained a copper-alloy buckle frame that can be dated to the late sixteenth or early seventeenth century.

A stone-lined drain or flue (2381) with intact capping stones appears to have been contemporary with the early phase of the building and apparently lay directly below the gravel floor. It ran at right angles to wall 2030 and had a possible opening at its west end, near the junction with the wall denoted by 'posthole' 2384 with its packing of large stones set in fired clay which had subsequently been filled with charcoal-rich silt. The drain/flue was filled with similar material and contained furnace or mould fragments together with a conical pedestal, possibly used to support a crucible. The eastern end of the drain had been removed by robber trench 2262, suggesting that it may have originally continued eastwards, perhaps through the wall.

Elsewhere within the northern rooms were a number of small, very shallow pits (2332, 2334, 2338) that may have been hearths serving some industrial purpose. All were less than 0.15 m in depth and had been lined with clay, and two had then been levelled with charcoal. However, the clay was largely unfired apart from around the upper rim of one of the features.

Three substantial postholes (2121, 2133, 2266), which formed a line along the inside of the west wall of the building, appear to be associated with this phase of activity though their purpose is unclear. They may have formed part of a temporary structure, perhaps for the maintenance or repair of the wall.

The southern room was given a surface of gravel (2173) which sealed a levelling dump containing crucible fragments and a drinking vessel dated to *c.*1550–1625. This predated robber trench 2144 and appears to be related to the earlier configuration of the room.

The area to the north of the building remained open and was utilised for pit digging. Large pit 2183/2192/2209 contained pottery dated to *c.*1580–1625, post-medieval window glass and an appreciable quantity of late-medieval roof tiles and scorched brick or quarry tile, perhaps from a hearth.

During the watching brief a south-west–north-east-aligned wall (Fig. 7.9, 1130 and 1147) was recorded that followed the same orientation as the north wall (2031) of the building in the basement excavation. It was constructed with limestone rubble bonded by a similar orange sandy mortar, with its south face pointed with white lime mortar. The wall cut earlier pit fills containing fourteenth-century pottery and was in turn abutted by a deposit containing pottery dated to 1550–1625 and late-medieval roof tile fragments.

Phase 6: Mid to Late Seventeenth Century (Fig. 7.8)

It appears that Building 2230 remained in use, though little survived relating to its internal layout from this period. A small rectangular well-house (2047) containing a stone-lined well was added to the north wall of the building. The walls of the well-house were constructed with limestone rubble bonded by mid yellowish-brown silt sand, the south ends of which directly abutted Building 2230. The area around the well was given a well-laid cobbled surface, which also overlay the lining of the well. Pottery dating to *c.*1600–50 was recovered from the construction pit of the well, though this is likely to have been derived from the fills of the underlying pits. The area to the west of the well-house remained external and contained a large rubbish pit (2048/2593) that produced pottery datable to *c.*1680–1750 along with late seventeenth-century clay tobacco pipe fragments. The pit also contained a clay mould for the production of a linear object, possibly a decorative handle or candlestick.

The area to the south of robber trench 2144 seems by now to have been external since a large rubbish pit (2141), 0.75 m deep, was dug in the area, slightly truncating the southern edge of the robber trench. It contained early to mid seventeenth-century pottery, late-sixteenth-century (or later) stemmed glass fragments and clay tobacco pipes datable to *c.*1610–40. Two large postholes (2102 and 2131) subsequently cut the backfilled pit, probably contemporary with postholes 2111

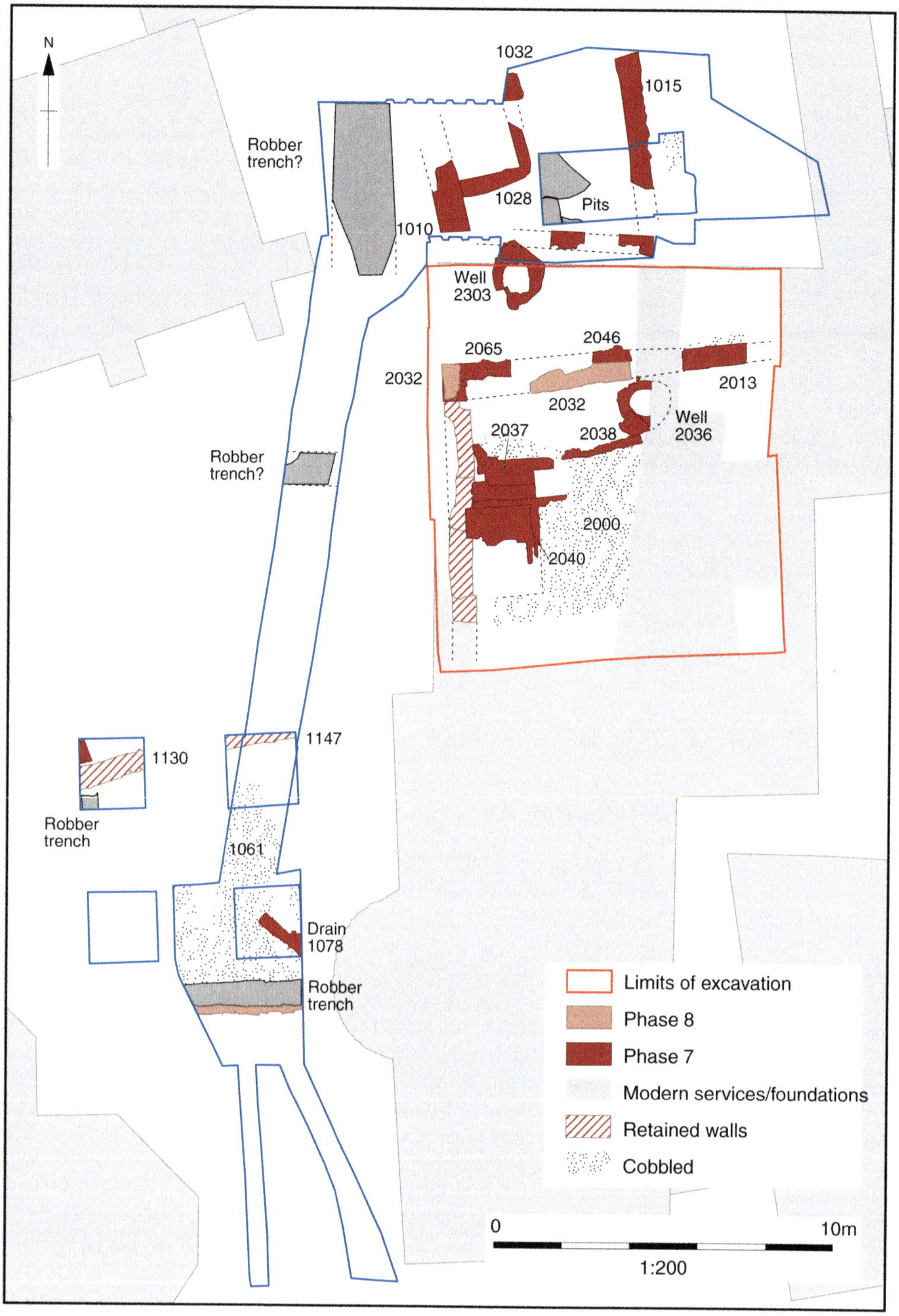

Fig. 7.9 Phases 7–8: late seventeenth to nineteenth century.

and 2115 to the north, the latter of which cut robber trench 2262. It is possible that they may have formed part of a structure. A series of dumps and possible occupation deposits within the footprint of the postholes may have been associated with them. The earliest of these contained a large part of a seventeenth-century mug and the latest, a levelling deposit over the earlier pit, contained a seventeenth-century clay pipe stem and a fragment of painted medieval window glass.

Phase 7: Late Seventeenth to Eighteenth Century (Fig. 7.9)
Possibly during the late seventeenth- or eighteenth century Building 2230 was either rebuilt or underwent substantial modifications. It appears that its west wall was retained and the north wall possibly entirely rebuilt on an alignment closer to east–west (2013, 2065 and 2046). The walls now enclosed what appears to have been a courtyard surface floored with a substantial layer of rounded cobbles and flagstones (2000) that sealed early to mid seventeenth-century dumps to the south. A rectangular area of brick paving against the west wall (2037) may have formed the floor of a building or lean-to structure built against the west wall (or a separate area within an internal space). There was a gap, approximately 0.24 m wide, between the bricks and stone cobbles to the east that may have been a beamslot (2040). The brick paving slightly overlapped the west wall, suggesting a threshold.

On the north side of this courtyard, a limestone-lined well at least 2 m deep was constructed (2036) that had cut slightly into the earlier north wall. The wall was probably rebuilt at this time although only a small fragment survived and possibly wall 2046 represents the remains of it. The well may have been enclosed within a small structure defined to the south by a low wall (2038) that also provided 'edging' to the northern extent of cobbled surface 2000.

Within the watching brief area to the north of the basement excavation, a number of limestone-built walls were revealed that probably date to this phase as they cut post-medieval garden soils and pit fills. They included part of a possible rectangular building whose west wall (1010) would have been aligned with the corresponding wall of Building 2230 to the south. Contained within the building was a stone-lined pit, possibly a small cellar (1028/1032). The area to the east and south appears to have been open and traces of a cobbled surface were recorded (1035). A well (2303) that respected the south side of the structure may have been contemporary. A large quantity of domestic pottery including bowls and dishes dated to *c.*1700–30 was recovered from the construction trench infill of the well together with some clay pipes dating to *c.*1690–1720.

Within the watching brief area to the south-west of the basement excavation, a further substantial and well-laid limestone cobble surface was recorded (1061), similar in nature to surface 2000. It may have formed part of a courtyard to the south of a pre-existing building (see Phase 5, walls 1130 and 1145). The cobbles sealed a stone-lined drain (1078) that ran approximately east–west and appears to have been either built at the same time or retained as the surface subsequently collapsed into it.

Phase 8: Nineteenth Century (Fig. 7.9)
The structures on the site were demolished to make way for the construction of the Fellows' and Rector's Gardens in 1808. The boundary wall between the two gardens appears on the 1876 Ordnance Survey map and had been built into the north wall of the Lecture Room and demolished prior to the excavations. Remains of a limestone wall bonded by a whitish mortar (2032), constructed on a slightly different alignment, were recorded overlying the north wall of the earlier building to the south.

POTTERY by JOHN COTTER

A total of 1785 sherds of pottery weighing 42.779 kg were recovered from all areas and stages of the fieldwork, though the focus here is on the material from the basement excavation, which comprises a total of 1579 sherds weighing 35.613 kg and with a total EVEs of 28.6 (Table 7.2). An additional quantification by rim count yielded a figure of 224 rim sherds. Of this 82 per cent

Table 7.2. Pottery types and quantities in approximate chronological order.

Fabric	Common name	Date	No. sherds	Weight (g)	EVEs	Rims
ROM	Roman pottery (residual)	AD 43–410	1	9		
OXR	St Neots-type ware (SE Midlands)	900–1100	12	74	0.05	1
OXZ	Stamford ware (Lincs)	850–1150	4	38	0.42	1
CRUC	Medieval crucible	850–1500	30	107	2.34	18
OXBF	SW Oxon ware (Kennet Valley A)	875–1250	11	126	0.1	3
CHALK	Chalk-tempered ware	1000–1350	1	15	0.05	1
OXAC	Cotswold-type ware	1050–1250	90	1485	1.37	20
OXY	Medieval Oxford ware	1075–1300	240	2907	1.79	21
OXAQ	East Wilts ware (Kennet Valley B)	1150–1350	76	1659	0.56	5
OXCG	Olney Hyde-type shelly ware (Bucks)	1150–1400	5	110	0.24	3
OXBH	East Midlands reduced ware	1175–1350	2	31		
OXAG	Ashampstead-type ware (Berks)	1175–1400	12	197		
OXAW	Early Brill ware (Bucks)	1175–1400	95	2014	0.95	7
OXBB	Minety ware (Wilts)	1225–1525	15	603	0.28	3
OXAM	Brill/Boarstall ware (Bucks)	1225–1625	463	8597	2.71	25
KING	Kingston-type ware (Surrey)	1240–1400	1	1		
CBW	Coarse border ware (Surrey/Hants)	1350–1500	3	41	0.05	1
CHEA	Cheam whiteware (Surrey/Hants)	1350–1500	3	144	0.4	2
TUDG	Tudor green ware (Surrey/Hants)	1375–1550	6	14	0.17	3
OXBX	Late medieval Brill ware (Bucks)	1400–1625	228	3965	4.06	33
RAER	Raeren stoneware (Germany)	1475–1550	2	15		
SNTG	South Netherlands maiolica	1480–1575	3	26		
PMRE	Early post-medieval redwares	1480–1600	8	363	0.07	1
CSTN	Cistercian-type ware (mainly Brill)	1480–1700	3	9	0.06	1
KOLS	Cologne stoneware (Germany)	1500–1580	2	38		
BEAU2	Beauvais double sgraffito ware (France)	1500–1630	1	30	0.07	1
FREC	Frechen stoneware (Germany)	1525–1750	67	2449	5.56	15
OXAP	Brill proto-stoneware (Bucks)	1540–1625	2	43		
BORDG	Border ware, green glazed (Surrey/Hants)	1550–1700	28	1196	1.53	11
BORDO	Border ware, olive glazed (Surrey/Hants)	1550–1700	2	153	0.22	2
BORDY	Border ware, yellow glazed (Surrey/Hants)	1550–1700	17	524	0.81	6
OLIV	Spanish olive jar	1550–1750	1	20		
PMR	Post-medieval red earthenwares	1550–1900	74	5033	2.01	18
TGW	English tin-glazed earthenware	1575–1825	21	1832	1.11	10

Fabric	Common name	Date	No. sherds	Weight (g)	EVEs	Rims
PMBL	Post-medieval black-glazed redwares	1580–1750	21	514	0.44	4
MART3	Martincamp III flasks (Normandy)	1600–1650	1	9		
BORDB	Border ware, brown glazed (Surrey/Hants)	1600–1700	2	36		
NIMS	North Italian marbled slipware	1600–1750	2	47	0.28	2
METS	Metropolitan slipware (Essex)	1630–1700	1	31	0.15	1
BRSL	Brill post-medieval slipware	1650–1800	2	426	0.2	1
LONS	London (salt-glazed) stoneware	1670–1850	2	24		
WBOT	Wessex-type bottles	1675–1750	7	391	0.4	1
STSL	Staffs-type combed slipware	1680–1900	3	68	0.1	1
SWSG	Staffs white salt-glazed stoneware	1720–1780	1	15		
STBL	Staffs fine blackware (Jackfield)	1740–1780	4	48	0.05	1
CREA DEV	Developed creamware (Staffs/Yorks)	1760–1830	2	50		1
PEAR	Pearlware (Staffs/Midlands)	1780–1830	2	86		
Total			1579	35,613	28.6	224

by sherd count is medieval and 18 per cent post-medieval (*c*.1480+). The percentages by weight differ somewhat (62 per cent and 38 per cent respectively). The pottery is in a fairly mixed and fragmentary condition although a small number of vessels are well-preserved.

The range of fabrics and vessel forms is fairly typical of sites along or near the main thoroughfares of central Oxford. Apart from three or four small residual Roman sherds the assemblage is medieval and post-medieval. A few possible (residual) late Anglo-Saxon sherds occur but no contexts here were dated to the late Anglo-Saxon period. Occupation on the present site appears to date from the later eleventh century onwards with pottery of the twelfth, fourteenth and sixteenth centuries being particularly plentiful.

Only a small number of late eighteenth- and nineteenth-century sherds occur from the site and the sequence seems to terminate around 1830, coinciding approximately with the demolition of Rotten Row in 1808. Most of the pottery is domestic in nature apart from a small but important assemblage of high medieval metalworking crucibles and one or two domestic pots probably adapted for industrial purposes. Nearly all the types present here also occur in a much larger assemblage of medieval and post-medieval pottery recently studied from the Brewer Street site where these types are described in more detail.[21] A similar range of pottery has also been published from Merton Street,[22] while a good range of post-medieval pottery has been published from the St Ebbe's area.[23] Medieval pottery fabrics were recorded using the system of codes developed for the Oxfordshire County type series.[24] Post-medieval fabrics were recorded using the codes of the Museum of London, which can be applied to most post-medieval types in south-east England.[25]

21 J. Cotter, 'Pottery', in S. Teague and B.M. Ford, 'Excavations in Oxford's South Suburb at Brewer Street, Littlegate Street and Rose Place', unpublished OA report (2019).
22 P. Blinkhorn, 'Pottery', in Poore, 'No. 4A Merton St.', pp. 258–78.
23 M. Mellor and G. Oakley, 'A Summary of the Key Assemblages ...', in 'St Ebbe's, Part II', pp. 181–219.
24 Mellor, 'Synthesis'.
25 Museum of London Archaeology, 'Medieval and Post-Medieval Pottery Codes' (2014) http://www.mola.org.uk//medieval-and-post-medieval-pottery-codes (accessed March 2017).

Phase 1 (*c.*1075–1225) is dominated by Medieval Oxford ware (OXY, 59 per cent by sherd count), followed by Cotswold-type ware (OXAC, 20.2 per cent) and East Wiltshire ware (OXAQ, 7.3 per cent), with some early Brill/Boarstall ware (OXAW) jugs appearing toward the end of the phase. One of the more interesting items from Phase 1 is the top of a yellow-glazed Stamford ware water-sprinkler, rarely found in Oxford, and hinting perhaps at the presence of a relatively wealthy household. Phase 2 (*c.*1225–1300) is dominated by fine Brill/Boarstall ware (OXAM) with jugs making up the bulk of the assemblage followed by jars. Phase 3 (*c.*1300–75) produced more than any other in terms of sherd count, and Brill/Boarstall ware jugs continued to dominate. It is worth noting that more than 50 per cent of the Phase 3 pottery came from the backfill of a single feature: a large rectangular stone-lined pit (2466), interpreted as a latrine. A highly decorated Brill 'tripledecker' strip jug could be reconstructed from this assemblage. The Phase 4 (*c.*1375–1525) assemblage contained the majority of the crucible fragments (16.4 per cent of the assemblage by sherds, 63.5 per cent by EVEs and only 3.8 per cent by weight), which are discussed separately below. Brill/Boarstall ware (OXAM) again dominated in Phase 4, including a conical jug with thick limescale-like deposits interpreted as a urinal. Phase 5 (*c.*1525–1625) was dominated by late-medieval Brill/Boarstall ware (OXBX) (44.5 per cent by sherds) with jugs continuing as the predominant form, if now among a wider range of vessel forms, including some sherds of imported German stoneware drinking jugs. Among these Frechen stoneware jugs (FREC) make up 41 per cent (by EVEs) of the pottery in use, although their durability tends to exaggerate their proportion. Other imported items include an attractive South Netherlands maiolica flower vase with polychrome decoration, and the rim of a Beauvais sgraffito ware dish also with polychrome glazes, both indicative of a fairly well-to-do sixteenth-century household. Ubiquitous post-medieval red earthenwares (PMR) make their appearance towards the latter part of this phase. Phase 6 (*c.*1625–1700) was again dominated by late Brill (OXBX) and Frechen stoneware. There was also a high number of black-glazed mugs (PMBL). Phase 7 (*c.*1700–1800) was characterised largely by post-medieval redware crockery (PMR, 20 per cent by sherds), followed by Border wares (BORD, 19.4 per cent by sherds), and English tin-glazed wares (TGW, 11.2 per cent). Finally, Phase 8 (*c.*1800–1900) was characterised almost entirely by redeposited earlier pottery, with just a few sherds of mass-produced Staffordshire-type tablewares (CREA DEV and PEAR).

Catalogue of Illustrated Pottery (Figs. 7.10–7.12):

1. Stamford ware (OXZ). Four joining sherds from neck and discoid top of a water-sprinkler. Ctx 2624, pit 2602, Phase 1.
2. Cotswold-type ware (OXAC). Jar shoulder sherd with cross-in-circle stamp. Tenth/eleventh century? Ctx 2484, pit 2235, Phase 1.
3. Medieval Oxford ware (OXY). Oil lamp rim (diameter 100 mm). Date *c.*1075–1300. Ctx 2356, residual in Phase 4.
4. Medieval Oxford ware (OXY)? Body sherd from ?storage jar with unusual decoration. Twelfth century? Ctx 2495, pit 2477, Phase 1.
5. Brill/Boarstall ware (OXAM). Tripledecker strip jug. Date *c.*1275–1350. Ctx 2597, latrine 2469, Phase 3.
6. Brill/Boarstall ware (OXAM). Near-profile biconical strip jug. *c.*1275–1350. Ctx 2597 with few joining sherds from 2494, both latrine 2469, Phase 3.
7. Brill/Boarstall ware (OXAM). Profile squat globular or sub-biconical jug with scrolling strip decoration. *c.*1275–1350. Ctx 2597, latrine 2469, Phase 3. Rim from 2361, pit 2075, Phase 2.
8. Early Brill/Boarstall ware (OXAW). Complete splayed flat base from baluster jug. *c.*1275–1350. Lower wall perforated. Ctx 2597, latrine 2469, Phase 3.
9. Early Brill/Boarstall ware (OXAW). Profile plain rounded jug probably copying metalware forms. *c.*1275–1350. Ctx 2597, latrine 2469, Phase 3.
10. East Wiltshire ware (Kennet Valley B ware) (OXAQ). Globular jar/cooking pot. *c.*1275–1350. Ctx 2597, latrine 2469, Phase 3.

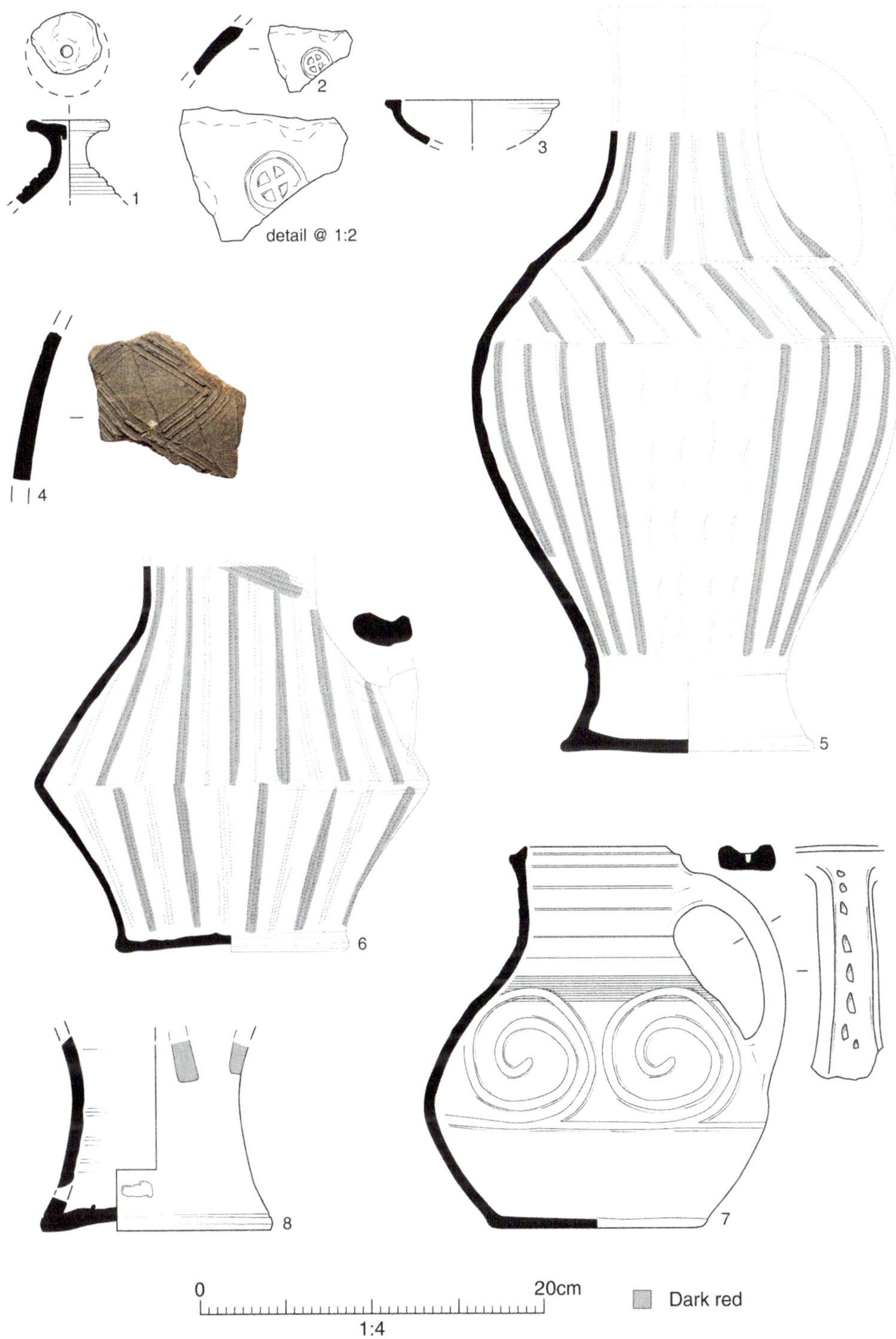

Fig. 7.10 Medieval pottery, nos. 1–8.

Fig. 7.11 Medieval pottery, nos. 9–11.

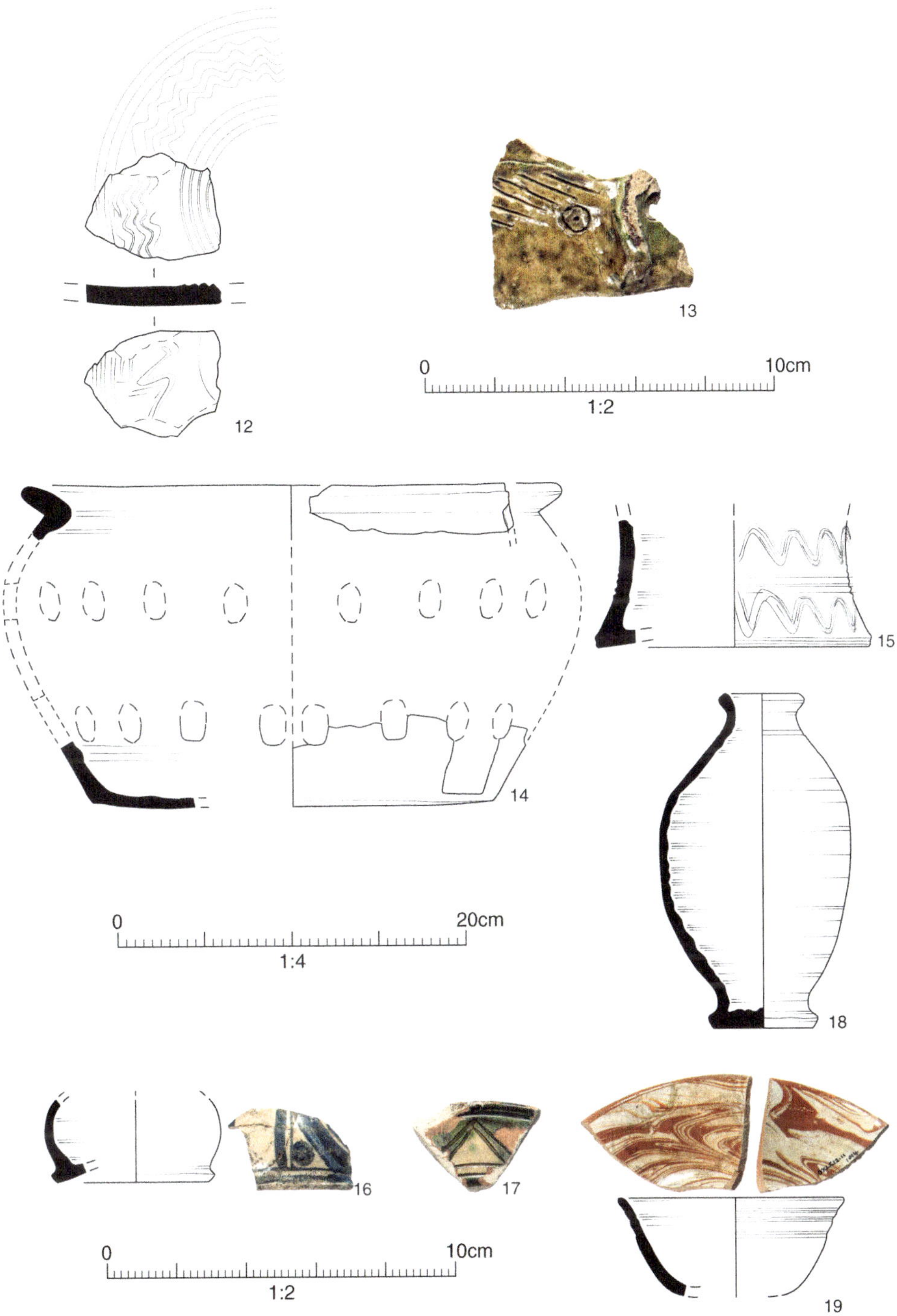

Fig. 7.12 Medieval and post-medieval pottery, nos. 12–19.

11. Brill/Boarstall ware (OXAM). Highly decorated stamped strip jug. *c.*1350–1400? Mainly Ctx 2420, pit 2424, Phase 4. Also Ctxs 2376, 2398 and 2447.
12. Brill/Boarstall ware (OXAM). Very unusual flattish ?base sherd from open vessel form – reversible dish/bowl or lid? Ctx 2360 (ash layer), Phase 4.
13. Brill/Boarstall ware (OXAM). Body sherd from cylindrical mug/tankard with applied 'Green Man'-style face. Late fourteenth/fifteenth century. Ctx 1043, Phase 4.
14. Minety ware (OXBB). Jar with crude (post-firing) perforations through wall (and base?). Probably industrial function (gold and silver traces detected in pXRF analysis). Rim: Ctx 2143, robber cut 2144; base: Ctx 2169; both Phase 5.
15. Late-medieval Brill/Boarstall ware (OXBX). Splayed pad base from a jug (or bunghole cistern?). Fifteenth/early sixteenth century? Ctx 2143, robber cut 2144, Phase 5.
16. South Netherlands maiolica (SNTG). Flower vase. Ctx 2263, Phase 5.
17. Beauvais double sgraffito ware (BEAU2). Dish rim. Ctx 2061, Phase 6.
18. Wessex bottle (newly identified fabric) (WBOT). Unglazed whiteware bottle. Ctx 2301, construction cut for well 2303, Phase 7. Ctx spot-date *c.*1700–30.
19. North Italian marbled slipware (NIMS). Small bell-shaped bowl. Ctx 2301. Pit 2300 (fill of construction cut for well 2303, Phase 7. Ctx spot-date *c.*1700–30.

CRUCIBLES by JOHN COTTER

Probably the most interesting objects within the ceramic assemblage are thirty sherds from around twenty-one small round-bottomed sandy crucibles with a pouring lip (Fig. 7.13). The earliest occurs in Phase 3 (context 2145) where it may be associated with the possible industrial ovens and stone-lined pits. Most however occur in Phase 4, where some may be residual from the previous phase. Most crucible sherds show evidence of use (scorching, internal and external slaggy deposits), and in one case the internal base of a crucible contains tiny droplets of gold embedded in a purplish glassy deposit. Several other sherds display dull grey globules which may be decomposed silver or lead.

Despite their firing differences, the crucibles form a cohesive group. They are in a very sandy brown or grey fabric and, although heat-altered in some cases, they most closely resemble the coarse sandy fabric of early Brill/Boarstall ware (OXAW, *c.*1175–1400, see above). No other groups of high medieval crucibles appear to have been published from Oxford, where most of those found previously are usually dated to the Saxo-Norman period. A couple of heat-altered sherds in non-crucible fabrics may be from jugs but were perhaps used as accessory vessels in an industrial process. Besides these, there are parts of two Minety ware vessels from Phase 5 with post-firing perforations potentially indicating reuse as industrial vessels.

Six crucible samples were submitted for scientific analysis using portable x-ray fluorescence (pXRF). There are problems with using pXRF on crucibles, including background signals from the ceramic material and the fact that different metals will be differentially absorbed into the ceramic fabric during use. Additionally, the crucible fabric may receive mobile metallic elements whilst buried – and presumably also lose others – at different rates according to their volatility and the specific burial environment. There are also more general drawbacks to pXRF, such as its limited usage for reading only the surface of an object at a relatively imprecise location. Nevertheless, of these six samples, four showed strong evidence for having been used to melt silver, and the one further crucible with visible droplets of gold showed positive evidence for that metal. A perforated Minety ware vessel (Fig. 7.12, no. 14) was also analysed, and showed traces of gold and silver.

The visible residues, the small size of the crucibles and the pXRF analyses all suggest that at least some of these crucibles had been used for the melting of precious metals. Potentially they derive from the workshop of a jeweller located somewhere in the vicinity, perhaps even the Aurifabers (Goldsmiths) mentioned in the historical record who owned property on Turl Street (see above). All in all, there are several strong indicators in the ceramic assemblage that some sort of metallurgical industry took place in the vicinity of the site during the fourteenth and possibly the early fifteenth century.

Catalogue of Illustrated Crucibles (Fig. 7.13):

1. Ctx 2363 (rubble dump or possibly fill of oven), Phase 4.
2. Ctx 2272 (occupation deposit/pit slump?), Phase 4.
3. Ctx 2248 (occupation deposit/pit slump?), From sieved sample 16. Phase 4.
4. Ctx 2231 (occupation deposit/pit slump?), From sieved sample 10. Phase 4.
5. Sherd showing gold droplets. Ctx 2220 (demolition deposit), Phase 5.
6. Sherd with slaggy coating externally. Ctx 2060 (levelling/occupation deposit), Phase 5.

Fig. 7.13 Crucibles.

FIRED CLAY by CYNTHIA POOLE

A small assemblage of fired clay amounting to 774 fragments (2,754 g) was recovered. The overall mean fragment weight (MFW) was 14 g. In Phases 1 and 2 fired clay was found in pits in dumps of domestic waste. In Phases 3 to 5 material was found in primary fills of hearth or oven bases, as well as discarded in associated occupation deposits. The single fired clay object from Phase 6 was discarded in a pit fill.

The fabric used for all pieces was a sandy micaceous clay, generally containing moderate to high densities of fine–medium quartz sand, rounded to subrounded, and sometimes with small riverine grits, *c.*2–8 mm, of flint or hard fine-grained rock. Some pieces of raw clay were retained and these were a pale yellowish cream/buff in colour. The fired clay was generally oxidised predominantly red or reddish brown in colour. Sandy clay fabrics were identified in previous excavations at Lincoln College as well as elsewhere in Oxford at St Ebbe's and Cornmarket.[26] In a few cases this clay contained the addition of fine organic inclusions either of chaff or crushed straw.

A number of different categories of items emerge including moulds for the casting of non-ferrous metals, a single pedestal of unknown function, and oven and hearth linings and structural elements. Of the mould fragments, none is of any easily identifiable object, though one fragment from Phase 6 (context 2137, fill of pit 2048) may have been used to produce a candlestick or handle. There were also unidentifiable fragments of piece mould from Phase 2, 3 and 5 contexts. Layer 2173 (Phase 5) produced a virtually complete pedestal of conical form, 82 mm high and 64 mm at the base tapering to 35 mm. The surface around the top was lightly vitrified, but the top surface itself appeared to have been protected from vitrification by an object resting on it, perhaps a crucible. It is an unusual item and no parallels are known to the author. It was most probably used in a metalworking context based on the evidence of vitrification and other evidence for metalworking from the site. Besides positively identifiable fragments of hearth linings, nearly two thirds of the fragments had only a single moulded surface that cannot be assigned to any function with certainty, but characteristics of moulding, wattle impressions and organic tempering suggest they are likely to derive from elements of oven or hearth structure. The assemblage is highly indicative of industrial activity.

BUILDING MATERIALS

Ceramic Building Material by John Cotter

A total of 506 pieces of ceramic building material (CBM) weighing 56.051 kg were recovered, the majority (338 pieces) being flat roof tile (also known as peg tile), of typically rectangular shape and fairly crude manufacture with a pair of circular nail holes at one end. There are no complete examples but one very fresh thirteenth- or fourteenth-century tile preserves a complete length of 278 mm. Other fresh and worn pieces of tile are associated with a number of pit groups containing thirteenth- or fourteenth-century pottery. Much of the roof tile is in a coarse, red, late-medieval fabric which probably dates to the fifteenth or sixteenth century and has been noted at other Oxford sites such as the Classics Centre.[27] A few pieces may be seventeenth century or later and one small fragment of twentieth-century tile has traces of a stamped maker's mark probably from Spain or Italy. The next most populous category is ridge tile (107 pieces), which occurs in similar fabrics, usually with a fairly extensive glaze coverage, dating between the thirteenth and sixteenth centuries. There are also thirty-two pieces of floor tile, though none was found in situ. Thirteen of these pieces were decorated though the condition was very worn

[26] K. Brown, 'The Fired Clay', in Kamash et al., 'Lincoln College, Oxford 1997–2000', pp. 240–2; J. Munby, 'Daub', in Hassall, 'St Ebbe's, Part II', p. 247; D. Sturdy and J. Munby 'Early Domestic Sites in Oxford: Excavations in Cornmarket and Queen St. 1959–62', *Oxoniensia*, 50 (1985), pp. 73, 89.

[27] J. Cotter 'Ceramic Building Materials', in Norton and Cockin, 'Excavations at the Classics Centre', pp. 187–9.

making most of the decoration obscure, but most of them are identifiable as being of the 'stabbed Wessex' tradition with 'inlaid' white slip decoration, dating to *c.*1280–1330. Identifiable designs include an imperial eagle and others with geometrical or floral designs including fleur-de-lys. Two decorated tiles are in the Penn/Chiltern tradition dating to *c.*1330–1400. The other floor tiles are plain late-medieval or early post-medieval 'quarry' tiles resembling imported Flemish tiles of the period. These are typically thick (*c.*34 mm) and have a plain white slip under a clear glaze, or are too worn to tell. Several of these are much thicker (to *c.*55 mm) and are burnt on the upper surface suggesting they were used as hearth tiles. Three of these came from a context with a good group of pottery of *c.*1680–1725 (2301) but the others are probably earlier than this. Additionally, there were 26 pieces of brick of Tudor and later dates.

Roofing Stone by Ruth Shaffrey

The majority of the worked stone comprises elements of roofing materials (33 fragments, weighing 12.4 kg), all fairly typical of medieval examples. Various types of stone are represented including shelly, oolitic and sandy limestones but most of these can be identified as being from the middle Jurassic Corallian beds.[28] Precise sources are not known, though they could have come from an old quarry near Buckland to the south-west of Oxford.[29] These roof stones came from a range of features, including ones conclusively dated to the thirteenth century (Phase 2). A clear increase in the discard of stone roofing from the early fourteenth century is a significant feature of the assemblage.

The discard patterns at this site generally mirror those seen elsewhere in Oxford. Stone roofing is found in small numbers on the majority of excavations of the medieval town suggesting that its use was widespread. Numbers are generally small, however, suggesting it was not used to the exclusion of other types of roofing and was probably not the preferred material. Although thatched roofing continued in use during the medieval period, stone roofing occurred from the twelfth century or early thirteenth century in Oxford.[30] As with the finds from this site, many of the pre-thirteenth-century examples are small fragments and not diagnostically definitely from roofing (for example Oxford Castle). However, a definite example with a perforation was found at Brewer Street in a context of late eleventh to mid thirteenth-century date and another at Corpus Christi College from a thirteenth-century context.[31]

GLASS by IAN R. SCOTT

The excavations produced 80 fragments of glass including 51 pieces of vessel glass, 24 pieces of window glass, four beads and a small possible intaglio, with most contexts producing no more than one or two pieces. The majority of the datable glass is post-medieval, although there is a piece of painted medieval window glass from context 2061 (Phase 6), which also produced two Nuremberg jetons dated to the first half of the sixteenth century. Glass from Phases 1 to 4 is minimal, but window glass begins to appear in Phase 5 and appears to be largely post-medieval in character. The vessels identifiable from these fragments include a beaker (Phase 1), a urinal or flask (Phase 2), a seventeenth-century shallow dish (Phase 5), a wine bottle (Phase 5), the foot of a stemmed glass and the rim of a dish or bowl (Phase 6), and a possible seventeenth-century pharmaceutical bottle (Phase 6), among a small number of other items including an unstratified sixteenth- or seventeenth-century lion mask baluster (Fig. 7.14).

28 W.J. Arkell, *Oxford Stone* (1947), p. 86.

29 Ibid. p. 150.

30 E.M. Jope and W.A. Pantin, 'The Clarendon Hotel, Oxford. Part 1: The Site', *Oxoniensia*, 23 (1958), p. 78.

31 R. Shaffrey, 'Worked Stone', in S. Teague and B.M. Ford, 'Excavations in Oxford's South Suburb at Brewer Street, Littlegate Street and Rose Place', unpublished OA report (2019); R. Shaffrey, 'Worked Stone', in R. Bashford et al., 'Medieval and Post-Medieval Remains from Excavations on the Site of the New Auditorium, Corpus Christi College, Oxford, 2008', *Oxoniensia*, 79 (2014), pp. 200–1.

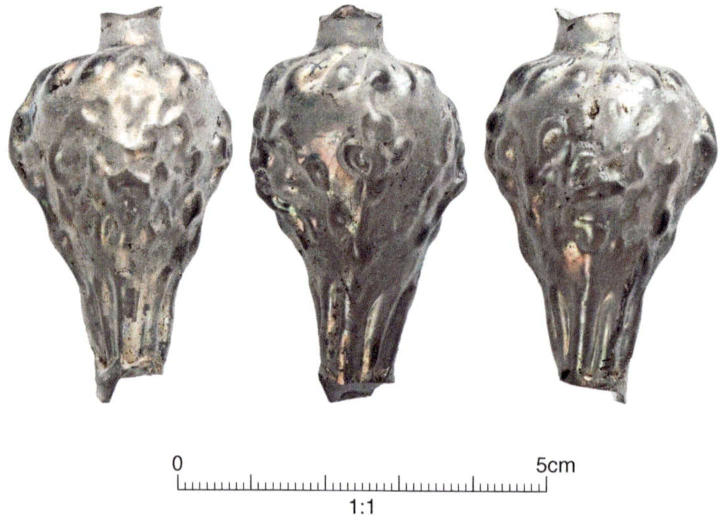

Fig. 7.14 Glass lion mask baluster.

CLAY TOBACCO PIPES by JOHN COTTER and DAVID A. HIGGINS

A total of 102 pieces of clay pipe weighing 1,065 g were recovered from 30 contexts. The pipes are mostly in good condition with a high proportion of complete bowls present (at least 47) and many quite long pieces of stem, some up to 140 mm long.

The two earliest pipe bowls date to *c.*1610–40 and include an example with what is probably intended as a 'crossed keys' mark on the base of a narrow circular heel (2140, fill of pit 2141, Phase 6; Fig. 7.15, no. 1). There are also five smallish Oxford Type A bowls of *c.*1630–55 with large circular or heart-shaped heels. Larger, slightly 'hipped', bowls of Oxford Type B (with a stubby spur) are clearly the most frequent type here with no less than 22 examples present. These are usually the most common seventeenth-century type found in Oxford and were initially dated by Oswald to *c.*1650–90.[32] More recent work, however, dates some examples slightly later to *c.*1730.[33] Type C (*c.*1690–1720) is also fairly common here and, taken together, Types B and C, plus a few rarer contemporary types, underscore the later seventeenth- to early eighteenth-century dating emphasis of the site assemblage as a whole. This fact may be related to the upsurge in domestic and collegiate building in this part of the city during the seventeenth century. A particularly interesting find was an extremely rare bowl of *c.*1690–1720 by the maker Robert Gadney of Oxford (1121, Phase 7; Fig. 7.15, no. 2). A flaring trumpet-shaped bowl seems to be a hybrid of two London-style bowls (AO19 and AO20, *c.*1680–1710). Other non-standard types of a broadly similar date include an unusual spur-less bowl of perhaps *c.*1690–1720 which appears to be an export style, a bowl type only rarely found in this country and then almost always at the ports from which they were exported (2180, modern garden soil; Fig. 7.15, no. 3). Only two bowls of Type D (*c.*1750–90) were found, both from the same context (2028). The fall-off in bowl numbers deposited after *c.*1720 is notable and suggests that rubbish disposal decreased

32 Hassall, 'St Ebbe's, Part II', fig. 51B.

33 D.A. Higgins, 'Clay Tobacco Pipes', in K. Brady et al., 'Excavations at Abingdon West Central Redevelopment: Iron Age, Roman, Medieval, and Post-Medieval Activity in Abingdon', *Oxoniensia*, 72 (2007), pp. 157–76; J. Cotter, 'Clay Tobacco Pipes', in '33–35 George Street, Oxford, Archaeological Watching Brief Report', unpublished OA report (2012), pp. 11–15, https://library.oxfordarchaeology.com/1015/.

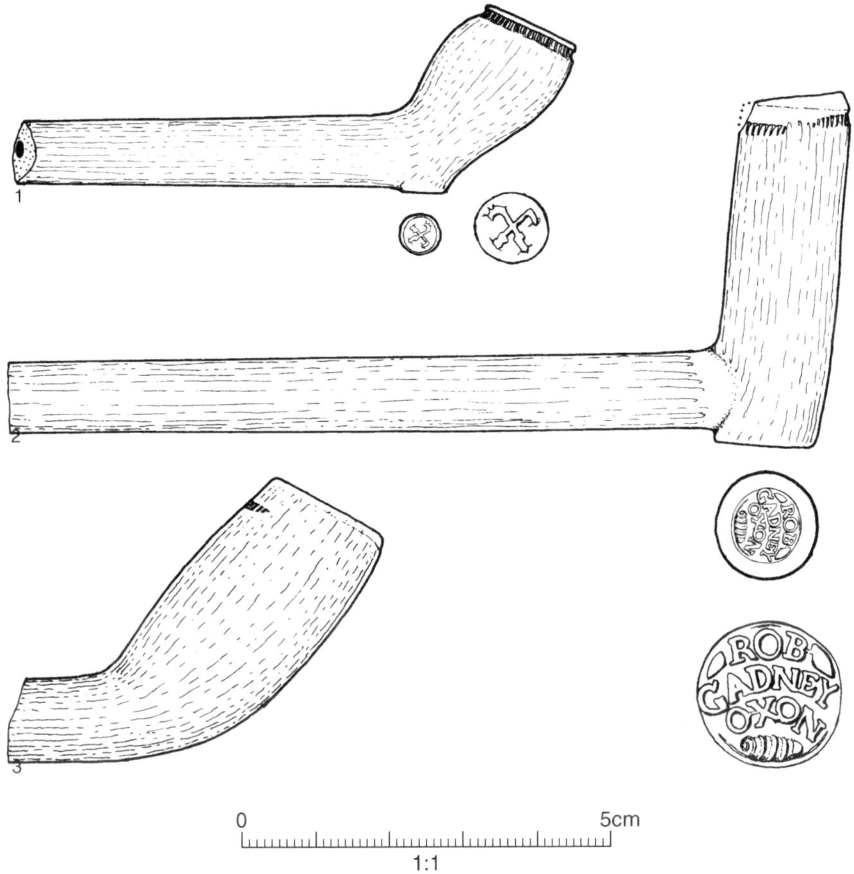

Fig. 7.15 Clay tobacco pipes. Stamp details at 2:1; burnished surface areas indicated with a fine broken line. Drawings by David A. Higgins.

in the area of the site after this date. The latest bowl is a single example of *c.*1820–60 but a few other contexts are also dated late by the presence of late eighteenth- or nineteenth-century pipe stems. One 75 mm-long stem fragment of this date has a (damaged) mouthpiece tipped with pink-red paint or sealing wax to protect the smoker's lips. It seems likely that most of the pipes are local Oxford products. A few might be from other Oxfordshire towns, or possibly beyond.

METALWORK by LEIGH ALLEN

A total of 349 metal objects were recovered. The majority were iron nails (228), with a further 66 examples of very common copper-alloy lace tags, pins and loop fasteners, and 32 unidentifiable fragments. Although large the assemblage is in very poor condition and was x-rayed to aid identification. The majority of the artefacts are late medieval or post-medieval in date and relatively utilitarian in nature, with the possible exception of a decorated hooked tag and possible casket fitting that date between the seventh and eleventh centuries and are therefore most likely residual. Other items include a segment of copper-alloy chain (Phase 3), sixteenth- or seventeenth- and eighteenth-century buckles, and a copper-alloy pin with a globular head (Phase 5).

COINS AND JETONS by IAN R. SCOTT

A worn and clipped silver long cross penny of the London mint of the late thirteenth century at the earliest, and a silver Tudor half groat, possibly of Edward VI, were recovered from Phase 5 contexts. Six jetons were recovered from Phase 5 and 6 contexts, including one English jeton of Edward II and a late fifteenth- or early sixteenth-century Tournai example, and four Nuremberg jetons. These comprise three 'Rose and Orb' jetons, two anonymous and one of Hans Krauwinckel II, and a Lion of St Mark jeton of his uncle Hans Krauwinckel I.

WORKED STONE OBJECT by RUTH SHAFFREY

A soapstone object was recovered from the backfill of well 2162 (Phase 8). One face has a crudely incised hatched pattern and the object has flat faces and a rounded terminus, perhaps serving as some form of rubber or polisher given that soapstone is too soft for use as a whetstone. Though we might assume a Norwegian source for the stone, it is not possible to determine a date for the object.

ANIMAL BONE by LENA STRID

The animal bone assemblage comprised an estimated total of 2,400 fragments from deposits dating from the late eleventh to the late seventeenth century. This number includes 308 fragments (13 per cent) from sieved soil samples, including several bones from birds and mice. The bones were generally in a good to fair condition. Gnawed bones were slightly more frequent in the post-medieval phases (7.8 per cent–9.8 per cent) than in the medieval phases (3.4 per cent–5.3 per cent), suggesting that scavengers had less access to the deposited butchery and kitchen waste in the medieval period. Burnt bones were rare throughout the assemblage.

As typical for a medieval and early post-medieval urban site, the assemblage is dominated by domestic livestock, mainly cattle and sheep/goat but also including some pig (Table 7.3).[34] No bones could be identified as goat, whereas sheep bones occurred in almost all phases, suggesting that most or all of the sheep/goat bones come from sheep. Apart from livestock, bones from other animals likely to have been butchered and eaten include rabbit, hare, red deer, fallow deer, roe deer, domestic fowl, goose, duck, teal, a possible pheasant, woodcock and small perching birds (passerines). Although it is uncertain whether the passerine bones represent wild fauna or kitchen waste, medieval records show that small birds such as thrushes were sold for consumption.[35] Other animals identified in the assemblage include pets and working animals such as cat, dog and horse, as well as wild fauna, represented by raven, brown/black rat, house mouse and frog/toad.

The faunal assemblage appears mainly to comprise a mixture of butchery waste and kitchen waste, but in addition, there are also small deposits of industrial waste from tanning/tawying. Age estimation for cattle and sheep/goat show a great variety of slaughter ages, ranging from very young to old, reflecting calves and lambs slaughtered for dairy production, sub-adult animals raised for meat and adult animals past their prime as breeding animals, draught oxen, milk and wool producers. Pigs were generally slaughtered as juveniles and sub-adults, for meat. There is an increase in juvenile cattle in the early post-medieval phases, which may relate to increased dairy production in the Oxford region.

34 N. Sykes, 'From *Cu* and *Sceap* to *Beffe* and *Motton*: The Management, Distribution and Consumption of Cattle and Sheep, AD 410–1550', in C.M. Woolgar et al. (eds), *Food in Medieval England: Diet and Nutrition* (2006), pp. 56–71.

35 D. Serjeantson, 'A Dainty Dish: Consumption of Small Birds in Late Medieval England', in H. Buitenhuis and W. Prummel (eds.), *Animals and Man in the Past: Essays in Honour of Dr. A.T. Clason, Emeritus Professor of Archaeozoology Rijksuniversiteit Groningen, the Netherlands*, ARC-Publicatie, 41 (2001), pp. 263–73.

Table 7.3. Number of animal bone fragments per taxon and phase. MNI (minimum number of individuals) in brackets.

	Phase 1 11th– E13th C	Phase 2 M– L13th C	Phase 3 E– M14th C	Phase 4 L14– E16th C	Phase 5 M16– E17th C	Phase 6 M– L17th C
Cattle	90 (4)	14 (2)	37 (2)	10 (1)	120 (4)	48 (2)
Sheep/goat	172 (11)	22 (3)	30 (3)	15 (3)	187 (15)	42 (5)
Sheep	19	2	1		8	2
Pig	60 (3)	8 (1)	31 (3)	3 (1)	36 (3)	20 (2)
Horse	1 (1)				2 (1)	
Dog	1 (1)		1 (1)	1 (1)	3 (1)	1 (1)
Cat	7 (2)	1 (1)	1 (1)		1 (1)	1 (1)
Dog/cat					1	
Rabbit				1 (1)	13 (3)	1 (1)
Hare	1 (1)	2 (1)			1 (1)	
Red deer	1 (1)					
Fallow deer		3 (1)				
Roe deer	1 (1)					
Domestic fowl	16 (3)	10 (3)	18 (3)	7 (3)	31 (6)	21 (5)
Goose	6 (2)	2 (1)	6 (1)	2 (1)	10 (1)	2 (1)
Duck	1 (1)			1 (1)	2 (1)	2 (1)
Teal	1 (1)					
?Pheasant	1 (1)					
Woodcock			1 (1)			
Raven	1 (1)					
Passerine	1	4				
Indet. bird	28	10	30	5	38	5
Rat sp.				1 (1)	1 (1)	1 (1)
House mouse	2 (2)				4 (2)	
Mouse sp.		1 (1)				
Micromammal	11	2	1	2	18	
Frog/toad	1				5	
Small mammal			1		3	
Medium mammal	109	13	21	19	174	53
Large mammal	88	23	24	16	159	40
Indeterminate	180	16	29	12	66	26
Total fragments	800	133	232	95	880	265
Total weight (g)	7725	1390	3743	961	12,462	4572

FISH REMAINS by REBECCA NICHOLSON

A small assemblage of identifiable and generally well-preserved fish remains was recovered comprising 459 identified bones, the great majority of which came from the sorted residues of bulk (flotation) soil samples. Most of the assemblage came from pit fills, charcoal spreads and occupation deposits from Phases 1, 3, 4 and 5, broadly reflecting the nature of the archaeology on the site. Most samples contained relatively small numbers of fish bones, which is likely to reflect the general mixing of material within features across the site. There was relatively little variation evident between phases with herring bones consistently comprising around 50 per cent of the identifiable bones and eel around 15 per cent, and some signs of a slight move from freshwater fish in Phase 1 toward sea fish from Phase 2, though both types were present in all phases. A great number of species were identified including clupeids, pike, perch, chub, ruffe, three-spined stickleback, trout, salmon, eel, rays, small shark or dogfish, flatfish, mackerel, several species of gadid (cod, whiting, haddock and ling), gurnard, sea bream and possibly grey mullet. Fish remains are less frequent in Phases 4 and 5 but the assemblages continue to be numerically dominated by bones from herring and, to a lesser extent, eel.

The regular occurrence of bones from both herring and eel is typical for medieval and post-medieval sites in Oxford as indeed for most English urban sites of these periods. These fish were evidently generally available and regularly eaten, as indicated by their relatively cheap price.[36] Herring transported into Oxford in the earlier medieval period is likely to have been preserved by pickling in brine, but fresh fish may also have been available. In 1276 fresh herrings were purchased by Bicester Priory,[37] so it is clear that even by this date all sea fish could be transported as far inland as Oxford quickly enough to remain fresh. For such a small assemblage the range of fish, which includes both sea fish and freshwater fish in all periods, is perhaps surprising, but this is typical for many sites in Oxford and indicates that a variety of fish was available in the marketplace.[38] By the fourteenth century (and probably from the mid twelfth century) Oxford had a busy fish market in the stalls below the Guildhall in St Aldate's (then Fish Street).[39]

PLANT REMAINS by SHEILA BOARDMAN

Forty-nine soil samples (20–50 litres in volume) were assessed for charred, mineralised and waterlogged plant remains as well as wood charcoal.[40] Of these, 14 samples from Phases 1–5 were selected for investigation of the charred plant remains, and one also for mineral-replaced plant remains. In the latter, plant tissues had been replaced by calcium phosphate. This typically occurs in environments with high concentrations of phosphate and calcium ions in solution such as, in this case, cesspits.[41]

Several cereal species were cultivated during the various phases, including bread wheat and rivet wheat, hulled six-row barley and rye. Cultivated oat is also presumed to be present as

[36] C. Dyer, 'The Consumption of Freshwater Fish in Medieval England', in M. Aston (ed.), *Medieval Fish, Fisheries and Fishponds in England*, BAR, BS 182 (1988), p. 31.

[37] C.J. Bond, 'Monastic Fisheries', in Aston, *Medieval Fish, Fisheries and Fishponds*, p. 77.

[38] For example, R.A. Nicholson, 'Fish Bones', in Norton and Mumford, 'Anglo-Saxon Pits and a Medieval Kitchen at The Queen's College, Oxford', pp. 210–4; R.A. Nicholson, 'Fish Remains', in Norton and Cockin, 'Excavations at the Classics Centre', pp. 192–3; R.A. Nicholson, 'Fish Remains', in Poore, 'No. 4A Merton St.', pp. 306–11.

[39] *VCH Oxon*. 4, pp. 3–73; see also chapter 4, above.

[40] S. Boardman, 'Charred, Mineralised and Waterlogged Plant Remains and Wood Charcoal', in 'Lincoln College Garden Building Oxford, Post-Excavation Assessment and Project Design', unpublished OA report (2014).

[41] L.M.E. McCobb et al., 'Phosphatisation of Seeds and Roots in a Late Bronze Age Deposit at Potterne, Wiltshire, UK', *Journal of Archaeological Science*, 30 (2003), pp. 1269–81.

this has been widely recovered elsewhere in Oxford during these periods. While most cereal crops probably reached towns in processed or part-processed form in the medieval period, the evidence suggests that whole cereal crops (in particular rye) and significant quantities of other early crop processing waste (cereal rachises, awns, straw), were reaching the town in the early to mid fourteenth century. This material is normally removed from the grain early on in processing, through threshing and winnowing, which generally take place close to cultivated fields because whole cereal crops are bulky and difficult to transport. The by-products of winnowing (straw, chaff, wild plants) may be traded, as they provide valuable fodder, bedding, thatching materials and so on, and this may account for some chaff and straw in the samples. However, the possibility that some rural crop-processing activities were taking place here in the fourteenth century remains possible.

A range of other cultivated plants are also evident including peas, small horse beans, flax and possible black mustard, plus several wild and cultivated fruits/nuts. None was particularly remarkable and all are known from other sites in Oxford for these periods. The types of remains do not point to such plants being cultivated or processed in this part of the town, although some may have been. Some small fragments of mineralised textile were also recovered and these seem to include some flax fibres, so there is a possibility that such goods were produced somewhere in Oxford or the surrounding area in this period. In terms of the textile fragments, similar material has been recovered from cess deposits at other sites, most recently at Gloucester Priory, and their use as lavatory paper is likely.

WOOD CHARCOAL by SHEILA BOARDMAN

Of the 49 samples assessed for wood charcoal and other plant remains (see above), 27 were selected for charcoal analysis. The Phase 1 samples were dominated by either oak, or hazel and hawthorn group. One Phase 2 sample had mostly hawthorn group charcoal. The Phase 3 samples were the most mixed in terms of the dominant taxa, which included oak, beech and hawthorn group. The Phase 4 samples were mostly beech dominated. Samples from this phase also had the narrowest range of taxa per sample. The more mixed sample came from an industrial hearth and had nine taxa groups. The Phase 5 samples had proportionally more oak charcoal, as compared to the Phase 4 samples, although 7 of 10 samples were again dominated by beech. The analysed samples from Phase 5 were quite mixed generally, with an average 7.5 taxa/sample, and the widest range of non-Fagaceae (beech/oak) charcoal taxa from the site.

Mixtures of timber and roundwood were present throughout the phases and the nature of the evidence suggests that both were being used as fuel in domestic and industrial contexts at the site. The main fuel species, oak and beech, both have good thermal capacities so they would have been suitable for most domestic purposes. In the bread oven samples, a large (or the largest) proportion of the fuels were from timber rather than roundwood. Roundwood may have been used predominantly to increase temperatures quickly. For bread ovens, generally, particular woods were sometimes preferred. Legume wood, in particular small gorse (*Ulex*) roundwood, which cannot be distinguished from broom (*Cytisus*), has been associated with Roman and later bread ovens.[42] Gorse is an abundant shrub that burns with a hot flame and ashes well, leaving little charcoal residue. Only one fragment of legume wood was recovered from these samples, from a Phase 5 ashy hearth fill (sample 4). The bread oven samples seem to have a more diverse range of taxa, as compared to the industrial hearth samples.

Evidence from a number of Oxford sites shows beech replacing oak as the principal fuel wood by the late fifteenth century. The evidence from the present site for the dominance of beech from the early to mid thirteenth century is therefore of interest. The wider context of this change from oak/mixed fuel sources to a dominance of beech in the late-medieval period is discussed in

42 C. Dickson and J. Dickson, *Plants and People in Ancient Scotland* (2000).

detail in the full report. By 1300, fuel wood was being transported in great quantities from the Chilterns along the Thames to London and had become a very valuable commodity. The beech wood reaching this site from the late fourteenth century was probably in the form of (waste) timber and faggots. The latter are bundles of (similar sized) twiggy wood or roundwood. The lengths and sizes of wood and bundles later became standardised. The mix of different ages of roundwood in the samples up to Phase 4 points to faggots cut from felled timbers, underwood, hedges or similar, rather than from similar aged coppice. However, different sized faggots may reflect different uses, the spent fuel from which later became mixed in refuse deposits. By the sixteenth century, with renewed clearances for cultivation and expanding timber sales, coppicing became the norm everywhere.

OTHER FINDS

Other finds included a residual prehistoric flint flake; small quantities of iron slag and fuel ash slag; and 243 pieces of marine shell, mainly oyster.

ACKNOWLEDGEMENTS

OA would like to thank Tim Knowles of Lincoln College for his and the college's assistance during the archaeological works, and for funding this report. Stephen Oliver, the project architect for Rodney Melville and Partners Ltd, and Mark Ketteringham, the Structural Engineer for SFK Consulting LLP, provided timely and important advice when necessary. William Tutcher, Peter McDonald, David Murphy of Stepnells Ltd provided helpful logistical support as the principal contractors during the excavations. The entire archaeological process was managed for OA by Ben M. Ford; on-site archaeological direction was provided by Robin Bashford, assisted by Jack Goodens, Lee Grana-Nicolaou, Michael McLean, Kevin Moon, Matthew Morgan, Benn Penny-Mason, Emily Plunkett, Chris Richardson, Alice Rose, Diogo Silva, Mike Sims, Lee Sparks and Jennifer Thurstan. Thanks are also due to the staff that processed the finds under the management of Leigh Allen, processed the environmental samples under the management of Rebecca Nicholson, and prepared the archive under the management of Nicola Scott. This report was edited by Toby Martin and Anne Dodd.

8.

Medieval and Later Activity at St Alban's Quad and Patey's Quad, Merton College

STEVEN TEAGUE and BEN M. FORD

with contributions by LEIGH ALLEN, PAUL BLINKHORN, LEE G. BRODERICK, JOHN GIORGI, DAVID A. HIGGINS, REBECCA NICHOLSON, CYNTHIA POOLE, IAN R. SCOTT and RUTH SHAFFREY

SUMMARY

Archaeological work at Merton College in St Alban's Quad and Patey's Quad revealed twelfth- to early thirteenth-century pits which predate the foundation of the college in 1264. The St Alban's Quad excavation apparently straddled the sites of two pre-college academic halls (Lomb Hall and Hertheved Hall), and the investigation revealed a possible boundary fence separating the two. The Patey's Quad site was located within the pre-college tenement of the Herprut family, and a pit here revealed tentative evidence for late twelfth- or early thirteenth-century horn-working. Gravel surfaces and a stone drain of later-medieval date were also revealed in Patey's Quad. Post-medieval evidence was limited to wall fragments from seventeenth- to nineteenth-century buildings belonging to the college and to St Alban Hall (a separate academic institution amalgamated with Merton College in the late nineteenth century), and a well that had been filled during the late eighteenth century.

Refurbishment of the basement area of the east wing of St Alban's Quad at Merton College to create a new music room led to an archaeological watching brief, which upon the discovery of significant archaeology became a controlled archaeological excavation. Additionally, the installation of a new lift pit within the yard known as Patey's Quad necessitated a programme of archaeological work including targeted excavation, watching brief and building recording (Fig. 8.1). Both sets of work were undertaken between July and September 2016.

This report summarises the results of both projects; further details can be found in the full reports, available via the OA Library.[1] The archives will be deposited with Oxfordshire County Museum Service under the accession numbers 2016.121 (Patey's Quad) and 2016.134 (St Alban's Quad).

[1] 'St Alban's Quad, Merton College. Oxford. Archaeological Watching Brief Report', unpublished OA report (2017), https://library.oxfordarchaeology.com/5762/; 'New Lift Pit, Patey's Quad, Merton College, Oxford. Excavation Report', unpublished OA report (2017), https://library.oxfordarchaeology.com/5761/; 'SCR Lift Installation, Merton College, Oxford. Historic Building Recording', unpublished OA report (2018), https://library.oxfordarchaeology.com/5761/.

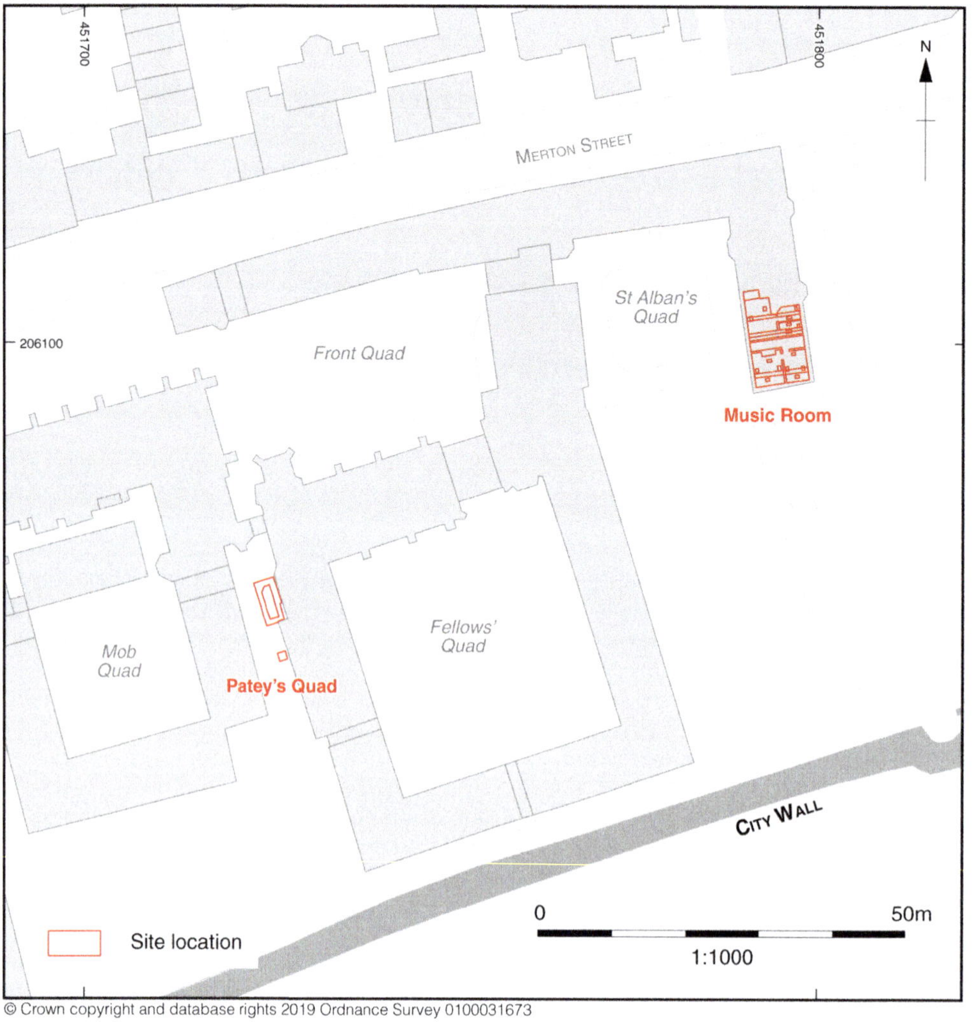

Fig. 8.1 Site location.

ARCHAEOLOGICAL AND HISTORICAL BACKGROUND

Merton College, founded in 1264, is located within the walled medieval town, and the southern boundary of the college is defined by a surviving section of the town wall. In 1970 an excavation was conducted on part of the town wall south-west of the college to establish whether it overlay an earlier, Anglo-Saxon rampart, but no such predecessor was found.[2] Recent excavations within Corpus Christi College to the west have indicated that the town wall was at least partially rebuilt in the early seventeenth century.[3] Historical evidence suggests that a late Anglo-Saxon

[2] T.G. Hassall, 'Excavations at Merton College, Oxford, 1970', *Oxoniensia*, 36 (1971), pp. 34–48. However, see Dodd, *Oxford*, p. 23 and appendix 1, no. 66 for David Sturdy's possible sighting of an Anglo-Saxon rampart under the new Warden's Lodgings.

[3] R. Bashford and A. Dodd, 'Medieval and Post-Medieval Remains from Excavations on the Site of the New Auditorium, Corpus Christi College, Oxford, 2008', *Oxoniensia*, 79 (2014), p. 186.

mural mansion lies beneath Mob Quad, although it has not been investigated by archaeological excavation.[4] Excavations in Mob Quad in 1922 recorded an early building and medieval pottery.[5] On the north side of Merton Street, excavations in 1961–2 at Logic Lane revealed evidence for continuous occupation from the late Anglo-Saxon period onwards.[6] Excavations at No. 4A Merton Street supplied evidence for domestic occupation from the eleventh to fourteenth centuries, and use of the site as stables during the late fourteenth to mid sixteenth centuries.[7]

Salter's plan of medieval landholdings predating the foundation of Merton College suggests that the area now occupied by both sites comprised part of a series of plots fronting on to St John's Lane (now Merton Street) that were occupied by academic halls.[8] The St Alban's Quad site possibly straddled two adjacent properties, Hertheved Hall (Salter SE 198) and Lomb Hall (Salter SE 196–7), which lay to the east. To the west of the site lay St Alban Hall (Salter SE 199), a medieval academic hall that survived as an independent hall until 1882, when it was incorporated into Merton College. Hertheved Hall was a tenement with houses in 1316;[9] once a hall and 'now a garden' *c.*1395,[10] and in 1497 a 'garden' leased by Balliol to Merton.[11] It was eventually bought outright by Merton College in 1804. Lomb Hall is first mentioned in a deed of 1310 when a messuage (house) with two tofts (vacant house plots) was given to Merton in 1331 (Salter SE 196–7). Patey's Quad lies within a property held by Henry Herprut in 1235–6 that had previously been held by Alured Herprut (Salter SE 203). It lay adjacent to a tenement belonging to Jacob the Jew known as Halegod's house (Salter SE 202) located to the east, and adjacent to the churchyard of St John the Baptist church (Salter SE 204). The two tenements and the church were purchased by Merton College *c.*1267. Herprut's house lay where the existing gatehouse stands.[12]

Agas' map of Oxford of 1578 shows the Music Room site occupying a narrow empty plot (probably the former Hertheved Hall property) located between St Alban Hall and the extensive Merton Gardens to the east. Loggan's map of 1675 shows a similar arrangement but the plot was by then a walled garden or orchard. The maps of Taylor (1750; Fig. 8.2) and Davis (1793) both show three small rectangular buildings within the northern part of the garden. A plan of St Alban Hall by James King (1848) shows one of these structures positioned in the south-west corner of the Principal's Garden and labelled 'parlour room'. The Ordnance Survey map of 1876 shows that these structures had been replaced by an apsed extension that projected eastwards from the south range of St Alban Hall. All but the frontage of St Alban Hall was demolished and replaced by the current St Alban's Quad during 1904–10. Within Patey's Quad, Taylor's map of 1750 shows a building linking the medieval Mob Quad with the 1610 Fellows' Quad.

DISCUSSION

The Site Before the College

No features that can be assigned to the late Anglo-Saxon period were identified although it is possible that some of the undated pits found on both sites are of this date. Single sherds of St Neots ware were found on each site, occurring residually in later pits. It is presumed that the

[4] E.M. Jope, 'Late Saxon Pits under Oxford Castle Mound: Excavations in 1952', *Oxoniensia*, 17–18 (1952–3), pp. 77–111 and fig. 39.

[5] *VCH Oxon.* 3, pp. 95–106.

[6] O.P. Radcliffe, 'Excavations at Logic Lane, Oxford. The Prehistoric and Early Medieval Finds', *Oxoniensia*, 26–7 (1961–2), pp. 38–69.

[7] Poore, 'No. 4A Merton St.'.

[8] Salter, *Survey*, vol. 1.

[9] Balliol College Archive, Deeds 171 (253).

[10] H.E. Salter (ed.), *A Cartulary of the Hospital of St John the Baptist*, 3 vols., OHS, 66, 68–9 (1914–17), vol. 3, p. 253.

[11] Balliol College Archive, Deeds 171 (254).

[12] Ibid.

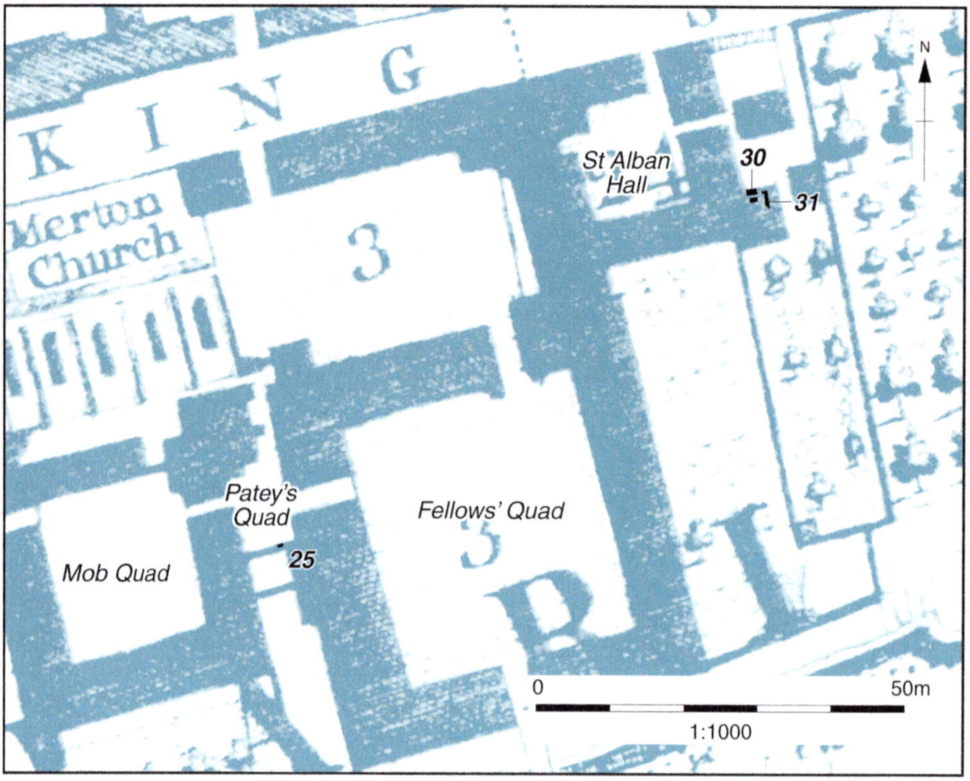

Fig. 8.2 Detail from Isaac Taylor's map of Oxford (1750) showing locations of walls 30/1 (Music Room) and 25 (Patey's Quad).

site lay within and close to the south-east corner of the *burh*, though to date no firm evidence has been found for the *burh* defences within this area. Indeed, the apparent lack of evidence from the site corresponds with the paucity of archaeological evidence along Merton Street.

The earliest evidence within both sites comprises several pits, that where dated contained medieval Oxford ware pottery dating to no earlier than the late eleventh or early twelfth centuries. Given their large size, some of the pits were probably utilised for the extraction of gravel for use in floors, yards and foundations before their eventual use for the disposal of refuse. At the Music Room, the pits were initially clustered within the north-eastern part of the excavated area before expanding westwards and southwards during the early thirteenth to fourteenth centuries. As such this follows a pattern of pits radiating outwards from buildings that presumably fronted St John's Lane located about 20 m to the north. No evidence for these frontage structures was found on either site. Two early postholes at the Music Room may hint at a fence possibly separating two properties, perhaps that between Hertheved Hall and Lomb Hall.[13] The apparent clustering of pits either side of this boundary may also support this suggestion.

Though the animal bone assemblage was small, the relative abundance of domestic fowl compared to the three principal domesticates (pig, sheep/goat and cattle) is comparable to other contemporary sites such as nearby No. 4A Merton Street.[14] A horncore and zygomaticus found

[13] Salter, *Survey*, vol. 1, SE 198 and SE 196–7.

[14] F. Worley and E.-J. Evans, 'Animal Bone', in Poore, 'No. 4A Merton St.', pp. 311–21.

in pit 68 at Patey's Quad tentatively suggests horn-working. Late twelfth- and thirteenth-century horn-working was identified at nearby No. 4A Merton Street suggesting such industries were present in the immediate area around this time.[15] The same pit was fairly rich in free-threshing wheat, suggesting bread making for the better off. The roof tile from this pit suggests that a building (possibly Herprut's house) on or near the property during the early thirteenth century was roofed with peg tiles, with the ridges covered with plain, probably glazed, ridge tiles.

The College

On both sites, the pits were sealed by garden soils, suggesting a change of land use. At the Music Room, this soil contained late-medieval pottery and a French jeton of late fourteenth- or early fifteenth-century date. At Patey's Quad, the soil developed earlier, probably during the mid to late thirteenth century. Both chronologies agree with the documentary evidence: the former site was a garden by *c.*1395, later being leased to Merton College, and the latter was acquired by the college in 1267. Exterior yard surfaces and a stone-lined drain at Patey's Quad certainly predate the construction of Fellows' Quad in 1610 and it is possible that they formed part of an access route leading from the new gatehouse and alongside the chapel and Mob Quad. The presence of hammerscale on the surfaces suggests smithing was occurring close by.

Little post-medieval evidence survived. The Music Room site probably remained open during the seventeenth century, as Loggan's map of 1675 shows an enclosed garden or orchard corresponding with the bounds of the former Hertheved Hall property and the extensive gardens of Merton to its east. Wall fragments broadly correspond with a structure projecting from the south-east corner of St Alban Hall depicted on Taylor's map of 1750 (Fig. 8.2). On James King's 1848 plan of St Alban Hall this is labelled as a 'parlour room'. The structure had been demolished by the time of the first edition Ordnance Survey map of 1876. At Patey's Quad, a wall fragment corresponds with the northern side of a structure depicted on Taylor's map linking Mob Quad and Fellows' Quad. On King's 1848 plan of Merton College this structure is labelled as comprising a 'water closet' and 'yard'. A stone-lined well found to the north may have served the adjacent kitchen in Fellows' Quad. It was filled in the late eighteenth century with deposits incorporating kitchen or table waste, such as mineralized fruit remains and fragments of glass decanters and drinking vessels.

STRATIGRAPHIC SUMMARY

Excavation of the Music Room site proceeded only as far as the impact level of the development (*c.*57.25 m OD, or *c.*0.50 m below the existing floor slab). At Patey's Quad, two trenches were excavated. In the larger, Trench 1, all archaeological deposits other than a post-medieval well were excavated to their base, while in Trench 2 a post-medieval wall was recorded but no further archaeological work was required. At the Music Room, natural yellowish orange silty sand, consistent with the Summertown-Radley (second) terrace, was revealed across the site at *c.*57.30 m OD. At the north-east corner of Patey's Quad it survived at 57.24 m OD.

Phase 1: Twelfth to Early Thirteenth Century (Figs. 8.3–8.5)

A number of pits and two possible postholes were located within the northern part of the Music Room. Two of the pits (53 and 57) remained unexcavated as they lay below the impact level. The remaining pits (20, 44, 49, 59, 82 and 99) were investigated to a maximum depth of 0.40 m and none were fully excavated to their base. Consequently, only their upper, probable secondary fills, were investigated. Pits 44 and 82 cut earlier pits (20 and 99), implying that they were not dug for extraction. Pit 44 contained large sherds of North-East Wiltshire ware and medieval Oxford ware, the latter type also being present in pit 82. The lack of the ubiquitous Brill/Boarstall

15 Poore, 'No. 4A Merton St.', pp. 216–9.

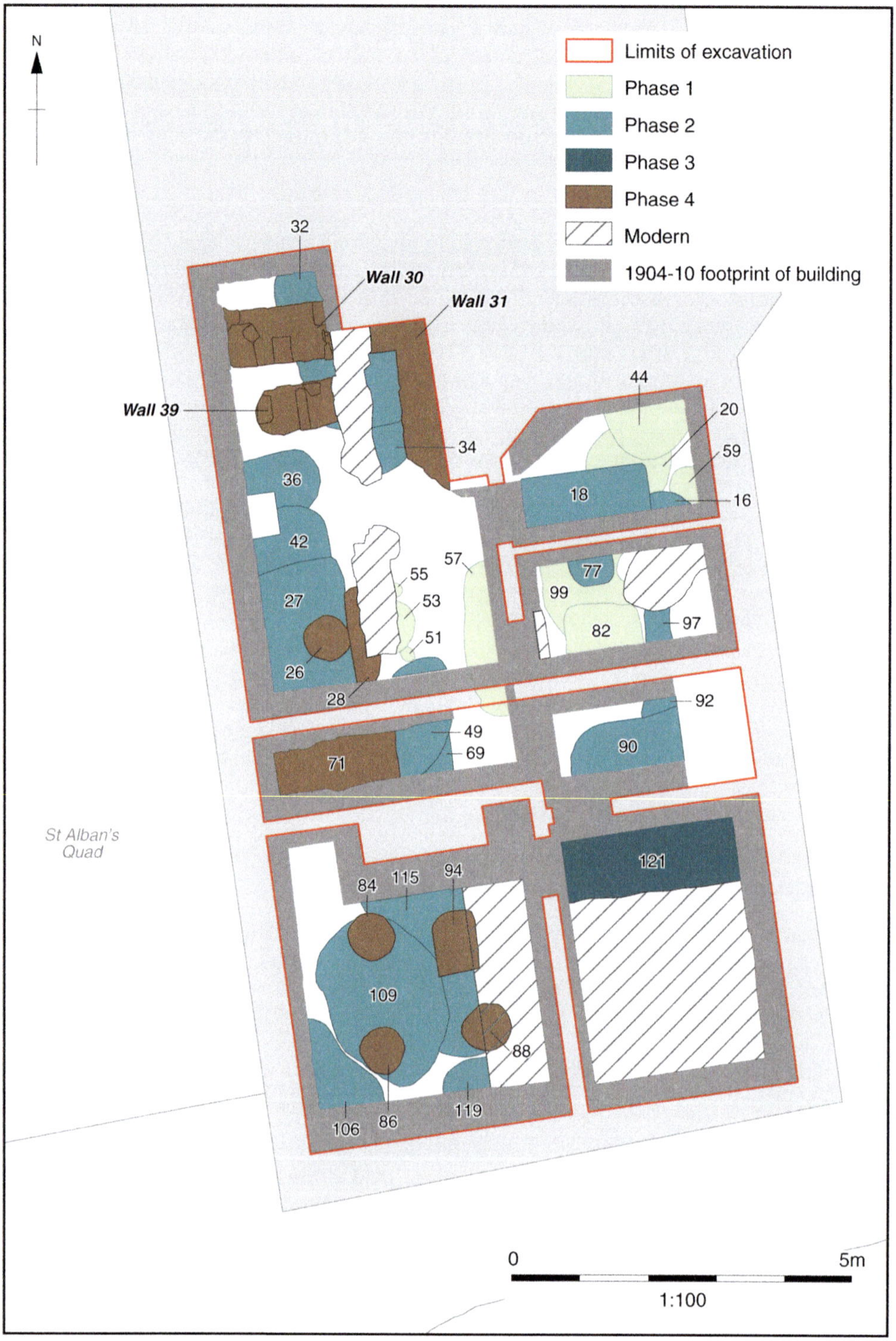

Fig. 8.3 Medieval and later features at the Music Room.

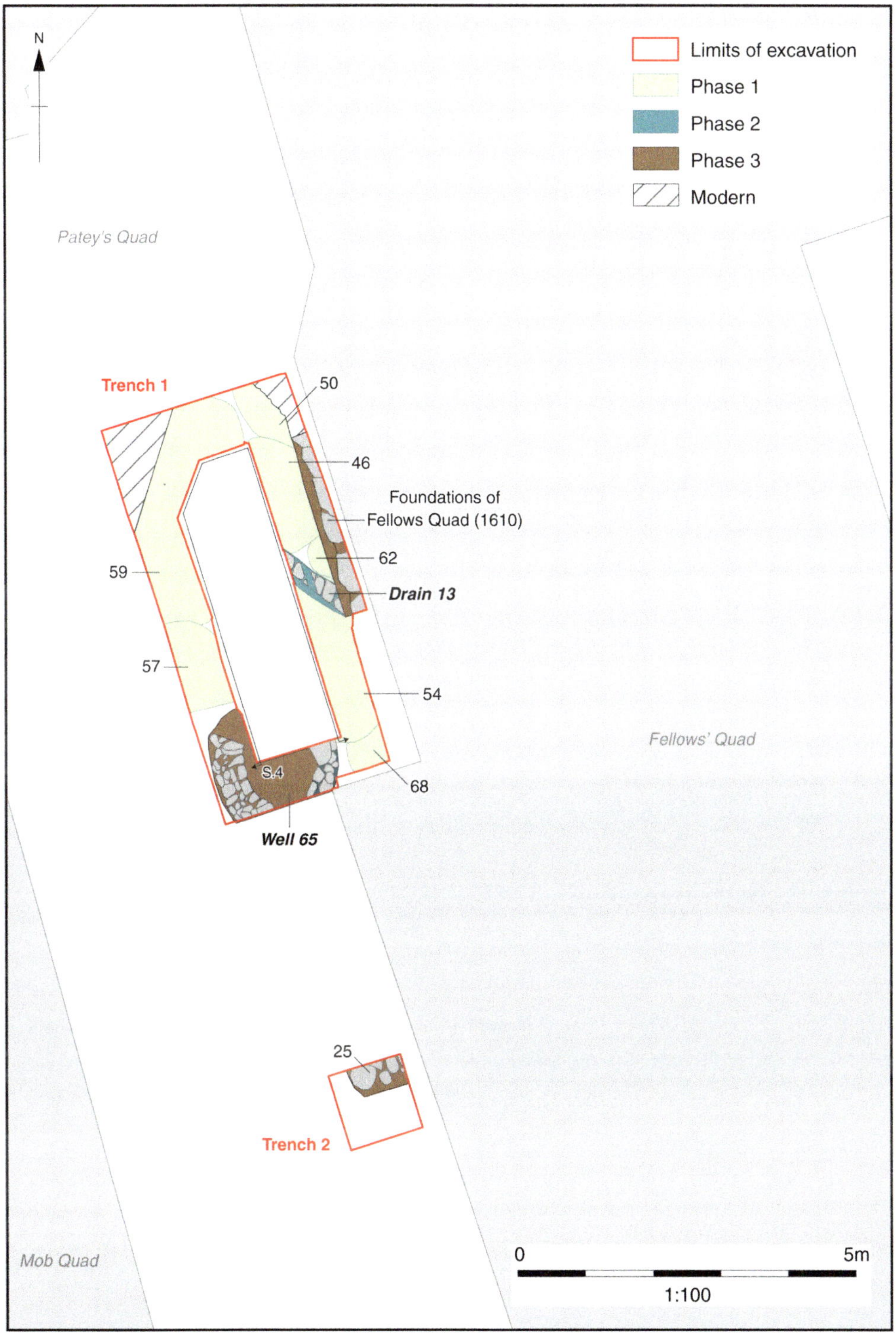

Fig. 8.4 Medieval and later features at Patey's Quad.

ware suggests both pits date to no later than the early thirteenth century. Although unexcavated postholes 51 and 55 are not dated, one was cut by pit 53, considered to be early in date. They may have formed part of a fence delimiting the pits the west.

Six pits were partially exposed within Trench 1 at Patey's Quad. The largest (59) measured at least 3.9 m by 2.0 m (east–west) and was 0.52 m deep and probably dug for gravel extraction since its relatively shallow depth precludes its use as a cellar. A second large pit (54) measuring at least 2.4 m across and of similar depth probably served a similar function though in contrast to the former pit it contained a noticeable quantity of animal bone, roof tile and medieval Oxford ware. It cut sub-rounded pit 68 that contained two ash/charcoal-rich fills (69 and 70), probably sweepings from a nearby hearth or oven. The dominant pottery was also medieval Oxford ware though several sherds of early Brill ware and Brill/Boarstall ware could suggest a late twelfth- or early thirteenth-century date for both pits. Rounded pits 46 and 50 both had clay linings, perhaps to prevent the seepage of ground water into them or to hold a liquid. The upper fill of pit 46 contained the only dating evidence, perhaps slumping of overlying layers, which included thirteenth-century roof tile, a large quantity of medieval Oxford ware, and a sherd of Brill/Boarstall ware, again suggesting an early thirteenth-century date.

Phase 2: Early Thirteenth to Fourteenth Century (Figs. 8.3–8.5)

The Music Room continued to be utilised for pitting, the degree of which intensified and spread outwards towards the western and southern part of the site. A total of up to 18 pits were revealed though none were excavated beyond depths of between 0.08–0.30 m. In contrast to those of Phase 1, the pits were somewhat larger or tended to be more rectangular and it is likely that the larger pits served as quarries before being utilised for the disposal of rubbish. Large rectangular pit 18 may have been lined with timber, given the regularity of its sides. Most of the

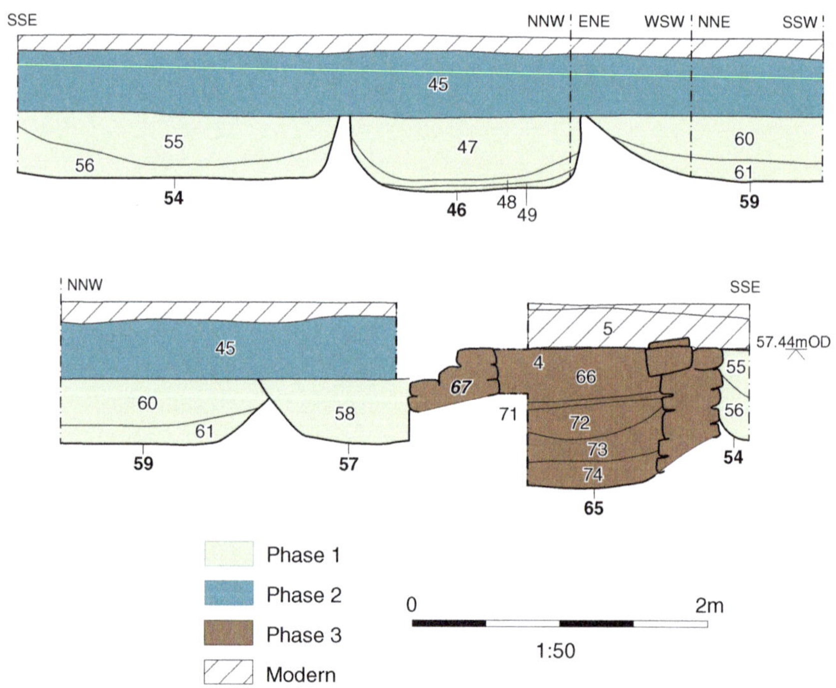

Fig. 8.5 Section 4 (Patey's Quad).

Fig. 8.6 Patey's Quad. Phase 2 drain 13 with contemporary gravel surface 16, looking south-east. Scale: 0.2 m.

pits contained a homogeneous fill of dark greyish brown clayish silt, likely to either represent deliberate backfill or in some cases accumulation of overlaying garden soils that could have slumped into them. Twelve of the pits contained Brill/Boarstall ware pottery, and the lack of discernible late-medieval wares suggests that the pits were filled between the early thirteenth and fourteenth centuries.

Sealing the pits in Patey's Quad was a 0.55 m-thick garden soil (Fig. 8.5, 45), suggesting a prolonged period of cultivation, although the pottery comprised unabraded medieval Oxford ware together with small quantities of Brill/Boarstall ware implying a date not later than the thirteenth century. Overlying this soil along the eastern arm of Trench 1 was a succession of thin gravel surfaces and silts that contained a few sherds of Brill/Boarstall ware. Contemporary with a later surface was a stone-lined drain (Fig. 8.6, 13) that ran at an oblique angle from and predated the west wall of the Fellows' Quad (constructed 1610).

Phase 3: Fifteenth to Mid Sixteenth Century (Fig. 8.3)
Sealing the pits within the southern part of the Music Room was an accumulation of garden soils (121). A French jeton dating to the late fourteenth- or early fifteenth-century and sherds of late-medieval Brill/Boarstall and reduced wares were recovered from the soils.

Phase 4: Late Sixteenth to Nineteenth Century (Figs. 8.3–8.5)
No post-medieval levels survived that predated the existing basement floor within the Music Room or the present pavement of Patey's Quad. At the Music Room were the remains of three limestone wall footings (30/31 and 39) that formed the north-east corner of a building that clearly predated the footings of the existing building (built 1904–10). It is possible that its southern extent was denoted by unexcavated rubble-filled feature 71, possibly a robber trench. No dating evidence was recovered from the structure, though the off-white mortar used is of post-medieval type. Robber trench 28 cut the upper fill of pit 27 that produced a clay tobacco pipe dated to 1610–40. The only other features were several circular rubble-filled pits (26, 84, 86, and 88) that may have represented tree holes, one of which cut possible robber trench 28.

Within Trench 2 in Patey's Quad a wall foundation (25) ran at right-angles to the west wall of Fellows' Quad. It was constructed with rough-squared limestone blocks bonded by a pale off-white 'cement' which supported a column base measuring *c.*0.40 m in diameter. A circular stone-lined well (67) was located immediately adjacent to the west wall of Fellows' Quad in Trench 1, and was excavated to a depth of 0.94 m. Pottery and clay tobacco pipes from throughout the excavated fill sequence indicate that the upper part of the well had been rapidly filled during the late eighteenth century. Various other refuse was recovered from these fills, including mineralised fruit remains.

POTTERY by PAUL BLINKHORN

The pottery assemblage from Patey's Quad comprised 239 sherds with a total weight of 2,892 g. The estimated vessel equivalent (EVE), by summation of surviving rim sherd circumference was 1.90. That from the Music Room consisted of 220 sherds with a total weight of 2,663 g (EVE = 1.03).

The pottery assemblages from both sites show broadly similar characteristics in that nearly 90 per cent of the material in each case broadly dates to the thirteenth to fourteenth centuries, with very little earlier material. At Patey's Quad, single small sherds of residual Roman and late Anglo-Saxon wares were the only pre-Conquest types present, and a solitary, small residual fragment of the latter was the only one noted at the Music Room. Patey's Quad produced a handful of sherds which may date to the eleventh to twelfth centuries, including a single fairly large and fresh sherd from pit 59.

The two relatively large groups of thirteenth- to fourteenth-century wares from the sites do exhibit quite different characteristics. The assemblage from Patey's Quad is dominated by Oxford ware (fabric OXY), which makes up 77 per cent (by weight) of the group, with Brill/Boarstall ware (fabric OXAM) comprising just 7.3 per cent. Conversely, at the Music Room, OXAM makes up around 68 per cent of the assemblage by weight, with OXY comprising only just over 18 per cent (by weight). At Patey's Quad, the rim assemblage is dominated by jars, with the rest of the assemblage made up of a few jugs, bowls and lamps, whereas at the Music Room, jars were not much more common than jugs. While both assemblages appear entirely domestic in nature, this suggests that this particular phase of activity at the two sites had quite different chronological characteristics.

The dominance of OXY and jars at Patey's Quad suggests that most of the pottery dates to the first half of the thirteenth century, as OXAM vessels are rare during that period, but very common, as are jugs, in the later thirteenth to fourteenth century.[16] This strongly suggests that the site was sealed from around the mid thirteenth century, when it was acquired by the college, until the post-medieval period. At the Music Room, it would appear that pottery deposition carried on more or less unchecked throughout the thirteenth to fourteenth century, with pottery deposition only dropping off once the site was given over to gardens, probably in the later fourteenth century or shortly thereafter.

There was very little post-medieval pottery present at either site, with a few sherds of mid sixteenth- to seventeenth-century material noted at both, and small groups of small sherds of eighteenth- to nineteenth-century wares occurring at Patey's Quad.

BUILDING MATERIALS

Ceramic Building Material by Cynthia Poole

A modest assemblage of ceramic building material (141 fragments, 6,251 g) was recovered, the majority of which (119 fragments, 5,225 g) came from Patey's Quad. It consists almost entirely of medieval roof tile apart from a few pieces of late nineteenth- to twentieth-century brick.

The roof tile comprises both peg tile and ridge tile, though a high proportion could not be assigned to either category. The peg tiles were identified by the circular tapering peg holes often punched at an angle rather than perpendicular to the surface. The peg tile ranged in thickness from 11–17 mm, sometimes thickening to the edge, and in general has a fairly rough, crude finish. The peg tile was made in standard Oxford fabrics, most in fabric VIIBB with smaller quantities in VIIB, IIIB and VIIIBB/IIIB. A small quantity was identified as ridge tile on the basis of glaze, profile or treatment of the edges such as knife trimming of the underside, but none had evidence of the ridge apex and no crests were found. Flat glazed fragments formed approximately a third of the assemblage and occurred in a variety of colours: pale green, dark green, olive green, amber or brown sometimes with brown mottles or speckles on the lighter colours. The glaze was generally thin, patchy, discontinuous or splashes rarely extending as far as the tile edge. The presence of glaze cannot be taken alone as an indicator of ridge tile, as it was noted that much of the peg tile at No. 4A Merton Street was also glazed.[17] A small number of tiles from Patey's Quad had impressions, including the imprint of a small hoof (pit 46), probably ovicaprid or deer, and others finger marks from handling during manufacture such as a large thumb print (pit 54) and three small contiguous fingertips (pit 46) which from their size are likely to be those of a child.

The tile derives from deposits largely predating the college and reflects the character of the property on this individual tenement. The tile at Patey's Quad suggests that the building occupying the tenement during the twelfth to thirteenth centuries was roofed with ceramic peg tiles with the ridges probably covered with plain glazed ridge tiles. The presence of roof tile in Phase 1 pits of twelfth- to early thirteenth-century date provides significant evidence for the early use of tile in the group VII fabrics. Flat roof tiles of plain rectangular form are known from documentary evidence and later twelfth-century contexts in several English towns and cities including London,[18] and in Oxfordshire at Eynsham abbey.[19] This assemblage provides evidence for the use of roof tile in a domestic setting and contrasts with the assemblage from No. 4A Merton Street, where the early phases were dominated by the early type A ridge tiles in fabric IB, virtually absent from the present excavation. The sandier fabrics of group III,

16 Mellor, 'Synthesis'.

17 J. Cotter, 'Ceramic Building Materials', in Poore, 'No. 4A Merton St.', pp. 292–305.

18 T.P. Smith, 'London's Earliest Medieval Roofing Tiles: A Comparative Study', *Medieval Ceramics*, 22–3 (1998–9), pp. 66–71.

19 N. Mitchell, 'The Floor and Roof Tile' in A. Hardy et al., *Aelfric's Abbey: Excavations at Eynsham Abbey, Oxfordshire, 1989–92*, Thames Valley Landscapes Monograph, 16 (2003), p. 214.

which formed a significant part of the later assemblage at No. 4A Merton Street, make their appearance in Phase 2 together with a few scraps of late fabrics (IIIA, IVA/B) of fourteenth- to sixteenth-century date.

Stone Roofing by Ruth Shaffrey
Nine pieces of likely or certain stone roofing were recovered from Patey's Quad from Phase 1 contexts onwards; all are made of beige sandstone (a Cotswold stone type such as Stonesfield Slate) and fine-grained oolitic limestone. Two pieces retain drilled circular perforations for the nails, and one of these (pit 68) appears to be from a small stone only 104 mm wide.

Window Glass by Ian R. Scott
The Phase 4 well in Patey's Quad produced 97 sherds of window glass. Most of the glass appears to be post-medieval in date.

VESSEL GLASS by IAN R. SCOTT

The Phase 4 well in Patey's Quad produced 61 sherds of vessel glass. From context 66 there is a thick-walled colourless sherd with etched floral decoration probably from the neck of decanter. The decoration is probably acid etched. The dating is likely to be later eighteenth or very early nineteenth century. Context 72 produced a small sherd from the applied and hand-tooled rim or finish of a wine bottle of late eighteenth-century date, and a small sherd from a colourless vessel, probably a decanter, with etched decoration. The extant decoration comprises two elongated links from a chain. The decoration of the decanter may have included an etched label indicating its contents. An etched label and chain was a device found on eighteenth-century decanters. From the same context are five thin-walled sherds of colourless glass probably from stemmed wine glass bowls, although the form of the bowls cannot be determined. Finally, context 73 produced small sherd of colourless glass from a fluted or facetted vessel and this may be of a later eighteenth-century or later date. The precise form of the vessel – whether a drinking glass or a bottle – cannot be determined.

CLAY TOBACCO PIPES by DAVID A. HIGGINS

The two excavations produced a total of 46 fragments of pipe. The Music Room produced two of these fragments, a bowl and joining stem, which were found together in pit 27 (context 40). The pipe has a rather squat, dumpy form but is very well made and has been neatly finished, the rim having been fully milled just below the lip and a good quality burnish applied all over its surface (Fig. 8.7, no. 1). The heel has been stamped with a star mark made up of a central dot with eight radiating arms, which are alternately straight and curved. This distinctive mark has previously been recorded from Jesus College, Oxford,[20] where it occurs on another good quality burnished pipe, but one that is clearly from a different mould, since it is much larger overall and with a different bowl profile (Fig. 8.7, no. 2).

The earliest pipemakers often used symbol marks, which makes them hard to identify or pin down to an exact manufactory. In this instance, however, a number of other examples are known from London, which suggests that this was their production place. Atkinson illustrates an example from the Thames foreshore with a similar bowl form to the Merton College find and with what is probably the same mark.[21] Another example from the foreshore, formerly in the

[20] R. Bashford and B.M. Ford, 'Eleventh-Century, Later Medieval and Early Post-Medieval Evidence from Investigations at Jesus College and Market Street, Oxford', *Oxoniensia*, 79 (2014), pp. 211–34.

[21] D.R. Atkinson, 'Makers' Marks on Clay Tobacco Pipes found in London, Part Two', *Archaeological Newsletter*, 7.11 (1965), pp. 249–56 and fig. 8.

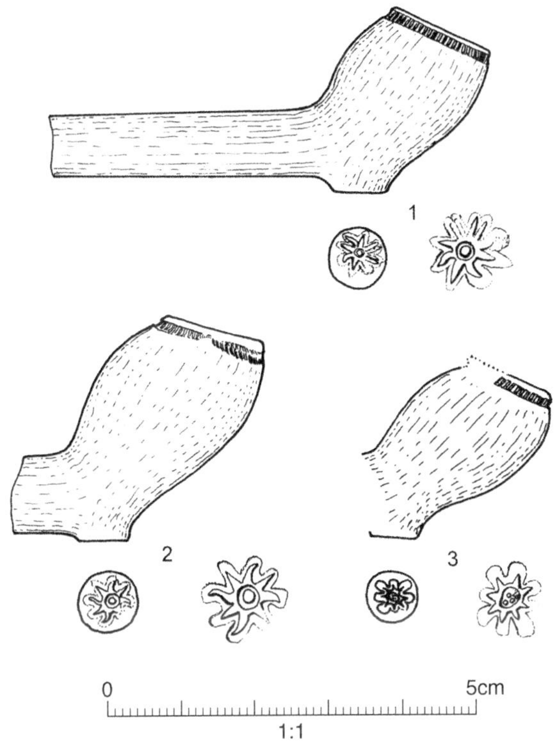

Fig. 8.7 Early seventeenth-century clay tobacco pipes with star marks. 1: St Alban's Quad Music Room, Ctx 40; 2: Jesus College, Oxford (OXJEKI09), Ctx 110; 3: Tong Castle, Shropshire (STC 79 JS/FS Pipe 2). Stamp details at 2:1. Drawings by David A. Higgins.

Le Cheminant Collection, has been recorded by the author and others have been excavated at Nos. 8–10 Crosswall (XWL 79 5169 <317>) and No. 118 Minories (MIO 86 1002 <121>), both of which are located just to the north of the Tower of London. There are also two examples from Queenhithe in the City of London (Elkins Collection in the National Pipe Archive, University of Liverpool) and there is an unprovenanced example in the Grosvenor Museum, Chester (but probably found there), which also has a finely burnished surface.[22] Finally, there is an example from the old fort excavations at Jamestown, Virginia (JR 1734 B). This latter example is particularly important for two reasons. First, the Jamestown settlement was largely financed by London investors and stocked with goods from the capital and, second, the pipe was found on the site of the early fort where many of the deposits date from *c.*1607–10. The first ships set out from London in 1606 and so the pipe could date from as early as that. The Jamestown evidence for the date of the mark together with the bowl form of the Merton College example suggest a range of *c.*1605–25 for the new Oxford find.

Although the name of the 'star' maker is not known, it is worth noting that this maker clearly operated on a considerable scale, as evidenced by the number of recorded examples and the fact that several different bowl forms are represented, some of which could date from as late as the middle of the seventeenth century. Given that several different moulds were being used and it appears that the workshop operated over a period of time, it is likely that there would have been several stamps for marking the pipes too. The Elkins collection includes a number of different versions of star marks from London and excavations at Tong Castle in Shropshire have produced a good quality early bowl with a similar star mark on the heel that could possibly have

22 J.A. Rutter and P.J. Davey, 'Clay Pipes from Chester', in P. Davey (ed.), *The Archaeology of the Clay Tobacco Pipe, III, Britain: The North and West*, BAR, BS, 78 (1980), fig. 30.6.

come from the same workshop (Fig. 8.7, no. 3). The distribution of the other identically marked pipes across England and to the New World shows that this workshop was able to market their goods over very considerable distances at an early date. They also appear to have specialised in making high-quality products, as evidenced by the finish of the pipes and the higher than average social status of the sites on which they have been found. The Merton College example therefore provides an important piece of evidence with regard to the understanding the broader patterns of trade and social status within early seventeenth-century society in general and, in particular, in relation to the emergent pipemaking industry.

The remaining pipe fragments came from Patey's Quad and, with the exception of one intrusive stem fragment from a medieval pit, all the pieces were recovered from various deposits within the Phase 4 well. There was no discernible difference in the pipe fragments from the lower and upper excavated fills, which suggests that the infilling of the well took place within a relatively short space of time. Although 42 pipe stem fragments and a mouthpiece were recovered, there was only one small bowl chip, which was not diagnostic enough to date accurately other to note that it was made of a fine sandy fabric type that probably dates from before *c.*1800. A number of different pipes were represented by the stems, all of which were very slender with a cylindrical cross section and typically with bores of 6/64″ or 5/64″. Fragments of up to 18 cm in length with barely any discernible taper survived, showing that they came from very long-stemmed pipes with essentially straight stems and simple cut tips. A couple of pieces have surviving traces of a red tip coating, probably paint or wax. The best example extends across a broken stem end, showing that even slightly damaged pipes were finished in this way for use. The stems suggest these were delicate, elegant pipes that were probably of a better than average quality. They are most likely to date from around 1760–1800.

METALWORK AND WORKED BONE by LEIGH ALLEN

Three metal objects were recovered from the Music Room, comprising a jeton (see below), a copper alloy strap-end and the shank from an iron nail. The composite strap-end is tongue-shaped with a pointed end and a single rivet at the top to secure it to the strap. It has a sheet spacer sandwiched between the front and back plates that occupies the whole width of the strap end but not the whole length. This form of strap-end dates to the fourteenth century and is relatively short lived.[23]

The assemblage from Patey's Quad comprises 61 objects of metal and one of worked bone. Phase 1 contexts produced two nails and part of a copper alloy pin with a wire wound head. Phase 2 produced three further nails. The majority of finds were recovered from Phase 4 well 67, including fragments from copper alloy pins with wire wound heads, a copper alloy buckle frame, fragments from an iron knife, numerous nail fragments, two pieces of lead waste and a bone button.

JETON by IAN R. SCOTT

French jeton, late fourteenth or early fifteenth century. *Obverse*: Shield of three lis with cross at top; shield with crown above, and flanked by annulets between pellets. Legend: + AVE MARIA o GRACIA PL. *Reverse*: Triple stranded straight cross feuilly within four-arched tressure with + A V S in spandrels. D: 24.5 mm. Music Room, ctx 108.

[23] G. Egan and F. Pritchard, *Medieval Finds from Excavations in London: 3, Dress Accessories c.1150–c.1450* (1991), pp. 146–8, and fig. 96.

ANIMAL BONE by LEE G. BRODERICK

A total of 181 animal bones were recovered, most of them from St Alban's Quad. More than half of the material (100 specimens) was from Phase 2, with another quarter (46 specimens) being associated with Phase 3.

Evidence from the twelfth to early thirteenth century was scarce, although domestic cattle (*Bos taurus taurus*), caprine (sheep – *Ovis aries* and goats – *Capra hircus*) and pig (*Sus scrofa domestica*) specimens were all identified from a pit (68) at Patey's Quad. Pig and cf. caprine were also identified from pits at the Music Room. The cattle specimens included a horncore and zygomaticus which may be relevant as previous excavations at No. 4A Merton Street, around 50 m to the north, identified evidence for a horner's workshop.[24] Animal bones were also recovered from excavations around 100 m to the south-west of Patey's Quad in the 1960s; these were comparable to the material recovered here in terms of both number and species, including another horncore, this time of a sheep.[25]

Phase 2 specimens from Patey's Quad came from garden soil deposit 45. These were in poor condition, the 13 specimens including unfused caprine femurs and tibiae as well as pig and cattle bones. A large mammal vertebra had been chopped through the centre axially. It was observed from the much larger assemblage recovered from No. 4A Merton Street that cattle carcasses were split in half lengthways from the eleventh century onwards and this would fit that observation.[26] The Phase 2 assemblage from the Music Room all came from pits. They again contained specimens of the three principal domesticates, including cranial, forelimb and hindlimb elements, and also specimens of domestic fowl (*Gallus gallus*) and greylag and/or domestic goose (*Anser* sp.). Three of the nine domestic fowl specimens came from juvenile individuals, suggesting summer to autumn use, and at least two adult birds were present. Despite being the phase that produced the most specimens, the assemblage is still small and it would be unwise to read too much into it. Broadly speaking, the relative abundance of species is consistent with patterns elsewhere in the town at this time, including at No. 4A Merton Street.[27] A medium mammal vertebra had been chopped axially through the centre in the same way as the large mammal vertebra from Patey's Quad, suggesting consistency in butchery practice, and a cattle metatarsal had been gnawed by rodents, perhaps rats, suggesting both that they were present on the site at this time and that that specimen, at least, had lain exposed for some time before being buried in the pit.

No material was recovered from later phases at Patey's Quad, whilst subsequent phases of activity at the Music Room produced progressively fewer specimens. The material recovered from Phase 3 came from a garden soil and contained the same range of species as Phase 2, with the addition of a domestic duck or mallard (*Anas platyrhynchos*) coracoid. Like the garden soil from Phase 2 at Patey's Quad the material was generally in poorer condition than the rest of the assemblage, and two of the specimens (a cattle calcaneum and a caprine humerus) also showed signs of having been gnawed by canids. A medium mammal vertebra showed the same pattern of butchery described in the previous phases. Other butchery marks recorded in this phase suggested additional processing – a chop through the medial side of the distal end of a caprine radius suggests heavy processing by a butcher and a domestic fowl ulna with multiple cutmarks may be evidence of meat being sold off the bone – cooked meat falling away far more easily. The specimens from Phase 4 at the Music Room consisted of cattle, pigs and caprines as well as medium and large mammals.

24 Worley and Evans, 'Animal Bone'.
25 Hassall, 'Excavations in Merton College'.
26 Worley and Evans, 'Animal Bone'.
27 Ibid.

FISH REMAINS AND MARINE SHELL by REBECCA NICHOLSON

A small assemblage of 76 identified fish bones and scales was recovered exclusively from the residues and flots of sieved soil samples from Patey's Quad. The great majority of bones (56) came from sample <10> taken from fill 70 within Phase 1 pit 68. The remains include bones and scales from small and tiny fish, particularly herring, but also including eel, pike, cyprinid, perch and small gadid (probably whiting). It is likely that the herring, which is exclusively marine and spoils quickly, had been preserved by pickling or smoking; the gadid may have been a dried fish, although fresh seafish were sold in Oxford at that time. The remaining fish are all likely to have been caught fairly locally in the surrounding rivers and ponds. Perch scales were also recovered from an eighteenth-century well fill (73) demonstrating continuity in the eating of fairly small freshwater fish. Bones from small and tiny freshwater fish have now been recovered from a number of sites in Oxford, for example from pit fills of similar date at No. 4A Merton Street.[28] The consumption of these small and bony freshwater fish seems to have been fairly commonplace. Certainly, in the fifteenth century, and perhaps before, the fishing in the River Cherwell as far as Magdalen Bridge belonged to Merton College as lords of Holywell.[29] The lack of bones from larger, potentially more expensive fish is probably a consequence of the small size of the excavations here rather than an indication of the status of the landowner.

A single European oyster (*Ostrea edulis*) valve was recovered from a Phase 2 gravel surface at Patey's Quad.

PLANT REMAINS by JOHN GIORGI

Ten samples from Patey's Quad produced identifiable plant remains; eight from medieval deposits and two from the post-medieval well.

Medieval Plant Remains

The fill (70) of a Phase 1 pit (68) produced the only significant charred plant assemblage from the site, consisting largely of poorly preserved cereal grains, the small number of identifiable grains mainly belonging to free-threshing wheat (*Triticum aestivum/turgidum*) including rachis evidence for bread wheat (*Triticum aestivum*). There was also evidence for rye (*Secale cereale*) (a few tentative grains and a rachis fragment) and a possible oat (*Avena*) grain in the pit fill as well as traces of possible free-threshing wheat, barley (*Hordeum vulgare*) and oat in the Phase 2 gravel/occupation surfaces (17, 28–9 and 31) and the drain fills (33–5).

These four cereals are the main grains found as archaeobotanical remains during this period in southern England,[30] as at No. 4A Merton Street,[31] free-threshing wheat often being the main cereal recovered from medieval sites in Oxford.[32] This was the preferred bread-making grain at the time and was mainly consumed by the better off.[33]

There were also a few fruit and nut remains in the medieval samples: a charred hazelnut (*Corylus avellana*) shell fragment and a plum/bullace (*Prunus domestica*) fruit stone in the pit fill

28 R.A. Nicholson, 'Fish Remains', in Poore, 'No. 4A Merton St.', pp. 306–11.

29 *VCH Oxon.* 4, pp. 327–31.

30 J. Greig, 'The British Isles', in W. van Zeist et al. (eds.), *Progress in Old World Palaeoethnobotany* (1991), p. 321.

31 R. Pelling, 'Charred and Waterlogged Plant Remains', in Poore, 'No. 4A Merton St.', pp. 323, 335.

32 W. Smith, 'Charred and Waterlogged Plant Remains', in Bashford and Dodd, 'Corpus Christi College', p. 206; W. Smith, 'Charred and Mineralized Plant Remains', in Bashford and Ford, 'Jesus College and Market Street', pp. 231–4; J. Giorgi, 'Plant Remains', in S. Teague et al., 'Late Saxon, Medieval and Post-Medieval Archaeology at the Nun's Garden, The Queen's College, Oxford', *Oxoniensia*, 80 (2015), p. 183.

33 P.W. Hammond, *Food and Feast in Medieval England* (1995), p. 2; B.M.S. Campbell et al., *A Medieval Capital and its Grain Supply. Agrarian Production and Distribution in the London Region c.1300*, Historical Geography Research Series, 30 (1993), p. 26.

and several non-charred blackberry/raspberry (*Rubus*) fruit seeds and a cherry (*Prunus avium*) fruit stone in the drain fills which may have survived as uncharred remains from this time.

Post-Medieval Plant Remains

Fill 74 of the Phase 4 stone-lined well contained uncharred fruit remains of cherry, grape (*Vitis vinfera*), fig (*Ficus carica*), raspberry (*Rubus idaeus*), blackberry (*Rubus* sect. *Glandulosus*), elderberry (*Sambucus nigra*) and strawberry (*Fragaria*) and hazelnut shell fragments. A few fig, blackberry/raspberry and possibly strawberry seeds and a hazelnut shell fragment were also found in the overlying well fill (73). Similar fruit remains have previously been recovered from earlier medieval deposits at No. 4A Merton Street.[34] and at other post-medieval sites in Oxford.[35] These fruits may have been garden cultivated, possibly close-by, although blackberries, raspberries and hazelnuts may have also been collected from the wild and the figs probably imported as dried fruit.

The fruit remains provide a partial insight into the diet of the inhabitants of the college during the late eighteenth century. The larger fruit remains may be refuse from food preparation taking place in the kitchen nearby and the smaller fruit seeds possibly part of human excrement backfilling the well.

ACKNOWLEDGEMENTS

OA would like to thank BGS Architects for commissioning this project on behalf of Merton College. The entire archaeological process was managed by Ben M. Ford; on-site archaeological direction was provided by Ben Attfield (Music Room) and Adam Fellingham (Patey's Quad), assisted by Robin Bashford, Sophie Bojadziev, Thomas Brook, Richard Kevill, Adam Fellingham, Javier Martinez-Jimenez and Adam Rapiejko. Thanks are also due to the staff that processed the finds under the management of Leigh Allen, processed the environmental samples under the management of Rebecca Nicholson, and prepared the archive under the management of Nicola Scott.

34 Poore, 'No. 4A Merton St.', p. 336.
35 Bashford and Dodd, 'Corpus Christi College', p. 207.

9.

Investigations in the Old Cloisters and Deer Park, Brasenose College

KATE BRADY, RICHARD BROWN and JULIAN MUNBY

SUMMARY

Archaeological work at Brasenose College comprised an excavation in the Old Cloisters and a watching brief in Deer Park. The watching brief encountered a well possibly of medieval date that may have been associated with the Old Kitchen nearby. The excavation uncovered a wall that may once have divided the medieval properties of St Mary's Entry and Little St Edmund Hall. It also revealed a series of garden soil layers, waste deposits and surfaces of late sixteenth- to mid seventeenth-century date, predating the construction of the Old Cloisters. Pottery and faunal remains from these deposits probably represent kitchen waste from the college. The pottery assemblage is notable for containing unusually large quantities of German stoneware drinking vessels, while the bone assemblage is rich in game animals and birds. These layers were later cut by graves within the Old Cloisters dating to c.1669–1754.

In 2015 an excavation was carried out within the Old Cloisters and a watching brief in Deer Park, Brasenose College (SP 515 063; Fig. 9.1). The Old Cloisters is a mid seventeenth-century building located on the western side of Radcliffe Square and forming the eastern side of the Deer Park quadrangle. At the time of the investigation, the building was used as a reading room on the ground floor, with the college library above. The excavation, which took place in February, was carried out in order to inform a proposed design for the refurbishment of the Old Cloisters, which included the re-use of a flagstone floor underlying the existing wooden flooring and the insertion of ducts below the flagstones. The Old Cloisters are known to have been used as a burial ground during the seventeenth and eighteenth centuries, and consequently the investigation was subject to the approval of the Consistory Court as advised by the Diocesan Advisory Committee and Diocesan Archaeological Advisor (Julian Munby). A significant aspect of the works was the use of archaeological techniques to locate the depth and location of burial cuts in order that any disturbance to the interments could be avoided during the redevelopment of the building. The impact level of the refurbishment and of the archaeological excavation was thus limited to 63.06 m OD (*c*.0.75 m below the base of the flagstones), above the level of the human remains. The watching brief, completed in November, took place during the laying of air vents in Deer Park. At the same time a further watching brief was carried out in the Stocker Room to the north; this revealed only a post-medieval cistern and is not discussed further here.

This report summarises the main results of the project. A full report providing details of the stratigraphy, artefacts and environmental evidence is available via the OA Library.[1] The archive will be deposited with Oxfordshire County Museum Service under the accession code 2014.263.

1 K. Brady et al., 'Brasenose College Oxford. Archaeological Investigation Report' (2016), https://library.oxfordarchaeology.com/5553/.

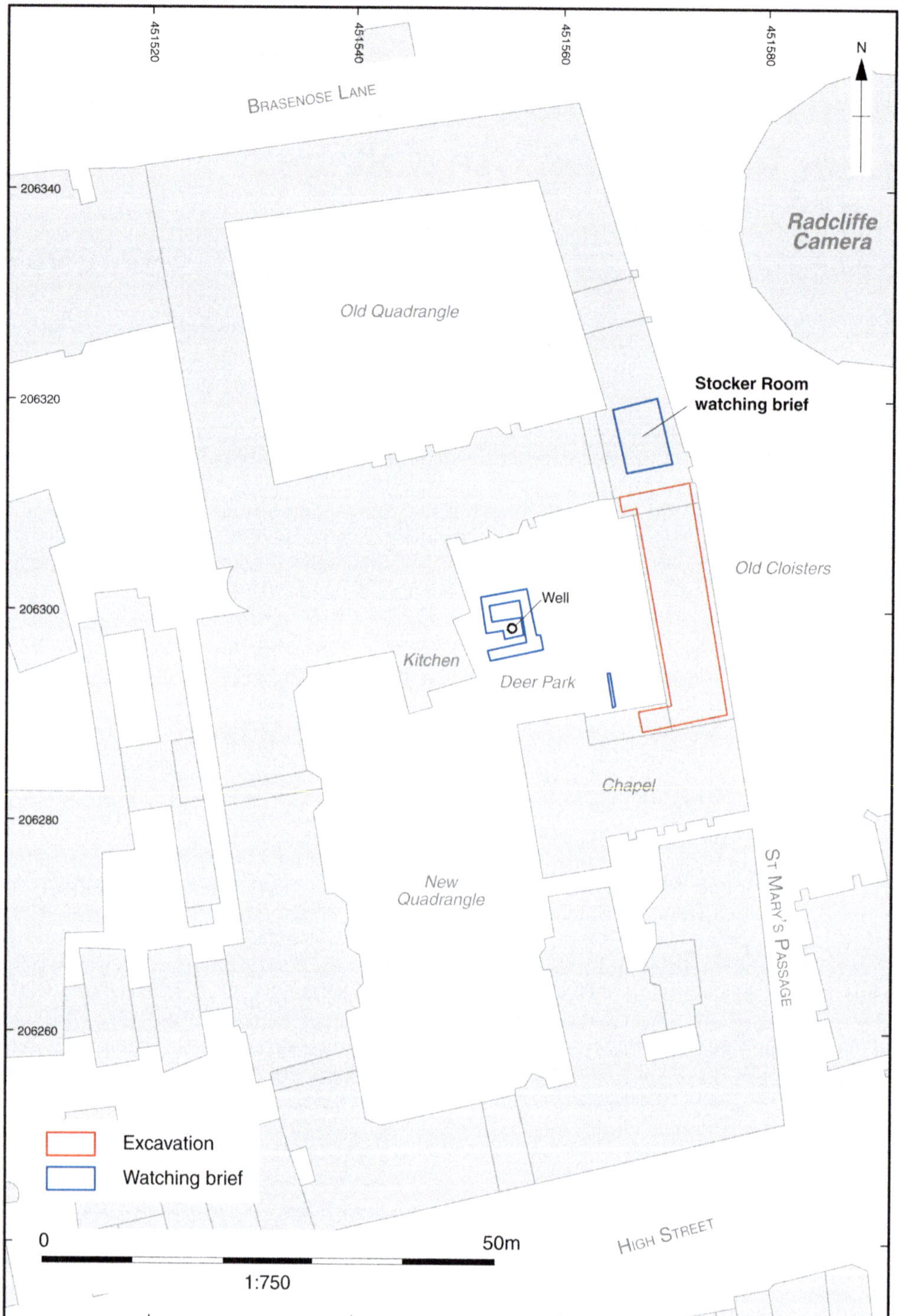

Fig. 9.1 Site location.

Fig. 9.2 H.E. Salter's reconstruction of medieval property boundaries, from his *Survey of Oxford*.

ARCHAEOLOGICAL AND HISTORICAL BACKGROUND

Prior to the foundation of the college, the site of the Old Cloisters and the back quadrangle (known as Deer Park) was during the fifteenth century occupied by three academic halls: Osney abbey's Little St Edmund Hall, on the south, and two properties of St Mary the Virgin Church, St Mary's Entry, in the centre, and Salissury (in 1333 'La Sale desyree'), on the north (Fig. 9.2).[2] Brasenose College was founded in 1508 on the site of Brasenose Hall, to the north of Salissury, where construction of the Old Quadrangle began in 1509. In 1510 the college acquired Salissury and St Mary's Entry from Oriel College, patrons of St Mary's,[3] and in 1530 it took a lease on Little St Edmund Hall from Osney (possibly having rented it previously). The earliest depiction of the college is on Ralph Agas' map of 1578, which shows the area to the south of the Old Quadrangle as open ground (Fig. 9.3). Little St Edmund Hall was only finally acquired from Christ Church (as successor of Osney) in 1656, being described as 'the ground whereon Brasenose chapel is built';[4] the hall was pulled down in the same year, and development of the Second Quadrangle

2 F. Madan, *The Site of the College Before its Foundation, Including Brasenose and Little University Halls*, Brasenose College Quatercentenary Monograph, 1 and OHS, 52 (1909), pp. 1–18; Salter, *Survey*, vol. 1, pp. 64–7, NE 88–92.

3 C.L. Shadwell and H.E. Salter (eds.), *Oriel Records*, OHS, 86 (1926), p. 108.

4 Madan, *The Site of the College*, p. 11; Salter, *Oseney*, vol. 1, p. 172.

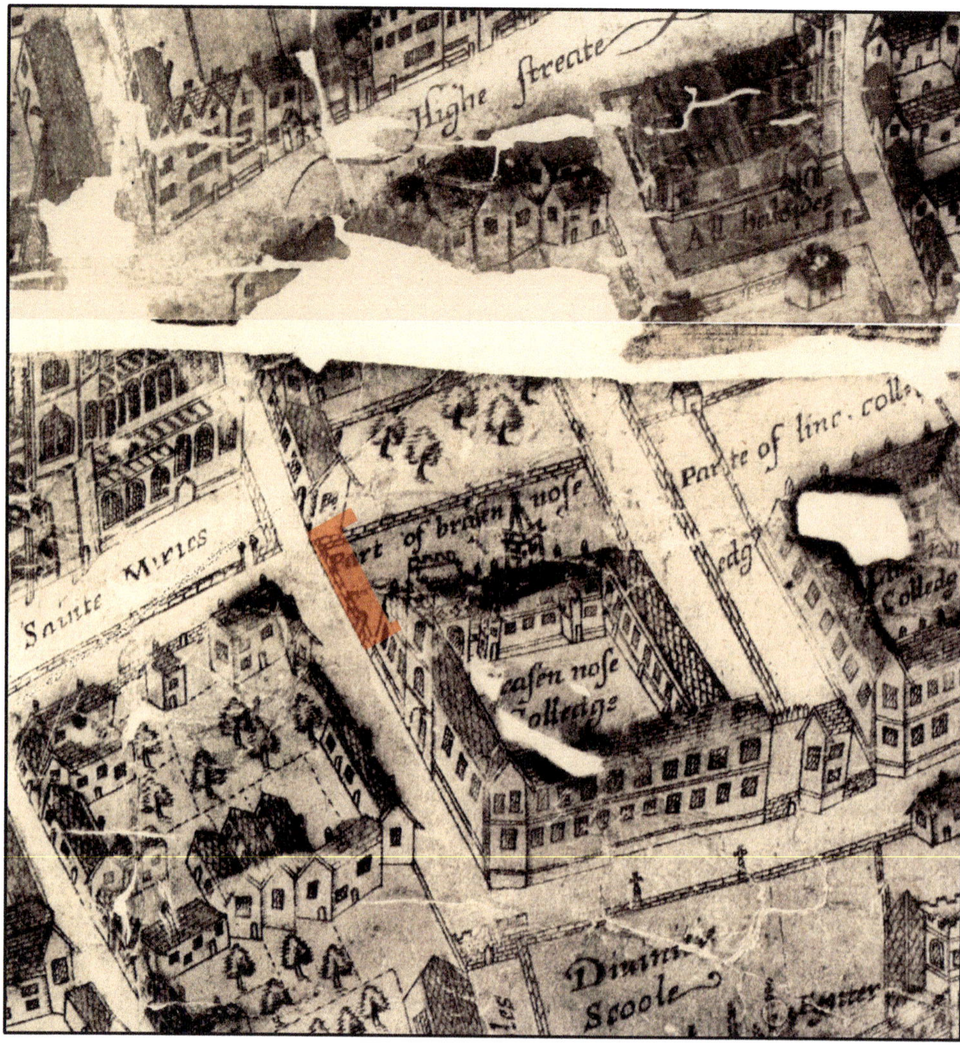

Fig. 9.3 Detail from Agas' 1578 map of Oxford.

(now Deer Park) began.[5] The name Deer Park was perhaps a jocular name for a small area or possibly derived from a deer hunt reported to have ended inside the college in 1820.[6]

Construction of the library on the eastern side of the quadrangle commenced in 1657.[7] The Old Cloisters, below the library, were open and used as a covered walkway between the college and chapel, and for college burials from *c.*1669 to 1754. College documents record sixty burials, and the location of most of these is indicated on a mid eighteenth-century plan of the

[5] E.W. Alfrey, *The Architectural History of the College*, Brasenose College Quatercentenary Monograph, III, OHS, 52 (1909); *VCH Oxon.* 3, pp. 207–19.

[6] *The Gentleman's Magazine*, Jan. 1820, p. 78, with an account of a stag hunt from Blenheim to Oxford on 21 December 1819.

[7] Alfrey, *Architectural History*, p. 20.

Old Cloisters.[8] In 1807 the Old Cloisters were divided off internally and converted into college rooms.[9]

Little previous archaeological work has taken place at Brasenose College. Between 2008 and 2011, OA carried out test pit excavation and building recording in and around the college kitchen to the west of Deer Park.[10] The earliest features encountered were two pits containing eleventh- to thirteenth-century pottery. A soil layer contained fifteenth- to sixteenth-century pottery, and a pit and a cesspit were dated to the sixteenth to seventeenth centuries.

The Old Cloisters excavation was preceded by an evaluation carried out in 2013. Four trenches were excavated, revealing five graves beneath the flagstone floor. A sequence of earlier deposits and surfaces survived between the grave cuts, the earliest dated to the late sixteenth to early seventeenth centuries.[11]

DISCUSSION

Summary of the Archaeological Sequence

Residual pottery suggests some activity at the site from the Saxo-Norman period onwards, but the earliest deposit encountered in the investigations was found in the Deer Park watching brief: a garden soil layer containing a single sherd of Brill/Boarstall ware pottery dated to the fifteenth to sixteenth centuries. This layer was cut by a circular stone-lined well (Fig. 9.1). The date of this feature is unclear, though as it is not mentioned in college records it seems likely to predate the construction of the Deer Park quadrangle in the mid seventeenth century.

The Old Cloisters excavation uncovered a limestone wall (687) on an east–west alignment, and a sequence of garden soils, surfaces and occupation layers (Figs. 9.4–9.5). The earliest deposits reached at the level of excavation were garden soils dated to *c.*1580–1600 (Phase 1), with subsequent layers dated to *c.*1600–30 (Phase 2) and from *c.*1630 up to the construction of the Old Cloisters in 1657 (Phase 3). Some Phase 1 and Phase 2 deposits abutted the wall and had clearly been laid down while this was still standing. Whether the wall was still extant in Phase 3 is unclear. The sequence of layers was sealed by the flagstone floor of the Old Cloisters, and cut by burials interred from *c.*1669–1754.

Later Medieval Halls

H.E. Salter showed that the Old Cloisters is built on the site of two medieval halls, St Mary's Entry (north) and Salissury (south), with the chapel constructed on part of Little St Edmund Hall. The divisions between these properties are unknown.[12] Agas' map of 1578 (Fig. 9.3) – which just predates the deposition in *c.*1580–1630 of the lowest layers uncovered by the excavation – shows an open area defined by a wall south of the existing front quadrangle, and labelled 'Part of brasen nose', to the south of which was a separate property with a building and garden behind, probably to be identified with Little St Edmund Hall. Since Agas shows the north end of the building aligned with the north wall of the churchyard of St Mary the Virgin, that would approximate also to the north wall of the new seventeenth-century Brasenose Chapel.

The absence of any buildings on the site of St Mary's Entry and Salissury suggests that they had been demolished by the time the map was produced. The 'entry' name for the property

8 Brady et al., 'Brasenose College Oxford. Archaeological Investigation Report', fig. 9.

9 Alfrey, *Architectural History*, p. 35.

10 A. Kelly et al., 'Building Recording and Test Pits at Brasenose College, Oxford', *Oxoniensia*, 81 (2016), pp. 247–52; 'Brasenose College Oxford: Historic Building Recording and Archaeological Investigations Report', unpublished OA report (2012), https://library.oxfordarchaeology.com/3520/.

11 'Old Cloisters Building, Brasenose College, Oxford. Archaeological Evaluation Report', unpublished OA report (2013), https://library.oxfordarchaeology.com/3518/.

12 The uncertainty is as shown on H.E. Salter, *Map of Mediaeval Oxford* (1934), and the firm outlines plotted by Madan are unwarranted.

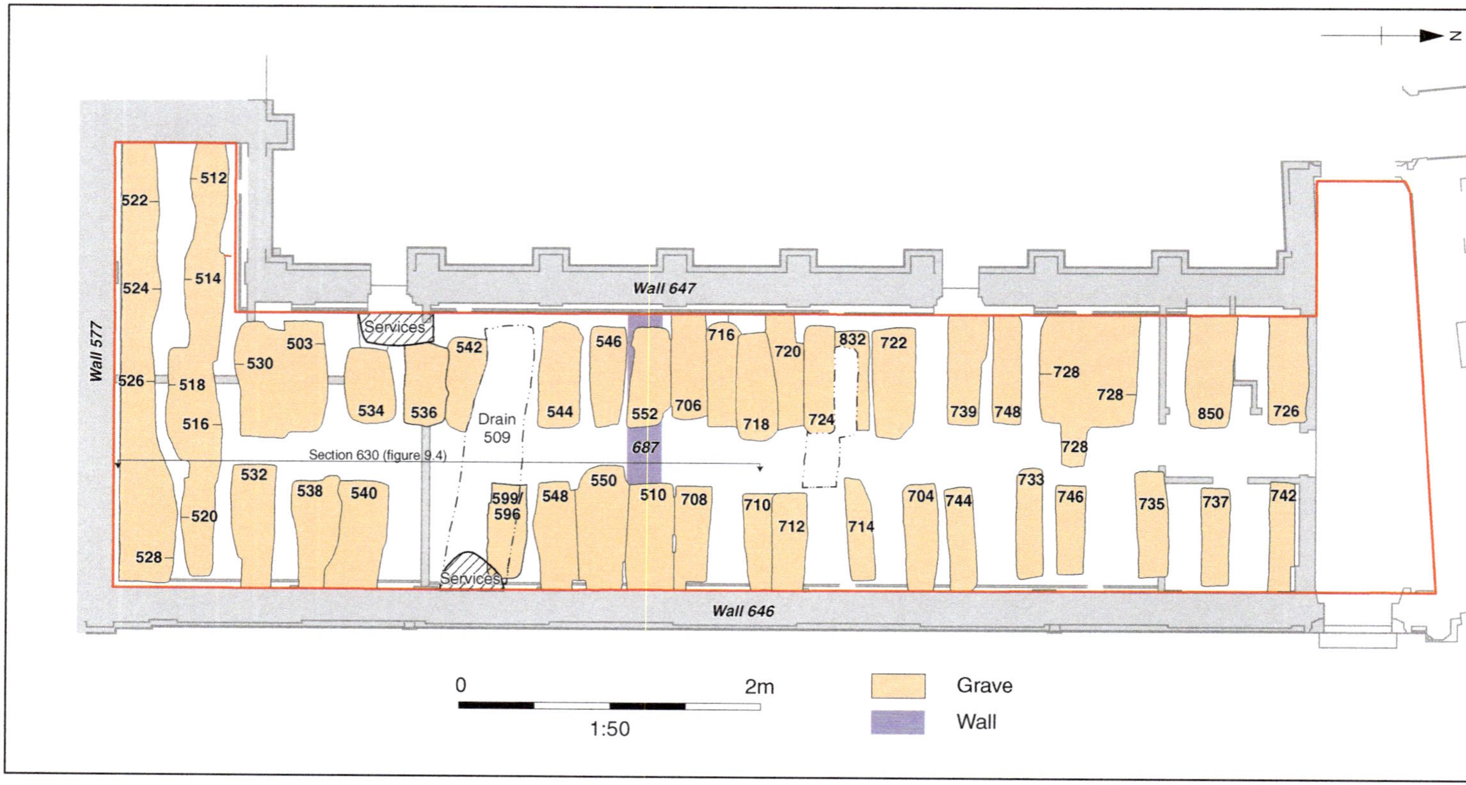

Fig. 9.4 Plan of the Old Cloisters excavation.

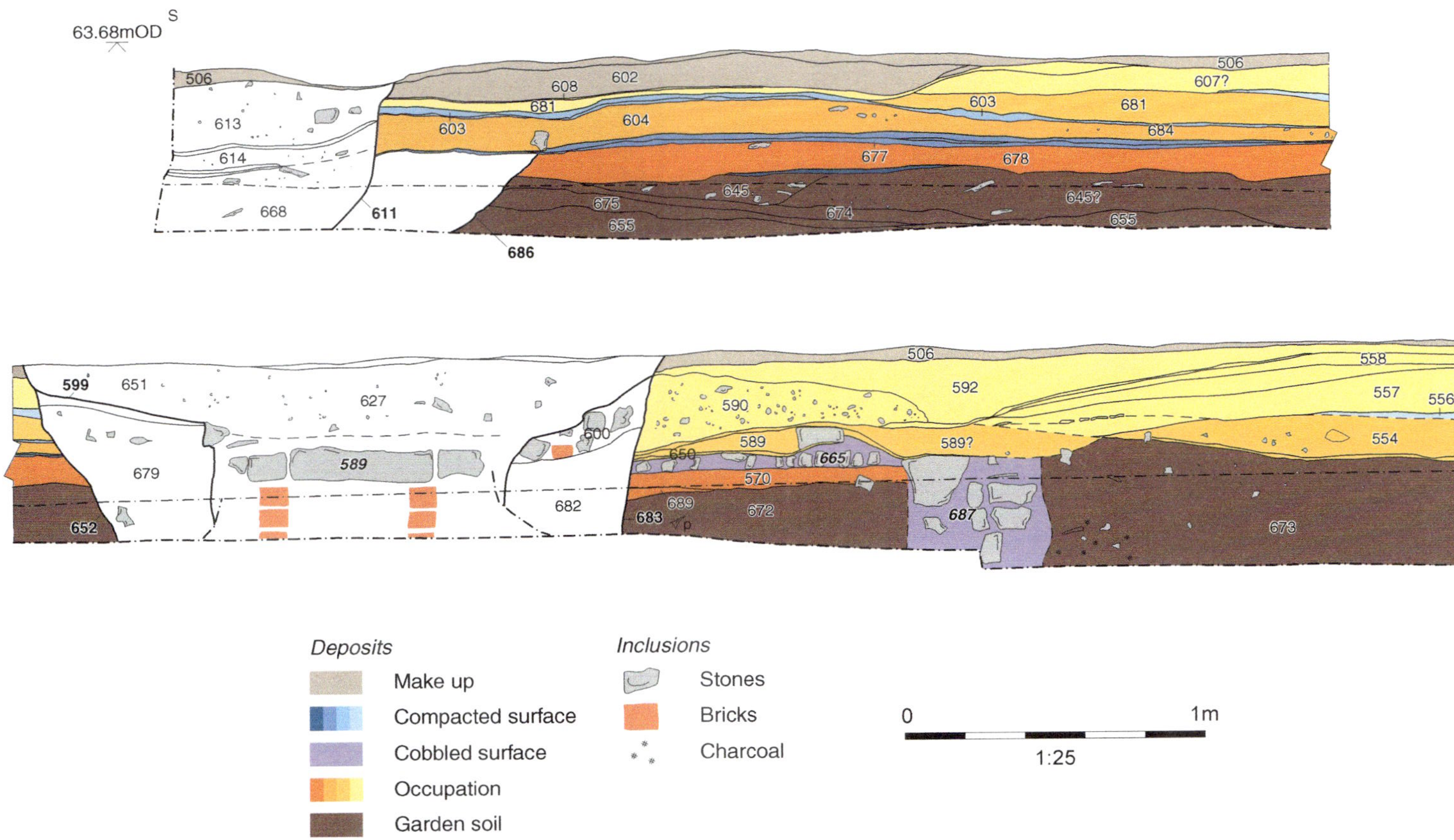

Fig. 9.5 Section of Old Cloisters excavation, showing wall 687.

(in 1392 it was recorded as the 'Entry of Juliana Glasier') implies an access to other land behind, as was the case when it was leased in 1275.[13] In 1451 it was described as a garden (*hortus*) between Salissury and Little St Edmund Hall, but by 1457 it was an academic hall, named 'St Mary's Entry', and the hall's principals were recorded until 1469.[14] It may be that the presence of a hall building was short-lived, as it was part of the constellation of halls annexed to Brasenose Hall before the foundation of the college,[15] and subsequently the space appears to have returned to use as a garden, as depicted on Agas' map of 1578.

The former medieval kitchen (now servery) still extant on the western side of Deer Park lay within the boundary of St Mary's Entry and is thought to date to at least the late fifteenth century.[16] Probably it was the kitchen serving Brasenose Hall and its satellites. The plot was granted to the founder of Brasenose in 1509–10, and subsequently the kitchen became the Brasenose College kitchen.[17] It is possible that the well uncovered in the Deer Park watching brief was associated with the kitchen.

Gardens c.1580–1600 (Phase 1)

Limestone wall 687 extended on an east–west alignment back from the frontage in the southern part of the site and predated the earliest layers recorded, continuing vertically below the level of excavation. Although only a small part of the wall remained, having been heavily truncated by grave cuts, it is possible that this is the wall depicted on Agas' map dividing the plots of St Mary's Entry and Little St Edmund Hall, and that it was constructed in the medieval period.

By the time the earliest deposits encountered during the excavation were laid down (in the late sixteenth century), the area right up to the frontage on both sides of the wall was garden. Medieval sherds were also recovered from the garden soil (more from the area south of the wall) and probably represent the reworking of the kitchen garden and its extension up to the frontage after the medieval building to the south of the wall was gone. On Agas' drawing the plot behind Little St Edmund Hall is depicted as a garden with trees, probably a small orchard, and St Mary's Entry is empty but may have functioned as a kitchen garden into which kitchen refuse was added and incorporated as it was worked over. If the boundary has been correctly located then the frontage building shown within Little St Edmund was gone by the time the earliest deposits were lain down at the southern end of the site, suggesting that it was demolished soon after Agas' drawing was made. The area may have become more fully a part of Brasenose College grounds, functioning as a garden to the south of the quad.

St Mary's Entry may have been empty but for the kitchen. The Front Quad of Brasenose College was built right up to its northern side in 1508, partially obstructing an original window, and subsequently became the college kitchen. The material collected from the garden soils was typical of late-medieval to early post-medieval kitchen deposits, with frequent charcoal from hearths, animal bone and pottery, including in this case many fragments of Frechen stoneware drinking vessels.

Surfaces and Rubbish Dumping c.1600–30 (Phase 2)

To the south of the assumed dividing wall between Little St Edmunds Hall and St Mary's Entry the earliest revealed surfaces were recorded. A make-up layer under a firm, laminated mortar layer suggests the transformation of the frontage from garden to an area that was trampled and possibly used as an uncultivated yard space. The two shallow pits found in this area may

13 Shadwell and Salter, *Oriel Records*, pp. 78, 149.

14 Madan, *The Site of the College*, p. 11; Salter, *Survey*, pp. 66–7.

15 J. Catto, 'The Triumph of the Hall in Fifteenth Century Oxford' in R. Evans (ed.), *Lordship and Learning: Studies in Memory of Trevor Aston* (2004), pp. 217–8, fig. 4. For the combined halls in 1462: H.E. Salter, *Registrum Cancellarii*, OHS, 94 (1932), p. 88.

16 'Brasenose College Oxford: Historic Building Recording and Archaeological Investigations Report'.

17 Madan, *The Site of the College*.

represent hollows in the ground infilled with rubbish to keep the surface somewhat level. There was no evidence of a structure.

To the north of the wall, similar dumping of refuse continued and this became trampled, forming more compacted laminated layers including trampled spreads of mortar. It is not clear whether these were formal surfaces or more informal spreads of mortar (originating from nearby construction) to firm the ground. There continued to be a strong component of Frechen stoneware drinking vessels in the pottery assemblage, suggesting that this material may have continued to come from the college dining hall.

During this period the area was still divided by wall 687 and two areas of limestone cobbled surface were laid. Surface 778 to the north of the wall covered an area *c*.5.5 m across, extending south from the northern limit of excavation. This was clearly a deliberately laid surface with regularly sized cobbles pushed into an underlying layer of bedding material. Wear was identified on some areas of the surface suggesting fairly prolonged use. The southern boundary of the surface appeared to be deliberate, with the surface laid in a shallow construction cut (861) through earlier layers that could be seen to the south and presumably once continued up to the northern limit of excavation. Immediately to the southern side of wall 687 was another area of cobbled surface (665), probably located within the former Little St Edmund Hall. It was truncated to the south by a modern drain but did not continue to the other side of this, suggesting it was originally a pathway or passage floor alongside the wall. The surface here was in a herringbone pattern and was present right up to the street frontage. It is not clear whether this was an external or internal surface, but no contemporary structural elements were identified. The use of both surfaces was fairly closely dated, with the underlying deposits dated to 1620–50 and the overlying to a similar date, confining its use to within this period. The space between the cobbled surfaces appeared to remain mainly as garden or yard areas where waste continued to be dumped and occasional thin layers of mortar (perhaps debris from nearby construction) were deposited.

Dumping and Levelling c.1630–57 (Phase 3)

From around 1630 the whole area north of wall 687 was again overlain by dumps of material alternating with layers of compacted mortar. Although these mortar layers were very firm, it is not clear if they were formal surfaces or trampled debris from nearby construction activity. Having said this, the sequence is consistent with the pattern of a floor layer (mortar) followed by occupation debris, and this pattern is repeated at least twice (Fig. 9.5). The pottery from these layers contained sherds with a date range beginning at *c*.1630, and therefore these deposits were probably laid down in the quarter of a century immediately before the construction of the Old Cloisters. No structural evidence for a frontage building was identified by the excavation and on balance it is likely that this was still an outside area. Neither the Deer Park watching brief trenches nor a previous test pit excavated just outside the southern wall of the kitchen[18] identified any similar mortar surfaces. This suggests that deposits were concentrated in the frontage area, although whether this was because there was a structure here or was for deliberate ground-raising for the Old Cloisters is not certain.

Although it is not certain that wall 687 was still extant in this period, the line of this boundary seems to have continued to divide the area into two plots. In the area to the south of the wall the deposits were characterised by thicker layers of more mixed material, including lumps of limestone, mortar and ceramic building material. This may represent the demolition of the building occupying Little St Edmund Hall. The recovery of an assemblage of unworn medieval tile, including crested ridge tile, from the backfill of a construction cut for one of the walls of the Old Cloisters does suggest that a nearby medieval building was demolished not too long before the new building was constructed.

18 'Brasenose College Oxford: Historic Building Recording and Archaeological Investigations Report'.

Fig. 9.6 Grave marker 'I W 1689'. From college records this can be identified as the grave of John Warburton, who matriculated in 1667 and died on 11 August 1689. Scale: 0.5 m.

The last deposits before the construction of the Old Cloisters levelled the ground again (which tended to slope from east to south), and then a layer of mortar was deposited as the bedding for the Old Cloisters' floor.

Burials in the Old Cloisters 1669–1754

Fifty-three grave cuts were recorded below the floor of the Old Cloisters, all on an east-west alignment (Fig. 9.4). The floor slabs appear to have been removed and replaced when a burial was inserted. No coffins or human remains were encountered at the level reached by the excavation. The location of each grave was marked by an inscription on the flagstone floor, usually consisting of the initials of the deceased and the year (Fig. 9.6). The locations of the grave markers correspond with the eighteenth-century plan held in the college archives.

SUMMARY OF FINDS AND ENVIRONMENTAL EVIDENCE

Almost all of the finds come from the Old Cloisters excavation. Most derive from deposits dated to *c.*1580–1657, or from the backfills of later graves. The grave fills mainly contained material redeposited from the earlier layers that they had been cut through, with some late seventeenth- to mid eighteenth-century material.

The pottery assemblage (2,329 sherds) is in a fragmentary and worn condition. Small amounts of residual medieval pottery are present, including a few sherds of St Neots ware dated to *c.*900–1100, but the bulk of the assemblage dates to *c.*1580–1650. An unusually high

Fig. 9.7 Frechen stoneware pottery of late sixteenth to early seventeenth century date. 1: Portrait medallion, probably chipped-down for use as a counter, from a girth-band jug of c.1550–80, Ctx 745; 2: Bellarmine jug with coat of arms, Ctx 511; 3: Bellarmine jug with date '1594', Ctx 511; 4: Bellarmine jug with lower part of bearded mask, and coat of arms, probably a variant of the arms of the House of Orange-Nassau, Ctx 753.

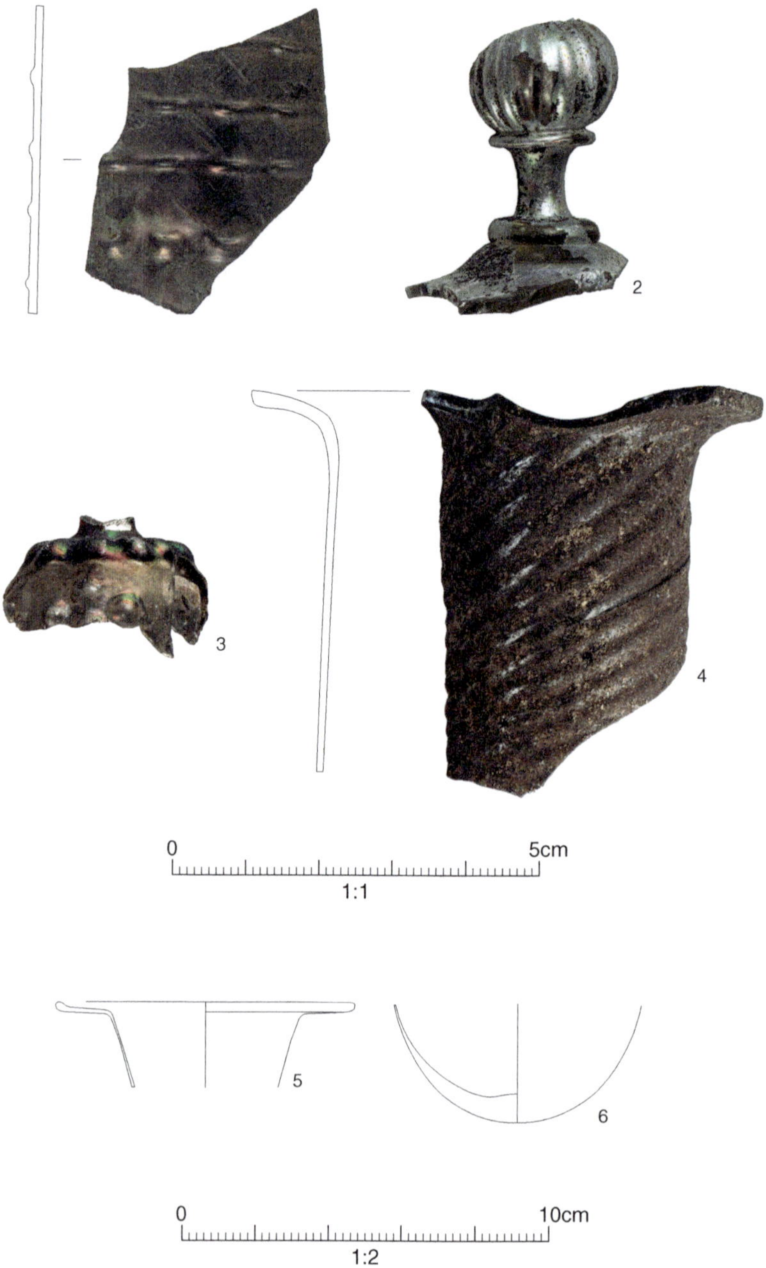

Fig. 9.8 Vessel glass. 1: Beaker with thin cut horizontal trails, colourless glass, façon de Venise, sixteenth or seventeenth century, Ctx 791; 2: Stemmed glass, lower part of stem with a small ribbed optic blown ball knop, colourless glass, sixteenth or seventeenth century, Ctx 485; 3: Fragment of optic-blown lion mask baluster, pale yellow glass, Venetian or façon de Venise, mid sixteenth to mid seventeenth century, Ctx 570; 4: Narrow-necked flask with wrythen optic blown ribs, pale green glass, Ctx 721; 5: Probable flask, colourless glass, Ctx 844; 6: Round base of urinal with pontil mark, pale green glass, medieval, Ctx 626.

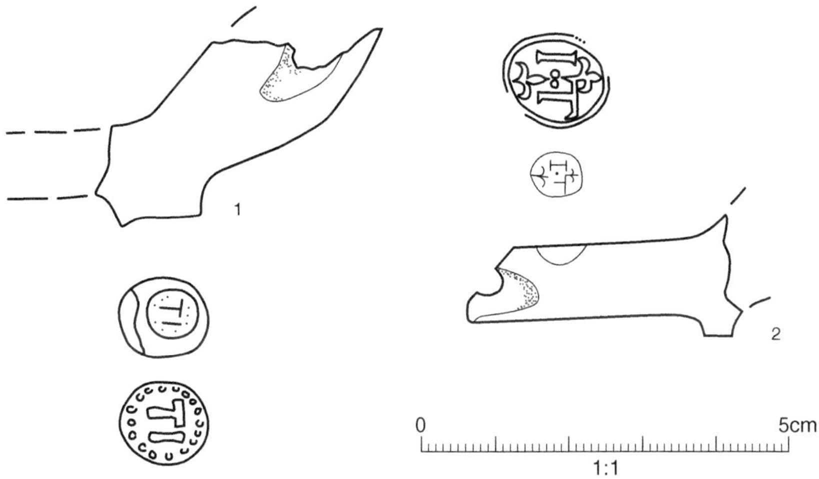

Fig. 9.9 Clay tobacco pipes of mid seventeenth-century date with maker's marks. 1: Ctx 784; 2: Ctx 783.

number of drinking vessels (local and imported) highlights an assemblage largely derived from social drinking activities, perhaps from college dining rooms. In particular, the assemblage is notable for its exceptionally large quantity of Frechen stoneware drinking vessels (906 sherds representing at least several dozen vessels), probably the largest quantity of German stoneware recovered from a single site in Oxford (Fig. 9.7). Single sherds of Italian tin-glazed ware and Beauvais yellow-glazed ware, both very rare types from Oxford, hint at elements of luxury within the early post-medieval assemblage. Sherds from at least fifteen post-medieval chafing dishes (plate-warmers or portable stoves) were also identified.

The small vessel glass assemblage (94 pieces) included six urinal bases of probable medieval date, and fragments of early post-medieval drinking vessels and flasks (Fig. 9.8). Late contexts produced wine bottle fragments of late seventeenth- and eighteenth-century date. There were also three black glass beads. The clay tobacco pipes (324 pieces) nearly all date to the period *c.*1630–60. Two pipes have maker's marks with no known local parallels (Fig. 9.9). An unexceptional range of metal objects were recovered, including pins, lace tags, nails, knives, keys, and a pair of dividers. There were three jetons: one was a France and the Dauphine type with a fleur-de-lys/dolphin design dated to the first quarter of the sixteenth century, while the other two were Nuremberg 'rose and orb' types of late sixteenth- to early seventeenth-century date. A crudely made perforated sandstone disc may have been a weight.

The ceramic building material assemblage (1,167 pieces, 71 kg) is mostly fifteenth- to seventeenth-century in date. Most consists of peg tile, but there are smaller amounts of brick, ridge tile, and floor tile. Three decorated medieval floor tiles are present, including a Penn product of *c.*1330–80. Some of the material may derive from buildings that once stood near the site, such as a large quantity of medieval peg tile recovered from a construction cut for one of the walls of the Old Cloisters. The condition of the assemblage suggests that most of it was brought to the site as building rubble. Other building materials included sandstone roofing (80 pieces, 8.6 kg) and a small amount of window glass, including two pieces with painted decoration.

The animal bone assemblage comprised 2,839 fragments. Aside from usual cattle, sheep/goat, pig and domestic fowl, the assemblage was notably rich in rabbit and game birds (goose, duck, possible pheasant, and passerines). The high occurrence of rabbit and game differs from most Oxford sites but does correspond with other late-medieval/early post-medieval college assemblages. Similarly, the small collection of fish remains includes a range of freshwater and sea species comparable to those identified in assemblages from other Oxford colleges. Some 2,871 fragments of marine shell were recovered, all from native European flat oysters, apart from a single whelk and a fragment of mussel shell. There were approximately similar numbers of left and right valves, indicating the deposition of the remains of complete shellfish rather than the remains of oysters served in the shell. Measurements taken on the shells from the late sixteenth-century garden soil suggest careful size selection with a marked difference in sizes seen between this and later assemblages (which were less uniform). The oysters in the slightly later deposits may have come from native, wild beds or less well managed beds, and were either purchased without pre-grading or purchased as several graded sizes and later mixed in refuse deposits.

Five bulk soil samples produced no plant remains other than wood charcoal. Beech charcoal dominated three of the four samples investigated, and co-dominated with oak in the fourth. This is comparable to other college sites in Oxford and consistent with the transition from oak to beech as the most commonly used wood for fuel by the late fifteenth to early sixteenth century.

ACKNOWLEDGEMENTS

OA would like to thank Philip Parker of Brasenose College and Tim Lee of Lee Fitzgerald Architects for the invitation to participate in the Brasenose Library project. The authors are grateful to library staff who contributed information for the Brasenose Archives. The project was managed by Richard Brown. The evaluation of the site was carried out by Dan Bashford and Mark Gibson. The subsequent excavation was carried out after lifting of the Old Cloisters' flagstone floor overseen by Roy Blakely of Knowles & Sons. The archaeological excavation was supervised by Vix Hughes with a team comprising Sophia Bojadziev, John Boothroyd, Ian Cook, Rose Grant, Victoria Green, Adam Fellingham, Christof Heistermann, Aaron Kulakiewicz, Michael McLean, Ben McAndrew, Meirion Prysor, Mike Sims, Jeremy Stone, Ashley Strutt, Pete Vellet, Leanne Waring, and Andrew Williams. A watching brief on the construction works carried out by Benfield and Loxley was carried out by Jim Mumford and Robin Bashford. The post-excavation work was managed by Lisa Brown and Richard Brown. The pottery, ceramic building material and clay tobacco pipe was analysed by John Cotter, the glass by Ian R. Scott, the metalwork by Leigh Allen, the jetons by Kate Brady, the stone by Ruth Shaffrey, the animal bone by Lena Strid, the fish bone and marine shell by Rebecca Nicholson and the charcoal by Sheila Boardman. Thanks are also due to the staff that processed the finds under the management of Leigh Allen, processed the environmental samples under the management of Rebecca Nicholson, and prepared the archive under the management of Nicola Scott.

PART 3

The Northern Suburb and Civil War Defences

10.
An Early Ditch, Medieval Boundary and Post-Medieval Quarrying at the President's Garden, St John's College

STEVEN TEAGUE, JULIAN MUNBY,
ANDREW SIMMONDS and CARL CHAMPNESS

with contributions by LEIGH ALLEN, PAUL BLINKHORN,
LEE G. BRODERICK, MICHAEL DONNELLY, DAVID A. HIGGINS, JULIA MEEN,
REBECCA NICHOLSON, IAN R. SCOTT, RUTH SHAFFREY and JOHN TIBBLES

SUMMARY

Excavations in the President's Garden at St John's College uncovered part of a substantial early ditch. The date of the feature is problematic and it is argued that it may have been a prehistoric feature or part of an early medieval defensive line, perhaps designed to protect the town from Viking assaults during the tenth century or during the Anarchy in the twelfth century. The ditch was recut on two occasions during the medieval period and formed the boundary between the parishes of St Mary Magdalen and St Giles, as well as the original northern boundary of the college. Other features pertained to gravel quarrying associated with construction work at the college during the mid sixteenth to mid seventeenth century and disposal of refuse. Notable finds from that period include rare decorated stove tiles and an exceptional assemblage of clay tobacco pipes.

Construction of a new library building in the President's Garden, St John's College, occasioned an archaeological investigation of the development site, which was undertaken between 2014 and 2016. The college is located in the historic northern suburb on the east side of St Giles' Street, and the new library building was to be constructed along the east side of the President's Garden, which lies to the rear of the main college quadrangles (NGR SP 5132 0669; Fig. 10.1). It was to be built against the western face of the Grade II Listed Sprott Wall, a garden wall of early seventeenth-century date. The topography of the site was generally flat, at *c.*63 m OD. The archaeological investigation comprised a trial trench evaluation, carried out in January 2014, and a main phase of excavation during 2016. The excavation area covered the whole footprint of the proposed building, comprising an area of 595 sq m, and, in addition, watching briefs were conducted during the excavation of a crane base, a pool plant, a soakaway and a new road that provided access into the site from Parks Road.

This report includes summaries of the analyses of the artefacts and environmental evidence. The full specialist reports and accompanying data can be downloaded from the OA Library.[1]

1 https://library.oxfordarchaeology.com/5765/.

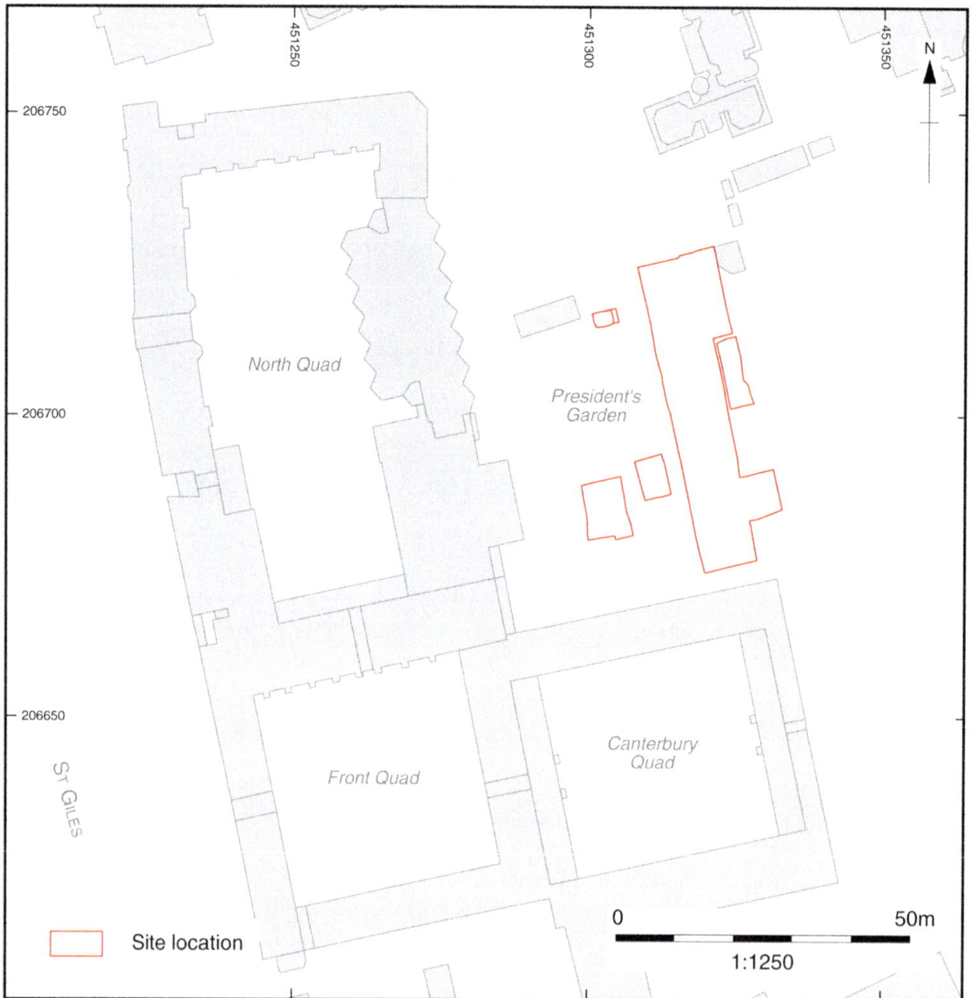

Fig. 10.1 Site location.

The excavation archive will be deposited with Oxfordshire County Museum Service under the accession code 2016.104.

FIELDWORK METHODOLOGY

The excavation areas were stripped using a 360° machine fitted with a toothless ditching bucket, under the supervision of an archaeologist. The overlying garden soils were removed until the first archaeological horizon was exposed and the archaeological features were then mapped and excavated by hand. At least 10 per cent of each linear feature was excavated and discrete features were half-sectioned; in the case of the complexes of intercutting features this was not possible and so they were investigated by means of hand-dug sondages that sought to characterise several pits and establish their stratigraphic sequence.

ARCHAEOLOGICAL AND HISTORICAL BACKGROUND

The site lies in close proximity to a complex of Neolithic and Bronze-Age monuments that lies beneath the northern part of the city centre (Fig. 10.2). The earliest element of this complex may have been a small square mortuary enclosure excavated at the Radcliffe Infirmary that has been radiocarbon dated to 3520–3360 cal BC.[2] A ditch at the Chemistry Laboratory on South Parks Road contained sherds that were tentatively identified as Peterborough Ware (*c.*3500–2800 BC) and has been interpreted as possibly being part of a cursus.[3] The most substantial monument in the complex is the Oxford Henge, which was uncovered during excavations at Kendrew Quad, St John's College, *c.*150 m north of the President's Garden.[4] During the Bronze Age the complex became dominated by monuments of a more clearly funerary character, comprising a linear barrow cemetery that extends across the University Parks and Radcliffe Infirmary with outliers at various locations from the Rex Richards Building to St Michael's Street and a possible example at Logic Lane.[5]

After the barrow cemetery fell out of use during the middle Bronze Age there appears to have been a hiatus in activity until the middle Iron Age, when occupation has been recorded north of the site in the University Parks and the Park Town area.[6] Evidence for Romano-British settlement has been uncovered nearby to the east of the site, between Parks Road and Mansfield Road.[7]

The site is located *c.*240 m north of the line of the medieval town wall, to the east of St Giles' Street, which was the main road into the town from the north. The hundred rolls survey of 1279 indicates that St Giles' Street was fully built up by this time, although the site is likely to have lain too far back to be within the tenements that fronted onto the road, and was situated in part of the open fields of St Giles parish.[8] A number of finds have been made within St John's that are likely to be associated with occupation of the tenements, including pits and a twelfth-century well along with wooden and ceramic vessels that were recorded during work in 1947 during the construction of Dolphin Quadrangle *c.*120 m south-west of the site; pits dating from the twelfth to fourteenth century found during excavations in 1959 *c.*50 m west of the site; and two pits dated to the fourteenth to fifteenth centuries uncovered in excavations at the Senior Common Room immediately to the west of the site.[9]

St John's College was originally founded to the south of the site in 1555 by Sir Thomas White, a former Lord Mayor of London, using the surviving buildings of the former Cistercian college of St Bernard, which had been established in 1437 and was dissolved in 1539 but continued as an academic hall; the buildings of St Bernard's were refurbished and partially rebuilt to form what is now Front Quad.[10] Features interpreted as quarry pits that have been uncovered in excavations at the President's Close and the Senior Common Room may have been associated

2 G. Lambrick, 'Prehistoric Oxford', *Oxoniensia*, 78 (2013), p. 9.

3 P. Bradley et al., 'Prehistoric and Roman Activity and a Civil War Ditch: Excavations at the Chemistry Research Laboratory, 2–4 South Parks Road, Oxford', *Oxoniensia* 70 (2005), pp. 141–202.

4 S. Wallis, *The Oxford Henge and Late Saxon Massacre: with Medieval and Later Occupation at St John's College, Oxford*, TVAS Monograph, 17 (2014).

5 Lambrick, 'Prehistoric Oxford', pp. 19–24.

6 D. Radford, 'Archaeological Work in Oxford, 2012', *Oxoniensia*, 78 (2013), p. 214; S. Thompson, 'Evidence for Iron Age Land Use and Settlement in the University Parks, Oxford', *Oxoniensia*, 80 (2015), pp. 97–109.

7 P. Booth and C. Hayden, 'A Roman Settlement at Mansfield College, Oxford', *Oxoniensia*, 65 (2000), pp. 291–331; Bradley et al., 'Prehistoric and Roman Activity and a Civil War Ditch'.

8 Salter, *Map of Mediaeval Oxford* (1934), map 1; Salter, *Survey*, vol. 2, NW 40–47; Dodd, *Oxford*.

9 E.M. Jope et al., 'Pottery from the Late 12th Century Well-Filling and Other Medieval Finds from St John's College, Oxford, 1947', *Oxoniensia*, 15 (1950), pp. 44–62; H. Case and D. Sturdy, 'Oxford, St John's College', *Oxoniensia*, 24 (1959), p. 101; S. Lawrence, 'Excavations at St John's College, Oxford, 2003', *Oxoniensia*, 70 (2005), pp. 325–31.

10 *VCH Oxon.* 3, pp. 251–64; W.H. Stevenson and H.E. Salter, *The Early History of St John's College, Oxford*, OHS, ns 1 (1939).

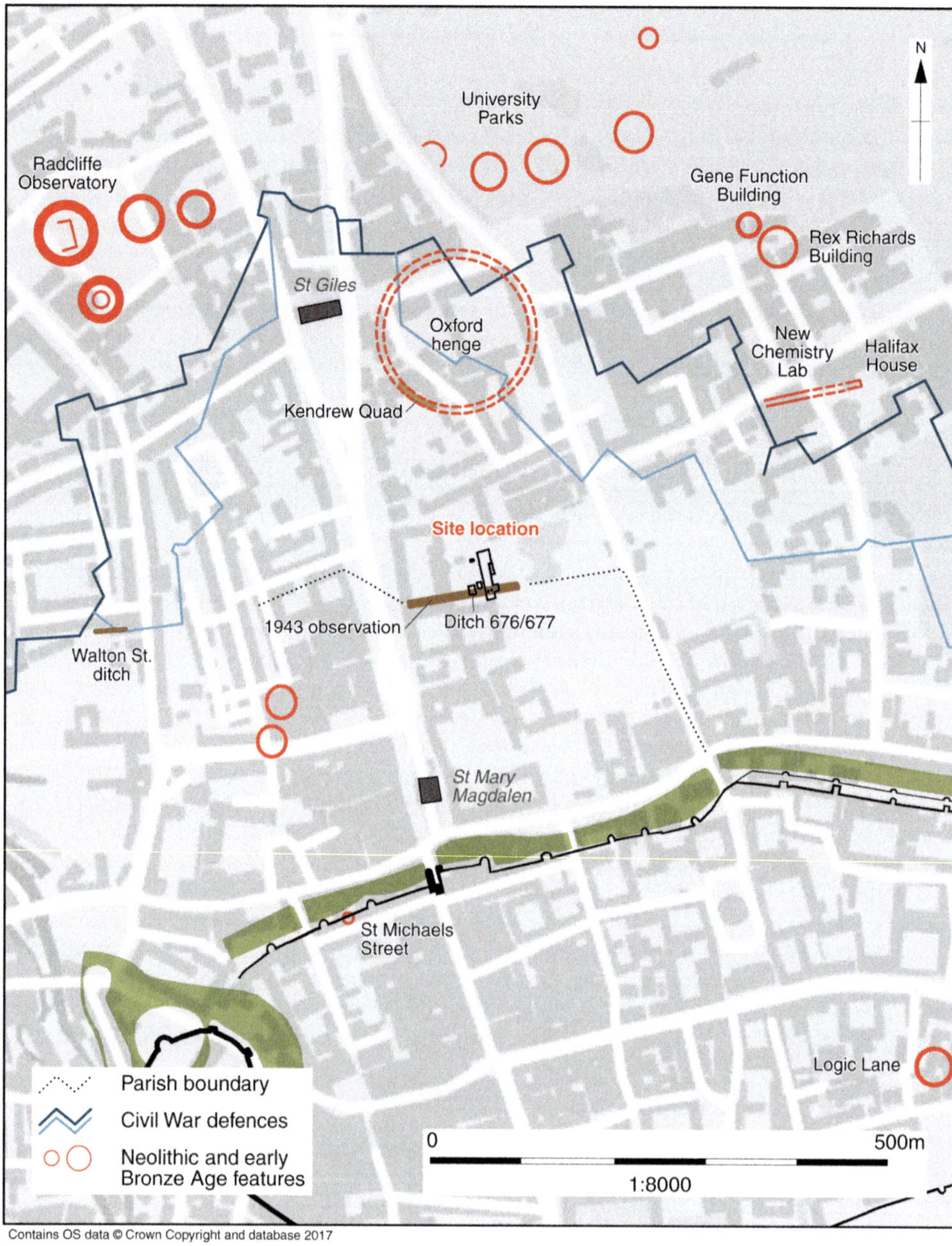

Fig. 10.2 Neolithic and early Bronze-Age monuments in north Oxford and other key topographic features.

with the acquisition of gravel for this work and subsequent development at the college during the sixteenth and seventeenth centuries.[11] However, the college property did not at first extend northwards beyond the boundary between St Mary Magdalen and St Giles parishes (marked by a ditch that occurs in college accounts) or further east than the tenements of St Bernard's College (marked by the east end of the Chapel and Senior Common Room buildings);[12] the story of its subsequent gradual expansion is well recorded.[13]

The area to the east of the tenements on St Giles' Street was part of Beaumont fields of St Giles and Mary Magdalen parishes. At the south end of the field was land of Godstow granted to Durham College (now Trinity) *c.*1286 that lay below the ditch 'across' Beaumont.[14] After the dissolution of the college in 1540, 'half of the garden of Durham College' was granted by the Crown to Christ Church in 1546 together with the site of St Bernard's College,[15] and when sold by Christ Church to Sir Thomas White in 1555 became the St John's College garden.[16] A small strip of land on the east side of St Bernard's College had been leased by the Cistercians since their foundation from Durham College and was granted to Christ Church in 1546 and so passed to St John's College on its foundation.[17] Trinity College was founded just before St John's and as a joint venture the two new colleges built a wall between their gardens, subject to an agreement in 1560 about making a door in the wall.[18]

The north side of the St John's garden may still have been bounded by a ditch, and in 1561 St John's leased from New College one acre of land next to the college, whose southern boundary was described as 'the chanell or watercourse coming out of Magdalen parish'.[19] This acre lay in the open fields of St Giles parish, and in the fourteenth-century terrier of St Giles/Walton Manor this furlong was called *Bemondefeld*. The New College acre at the south end was 'next the wall' (*iuxta murum*) of Durham College and the field extended as far north as 'Rome' at the junction of Parks and the Banbury Road.[20] The next three acres to the north belonged to Godstow abbey, but were granted to St John's by Richard Owen of Godstow in 1558 (and separately from his sale of the whole of Walton Manor to the college in 1573).[21] None of this land had been taken into the college by the time of Ralph Agas' map of 1578, and it was then shown as open ground, possibly representing pasture, while the southern end of the site extends into a walled garden at the rear of the college; there is no sign of any ditch (Fig. 10.3). However, the New College lease had expressly included the right to use an existing gravel pit as much as was wished, and then to dig another one.[22] The boundary ditch between St Giles and St Mary Magdalen parishes had no doubt been necessary to prevent cattle grazing the open fields from straying outside the parish, and now as the college boundary it continued to be maintained (although not shown by Agas). The college accounts refer to 'scowringe the diche by Mr President's Garden' (1569), 'skowringe

11 B. Durham and C. Bell, 'Oxford, Former Department of Rural Economy, Parks Road', *SMidlA*, 23 (1993), p. 74; Lawrence, 'Excavations at St John's College'.

12 Stevenson and Salter, *The Early History of St John's College*, plan opposite p. 501, and p. 53 for the tenements of St Bernard's College (Salter, *Survey*, vol. 2, NW 43–44).

13 Stevenson and Salter, *The Early History of St John's College*.

14 A. Clark, *The English Register of Godstow Nunnery*, EETS 130 (1906), p. 500 (675); E. Amt, *The Latin Cartulary of Godstow Abbey*, British Academy (2014), p. 256 (539); original charter Bodleian Library MS Ch. Oxon. A.11 no. 205, with its counterpart in Durham Cathedral Archives: Eboracensia 1.5.Ebor.8. The Latin text reads '*a quodam fossato extransverso in Bello monte*', translated for the nuns as 'thurte over in Bewmont'.

15 Stevenson and Salter, *The Early History of St John's College*, p. 91, app. XIV.

16 Stevenson and Salter, *The Early History of St John's College*, p. 375, app. XVIII.

17 *VCH Oxon.* 3, p. 238; H.E.D. Blakiston, 'Some Durham College Rolls', *Collectanea III*, OHS, 32 (1896), p. 61; Stevenson and Salter, *The Early History of St John's College*, pp. 23, 50, and map opposite p. 501.

18 Stevenson and Salter, *The Early History of St John's College*, p. 125.

19 Ibid. 127–8; it was finally purchased in 1785.

20 Ibid. pp. 514–5.

21 Ibid. p. 123; Walton Manor cost £1,566 13s. 4d.: the deed is printed in Stevenson and Salter, *The Early History of St John's College*, p. 527.

22 Ibid. p. 128.

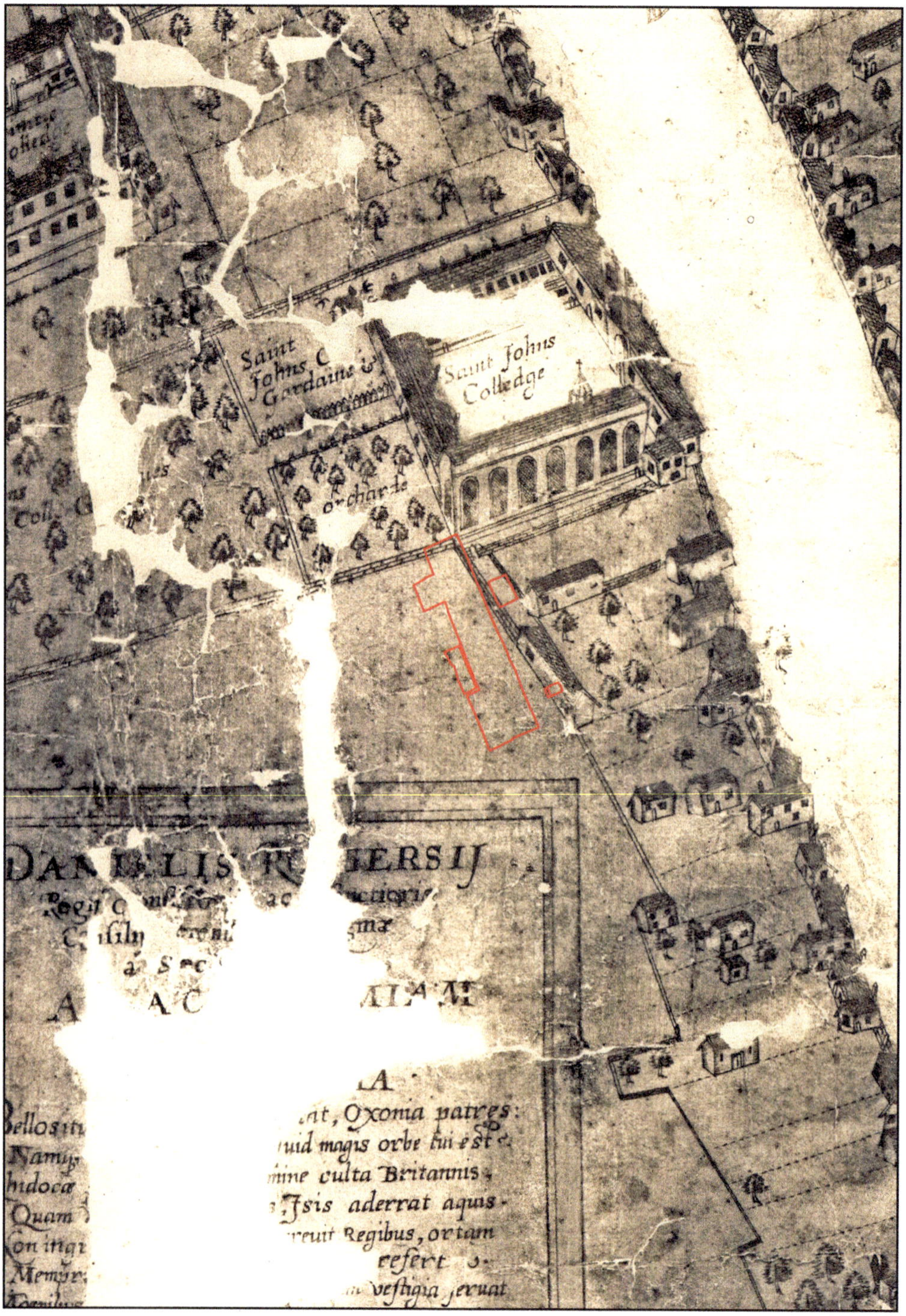

Fig. 10.3 Detail from Agas' 1578 map of Oxford. North to bottom.

the diche by the kitchin' (1571) and 'making clean the diche in the grove' (1579), 'scouring the ditche toward the privies' and 'scouring the ditch along the grove wall' (1582), so evidently it was kept clean, and was perhaps drawing water from the roadside ditches in St Giles' Street.[23]

The land north of the ditch, including most of the excavation area, was formally taken into the college following a decision in 1600 that four acres in the open fields 'lying on the north side of the Grove' should be enclosed by a wall as an addition to the Grove;[24] with the £200 benefaction of the former fellow Edward Sprott in 1612,[25] the new garden could be enclosed, with the 'Sprott wall' including the north–south length dividing the President's Garden from the Fellows' Garden being built in 1613. While the configuration of the President's Garden later changed, from the walled gardens and yards shown on Loggan's 1675 map of Oxford to the extensive garden and adjoining President's Close mapped in 1875, the eastern boundary of the Sprott Wall remained, and the site remained part of the garden until the construction of the new library.

A trial trench evaluation of the site, comprising three trenches, was undertaken in 2014 and uncovered pits of various sizes dating from the twelfth to seventeenth centuries, representing quarrying and possibly domestic activity.[26]

DISCUSSION

The remains uncovered by the excavation can be divided into three aspects, comprising the poorly dated but evidently early ditch 677, the medieval boundary represented by ditches 675 and 676, and the post-medieval quarry pits and the refuse with which they were backfilled (Fig. 10.4).

Early Ditch

The substantial early ditch (677) that crossed the southern part of the site was evidently a significant feature, but its date is problematic. It had massive proportions, surviving to a depth of up to 2.38 m and a width of 3.4 m, and its fills comprised sterile weathered sands and gravels that derived from the surrounding natural strata. It had clearly silted over an extended period of time before it was cut (or recut) by medieval ditch 676, but it lacked artefactual material or any charred plant remains that could be used for radiocarbon dating. Two samples taken for optically-stimulated luminescence (OSL) dating produced date ranges of 4695 ± 435 years before 2017 (3113–2243 BC) for the bottom fill and 3645 ± 865 years before 2017 (2493–763 BC) for the second fill. The date for the lower sample was not considered reliable as it was based on a single measurement but the date ranges for the two samples are nevertheless consistent with the stratigraphic sequence and, if taken at face value, would indicate that the ditch was dug during the late Neolithic period and silted gradually during the Bronze Age and perhaps beyond. Such a date is not implausible for a feature in this location, since the gravel ridge on which north Oxford is situated contains a complex of late Neolithic and early Bronze-Age ceremonial monuments (Fig. 10.2). Neolithic elements include the henge monument uncovered at Kendrew Quad, *c.*220 m north of ditch 677, a square mortuary enclosure at Radcliffe Infirmary, a linear ditch parallel to South Parks Road, part of a second linear ditch at Logic Lane, and an unexcavated enclosure identified as a cropmark in Christ Church Meadow, while Bronze-Age features comprise ring ditches identified as cropmarks or excavated evidence as well as some flat burials.[27]

23 Ibid. pp. 174, 177, 217, 237–8.

24 Ibid.; *VCH Oxon.* 3, p. 257 (decree of 1 Dec. 1600).

25 A. Hegarty, *A Biographical Register of St John's College, Oxford 1555 to 1660*, OHS, ns 43 (2011), p. 140.

26 'President's Garden, St John's College, Oxford. Archaeological Evaluation Report', unpublished OA report (2014), https://library.oxfordarchaeology.com/3404/.

27 Lambrick, 'Prehistoric Oxford', pp. 9–26.

Fig. 10.4 Phases 1–4: undated to mid sixteenth century.

The form of the feature represented by ditch 677 is uncertain, not least because the full extent of the ditch is not known, although it extended for at least the 33 m width of the excavation area. A substantial ditch had previously been encountered in 1943–4 during the insertion of a water tank in North Quad, a short distance west of the President's Garden, but the feature was not bottomed and it is uncertain whether it represents a continuation only of the later ditch 675/676 or whether the earlier ditch also continued on this alignment.[28] Either way, ditch 677

[28] 'Archaeological Finds in the City of Oxford', *Oxoniensia*, 8/9 (1943–4), p. 203.

was clearly part of a substantial and potentially extensive monument, as may the ditches at South Parks Road and Logic Lane. The ditch at South Parks Road was identified at the Chemistry Laboratory site and may have extended as far as Halifax House, 50 m further east, where a terminus of comparable form was recorded.[29] Its extent to the west has not been established. The ditch was considerably smaller than the ditch at St John's, measuring 2.20 m wide and 1.05 m deep, but pottery from its middle fill identified as Peterborough ware (*c.*3500–2800 BC) may indicate a broadly contemporary date. Ditch 2 at Logic Lane was of similar dimensions and produced a sherd that may also be Peterborough ware.[30] Linear monuments, of which these ditches may form part, were a common part of the Neolithic/early Bronze-Age repertoire, as exemplified by the numerous long mortuary enclosures, cursus monuments and bank barrows recorded within the upper Thames valley. The possible mortuary enclosure in Christ Church Meadow measures *c.*100 m long and other similar monuments include North Stoke, at more than 20 m long, Dorchester Site VIII, at 63 m, and Yarnton Site 5, at more than 52 m.[31] However, the enclosure ditches were all considerably smaller than ditch 677, the ditch at North Stoke measuring 1.8 m wide and 1.5 m deep, that at Dorchester measuring 2.1 m wide and 0.9 m deep and that at Yarnton measuring up to 2.2 m wide and 1.08 m deep. Cursus monuments and bank barrows represent two closely similar classes of monument, the former comprising a pair of parallel ditches 45–75 m apart with corresponding internal banks and the latter defined by more closely spaced ditches with a single intervening mound. At least nine such monuments are known along the 60 km stretch of the River Thames between Lechlade and Goring.[32] Again, the ditches are typically less substantial than ditch 677, rarely significantly exceeding 1 m in depth, although the ditches of the bank barrow at North Stoke were more substantial with a width of up to 2.45 m and a depth of up to 2.30 m.[33] These monuments are therefore more closely similar to the ditches at South Parks Road and Logic Lane than to the more massive ditch 677.

A closer parallel for ditch 677, at least as regards the form and scale of the ditch, is provided by the ditch of the henge monument that lies beneath Kendrew Quad and Keble College, which measured *c.*5–8 m wide and up to 2.8 m deep, forming a monument with a projected diameter of *c.*150 m.[34] Furthermore, the lower fills of the henge ditch (Key Layers E and F) are similar in composition to the surviving fills of ditch 677. In addition to this, sherds of late Neolithic and Beaker pottery were recovered from the later Key Layer E, suggesting that it had silted up to a similar level by the early Bronze Age. Although the projected shape of the henge is approximately circular, the part that was exposed in excavation at Kendrew Quad in fact comprised a linear segment *c.*40 m long, curving at either end to meet what are presumably similar segments to form a monument that is more strictly polygonal in form. While it is conceded that henges more typically occur as individual examples, and there are no known instances of pairs or larger groups within the Thames Valley region, groups are occasionally found elsewhere; the group at Priddy, Somerset, for example comprises an alignment of three henges separated by intervals

[29] Bradley et al., 'Prehistoric and Roman Activity'; S. Anthony, 'Prehistoric and Early Roman Field Systems at Halifax House, South Parks Road, Oxford', *Oxoniensia*, 70 (2005), pp. 129–39.

[30] F. Radcliffe, 'Excavations at Logic Lane, Oxford. The Prehistoric and Early Medieval Finds', *Oxoniensia*, 26/27 (1961/2), pp. 39–43.

[31] Lambrick, 'Prehistoric Oxford', p. 14; H.J. Case, 'The Linear Ditches and Southern Enclosure, North Stoke', in H.J. Case and A.W.R. Whittle (eds.), *Settlements Patterns in the Oxford Region: Excavations at the Abingdon Causewayed Enclosure and Other Sites*, CBA Research Report, 44 (1982), p. 66; A. Whittle et al., 'Excavations in the Neolithic and Bronze Age Complex at Dorchester-on-Thames, Oxfordshire, 1947–1952 and 1981', *Proceedings of the Prehistoric Society*, 58 (1992), p. 148; G. Hey et al., *Yarnton: Neolithic and Bronze Age Settlement and Landscape* (2016), p. 405.

[32] G. Hey and A. Barclay, 'Inscribing the Landscape: Neolithic Funerary and Ceremonial Monuments', in A. Morigi et al., *The Thames Through Time: Early Prehistory to 1500 BC*, Thames Valley Landscapes Monograph, 32 (2011), p. 293.

[33] Case, 'The Linear Ditches and Southern Enclosure', p. 66.

[34] Wallis, *The Oxford Henge*.

of *c.*80 m with a fourth a further 475 m away, while the three henges at Thornborough, North Yorkshire, are *c.*750 m apart.[35]

Alternatively, a historical context might be sought for the ditch. The ditch observed in North Quad was interpreted as part of the city's Civil War defences,[36] but it does not correspond with the known alignments of this date and is likely to be earlier. Sturdy had previously postulated a late Anglo-Saxon defensive earthwork on this alignment, which would most plausibly have been constructed against Viking incursions during the late tenth and early eleventh centuries that included the sacking of the town in AD 1009.[37] Another possibility is that the ditch was part of a defence designed to protect the fledging northern suburb and the newly constructed Beaumont Palace during the Anarchy and the associated siege of Oxford during 1142.[38] In either case, the ditch would presumably have comprised part of a forward defensive line that extended across the gravel promontory between the Thames and Cherwell. A further part of such a defence might be represented by a ditch of similar proportions and on the same alignment that was recorded 380 m to the west on the former Ruskin College site in Walton Street.[39] Although interpreted as part of the Civil War defences, it continued east beyond the projected line of these defences and only contained pottery and brick/tile of medieval date, suggesting that it may represent an earlier ditch that was subsequently partly followed by the Civil War line. To the east of St John's, the alignment is continued by the ditch 'across Beaumont' forming the northern boundary of Durham College described above, and its alignment was continued into Holywell parish as a field boundary that was later used for the inner line of Civil War defences.

Medieval Boundary

A twelfth-century date for ditch 677 would require it to have silted quite rapidly before it was recut as ditch 676. The latter was less substantial, with a depth of about half that of the earlier ditch, but survived to a greater width of up to 4.1 m. In contrast to the earlier ditch its fills were soil rich and contained an appreciable quantity of animal bone, small amounts of pottery and a fragment of tile. The pottery comprised a single sherd of Cotswold ware together with seven sherds of Oxford medieval ware. A radiocarbon date of cal. AD 1043–1245 was obtained from fill 666, with a 73.4 per cent probability that the date falls after cal. AD 1118. On balance, considering the pottery and tile fragment, a date somewhere in the twelfth century is most likely. Its occurrence as a boundary feature in medieval documentation has been described above, and its correspondence with the parish boundary between St Mary Magdalen and St Giles is significant (it was also the boundary of the Northgate hundred in its late-medieval, reduced, extent, as indicated by the boundary stone in Parks Road). St Giles' church was built by Edwin son of Godgose between 1123–33 after which it soon gained parochial rights.[40] Such a date corresponds with the northwards expansion of the suburb as evidenced by occupation recorded at Kendrew Quad, adjacent to the church.[41]

Ditch 676 remained open during the later medieval period and appears to have been recut as ditch 675, perhaps at the time that Durham College was founded in the late thirteenth century, which would accord with the thirteenth- to fourteenth-century pottery recovered from its fills. The recut ditch contained the remains of three dogs and a small quantity of kitchen waste.

35 C. Taylor and E.K. Tratman, 'The Priddy Circles: Preliminary Report', *Proceedings of the University of Bristol Spelaeological Society* 8:1 (1957), p. 8; J. Harding and B. Johnson, 'The Neolithic and Bronze Age Monument Complex of Thornborough, North Yorkshire, and its Landscape Context: Desk-Top Assessment', unpublished report (2008), https://doi.org/10.5284/1000080.

36 'Archaeological Finds in the City of Oxford', p. 203.

37 D. Sturdy, *Historic Oxford* (2004), pp. 27–9; *VCH Oxon*. 4, p. 300.

38 *VCH Oxon*. 4, p. 11.

39 R. Bashford, 'Exeter College, Ruskin Building, Walton Street, Oxford: Archaeological Watching Brief', unpublished OA report (2015), https://library.oxfordarchaeology.com/3521/.

40 *VCH Oxon*. 4, p. 381.

41 Wallis, *The Oxford Henge*, pp. 235–8.

The presence of dogs (and gnawed food bones) suggests that the boundary ditch served as a rubbish dump from its north side and as well as for the disposal of food waste from the monks residing at Durham College or from the adjacent tenements. Similarly, the small quantity of roof tile recovered could have been deposited either during construction works within the college or from the houses occupying the nearby tenements.

By the time that the Benedictine Durham College and Cistercian St Bernard's College had surrendered to the Crown in the 1540s, the ditch had seemingly been levelled, possibly being replaced by a much smaller ditch (645) immediately to the south. This later ditch appears to have been filled during the second part of the sixteenth century, corresponding to the founding of St John's College in 1555, or its acquisition of land to the north shortly after. The periodic scouring of the ditch by St John's College is recorded in college accounts in the late sixteenth century, as noted above, and the ditch would only have become redundant when the wall separating the President's Garden from the yard alongside Canterbury Quad was built in 1612.

Post-Medieval Quarrying and Rubbish Disposal

For the medieval period onwards, the site has to be seen in two contrasting contexts: first in the open fields of St Giles parish, and secondly, after 1600, as an enclosed space in the college garden. It is clear from the archaeological record that the division of activity is not quite so clear cut, and while Agas' map of 1588 shows open fields outside the college garden, as has been shown above from the historical records the college had acquired land outside the garden with consent to use it for gravel digging, and the archaeological record demonstrates that the area was used for periodic episodes of gravel extraction and waste disposal in the field. The distribution of these pits perhaps suggests they were located with regard to east–west strips of ridge and furrow, and while this alignment is implied by the historical records, no other evidence of this was detected. Perhaps, in association with clearance of the ditch, the pits were opened, extracted, and filled in order to clear accumulated middens of domestic rubbish. Although there were a few earlier pits, the main phase of quarrying dated from the mid sixteenth to mid seventeenth century and is likely to have been associated with the acquisition of gravel for building works during the early years of the college. This is less likely to have occurred after the land was incorporated in the President's Garden, though not impossible if carried out as a single episode of short duration. The nature and quality of the post-medieval finds is certainly suggestive of a collegiate origin.

The post-medieval pottery reflects drinking and entertaining in the types of vessels and better quality tableware, as should be expected in college waste disposal. Decorative stove tiles – a rare find from Oxford – were probably continental imports, and were perhaps for use in the president's lodgings. An exceptional collection of clay pipes shows the prevalence of tobacco smoking,[42] and includes examples of the earliest pipe forms from the late sixteenth century and a fine group of the Civil War and Commonwealth period.

While the medieval small finds had an agricultural flavour, including the tip of a livestock goad, the post-medieval finds belong more to domestic life appropriate to the college, including dress accessories and items reflecting academic study (book clasps), leisure (riding), and domestic consumption (eating, drinking and lighting), while in Phase 6 there is evidence of the building work. Remains of glassware include good-quality flask beakers amongst a variety of drinking vessels, and a college common room bottle seal of 1759, at which date wine was still being decanted into marked bottles for fellows' use.[43] There is a difference between the medieval and later food remains, and once more a suggestion of the distinction between earlier rubbish deposits (some of which had lain long enough in the ditch to be gnawed by rats) and the post-medieval deposits which are from a collegiate context and the subject of deliberate

42 Below-floor deposits recovered in 1975 from the rooms below the Old Library included a large number of pipes of early eighteenth-century date: personal communication from J. Munby.

43 J. Haslam, 'Sealed Bottles from All Souls College', *Oxoniensia*, 35 (1970), pp. 27–33.

disposal. While the medieval cattle remains suggest horn-working, in the post-medieval period the emphasis is on food waste, with high numbers of sheep and chicken bones, along with a variety of fish remains and garden fruits.

A further topic of interest, which requires more exploration in historical sources, is the source of fuel evidenced by charcoal remains. The prevalence of beech, noted here, as on other sites in Oxford, may suggest that the town (like London) obtain significant quantities of fuel from the Chilterns rather than from more local sources.

EXCAVATION RESULTS

Phase 1: Undated (Prehistoric?)

This phase comprised a large ditch (677), the earliest of a sequence of three ditches that extended across the southern part of the site (Figs. 10.4–10.6). Although the subsequent ditches (676 and 675) were dated by pottery and radiocarbon to the medieval period, the date of the earliest ditch could not be established with any certainty. No finds were recovered and soil samples taken from its fills to retrieve material suitable for radiocarbon dating proved to be completely sterile. A possible prehistoric date was suggested by OSL dating.

The ditch had been partially removed by later ditch 676, although its lower profile survived (Fig. 10.5). Part of its upper profile was revealed further to the west in the soakaway trench. The ditch was exposed for a length of 10.9 m and seems to have followed the alignment of the later ditch (676) between these excavated sections. There is some degree of uncertainty regarding the identification of its profile within the two interventions in the soakaway trench given the lack of full excavation in this area. Furthermore, its northern lip appears to have been revealed near the western edge of the soakaway trench. The ditch had a very sharp 'V'-shaped profile, the lower half of which was straight and steep-sided forming an almost perfect 'V'. Its upper part was slightly less steep and where surviving was also straight and unweathered. It full depth was 2.33–2.38 m and it survived to a width of *c.*3.40 m. Two fills survived, the earlier of which (672) was the main deposit and comprised laminated redeposited natural gravel with lenses of greyish yellow or pinkish grey sands. The composition of this deposit suggested that it represented an accumulation over an extended period, probably as the result of natural silting. A sample taken from this deposit for OSL dating (SJC16–01, Fig. 10.5) produced a date of 4695 ± 435 years before 2017. The second fill (671) comprised reddish yellow/grey sand that contained less gravel than the underlying fill, although it was probably also deposited as a result of natural silting. A sample from this deposit (SJC16–02, Fig. 10.5) returned an OSL date of 3645 ± 865 years before 2017.

Phase 2: Eleventh to Twelfth Century

Ditch 677 was cut by ditch 676, which was exposed for a length of 33 m. It had moderately sloping sides with a concave or slightly rounded base and measured up to 4.1 m wide and 1.20–1.31 m deep (Figs. 10.4 and 10.5). It contained at least four fills, although the upper fills had been truncated by the subsequent ditch 675 (see below). The fills all appeared to have been deposited naturally as a result of weathering and largely comprised gravel-rich dark grey silty sands. Only a limited amount of dating evidence was recovered; fill 666 contained pottery dating from the mid eleventh to twelfth century, and medieval Oxford ware of similar date was recovered from the western end of the ditch. Ceramic building material and animal bone were also present, suggesting the proximity of occupied areas. A cattle metacarpal from fill 666 produced a radiocarbon date of cal. AD 1043–1245 (Table 10.6).

Phase 3: Thirteenth to Fourteenth Century

During this phase the ditch was recut for a second and final time and a small number of pits were dug to the north (Fig. 10.5).

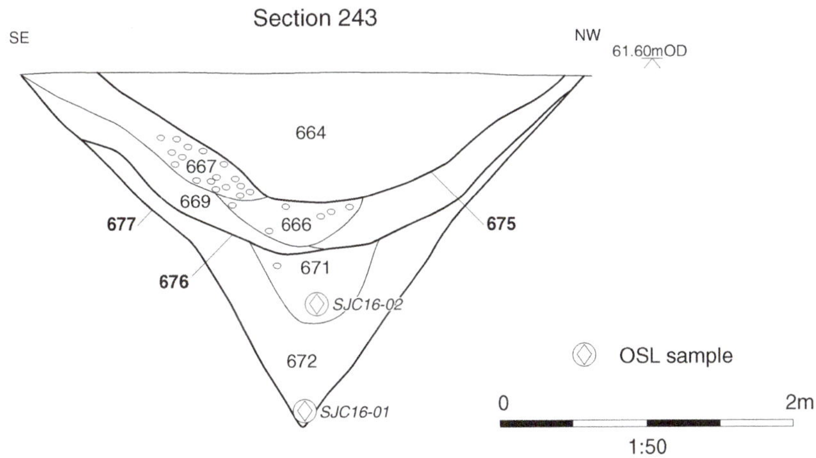

Fig. 10.5 Section of ditches 675, 676 and 677.

Fig. 10.6 Ditches 675, 676 and 677, looking west. Scales: 1 m and 2 m.

Ditch 675 Ditch 676 was recut as ditch 675. Within the soakaway pit it was largely truncated by Phase 5 pits but in the main excavation area it was found to be 3.2 m wide and 0.86m deep (Figs. 10.4 and 10.5). Its profile was similar to that of ditch 676, comprising gentle, slightly concave sides and a concave base. It contained a single homogeneous fill of greyish red, slightly clayey sand (664) which was very distinct from the fills of the earlier ditches and may have been deliberately deposited to level the ditch. This material contained animal bone together with pottery that predominantly comprised Brill/Boarstall ware, suggesting a thirteenth- to fourteenth-century date.

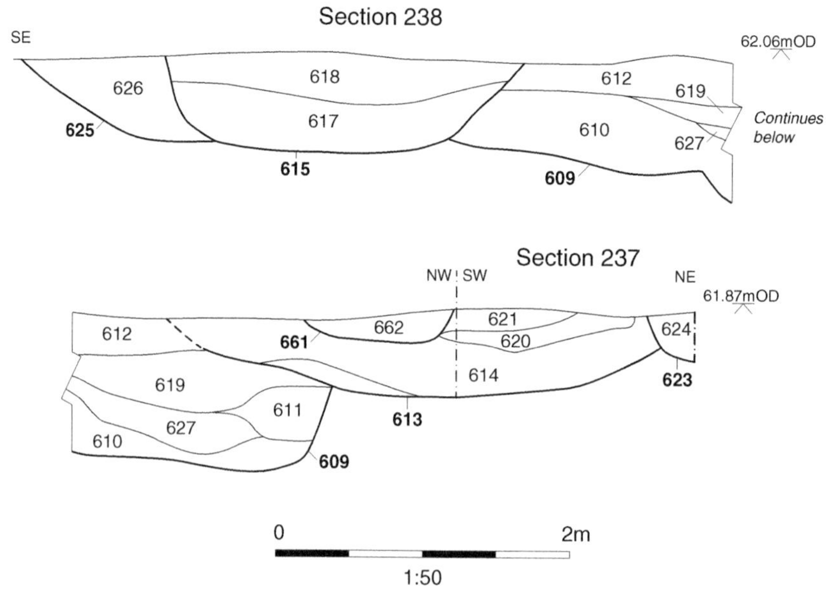

Fig. 10.7 Sections of Phase 3 and 4 quarry pits 609, 613, 615, 623 and 625.

Quarry Pits The earliest features north of ditch 675 comprised a number of pits, which had an early stratigraphic position and/or contained assemblages of thirteenth- to fourteenth-century Brill/Boarstall ware that indicated that they predated the main phasing of pitting during Phase 5 (Fig. 10.4). The pits were all either circular or ovoid in shape and the majority measured less than 2.5 m in diameter and were 0.36–0.68 m deep. Their intercutting nature suggests that the earliest pit remained partially open whilst the next pit was being excavated, and they may have been dug as quarries to extract the natural gravel and sand.

Three distinct clusters of pits were apparent, separated by approximately equal intervals. The northern group comprised three intercutting pits (210, 216 and 388) that were dug in sequence from east to west before being truncated by larger Phase 4 pits. The central group comprised a larger number of pits, possibly representing two or three smaller clusters, each containing two or three intercutting pits. They probably served the same purpose (e.g. pits 348, 366 and 468). The southern cluster (Fig. 10.7) was situated adjacent to ditch 675 and respected the line of the ditch, suggesting that it remained a discernible boundary at the time the pits were dug. This group consisted of somewhat larger pits, measuring in excess of 3.9 m across (114, 609 and 625), of which pit 609 was the deepest at 1.0 m depth. This suggests that gravel/sand extraction was undertaken on a larger scale within this area.

Most of the pits contained several fills, the earliest of which tended to comprise redeposited loose gravel and sand suggesting that they had remained open for some time. Their upper levels comprised deliberate infill of dark greyish sand silts with lenses of redeposited gravel/sand. Most pits contained animal bone in small quantities, suggesting rubbish was disposed of during backfilling or whilst the pits were still open.

Phase 4: Fifteenth to Mid Sixteenth Century

Three pits (374, 613, 615) were tentatively attributed to this phase (Fig. 10.4). Pits 613 and 615 both cut Phase 3 pit 609, the upper fill of which contained late-medieval Brill/Boarstall ware, which was introduced from the early to late fifteenth century. Both pits were of a similar depth to pit 609 and may have represented the continuation of the quarrying in this pit cluster that had commenced during Phase 3. Similarly, pit 374 may represent a southern extension of the northern pit cluster, which was subsequently extensively truncated by Phase 5 pits.

Phase 5: Mid Sixteenth to Mid Seventeenth Century

Ditch 675 is likely to have been levelled by this time and the boundary it had represented was now defined by the smaller ditch 645, which was located slightly further south (Fig. 10.8). The phase was marked by an enormous increase in the intensity and extent of pit digging that probably represented a more intensive level of quarrying compared with the preceding Phases 3 and 4.

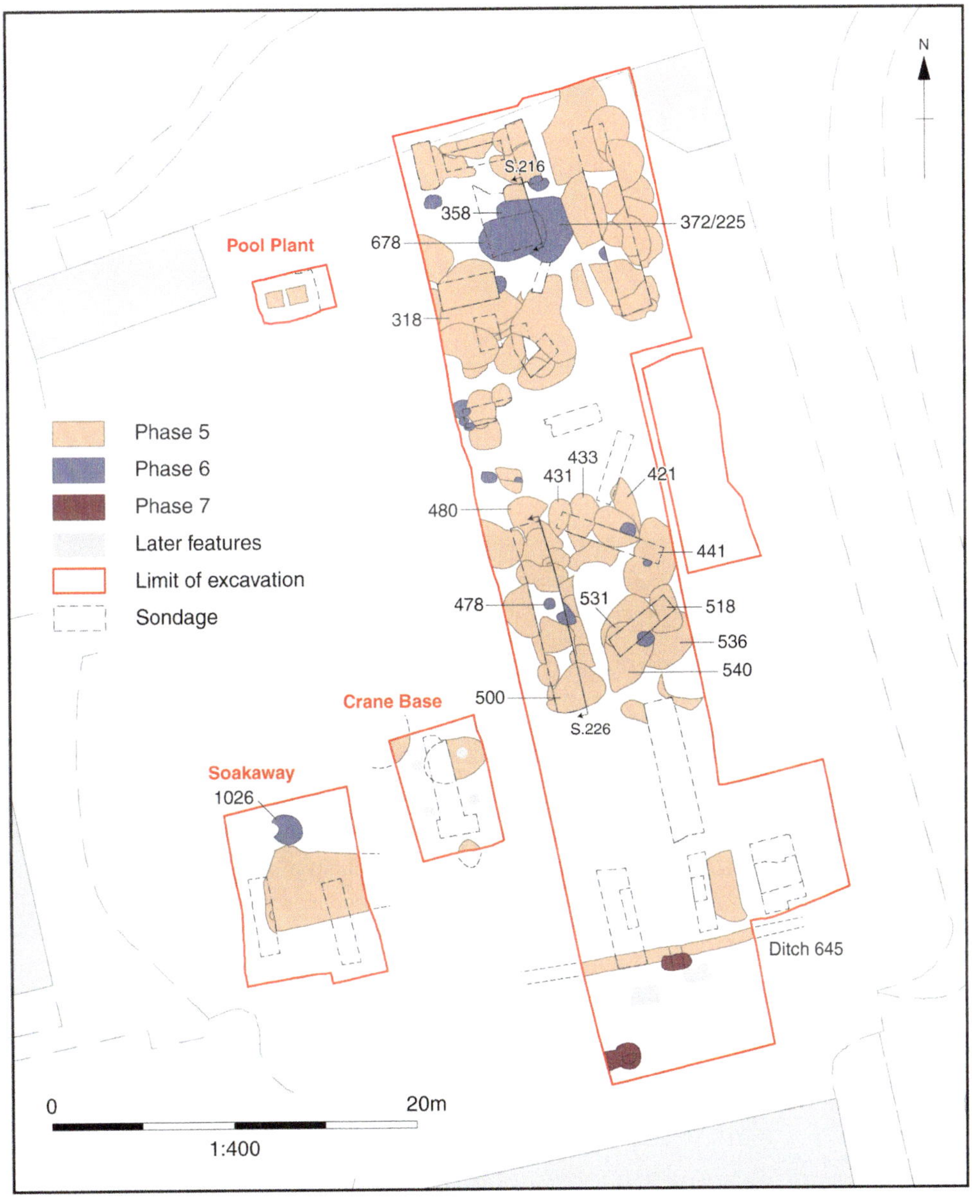

Fig. 10.8 Phases 5–7: mid sixteenth century to modern.

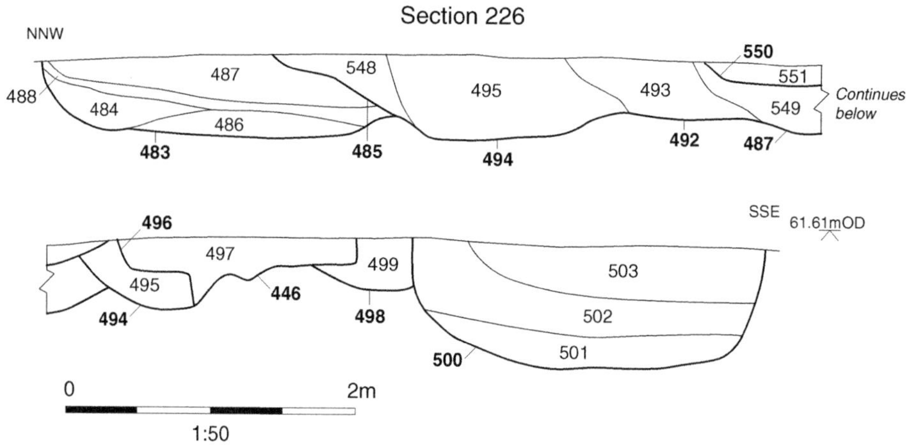

Fig. 10.9 Section of Phase 5 and 6 quarry pits 446, 483, 485, 487, 492, 494, 498 and 500.

Ditch 645 The ditch ran parallel to and *c.*1 m south of Phase 4 ditch 675. It measured 0.60–0.62 m wide and 0.28–0.30 m deep and had a concave profile. It was filled with dark grey clayey silt that contained a sherd of mid to late sixteenth-century pottery and animal bone.

Quarry Pits Most of the pits were contained within three large clusters and were largely dug within those areas that had not been utilised during Phases 3 and 4. The two clusters at the northern end of the excavation area comprised an eastern group of eighteen pits and a western group of eleven pits with an additional five isolated pits located between them and the southern cluster. In the north-eastern group the easternmost pits appeared to be the earliest features, and ended in a distinct alignment close to the eastern boundary of the excavation area. This could suggest that quarrying here proceeded from east to west. No such sequence could be determined for the western cluster, although there was a clear alignment along their northern extent that avoided the earlier quarries from Phases 3 and 4.

The southern group comprised a cluster of up to thirty intercutting pits (Fig. 10.9). They had been dug sequentially from north to south. Therefore, the earliest pits within this group were the northernmost pits, represented by pits 421, 431, 433 and 480. Most of the pits in this group were ovoid or circular, with sloping sides and slightly rounded bases. They typically measured just over 2 m in diameter and ranged in depth from 0.55–0.80 m, although the largest (421) measured 3.9 m across and 1.05 m deep.

Most pits contained no more than three fills, which largely comprised deliberate backfill of dark greyish brown silty sandy clays, often containing a considerable quantity of animal bone, pottery, roof tile and other material, suggesting that they were filled with refuse. The pits can be dated generally by the pottery to the mid sixteenth to mid seventeenth century. Early to mid seventeenth-century fabrics were found almost exclusively within the southernmost pits of the southern cluster (500, 518, 531, 536 and 540), suggesting that they represented the latest features. One of these pits (518) produced a jeton dated to 1586–1635. Seventeenth-century pottery, clay pipe and glass fragments were present in the upper fills of pits 318 and 358 within the northern clusters.

Phase 6: Mid Seventeenth to Eighteenth Century

This is no firm evidence that quarrying continued beyond the early to mid seventeenth century. By 1675, Loggan's map shows the site as an enclosed formal garden or orchard, and many of the earlier quarry pits were cut by small, shallow pits that are likely to represent planting pits. Most

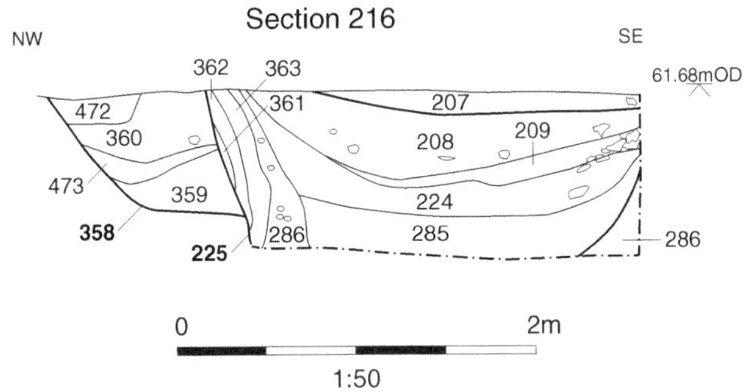

Fig. 10.10 Section of Phase 6 pit 225.

were oval or circular, measuring 0.70–0.90 m across and no more than 0.20 m in depth. No clear arrangement can be deduced from the surviving evidence, although it is likely that many shallower features did not survive later truncation. Only three pits contained any finds, with pit 478 producing pottery dating from the early to mid seventeenth century.

Towards the northern end of the site intercutting pits 225/372 and 678 represented the latest in the sequence of pits in this area and were used for the disposal of an exceptionally large amount of rubbish. This amounted to 20.3 kg of animal bone, 5.4 kg of pottery, 2.3 kg of shell and 803 fragments of clay tobacco pipes together with quantities of metal objects, glass and tile. The earlier pit (225/372, Fig. 10.10) was sub-circular with steep sides and measured *c.*3.5 m across. It was excavated to a depth of 0.78 m without reaching the base. It contained a number of fills, the earliest of which comprised almost vertical slumps of weathered natural against the edge of the pit that suggest that, unlike the earlier quarries, it was of considerable depth and remained open for a significant period. The rubbish was all contained within its upper fills, which comprised dark grey silts and charcoal dumps. The pottery and clay tobacco pipes can be dated to the mid to late seventeenth century. Also recovered from these fills were sixteen farthings of Charles I, the latest of which can be dated to 1639–43, as well as three coins of James I and two jetons. Pit 678 was shallower and similarly contained a large amount of rubbish, including pottery of similar date.

Circular pit 1026, located in the soakaway trench, also contained a large amount of domestic refuse throughout its fills and was probably, given its size, dug specifically as a rubbish pit. It lay directly to the north of earlier quarries and contained pottery dated to the early to mid seventeenth century.

Phase 7: Nineteenth to Twentieth Century
Few modern features were encountered, reflecting the continued use of the site as a garden.

POTTERY by PAUL BLINKHORN

The pottery assemblage comprised 1,271 sherds with a total weight of 17,916 g. The late Anglo-Saxon and medieval material was recorded using the conventions of the Oxfordshire County type-series,[44] as follows:

[44] M. Mellor and G. Oakley, 'A Summary of the Key Assemblages …', in 'St Ebbe's, Part II', pp. 181–219; Mellor, 'Synthesis'.

OXR	St Neots ware, 850–1200. 2 sherds, 21 g.
OXAC	Cotswold-type ware, 975–1350. 42 sherds, 378 g.
OXBF	North-East Wiltshire ware, 1050–1400. 15 sherds, 160 g.
OXY	Medieval Oxford ware, 1075–1350. 77 sherds, 504 g.
OXAM	Brill/Boarstall ware, 1200–1600. 176 sherds, 1618 g.
OXBG	Surrey whiteware, mid thirteenth–mid fifteenth century. 1 sherd, 7 g.
OXBN	Tudor green ware, late fourteenth–sixteenth century. 6 sherds, 32 g.
OXBX	Late-medieval Brill/Boarstall ware, fifteenth–early seventeenth century. 103 sherds, 1,639 g.

The late-medieval and early post-medieval wares were recorded using the conventions of the Museum of London Type-Series,[45] as follows:

CSTN	Cistercian ware, 1470–1600. 5 sherds, 7 g.
RAER	Raeren stoneware, 1480–1600. 3 sherds, 63 g.
FREC	Frechen stoneware, 1550–1750. 275 sherds, 4938 g.
MPUR	Midland purple ware, 1400–1700. 1 sherd, 49 g.
MY	Midland yellow ware, 1550–1700. 1 sherd, 39 g.
TGW	English tin-glazed ware, 1600–1800, 1613–1800. 174 sherds, 1,366 g.
WEST	Westerwald-type stoneware, 1590–1800. 1 sherd, 15 g.
PMR	Post-medieval redware, 1550+. 182 sherds, 4,947 g.
PMBL	Post-medieval black-glazed redware, late sixteenth–seventeenth century. 32 sherds, 410 g.
DERBS	Derby stoneware, 1700–1900. 1 sherd, 28 g.
CHPO	Chinese porcelain, 1650+. 1 sherds, 7 g.
LONS	London stoneware, 1680 +. 3 sherds, 90 g.
SWSG	Staffordshire white salt-glazed stoneware, 1720–1800. 2 sherds, 5 g.
BORDY	Yellow-glazed Border ware, 1550–1700. 57 sherds, 574 g.
BORDG	Green-glazed Border ware, 1550–1700. 20 sherds, 176 g.
BORDB	Brown-glazed Border ware, 1600–1700. 11 sherds, 162 g.
WHEW	Mass-produced white earthenwares, nineteenth–twentieth century. 78 sherds, 661 g.

Each stratified, context-specific pottery assemblage was given a ceramic phase date (CP) based on the range of ware and vessel types present, and adjusted based on the stratigraphic evidence. The results are summarized in Table 10.1 and show that the main period of activity (in terms of pottery deposition) was the mid sixteenth–late seventeenth century. The paucity of St Neots ware (OXR) and the complete absence of Oxford shelly ware (OXB) indicates very strongly that there was no significant activity at the site before the beginning of the eleventh century, as either or both of these fabrics usually occur in fairly large quantities at late Anglo-Saxon sites in the town.[46]

The pottery occurrence per ceramic phase by fabric type, expressed as a percentage of the total weight per phase for the major fabrics, demonstrates a fairly typical pattern for sites in Oxford in terms of the occurrence of ware types, although with some possibly significant differences (Table 10.2).

[45] A.G. Vince, 'The Saxon and Medieval Pottery of London: A Review', *Medieval Archaeology*, 29 (1985), pp. 25–93.

[46] For example, P. Blinkhorn, 'The Pottery', in Z. Kamash et al., 'Late Saxon and Medieval Occupation: Evidence from Excavations at Lincoln College, Oxford 1997–2000', *Oxoniensia*, 67 (2002), pp. 234–40.

Table 10.1. Ceramic phase chronology, occurrence and defining wares.

Phase	Defining wares	Date	No. sherds	Weight (g)
LSAX	OXR	10th C	1	1
SN	OXAC, OXBF	11th C	9	64
M1	OXY	L 11th–12th C	9	57
M2	OXAM	13th–14th C	97	766
M3	OXBX, OXBN	E–L15th C	22	328
M4	CSTN, RAER	L 15th–M 16th C	7	47
PM1	PMR, FREC, BORDY, BORDG	M–L 16th C	218	3160
PM2	TGW, WEST, PMBL	E–M 17th C	264	5459
PM3	TGW*	M–L 17th C	395	5332
PM4	LONS	L 17th–E 18th C	2	23
PM5	DERBS, SWSG	18th C	64	730
MOD	WHEW	19th C	183	1953
Total			1271	17,916

Ditch 676

The ditch only produced pottery from a single context (666). The assemblage consists of just six sherds (53 g), of which five are in fabric OXAC (35 g) and the other is a residual Roman sherd. Ascribing a date to the feature on the basis of this pottery assemblage is very difficult. The five pieces of OXAC are all from the same sherd which was smashed during excavation. Part of it is missing, but it reconstructable and is from the rim of a small jar (Fig. 10.11, no. 1). It has patches of sooting on the outer surface, and was clearly well-used before breakage. Dating such pottery in Oxford is notoriously difficult.[47] Generally, it does not occur reliably in the town until the mid eleventh century, though a vessel of this type is known from a securely dated early tenth-century context at Trill Mill.[48] However, large quantities of OXR and OXB, both fairly common late Anglo-Saxon fabrics in the town, also occurred in association with it, which was not the case here, suggesting a late Anglo-Saxon date for this feature is very unlikely.[49] Overall, only two sherds of OXR occurred at this site, although one of them, a fairly large sherd weighing 20 g, occurred nearby in the fill of ditch 675. Just three more possible stratified sherds of OXAC occurred at the site, all single sherds weighing 4 g or less which could easily be residual, suggesting there was very little activity here in the eleventh century. The balance of ceramic evidence would therefore suggest a backfill date for the ditch of the late eleventh century or thereabouts, but this must be regarded as tentative; given the paucity of pottery dating to before the thirteenth century on the site, a date of a century later cannot be entirely discounted.

The Rest of the Assemblage

The fact that just nine sherds of pottery, from two contexts, can be dated to CP M1, lasting over one hundred years, indicates that there was very little activity at the site at this time.

Ceramic phase M2 sees the first real evidence of activity at the site, mainly in the form of small assemblages from pits, although given the length of the ceramic phase, this activity can

47 Mellor, 'Synthesis', pp. 51–2.
48 Ibid.
49 Dodd, *Oxford*, p. 292.

Table 10.2. Pottery occurrence per ceramic phase by fabric type, expressed as a percentage of the total weight per phase, major fabrics only. Shaded cells: residual material.

Fabric	SN	M1	M2	M3	M4	PM1	PM2	PM3	PM4	PM5	MOD
OXAC	71.9%	0	10.3%	0	0	2.5%	1.8%	0.9%	0	0	1.3%
OXBF	0	14.0%	0.9%	4.3%	10.6%	1.1%	0	0	0	3.0%	3.6%
OXY	–	86.0%	22.5%	0	12.8%	3.7%	1.0%	0.1%	0	8.1%	2.0%
OXAM	–	–	66.3%	20.1%	63.8%	5.9%	3.9%	1.3%	0	68.4%	2.2%
OXBX	–	–	–	60.1%	0	6.1%	8.4%	5.4%	0	0	25.7%
FREC	–	–	–	–	–	32.1%	28.0%	43.7%	0	0	3.3%
PMR	–	–	–	–	–	42.7%	45.7%	13.9%	0	7.0%	16.0%
BORDG	–	–	–	–	–	2.4%	0.2%	0.6%	0	0	2.0%
BORDY	–	–	–	–	–	2.0%	1.6%	8.0%	17.4%	1.8%	0
TGW	–	–	–	–	–	–	1.0%	22.6%	0	0.7%	5.0%
PMBL	–	–	–	–	–	–	7.1%	0.3%	0	0	0.5%
BORDB	–	–	–	–	–	–	0.5%	2.4%	0	0	0.4%
LONS	–	–	–	–	–	–	–	–	82.6%	0	3.6%
DERBS	–	–	–	–	–	–	–	–	–	3.8%	0
WHEW	–	–	–	–	–	–	–	–	–	–	33.8%
Total weight (g)	64	57	766	328	47	3160	5459	5332	23	730	1953

probably best be described as marginal. The assemblage is dominated by OXAM, along with smaller quantities of OXY, OXAC and OXBF. This is very typical of pottery assemblages of the thirteenth to fourteenth century in the town. Most of the OXAM was from glazed jugs, with the other wares being fragments of unglazed jars.

The assemblage from ceramic phase M3 is once again very small, with most of the pottery coming from pits 373 and 609. This period corresponds with the founding of St Bernard's College. The assemblage is once again dominated by Brill/Boarstall wares in the form of OXBX and OXAM. Other contemporary wares are present in small quantities, specifically single sherds of MPUR, OXBN and CIST. A dripping dish in OXBX is worthy of comment. Such pottery, which is typical of the later medieval period, had a specific use for catching the fat dripping from spit-roasted meat and occurred in unusually large quantities during excavations at 4A Merton Street, along with drinking pottery and lamps, and may be evidence of mass catering.[50]

Very little pottery was deposited during ceramic phase M4, with just over a third of that which did occur being residual, suggesting that there was very little activity at the site which involved pottery deposition, despite St Bernard's College still being in existence.

Ceramic Phase PM1 corresponds with the foundation of St John's College and sees a considerable increase in the amount of pottery deposited. Residuality is fairly low, suggesting that the lack of stratified medieval material is not due to disturbance by later activity. All the assemblages appear to be the product of secondary deposition, comprising small groups of reasonably well-preserved sherds, with no single vessel particularly well-represented and refits rare. The assemblage is dominated by PMR, along with relatively large quantities of German stonewares in the form of FREC. Other early post-medieval wares were rather scarce, with only Border wares and late Brill/Boarstall ware being present in any quantity. The PMR assemblage appears entirely utilitarian, comprising fragments of large bowls and jars with internal glazing, which is fairly typical of the tradition but offers little insight into any functional activity on the site at the time. The large assemblage of FREC entirely comprises drinking jugs or bottles, and while these were the main products of the industry at that time, the large number of them present is unusual and suggests that drinking was one of the commonest activities at the site at this time. However, large quantities of cooking pottery are absent, suggesting that the material does not derive from mass catering, as it appears to have done at 4A Merton Street. Given that this phase corresponds with the founding of St John's College and major building works, it is possible that much of this drinking pottery was used by builders rather than the inhabitants of the college.

The large assemblage from ceramic phase PM2 is of a similar nature to that from the mid to late sixteenth century, although the sherds are on the whole somewhat larger and some vessels reasonably well represented. In addition, a small number of sherds from vessels associated with cooking were also noted. The material mostly consisted of drinking pottery in FREC and PMBL (Fig. 10.11, no. 2). Most of the fragments of Border ware were too small to allow confident identification of the vessel, although pit 330 produced a fragment of a brown-glazed mug with encrusted decoration (Fig. 10.11, no. 3). These are generally of mid seventeenth-century date in London.[51] A very large dripping dish in OXBX, although incomplete, is unusually thick and heavy, and appears much larger than ordinary domestic vessels, suggesting it may have been used for mass catering (Fig. 10.11, no. 4).

Most of the pottery from ceramic phase PM3 came from pit 216 and much from pit 678. There are cross-fits between the two pits, and so it seems that both features were back-filled with pottery from the same source. The major ware during this phase was FREC, with TGW also very common. The small representation of PMR is somewhat unusual, as such pottery

50 P. Blinkhorn, 'Pottery', in Poore, 'No. 4A Merton St', pp. 258–78.

51 J. Pearce, *Border Wares* (1988), pp. 27–9.

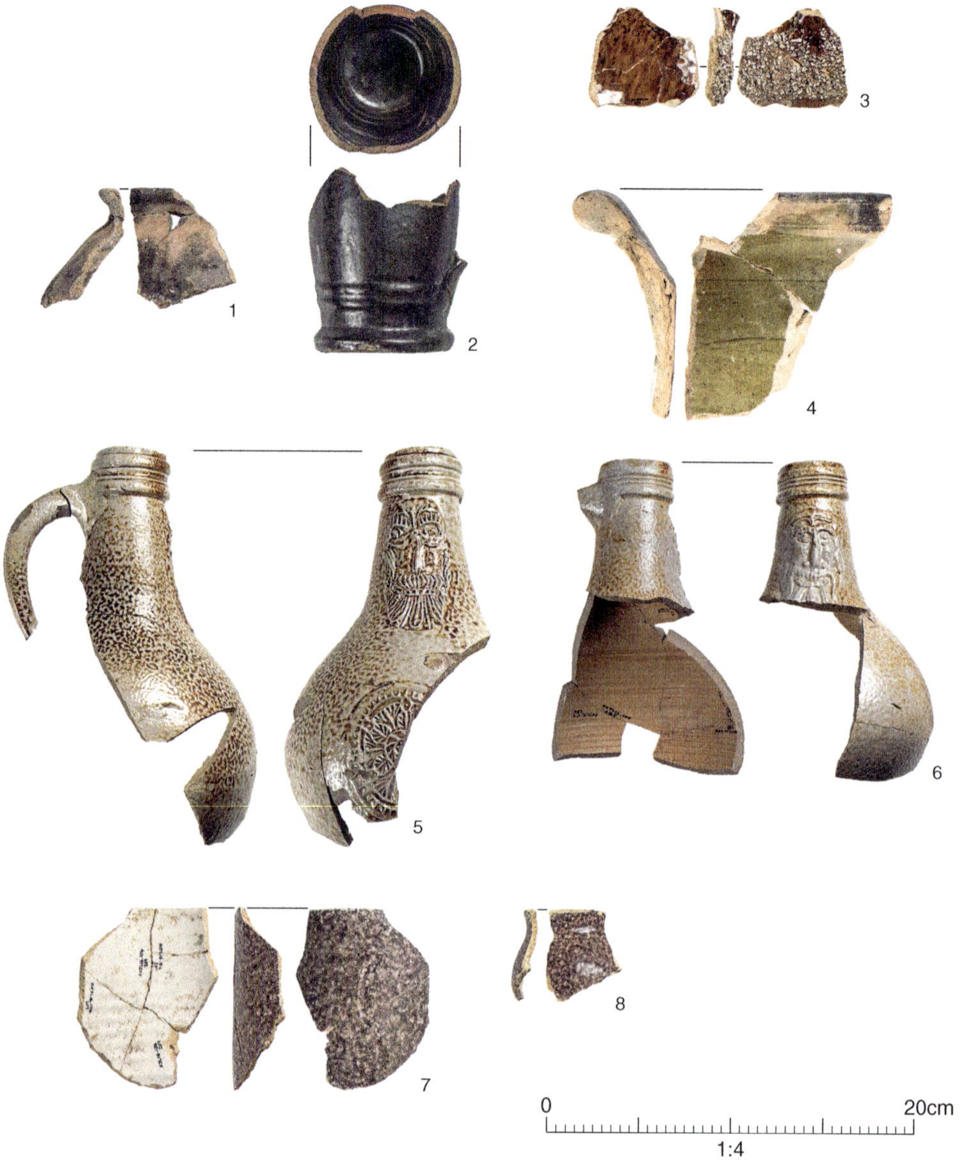

Fig. 10.11 Pottery.

normally dominates assemblages of this date.[52] The assemblage of FREC once again comprises drinking pottery in the form of bottles and jugs, some with Bartmann decoration and embossed floral prints (Fig. 10.11, nos. 5 and 6). There are large numbers of fragments of TGW, almost entirely in the form of cups and mugs with manganese-sponged decoration (Fig. 10.11, nos. 7 and 8). Such vessels are generally rare at contemporary sites in Oxford. The rounded forms and straight-sided mugs that make up much of the assemblage from here are dated to the third quarter of the seventeenth century.[53] It is also worthy of note that other vessel forms in this fabric are far less common here, which is somewhat unusual for contemporary Oxford sites, where painted, good-quality tablewares are fairly common.[54] Nearly all the pottery is vessels associated with drinking. The presence of large quantities of similar tin-glazed mugs suggests that they were a job-lot which was purchased for mass catering with a degree of formalization.

Ceramic Phase PM4 produced just two sherds of pottery and Phases PM5 and MOD both included a substantial proportion of residual material.

Catalogue of Illustrated Vessels (Fig. 10.11):

1. Cotswold-type ware (OXAC). Rim sherd from a small jar. Grey fabric with orange-brown surfaces, patches of sooting on the outer surface. Ctx 666, ditch 676, Phase 2.
2. Post-medieval black-glazed redware (PMBL). Base and lower body from a cup. Orange-red fabric with thick black glaze on both surfaces. Ctx 537, pit 535, Phase 5.
3. Brown-glazed Border ware (BORDB). Fragment of a mug with encrusted decoration. Buff fabric with streaky brown glaze, angular white flint decoration. Ctx 333, pit 330, Phase 5.
4. Late-medieval Brill/Boarstall ware (OXBX). Rim and base of a dripping dish. Buff fabric with darker surfaces, glossy apple-green glaze on the inner surface. Outer surface of the body has thin, even sooting. Ctx 503, pit 500, Phase 5.
5. Frechen stoneware (FREC). Bartmann jug. Grey fabric, mottled grey and brown glaze on outer surface, brown iron-wash on inner. Ctx 285, pit 225, Phase 6.
6. Frechen stoneware (FREC). Bartmann jug. Grey fabric, mottled grey and brown glaze on outer surface, brown iron-wash on inner. Ctx 285, pit 225, Phase 6.
7. English tin-glazed ware (TGW). Rim and body from a straight-sided mug/tankard. Buff fabric with white glaze on both surfaces, purple sponged decoration on the outer. Ctx 207, pit 678, Phase 6.
8. English tin-glazed ware (TGW). Rim and body from a mug. Buff fabric with white glaze on both surfaces, purple sponged decoration on the outer. Ctx 209, pit 225, Phase 6.

STOVE TILE by PAUL BLINKHORN

Four fragments of stove tiles occurred in fill 447 of pit 441, with a further small fragment from fill 446. The fragments appear to be from at least two tiles, one with a buff fabric with sparse quartz and rare red iron oxide and the other in an orange-red fabric with slightly dense, finer inclusions of the same type. The fragments of the tile with the red fabric have a black glaze, as does one of the pieces with a buff fabric. The other two fragments of buff tile have a very dark green glaze. The buff fabric is very similar to that of the stove tiles from Camber Castle, and probably of Rhenish or central German origin.[55]

[52] Mellor and Oakley, 'A Summary of the Key Assemblages', p. 191.
[53] Ibid. p. 315.
[54] Ibid. p. 195.
[55] D. Gaimster, 'The Continental Tile-Stove', in M. Biddle et al., *Henry VIII's Coastal Artillery Fort at Camber Castle, Rye, East Sussex* (2001), p. 152.

The two fragments in the red fabric (Fig. 10.12, no. 1) do not join, but appear to be from the same figurative tile. The mould was clearly very worn when it was made and the detail is indistinct but they are from the edge of the tile, with the moulded decoration being of a herm with a robed, bearded head and shoulders on a plinth with floral decoration. They appear to be identical to, and almost certainly from the same mould as, the herms on a partially complete tile in the British Museum which was made in Cologne and has the date '1561' incorporated into the design.[56] The British Museum example, which shows a female figure holding scales, flanked by bearded herms, differs from the one from this site in that it is in a much paler, buff fabric, and has a green glaze and is also much more sharply cast, suggesting that the mould was much newer when it was made. This does not mean that the tile from this site was not made from the same mould, however. It has been shown that stove tile moulds were widely traded with, for example, seventeenth-century German moulds known from sites in Sweden, such as Lund.[57]

The red fabric suggests a number of possible sources. The only known English manufactory of stove tiles, Cove in Hampshire, did produce tiles in such a fabric, although the tiles from that source have exclusively armorial designs.[58] Red earthenware stove-tiles were very common products of the lower and middle Rhineland and also Flanders, the northern Netherlands and northern Germany, and this seems to be the most likely area of origin of this tile.[59]

The three fragments of buff tiles include a small fragment which has survived to its full width (Fig. 10.12, no. 2), and appears to have been a spacer tile. One of the other two is from a corner (Fig. 10.12. no. 3) and the third, very small fragment also appears to be from an edge, and has two small moulded flowers, probably part of a border, surviving (Fig. 10.12, no. 4).

The presence of stove tiles at this site is of some significance. If the tile is indeed made from the same mould as the British Museum example with the 1561 date, then the stove must have been installed not long after the foundation of St John's College. Evidence of tiled stoves of this date in England is largely restricted to sites of high status, particularly religious houses and those of wealthy urban merchants, although they became more common during the sixteenth century.[60] Contemporary records suggest that in England they were used occasionally for steam-baths, rather than continuously as central heating, as was the case on the continent.[61] The fact that these tiles occurred in a context of early to mid seventeenth-century date is perhaps to be expected. Gaimster noted that, in England, tiled stoves rapidly fell from fashion at the beginning of the seventeenth century due to high prices and official restrictions on the use of wood for domestic heating purposes.[62] Presumably the stove was removed about that time, which also corresponded with extensive rebuilding at the college.

Catalogue of Illustrated Stove Tiles (Fig. 10.12):

1. Two non-joining fragments from the edge of a stove tile. Orange-red fabric with thick black glaze on the upper surface. Ctx 447, pit 441, Phase 5.
2. Fragment in buff fabric with a very dark green glaze on the upper surface. Ctx 447, pit 441, Phase 5.
3. Fragment in buff fabric with a black glaze on the upper surface. Ctx 446, pit 441, Phase 5.
4. Fragment in buff fabric with a black glaze on the upper surface. Ctx 447, pit 441, Phase 5.

56 British Museum, number OA7397.

57 D. Gaimster, 'An Imported Renaissance Stove-Tile from Dover in the Collections of the Society of Antiquaries', *Antiquaries Journal*, 69 (1989), p. 301.

58 Gaimster, 'The Continental Tile-Stove', p. 152.

59 D. Gaimster, 'Armorial Stove-Tiles Excavated in 1939', in S. Thurley, *Whitehall Palace. An Architectural History of the Royal Apartments, 1240–1690* (1999), p. 163.

60 Gaimster, 'The Continental Tile-Stove', p. 151.

61 Ibid. p. 152.

62 Ibid.

Fig. 10.12 Stove tiles.

BUILDING MATERIALS

Ceramic Building Material by John Tibbles
An assemblage of 413 fragments of ceramic building material (*c*.27.9 kg) was recovered. The assemblage in general is made up from quality materials which would be associated with buildings of high status or religious houses. The bricks appeared to be of good quality with only two examples being classed as seconds. Most of the bricks displayed thicknesses compatible with early medieval date, but the dimensions of the bricks were fairly evenly spread throughout the site phases suggesting that no direct correlation can be made between phase and brick size. The continual reuse of brick as a building material may act as a contributing factor to this evenness. A total of thirty floor tiles was identified, of which twenty-four bore evidence of glaze, seven displayed heavy footwear, and the majority residual mortar adhesions. Although it is likely that decoration may have existed on some of the tile, the heavy wear has destroyed any evidence. The floor tiles are of a probable fourteenth-century date of manufacture. A single fragment of a patterned glazed Delft wall tile came from pit 225. The small amount of glazed flat roof tile recovered suggests that only the eaves of a building had glazed flat tiles, possibly in association with glazed ridge tiles. Fourteen fragments of ridge tile were identified, including examples that bore evidence of either an olive green or reddish brown glaze.

Roofing and Architectural Stone by Ruth Shaffrey
A total of 36 fragments (5.8 kg) of stone roofing was recovered. Most of this was found in Phase 5 pits but there were two fragments in Phase 3 ditch 675 and a few pieces from other features. Approximately half the roofing is made from a calcareous sandstone of Stonesfield slate type, including three fragments from Phase 3 features, although not necessarily from Stonesfield itself. The early date of some of the examples indicates another unfrosted Cotswold stone source, since there was little stone exposed at Stonesfield suitable for roofing prior to the discovery of frosting in the seventeenth century.[63] The rest of the stone roofing is made from shelly oolitic limestone, probably from the Pusey Flags.[64] Both stone types are typical of Oxford roofs. Other pieces of building stone include a small piece of moulded oolitic limestone from Phase 6 pit 225.

Window Glass by Ian R. Scott
There are 382 fragments of window glass, much of it from Phase 5 and 6 contexts. One sherd of weathered and laminated green window glass possibly of medieval date was recovered from pit 114 and three opaque sherds of de-vitrified window glass probably of medieval date were recovered from pit 132. The glass from pit 373 comprises a partly melted sherd with opaque weathering.

VESSEL GLASS by IAN R. SCOTT

The assemblage comprises 157 sherds of vessel glass, much of it from Phase 5 and 6 contexts. It is worth noting that evidence for wine bottles is limited.

The only vessel glass from a medieval context was the neck and rim of a free-blown, wide-necked flagon in green glass from pit 1009 which could be medieval or post-medieval in date. There is, however, a sherd of this date, probably from a fine quality goblet of French or perhaps Italian manufacture, from Phase 6 pit 1026 (Fig. 10.13, no. 1).

Glass was recovered from a number of early post-medieval contexts, but no contexts or features produced any large quantities. Pit 1200 produced the most, with nineteen sherds

63 W.J. Arkell, *Oxford Stone* (1947), p. 131; M. Aston, *Stonesfield Slate*, Oxfordshire County Council Department of Museum Services Publication, 5 (1974), p. 22.
64 Arkell, *Oxford Stone*, pp. 149–50.

including five sherds of vessel glass. The latter included the base of a small flask or phial with conical kick and opaque weathering, the base from a flask in green glass with pontil mark and the base of a badly weathered and laminated pedestal beaker of mid sixteenth- to mid seventeenth-century date. Another pedestal beaker base fragment was recovered from pit 581. This example was in greyish, colourless glass decorated with thin white trails and is probably an imported vessel dating from the first half of the seventeenth century (Fig. 10.13, no. 3).

Most of the diagnostic vessel glass dates to the later sixteenth or early seventeenth century, although there are a few small pieces which would fit better in a slightly later context. For example, pit 318 produced a rim and body sherd from a drinking vessel with optic blown ribs probably of mid sixteenth- to mid seventeenth-century date, but also a merese from the stem of a drinking vessel in colourless glass that may well be of seventeenth- or even early eighteenth-century date. Pit 518 produced two sherds from a cylindrical vessel in colourless glass, a rim sherd from a drinking vessel in colourless glass and a piece of a foot with folded edge from a stemmed vessel in colourless glass. These pieces suggest a later seventeenth- or early eighteenth-century date. Pit 537 produced the neck and shoulders of a small oval section flask with optic blown wrythen ribs, which would date comfortably to the sixteenth century (Fig. 10.13, no. 4). A body sherd with optic blown ribs from a similar flask was recovered from pit 540. From pit 437 there is a body sherd from a colourless cylindrical beaker with optic blown ribs and a thin diagonal trail, which dates to the late sixteenth or early seventeenth century (Fig. 10.13, no. 2).

The Phase 6 glass assemblage is much smaller than that from Phase 5 and mostly came from pits 225 and 1026. Much of the vessel glass from pit 225 comprised undiagnostic sherds, but included a number of fragments from eighteenth-century cylindrical phials, sherds from flasks or bottles and some sherds from wine bottles. There were also some sherds from stemmed vessels. Similar vessel glass was recovered from pit 1026.

A small quantity of glass was either unstratified or from unphased contexts. Amongst the vessel sherds was a college wine bottle seal dated 1759 (Fig. 10.13, no. 5) and an elongated inverted baluster (so-called 'cigar' baluster) in greyish colourless glass from a stemmed vessel, either goblet or dish. This could be Venetian or in the Venetian style (*façon de Venise*).[65]

Catalogue of Illustrated Glass (Fig. 10.13):

1. Goblet. Sherd from lower angle of a goblet with a vertical-sided or barrel-shaped bowl. A pincered trail has been applied around the bowl at the bottom angle. Greyish colourless glass. Late thirteenth or fourteenth century. Probably of French make.[66] Ctx 1028, pit 1026, Phase 6.
2. Cylindrical beaker with optic blown ribs and spiral trail. Colourless glass with opaque weathering. Early seventeenth century.[67] Ctx 440, pit 437, Phase 5.
3. Pedestal beaker, with applied foot. Greyish colourless glass with thin white trails. Venetian or façon de Venise. Late sixteenth or early seventeenth century?[68] Ctx 582, pit 581, Phase 5.
4. Flask with optic blown wrythen ribs on its oval section body. Everted fire polished rim. Colourless glass, opaque iridescent weathering. Sixteenth century.[69] Ht extant: *c.*65 mm. Ctx 537, pit 536, Phase 5.
5. Wine bottle seal in olive green glass, reading 'St I *c* R 1759', for St John's Common Room. Ctx 1000, unphased.

65 H. Willmott, *Early Post-Medieval Vessel Glass in England c.1500–1670*, CBA Research Report, 132 (2002), p. 60 and fig. 58.

66 Type A8.1 in R. Tyson, *Medieval Glass Vessels Found in England c.AD 1200–1500*, CBA Research Report, 121 (2000), p. 63 and fig. 7, g34.

67 Wilmott, *Early Post-Medieval Vessel Glass*, p. 39 and fig. 10.

68 Ibid. p. 50 and fig. 37; P. Courtney, 'Vessel Glass', in K. Rodwell and R. Bell, *Acton Court: The Evolution of an Early Tudor Courtier's House* (2004), p. 337 and fig. 9.13, 16.

69 Wilmott, *Early Post-Medieval Vessel Glass*, p. 82 and fig. 102.

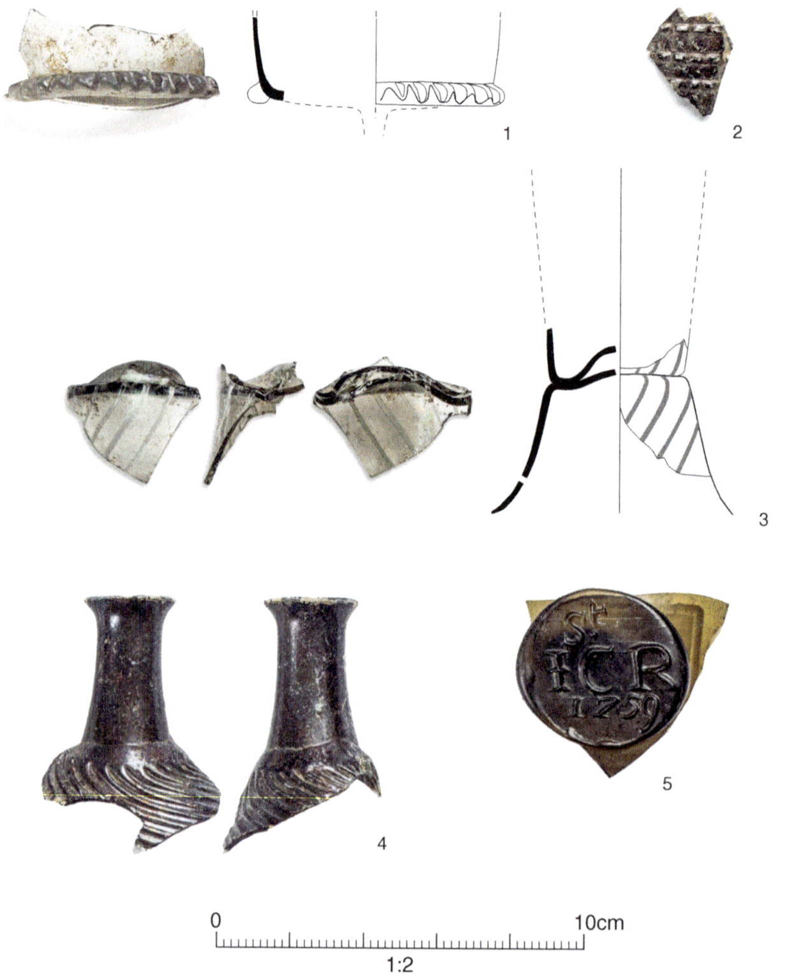

Fig. 10.13 Vessel glass.

CLAY TOBACCO PIPES by DAVID A. HIGGINS

The excavations produced a total of 878 fragments of pipe, comprising 172 bowl, 667 stem and 39 mouthpiece fragments. The assemblage as a whole is significant for three reasons. Firstly, it has produced some of the very earliest pipe forms, dating from *c.*1580–1610, which are nationally rare. Secondly, pit 225 has produced a sequence of large pipe groups ranging from *c.*1640–60 in date that provide what are probably the best Civil War and Commonwealth assemblages to have been recovered from Oxford to date. Finally, the marked and decorated pipes include some previously unrecorded types and add to the corpus of known types from the city. The following is a summary of the full report, which is available via OA Library.

Early Pipes

Two fragments of the earliest recognisable pipe forms were recovered.[70] Tobacco during this period was very expensive and smoking a new introduction that was largely confined to those who could afford it or had access to foreign ships or ports where tobacco could be obtained. Examples of these early pipes are very rare and very few have previously been recorded from Oxford,[71] despite the concentration of wealthy and well-connected individuals who visited or lived in the city.

One of the early examples was the only pipe find from pit 318 and is a finely burnished piece stamped with the maker's initials TB (Fig. 10.14, no. 1). It is stylistically similar to the incuse initials RC that are attributed to the early pipemaker Robert Cotton, who left England in 1607, suggesting that it may belong to the latter part of the 1580–1610 date range.[72] The other piece is more fragmentary (Fig. 10.14, no. 2). Although this is also polished, the burnish is only of a poor quality and this appears to have been a much less accomplished piece. It is also likely to date from towards the end of the 1580–1610 range. The presence of these two pieces is significant in providing evidence for the early adoption of smoking in Oxford and, in particular, on this site.

Pit 225

The majority of the pipes came from just four fills (209, 224, 285 and 286, Fig. 10.10). Taken together, these contexts produced 759 pipe fragments (155 bowl, 569 stem and 35 mouthpieces). All four groups include large numbers of complete bowls, often with reasonably long stem sections surviving, and their generally crisp and unabraded nature points to this material being freshly discarded waste. Despite this, very low levels of joins were found within or between these contexts so that it is unlikely that complete pipes are present, particularly since mouthpieces are under-represented in the sample collected. Equally, the very low level of stem junction to bowl joins shows that the material recovered only represents a small proportion of that which originally existed.

There was a marked division between the material from the earlier three fills (Figs. 10.14–10.16, nos. 3–26, which contained very similar-looking bowl forms and shared several mould types in common, and fill 209 (Figs. 10.17–10.18, nos. 32–44), which contained a different-looking range of bowl forms, none of which can be exactly matched in the earlier three deposits. These three contexts clearly form a contemporary, or near-contemporary, series of deposits and so can be considered collectively. In terms of absolute dating, the earliest context stratigraphically is 286, which produced a farthing issued in 1636, thus providing a *terminus post quem*. Furthermore, the next fill (285) included a farthing issued between 1639 and 1643, which suggests that these deposits are unlikely to be any earlier than *c.*1640 in date. At the other end of the range, the bowl forms themselves are unlikely to be any later than *c.*1650. The earlier group also includes an MH mark (Fig. 10.16, no. 19) which can be attributed to Miles Higges of Oxford or his widow and should date before 1649, and so these contexts fall neatly within the decade 1640–50, thus spanning the Civil War period. The later deposit (209) includes a mark of John Taylor, who took his freedom in 1649,[73] but cannot be any later than *c.*1670, based on the bowl forms. There is, however, a pit group from Queen's College that can be compared with this group.[74] The Queen's College finds show a number of differences (in particular slightly larger bowl forms and heel

[70] Types 1–3, dating from *c.*1580–1610, in D. Atkinson and A. Oswald, 'London Clay Tobacco Pipes', *Journal of the British Archaeological Association*, 3rd series, 32 (1969), pp. 171–227.

[71] For example, J. Cotter 'Clay Pipes', in S. Teague et al., 'Late Saxon, Medieval and Post-Medieval Archaeology at the Nun's Garden, The Queen's College, Oxford', *Oxoniensia*, 80 (2015), p. 170; 'Electricity Substation and Cable Trenching, University Parks, Oxford, Archaeological Investigation Report', unpublished OA report (2011), https://library.oxfordarchaeology.com/611/.

[72] D.A. Higgins, 'The Earliest Known Clay Tobacco Pipe Mould', *Post-Medieval Archaeology*, 46/2 (2012), pp. 361–6.

[73] D.A. Higgins, 'Clay Tobacco Pipes', chapter 6, above.

[74] Ibid. context 1085.

sizes), which suggests that that group must be later in date. Given that both deposits are broadly datable to *c.*1650–70, it seems that the St John's College group must be earlier within this range, say 1650–60, while the Queen's College group can be pushed back to *c.*1660–70. The Queen's College excavations also produced an earlier closely dated pit group of *c.*1630–45. This gives an unusually precise dated sequence whereby four key groups (two from St John's and two from Queen's) can each be attributed a 10- to 15-year period of deposition, collectively spanning the 1630–70 range.

There are two instances where very similar forms occur in the two groups (Fig. 10.15, no. 15 and Fig. 10.17, no. 37; Fig. 10.16, no. 25 and Fig. 10.18, no. 43), but the mould types are not exact matches. This shows that the moulds must have had relatively short lives, so that there was a complete turnover between the two groups, which are only a decade apart. This rapid turnover is why pipes provide such sensitive dating indicators and makes it important to understand the subtle differences that distinguish those produced in one decade from another.

The pipes from this pit are discussed in greater detail in the full report.

Marked Pipes

Ten pipes had stamped maker's marks, some of which are of previously unrecorded types. One partial stamp was recovered which had a leaf-like or stylised fleur-de-lys motif under the (presumed) initials. The marks are listed and described in alphabetical order (by surname initial):

BEN/ABB/OTT One example of a rectangular relief stamp across the stem reading BEN/ABB/OTT was recovered (Fig. 10.19, no. 48). An average quality burnish has been applied to the stem, but avoiding the mark. A similar mark reading BENJ/ABB/OTT, but with a shaped border and no dividing lies between the text, has been illustrated from the St Ebbe's excavations.[75] These stamps can now be dated to around 1740–70, even when they occur separately from their bowls. Benjamin Abbott is recorded at Ramsden, Oxfordshire, in 1746 and 1757 (marriages) and 1758 (took William Hopkins apprentice).

ED/BEAS/TEN A fairly thick stem fragment of *c.*1690–1730 with an incuse ED/BEAS/TEN stem stamp (probably Die 2124) was recovered (Fig. 10.19, no. 46). The stamp has large letters and has been poorly impressed. This maker is well known from his marks but has proved difficult to pin down in documentary sources. Cannon notes that the largest concentration of his marks has been found in the Newbury area, about 38 km south of Oxford.[76]

TB The larger part of a very early bowl type stamped with a previously unrecorded version of a TB mark was recovered from pit 318 (Fig. 10.14, no. 1). The bowl form dates from *c.*1580–1610 and is finely burnished with the incuse mark comprising simple unbordered letters. The style of the pipe and mark both suggest a London origin. The new find from these excavations pushes back the earliest evidence for the first 'TB maker' and adds to the known distribution of his products.

Gauntlet mark Two examples of gauntlet marks were found, both of which occur on West Country style heel fragments with their bowls missing. One of these is of typical form and quality (Fig. 10.19, no. 45). The other is of much finer quality (Fig. 10.18, no. 44). The bowl itself is missing but the tailed (tear-drop) shaped heel cut flush with the stem survives with an impressed gauntlet symbol on it, the thumb facing to the right. There is no doubt that this is an extremely well-produced and finished pipe that would have been a 'top of the range' product and which would have cost significantly more. There can be little doubt that this second marked example is a product of the Gauntlet(t) family of Amesbury in Wiltshire, who were famous during the

75 A. Oswald, 'Clay Pipes', in Hassall, 'St Ebbe's, Part II', fig. 54.25b.

76 P. Cannon, 'Clay Tobacco Pipes', in C. Bateman et al., 'Medieval Oxford's Northern Suburb: Evidence from Recent Work at 1–12 Magdalen Street', unpublished Cotswold Archaeology report (2000), http://reports.cotswoldarchaeology.co.uk/report/debenhams-1-2-magdalen-street/.

seventeenth century for their production of high-quality pipes and who used the gauntlet mark as a rebus for their surname.

MH Two bowls with identical heel stamps reading MH were recovered. The circular stamp comprises the initials MH with a single rather crudely executed star above and below (Die 2125). These pipes can be attributed to the Oxford pipemaker Miles Higges, who died in 1643, though the mark may well have continued in use until 1649 when his widow's new husband took his freedom. This particular die occurs in the closely dated 1640s deposit (Fig. 10.16, no. 19) and on a bowl form that is also likely to date from *c.*1640 or later (Fig. 10.17, no. 27). In contrast, the Queen's College excavations produced two examples from a pit group of *c.*1630–45, both of which are different die types with ligatured initials (Dies 339 and 1120).[77] This hints at a chronological distinction between the ligatured marks, which perhaps date from the 1630s, with the particular die type found on these excavations dating from the 1640s.

BCS This is a distinctive and unusual three letter mark, with the letter S placed above the letters BC within a circular mark on the heel of a burnished pipe from a pit fill of *c.*1650–60 (Fig. 10.15, no. 17). The English convention for three letters arranged in this way is that the top letter represents the surname with those of a husband and wife beneath. Oswald notes this mark as dating from *c.*1620–45 and suggests Belier Sacheverell and his wife as the possible makers, a suggestion repeated for an identical example of this mark excavated at St Ebbe's.[78]

IT A stem stamp with the relief initials IT within a plain border was found (Fig. 10.17, no. 35). There are two small dots between the initials and a fleur-de-lys above and below (Die 1012). The mark occurs on a finely burnished spur bowl. There is an identical example in the World Museum, Liverpool, which was found in Broad Street, Oxford, in 1915. This mark can be attributed to John Taylor of Oxford, who took his freedom in 1649 and died in 1684. His life has been extensively documented by Price.[79]

Kiln Debris

A modern deposit produced a clay roll that is almost certainly debris from a pipe kiln (Fig. 10.19, no. 49). The fragment has been simply hand-rolled and then one end pinched off to break it. Rolls such as this were typically used to help bed and stabilise the unfired pipes when loading the kiln but were discarded afterwards, since they could not be reused.

Summary and Conclusions

These excavations have produced some of the earliest evidence for smoking yet recorded from Oxford, comprising two pipes of *c.*1580–1610, one of which was probably produced in London and has a previously unrecorded mark on it. There are also a number of later marks, including a gauntlet stamp on an exceptionally fine pipe from Amesbury that can now be used to identify other examples of these outstanding products.

Perhaps the most significant result of the excavations was the recovery of two large deposits of closely datable mid seventeenth-century pipes. Together with key groups recently excavated from Queen's College it is now possible to establish a tightly dated narrative for the pipes produced and used in Oxford between about 1630 and 1670 (Table 10.3).

With regard to the three basic types of bowl forms, it appears that spur types were very common during the earliest period but that they dropped in frequency during the Civil War and Commonwealth periods before enjoying a resurgence in the 1660s. This may be in part

77 Higgins, 'Clay Tobbaco Pipes', chapter 6, above.

78 Oswald, 'Pipe Stamp Index'; Oswald, 'Clay Pipes', p. 253.

79 R. Price, 'John Taylor of Oxford', *Society for Clay Pipe Research Newsletter* 72 (2007), pp. 18–21; R. Price, Bristol Pipemaking Families of the 17th to 20th centuries (2013), working draft held at the National Pipe Archive, which is currently housed at the University of Liverpool.

Table 10.3. Comparison of the four key groups of clay tobacco pipes from Oxford, 1630–70. SP: spur; TH: tailed heel; RH: round heel; Tot: group total; S Fab: the number made of a visibly sandy fabric under a 10x lens; Bur: number of burnished examples; 6/64″ to 9/64″: bore size; M0–M4: the amount of rim milling, to the nearest quarter (M0 = no milling to M4 = fully milled).

Group (date)	Sp	TH	RH	Tot	S Fab	Marks	Bur	6/64″	7/64″	8/64″	9/64″	10/64″	M0	M1	M2	M3	M4
Queen's College Provost's Garden, pit 1475 (1630–45)	21 (42%)	7 (14%)	22 (44%)	50	32 (64%)	7 (14%)	9 (18%)	1	2	17	26	3	7	0	0	1	42
St John's College President's Garden, pit 225 fills 224, 285 and 286 (1640–50)	8 (12%)	24 (35%)	36 (53%)	68	30–32 (44–47%)	3 (4%)	6 (9%)	1	32	25	8	0	0	0	1	11	48
St John's College President's Garden, pit 225 fill 209 (1650–60)	7 (13%)	1 (2%)	45 (85%)	53	2–3 (4–6%)	2 (4%)	6 (11%)	0	16	31	2	0	2	0	2	3	42
Queen's College Provost's Garden, pit 1085 (1660–70)	12 (32%)	0 (0%)	26 (68%)	38	0 (0%)	2 (5%)	6 (16%)	1	23	12	0	0	0	0	3	13	13

because they were generally better quality pipes (more expensive and prestigious) that may not have been as readily available or fashionable during these periods. Pipes with tailed heels were generally imported into Oxford; 1640–60 was the only period with locally produced forms of this type, perhaps filling a gap in the market created by disruption in trade as a result of the war. Alternatively, perhaps the college itself purchased pipes corporately and there was a preference for this particular style.

Pipes with round heels were the most common form at all periods, but with higher percentages in use during the 1650s and 1660s than previously. A few examples were imported from elsewhere and these tend to be evident from their marks, form or finish. The local round heel forms were very rarely burnished and, although competently made and usually fully milled, appear to have been the 'everyday' types in use rather than anything special.

A progressive trend over time is the decreasing use of the local sandy fabric (probably obtained from Shotover Hill). Use of this clay fell dramatically during the Commonwealth period and it was not seen at all in pipes of the 1660s. The changing exploitation of this clay over time is certainly something that would repay further study, especially if a more reliable petrological method of identifying it could be employed.

Stamped marks were rather more frequent in the earliest group studied than the later three but quite a number of these at any given period were imports to the city. The local makers rarely seem to have marked their products. The most common early mark in Oxford is that of Miles Higges, but even he only marked a small proportion of his pipes. Burnishing was relatively rare amongst the locally produced pipes in the earliest periods, the overall percentage being inflated by larger numbers of burnished West Country imports, and increases gradually during the 1650s and 1660s.

The final trend can be seen in rim milling. The earliest group had almost entirely fully milled rims, the notable exception being seven imported West Country forms that had no milling at all. The overall quality dropped a little during the Civil War period, perhaps as a result of disruption to the labour force due the to the demands of the war, with a higher percentage of rims being only three-quarters milled. Rims were once again almost all fully milled during the 1650s period but the 1660s sees a marked change with as many being three-quarters milled as fully milled.

The detailed observations made possible by comparing these well-dated groups show how many different strands of the information it is possible to follow to help interpret these assemblages. The pipes being consumed at any one period were made up of a mix of locally produced and imported pieces, with different styles and qualities being represented. Individual workshops had different ways of manufacturing, decorating, finishing and marking their products, in addition to which the preferences of individual consumers or corporate purchasers can influence the final mix that creates the archaeological record. The individual attributes of any given pipe can often narrow its place and date of origin to within a few decades but, when larger groups such as these are available, it is possible to refine their dating to within a few years and to interpret the significance of the assemblage in much greater detail.

Catalogue of Illustrated Pipes (Figs. 10.14–10.19):

1. Very early bowl type stamped with a previously unrecorded version of a TB mark (Cast 744.30; Die 2230). The bowl form dates from *c.*1580–1610 and is finely burnished with the incuse mark comprising simple unbordered letters. The style of the pipe and mark both suggest a London origin. The pipe has a reduced grey core (a feature characteristic of the earliest pipes) and a stem bore of 7/64". Ctx 319, pit 318, Phase 5.
2. Very early pipe fragment from *c.*1580–1610 with the heel trimmed flush with the stem. This piece has a poor quality burnish and is quite roughly made when compared with no. 1. There are some fine gritty inclusions in the fabric, which does not have a reduced core. Stem bore just over 7/64". Ctx 1205, pit 1204.
3. Spur bowl with a half milled rim and a fine burnish. Stem bore 8/64". Ctx 286, pit 225, Phase 6.

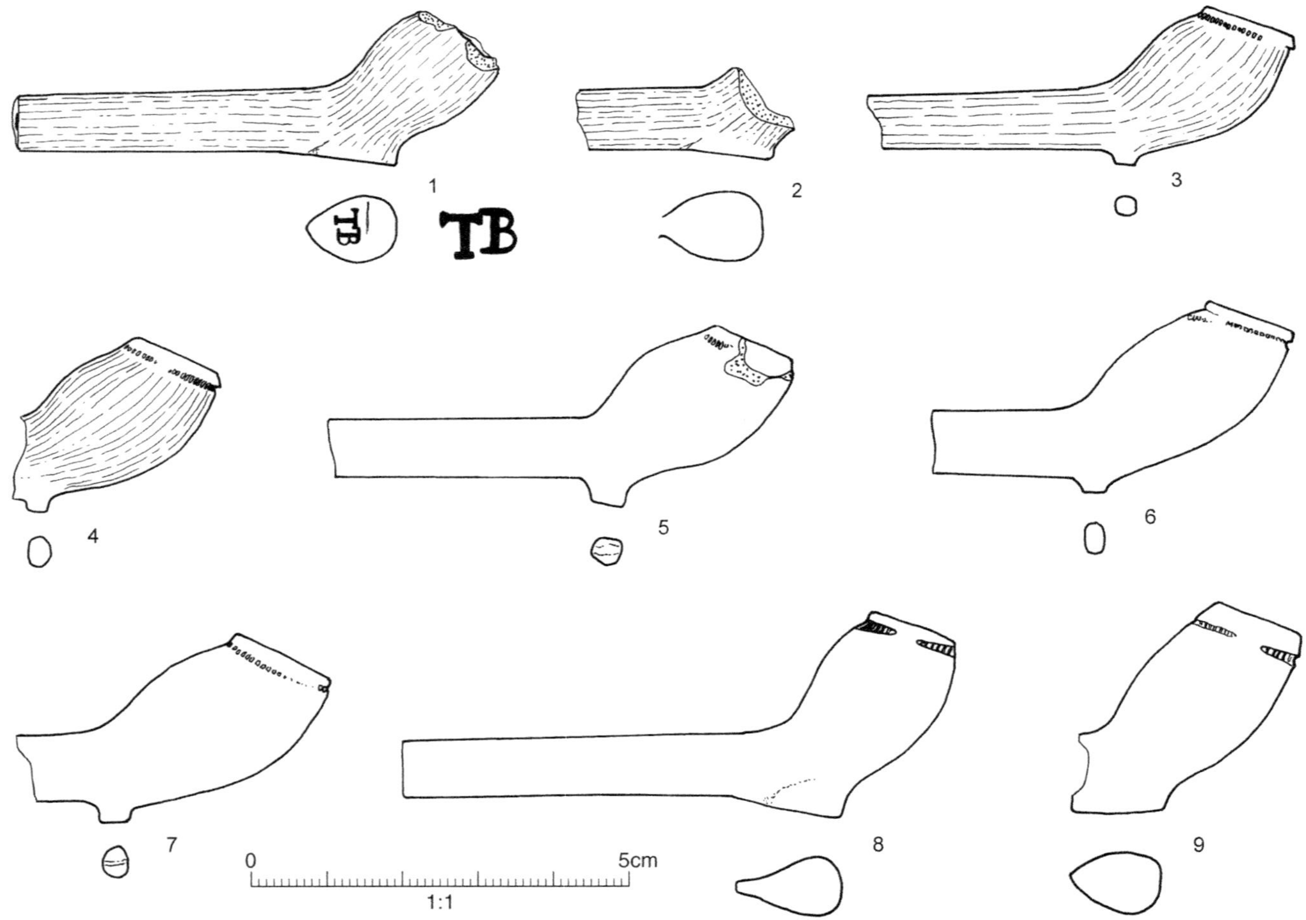

Fig. 10.14 Clay tobacco pipes, nos. 1–9. Drawings by David A. Higgins.

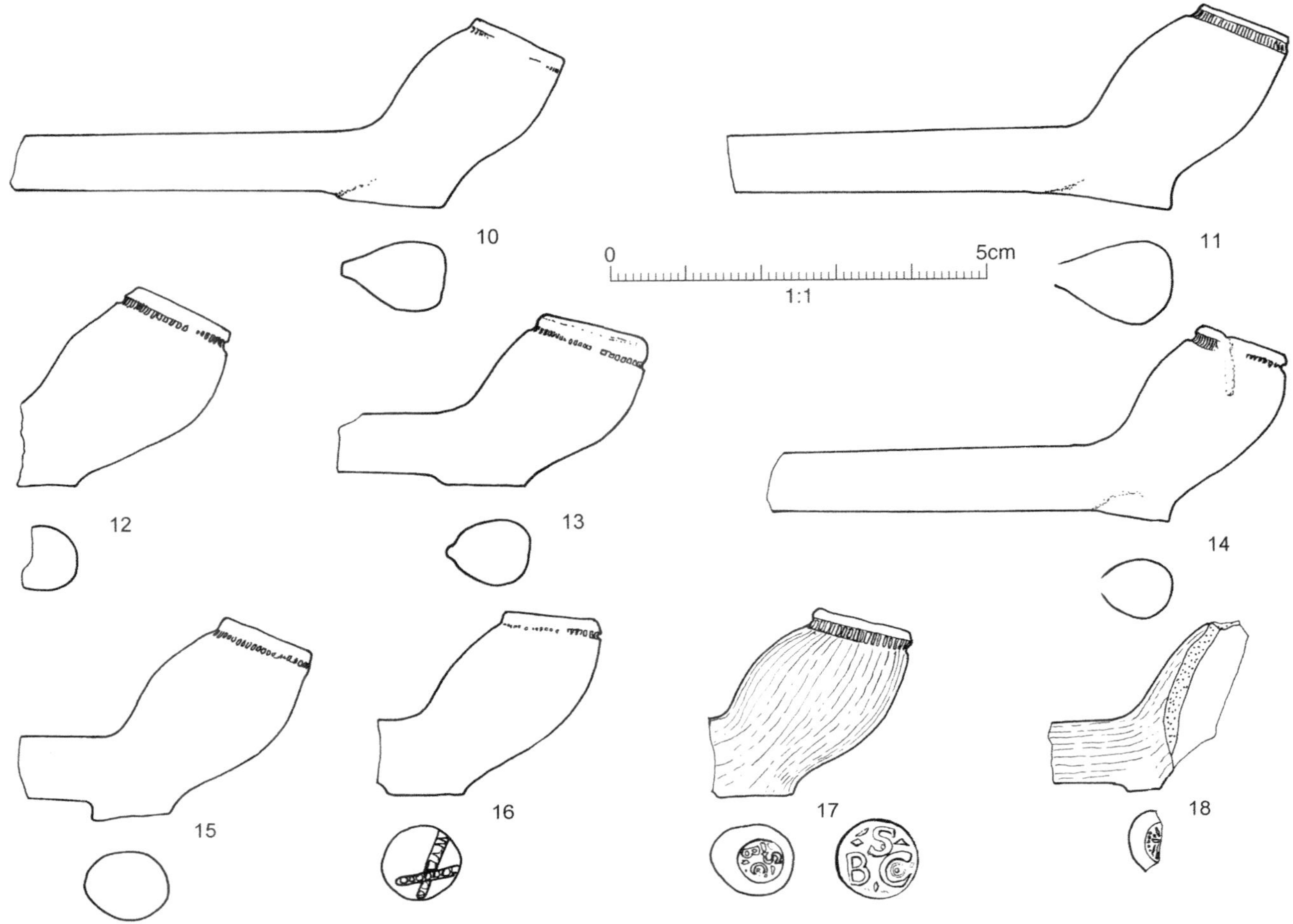

Fig. 10.15 Clay tobacco pipes, nos. 10–18. Drawings by David A. Higgins.

4. Spur bowl with a fully milled rim and a finely burnished surface. Stem bore 8/64". Ctx 285, pit 225, Phase 6.
5. Spur bowl made of a fine sandy fabric with a fully milled rim. Stem bore 8/64". Ctx 224, pit 225, Phase 6.
6. Spur bowl with a fully milled rim. Stem bore 7/64". Ctx 224, pit 225, Phase 6.
7. Spur bowl with a fully milled rim. Stem bore 9/64". Ctx 224, pit 225, Phase 6.
8. Bowl with a tailed heel made of a sandy fabric and with a fully milled rim. Stem bore 8/64". Ctx 286, pit 225, Phase 6.
9. Bowl with a tailed heel and a fully milled rim. Stem bore 7/64". Ctx 286, pit 225, Phase 6.
10. Bowl with a tailed heel and a three-quarters milled rim, sandy fabric. Stem bore 8/64". Ctx 224, pit 225, Phase 6.
11. Bowl with a tailed heel and a fully milled rim, sandy fabric. Stem bore 8/64". Ctx 224, pit 225, Phase 6.
12. Bowl that probably had a tailed heel. Fully milled rim. Stem bore 7/64". Ctx 224, pit 225, Phase 6.
13. Bowl with a round heel and a fully milled rim. Stem bore 7/64". Ctx 285, pit 225, Phase 6.
14. Bowl with a round heel and a fully milled rim, sandy fabric. Stem bore 8/64". Ctx 286, pit 225, Phase 6.
15. Bowl with a round heel and a fully milled rim. Stem bore 7/64". Ctx 224, pit 225, Phase 6.
16. Bowl with a round heel and a fully milled rim. There are also two crossed lines of milling on the base of the heel, the significance of which is unknown. Milled heels occasionally occur in many parts of the country but they tend to be most common in Yorkshire and East Anglia. Stem bore 8/64". Ctx 285, pit 225, Phase 6.
17. Bowl with a round heel, a finely burnished surface and a fully milled rim. There is a three-letter maker's stamp on the heel, probably for a husband and wife with the Christian name initials B and C respectively and a surname beginning with an S (Cast 744.29; Die 2232). Probably a London product. Stem bore 8/64". Ctx 224, pit 225, Phase 6.
18. Damaged bowl with a round heel and the very bottom of a maker's mark on the heel. This has a little foliage or fleur-de-lys motif below the initials and a finely beaded border (Cast 744.31). Stem bore 7/64". Ctx 285, pit 225, Phase 6.
19. Bowl with a round heel stamped with an MH mark and a fully milled rim (Cast 744.27; Die 2125). This can be attributed to the Oxford pipemaker Miles Higges. The mould type has a distinctive profile and can be identified by a clear horizontal flaw on the left hand side of the heel, near the stem/heel junction. There are fourteen other examples of this mould type from contexts 224, 285 and 286, showing that Higges only marked a small proportion of his products. What appears to be the same mould type was also recovered at the Ashmolean Museum,[80] where one example was found stamped with this same die type and another was found without. This mould type is also very similar to the bowl forms nos. 20 and 22, which have a similar flaw on the left-hand side of the heel. They also seem to have additional flaws on the right hand side, perhaps suggesting that it is the same mould that has been modified. The illustrated example appears to have some very fine sandy particles in its fabric. Stem bore 7/64". Ctx 224, pit 225, Phase 6.
20. Bowl with a round heel and a fully milled rim (one of ten bowls made in this mould from contexts 224, 285 and 286). The design is very similar to no. 20, and it may well be the same Miles Higges mould that has been modified. There are distinctive flaws on both sides of the heel. Stem bore 7/64". Ctx 286, pit 225, Phase 6.
21. Two joining stem sections with 'barley twist' decoration. Perhaps from the same pipe as no. 22. The mouthpiece itself is broken off, but the decoration clearly stopped a short way from this. Stem bore 7/64". Ctx 286, pit 225, Phase 6.

80 D.A. Higgins, 'Clay Tobacco Pipes', chapter 11, below.

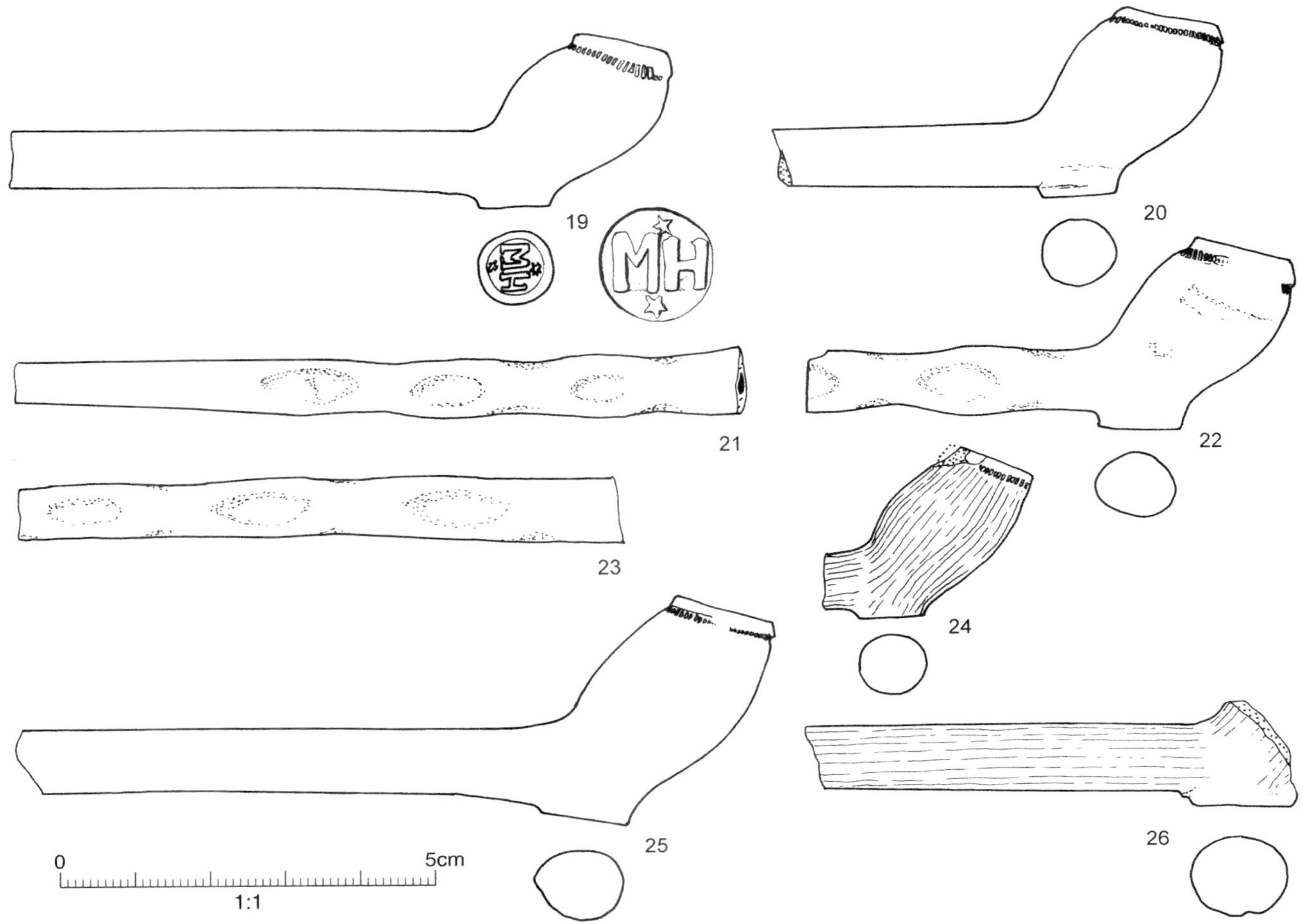

Fig. 10.16 Clay tobacco pipes, nos. 19–26. Drawings by David A. Higgins.

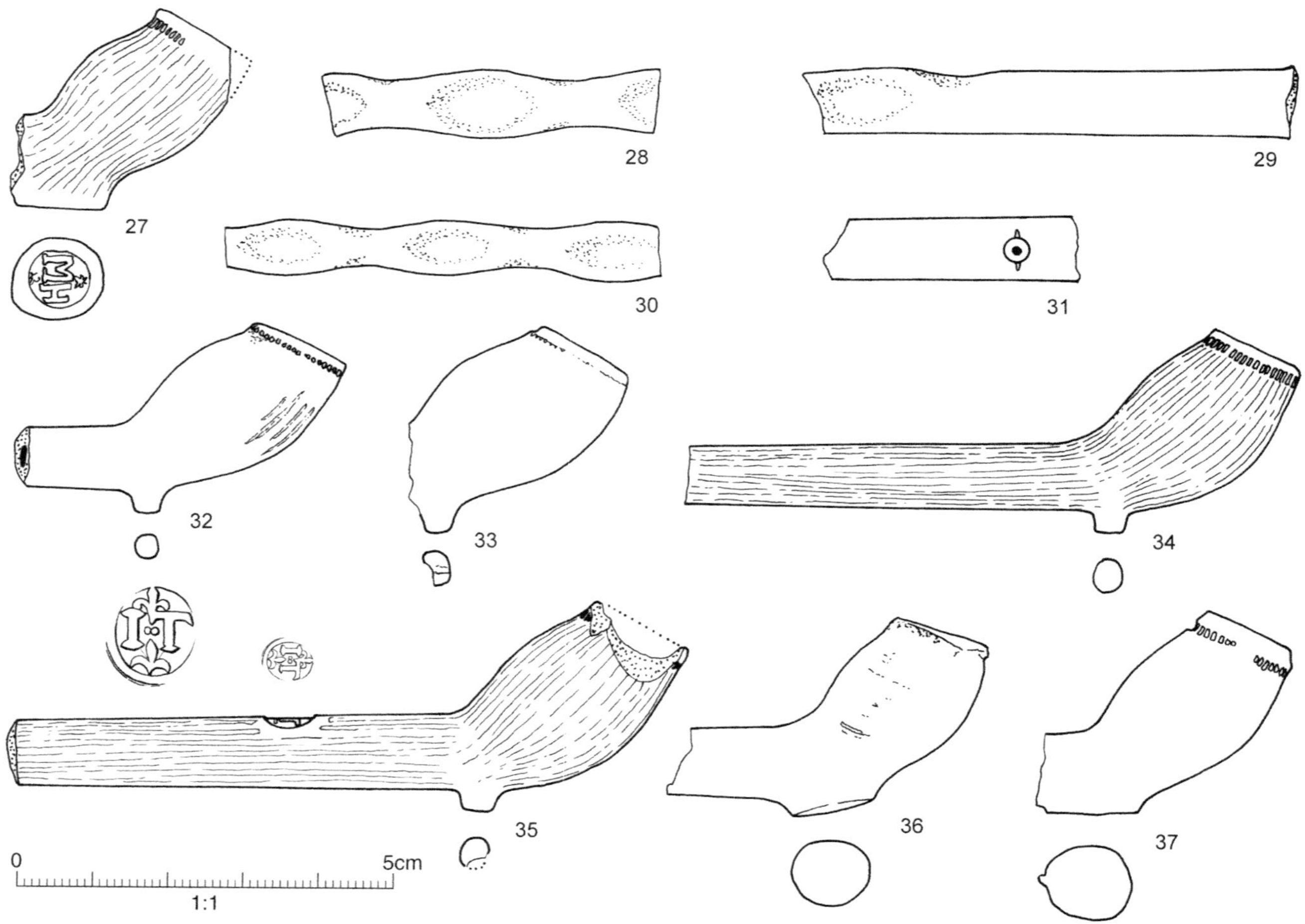

Fig. 10.17 Clay tobacco pipes, nos. 27–37. Drawings by David A. Higgins.

22. Bowl with a round heel and a three-quarters milled rim. The bowl is poorly moulded with surface folds in the clay forming the bowl but it is almost certainly from the same mould as no. 20 and most likely from the Higges workshop (see nos. 19–20). The stem has 'barley twist' decoration and it is perhaps from the same pipe as stem sections no. 21. Stem bore 8/64″. Ctx 286, pit 225, Phase 6.
23. Stem section with 'barley twist' decoration. Stem bore 7/64″. Ctx 285, pit 225, Phase 6.
24. Miniature pipe bowl with a round heel and what was almost certainly a fully milled rim (one small section chipped away). The bowl is finely burnished and has a stem bore of 7/64″. Ctx 285, pit 225, Phase 6.
25. Bowl with a round heel and a fully milled rim. The bowl is much larger than any others from the early group but comparable with no. 43 from the *c.*1650–60 group, suggesting that it may be intrusive. Stem bore 7/64″. Ctx 224, pit 225, Phase 6.
26. Round heel fragment with a good burnish. Some fine sandy particles in the fabric. The heel is much larger than any others from the early group suggesting that it may be intrusive. Stem bore 7/64″. Ctx 285, pit 225, Phase 6.
27. Bowl with a round heel stamped with an MH mark for Miles Higges of Oxford (Cast 744.26; Die 2125). The bowl form would normally be dated *c.*1640–1660, but Higges died in 1643 and the mark is unlikely to have been used after 1649 (see no. 19), so this piece can be dated to *c.*1640–50. The pipe is made of a fine sandy fabric and has a good burnish and three-quarters milled rim. Stem bore 8/64″. Ctx 360, pit 358, Phase 5.
28. Stem fragment with 'barley twist' decoration. Stem bore about 8/64″. Ctx 209, pit 225.
29. Stem fragment with possible 'barley twist' decoration. This piece has just two clear indentations and they are at a distance from the bowl junction and so it is possible that this is some form of accidental damage rather than intentional decoration. Stem bore 7/64″. Ctx 209, pit 225, Phase 6.
30. Stem fragment with 'barley twist' decoration. Stem bore about 8/64″. Ctx 209, pit 225, Phase 6.
31. Stem fragment that has been modified after firing by having a small hole drilled through to the bore with a narrow point. There is also a sharp knife cut across the stem at this point. It is not clear where the mould seams are on this piece of stem, so it is unclear which orientation the hole is in relation to the top. Stem bore 8/64″. Ctx 209, pit 225, Phase 6.
32. Spur bowl with a fully milled rim. Some scrape marks caused during manufacture on the front right-hand side of the bowl. Stem bore 8/64″. Ctx 209, pit 225, Phase 6.
33. Spur bowl with a half milled rim. Stem bore 8/64″. Ctx 209, pit 225, Phase 6.
34. Spur bowl with a fully milled rim and a good burnish. Stem bore 8/64″. Ctx 209, pit 225, Phase 6.
35. Spur bowl with a fine burnish and a milled rim (probably fully milled originally, but now partially chipped away). There is a relief IT stamp across the stem, 20mm from the bowl, for John Taylor of Oxford (Cast 745.5; Die 2285). Stem bore 8/64″. Ctx 209, pit 225, Phase 6.
36. Heel bowl with a bottered rim, but no milling. Rather poorly made with scrape marks on the right-hand side of the bowl and the heel trimmed at an odd angle. Unusually small form for this group. Stem bore 8/64″. Ctx 209, pit 225.
37. Heel bowl with a fully milled rim. Stem bore 8/64″. This bowl represents a common type in this group, with a total of ten examples present. These are typically well-made and finished and cannot be separated into individual mould types, even though several are likely to be represented. Ctx 209, pit 225, Phase 6.
38. Heel bowl, neatly designed and manufactured with a fully milled rim but the heel trimmed at an odd angle. Stem bore 7/64″. Ctx 209, pit 225, Phase 6.
39. Heel bowl with a bottered rim, but no milling. Rather poorly made from a fabric with very fine sandy inclusions. Stem bore 7/64″. Ctx 209, pit 225, Phase 6.
40. Heel bowl with a fully milled rim. Unusually large and heavy bowl with a chunky form and thick stem. Made from a fine sandy fabric, which is now a slightly greyish colour (possibly burnt). Stem bore 8/64″. Ctx 209, pit 225, Phase 6.

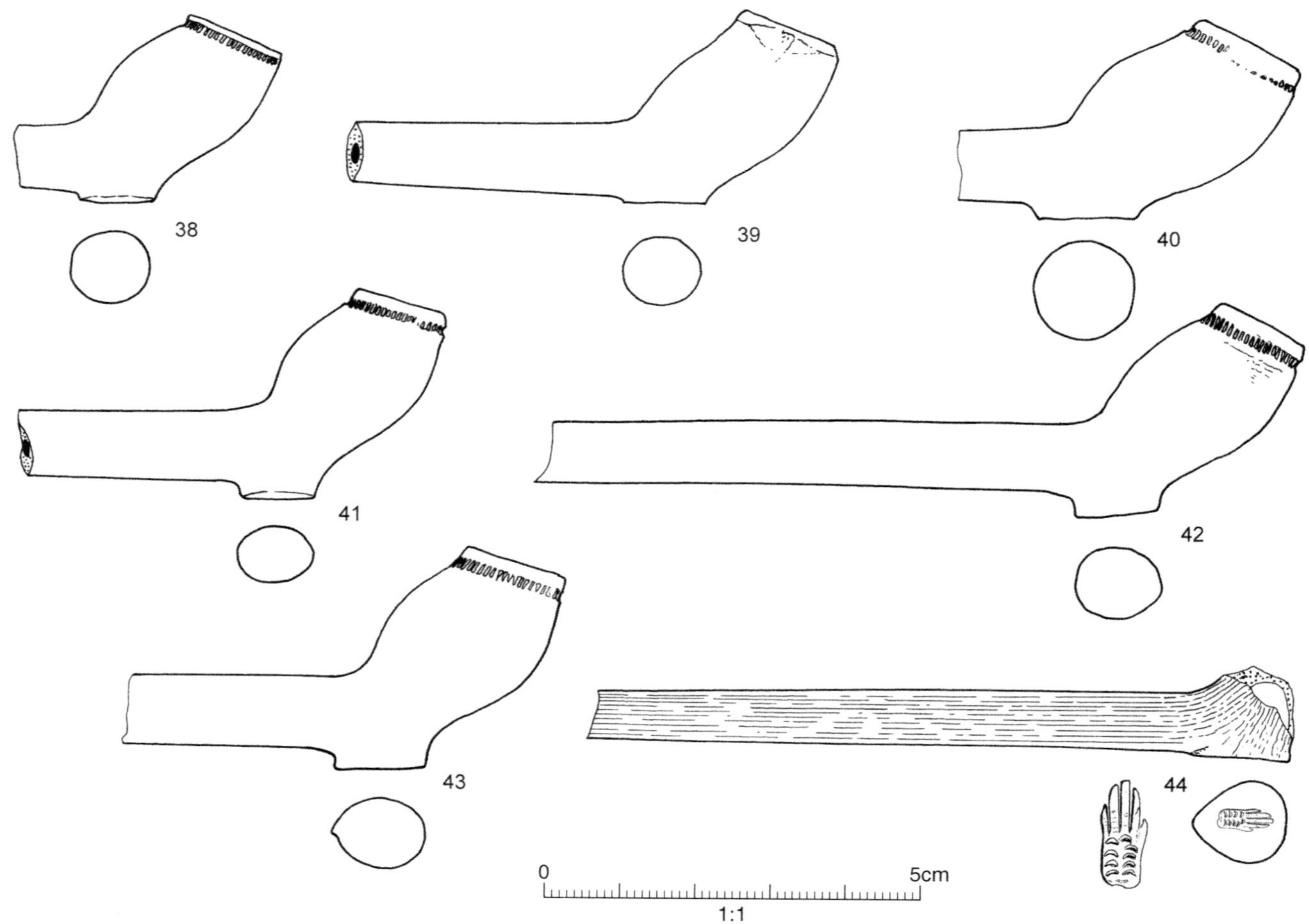

Fig. 10.18 Clay tobacco pipes, nos. 38–44. Drawings by David A. Higgins.

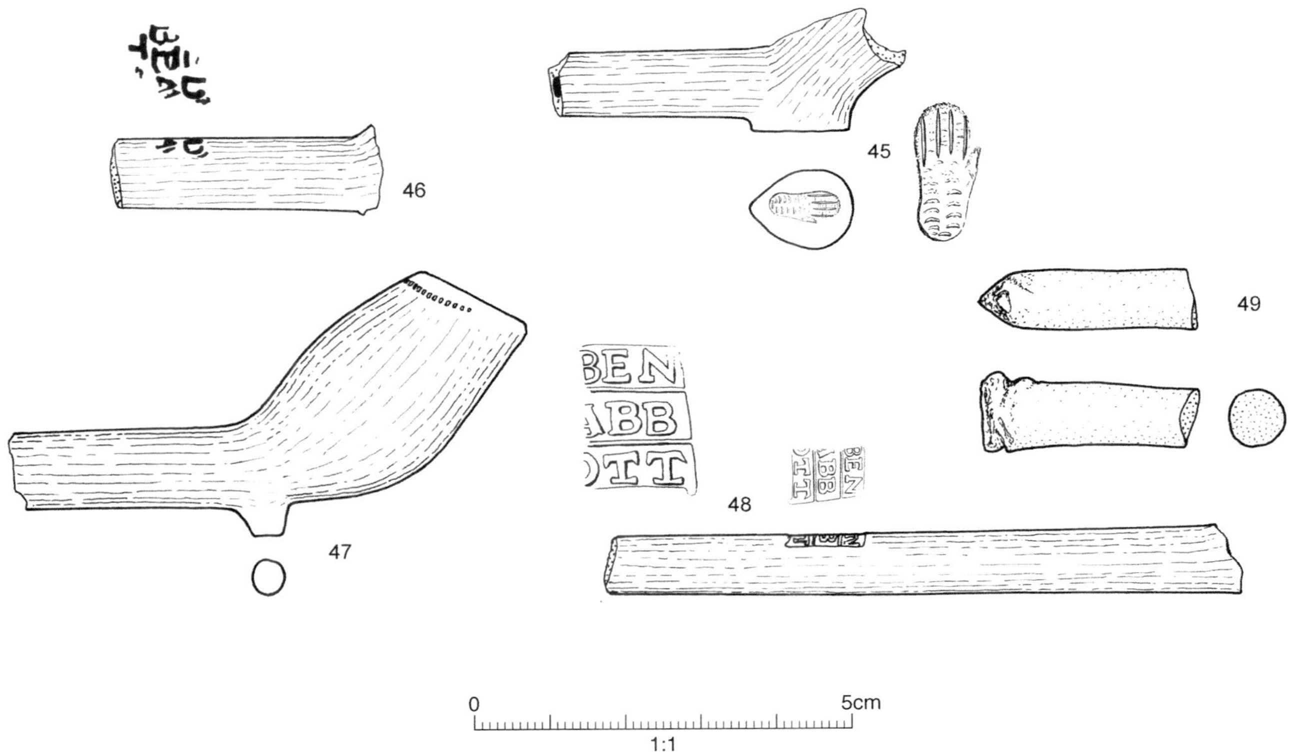

Fig. 10.19 Clay tobacco pipes, nos. 45–9. Drawings by David A. Higgins.

41. Heel bowl with a fully milled rim. Stem bore $^{8}/_{64}$". This is the most typical form in the *c.*1650–60 group, with 21 similar examples in total. These exhibit a range of minor differences, suggesting that several different moulds are represented, but these cannot be distinguished from flaws into individual mould types. They are typically well-made and finished in a hard-fired fabric and with fully milled rims – a very uniform and competently made product. Ctx 209, pit 225, Phase 6.
42. Heel bowl, neatly made with a fully milled rim. Stem bore $^{7}/_{64}$". Ctx 209, pit 225, Phase 6.
43. Heel bowl, neatly made with a fully milled rim. Stem bore $^{7}/_{64}$". This is the largest size represented in the *c.*1650–60 group and would normally be dated to *c.*1650–70 when found in isolation. There are, however, five examples of this type in the group and it fits well with being at the larger end of the range represented by nos. 37 and 41–42. Ctx 209, pit 225, Phase 6.
44. Bowl fragment from a West Country style fragment of *c.*1650–60. The bowl is missing but the tailed (tear-drop) shaped heel cut flush with the stem survives with an impressed gauntlet symbol on it, the thumb facing to the right (Cast 745.4; Die 2231). Can be attributed to the Gauntlet(t) family of Amesbury in Wiltshire. Stem bore $^{8}/_{64}$". Ctx 209, pit 225, Phase 6.
45. Heel fragment from a West Country style bowl stamped with a gauntlet mark depicted with its thumb to the right (Cast 745.3; Die too abraded to allocate a unique number). The bowl was burnished originally but is now too weathered to grade the quality of the burnish. Either a product of the Gauntlet(t) family, or a copy of one of their products. Stem bore just over $^{7}/_{64}$". Ctx 1000, unstratified.
46. Stem of *c.*1690–1730 with a good burnish and a poorly impressed Edward Beasten mark (Cast 745.2; probably Die 2124). Stem bore $^{6}/_{64}$". Ctx 1000, unstratified.
47. Spur bowl, a large, chunky, local style piece of *c.*1670–90 made of a fine sandy fabric and with an average burnish. The rim is bottered and half milled. Stem bore $^{8}/_{64}$". Ctx 1000, unstratified.
48. Stem fragment of *c.*1740–70 with a rectangular relief stamp across the stem reading BEN/ABB/OTT (Cast 745.1; Die 2233). The stem is made of a local fabric with fine sandy inclusions. The stamp has been placed about 48 mm from the bowl junction and an average quality burnish has been applied to the stem, but avoiding the mark, which shows that the pipe was burnished after the stamp had been impressed. Stem bore just over $^{5}/_{64}$". Ctx 1000, unstratified.
49. Piece of pipe kiln supplement, comprising a hand-formed roll of white pipeclay that has been pinched together at one end to cut it while still soft. This piece most likely dates from the seventeenth or eighteenth century. Ctx 1003, modern.

METALWORK AND WORKED BONE by LEIGH ALLEN

The metalwork assemblage comprises 127 copper alloy objects (including 45 lace tags and 59 pins), 243 iron objects (including 168 nails) and nine lead objects. A small number of unidentifiable fragments of sheet and strip were recovered but are not reported on here. Three objects of worked bone were also recovered.

The earliest finds from the site come from Phase 3 pits; they include horseshoe nails and a goad for guiding livestock and indicate the use of land in the vicinity for agricultural purposes. Phase 4 contexts produced only nails (including horseshoe nails), pins and lace tags. The bulk of the assemblage came from Phases 5 and 6, mostly from pit fills dating to the mid sixteenth to eighteenth centuries.

Phase 5 saw a huge increase in pit digging compared to earlier phases and the subsequent infilling of these pits with refuse. Structural nails, relating to the rebuilding and refurbishment of college buildings during this period, were recovered in large quantities. Numerous lace tags and pins were also recovered; these dress accessories are common finds in late-medieval and post-medieval contexts. Phase 5 pits also produced objects associated with books and writing, riding, dining, and lighting – items relating to college life in the sixteenth and seventeenth century. A catch plate from a book clasp came from pit 278 and a seal matrix from pit 441 (Fig. 10.20, nos. 1 and 2). The catch plate has a scalloped outside edge and is decorated with a concentric circle design. It would have been attached to a book cover and a hooked plate attached to the opposing cover would have hooked over the catch plate bar. Heavy clasps on books helped to keep them closed. The seal matrix has a circular stamp, a slender shank with a rectangular section and a trefoil knop. The top loop is pierced for suspension. The seal bears the image of a hare or rabbit. It is almost identical in form to a seal matrix recovered from St Ebbe's.[81] The domestic items comprise five knives, two forks, a vessel rim fragment and a candle snuffer. The knives comprise three whittle-tang knives, a scale-tang knife and a decorative iron knife handle. The whittle-tang knives include a complete knife with worked bone handle from pit 540 (Fig. 10.20, no. 3). The knife has a bolster of oval section between the blade and the tang, and a 'through' tang that runs the whole length of the handle, protruding from the end. The simple bone handle expands towards the butt end, where it is cut straight. The bolster, a thickening at the junction of the blade and the handle, was an innovation in hafting introduced in the sixteenth century. It added strength to the knife at the point where the most force was applied, and contributed to a better balance between the knife and the handle, thus improving control. The other two whittle-tang knives, both from pit 318, are very damaged with only short sections of the tang and blade surviving either side of the bolster.

The scale-tang knife (folded in half) was recovered from pit 483. It is in very poor condition but there are two rivet holes visible in the tang for attaching the scales. The corroded remains of a decorative knife handle dating to the late sixteenth century came from pit 1200. It would have abutted the bolster and has a decorative discoidal end with a small protruding pommel.[82] Two forks were recovered from Phase 5 contexts; the example from pit 1011 is complete, with long, straight prongs, a moulded shaft with a slender bolster and a worked bone handle with an octagonal section that expands to a rounded butt (Fig. 10.20, no. 4). The second fork has shorter prongs and a larger, more robust bolster. The tang survives but the handle is missing. Forks only came into common use in the latter half of the seventeenth century.

An almost complete candle snuffer/wick cutter of 'scissor' form came from pit 318 (Fig. 10.20, no. 5). Designed for trimming the wicks of burning tallow candles to prevent guttering, the snuffer has a box and plate mounted on the blades so that the wick could be cut and captured in the box. The sharp point at the front was useful for spearing scraps of burnt wick that fell into the hot tallow. Snuffers are recorded in the privy purse expenses of Henry VIII (1509–47) but they do not appear in common use until the seventeenth century.[83]

Two small badges/button covers decorated with religious motifs are a reminder that St John's College was founded in 1555, during the reign of Mary I, for the purpose of training Catholic priests. They comprised very worn copper alloy discs recovered from pits 135 and 441, stamped with a central motif of Christ on the cross, flanked by the letters 'I' and 'C' for Jesus Christ. Badges or medallions showing religious scenes or saints are found quite widely in the Catholic world.

Phase 6 contexts produced the largest number of finds from the site, all from three substantial pits (225, 678 and 1026) used for the disposal of an exceptional amount of rubbish. Nails, pins and lace tags are again the most common finds. Structural items, fixtures, fittings and lock furniture (presumably from college buildings) predominate. There are no items in the assemblage that could be considered as high status, and the number of dress accessories other than lace tags and pins is small. Items often found on college sites, such as writing implements and objects associated with musical instruments, are absent. Eight small 'L'-shaped hooks came

[81] A.R. Goodall, 'Copper Alloy and Silver Objects', in Hassall, 'St Ebbe's, Part II', p. 221 and fig. 31 no. 2.

[82] S. Moore, *Cutlery for the Table: A History of British Table and Pocket Cutlery* (1999), p. 110, second knife down on the lower plate.

[83] D.J. Eveleigh, *Candle Lighting*, 2nd edn (2003), p. 16.

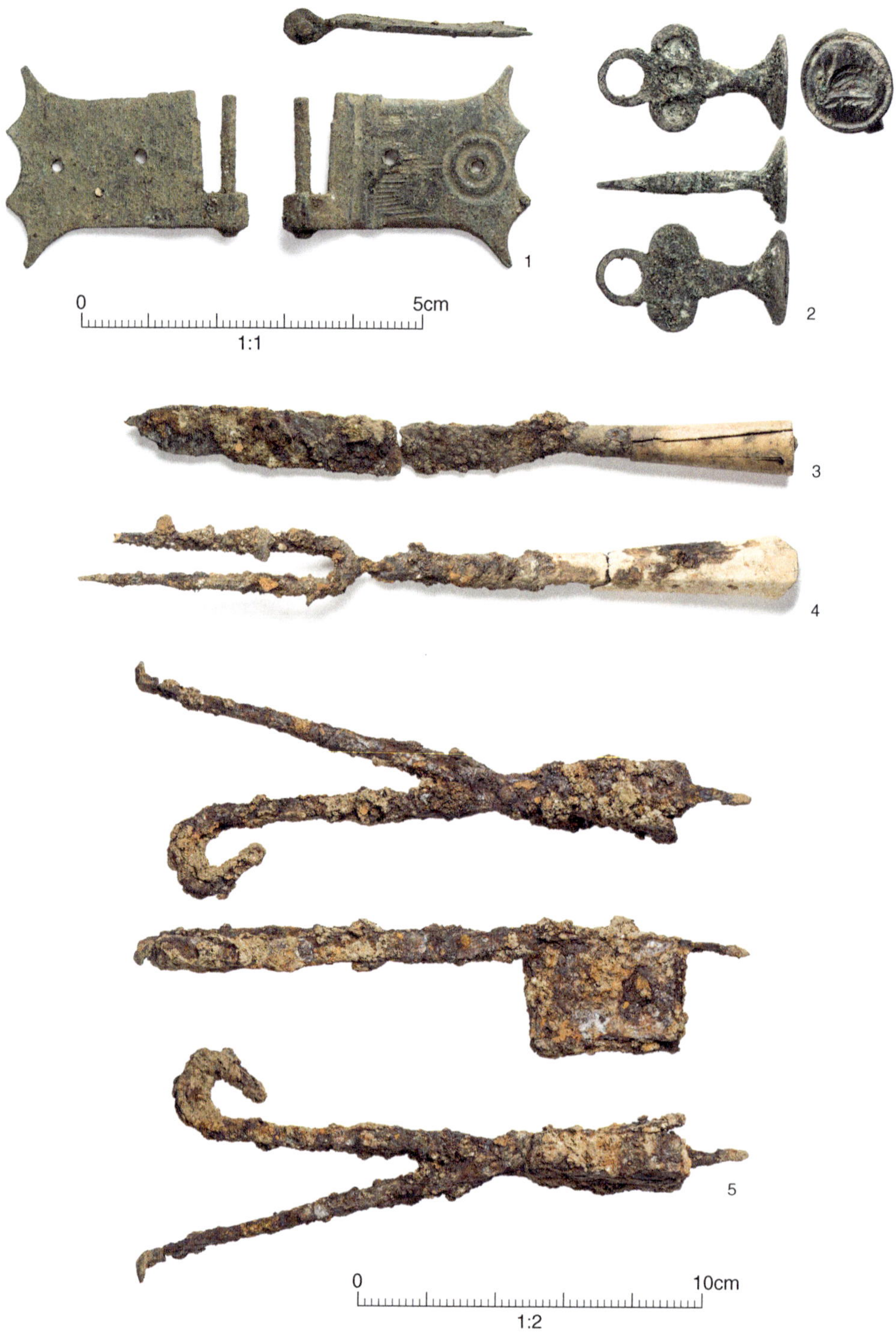

Fig. 10.20 Metalwork.

from pit 225. They have tapering shanks and hooks and vary in length from 30 to 47 mm. They could be tenter-hooks used on tenters (a post and rail construction) to stretch cloth out to dry after fulling. Alternatively, and perhaps more likely considering the setting, they could have been used to support wall hangings and tapestries.[84]

The objects from Phase 7 contexts comprised six nails, a fragment from a knife blade and a length of window came.

Catalogue of Illustrated Pieces (Fig. 10.20):

1. Book clasp catch plate, copper alloy, complete. Scalloped outside edge and concentric circle decoration. L: 34 mm. Ctx 279, pit 278, Phase 6.
2. Seal matrix, copper alloy, circular stamp bearing the image of a hare or rabbit, slender shank with rectangular section and a trefoil knop. The top loop is pierced for suspension. L: 22 mm. Ctx 446, pit 441, Phase 5.
3. Knife, iron and bone, complete. Whittle-tang knife with worked bone handle. Oval shaped bolster, 'through' tang, simple bone handle. L: 196 mm. Ctx 542, pit 540, Phase 5.
4. Fork, iron and bone, complete. Two straight prongs, moulded shaft with slender bolster. Bone handle with octagonal expanding a rounded butt. L: 202 mm. Ctx 1014, pit 1011, Phase 5.
5. Candle snuffer, iron, complete. 'Scissor form', box and plate mounted on the blades and sharp point at front. L: 166 mm. Ctx 319, pit 318, Phase 5.

COINS AND JETONS by IAN R. SCOTT

There are sixteen early Stuart farthing tokens and four jetons. Most of the coins and jetons come from pit 225. Most of the farthing tokens date from the reign of Charles I and comprise three Richmond farthings (dated 1625–35) and ten Rose farthings (1636 and after). Rose farthings are by far the most commonly found of the farthing tokens of Charles I. The other three farthings date to the reign of James I and comprise Lennox farthings (*c.*1616–23), one possibly and one probably counterfeit. The jetons comprise three 'rose and orb' jetons of Hans Krauwinckel II (1586–1635) and an anonymous Nuremberg jeton of *c.*1500–70.

WORKED STONE ARTEFACTS by RUTH SHAFFREY

An inscribed piece of slate was found in fill 644 of Phase 3 ditch 675 (Fig. 10.21). It is a very small fragment, measuring 27 x 24 x 2 mm, and is inscribed on one face with two parallel lines forming part of a circle and inside these two curved lines, the numbers 4, 5, 6. There are also a row of short lines incised at right angles to the broken edge, which appear to have been carved later than the circle. The style of the numerals indicates a post-medieval date for the object, implying that it was intrusive in its context of discovery. Slates inscribed with graffiti are not common, although a seventeenth- to eighteenth-century example lightly incised on both sides with a continuous cruciform pattern was found at Queen's College.[85]

FLINT by MICHAEL DONNELLY

The excavation yielded just five flints, of which one may be modern in date, all from post-medieval features. Three of the flints were recovered from pit 225, fill 209. These were in varying states and included the possible modern split flake that may have been struck with a metal hammer. One probable crested bladelet was also recovered, although it could alternatively relate to core tool

[84] Goodall, 'Copper Alloy and Silver Objects', pp. 234–5.
[85] R. Shaffrey, 'Worked Stone Objects', chapter 6, above.

Fig. 10.21 Inscribed slate.

shaping rather than being a crest from blade core production. The final piece from context 209 was a probable scraper fragment that is quite badly rolled. A preparation flake from the initial stages of core working was also recovered, while the largest flint by far was one that may also be a flake from axe/adze production, since it has the very typical short, squat plunging profile from the preform stage of core tool production.

The flint recovered from this site is fairly poor in terms of assemblage size, condition and potential and contrasts with some other urban excavations in Oxford that have produced considerable assemblages of flint.[86] However, the volume of flintwork can be a poor indicator of prehistoric activity, as is demonstrated by the assemblage of just three flakes recovered from the henge site a short distance to the north of this excavation.[87] The two possible axe-adze working flakes are potentially Neolithic in date but these pieces could just as easily be Mesolithic finds; indeed, one may simply be squat core working flake of the later prehistoric period and the other a crested bladelet of early prehistoric date.

ANIMAL BONE by LEE G. BRODERICK

The excavation recovered a small assemblage of animal bone, mostly dating from the medieval and post-medieval periods (Table 10.4).

Medieval Period

The assemblage from Phases 2 and 3 comprises 651 specimens, of which 638 (98 per cent) were recovered by hand and 13 were from environmental samples. The assemblage came principally from ditches 675 and 676. The most notable feature of these was an associated bone group (ABG)

86 For example, H. Lamdin-Whymark, 'Flint', in P. Bradley et al., 'Prehistoric and Roman Activity and a Civil War Ditch: Excavations at the Chemistry Research Laboratory, 2–4 South Parks Road, Oxford', *Oxoniensia*, 70 (2005), pp. 151–4; D. Mullin and M. Donnelly, 'Flint', in Munby, *Oxford Castle*, pp. 292–4.

87 S. Ford, 'Struck Flint', in Wallis, *The Oxford Henge*, pp. 25–6.

Table 10.4. Quantification of animal bone by phase. NISP: Number of Identified SPecimens), NSP: Number of SPecimens. Material from soil samples are included in their own columns, separate from the hand-collected data.

	Phase							
	2	**3**	**4**	**5**	**6**	**7**	**2 (sieved)**	**3 (sieved)**
Domestic cattle	6	18	4	76	68	7	2	1
Domestic cattle?		1						
Caprine	13	22	14	221	357	14		
Caprine?		1						
Caprine/roe deer							2	1
Pig	1	4	1	13	12	7		
Horse	1	2		4	1			
Dog	6	68	2	12	2			
Dog?								1
Domestic cat		1		1	1			
Domestic cat?	1							
Rabbit			2	9	17	2		
Small mammal	29	4						
Medium mammal	6	349					1	
Large mammal	13	52						
Total mammal	76	522	23	336	458	30	5	3
Amphibian						7		
Frog/toad								1
Total amphibian	0	0	0	0	0	7	0	1
Bird				4	29	3		
Swan				1				
Swan?					1			
Greylag/domestic goose		1		5	3	1		
Domestic fowl		2	3	60	108	1		
Domestic fowl?		1						
Crow/rook				2	1			
Total bird	0	4	3	72	142	5	0	0
Total NISP	76	526	26	408	600	42	5	4
Total NSP	106	532	88	2048	3121	258	5	8

from ditch 675 that contained 63 dog specimens (*Canis familiaris*), including cranial, forelimb and hindlimb elements of both sides from at least three individuals (based on the left humerus). One of the individuals was considerably more complete than the other, with duplicate elements limited to the left mandible, axis, atlas, right scapula, left humerus, left second metacarpal, a fourth metacarpal and the left tibia. This animal, as well as one of the other two dogs in the ditch, was around 55 cm tall at the shoulder, representing a medium-sized dog, with the least represented individual being around 15 cm taller. A bacculum (suggesting that the ABG included a male dog) was also recovered from the ditch, along with six cervical vertebrae, ten thoracic vertebrae, three lumbar vertebrae and ten caudal vertebrae and 124 rib fragments of medium mammal, probably mostly from the same individual.

Leaving aside the dog specimens, the most commonly represented species in each phase were domestic cattle (*Bos taurus taurus*) and sheep (*Ovis aries*) and/or goats (*Capra hircus*) distantly followed by pig (*Sus scrofa domesticus*), a pattern which is consistent with the larger assemblage recovered from Kendrew Quad, a short distance north of this site, which was interpreted as being characteristic of horn-working or of primary butchery waste.[88] Also similar to that assemblage was the relatively large number of cranial elements of domestic cattle recovered from Phase 3 (nine out of eighteen), including three horncores. Of the remaining specimens from this phase, five elements were foot elements (phalanges and metapodials), as were five of the six domestic cattle specimens from Phase 2. These figures are in contrast to those for caprines: just five of the thirteen Phase 2 caprine specimens and six of the twenty-one Phase 3 caprine specimens were head or foot elements. At least three individual caprines were represented in the assemblage in each phase and at least two domestic cattle in the Phase 3 component.

The pattern fits with sites peripheral to the town in Wilson's spatial distribution patterns for animal bone disposal, partly modelled on the archaeology of Oxford, but we can also use this dataset, small as it is, to tentatively suggest some supporting evidence for the interpretation of the Kendrew Quad site.[89] The lack of any bias towards head or foot elements for caprines argues against this site being one of primary butchery waste, with fourteen specimens (64 per cent) of meat-yielding limb elements (humerus, radius, femur and tibia) instead suggesting that the assemblage results primarily from domestic (kitchen) waste.

Butchery evidence was, in fact, sparse – a caprine femur from Phase 3 was chopped through mid-shaft and a caprine humerus from Phase 2 had an oblique cutmark on the cranial side near the distal end. Both are likely primary butchery marks, the latter from breaking the carcass down by following the anatomy of the animal and the former from breaking one of the resultant pieces into a smaller one. By contrast, butchery marks were slightly more common on domestic cattle specimens and large mammal ribs (a cut and a chop) and vertebrae (a chop). A domestic cattle metatarsal from Phase 2 had superficial chopmarks on the lateral side and a first phalanx from the same phase had oblique cutmarks around the cranial and caudal surfaces. These marks would be consistent with some processing for skins taking place near the site at this time whilst cutmarks on the caudal side of a horncore base would seem to support the idea that a horner may have been practising his craft in the vicinity in Phase 3.

Six specimens from Phase 3 had been gnawed by canids, which is a much lower proportion than was reported at Kendrew Quad, but nonetheless paints a picture of disposed refuse in pits and ditches being left open and exposed for some time to scavengers. A chicken bone from this period, gnawed by a rodent, adds to this impression. Unusually, a dog ulna had also been gnawed by canids. This particular specimen was from the same ditch as the ABG(s) discussed above.

The evidence from this period suggests a town-edge refuse disposal site frequented by scavengers, possibly including the dogs in this assemblage. At this time the site appears to have

88 M.A. Holmes, 'The Animal Bones', in Wallis, *The Oxford Henge*, pp. 222–6.

89 B. Wilson, 'Mortality Patterns, Animal Husbandry and Marketing in and Around Medieval and Post-Medieval Oxford', in A.R. Hall and H.K. Kenward (eds.), *Urban-Rural Connexions: Perspectives from Environmental Archaeology* (1994), pp. 103–16.

been used for disposal of kitchen waste from the nearby tenements as well as from a possible horner, similar to the Kendrew Quad site.

Post-Medieval Period

The most striking feature of the assemblage from these phases is the large proportion of caprine specimens. This is above 50 per cent in Phases 4, 5 and 6, reaching a peak of 59.5 per cent in Phase 6. Almost as dramatic, especially when compared with the medieval phases, is the proportion of bird remains on the site, particularly domestic fowl (*Gallus gallus*). Domestic fowl are the third most common taxon by NISP in Phases 4 and 5 and the second most common in Phase 6. This is in stark contrast to the diverse Civil War assemblage from Mansfield College,[90] and to the post-medieval assemblage from Kendrew Quad, in which caprines and domestic cattle are present in similarly large proportions and domestic fowl are a minor component or else absent. The continued presence of dog and cat specimens in the assemblage, albeit in small quantities, as well as those of crow (*Corvus corone*) or rook (*Corvus frugilegus*), suggest that disposed rubbish continued to be left exposed, at least at times. The large proportion of caprine and domestic fowl is suggestive of a different diet, particular to the college, compared to surrounding sites such as Kendrew Quad.

FISH BONE by REBECCA NICHOLSON

A small collection of 152 fragments of fish bone and scales was recovered, virtually entirely by the sieving of soil samples from post-medieval features. Of these, 53 bones were identifiable at least to family. The bones include both marine and freshwater species, as well as bones from the catadromous eel (*Anguilla anguilla*) and either salmon (*Salmo salar*) or sea trout (*Salmo trutta*). Hand-retrieved bones include a haddock (*Melanogramus aeglefinus*) post temporal from Phase 3 pit 1020, a vertebra from a fairly small shark (Scyliorhinidae), probably tope (*Galeorhinus galeus*), from Phase 5 pit 318 and two supracleithra from at least one cod (*Gadus morhua*) of around 60 cm found in Phase 6 pit 225. The most commonly identified fish in the sieved samples were eel and herring (*Clupea harengus*), the former likely to have been caught fairly locally and the latter likely to have been imported as salted or pickled fish from the ports of south-east England or East Anglia.[91] Both herrings and eels would have been fairly cheap and their bones are ubiquitous in medieval urban rubbish and cesspit deposits where fish remains survive. The freshwater fish identified in the assemblage include bream (*Abramis brama*), probable chub (*Leuciscus cephalus*), pike (*Esox lucius*) and perch (*Perca fluviatilis*). None are particularly large and all could have been caught in the River Thames or Cherwell.

MARINE SHELL AND AVIAN EGGSHELL

Some 6.6 kg of marine mollusc shell was recovered. This was dominated by oyster, with occasional mussel and a single cockle. Small quantities of avian eggshell were extracted from environmental samples from pits dating to Phases 5 and 6.

CHARRED PLANT REMAINS AND CHARCOAL by JULIA MEEN

Twelve bulk samples were collected; many of the samples contained little charcoal, but a representative selection of charcoal fragments from each sample was examined to determine the range of wood taxa present in samples 205 and 208 (from ditch 675) and samples 200 and

[90] Chapter 13, below, and full archive report.
[91] *VCH Oxon.* 4, pp. 305–12.

207 (from mid sixteenth- to mid seventeenth-century pit 571 and early to mid seventeenth-century pit 1026).

Ditch 675

The bulk samples from the ditch were very poor in charred plant remains. Only fills 601 and 664 contained any identifiable material. Each produced a single, tiny fragment of charred hazelnut shell and, in context 601, two cereal grains that were too poorly preserved to identify to genus. A very small number of charcoal fragments were also recovered from these two contexts, dominated by oak (*Quercus*). With so little material recovered from the ditch, it is not possible draw any further conclusions, especially as these sparse, fragmentary remains may well have undergone reworking.

Pits 571 and 1026

The three bulk samples from post-medieval pits contained only sparse charred plant remains. These were mostly oddments of poorly preserved cereal grain, including a small number of better preserved free-threshing wheat grains (*Triticum aestivum/turgidum*). A fragment of charred fruit stone is provisionally identified as *Prunus domestica* (plum/damson) or possibly apricot (*Prunus armeniaca*). Apricot is believed to have been introduced to Britain in the sixteenth century, and in the seventeenth and eighteenth centuries it was a popular garden fruit, being cultivated against sunny walls.[92] Material including animal bone, eggshell, marine shell and pottery was recovered from the three sampled pits, so it seems that the pits were being used to dispose of domestic waste. However, if any food plants were amongst the kitchen waste thrown into the pit they were presumably uncharred and have not been preserved. The pits were quite rich in wood charcoal, suggesting these pits were used to dispose of fuel, perhaps also from the kitchen. The charcoal includes frequent beech (*Fagus sylvatica*), much of it roundwood. Several other sites in Oxford including Lincoln College, Queen's College and Merton College have also shown a preference for beech as the main fuel wood, with a shift from mainly oak utilisation occurring in the early post-medieval period or even earlier.[93]

SCIENTIFIC DATING EVIDENCE by ANDREW SIMMONDS

OSL Dating

Two samples were taken from the lower fills of ditch 677 and processed at the Luminescence Dating Laboratory of the University of Oxford by Dr Jean-Luc Schwenniger (Fig. 10.5; Table 10.5). The dating of the lower sample (X7236) was problematic due to large over-dispersion of individual OSL measurements, indicative of partial bleaching of the sediment, and is not considered reliable as it is based on a single measurement. Nevertheless, the date ranges of the two samples are consistent with the stratigraphic sequence and may indicate a late Neolithic date for the digging of the ditch.

Radiocarbon Dating

A sample of cattle bone from fill 666 of ditch 676 was submitted to the Scottish Universities Research Centre for radiocarbon dating and returned a date range of cal. AD 1043–1245 (Table 10.6).

92 F.A. Roach, *Cultivated Fruits of Britain: Their Origin and History* (1985).

93 D. Challinor, 'The Wood Charcoal', in Kamash et al., 'Late Saxon and Medieval Occupation: Evidence from Excavations at Lincoln College', pp. 271–4; S. Boardman, 'Wood Charcoal', chapter 6, above; Poore, 'No. 4A Merton St.', pp. 227, 247.

Table 10.5. Summary of OSL dating.

Field code	Laboratory no.	Context	OSL age estimate (years before 2017)	Calibrated date range
SJC16–01	X7236	672	4695 ± 435	3113–2243 BC
SJC16–02	X7237	671	3645 ± 865	2493–763 BC

Table 10.6. Summary of radiocarbon date.

Laboratory no.	Context	Feature	Material	δ¹³C (‰)	Radiocarbon age (BP)	Calibrated date (95.4% confidence)
SUERC-70159	666	Ditch 676	Cattle bone	−21.5	873 ± 32	Cal AD 1043–1104 (22.0%) Cal AD 1118–1245 (73.4%)

ACKNOWLEDGEMENTS

The fieldwork, post-excavation programme and publication were funded by St John's College, Oxford. The authors are grateful to Stepnells and Wright and Wright Architects for commissioning the archaeological work, and special thanks are owed to Ronan Barry of Stepnells and James Taylor of Wright and Wright Architects for their support. The authors are also grateful to David Radford, archaeologist for Oxford City Council, for his advice and guidance. The fieldwork was managed for OA by Carl Champness, and the site supervisors were Peter Vellet and John Boothroyd, assisted by Natalie Anderson, Tom Black, Sophie Bojadziev, Anne-Laure Bollen, Diana Chard, Christopher Clark, Maria Diaz Tena, Adam Fellingham, Raul Gonzalez, Victoria Green, Camille Guezennec, Vix Hughes, Martin Locker, Javier Martinez-Jimenez, Michael McLean, Conan Parsons, Benjamin Slader, Ashley Strutt and Peter Vellett. The post-excavation project was managed by Andrew Simmonds. Thanks are also due to the staff that processed the finds under the management of Leigh Allen, processed the environmental samples under the management of Rebecca Nicholson, and prepared the archive under the management of Nicola Scott. David A. Higgins would like to thank Dr Susie White, who helped with drawing the clay pipes.

11.

Medieval and Post-Medieval Tenements at the Ashmolean Museum Extension Site

STEVEN TEAGUE and BEN M. FORD

with contributions by LEIGH ALLEN, MARTIN ALLEN, PAUL BLINKHORN, JOHN COTTER, ALISON DE TURBERVILLE, DAVID A. HIGGINS, REBECCA NICHOLSON, RUTH SHAFFREY, WENDY SMITH, LENA STRID and HUGH WILLMOTT

SUMMARY

Excavations in advance of an extension to the Ashmolean Museum revealed evidence dating from the middle Anglo-Saxon period to the nineteenth century. A small group of middle Anglo-Saxon Ipswich ware pottery adds to growing evidence for occupation of this period in the vicinity, and is only the second group of such pottery recovered to date in Oxford. From the late twelfth century the area formed part of the developing northern suburb of the medieval town, and evidence was recovered for three tenements extending from St Giles' Street through to the boundary of the royal palace of Beaumont to the west. Most of the excavated area fell within a tenement identifiable with a property documented from the early thirteenth century. Between 1240 and 1260 this was held by Master Ralph of Swalcliffe, one of the earliest medical doctors known from the university, and subsequently by his brother, John. A fragment of window tympanum recovered during the excavations is likely to have come from a stone house constructed at the site by c.1200. This might be identifiable with the documented houses of Andrew Rufus, the earliest known owner of the property, who was alive in the last decade of the twelfth century. Clear evidence for long-lived property boundaries was seen in the excavations, and this suggests some revision of Salter's mapping of the area. Numerous thirteenth- to fifteenth-century features included wells, quarries and rubbish pits, and an unusually high number of medieval coins were recovered. There was some evidence for retrenchment in the later medieval period and for the subdivision of properties into the smaller holdings that are evident on early maps. Nevertheless, as on many sites of this period, the finds and environmental evidence from the fifteenth to the seventeenth centuries also point to a rising standard of living. Fishing is suggested by an unusually rich assemblage of bone from freshwater fish and eels and a group of fishing net weights. Other unusual finds include a coin weight for a James I gold half angel, and an assemblage of musket balls and a powder holder cover that are likely to date from the Civil War. In the eighteenth century, an assemblage of malting kiln tiles and glass drinking vessels suggests that an inn that brewed ale existed on the site.

Between December 2006 and March 2007 an excavation and watching brief were carried out on land formerly occupied by a late nineteenth-century extension to the rear of the Ashmolean

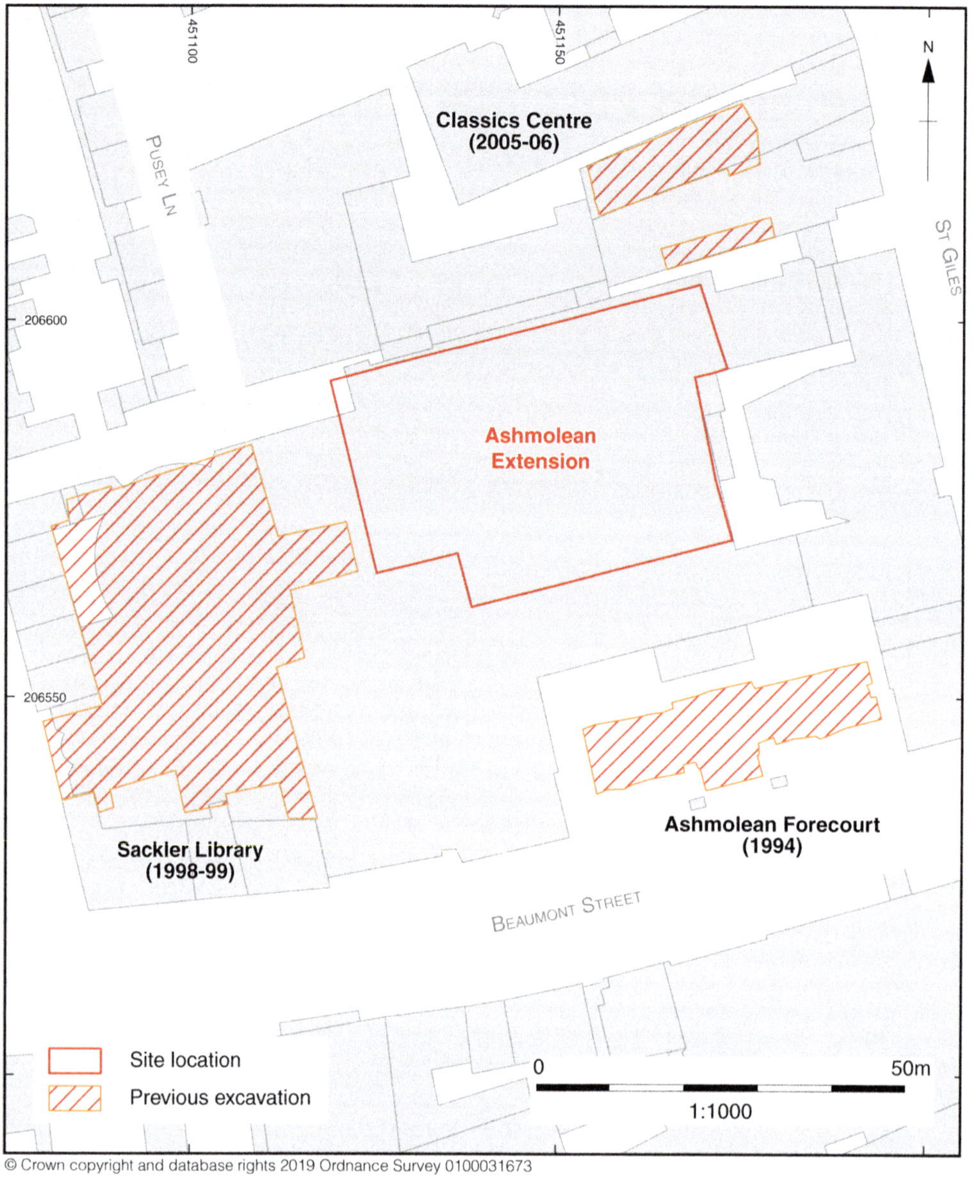

Fig. 11.1 Site location with previous excavations in the area.

Museum, Beaumont Street (NGR SP 5114 0659).[1] A watching brief on contractor's test pits in 2005 and an evaluation trench in 2006 had previously confirmed that archaeological deposits survived between the foundations of the existing building.[2] The work was carried out in advance of a complete rebuilding of the extension. The development site is bounded by the Sackler Library to the west, St Giles' Street to the east, the Classics Centre/Cast Gallery to the north and the older part of the Ashmolean Museum to the south. It covers an area of approximately 0.20 ha. and lies at *c*.64 m OD (Fig. 11.1).

This report includes summaries highlighting the most important aspects of the finds and environmental assemblages recovered during the excavations. The full original reports, catalogues and data tables are available via the OA Library.[3] The archive will be deposited with the Ashmolean Museum under accession number 2006.68.

ARCHAEOLOGICAL AND HISTORICAL BACKGROUND

Important early prehistoric remains and evidence for settlement in the Iron Age and Roman period are known from the general area of central north Oxford.[4] Ring ditches of two Bronze Age barrows have been excavated immediately to the west of the site at the Sackler Library (Fig. 11.1).[5]

The site lies within the former northern suburb of medieval Oxford, *c*.200 m to the north of the town wall and adjacent to the precinct of the royal palace of Beaumont (later the Carmelite friary), which was built for Henry I by *c*.1132. There is no evidence that a northern suburb existed in the late Anglo-Saxon period. The church of St Mary Magdalen, which stands a short distance outside the north gate, was in existence by the early to mid twelfth century.[6] The surrounding lands north of the town fell within the Northgate Hundred, which belonged to the manor of Headington. This was a royal estate in the eleventh century, but by 1142 at the latest it had been granted away by the Crown, initially to Hugh de Pluggenait, a Breton follower of the Empress Matilda.[7] Beaumont Palace became a favourite resting-place for the Angevin kings en route from London or Windsor to the royal hunting lodge at Woodstock. References in royal building records suggest it originally consisted of a hall, a kitchen, at least two chambers, a chapel and a cloister, with a number of well-documented additions throughout the thirteenth century.[8] Royal visits to Beaumont ceased in the late thirteenth century, and in 1318 the site was granted by Edward II to the Carmelite (or White) Friars, who occupied it until its surrender at the Dissolution in 1538. Excavations at the Sackler Library immediately west of the present site revealed a grid of tree planting pits, which may have formed part of a royal orchard on the east side of the palace complex, along with a number of contemporary rubbish pits. Between the orchard and the palace precinct boundary was part of a robbed north–south wall associated with twelfth to thirteenth century window glass, which was interpreted as the remains of a demolished building of some status. The remains of a second substantial building were revealed

1 This report was largely completed in 2011 and has undergone only minor subsequent revision. For details of fieldwork methodology, see below.

2 'Ashmolean Museum, Oxford: Archaeological Watching Brief Report', unpublished OA report (2005), https://library.oxfordarchaeology.com/3913/; 'Ashmolean Museum, Beaumont Street, Oxford: Archaeological Evaluation Report', unpublished OA report (2006), https://library.oxfordarchaeology.com/1306/.

3 https://library.oxfordarchaeology.com/5767/.

4 G. Lambrick, 'Prehistoric Oxford', *Oxoniensia*, 78 (2013), pp. 1–48. For Roman settlement in north Oxford: chapter 13, below.

5 Poore, *Beaumont*.

6 The church of St Mary Magdalen belonged to the collegiate church of St George in the castle and passed with St George's into the ownership of Osney abbey in 1149.

7 For the manor of Headington: *VCH Oxon*. 5, pp. 157–68.

8 H.M. Colvin et al., *The History of the King's Works, Vol II, The Middle Ages: The King's Houses 1066–1485* (1963), p. 986.

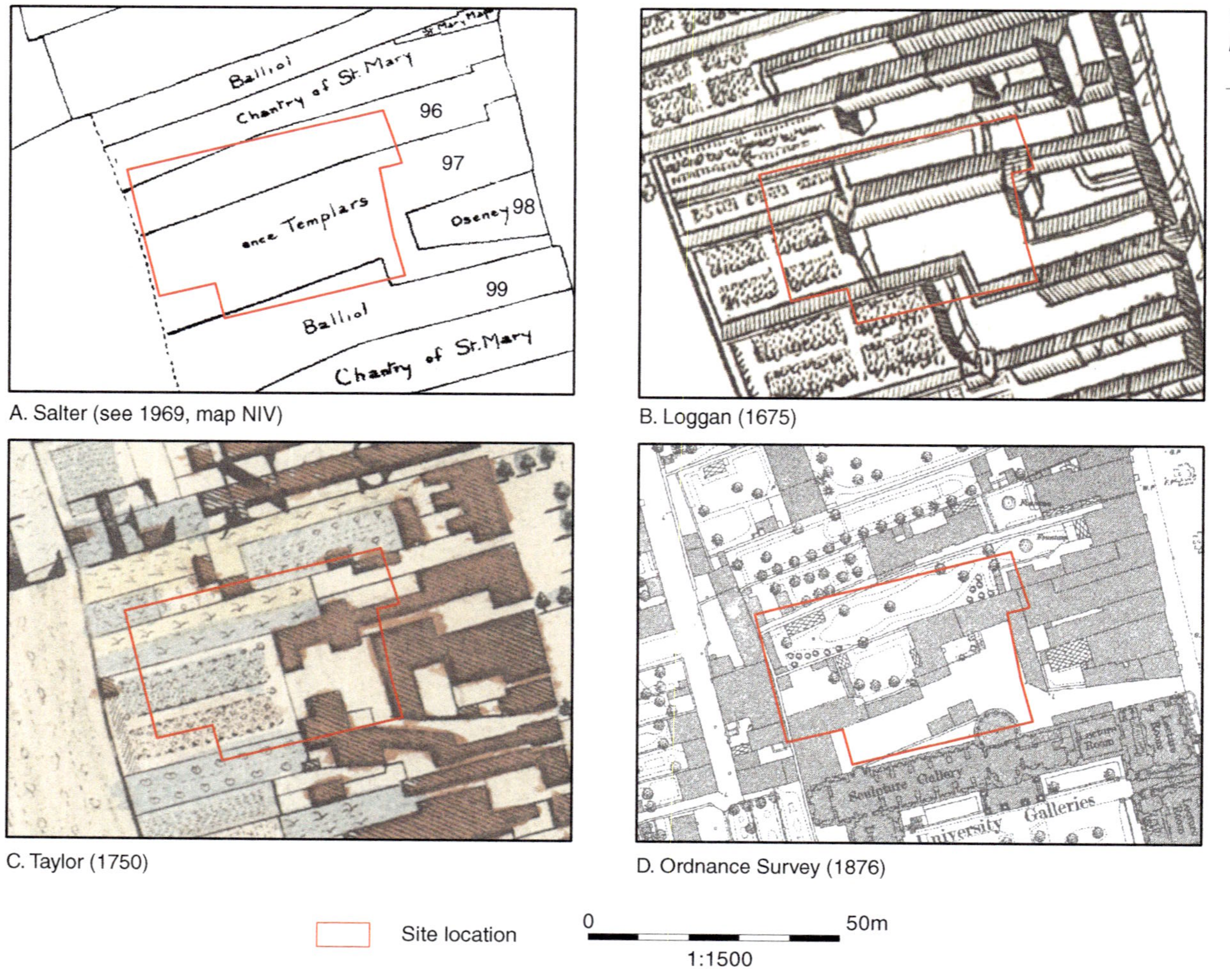

Fig. 11.2 Site located over historic mapping.

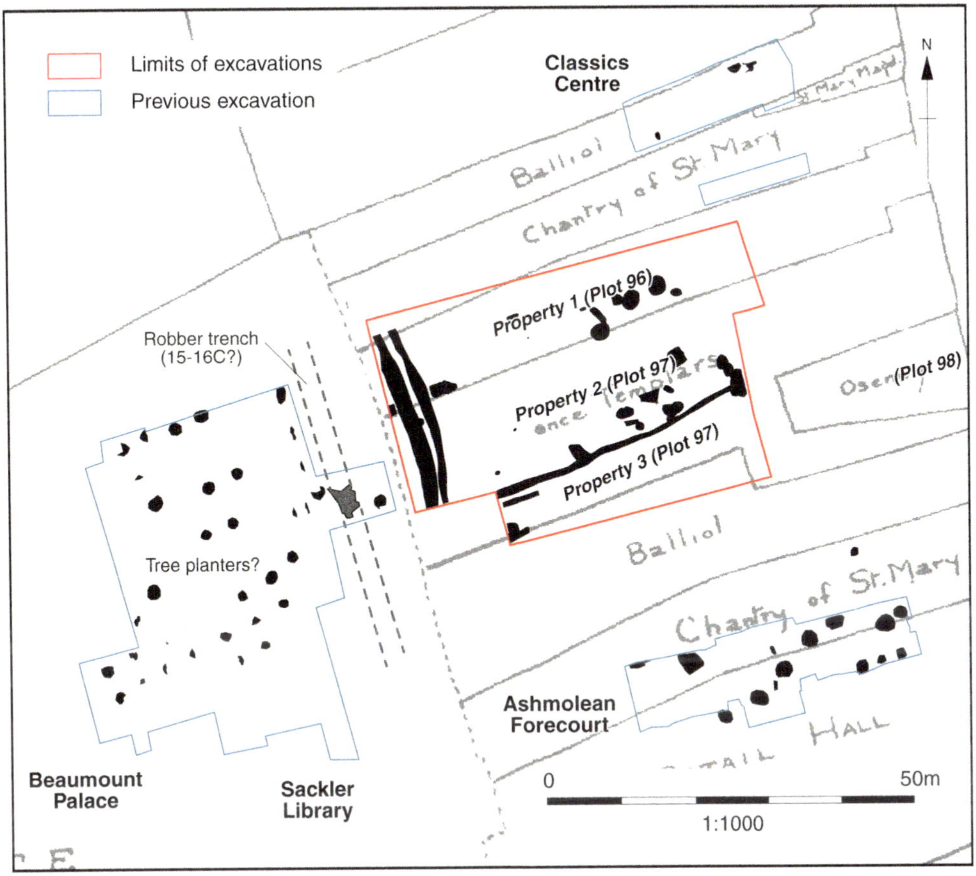

Fig. 11.3 H.E. Salter's reconstruction of medieval property boundaries, from his Survey of Oxford.

a short distance to the south-west; its origins were unclear but it seemed likely that it had ultimately been used as a church or chapel by the White Friars.[9]

The site of the present excavations extends 26–78 m back from the modern frontage of St Giles' Street, which appears to have been fully built up by the time of the 1279 hundred rolls survey, and the excavated area can be equated with three medieval properties here (Fig. 11.2a).[10] Most of the excavated area was mapped by Salter as falling within the rear part of the large tenement N97–8, which can be broadly equated with the area designated Properties 2–3 in the excavations (Fig. 11.3). These properties are first recorded *c.*1220–40, when N97 was granted by Andrew Marshal to the Templars; the grant describes it as 'the houses' that had been given to Andrew Marshal by his uncle Andrew Rufus. Around 1240, what appears to be the neighbouring property to the south, N98, was acquired by Ralph of Swalcliffe, one of the earliest medical doctors known by name at the University of Oxford, paying an annual rent of 4*s.* to John Plumbar. Shortly afterwards, *c.*1245, Ralph of Swalcliffe also acquired the larger property, N97, from the Templars, for a rent of 2 marks, and in *c.*1250 he bought out the remaining interests of John Plumbar and John Halegod in N98. The history of these properties in the middle of the

9 Poore, *Beaumont*, pp. 29–35.
10 For the following section: Salter, *Survey*, vol. 2, pp. 215–17 and map N IV; and Salter, *Oseney*.

thirteenth century becomes rather confused. According to a charter in the cartulary of Osney abbey, Ralph of Swalcliffe seems to have granted his whole property here to the abbey in 1259–60, in a deed that preserves an unusual amount of topographical information:

> … *illam terram meam cum pertinenciis que est inter terram Iohannis Gamage & mansionem illam que fuit Rogeri le Sauser in parochia sancte Marie Magdalene, ubi aliquando molendinum meum situm fuit, & extendit se a regio vico usque ad murum regium, qui dividit terram illam & curiam domini regis* … (Salter, *Oseney*, vol. 5, no. 857)

> … that land (of) mine with appurtenances, which is between the land of John Gamage, and the mansion formerly of Roger le Sauser in the parish of St Mary Magdalen, where my mill was once located, and extends from the king's highway to the king's wall, which divides that land from the king's court …

Whether the entire property was granted to Osney, or only the part of it that can be equated with N98, is unclear; however, by the time of the hundred rolls survey N97 was occupied by John of Swalcliffe, brother of Ralph, still holding of the Templars, while N98 was held of Osney by Henry of Eynsham, a tiler ('slatter'). In 1353 N98 is recorded as two tenements, and a northern and a southern tenement within the property are recorded in the fifteenth century, although sometimes held jointly.

To the north of Ralph of Swalcliffe was N96, which can be equated with the area of Property 1 in the excavations (Figs. 11.2a and 11.3). This property was held by Andrew le Sauser in 1279, in succession to his father Roger. The Swalcliffe grant to Osney (above) refers to this property as the 'mansion formerly of Roger le Sauser', which would imply the presence of a substantial dwelling here. To the south of Ralph of Swalcliffe was N99. Salter's account suggests that here, too, there had been some complexity and subdivision of a larger tenement, with one holding on the northern part of the frontage, and the other occupying the south part of the frontage and the whole of the back. The smaller northern tenement on the frontage can be associated with the southern abuttal recorded in the Swalcliffe deeds, since in 1279 it was held by John Brun who had bought it from Henry Gamage. Salter suggests, however, that the remainder of the tenement can be equated with a property held in 1279 by Thomas of St Andrew, paying 3s. to Godstow and 1s. to Agnes Halegod. The connection with Halegod is interesting, since Ralph of Swalcliffe had bought out the interest of John Halegod in N98 in *c.*1250 and Salter's mapping suggests an odd intrusion of the Balliol property northwards into N97 (Fig. 11.2a). Very little of this property, however, fell within the area of the excavations.

Two previous archaeological excavations immediately adjacent to the present site, at the Ashmolean Forecourt and the Classics Centre (Fig. 11.1), have also revealed evidence of the medieval tenements of the area.[11] Excavations at the Classics Centre revealed part of two tenements, including five eleventh to thirteenth century pits containing butchery or tanning waste, overlain by a cultivation soil. Evidence for a thirteenth- or fourteenth-century stone structure was seen within the northern tenement. The pottery assemblage from the site was notable for the presence of a large collection of medieval ceramic oil lamps and it was suggested that this might be a sign that the property was in use as an academic hall. Yard areas of a further two tenements were excavated at the Ashmolean Forecourt. Here, in addition to back yard rubbish pits, the southern tenement contained a thirteenth century sunken building of timber and stone that may have been a cellar. This was succeeded in the fourteenth century by a more substantial stone structure extending back from the street frontage, which was probably part of the documented Batayl Hall, a property of Exeter College from 1320. Two large fourteenth-century bread ovens were found in the northern tenement.

11 P. Andrews and L. Mepham, 'Medieval and Post-Medieval Extra-Mural Settlement on the Site of the Ashmolean Museum Forecourt, Beaumont Street, Oxford', *Oxoniensia*, 62 (1997), pp. 179–223; A. Norton and G. Cockin, 'Excavations at the Classics Centre, 65–67 St Giles', Oxford', *Oxoniensia*, 73 (2008), pp. 161–94.

Loggan's map of 1675 (Fig. 11.2b), as with Agas' earlier map, shows the site within the central part of three long tenement plots, located within the back yards/gardens immediately behind the properties fronting St Giles' Street to the east. The map shows open yards with gardens at the very rear of the plots, which back onto the precinct of the ruined palace and friary. From the seventeenth century, the expanding population of the town resulted in the creation of living space in the backs of most of the properties fronting St Giles' Street. Taylor's map of 1750 (Fig. 11.2c), shows what are probably two rows of cottages, extending westwards from the main properties fronting St Giles' Street, into what had previously been open yards. Contemporary title deeds describe No. 68 St Giles' Street (the northern tenement) as two messuages in *c.*1770.[12]

The first half of the nineteenth century saw considerable change to the topography of the area, with the construction of Beaumont Street in the 1820s and the opening up of St John's Street, Pusey Street and Pusey Lane. In 1841–5 the Taylor Institution and the University Galleries (later the Ashmolean Museum), designed by Charles Robert Cockerell, were constructed immediately south of the present site. The Ordnance Survey 1st Edition 1:500 map of 1876 (Fig. 11.2d) shows that part of the galleries known as the hemicycle or exedra extended into the southern part of the site. In the rest of the site, the map shows the back of at least two properties fronting St Giles' Street, a number of possible cottages and outbuildings, and open space. These buildings were demolished in the late nineteenth century for an extension to the rear of the Taylor Institution and the University Galleries, built in 1892–5.

DISCUSSION

Prehistoric and Roman Evidence

A single struck flint, possibly an arrowhead, broadly datable to the Neolithic or early Bronze Age was found within a later feature. This may be related to the ring ditches immediately to the west. Three Roman coins (dating from the first to early second century, 270–273? and 364–378?) and five sherds of Roman pottery were also found on the site. No features attributable to the Roman period have been found in the immediate area, though small quantities of residual pottery have occurred on all the excavated sites in the vicinity. The nearest known settlement lies *c.*0.5 km to the north-east.[13]

The Anglo-Saxon Period

A small assemblage of middle Anglo-Saxon Ipswich ware (*c.*720–850) was found, together with four sherds of undecorated hand-built pottery of early to middle Anglo-Saxon type. All occurred residually within later features. A few sherds of Ipswich ware were also recovered during the earlier excavations at the Sackler Library;[14] no pottery of this date was identified at the Ashmolean Forecourt, but a single sherd of early to middle Anglo-Saxon undecorated pottery was found at the Classics Centre. During the present excavations, a pair of tweezers with ring and dot decoration were found with one of the Ipswich ware sherds in fill 778 of Phase 5 pit 1017 (Fig. 11.23, no. 8). Tweezers of this kind are very characteristic of the early to middle Anglo-Saxon period, and occur commonly on settlement and cemetery sites. Two very early finds are also known from this area, a gold bracteate found in 1646 in the Civil War defences in St Giles Field, and two graves, one of them containing a silver plated disc, found in the grounds of the Radcliffe Infirmary in 1770.[15] Recently, a sunken-featured building has been found close to the Walton Street frontage of the Radcliffe Infirmary, associated with sixth

12 Salter, *Survey*, vol. 2, p. 215.
13 Chapter 13, below.
14 P. Blinkhorn, 'Pottery', in Poore, *Beaumont*, p. 42.
15 T. Dickinson, 'The Anglo-Saxon Burial Sites of the Upper Thames Region', Oxford University D.Phil. thesis (1976).

century decorated pottery and loomweights.[16] The assemblage of Ipswich ware from the Sackler Library excavation and the present site is the only occurrence of this particularly diagnostic pottery known from Oxford to date. Its concentration within this relatively small area implies a focus of activity here during the eighth and ninth centuries, and possibly earlier. By this time there was an established crossing of the Thames at Oxford, and there is increasing archaeological evidence for the existence of the minster of St Frideswide, traditionally believed to have been founded on what is now the site of Oxford Cathedral in the early eighth century.[17] More widely, early to middle Anglo-Saxon pottery and a fragmentary finger ring of sixth- or seventh-century date have been found in excavations at Oxford Castle, along with the remains of a building and associated features that predate the foundation of the defended *burh* of the late ninth or early tenth century.[18] Excavations at Nos. 6–7 High Street have uncovered a pit radiocarbon dated to the late eighth to ninth century cal. AD.[19]

The only possible evidence for late Anglo-Saxon activity on the present site comprised single sherds of St Neots ware (850–1100) and Stamford ware (850–1150), both of which occurred redeposited in much later features. The earliest stratified features (Phase 2; Fig. 11.5) contained small quantities of Cotswolds-type ware (975–1350). Though this could feasibly indicate a date in the first part of the eleventh century, the assemblage, given its small size, may simply lack the defining wares of Phase 3. Indeed, the scarcity of late Anglo-Saxon pottery and other objects from the present site and the nearby excavations would strongly suggest that the area was not built up at this time. It has been suggested that before the late twelfth century there was still adequate room for expansion inside the walls of the town, with no great pressure for new suburban development.[20]

The Early Development of the Site (Late Eleventh to Twelfth Centuries)

The earliest features (Phase 2) included two parallel small ditches or gullies (514 and 1275) aligned perpendicular to St Giles' Street (Fig. 11.5). Unfortunately, their relationship with the larger Phase 3 ditches (1387 and 1388) could not be determined, which makes it difficult to interpret their function. Ditches 514 and 1275 may have been associated with an early entrance to Beaumont Palace from St Giles' Street, but if they did continue westwards beyond the larger Phase 3 ditches, no evidence for them was found on the Sackler Library site. Alternatively, both sets of ditches may have formed part of a rectilinear enclosure whose south-west corner lay just outside the excavated area, though this seems less likely given that the Phase 3 ditches were significantly more substantial. A third possibility is that they may have been associated with early land apportionment between the boundary of Beaumont Palace and St Giles' Street. The line of ditch 1275 subsequently became established as a long-lived property boundary (see below). Ditches 514 and 1275 contained some animal bone (cow, sheep and pig), with ditch 514 also containing fish bone and charred free-threshing wheat, suggesting food preparation and consumption nearby, but there was very limited dating evidence for this activity.

It seems likely that the two parallel ditches 1387 and 1388 (Phase 3), which both appear to have been open at the same time, marked the initial rear boundary of properties fronting onto St Giles' Street. They represented, stratigraphically, the earliest features along the western side of the excavated area. They contained sherds of medieval Oxford ware (1075–1350) and were cut by thirteenth to fourteenth century pits (Phase 4). These ditches are within 3 m of the boundary of the Beaumont Palace/Whitefriars precinct as depicted by Salter, Agas (1578), Hollar (1643), Loggan (1675) and later maps. It seems unlikely, however, that these relatively

16 D. Radford, 'Archaeological Work in Oxford City, 2009', *Oxoniensia*, 75 (2010), p. 219.

17 Dodd, *Oxford*, pp. 13–19.

18 Munby, *Oxford Castle*.

19 '6–7 High Street, Oxford, Archaeological Excavation Report', unpublished OA report (2014), https://library.thehumanjourney.net/998/.

20 Dodd, *Oxford*, pp. 61–2.

insubstantial ditches would have been the palace boundary, and the Swalcliffe grant to Osney noted above refers to the existence of a wall. It is possible that a boundary wall for the palace precinct lay within the *c.*2.5 m unexcavated strip between the present site and the Sackler Library excavations. However, it also seems possible that the north–south robber trench that was found on the Sackler Library site, some 9 m to the west of the ditches, may have marked the position of a boundary wall, although it was considered by the excavators to have been part of a building. The robber trench in fact corresponds exactly with the boundary shown on Faden's map (1789), which may be the same as the boundary shown on Agas' map.

The fills of ditch 1388 on the present site contained abundant mortar that is likely to have come from the construction or repair of a nearby wall. These fills did not contain the Brill/Boarstall wares that dominate medieval pottery assemblages of the thirteenth century and later in Oxford, and the construction or repair of the nearby wall is therefore likely to have taken place before *c.*1200. All the pits interpreted as tree-planting pits from the palace orchard (see above) were situated to the west of the robber trench, apart from a single pit located *c.*2 m to its east. Poore and Wilkinson considered that the existence of this eastern pit meant that the palace precinct extended beyond the line of the robber trench.[21] However, the published plan shows a row of four equally spaced pits that would have run parallel to, and *c.*2 m inside, the robber trench, suggesting that their placing had been influenced by a pre-existing boundary. In addition, the easternmost pit (details of which were not published) does not fit easily within the grid pattern of those found to its west. It could pertain to the rear of Property 2 on St Giles' Street, an area that had become densely pitted during the thirteenth to fifteenth centuries (see below).

The area of the present excavations lay some distance from the St Giles' Street frontage and throughout the medieval period the principal buildings would have been to the east of the excavated area, which would have remained largely open yard or garden space where pits and wells could be dug. Relatively few pits were datable to the period before *c.*1200 (Phases 2 and 3; Fig. 11.5); most were under 1 m in depth and were used to dispose of domestic rubbish. These have been dated to the twelfth century on the basis that they do not contain Brill/Boarstall pottery, but numerous pits produced fragments of plain, flat roof tiles, which are not thought to have been in use in Britain prior to the mid to later twelfth century.[22] The presence of the tile, together with the absence of Brill/Boarstall ware, therefore supports the conclusion reached at the Ashmolean Forecourt site, that the development of occupied tenements in this area can probably be dated to the late twelfth century onwards.[23] A number of the pits can be seen to follow the alignment of the later property boundaries. Pits were commonly located along tenement boundaries in this way in medieval towns, and this provides evidence that boundaries had been established by this time between Properties 1, 2 and 3.

Two of the pits in Property 1 (1050 and 1068) and a third within Property 2 (1285) were over 4 m deep and are likely to have been wells, though the modern water table was not reached at this depth. Given their circular shape, pits 1050 and 1068 may have been lined with reused and stacked barrels, whose remains have subsequently decayed. A similar method of lining medieval wells has been found at York[24] and Bristol.[25] However, the pits had diameters in excess of 2.1 m, considerably greater than the largest barrel (tun) used for beer/ale, so perhaps the barrels were placed free-standing in the pit with packing around their sides. Such a method of construction could be proposed for thirteenth or fourteenth century well 663 (Fig. 11.8).

21 Poore, *Beaumont*, fig. 14.

22 J. Schofield and A. Vince, *Medieval Towns: The Archaeology of British Towns in their European Setting*, 2nd edn (2005), p. 129.

23 R. Montague and L. Mepham, 'The Ceramic and Stone Building Material', in Andrews and Mepham, 'Ashmolean Museum Forecourt', pp. 208–10.

24 R.A. Hall, *Book of York* (1996).

25 B.M. Ford et al., *From Bridgehead to Brewery. The Medieval and Post-Medieval Archaeological Remains from Finzel's Reach, Bristol*, Oxford Archaeology Monograph, 27 (2017).

Finds and environmental evidence was limited for these early phases, but one notable find was a stylus of thirteenth to fourteenth century type from a mortar-rich fill (597) of ditch 1388. Elsewhere, the presence of the appreciable quantities of plain roof tiles within the pits in Property 2 suggests construction or modification of substantial buildings on the property from the later twelfth century; such buildings were presumably located towards the street frontage. Roof tiles were largely absent from the pits within Property 1 in this phase. Occupation appears to have been domestic, and is comparable with the evidence from the contemporary pits at the Ashmolean Forecourt. The majority of the animal bone came from the boundary ditch/gully between Properties 2 and 3 and represented a mixture of butchery and kitchen waste.

Rising Fortunes: Tenement Development in the Thirteenth and Fourteenth Centuries (Fig. 11.7)
The thirteenth and fourteenth centuries saw a significant rise in the intensity of use of the site and the properties expanded westwards across the former ditches 1388 and 1387; as before, it is assumed that the contemporary buildings were located towards the St Giles' Street frontage. The boundaries between the three properties became more clearly defined, especially the boundary between the rear of Properties 1 and 2, which was marked by a narrow wall (325). The division between Properties 2 and 3 was marked by a fence that followed the line of the earlier ditch 1275 (see above).

Two distinct phases of pit digging had taken place on Property 2, the earlier consisting of large rectangular pits interpreted as quarries, and the later of small round rubbish pits and wells. Both phases contained the defining pottery of the thirteenth century, Brill/Boarstall ware (*c*.1200–1600), though the scarcity of exclusively fourteenth century pottery meant that many features cannot be dated more closely than to the thirteenth to fourteenth centuries. At the east end of the site, however, a closer dating sequence can be proposed (see below). The quarries at this end of the site (Group 1404) were large and of some depth suggesting that substantial quantities of gravel had been excavated, prior to the construction of successive wells within a well house. The gravel may have been used for yards to the rear of houses, although it could also have been used for the resurfacing of the street outside, since the duty of street maintenance in medieval towns fell on the citizens. Similar pits were found at the Classics Centre and at the Ashmolean Forecourt.[26] The shallower quarry pits of Group 1400 may also have been used to extract soil for beaten earth flooring. Postholes forming a rectilinear structure at the east end of Property 2, Structure 1402, were probably for a well house attached to the rear of a building, and represented the only medieval building within the excavated area. Two wells, 663 and 1176, one probably a successor to the other, appeared to be contained within this structure. The continuing presence of ceramic and stone building material in pits suggests that there were more substantial buildings elsewhere on the properties. Roof tiles, including some glazed ridge tile fragments, were more abundant on Property 2 than Property 1, but it is unclear whether this reflects a genuine difference in building styles and materials at this date, or whether it simply reflects the fact that much less of Property 1 was excavated. The pottery assemblage from Property 1 did, however, include an unusual modelled deer's antler, which may have come from a decorative roof finial (Blinkhorn, below).

The backfills of well 663 (Fig. 11.8) contained a number of items of particular interest. Three of these were fragments of architectural stonework, all found in fill 662. The finest was a fragment of limestone window tympanum with an outer roll moulding forming an overall arch and an inner roll which forms the head of a window light (Fig. 11.16). The second fragment was from a quoin with a plain chamfered corner; the weathered surface suggests this was a jamb for an external door or window. The third piece appears to be a corner section of a window frame.

26 Norton and Cockin, 'Classics Centre', p. 176; Andrews and Mepham, 'Ashmolean Museum Forecourt', p. 195.

This is a roughly made piece and probably came from a lower status building. In the underlying fill (1151) was a group of complete and nearly complete stone roof tiles.

It is possible that this stonework derives from buildings at the adjacent palace, although there is no other evidence that material from there found its way onto the present site in the thirteenth and fourteenth centuries; conversely, the presence of medieval stained window glass fragments in late sixteenth to seventeenth century deposits suggests that this did happen when the redundant buildings of the friary were demolished after the Dissolution (see Phase 6, below). This raises the possibility that there was a medieval stone house on the present site, perhaps similar to that at No. 4A Merton Street. At that site a similar though more elaborate window moulding was recovered, which had demonstrably come from one of the original windows of a stone house built there around 1200. A number of other contemporary examples have been noted by Munby;[27] closer to the present site a stone building was seen in the excavations at the Classics Centre, and at the Ashmolean Forecourt a building of timber and stone was replaced by a substantial masonry building in the fourteenth century.

The window tympanum is not closely datable, but it is likely to have come from a building constructed in the twelfth century or (as at No. 4A Merton Street) at the latest *c.*1200. Its presence in the well fill, along with the other architectural fragments and the stone roof tiles, suggests that there was a phase of building alterations nearby at around the time that well 663 was decommissioned and backfilled, and the replacement of the well may have formed part of this. Although the well could not be excavated to its base, its earliest excavated fill (1150) contained a Scottish silver cut halfpenny that would have been in circulation in England between *c.*1210–50; a second coin of the same type and date was found in a shallow pit (1210) located a short distance to the north of the well. The pottery from the excavated fills of well 663 was contemporary with these coins, and taken together this evidence suggests that the well was decommissioned around the middle of the thirteenth century.

The earliest documentary reference that can be equated with the excavated Property 2 dates from the period *c.*1220–40, when Andrew Marshal granted the Templars the 'houses' that had been given to him by his uncle Andrew Rufus (see above). Andrew Rufus appears as a witness to three charters of Osney abbey dated *c.*1195 concerning properties on the corner of what are now George Street and Magdalen Street,[28] and the tympanum fragment found in the excavations could plausibly have come from his 'houses' built by, or around, this date. The presence of roof tile on this property in what are probably pre-thirteenth-century contexts supports this suggestion (see above).

Little is known about Andrew Marshal's tenure of the property, but the next owner, magister Ralph of Swalcliffe, *medicus*, clearly had a considerable interest here. His first acquisition in the vicinity seems to have been N98, which perhaps corresponds to Property 3 of the excavations, around 1240 (see above). A few years later, *c.*1245, he acquired the larger holding N97 from the Templars, and around 1250 he appears to buy out the residual interests of John Plumbar and John Halegod in N98 (see above), thus consolidating the two properties into a single holding. This would provide a convincing context for a campaign of building and renovation at the site, which the archaeological evidence suggests could have included the decommissioning of an old well and the replacement of old windows, perhaps with a more fashionable style.

Clear evidence was recovered in the excavations for property boundaries of this period (see above) and this evidence strongly suggests that N98 may not originally have been the small frontage property suggested by Salter (Fig. 11.2a) but a full-length tenement running from St Giles' Street to the palace wall (Fig. 11.3). No evidence was recovered for the mill mentioned in Ralph of Swalcliffe's grant to Osney, although it is possible that this was located on Property 3,

27 J. Munby, 'Worked Stone' and 'Stone Houses in Oxford', in Poore, 'No. 4A Merton St.', pp. 305, 340–1, fig. 5 and plate XI.

28 Salter, *Oseney*, vol. 2, pp. 275–7.

very little of which was actually seen in the excavations. The grant confirms that the property extended from St Giles' Street all the way back to the palace wall, which is explicitly mentioned (see above).

Evidence from the finds and environmental assemblages is consistent with domestic occupation, with relatively little to distinguish between the three properties. However, there was an unusually high representation of ceramic lamps in the pottery from Property 2. At the Classics Centre the high incidence of such lamps was interpreted as evidence for the use of the property as lodgings for scholars, and unusually large numbers of ceramic lamps have also previously been noted in excavations at Merton College.[29] Here, however, the occurrence of lamps in the backfill of well 663 suggests that they may have been in use during Ralph and John of Swalcliffe's ownership of the property.

Fifteenth to Mid Sixteenth Centuries (Fig. 11.9)

The population of England fell by between a third and a half following the agricultural crises and plagues of the fourteenth century. In medieval towns this is often reflected in the suburbs, which expanded when population levels were high in the thirteenth century, but were vulnerable to depopulation once the demand for housing had fallen. The archaeological evidence for this is hard to interpret, however, and while a falling level of occupation could lead to abandonment and ruin, it could also provide opportunities for improved living conditions. At the present site, the pottery assemblage contains very little material of late-medieval date such as Tudor green ware (*c.*1475–1500) and Cistercian ware (1475–1700), and this is consistent with a reduction in the intensity of use of the site at this time. There were far fewer pits in this period in Property 2, and a garden soil accumulated in the northern part of the excavated area, which was to persist until the nineteenth century. However, there are signs that the properties continued to be occupied. Appreciable quantities of roof tiles were still being deposited in the pits, with an increasing number at Property 1, amongst them an unusual green-glazed ridge tile with a thumbed lower edge. The former well house at Property 2 seems to have remained in use, although now probably serving as a latrine. Continuing evidence for gravel quarrying would imply that buildings, yards and possibly even the street outside, were still being maintained, and the finds assemblages include numerous domestic items such as pins and lace tags, and a glass urinal of fifteenth century date was found on Property 1. Fragments of window glass on both Property 1 and Property 2 are also likely to come from glazing of this date, and the appearance of rabbit and swan in the animal bone assemblages suggests a more diverse diet. Nevertheless, the relative sparsity of occupation at this time is underlined by the fact that a coin and a jeton found, probably in situ, in pits on Property 1, are separated by nearly a century in date, the coin, of 1421–2, in quarry pit 412 and the jeton, of 1500–25, in nearby pit 815. A possible steelyard weight found within Property 2 would have been used by traders to weigh small ounce-sized items of merchandise so perhaps a shop operated on the property. A hiatus of occupation from *c.*1400–75 was suggested at the Classics Centre, and lulls in activity from the fourteenth century onwards have been identified elsewhere in the northern suburb at 1–12 Magdalen Street and the Kendrew Quadrangle, St John's College. However, occupation apparently continued unabated during the late fourteenth to fifteenth century at the Ashmolean Forecourt.[30]

[29] Norton and Cockin, 'Classics Centre', p. 169; P. Blinkhorn, 'Pottery', in Poore, 'No. 4A Merton St.', p. 261.

[30] Norton and Cockin, 'Classics Centre', p. 169; C. Bateman et al., 'Medieval Oxford's Northern Suburb: Evidence from Recent Work at 1–12 Magdalen Street', unpublished Cotswold Archaeology report (2000); S. Wallis, *The Oxford Henge and Late Anglo-Saxon Massacre, with Medieval and Later Occupation at St John's College, Oxford* (2014); Andrews and Mepham, 'Ashmolean Museum Forecourt', pp. 188–95.

Urban Pressures and Sub-Divided Tenements: Late Sixteenth to Eighteenth Century (Figs. 11.11–11.12)

From the seventeenth century, the expanding population of the town resulted in the creation of living space in the backs of most of the properties fronting St Giles' Street, and this can be seen on Loggan's map of 1675 (Fig. 11.2b). The sub-division of these back yard and garden areas is also evident on the earlier maps of Hollar (*c.*1643) and Agas (1578), though few buildings are depicted and N68 (Property 1) is described as two messuages in *c.*1770.[31] Due to the inherent inaccuracies of both Agas' and Hollar's maps, it is not possible with any degree of certainty to overlay these early maps onto the modern topography. However, Loggan and later maps do correspond reasonably well to the archaeological evidence.

The rear part of Property 2 was divided by the construction of a wall, which seems to have had the effect of dividing this part of the property into two areas or tenements (2E and 2W). The dating evidence from the associated clay pipe fragments suggests that this had happened by the second half of the seventeenth century. The wall seemed to stop at its junction with Property 3, implying that the width of the property remained unchanged at this point. Traces of a large rectangular stone structure (Building 1379) abutted its east side, which corresponds to an extended structure depicted by Loggan (1675). Given its shallow wall foundations it is likely that this building was timber-framed, possibly a house or cottage. Loggan appears to show another smaller structure at right-angles to the west end of Building 1379, which is linked on its south side to a wall corresponding to wall 1384.

The finds and food remains offered a good insight into the life of the inhabitants in the late sixteenth and seventeenth centuries. Curiously, the evidence for subdivision of the tenements into smaller houses is nevertheless accompanied by signs of a rising standard of living. Samples from latrine pit 1373 were rich in fruit remains, predominantly fig and wild strawberry, and notably included quince. This is a bitter fruit that was used to make quince jelly, and in medieval Europe was praised by physicians for aiding digestion and as a cure for heartache.[32] Other finds from Property 2W included a glass flask, drape rings, and a decorated hooked clasp. Three further hooked clasps (Fig. 11.24, nos. 18–20) of sixteenth century or later date used as book cover attachments were found in garden soils within the property, suggesting a degree of literacy. A coin weight (Fig. 11.24, no. 16) from the same soil, for weighing a James I gold half angel (1612–25), would imply that the premises continued to be used for trading, perhaps selling merchandise of some value. The garden soils also contained a group of musket balls and a powder holder cover, which are likely to date from the Civil War period, together with fishing net weights that can be associated with the distinctive freshwater fish remains from latrine pit 1373 to suggest occupants who fished in the River Thames nearby.

Despite the apparent lack of expansion of buildings into the rear area of Property 1, there is evidence for increased prosperity. The bird bone assemblage included both swan and the newly introduced turkey, the former considered the height of luxury cuisine in medieval and Elizabethan times.[33] There is less certainty, however, about the provenance of some of the other objects found in pits of this phase, since the fragments of late-medieval window glass are highly likely to have come from demolished buildings of the friary nearby, and the same possibility has to be considered for the late-medieval glass urinal and the fragment of fourteenth-century printed floor tile. During the 1770s, the inhabitants of the property may have had connections with All Souls College since a complete mallet wine bottle was recovered impressed with a seal of the college.

During the late seventeenth and eighteenth centuries, substantial stone cellars were constructed within the eastern and western divisions of Property 2 (Figs. 11.11–11.12). The larger

31 Salter, *Survey of Oxford*, vol. 2, p. 215.
32 M.W. Adamson, *Food in Medieval Times* (2004), p. 20.
33 Ibid. p. 39.

(vaulted cellar 1354) was constructed within the earlier house 1379, suggesting a growing requirement for storage, and can be dated to 1752 by a marked quoin stone on its entranceway. Taylor's map (1750) shows a small structure attached to the south side of the house, which probably corresponds to the building containing cellar 176, which dating evidence suggests was constructed after *c.*1660. Much glass associated with wine consumption was found within Properties 1 and 2 suggesting that a tavern or inn existed on or near the site in the eighteenth century. Part of a stoneware tavern-mug with a Queen Anne (1702–14) stamped assay ale-mark was found in a pit within Property 2W, together with 22 perforated oast or malting kiln tiles of eighteenth-century type (Fig. 11.17, no. 4). Such tiles would have formed the raised floors of oast houses or malting kilns and are usually associated with the brewing of ale. If such production occurred on the site then no such malting structure was identified, unless cellar 176, which contained evidence of a suspended floor, was suitably adapted. No firm documentary evidence has been identified for a tavern or inn on the site at this time, though the Hare and Hounds was recorded at No. 66 St Giles' Street (the site of the Classics Centre) in 1697. Pigot's 1830 directory lists a pub on the west side of St Giles' Street called the Chequers, with the landlord being William Jannaway, and the Robin Hood at No. 78 was demolished in 1841 to make way for the Ashmolean Museum.[34] The same directory also lists a maltster, Wm. Eaton Burrows, with premises somewhere on St Giles' Street. This may have been the same person as, or a descendant of, the William Burrows who is listed as a maltster in the Universal Business Directory for Oxford 1794–5.[35]

The depictions of the site from Loggan (1675) to Faden (1789) show that the rear part of the site remained open and contained gardens or open spaces, attached to the houses located towards the frontage.

Nineteenth Century (Fig. 11.14)

By the time of the first Ordnance Survey map (1876), much of the rear of Property 2 contained structures which overlooked a yard to their south, which was accessed from St Giles' Street by a wide passage. The yard was bounded to the south by the rear part of the University Galleries (built 1841–5) and it would appear that by this time Property 3 had been amalgamated with Property 2. This area was known as Wyatt's Yard (No. 74 St Giles' Street) and was contained within a large plot to the rear of Nos. 70–73. It contained the premises known as G. Wyatt & Son (masons and builders) owned by Margaret Wyatt from 1846–61, and later, according to the 1881 census, by Thomas Wyatt who was also in residence.[36] It is in this context that the excavated nineteenth century structures within this property should be seen. Elongated cellared structure 107 possibly served some storage purpose, perhaps for building materials such as lime and sand. During this time cellars 176 and 1354 appear to have been combined into a single structure and probably incorporated the residence and offices of the company's owner.

In contrast, the rear of Property 1 (No. 68 St Giles' Street) remained largely unchanged and is depicted on the first Ordnance Survey map as a garden containing a large glasshouse with a fountain immediately behind a large house on the frontage. During the period 1839–52 it was the premises of George Rackstrow (solicitor) and from 1861–90 of Hawkins & Sylvester (accountant).[37]

[34] 'St Giles, Oxford: Inns and Public Houses', available at http://www.headington.org.uk/oxon/stgiles/history/inns.htm, accessed Dec. 2010.

[35] Some of the principal inhabitants of Oxford in 1794, http://www.headington.org.uk/oxon/people_lists/oxford_1794_universal/index.htm, accessed Dec. 2010.

[36] 'St Giles, Oxford: Nos. 68–73: Extension to Taylorian', http://www.headington.org.uk/oxon/stgiles/tour/west/68_73_taylorian_new.htm, accessed Dec. 2010.

[37] Ibid.

A structure corresponding to the hemicycle of the University Galleries (built 1841–5) was located, although only the red brick foundation of its basement survived.[38] This was demolished and the site of G. Wyatt & Son's premises (No. 74) cleared to make way for the extension to the University Galleries in 1894.[39]

EXCAVATION METHODOLOGY

The development entailed the removal of all deposits to *c.*58.73 m OD in the northern half of the site, or *c.*59.68 m OD in the southern half of the site, to depths of approximately 4.3–5.3 m respectively. This necessitated the destruction of all archaeological deposits except the deepest pits or wells and their preservation by record.[40] The excavation covered the entire footprint of the nineteenth-century extension to the rear of the Ashmolean Museum (Figs. 11.1 and 11.4). Machine excavation, utilising a toothless bucket, was employed to the first significant archaeological horizon. These levels were hand-cleaned exposing seventeenth- to mid nineteenth-century structures and pits that were then fully hand-excavated and recorded, except the large stone cellars, which were excavated by machine. Further machine excavation was used to remove earlier soil formations to a level where negative features such as pits could be identified and then hand-cleaned. All pits were hand-excavated, usually half sectioned, the deepest initially to a maximum depth of 1.2 m. Linear features were subject to 15 per cent sample excavation and all structural features were fully recorded. Those deeper pits that could not be fully excavated by hand were machine excavated and 'grab sampled' for finds and environmental evidence. The very deepest pits such as wells were further investigated during subsequent ground reduction for initial construction works to enable the installation of the 'pile mat'. During the machine-assisted excavation of the earlier soil formations spoil was monitored by a qualified archaeologist, and metal detecting was carried out as part of this process. Wherever possible finds from these soils were assigned to the corresponding contexts identified during partial hand-excavation.

DESCRIPTION OF ARCHAEOLOGICAL DEPOSITS

The site sequence was divided into nine phases, based on stratigraphic relationships and finds dating evidence. For the later periods cartographic evidence provides a *terminus ante quem* for some features.

Phase 1: Undated Natural Features

The surface of the Quaternary River Gravels rose gently from 62.26 m OD to 62.46 m OD from east to west across the site and where not truncated was overlain by up to 0.25 m of reddish brown loessic loam. A small number of features containing sterile fills similar to the loessic loam were revealed. Some were sealed by it and were therefore probably periglacial, while others were cut through it and can only be broadly dated to the Holocene.

Phase 2: Late Eleventh to Twelfth Century (Fig. 11.5)

Phase 2 features comprise up to four ditches and a scatter of seven other features. The most significant feature was a narrow and shallow south-west to north-east aligned ditch (1275) that ran along the south side of the site and perpendicular to St Giles' Street to its east. It had a slightly concave profile and where its full extent survived, measured 0.60–0.80 m in width.

38 A cross-section of the basement is shown on a drawing by Cockerell of *c.*1842: Oxford University Estates Service, 'Ashmolean Museum Conservation Plan' (2012), fig. 4.

39 History of the Ashmolean, http://www.ashmolean.org/about/historyandfuture/, accessed Dec. 2010.

40 The brief and methodology of the fieldwork are described in 'Ashmolean Museum, Beaumont St. Oxford: Post-Excavation Assessment and Updated Project Design', unpublished OA report (2008).

Fig. 11.4 The excavation in progress (looking east).

Fig. 11.5 Phases 2–3: late eleventh to twelfth century.

It varied in depth from 0.20–0.60 m and was filled with reddish brown silt similar to that of the loessic loam that it cut, suggesting that it silted up naturally. It was largely devoid of finds apart from a section that was cut towards its west end from which two sherds of Cotswold-type ware and very small quantities of cow, sheep and eel bones were recovered. Two further ditches (1020 and 514) ran parallel to it on either side, both of similar dimensions and fills, suggesting some degree of contemporaneity or association. Ditch 514 contained a single sherd of early-middle Anglo-Saxon pottery, a small quantity of animal bone including cow, sheep and pig, and charred free-threshing wheat grains, suggesting occupation fairly close-by. The other features, all located to the north of the ditches, were small shallow pits of indeterminable function but probably not of natural origin on account of their regular shape. Several (566, 695 and 1268) contained a few sherds of Cotswold-type ware. Pit 566 also contained parts of a sheep and of a cattle skull. The undated features are assumed to be broadly contemporary based on having almost identical fills (redeposited loessic silt and river gravels) to the dated features. The most significant of these was vertical sided sub-rectangular pit 585, which was cut by twelfth century ditch 1388 (see below). It was at least 1.2 m deep, and compact green-stained sandy silts within its upper fills suggest it had been used as a cesspit.

Phase 3: Twelfth Century (Fig. 11.5)

Boundaries Two parallel ditches (1388 and 1387) at the western edge of the site were dated to this phase and were shown stratigraphically, with the exception of pit 585 (see above), to represent the earliest activity on this part of the site. A further 24 features, mainly pits, were also allocated to this phase given their early stratigraphic position and the presence of the defining pottery fabrics of medieval Oxford ware and North-East Wiltshire ware that are datable to 1075–1350 and 1050–1400 respectively. Although the date ranges of these fabric traditions are very wide, the complete absence from these features of Brill/Boarstall ware (1200–1600), a fabric that occurs extensively in Oxford, supports a twelfth-century date. The western ditch (1388) was aligned approximately north-west to south-east, parallel to St Giles' Street to the east, and was traced along the full length of the excavated area. Although extensively disturbed by later pits (and perhaps by general truncation) its full width was found to vary widely from 1.1–2.0 m. Excavated sections typically revealed that the ditch was flat-bottomed with concave shallow sides and varied in depth from 0.50 m at its southern end becoming shallower towards the north to 0.35 m (Fig. 11.6, Section 172). Over most of its length it had a single sterile fill of firm reddish-brown sandy silt probably derived from the weathering of its edges, though one section contained a sherd of medieval Oxford ware, and cow and sheep bones including the base of a horncore. A section close to its southern end revealed more deliberate in-filling of compact greyish brown clay silt containing much mortar and a lead stylus, above which was a very compact deposit of gravel and mortar. The compaction of the latter fill suggests that it may have acted as a surface that had been laid over the ditch, possibly, given the lack of silting at this point, when the remaining part of the ditch remained open. The abundance of mortar in these fills implies the existence of a masonry wall nearby. Ditch 1387 ran approximately parallel to ditch 1388, some 1.0 m to its east, though the gap narrowed to less than 0.3 m at its southern end at the point where both ditches survived to their deepest extent, possibly because less truncation had occurred here. It was somewhat narrower, measuring 0.75–1.1 m in width but with a similar profile and varied in depth from 0.30 m at its north end to 0.90 m at its southern extent (Fig. 11.6, Section 172). It also contained a single sterile fill of weathered natural throughout most of its length, from which a sherd of medieval Oxford ware and articulated pig bones were recovered (excavated sections 871 and 605). However, at its south end the fill was somewhat darker and more mottled suggesting deliberate infilling, and the lack of weathered silts suggests, as with ditch 1388, that it had been similarly filled at this point before the remaining part of the ditch had silted up. This would suggest that both ditches had been open at the same time. The pits were confined to the east of the ditches, and the majority were located towards the eastern half of the

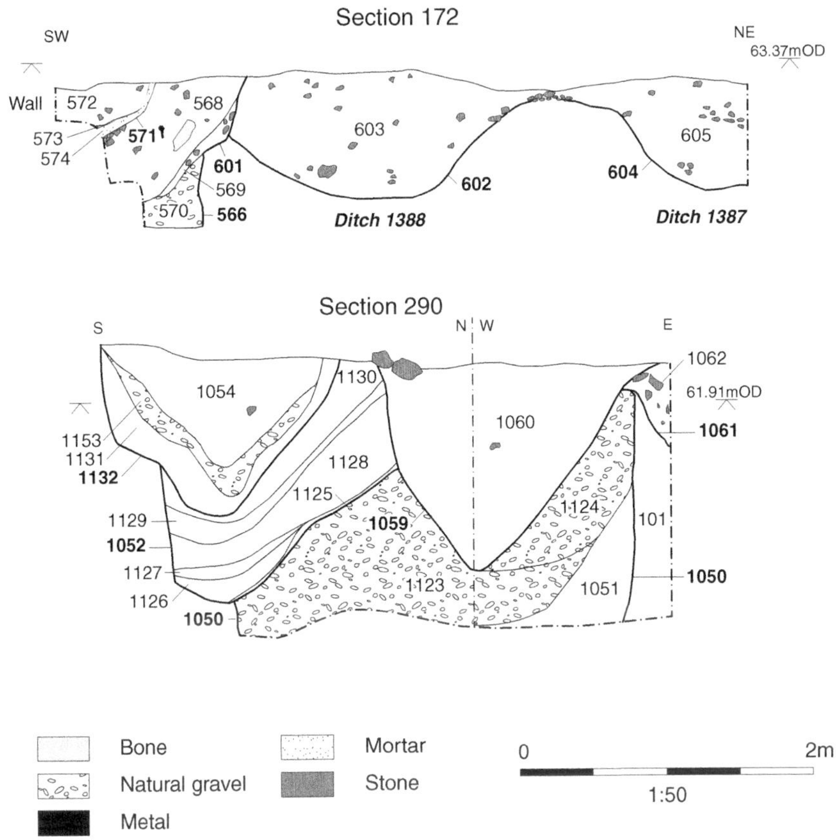

Fig. 11.6 Sections 172 and 290.

site suggesting that they were associated with occupation focused towards the St Giles' Street frontage. A clear line of pits and possible wells occurs alongside the line of the later boundary between Properties 1 and 2, although the pits within what was to become Property 2 seem to be spread over a rather wider area. The boundary between Properties 1 and 2 became more defined during Phase 4 but the pit alignment suggests that it existed by this point. Ditch 1275 seems to have gone out of use in this phase, since it was cut by pits 765, 1272 and 1215.

Property 1 Circular pits 1050 (Fig. 11.6, Section 290) and 1068 measured 2.1 m and 2.55 m in diameter respectively and represent the earliest in a sequence of a dense cluster of pitting. Mechanical excavation showed that they were both more than 4.1 m in depth suggesting that they may have served as wells. If so, they would presumably have been lined though no remains of the linings survived; greyish brown silty clay was observed to adhere to the sides of pit 1050 and could indicate decayed timber. In addition, the sides of each feature were straight and vertical suggesting they had both been protected from the elements. Pit 1050 had been rapidly filled with natural sand largely devoid of finds and gravel apart from a few fragments of slag. However, the upper fills of pit 1068 contained an appreciable quantity of pottery and animal bones (sheep, cattle, pig and roe deer) suggesting that it had been used as a rubbish pit. It is possible that 1050 was filled with the upcast from adjacent well 1068 and as such may have been the direct precursor to it. The remaining pits towards the east of the property were too fragmentary to warrant further comment though both 852 and 1094 contained fragments of roof tile suggesting the presence of a structure nearby. Ovoid pit 704 was located at the west end of the property immediately to the east of ditch 1387 though any interception with it had been removed by a modern foundation. The pit was 1.38 m deep and had been filled with dumps of redeposited natural sand and gravel with relatively little rubbish given the size of the pit. It may have served as a quarry since its position against the edge of the ditch could have facilitated the extraction of the gravel.

Property 2 The majority of pits were clustered towards the south side of the property and these comprised mainly small and shallow circular or rectangular pits (656, 765, 973, 1108 and 1178). These appear to have been dug for the disposal of rubbish, predominantly cattle, pig and sheep bones. Many also contained a fair amount of Cotswold-type and medieval Oxford ware suggesting a date in the twelfth century. All the pits contained fragments of ceramic roof tiles, some with evidence of faint glaze, which seem likely to derive from the construction of buildings towards the St Giles' Street frontage. Vertical-sided sub-rectangular pit 1285 may have served as a well since machine excavation revealed its depth to have been more than 3.5 m. The easternmost pit (1215), at 1.8 m in depth, was somewhat deeper than the other rubbish pits and contained a 0.50 m thick layer of greenish-grey silty clay at its base. Given its position and the nature of its primary fill, it may have served as a cesspit possibly positioned immediately to the rear of structures located towards St Giles' Street.

Property 3 Two features occurred within the limited area excavated: a linear feature, 673, which cut shallow pit 679. Both produced medieval Oxford ware. Linear feature 673 measured 0.8 m in width and 0.8 m in depth and given its vertical profile may represent a robbed wall, though no evidence was found for this in its fills.

Phase 4: Thirteenth to Fourteenth Century (Fig. 11.7)

Boundaries During this phase the two parallel ditches (1388 and 1387) located at the western edge of the site had gone out of use and had been cut through by a number of pits pertaining to the rear of properties fronting St Giles' Street. This would imply that a new boundary was established further to the west and outside the excavated area. At the same time the boundary between Properties 1 and 2 became more defined by the construction of a narrow east–west-aligned stone wall foundation (325) that extended over the line of the former parallel ditches 1388 and 1387. This boundary would remain essentially unchanged throughout Phases 5–8, the immediate area to its north and south remaining mostly devoid of pits. It may have replaced a timber fence, located slightly further south, possibly defined by stratigraphically early postholes 825, 336 and 1288. Posthole 825 cut boundary ditch 1387 (Phase 3) and contained Brill/Boarstall pottery datable to 1200–1600. The southern boundary of Property 2 may have been delimited at this stage by a fence marked by shallow postholes 523, 197, 1264, 1262 and 1260 located slightly south of Phase 2 ditch 1275. Large parts of the area immediately to the north of this line remained devoid of pits and (with the exception of pit 478) pits did not intercept its line until Phase 7.

Property 1 Fifteen pits were identified, arranged in three groups spread widely along the property and with large areas between them apparently devoid of pitting. There was no evidence for structures or other features. Seven pits were located at the west end of the site, six of them stratigraphically later than the filling of the boundary ditches of Phase 3, suggesting that the tenement extended at least this far west by this time. Two of the pits (877 and 901) were shallow and contained no finds whilst pit 773 appears to have been dug to dispose of a dead dog. Circular pit 870 was significantly deeper at 2.7 m, and was possibly a well. Although there were no remains of a lining, its straight and vertical sides suggest either that the pit was not left open to the elements for any length of time or that they were otherwise protected by timber. It appears to have been rapidly filled with yellowish sandy silt before being levelled

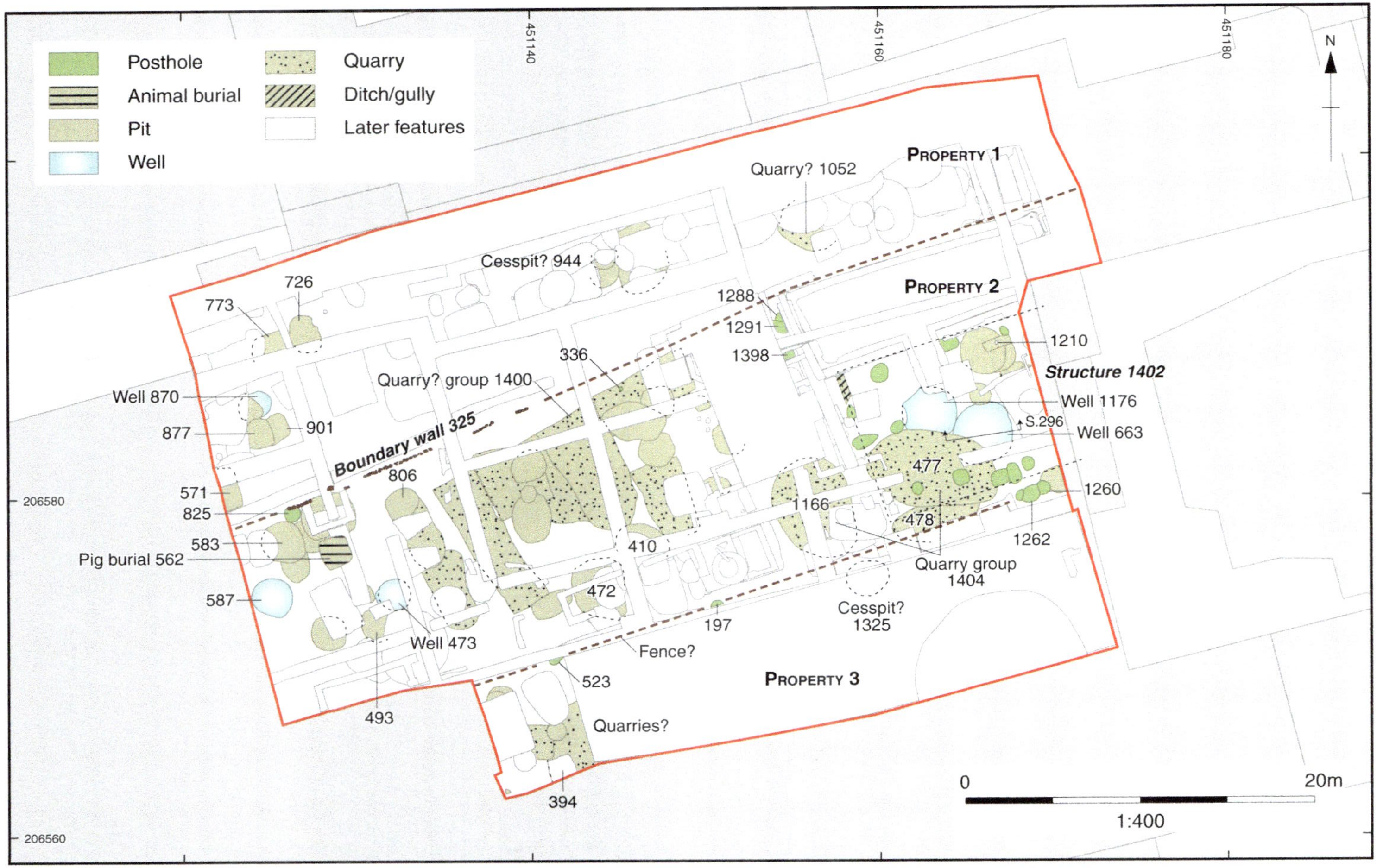

Fig. 11.7 Phase 4: thirteenth to fourteenth century.

with a darker grey-brown sandy silt containing much animal bone, an iron table knife and pottery including much Brill/Boarstall ware. Pit 571 included dumps of whitish-grey and brown mortar, presumably construction debris from a nearby wall. The central group comprised five similarly sized pits, four of which were rectangular and measured 0.42–0.55 m in depth and contained small quantities of animal bone and pottery. Pit 944 contained rich greenish-brown 'organic' fills that may indicate use as a cesspit. The only notable pit from the eastern group was rectangular feature 1052, which at 5.0 m across was significantly larger than the other pits within the property. The pit was 1.58 m deep with very irregular sides, possibly because of quarrying of the natural gravel. The basal fills of the pit comprised thick redeposited gravel with few finds, although a sherd of Surrey whiteware (mid thirteenth to mid fifteenth century) was recovered. The pit was eventually levelled with dumps of dark grey silty clay containing domestic refuse.

Property 2 The thirteenth and fourteenth century saw a marked increase in pit digging in Property 2, which resulted in a dense distribution across most of the excavated area. Although it was not possible using the dating evidence to suggest a close chronological sequence it is clear that two types of pits were present. Where stratigraphic relationships existed, the earlier pits (for example Group 1400 and 1404) were significantly larger, rectangular and arranged in two groups, clustering towards the property boundaries. The remaining pits were mainly smaller, circular and generally contained more finds. They included up to three wells, two of which may have been located within a timber structure (Group 1402).

Pit group 1400 comprised a tight cluster of eight large and shallow elongated rectangular pits. Their northern extents formed a straight line close to, but askew, to boundary wall 325 suggesting that they were aligned on an earlier precursor to the boundary or that space for access was left between the boundary wall and the pits. The pits were roughly the same width (2.4–3.0 m) and depth (*c.*0.40–0.50 m) but varied in length from 3.0–7.5 m and were all flat-bottomed. Most were filled with a single homogenous dark grey sandy silt suggesting that they had all been deliberately and rapidly infilled shortly after digging. Some contained animal bone and pottery, but not in sufficient quantity to suggest that they functioned primarily as rubbish pits. All penetrated the base of the natural loessic loam. Many of the pits contained quantities of roof tile suggesting that they derive from a period of building construction, presumably from structures located towards the St Giles' Street frontage.

Pit group 1404 comprised three large pits (477, 478, 1166) measuring 5.2–6.8 m across and located alongside the southern boundary of the property; pit 1166 cut the backfill of possible well 1285 (see Phase 3). The pits were slightly irregular in plan and 1.1–1.8 m in depth, and were filled with a succession of dark grey sandy silts containing tips of domestic refuse such animal bone, pottery and burnt grain (largely wheat; samples 164 and 165). At the base of pit 477 were the articulated remains of a dog. However, as with pit group 1400, the material was not present in any great quantity given the size of the pits. The pits dug deep into the underlying gravel and therefore may originally have served as quarries to extract gravel for use elsewhere.

A further 32 pits have been assigned to this phase. Although a number clearly post-dated the filling of quarry group 1400, others may have been contemporary with the quarries. The pits were significantly smaller than the possible quarry pits and were distributed more densely towards the rear of the property. Most were circular and measured less than 2 m across and *c.*1.0 m in depth, the majority being less than 0.6 m in depth. Many contained appreciable amounts of animal bone and pottery suggesting that they were dug to dispose of domestic refuse, most notably pits 410, 472, 473 and 493, three of which also contained fragments of sheep, pig and cow skulls and mandibles suggesting the utilisation of head meat. They do not appear to have been used as cesspits though dumps of cesspit-like silt (night waste?) were noted in pit 472, from which a few herring and cod bones were also recovered. Many of the pits, particularly 472 and 583, contained roof tile suggesting construction/demolition waste from nearby structures. Shallow pit 562 seems to have been dug to bury the remains of a pig (Fig. 11.8).

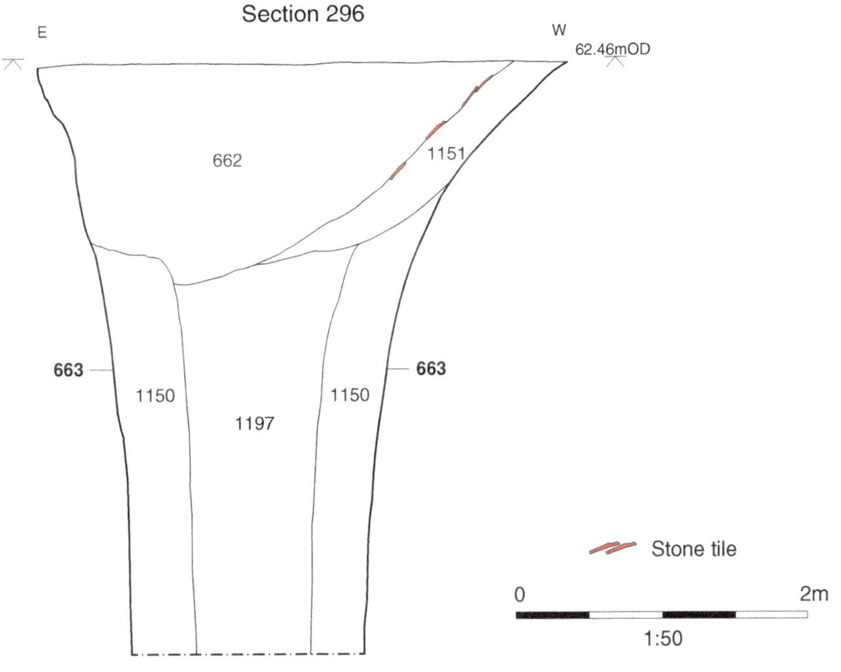

Fig. 11.8 Top: pig burial 562, facing east (scale 0.5 m); bottom: section 296.

It is probable that pits 587 and 473 (located towards the west) and 1176 and 663 (located towards the east) functioned as wells, given their depths. The lower levels of these pits were subject to mechanical excavation and all remained un-bottomed at depths of 3.0 m (4 m for pit 663). All were circular in plan, though pits 473 and 587 were smaller in diameter, at 1.8 and 2.1 m respectively, than pits 663 and 1176, which were 3.4 and 3.2 m in diameter respectively. None had any surviving timber or masonry lining although the edges of pit 1176 seem to have been lined with thin hard orange-brown clay. This could have functioned as a lining to the shaft to stop collapse and the seepage of water or contaminants, or alternatively it may have been infill behind a timber lining that had subsequently decayed. All the pits seemed to have been rapidly filled with single homogeneous deposits of gravelly clay, which would support their interpretation as wells. Their upper levels often contained dumps of refuse, probably as final levelling as the infill settled. The upper levels of pit 663 in particular contained significant quantities of pottery and animal bone, including fragments from at least five ceramic lamps and Potterspury ware datable to the late thirteenth to seventeenth centuries. The earliest recorded fill of the pit contained much Brill/Boarstall pottery (1200–1600) and a Scottish silver cut halfpenny datable to 1195–*c.*1249.

A rectangular arrangement of postholes (Group 1402) around pits 663 and 1176 suggests that these wells were contained within a timber structure, perhaps a well house attached to the rear of buildings towards the street frontage. The postholes were mostly large and circular measuring 0.8–1.1 m across and up to 1.1 m deep; two showed evidence for stone packing. The structure extended up to the boundary with Property 3 and may have measured *c.*8.5 m across and extended at least 10.0 m from the east.

Property 3 Six pits were contained within the excavated area of the property. Only the largest pit was of note (394); with a width of at least 3.5 m this may have been a quarry, but it was only excavated to a depth of 0.90 m. It contained few finds apart from a dump of rubble that contained ceramic and stone roof tiles and a fragment of brown-glazed floor tile. Pit 1325 may have served as a cesspit since its basal fills showed evidence of having been stained with ordure. A large fragment of limestone shouldered roof tile was recovered from its upper fill and together with the material found in pit 399 may attest to the presence of a substantial building nearby.

Phase 5: Fifteenth to Mid Sixteenth Century (Fig. 11.9)

This period was characterised by continued, but less extensive, pit digging for gravel extraction and refuse/cess deposition, and the accumulation of a garden soil horizon within Property 2. Further possible wells were dug within Property 2 and the well house in Property 2 probably continued in use. No features were found in Property 3, and from this phase onwards it is not certain that it continued as a separate tenement plot.

Property 1 The density and distribution of pits remained similar to the preceding phase though they tended to be larger. Eleven pits were assigned to this phase, most of which contained domestic refuse. It is possible that the larger pits were originally quarries, though this is unlikely to be true of the eastern group of pits since they had cut through Phase 4 pits including quarry pit 1052. The most notable pits were rectangular pits (412, 815 and 1017), all of which contained large amounts of animal bone. Pit 412, measuring 3.2 x 2.3 m, was at least 1.2 m deep and had weathered edges suggesting that it had remained open for an appreciable amount of time although it appears finally to have been infilled rapidly, suggesting a quarry or perhaps a well. A French billon coin dated to 1421–2 was found within the upper fill of the pit. Pit 1017 was of a similar size but was bottomed at a depth of 0.86 m and also appears have to have been rapidly filled, suggesting it may originally have been a quarry. Pit 815 was 1.3 m deep and contained part of a fifteenth century glass urinal, a number of bronze pins, a Nuremberg jeton dating to *c.*1500–25 and the remains of a dog and a jackdaw. The only notable finds from the eastern group of pits were from pit 1087, which produced several horncores suggesting bone working.

Property 2 Unlike Property 1, the density of pitting was significantly less than in Phase 4, with only nine pits that could be assigned to this phase. The two wells located towards the east had been filled in. It is possible that the well house structure around them continued in use since a small pit (1214), 1.2 m in depth, was contained within its footprint. It contained thick yellowish green sandy silt at its base that also adhered to its sides, suggesting it had been used as a cesspit, though no mineralised remains were found. The pit was capped with dark grey clay, probably to seal off the odours, and levelled with rubble containing a quantity of roof tiles that might derive from the enclosing structure. A similar sized pit (576; Fig. 11.10, Section 169), 1.66 m in depth, was located at the west end of the site and contained a thin greyish silt at its base over which thick deposits of green-stained weathered natural gravel had developed against

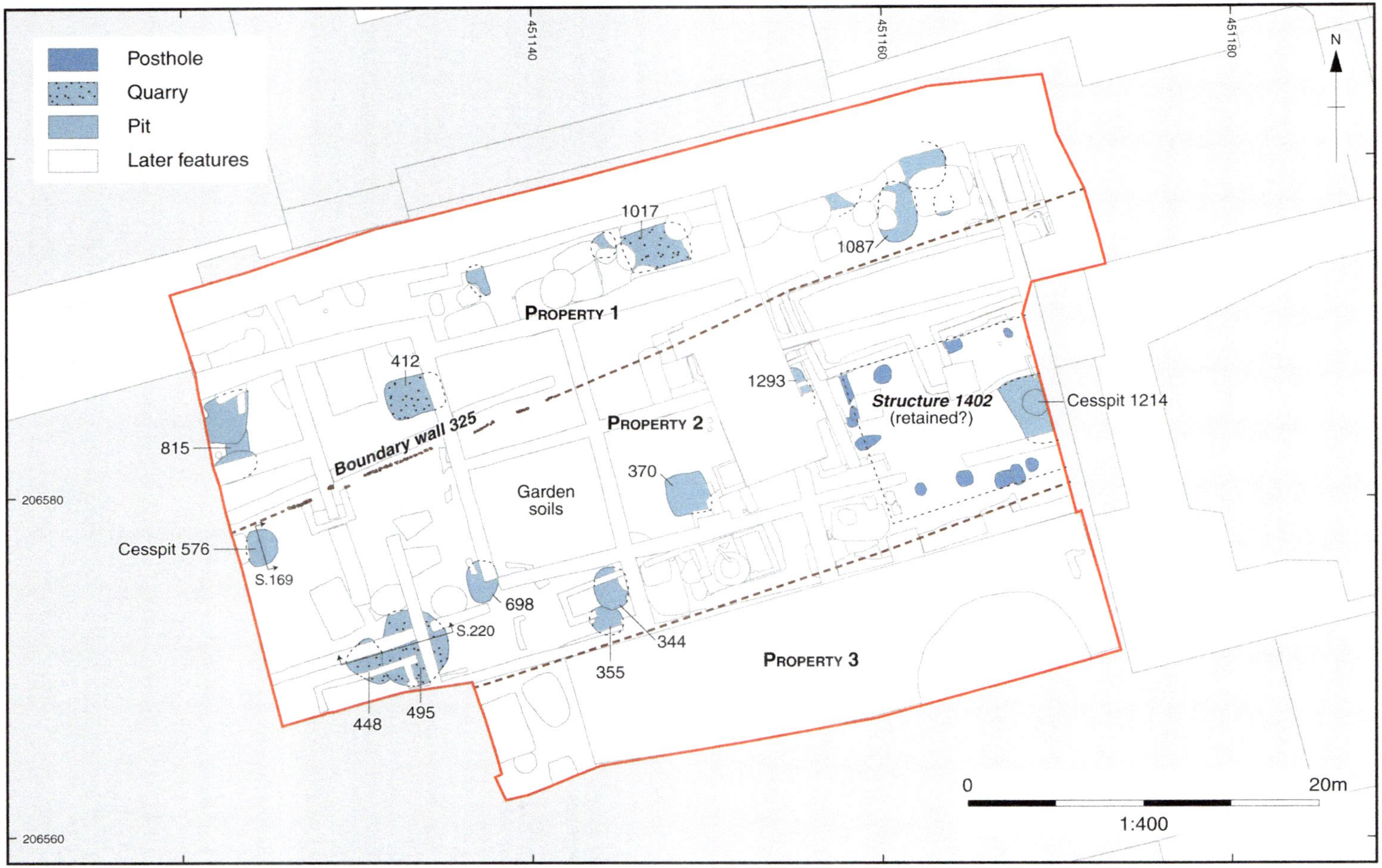

Fig. 11.9 Phase 5: fifteenth to mid sixteenth century.

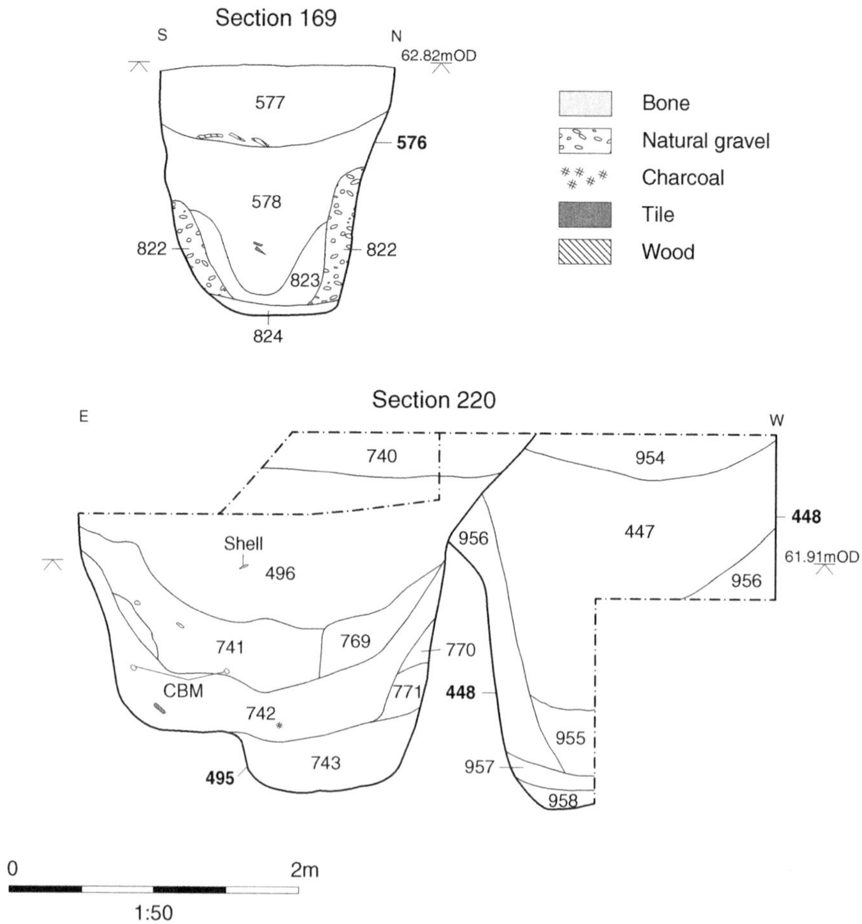

Fig. 11.10 Sections 169 and 220.

its sides. This may suggest that the pit had been left open to the elements before its apparent rapid infilling with dark grey silt that contained a sherd of Tudor green ware (*c.*1450–1550). It was finally levelled with compact dark brown clay that contained a quantity of roof tiles and badly decayed wood fragments, perhaps the remains of a structure around the pit. Vertical-sided oval pits 355 and 698, given their depths of more than 1.4 m and 1.65 m respectively, may have served as wells though no evidence for any linings was found. Both appear to have been rapidly filled (to their excavated depths) with relatively small amounts of refuse though pit 698 contained a large quantity of rubble including many roof tiles. Pit 355 was clipped on its north side by circular pit 344, which was 1.50 m deep and contained a deposit of dark brown-green sandy silt on its sides and base possibly derived from ordure. It was subsequently rapidly filled with rubbish that included sherds of Surrey white ware and Tudor green ware suggesting a mid fifteenth to mid sixteenth century date.

Sub-circular pit 495 (Fig. 11.10, Section 220) measured 4.2 m across and given its depth (2.4 m) may have served as a gravel quarry. Its sides had been slightly undercut suggesting that the underlying gravel had been extracted and its base was somewhat irregular. It contained a thick deposit of loose dirty gravel at its base that accumulated while the pit was open and possibly represents debris left over during the extraction of the gravel. The pit was subsequently used for the disposal of rubbish, including eel and cod/whiting remains. It clipped pit 448 (Fig. 11.10, Section 220), which was of similar depth and may also initially have been a quarry before being used as a rubbish pit. Its upper fills contained sherds of Frechen stoneware suggesting a sixteenth century date.

The only other pit of note was vertical-sided rectangular pit 370 that measured 2.3 m by at least 1.4 m in plan. Its straight sides suggest that it was either lined or otherwise protected from the elements, possibly as a well or a cesspit. It appears to have remained open for a sufficient length of time for a sequence of fills comprising thin alternating layers of soil and redeposited gravel to accumulate. These contained domestic refuse, notably swan bones. In addition, its upper fill contained a fragment of sixteenth century window glass.

By the start of this phase a garden soil had begun to accumulate over the western part of the property. This deposit was mechanically investigated but was seen to abut the south side of wall 325 that defined the boundary with Property 1 (see Phase 4 above). The deposit, a friable brown sandy silt (906), was up to 0.30 m thick and micromorphological analysis confirmed it as strongly amended and biologically worked soil, enriched in ash and phosphate-rich waste, probably derived from domestic waste.[41]

Phase 6: Late Sixteenth to Mid Seventeenth Century (Fig. 11.11)

This period was characterised by the construction of a drystone wall (1384) that sub-divided Property 2 into two areas, 2W to the west and 2E to the east. Subsequently two stone-lined pits (Structures 288 and 186) were built on either side of wall 1384 and probably served as cesspits for the individual properties. A third such pit (Structure 1373) was located on the south side of Property 2W. Remains of a building (Structure 1379) predating mid eighteenth-century cellar 1384 (see Phase 7 below) were found within Property 2E, abutting the boundaries with Properties 1 and 2W. It is possible that this structure is stylistically shown on Loggan's map of Oxford, dated 1675 (Fig. 11.2b).

Wall 1384, measuring 0.6–0.7 m in width, comprised unmortared and roughly hewn limestone blocks set in a shallow foundation trench. Towards the south, where it crossed early pits, the foundations were deeper and comprised larger pitched stones, presumably to create a relieving arch within the foundations to counteract the soft ground. The wall had largely been robbed at the southern extent though a small area of undisturbed natural survived where it would have met the postulated boundary with Property 3. This would imply that the wall terminated before this point suggesting that the boundary with Property 3 was still extant. No dating for its construction was recovered though it cut through Phase 4 pit 1398, which produced Brill/Boarstall pottery broadly datable to 1200–1600. However, it predates the construction of stone-lined pit 1383, which was eventually filled with material containing clay pipes datable to 1660–1720. This could suggest that the wall was in existence by the mid seventeenth century.

Property 1 Most of the excavated area of this property seems to have remained open and set aside for the digging of pits. However, an area adjacent to the boundary with Property 2W, measuring *c.*3–4 m in width, remained free of pits, perhaps to allow access from the east side of the property. Many of the pits contained appreciable quantities of animal bone and pottery suggesting use for the disposal of refuse. Several may originally have been dug as quarries, although one (1143) could have served as a well.

Most of the features to the west had been dug in areas that had previously been free of pits, mostly notably adjacent pits 799 and 859. Both pits were rectangular and of similar size, measuring 2.7–2.8 m across, though pit 859 was somewhat shallower at 0.65 m than pit 799, which was 1.36 m deep. Both contained sequences of gravel-rich silty fills interlaced with thick dumps of rubbish-rich dark silts, with notably high proportions of neonatal sheep and cattle remains, suggesting that both had remained open for an appreciable period of time. Pit 799

41 Report by Macphail and Crowther.

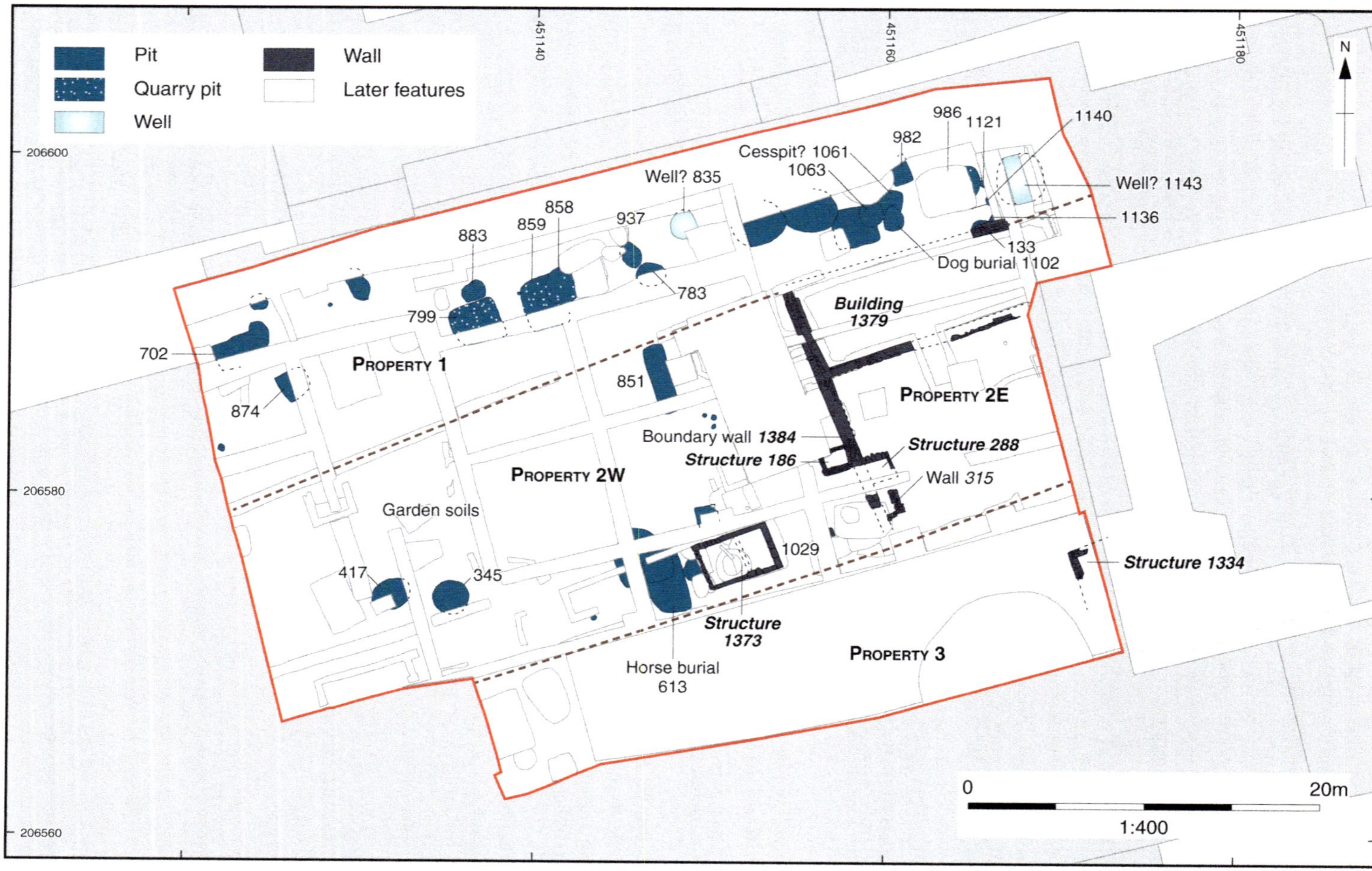

Fig. 11.11 Phase 6: late sixteenth to mid seventeenth century.

contained post-medieval pottery but no clay pipes, and may therefore have been earlier than pit 859, which contained clay pipes datable to 1660–1710; an absence of clay pipe would be consistent with, but does not prove, a date prior to the early seventeenth century. As before, these pits may have originated as quarries prior to being used for refuse disposal. Somewhat irregular and shallow pits 702 and 874, located to their west, may be earlier since they contained clay pipes datable to 1630–55 and 1650–90 respectively. They may have represented quarrying activity though pit 702 contained a rich assemblage of animal bones including sheep skulls and the remains of a cat. The pit also contained fragments of thirteenth to fourteenth century window glass, painted with a foliage design, and many ceramic medieval/early post-medieval roof tiles suggesting a nearby medieval building of some status was being cleared or altered. Probably at some point late in this phase pit 859 was cut through by circular pit 858 which was, at 2.0 m, considerably deeper. It had been rapidly filled with dark grey-brown clayey silt with few finds. Shallow, irregular pit 883, located adjacent to quarry pit 799, had a high charcoal and animal bone content. The pit also contained a Rose farthing of 1639–43 and part of a glass pedestal beaker dateable to the sixteenth to early seventeenth centuries.

The pits to the east are unlikely to have served as quarries given that they had largely cut into earlier pits and overall were shallower in depth. The smaller pits (1102, 1063, 982, 937, 783) were all less than 1.0 m deep and contained relatively few finds; some of these may simply have represented levelling of the top of earlier pits. It is possible that rectangular pit 1061 served as a cesspit given the yellowish stained sandy silt found at its base. Pit 1102 appears to have been dug to bury the remains of a dog.

It is likely that pit 1143 served as a well since machining revealed its depth to have been at least 3.5 m. The pit may have been circular with irregular sides and measured *c.*2.6 m in diameter. However, at a depth of *c.*2.5 m it was observed to have narrowed to a vertical shaft though no evidence for any lining was noted. It is possible that the upper levels of the pit had originally been lined and had subsequently been robbed since the upper fill included a dump of stone rubble. The upper fills of the pit also contained a rich assemblage of animal bones including the articulated remains of a piglet, goose, swan and turkey bones. The fills also contained fragments of a small glass case bottle of seventeenth century date, part of a late-medieval glass urinal as well as tin-glazed pottery dating to *c.*1616–1800. It is possible that the well was contained within a timber structure whose west side was defined by an alignment of three equally spaced small pits (1121, 1140 and 1136). Though mostly removed by later activity, the pits were probably circular, each measuring *c.*0.5–0.6 m in diameter and 0.7–1.16 m deep. The structure could have represented a well house, presumably attached to the rear of a building that fronted St Giles' Street. It is possible that circular pit 835 located to the west also served as a well. Although only investigated to a depth of 1.2 m, its fills tipped down sharply suggesting it may have been substantially deeper than its excavated depth.

Property 2W Located immediately adjacent to the conjectural boundary with Property 3, Structure 1373 was a large rectangular stone-lined pit that may originally have served as a small cellar but was later used as a latrine. It measured 3.8 m in length and 2.2 m in width and approximately 2.0 m in depth, though due to the site conditions the structure was not fully exposed and could not be recorded in detail. However, it was apparent that it was originally approximately *c.*2.2 m square and lined with squared limestone blocks (0.3 x 0.1 x 0.2 m in size) bonded with a yellow clayey sand mortar. It had subsequently been enlarged westwards; this involved the removal of the original west wall, though a protruding block belonging to the original wall was noted on the south-facing wall. The walls of the extension were built of larger, well-coursed, green stone blocks, 0.45 x 0.2 x 0.3 m in size, with pale green/yellow bonding. The basal fill of the pit comprised a 0.40 m thick, grey, very fine clayey silt, that contained mineralised fruit remains, mostly fig and wild strawberry, though grape, quince, elderberry and apple/pear were also present in small quantities. The presence of mineralised fly remains including the 'latrine fly' suggests the use of the structure as a latrine. The deposit also contained the articulated remains of a cat, a lamb and a hedgehog as well as a large quantity of well-preserved fish remains, though it is possible that these remains had been dumped after the latrine had gone out of use and had sunk in the liquid ordure. The structure had been backfilled with rubble containing much stone, presumably from its wall, as well as a large quantity of stone and ceramic roof tiles, the latter implying that it may originally have been roofed. The infill also contained much Brill/Boarstall ware (1200–1600) and two large sherds of red earthenware (1550+), as well as weathered fragments from a glass flask, datable to the fifteenth to early sixteenth centuries. The lack of clay pipes suggest that it had been filled prior to *c*.1600. The date of its filling suggests that the structure was constructed early during Phase 6; a date during Phase 5 cannot be ruled out, though unfortunately this cannot be established on the stratigraphic evidence alone.

Structure 186 was a small rectangular sunken stone structure that abutted the west side of wall 188 but had been cut on its north-west corner by cellared building 176 (see Phase 7). It comprised roughly hewn limestone blocks bonded with orange sandy clay that lined a pit *c*.0.80 m in depth which formed a shaft measuring 1.3 m x 0.9 m. The purpose of the structure is uncertain, since there was no evidence that it ever served as a latrine, although it could have been used as a storage chamber. The structure had been rapidly filled with gravel and rubble that included ceramic roof tiles, suggesting that it may have been roofed. Its latest fill also contained clay pipes datable to *c*.1660–1720 and pottery, together suggesting a date within the second half of the seventeenth or early eighteenth century for its destruction.

Ten predominantly shallow pits were largely confined to the southern side of the property. Apart from pit 851, located close to the NE corner of Property 2W, the northern side of the property remained free of pits, and a 0.7 m-thick garden soil accumulated above the Phase 4–5 pits within this area. Several of the pits were rich in rubbish and contained closely datable material. Elongated rectangular pit 851 was 2.5 m in length and 0.70 m deep, and abutted the boundary with Property 1. It contained clay pipes datable to 1640–60, a farthing of Charles I dated to 1639–43 and fragments from a square case bottle of seventeenth century date, all of which could suggest that the pit was in use during the 1640s. The pit also contained a large amount of animal bone, including the articulated remains of a piglet. Shallow rubbish pit 417 contained material of a similar date including clay pipe datable to 1630–70, a Nuremberg jeton datable to 1586–1635 and fragments of a glass bottle or jar of mid to late seventeenth-century date. Large shallow pit 613, located immediately to the west of Structure 1373, was dug to bury the remains of an immature horse. The fill of the pit also contained sherds of Frechen stoneware (1550–1700).

Property 2E Given the lack of pits, the area to the east of wall 1384 seems to have been set aside for structures or as a yard, though only fragmentary remains of two structures survived (288 and 1379). Building 1379 occupied the north-west part of the property with its west wall built upon the top of wall 1384, maintaining its alignment. The building had shallow wall foundations *c*.0.50 m in width comprising limestone blocks bonded with light orange clay, their slight nature suggesting sleeper walls supporting a timber-framed building. In all, the building measured *c*.5.0 m in width and perhaps *c*.12.7 m in length since slight evidence for a return southwards was found at the surviving east end of the north wall suggesting that it followed the footprint of eighteenth century cellar 1354 that was later inserted within it (see Phase 7 below). Any internal deposits had been removed by the later cellar and no dating evidence was found for its construction, although the cellar seems to have been constructed in or after 1752 (see Phase 7 below).

Structure 288 was a small stone-lined pit attached to the east side of wall 1384, located to the south of Building 1379. The walls that lined its north and east sides were constructed of roughly hewn stone blocks bonded with clay. The wall on its south side had been removed by an Ashmolean foundation and its west wall had apparently collapsed into the pit. The shaft was probably square measuring *c*.1.3 m across and 1.6 m in depth. A compact clay surface was noted at the base of the shaft and had been stained greenish-yellow; otherwise no other deposits were found to suggest that it had served as a latrine. A 0.3 m thick accumulation deposit of sand, silt and rubbish at the base probably formed after the pit had gone out of use. It was finally levelled with stone rubble that contained a large quantity of late/post-medieval ceramic roof and floor tiles. Immediately to the south of Structure 288 were traces of a ground-level square structure (wall 315) that also abutted the north side of wall 1384. It may have been associated with Structure 288, though its relationship with it had been removed by the Ashmolean foundation.

Property 3 Only one feature, stone-lined pit 1334, was allocated to this phase though it is possible that pit 393 (see Phase 7) may also date to this phase if the sherd of eighteenth-century pottery found within it is considered intrusive. Only its north-west corner and the lowest 0.40 m of the pit had survived truncation, though its full depth would have been in excess of 2.7 m. The pit was constructed with roughly hewn limestone slabs, with no evidence for mortar bonding. A compacted deposit of gravel and lime/chalk may have formed a rudimentary surface at the base of the feature. This supported a 0.12 m thick deposit of mid greenish grey silt, possibly remnants of ordure though no mineralised remained were found. Although no dating evidence was recovered, it has been placed within this phase given its similarity to the stone-lined pits found in Properties 2W and 2E.

Phase 7: Late Seventeenth to Eighteenth Century (Fig. 11.12)

Property 1 Wall 140 may have formed the rear of a building that lay mostly to the east of the excavated area. It was 0.40 m wide and comprised two courses of squared limestone blocks bonded with a yellow mortar. It was aligned at right-angles to, and abutted, wall 139 that formed the north wall of Phase 6 Building 1379 within Property 2E. The wall ran northwards for a length of 4.2 m before it abruptly terminated, which presumably marked the point of its return eastwards although later disturbance had removed any evidence for this. The wall cut a 0.46 m thick levelling dump of dark greenish-brown silt-sand. This contained seventeenth century pottery and an assemblage of clay pipe that could be dated to 1670–90. Pit digging continued throughout Property 1 at much the same level as in the preceding phase, mostly within those areas that had not been dug during the previous phases. No pits occurred east of wall 140.

As with Phase 6, an area *c.*1.5 m wide to the north of the boundary with Properties 2W and 2E remained clear of pits, and was perhaps maintained for access. Elsewhere, a total of 11 pits were identified, which can be divided into two main types: large rectangular pits (380, 777 and 1077) that may originally have been for gravel extraction, and smaller, more oval pits, that may have been dug to dispose of rubbish, particularly the group that occurred within the centre of the property (857, 920, 946 and 963). Possible quarry pit 380 measured at least 3.2 m in length, was 2.5 m in width, and mechanical excavation revealed it to be at least 3.5 m in depth. Its edges were straight and vertical suggesting that it must have been shored in order to prevent the collapse of the loose gravel that was extracted, though no evidence for any such lining was observed. The pit was rapidly levelled with rubbish that contained significant quantities of late seventeenth to eighteenth century wine bottles, including a complete wine bottle dating to the 1760s and impressed with a seal of All Souls College (Fig. 11.19). Pit 1077 was only 0.45 m deep, and appears on clay pipe evidence to have been filled after 1660–80. The other pits were no more than 1.6 m in depth, the deepest comprising a sequence of four intercutting pits within the central area of the property (857, 920, 946 and 963). Unlike the possible quarry pits, the fills of each of these pits suggested that they were filled over a period of time and contained higher quantities of animal bone. It is possible that this part of the property had been set aside for rubbish disposal for a sustained period of time, which on the evidence of the clay pipes would have been between the late seventeenth and mid eighteenth centuries.

Property 2E Within Property 2E this phase saw the construction of a vaulted cellar (1354) within Building 1379 (Phase 6 above), with stairs down to the cellar on its southern side. A dated facing stone built into its south wall would seemingly date this event to 1752 (Fig. 11.13B).

Cellar 1354 was fully exposed, though modern disturbance had removed part of its south-east corner. It is unclear if the construction of the cellar involved the demolition of Building 1139 or

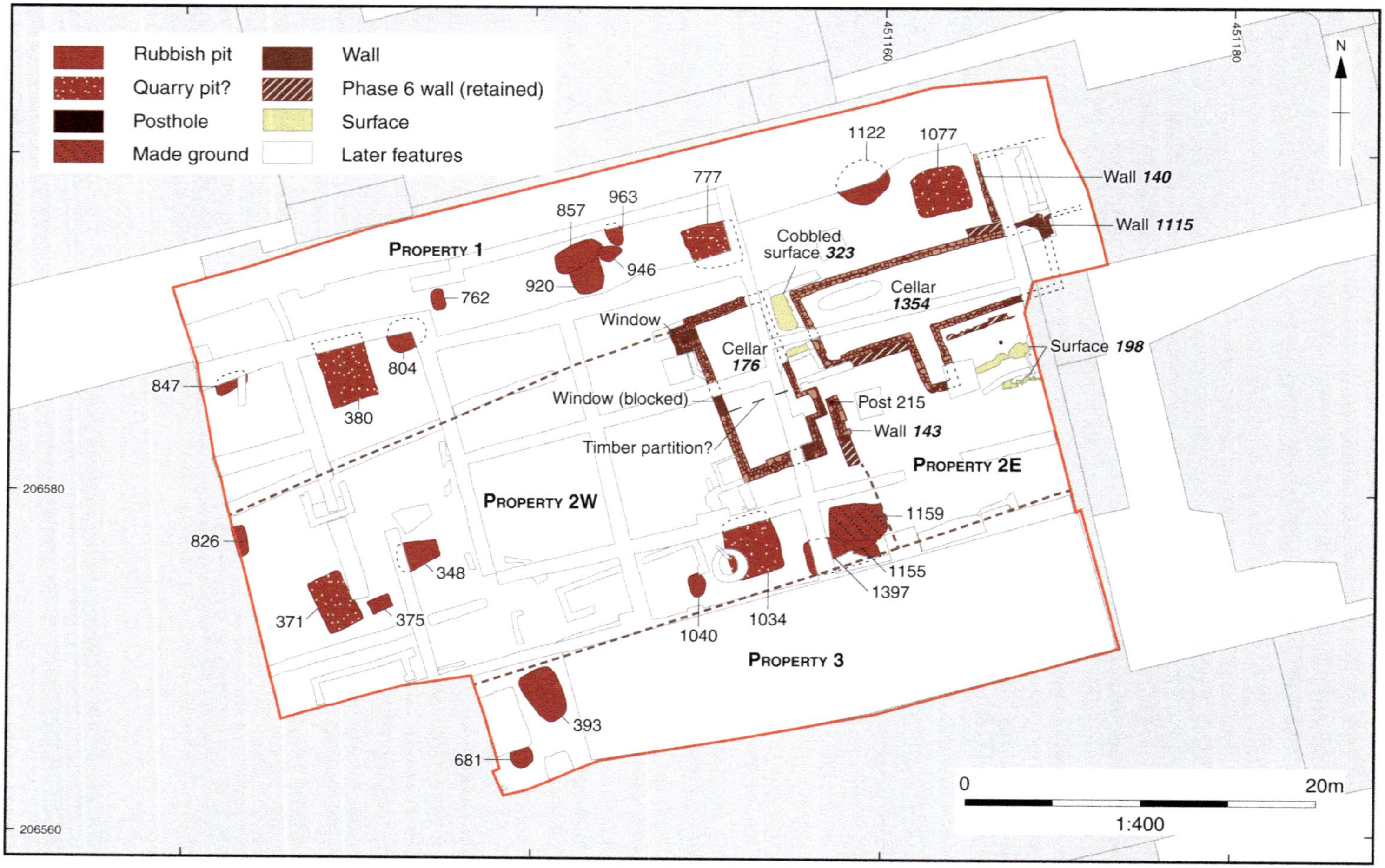

Fig. 11.12 Phase 7: late seventeenth to eighteenth century.

Fig. 11.13 A: Cellar 176, south-west corner showing timber partition (scale: 2 m); B: Cellar 1354, south wall with inserts for shelving and dated stone on entrance corner.

alternatively if it had been built within the standing structure. The fact that the cellar is smaller than the original building perhaps supports the idea that the earlier building was left intact. The cellar was rectangular in plan and measured 14.0 x 3.6–3.8 m internally, the variation in its width being due to a bow in its north wall possibly as a consequence of the north wall of the earlier structure not being built straight. It survived to a depth of up to 2.4 m and was lined with walls 0.50 m thick, comprising roughly coursed and squared limestone blocks (typically 0.25 m x 0.13 m) bonded with white lime mortar. The internal face of the cellar had been rendered with a hard, grey mortar. At the top of the north wall (and possibly the west wall) was a slight overhang and the stones were pitched at an angle of 45 degrees, suggesting springing for a vaulted arch. Evidence for an arch was also seen on the north-east corner of the cellar. The staircase comprised a rectangular cut with a base sloping at *c.*45 degrees that projected 3.4 m from the south wall of the cellar; the north and south sides of the cut were lined with roughly squared limestone blocks similar to the main cellar walls and also rendered with hard, grey mortar. The internal width of the staircase was 1.1 m and its steps appeared to have been robbed, though a step was recorded during the evaluation at its southern (upper) end. The walls of the stairs were keyed into and therefore contemporary with the construction of the south wall of the cellar. The limestone quoins at the intersection with the south wall of the cellar had been more carefully dressed and had squared recesses on their corners (0.07 m x 0.1 m), presumably to accommodate a door. The uppermost surviving quoin stone on the western intersection also had the date '1752' carved onto its north face (Fig. 11.13B). Two horizontal grooves, 0.76 m apart, measuring 1.26 m in length, were cut into the west wall against its south end. These were at the same height as two rows of rectangular holes in the south wall (west of the entrance), which were spaced 0.85 m apart (horizontally). They may have formed part of a timber structure attached to the south-west corner of the cellar, perhaps for shelves or wine racks. No evidence was found for a floor, implying that it had been made of stone slabs or wooden planks, either of which could have been removed prior to its demolition along with the stone steps from the staircase.

Wall 1115, located immediately to the east of cellar 1354, formed part of a second cellared structure, though only its north-west corner was exposed within the excavation area. No relationship with cellar 1354 was established, although, given its position, it may have been abutted by it and therefore predated its construction. The wall, 0.45 m thick, was constructed with limestone blocks bonded with yellowish brown sandy clay mortar whose internal faces (east and south) were very well hewn and finished. Its internal fill was not investigated beyond a depth of 0.2 m, which comprised rubble suggesting the structure remained in use into the twentieth century.

The area to the south of cellar 1354 appears to have remained open and free of pits and structures. Immediately to the east of the staircase were two areas of limestone blocks (198) that appeared to have been roughly shaped and laid flat to form a rough cobbled surface, laid upon a bedding of gravel. It was not possible to ascertain whether these surfaces were contemporary with the cellar or with its predecessor, Building 1379. A 1.2 m-wide gap lay between the buildings that would have contained cellar 1354 and cellar 176 at ground level; in the gap was a surface of rounded cobbles and bricks (323) supported on a base of loose orange gravel, which contained clay pipe fragments datable to 1680–1760. The construction of this surface necessitated the levelling of wall 1384 in the area between the two cellars, since the cobbles partially lay over it. It is unclear whether the full length of wall was removed at this time though it would appear that it may have been rebuilt since wall fragment 143 lay over it on a slightly different alignment. The wall was 0.78 m thick and poorly built, with roughly hewn limestone blocks, bonded by clay. It terminated at the north end at a contained circular posthole (215), 0.22 m in diameter and 0.45 m deep. It is possible that this was the setting for a post that formed part of a gate attached at ground level to the south-west corner of cellar 1354, allowing access to the open area to its south.

Property 2W Rectangular cellared Structure 176 was constructed *c.*1.0 m west of the wall that sub-divided Property 2 during Phase 6; its north wall respected and therefore maintained the boundary with Property 1. Its south-east corner cut into the fills of stone-lined pit 186 (see Phase 6 above) that contained clay pipes suggesting a *terminus post quem* of *c.*1660 for the construction of the cellar and perhaps no later than 1720. The cellar measured 9.1 x 3.9 m and was *c.*2.0 m in depth. Its walls were 0.58–0.68 m thick and constructed with coursed, roughly squared limestone blocks, which were faced on their internal sides, set in a yellow/brown mortar. The interior faces of the east, west and south walls had been rendered with a thin layer of plaster which in places had traces of blue/grey paint adhering to it. However, this paint was not an original feature of the cellar since in some areas, where the plaster did not survive, it directly overlay the facing stones. A vertical scar, 0.06 m wide, ran up the full height of the west wall, 3.67 m from the south wall, and may have indicated the position of a timber partition, though no corresponding scar was recorded in the east wall (Fig. 11.13A). A 0.65 m-wide recess in the north end of the west wall projected 1.0 m outwards from its inner face and may have formed part of a light well. A second such opening located 3.5 m further south along the wall had subsequently been blocked with brick, in order to create a door at ground level (see Phase 8 below). Another opening was found on the east wall and this may have served a similar purpose. In addition, a narrow sloping chute on top of the west wall could have offered further ventilation within this partition. No evidence for the floor of the cellar survived and it is assumed to have been constructed with tile or stone that had been removed during its demolition.

As in Phase 6, much of the area to the west of cellar 176 remained devoid of pits and a garden soil continued to develop. This deposit (223) was mechanically excavated but was observed to abut the west wall of cellar 176 and was cut by walls of nineteenth century date, though no relationship with other features of this phase was established. It was recorded as a greyish brown sandy silt, 0.3–0.7 m thick, and contained a mix of material ranging from medieval to modern in date, although it is likely that the latter was intrusive. Metal detecting undertaken before its removal recovered 15 coins and jetons datable from 1184–1654, though the majority were of mid sixteenth century or later date. The clay pipe evidence, which comprised 57 predominantly fresh fragments, was of a similarly mixed date. Although the majority was datable to 1680–1720, there were smaller groups represented that dated to 1640–80 and 1720–70.

Pits were confined to two clusters in the same areas as during Phase 6, towards the west and alongside the boundary with Property 3. The western group comprised four rectangular pits (348, 371, 375 and 826), that were not bottomed but ultimately appeared to have served as rubbish pits. The largest, pit 371, measured 3.4 m x 2.0 m and had vertical sides suggesting either that it had been lined or that it did not remain open long enough to allow for its sides to become weathered. Its size suggests that it could have served as a gravel quarry especially since its depth was in excess of 1.5 m. It was filled with rubble containing a large quantity of post-medieval ceramic tiles, including eighteenth century floor tiles, possibly from the demolition or modification of nearby buildings. A large assemblage of clay pipe dates this event to 1720–50. Adjacent pit 375 measured 1.3 m in length, was 0.65 m deep, and had a stepped base. Its fill contained ceramic tiles, eighteenth century pottery, glass, and a large quantity of animal bone.

The area to the east effectively contained two pits (1397 and 1155) since the remaining features (1034 and 1159) were consolidation deposits over earlier pits, the former including Phase 6 Structure 1373. Both of these consolidation events can be dated by the clay pipe and glass evidence to the late seventeenth century. The upper part of this levelling episode contained 25 fragments of oast/malting kiln tiles of eighteenth-century date (context 301). Rectangular pit 1397 could only be investigated to a depth of 0.70 m but was of similar size to broadly contemporary pit 371 to the west and may have served a similar purpose. It had been filled with rubble including four fragments of eighteenth-century malting kiln tiles and clay pipes suggesting a date of 1690–1730. Small rectangular rubbish pit 1155, at least 0.85 m in depth, seems to have been dug shortly afterwards since it contained material of similar date.

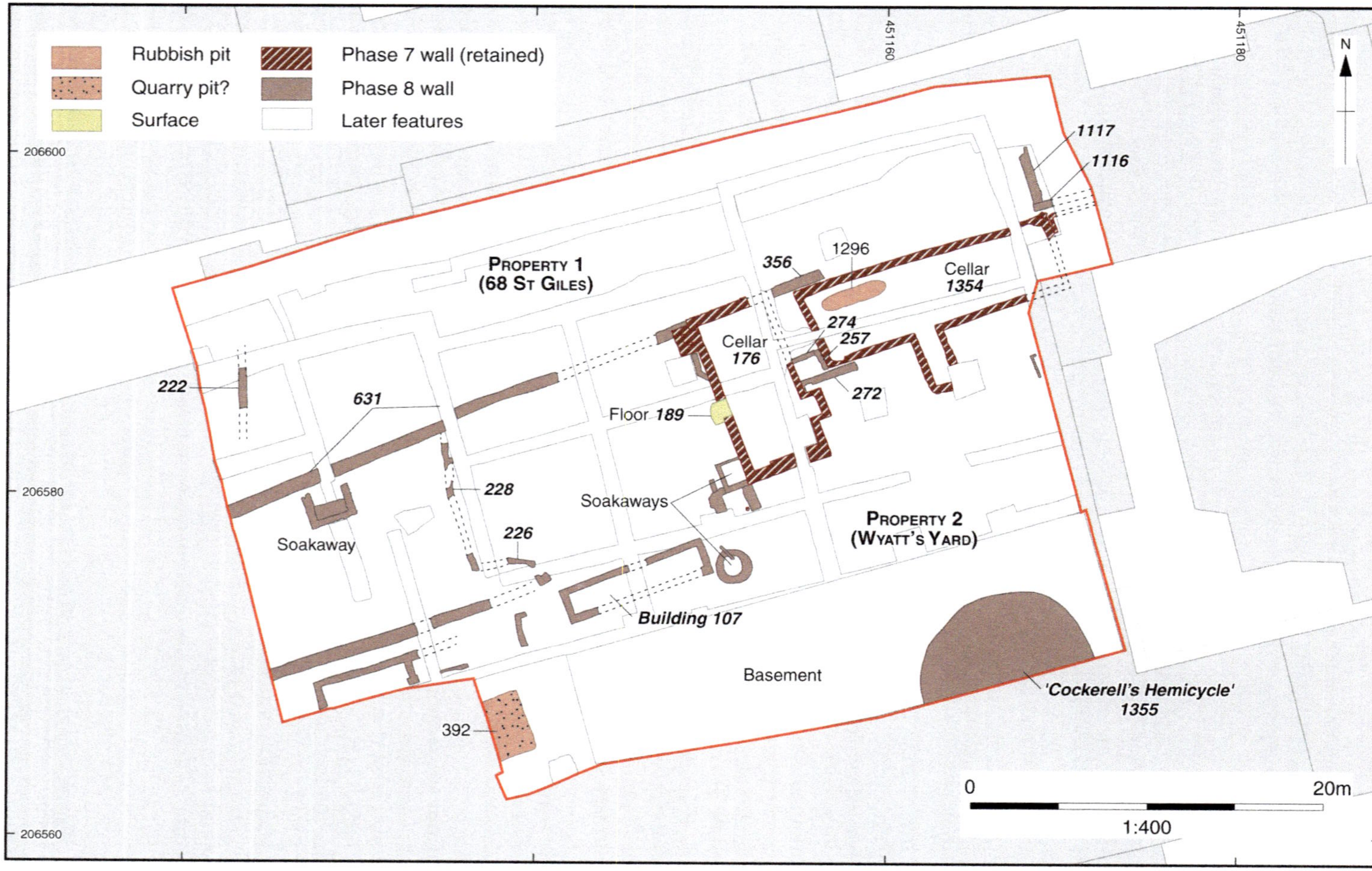

Fig. 11.14 Phase 8: 1800–92.

Property 3 Only two features could be assigned to this property within the area investigated, one of which (393) represented the upper fills of possible quarry pit 1298, that was in use during Phase 6. Its fills contained dumps of building material including medieval and post-medieval ceramic roof tiles and eighteenth-century pottery.

Phase 8: c.1800–92 (Fig. 11.14)

The boundary between Properties 1 and 2 was renewed with the construction of wall 631, visible on the Ordnance Survey map of 1876 (Fig. 11.2d). The map shows the area of Property 1 as a garden. This is reflected in the dearth of features seen in the excavation, though wall fragments at its eastern (1116 and 1117) and western ends (222) correspond to structures depicted on the map.

In Property 2, cellars 176 and 1379 continued in use and underwent only slight modifications. The Ordnance Survey map shows that they lay within two conjoined buildings on the northern side of an open yard (Wyatt's Yard). The map also shows a number of other buildings around the yard, some of which broadly correspond with excavated foundations. To the east of cellar 176, the map depicts a garden bounded to its east by a wall, corresponding with stone walls 226 and 228.

By this time, Property 3 had been amalgamated with Property 2, and formed the southern part of Wyatt's Yard. A rectangular pit (392) in this area contained a large quantity of vessel glass, mostly of eighteenth-century types, but clay pipe and pottery evidence suggests a nineteenth-century date for the deposit. At the southern edge of the excavation a semi-circular paving of red bricks (1355), three courses thick, represents the basement of the hemicycle of the University Galleries (built 1841–5).

Phase 9: 1892 Onwards

This phase represents the demolition of all the earlier buildings, the deposition of thick makeup layers and the construction of the extension to the rear of the University Galleries in 1892–5 (Fig. 11.14).

POTTERY by PAUL BLINKHORN

The pottery assemblage comprised 2,979 sherds with a total weight of 55,675 g. The estimated vessel equivalent (EVE) by summation of surviving rim sherd circumference was 19.76. The assemblage is noteworthy for the presence of a small group of early/middle Anglo-Saxon hand-built wares and Ipswich ware. The medieval and later pottery is typical of domestic assemblages from Oxford, with a notable group of sherds from at least five ceramic lamps from the backfill of early to mid thirteenth century well 663.

Fabrics

The pottery was recorded using the coding system and chronology of the Oxfordshire County type-series,[42] as follows:

F100	OXR	St Neots ware type T1(1), AD 850–1100. 1 sherd, 21 g, EVE = 0.
F200	OXAC	Cotswold-type ware, 975–1350. 277 sherds, 3,115 g, EVE = 2.29.
F202	OXBF	North-East Wiltshire ware, 1050–1400. 193 sherds, 2707 g, EVE = 1.52.
F205	OXZ	Stamford ware, 850–1150. 1 sherd, 5 g, EVE = 0.
F300	OXY	Medieval Oxford ware, 1075–1350. 799 sherds, 8,324 g, EVE = 4.96.
F329	OX68	Potterspury ware, late thirteenth to seventeenth century. 2 sherds, 447 g, EVE = 0.10.
F330	OXBK	Medieval shelly coarseware, 1100–1350. 11 sherds, 241 g, EVE = 0.46.

42 M. Mellor and G. Oakley, 'A Summary of the Key Assemblages …', in 'St Ebbe's, Part II', pp. 181–219; Mellor, 'Synthesis'.

F352	OXAM	Brill/Boarstall ware, 1200–1600. 959 sherds, 16,161 g, EVE = 7.96.
F355	OXBB	Minety ware, early twelfth to fifteenth century. 2 sherds, 27 g, EVE = 0.
F356	OXBG	Surrey whiteware, mid thirteenth to mid fifteenth century. 12 sherds, 165 g, EVE = 0.
F362	OXAG	Abingdon ware, mid/late eleventh to mid fourteenth century. 14 sherds, 109 g, EVE = 0.08.
F403	OXBN	Tudor green ware, late fourteenth century to *c*.1500. 21 sherds, 87 g, EVE = 0.15.
F404	OXCL	Cistercian ware, 1475–1700. 37 sherds, 602 g, EVE = 0.
F405	OXST	Frechen stoneware, 1550–1700. 51 sherds, 2,251 g, EVE = 1.54.
F408	OXAM	Brill/Boarstall 'Tudor green' type ('BBTG'), late fifteenth to sixteenth century. 5 sherds, 10 g, EVE = 0.08.
F410	OXCE	Tin-glazed earthenware, 1613–1800. 91 sherds, 1,367 g.
F412	OXRESWL	Polychrome slipwares, seventeenth to early eighteenth century. 24 sherds, 1032 g.
F413	OXSTW	Westerwald stoneware, *c*.1590–1800. 2 sherds, 27 g.
F425	OXDR	Red earthenwares, 1550+. 236 sherds, 11,855 g.
F431	OXFI	Chinese porcelain, *c*.1650+. 16 sherds, 310 g.
F436	XBEWSL	Staffordshire-type slipwares, *c*.1650–1800. 10 sherds, 136 g.
F437	OXBEW	Staffordshire manganese wares, *c*.1700–1800. 34 sherds, 2,041 g.
F438	OXEST	English stoneware, *c*.1680+. 34 sherds, 2041 g.
F443	OXFM	White salt-glazed stoneware, 1720–80. 39 sherds, 442 g.
F448	CRM	Creamware, mid eighteenth to early nineteenth century. 7 sherds, 130 g.
F451	OXFH	Border wares, 1550–1700. 83 sherds, 1,433 g.
F1000	WHEW	Mass-produced white earthenwares, mid nineteenth to twentieth century. 27 sherds, 1,868 g.

The following, not included in the Oxford type-series, were also noted:

F2	Early-middle Anglo-Saxon handmade wares, AD 450–850. 4 sherds, 71 g, EVE = 0
F95	Ipswich ware, 720–850. 4 sherds, 114 g, EVE = 0.62. One of these is an uncertain identification and is discussed further below.
F1001	Romano-British wares. 5 sherds, 208 g

Chronology

Each context was given a seriated ceramic phase (CP) date, based on the wares present (Table 11.1). The dating has been adjusted with reference to the stratigraphic matrix to allow identification of assemblages which are lacking contemporary wares. As elsewhere in Oxford, pottery deposition begins in earnest in the late eleventh or twelfth century (CP2), which covers the period of the establishment of the nearby Beaumont Palace. The peak comes during the thirteenth century (CP3), when tenements were known to be present to the east of the palace, with around 25 per cent of the pottery from this site being of that date. The rate of pottery deposition afterwards remains at a reasonably constant rate up to the nineteenth century, although there is something of a decrease in CP4–CP6, which is not untypical of sites in the town and may reflect retrenchment in population and occupation before pottery deposition rates increase again from the mid sixteenth century.

The Assemblage

Early/Middle Anglo-Saxon, c.AD 450–850 The early and middle Anglo-Saxon pottery from the site is residual. The small assemblage of hand-built material is a further addition to the growing

Table 11.1. Ceramic phase chronology and defining wares.

Ceramic phase	Site phase	Date	Defining fabrics	No. sherds	Weight (g)	EVE
CP 1	2	E–L 11th C	OXAC	19	306	0.18
CP 2	3	L 11th–12th C	OXY, OXBF	257	2649	1.44
CP 3	4	13th C	OXAM, OXBG	1098	12,860	9.06
CP 4	4	14th C	OXAM	162	3137	1.94
CP 5	5	15th–L 15th C	OXBN	190	2014	1.13
CP 6	5	L 15th–M 16th C	OXCL, BBTG, OXST	170	3016	2.23
CP 7	6	M 16th–17th C	OXDR, OXFH	297	6421	1.52
CP 8	6	17th C	OXREWSL, OXCE	234	5878	0.87
CP 9	7	L 17th–M 18th C	OXBEW, OXFI	203	4620	0.31
CP 10	8	M–L 18th C	OXFM, CRM	276	8920	1.00
MOD	8	19th C+	WHEW	72	5845	0.08

corpus of such pottery from Oxford.[43] All the sherds from the present site are undecorated, and thus can only be dated to the broad early/middle Anglo-Saxon period.

The group of Ipswich ware from this site is only the second from Oxford, the only other material being from the neighbouring Sackler Library site, where four sherds were found.[44] This suggests very strongly that there was a focus of middle Anglo-Saxon activity in this area of Oxford. The Ipswich ware assemblage included a fragment from the rim of a fairly large jar (Fig. 11.15, no. 1), which is a typical find at sites outside the kingdom of East Anglia, where vessels used for the transportation of trade-goods, probably salt, are more common than small jars. One of the sherds (Fig. 11.15, no. 2) appears to be from the rim of a Buttermarket-type bottle, but the piece is heavily burnt, with a thick black residue adhering to the inner surface, and the identification is tentative. It has been suggested that the piece could be a twelfth- to thirteenth-century curfew/firecover apex in OXY.[45]

Mid to Late Eleventh Century (Ceramic Phase 1; Site Phase 2) The assemblage from this phase comprised entirely Cotswolds-type wares (fabric OXAC). It consisted of plain body sherds apart from a single jar rim sherd and another from a pitcher. The latter is rather unusual, as such vessels in this fabric are relatively rare, although others have been noted at other sites in the town.[46] None of the context-specific assemblages of this date numbers more than four sherds, so it is entirely possible that at least some of them are later, and lack the defining wares, as it is a relatively long-lived ceramic tradition. The fact that only a single sherd of St Neots ware occurred at the site indicates that there was virtually no activity before the early to mid eleventh century. This broadly supports the chronological picture gained from the Sackler Library excavations. There, a small assemblage of eleventh century material (nine sherds) was noted, and no St Neots ware, with activity (in terms of pottery deposition) only really beginning in the late eleventh to twelfth century.

Late Eleventh and Twelfth Century (Ceramic Phase 2; Site Phase 3) The mean sherd weight for the pottery from this phase is quite low for a medieval assemblage (10.2 g) and suggests

43 P. Blinkhorn, 'Pottery', in Norton and Cockin, 'Classics Centre', p. 180.
44 P. Blinkhorn, 'Pottery', in Poore, *Beaumont*, pp. 42–4.
45 Personal communication from John Cotter.
46 For example, Mellor, 'Synthesis', fig. 14, no. 2.

that a large proportion of the pottery is the product of secondary deposition, perhaps due to midden material being used to backfill earth-cut features during the re-organisation of the site around this time. The assemblage is characteristic of sites of this period in Oxford. It was dominated by early medieval Oxford ware (fabric OXY, 65.7 per cent by weight) along with smaller assemblages of OXAC (21.0 per cent) and North-East Wiltshire ware (OXBF, 10.1 per cent). A few sherds of medieval Shelly ware (1.5 per cent), two sherds of Abingdon ware and a single residual early/middle Anglo-Saxon hand-built sherd were also present. The rim sherd assemblage was dominated by jars (61.1 per cent), along with smaller quantities of jugs (26.4 per cent) and bowls (12.5 per cent). The handles included a single example from an OXY skillet. These generally occur in small numbers amongst the larger assemblages of the period. Decorated sherds were extremely rare, other than glazed body sherds from OXY pitchers. Just one other was noted, a fragment of an OXBF storage jar with thumbed applied strips.

Thirteenth Century (Ceramic Phase 3; Site Phase 4) Property 1 produced entirely plain body sherds apart from two small fragments of OXY jar rims and a very unusual modelled piece (Fig. 11.15, no. 4), which is glazed and slipped, and appears to be an antler from a modelled deer's head. Such decoration is very rare on the products of the Oxford ware industry, although it is possible that this piece is from a roof finial in Abingdon ware (fabric OXAG).[47] The large Property 2 assemblage is not unusual for this date in Oxford. The relative occurrence of jars, bowls and jugs is as expected although the fairly large quantity of lamps is a little unusual, and not seen in the other properties, suggesting that this tenement may have had a different function to the others. The small assemblage from Property 3 comprised entirely body sherds.

Fourteenth Century (Ceramic Phase 4; Site Phase 4) This phase produced a generally smaller assemblage than that which preceded it, but a wider range of regional imports such as Potterspury and Surrey wares were noted. This is consistent with sites of the period elsewhere in Oxford. The pottery from Property 1 comprised entirely plain body sherds, apart from a OXAM lamp base. The data are distorted somewhat by the presence of the single, very large sherd from a Potterspury ware jug (Fabric OX68) but otherwise the dominance of OXAM in the assemblages for both properties is characteristic of the period. This Property 2 group also shows a fairly wide range of vessel types, with stems from two further lamps. No pottery of this phase was recovered from Property 3.

Fifteenth Century (Ceramic Phase 5; Site Phase 5) This phase generally sees the end of many of the earlier medieval traditions, such as fabrics OXAC, OXBF, OXY and OXBK, and the start of the later-medieval tradition, particularly cooking and drinking pottery, and Surrey 'Tudor green' whitewares. Residuality is quite high at this time, with at least 29.3 per cent of the pottery in Property 1 being redeposited. The actual figure is likely to be higher, as at least some of the OXAM is also likely to be residual. This may explain why so little pottery occurred in earlier features, and there seems to have been a degree of disturbance, presumably due to quarrying. All the rim sherds were from OXAM jugs, apart from a single OXBN example, from a lobed cup or bowl, a common product of the tradition. Some 37.3 per cent of the Property 2 pottery in this phase is also residual, and in addition, a single sherd (25 g) of residual middle Anglo-Saxon Ipswich ware occurred with this group. This again suggests disturbance of earlier strata due to gravel extraction. Eight rim sherds occurred, comprising jars (EVE = 0.24), bowls (EVE = 0.10), jugs (EVE = 0.16) and two small fragments of 'Tudor green' lobed cups (EVE = 0.07). Two of the jar rims were residual (EVE = 0.16). All the others, the 'Tudor green' apart, were in OXAM. No pottery of this phase was recovered from Property 3.

Late Fifteenth to Mid Sixteenth Century (Ceramic Phase 6; Site Phase 5) For Property 1, the data are somewhat distorted by the presence of a near-complete German stoneware jug. The

[47] Personal communication from John Cotter.

vessel is somewhat unusual in that it has a hole through the centre of the base which appears to have been made after firing but before deposition. It is possible that this was to enable the vessel to be used as a watering-pot, but this is by no means certain. Residuality is still fairly high, with 18.4 per cent of the assemblage consisting of such types. Three jug rims occurred, two of which were in OXST and the other OXAM, along with two jar rims, one OXAM, the other residual. Property 2 produced only a small assemblage with a very high level of residuality (at 61.9 per cent). The actual figure is probably even higher, given that some of the OXAM is likely to be residual. The only stratified rims were a single example from an OXAM jar and another from an OXST mug. A fragment of a residual lamp in OXY also occurred. Property 3 did not produce any pottery of this date.

Mid Sixteenth to Seventeenth Century (Ceramic Phase 7; Site Phase 6) The Property 1 assemblage is dominated by utilitarian red earthenware fabric OXDR, as is fairly typical of sites of the period, with OXAM also fairly common, although some of this is likely to be residual. The rest of the contemporary pottery is OXCL, OXST and OXFH, again, a fairly typical pattern, with residuality much lower than in the previous phase, at 11.6 per cent. Just four rims were noted, two from OXST mugs, one from an OXAM jar, and one residual. In addition to those listed, a single sherd of Ipswich ware (17 g) also occurred. For Property 2E, the entire assemblage was dominated by OXDR, with very little residual pottery, and just a few sherds of OXAM and OXST making up the rest. For Property 2W, residual pottery comprised 15.3 per cent of the assemblage, although some of the OXAM is also likely to be residual, such as two lamp fragments. There is also a rather unusual stamped OXY jar rim (Fig. 11.15, no. 5). An OXAM skillet handle is also present, which may be residual although such vessels were still in use at this time. Two cup rims, one in BBTG and the other in OXBN, were noted and are probably also residual. Most of the rim assemblage consisted of redeposited medieval examples, with three OXAM jars (EVE = 0.28) and a jug in the same fabric (EVE = 0.20) probably being the only contemporary pottery. Red earthenware (OXDR) formed a smaller part of this assemblage when compared to Property 2E in the same period, although this may be due to higher levels of residuality. Property 3 did not produce any pottery of this date.

Seventeenth Century (Ceramic Phase 8; Site Phase 6) Residuality is again high for Property 1 in this phase, with 37.8 per cent of the assemblage by weight comprising such wares. The contemporary pottery is typical of reasonably well-to-do household in Oxford in the seventeenth century, comprising a mixture of utilitarian wares such as red earthenware OXDR and OXFH along with finer display and tablewares, such as tin-glazed earthenware OXCE, and the slipwares, and drinking pottery in the form of German stonewares. One tin-glazed sherd, the rim of a dish, has polychrome decoration and is of better than usual quality. At Property 2W, residuality is low, comprising just 7.0 per cent of the assemblage. The contemporary wares demonstrate a similar range to the material from Property 1 in this ceramic phase, suggesting a similar level of wealth and social standing. No pottery of this date was recovered from Properties 2E or 3.

Late Seventeenth to Mid Eighteenth Century (Ceramic Phase 9; Site Phase 7) In Property 1, residuality is reasonably low at 14.8 per cent. The contemporary assemblage is dominated by utilitarian red earthenware (OXDR), with small quantities of display and drinking and tablewares. In Property 2W, residuality is again at reasonable levels, at 8.0 per cent of the assemblage. This assemblage is also dominated by red earthenware (OXDR), along with small quantities of drinking pottery and tablewares. Some of the drinking pottery, particularly the German stoneware, is quite ornate. Two of the vessels have decorated moulded medallions, and another, moulded oak leaves. The latter is very typical of the Cologne potteries of the first half of the sixteenth century, with the former used extensively in most of the German industries in the sixteenth and seventeenth centuries. One of the medallions is nearly complete, and is of a floral design which is reasonably common. A Frechen vessel with a similar medallion is known from Norwich and dated to the mid sixteenth to mid seventeenth century.[48] A fragment of an English (Nottingham or Derby) stoneware gorge (tavern-mug) with an 'AR' assay mark was also present (Fig. 11.15, no. 6). These marks were introduced in June 1700 after parliament passed an act for ascertaining the measures for retailing ale and beer. This made it illegal to retail ale or beer in vessels without a stamped assay mark.[49] The 'AR' ale-mark dates from the reign of Queen Anne (1702–14) although pots with these marks were sometimes still in use at the end of the eighteenth century. The vessel may be evidence of an inn on or near the site, although gorges with ale-marks do occur in pottery assemblages from domestic dwellings. Another fragment worthy of note is a handle from an Anglo-Dutch tin-glazed posset-cup, with high-quality blue-painted decoration. The pottery from Property 2E was entirely residual apart from a single sherd (4 g) of OXBEW. Property 3 produced 2 sherds with a total weight of 68 g (EVE = 0). One sherd (26 g) was OXCE, the other, OXBEW.

Mid to Late Eighteenth Century (Ceramic Phase 10; Site Phase 8) In Property 1, residuality is very high, with 54.0 per cent of the pottery falling into this category. These figures are perhaps artificially increased by the presence of a number of large sherds of OXAM jugs, including virtually all of the lower half of a baluster vessel. It seems very likely that the OXAM is from an earlier feature, probably of fourteenth-century date, which was not recognised during excavation. Amongst the contemporary pottery, OXDR is again the dominant assemblage, with small quantities of finer tablewares, such as fragments of white and brown stonewares (OXEST and OXFH). One fragment of note is a large sherd from the base of a plain tin-glazed bowl. It is possible that this is from a vessel of Iberian origin, although such pottery is quite rare at sites in the Thames valley to the west of London, despite being a common find in small quantities in the capital. However, it is also possible that this is an English product, from Bristol.[50]

Some 67.8 per cent of the assemblage from Property 2W is residual. This is due to the presence of a small number of large sherds of Border ware (OXFH). It is possible that this material, which had more or less ceased to be made by the end of the seventeenth century, was contemporary in the sense that it was a group of old pots which had been in use up until this time. It is not unusual to see fairly large dumps of domestic pottery from this period, as it was a time of rapidly changing technology and tastes, with new wares being introduced at fairly regular intervals from around 1720 onwards, and some fashionable households seem to have responded to this by clearing out old pottery and replacing it with the new. The contemporary assemblage is fairly small, and again comprises mainly OXDR, along with small quantities of stonewares and Staffordshire tablewares. There was no pottery of this date from Properties 2E or 3.

Nineteenth century (Ceramic Phase MOD; Site Phase 8) This phase produced 72 sherds with a total weight of 5845 g. The assemblage is dominated by mass-produced white earthenwares, along with residual medieval and earlier material. Two large (56 g) sherds of early/middle Anglo-Saxon hand-built pottery occurred in the phase, as did the middle Anglo-Saxon Ipswich ware rim sherd (Fig. 11.15, no. 1).

Discussion

The pottery assemblage from this site is large although there are high levels of residuality. Apart from the unusual early and middle Anglo-Saxon pottery, the assemblage is generally consistent with domestic pottery from elsewhere in medieval and post-medieval Oxford. The general range of fabrics and forms is similar to that from earlier excavations at the Ashmolean Forecourt, with much of the medieval pottery dating to the earlier part of the period, and late-medieval pottery

48 S. Jennings, *Eighteen Centuries of Pottery from Norwich*, East Anglian Archaeology, 13 (1981), fig. 49, no. 811.
49 M. Bimson, 'The Significance of 'Ale-Measure' Marks', *Post-Medieval Archaeology*, 4 (1970), pp. 165–6.
50 Personal communication from John Cotter.

scarce.[51] Skillets and lamp fragments were also noted at that site, together with an unusual (for Oxford) sherd of a thirteenth century London ware imitation Rouen-style jug. The range of post-medieval wares was also very similar, with most of the material dating to the eighteenth century. The range of vessel types and consumption patterns at the nearby Classics Centre site is also very similar.[52] Most of the medieval pottery there occurred in contexts of the thirteenth century, with otherwise low levels of pottery deposition until the late fifteenth to sixteenth century. Large quantities of lamps were noted in the main medieval groups. In contrast to the present site, however, the latest medieval groups from the Classics Centre produced a fairly large assemblage of drinking pottery.

The small group of Ipswich ware is of considerable importance. Together with the four sherds of the same type from the adjacent Sackler Library site, it provides evidence for settlement in this area of Oxford in the early eighth to ninth century. The small group of hand-built pottery may be contemporary with the Ipswich ware, but could be earlier. It is entirely possible that the middle Anglo-Saxon inhabitants of Oxford were not using hand-built pottery, and the only ceramics in use were imported wares, by-products of trade rather than desired objects in their own right. Evidence from the middle Anglo-Saxon levels at Yarnton and Eynsham abbey indicates very strongly that there was a hiatus in the making and using of pottery in this area of the Thames valley at that time.[53] Thus, a fairly extensive middle Anglo-Saxon settlement may not leave much evidence in the form of pottery, especially if the strata of that date have been heavily disturbed. At both this and the Sackler Library site all the Ipswich ware was residual, and occurred in much later contexts.

Pottery only begins to be deposited at the present site in any significant quantities in the late eleventh or twelfth century, but the assemblage of this period is fairly mundane, and appears entirely domestic in nature, comprising largely undecorated jars, along with smaller quantities of bowls and jugs, and a single skillet handle. The thirteenth to fourteenth century saw the development and occupation of three tenements. The most interesting medieval assemblages came from Property 2 where there was a large assemblage of thirteenth-century pottery, dominated by OXAM, as would be expected; there was also a fairly wide range of common coarsewares, but also a few regional glazed wares such as Abingdon ware and Surrey whiteware, which often occur in small quantities at sites of the period in the town. Much of the assemblage comprised jars, bowls and jugs, with the first-named the most common, but 11.5 per cent of the rim sherds (by EVE) were OXAM lamps, which although not uncommon, do not usually occur in such large numbers. However, these vessels are sometimes unusually numerous in Oxford, particularly at medieval educational establishments such as Merton College.[54] Most of the lamps came from the backfills of pits or wells and were fairly well spread out and occurred singly. Significantly, none were from the earlier pits along the boundary with Property 1. This would suggest that the lamps were used by the inhabitants of Property 2 rather than having been brought in with soil to backfill existing features when the tenements were being laid out. Lamps are also well represented in the assemblage from the fourteenth century features in Property 2, with lamps making up at least 9.3 per cent of the rims. Also worthy of note is a rather unusual rim from an OXAM jug with what appears to be a modelled owl face-mask (Fig. 11.15, no. 3). Very little pottery occurred in the period from the late fifteenth to mid sixteenth century (38 sherds), and nearly two-thirds of it (61.9 per cent) was residual, indicating that there was a fairly

51 Mepham, 'The Pottery', in Andrews and Mepham, 'Ashmolean Museum Forecourt', table 3.

52 Blinkhorn, 'Pottery', in Norton and Cockin, 'Classics Centre'.

53 P. Blinkhorn, 'Early and Middle Anglo-Saxon Pottery', in G. Hey, *Yarnton. Anglo-Saxon and Medieval Settlement and Landscape*, Oxford Archaeology Thames Valley Landscapes Monograph, 20 (2004), pp. 267–72; P. Blinkhorn, 'The Pottery', in A. Hardy et al., *Aelfric's Abbey. Excavations at Eynsham Abbey, Oxfordshire, 1989–92*, Thames Valley Landscapes Monograph, 16 (2003).

54 Blinkhorn, 'Pottery', in Poore, 'No. 4A Merton St.'.

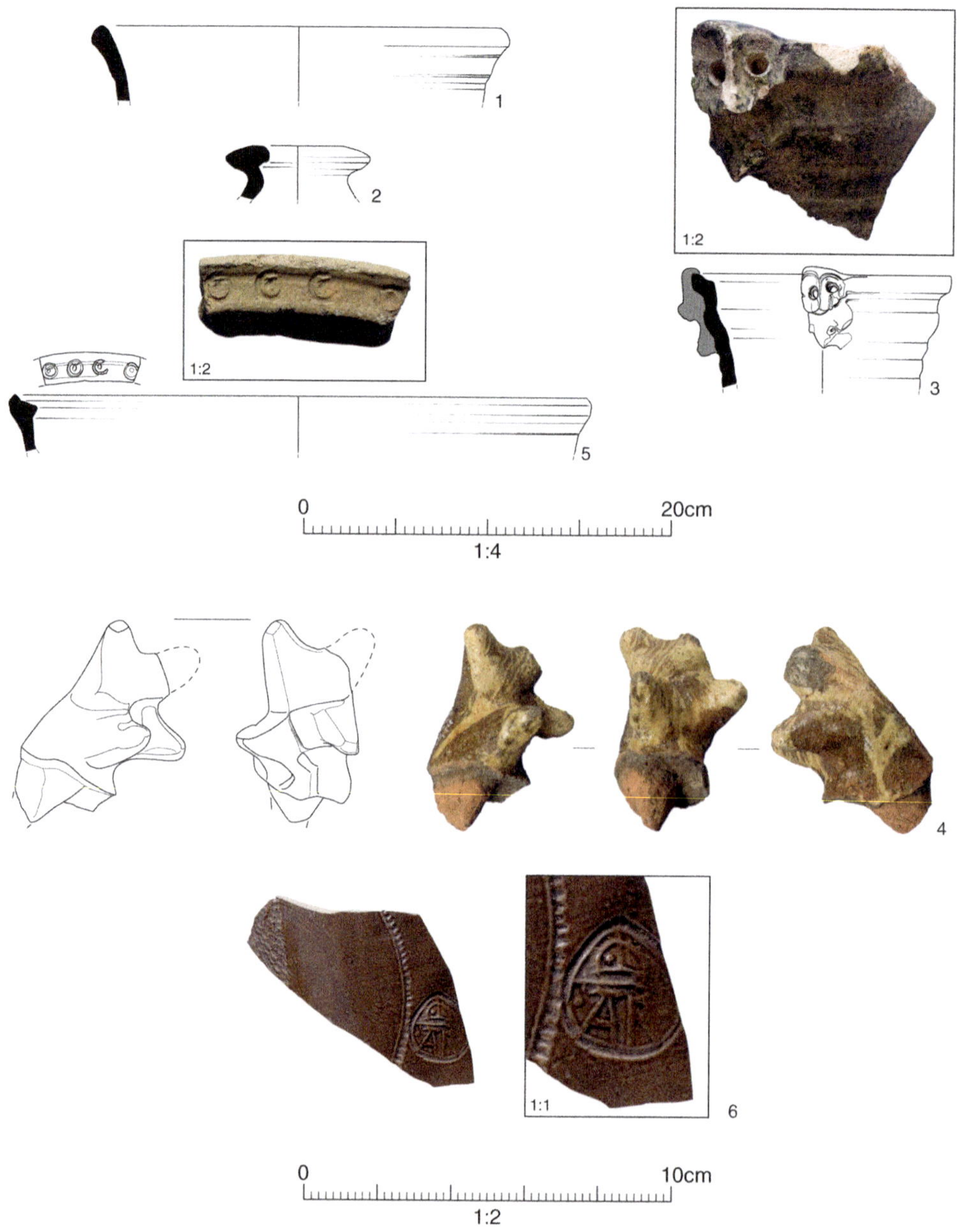

Fig. 11.15 Pottery.

sharp drop-off in occupation activity at the time, a suggestion supported by the small amounts of pottery of this date as residual material in later contexts.

The mid sixteenth to seventeenth century saw the property divided in two. The easternmost tenement, 2E, produced just 18 sherds dating to this time, with around 5 per cent of it residual. The western tenement, 2W produced a much larger assemblage, 177 sherds, with residual material comprising just over 15 per cent of this. Most of the contemporary material was utilitarian earthenwares, but lamps and a few sherds of later-medieval drinking pottery were noted amongst the residual group. The seventeenth-century pottery from Property 2W, as with Property 1 at this time, consisted mainly of utilitarian earthenwares along with small quantities of drinking and display vessels. The eighteenth-century pottery from the property was largely red earthenware, but some of the drinking pottery, particularly the German stonewares, was quite ornate, with oak leaf or moulded medallions. These could be residual, however, as such decoration was more common in the sixteenth and seventeenth centuries. A Nottingham/Derby stoneware tavern-mug ('gorge') fragment occurred with a Queen Anne ale-mark (within Phase 7 pit 1159), offering a secure *terminus post quem* of 1702 (Fig. 11.15, no. 6). Property 2E produced very little post-medieval pottery. Property 3 produced very little evidence of activity in the thirteenth century, and there was no pottery at all from the fourteenth to late seventeenth century, and just two sherds from the late seventeenth to mid eighteenth century.

Catalogue of Illustrated Pottery (Fig. 11.15):

1. Ipswich ware. Rim sherd from a medium to large jar. Uniform dark grey fabric, surfaces somewhat abraded. Ctx 223, Phase 7 (residual).
2. Light grey fabric with darker surfaces, inner surface sooted and with a heavy black burnt residue. Ipswich ware bottle rim or possibly OXY curfew apex. Ctx 662, well 663, Phase 4.
3. Fabric OXAM. Rim sherd from a jug with applied 'owl' mask. Pale grey fabric with buff surfaces, dark green, copper-rich glaze on outer surface. Ctx 662, well 663, Phase 4.
4. Fabric OXY or OXAG. Modelled spike, possibly a deer antler? Grey fabric with an orange core, olive green glaze over yellow slip decoration. Ctx 774, pit 773, Phase 4.
5. Fabric OXY. Rim sherd from a jar. Pale yellow-green glaze on upper rim over ring-and-dot stamp impressions. Ctx 1027, Phase 7 (residual).
6. Fabric OXEST. Body sherd from a mug with an 'AR' ale-mark. Grey fabric with brown salt-glaze on outer surface. Ctx 300, pit 1159, Phase 7.

BUILDING MATERIALS

Architectural Stone by Alison de Turberville

Over 100 fragments of stone were recovered during the excavation with less than a third showing any sign of worked surface. The vast majority of pieces were located in contexts that involved the reuse of stonework as fill or hardcore. The recovered stone is of varying quality and the 29 pieces of worked stone within the assemblage show little duplication of moulding detail, as might be suggestive of a definite style or building which may have formerly occupied the site.

The most significant piece came from the Phase 4 fill (662) of well 663 (Fig. 11.16). This was an oolitic limestone fragment of a tympanum above a window with an outer roll moulding forming an overall arch and inner roll which forms the head of the window light. This fragment is part of a window for a stone house probably dating to the twelfth century. It is similar to, although simpler in design than, a fragment recorded during an excavation at No. 4A Merton Street.[55] Several depictions of stone houses in visual records and mentions in property documents suggest that this style of house was not concentrated in a particular area, but occurred across

55 Munby, 'Worked Stone'.

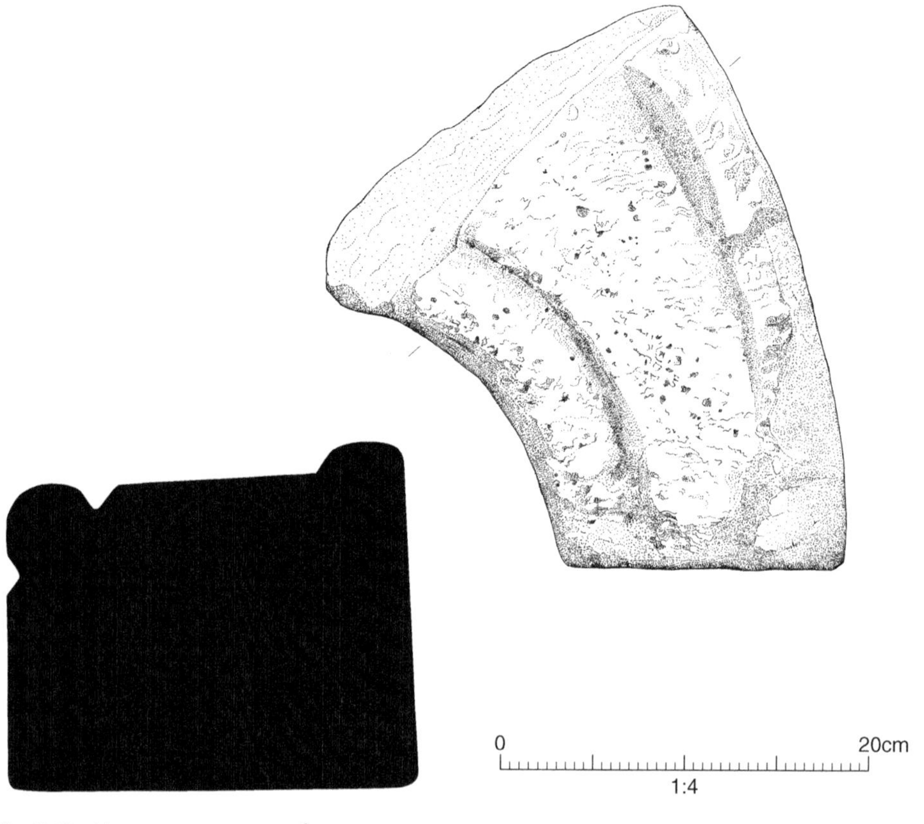

Fig. 11.16 Limestone tympanum fragment.

all of Oxford during the twelfth century.[56] The present fragment is likely to be from a house either on or very close to the excavation site. Another fragment, found within the same context, was a corner section of a limestone window frame with the remains of corroded metal bars set within a rebate. This is a roughly made piece and probably comes from a lower status building. Another Phase 4 find (layer 263) was a fragment of limestone with bead moulding and a recessed flat panel which is probably the corner section of an external doorway. The later phase contexts included further fragments of stone that had evidently been used. A section of window lintel with hollow chamfer moulding with a rebate within the chamber and the remains of two wooden pegs within was removed from context 547, reused stonework forming the lining of an early nineteenth-century soakaway. This suggests there was a later external lean-to structure adjacent to this window when it was in situ, as the chamfering at this point is weathered showing it was originally an external face.

Ceramic and Stone Tile by John Cotter and Alison de Turberville

Roof tile forms over 90 per cent of the assemblage, with 1673 fragments recovered from the site. By far the commonest category are flat clay roof tiles, which represent 80 per cent of the assemblage by fragment count. These are traditional medieval/post-medieval flat roof tiles (peg tiles) with a pair of circular nailholes at one end. Glazed examples are rare, though 17 fragments

56 Ibid.

Fig. 11.17 Ceramic and stone tiles.

retaining traces of glaze are present. All but a handful of tiles are in red-firing sandy fabrics, with small numbers of fragments from distinctive thirteenth to fourteenth century pink or cream fabric tiles. There are around 80–100 fragments of stone roof tile, which are of roughly hewn limestone with a single drilled nail hole at one end (illustrated example from latrine pit 1373, context 1026; Fig. 11.17, no. 1). Some 27 fragments of ceramic ridge tile were present, mainly of medieval date, although a few examples appear to be post-medieval. Most examples are glazed or partially glazed, usually greenish-brown or brown, and most are in red- or grey-firing sandy fabrics; two small pieces are in the rarer Oolitic limestone-tempered fabric which is thought to be of thirteenth- and early fourteenth century date. The majority of the assemblage consists of edge fragments, though there is a small piece with triangular crests from pit 370 (context 368, Phase 5; Fig. 11.17, no. 2), and a well-preserved example with black glaze from pit 1034 and context 1027, Phase 7. A small piece of ridge tile from pit 412 is unusual in having a green glaze and a thumbed lower edge.

Only 26 fragments of floor tile were recovered from Phase 4 to 8 contexts, which is perhaps surprising given the proximity of the site to Beaumont Palace and the later Carmelite friary.

Fragments of glazed tile occurred in contexts of Phase 4, a greenish-glazed fragment in pit 1166 and a fragment of brown-glazed tile in pit 394. There were no floor tiles within the assemblage from Phase 5. The majority of the assemblage was recovered from Phase 6 contexts with a late sixteenth to mid seventeenth century date. A single corner fragment from a decorated medieval 'printed' floor tile was recovered from pit 1143 (context 1145; Fig. 11.17, no. 3). This is likely to be a Penn/Chiltern or south-east Oxfordshire piece dating from the fourteenth century.

The most unusual element of the assemblage was the collection of 29 fragments of oast or malting kiln tiles, 25 of which came from context 301 (Phase 7; Fig. 11.17, no. 4). These are smaller than Victorian examples and less regular in appearance and therefore probably earlier in date, possibly eighteenth century. Two complete widths of 142 mm and 144 mm and a broken length of 178+ mm were recorded from context 301. Another complete width of 140 mm with a broken length of 156+ mm was recorded from pit 371. Thicknesses vary from 24–26 mm and both straight and bevelled edges are present. The tiles have a soft orange brick-like fabric and many have a thin pale grey ?ash glaze along their edges; most show traces of white mortar on their undersides – usually along the edges. The surfaces are perforated with circular 'socket'-like perforations typical of oast kiln tiles – each main circular perforation exiting on the other side of the tile as a group of three smaller perforations. Alternating main perforations exit as a single small perforation thus creating a regular pattern of perforations on both sides of the tile, large perforations on one side and a sieve-like pattern of finer perforations on the reverse side. Tiles of this sort formed the raised floors of oast houses or malting kilns with the perforations allowing the circulation of heat and air throughout the kiln. Malting kilns were usually for the malting of barley and are often associated with brewing. Their presence in some quantity on this site may indicate the presence of a brewing industry either here or in the vicinity. Oast kiln tiles are known to have been produced at the Nettlebed potteries in south-east Oxfordshire during the eighteenth and probably the nineteenth century, but may have been produced elsewhere in the county too.

Other Objects by John Cotter

A worn sherd from context 455 (unphased; max width 60 mm) appears to be from a thick-walled cylindrical object with an oblique perforation through the wall – most likely part of a rare medieval chimney pot. This occurs in late Anglo-Saxon/early medieval calcareous gravel-tempered ware, also known as Cotswolds-type ware (fabric OXAC), dating to *c.*900–1250, most likely from the later end of this range. Only one or two other examples of this form have been noted from Oxford before. A lump of painted wall plaster was recovered from layer 1274 (Phase 8). This is white, on a backing of grey render, with crudely painted bands of red ochre just about distinguishable. It could be late medieval or early post-medieval in date.

GLASS by HUGH WILLMOTT

The glass assemblage comprised 440 fragments from both vessels and windows; much was relatively recent in date or in a very fragmentary condition. All the glass was assessed and the most interesting items are discussed here.

Phase 4 (Thirteenth to Fourteenth Century)

Only two fragments of glass were recovered, both from pit 1091 (ctx 1088) in Property 1. These are both fragments of green devitrified plain window glass which are roughly datable to the thirteenth to fifteenth centuries.

Phase 5 (Fifteenth to Mid Sixteenth Century)

Property 1 Pit 745 contained a single fragment of green devitrified plain window glass, which although difficult to date precisely is likely to be fifteenth rather than sixteenth century in date. More diagnostic are fragments of curved base from a urinal, found in pit 815 (Fig. 11.18, no. 1).

Urinals were a commonly used tool for the diagnosis of health problems in the late medieval period, and are often associated with higher-status properties.[57]

Property 2 A fragment of green-tinted plain window glass was found in pit 370. This is slightly lighter in colour and of better quality suggesting that it dates to the sixteenth, rather than the fifteenth, century.

Phase 6 (Late Sixteenth to Mid Seventeenth Century)

Larger assemblages of glass were found in association with Properties 1 and 2W.

Property 1 Glass was found in four pits. Pit 883 contained fragments of folded tubular base-ring from a pedestal beaker. The glass is green and potash-rich with medium weathering. This was a form produced at a large number of regional glassmaking sites in England throughout the late sixteenth and early seventeenth centuries.[58] Three other pits from this phase contained residual material, or glass that was deposited many years after it was manufactured. Pit 702 included a fragment of thirteenth to fourteenth century window glass decorated with a painted grisaille design, as well as two fragments of plain late-medieval window glass. Possible well 835 contained fragments of late-medieval window glass which, although plain, retain their original grozed edges. Pit 1143 contained the upturned rim from a late-medieval urinal (Fig. 11.18, no. 2), as well as part of a later seventeenth century case bottle (Fig. 11.18, no. 3). Interpreting these finds is difficult, but the presence of so much earlier glass might suggest that during the late sixteenth to mid seventeenth century a late-medieval building of some status was being altered or demolished.

Property 2W A number of glass finds dating to the seventeenth century were recovered. Late-medieval window glass came from horse burial pit 613, although this may well be a residual find. Two other features did contain glass contemporaneous with Phase 6. Pit 417 included a small fragment of better-quality plain window glass, as well as the portion of an ordinary storage jar decorated with an optic-blown mesh design. Such vessels are commonly found on seventeenth-century sites.[59] Of similar date was the rim and neck from a small square-section case bottle from pit 851, another common type of storage vessel.[60] Slightly earlier in date, but probably still post-medieval, were several finds from latrine pit 1373. These include the base, neck and rim from a flask, and two plain fragments of window glass. Although small in size, the presence and domestic character of the assemblage does seem to indicate that there were buildings on the property at this time. However, all the glass is very ordinary in character, with there being no definitive suggestion that this was high-status in nature.

Phase 7 (Late Seventeenth to Eighteenth Century)

The bulk of the glass came from Phase 7 contexts across Properties 1, 2W and 3. A wide range of vessel and window glass was found on Property 1. In pit 380 was found one of the most interesting of these, the rim from a good-quality lead crystal wine glass that is eighteenth century in date. In association were a significant number of wine bottle fragments of the late seventeenth- to early eighteenth-century onion form. Other glass present in this feature includes a portion of cylindrical phial and two fragments of window glass. Pit 777 contained a small number of fragments from a similar onion wine bottle, whilst pit 847 included a phial, wine bottle and window glass. Pit 918 also had a small number of window glass fragments in its fill. The remaining glass was more diverse. Pit 920 contained a fragment of rim and neck from a

57 R. Tyson, *Medieval Glass Vessels Found in England c.AD 1200–1500*, CBA Research Report, 121 (2000), pp. 149–53.
58 H. Willmott, *Early Post-Medieval Vessel Glass in England c.1500–1670*, CBA Research Report, 132 (2002), p. 68.
59 Ibid. pp. 97–9.
60 Ibid. pp. 87–8.

sandglass. These vessels are surprisingly common in seventeenth-century contexts, although it is often unclear why people were so concerned with measuring time in this way.[61] Pit 1122 included a portion of a flattened oval bottle (Fig. 11.18, no. 4), which differs from normal in that it has an intentionally sheared, rather than the usual out-turned, rim. The final vessel (Fig. 11.19, no. 9) is rather more remarkable, being a complete mallet wine bottle dating to the 1760s and impressed with a seal of All Souls College (pit 380). The glass finds from Property 1 suggest that there was a fairly dense level of occupation here during Period 7. Furthermore, whilst the increased level of evidence for wine consumption might indicate a domestic function, it is just possible that it could have derived from an inn. Property 2W produced a very similar assemblage to Property 1 with quite a high proportion of glass associated with wine consumption, and it therefore could have derived from a similar source. These include a single wine bottle from pit 287, and several different examples from pit 371. This latter feature also contained the base from a small lead glass decanter, another decorative ribbed bottle, and a small phial (Fig. 11.18, no. 5). Pit 1159 contained portions of a shaft and globe bottle (the earliest type of wine bottle) dating to *c.*1650–80, as well as a slightly later onion wine bottle and five fragments of window glass. Just one glass vessel, from pit 393, was recovered from Property 3, this being two fragments of base from a seventeenth-century shaft and glove wine bottle.

Phase 8 (1800–92)

A very interesting assemblage of glass came from Property 2. Although apparently deposited during the nineteenth century, without exception all the glass was manufactured during the preceding century. This might suggest that there was significant clearance or redevelopment of earlier buildings taking place that this time. The glass includes a mixture of drinking and dining wares, storage vessels and some interesting gardening items. The lack of window glass in this phase is also notable. The largest group came from pit 392 and can be closely dated to the first half of the eighteenth century. These include the base and lower body from a fashionable lead crystal jelly glass (Fig. 11.18, no. 6), and a portion of bevelled edge mirror, an expensive item in the eighteenth century. More ordinary vessels include a large bottle-shaped phial (Fig. 11.18, no. 7), and two near-identical square medicine bottles. More unusual were portions of folded edge from two different green glass cloches or 'bell glasses' (Fig. 11.18, no. 8). Although documentary sources suggest these became increasingly popular during the eighteenth century for the cultivation of delicate and often exotic plants,[62] they are rarely identified on sites, presumably because of their similarity to wine bottles when fragmented. The remaining thirty-four fragments from this pit were from eighteenth century wine bottles. Glass was recovered in much smaller quantities from two other contexts. Rubble layer 1274 contained a fragment of lead crystal wine glass base, although its precise form could not be reconstructed, and part of the moulded stem from another jelly glass. Pit 1296 contained fifty-two fragments of wine bottles, all forms datable to the first half of the eighteenth century.

Catalogue of Illustrated Glass (Figs. 11.18 and 11.19):

1. Convex base with external pontil mark from a urinal base. Clear green potash glass with quite light weathering. Fifteenth century. Ctx 814, pit 815, Phase 5.
2. Flat rim with up-turned edge from a urinal. Green clear potash glass with heavy weathering. Rim diameter 90mm. Fifteenth to early sixteenth century. Ctx 1144, pit 1143, Phase 6.
3. Rim, body and base from a small square case bottle. Green clear mixed alkali glass with medium weathering. Rim diameter 26 mm, base diameter 47 x 47 mm. Seventeenth century. Ctx 1147, 1148 and 1149, pit 1143, Phase 6.

61 Ibid. p. 91.

62 A. Noël Hume, *Archaeology and the Colonial Gardener*, Colonial Williamsburg Archaeological Series, 7 (1974), pp. 62–3.

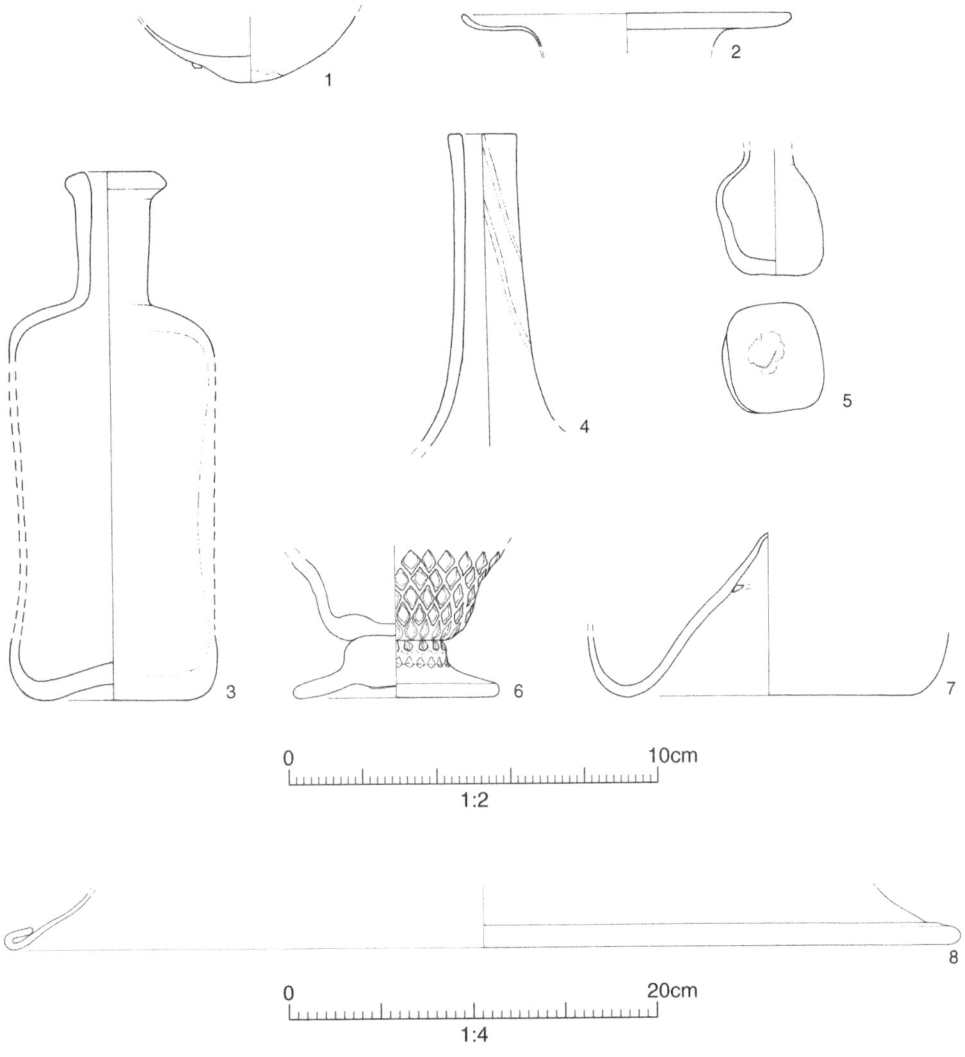

Fig. 11.18 Vessel glass.

4. Long tapered neck with a sheared rim from a flattened oval bottle. Green mixed alkali glass with little weathering. Early to mid eighteenth century. Rim diameter 18 mm. Ctx 983, pit 1122, Phase 7.
5. Flat base and squared body from a very small rectangular phial. Green mixed alkali glass with very little weathering. Base diameter 22 x 20 mm. Late seventeenth to early eighteenth century. Pit 371, Phase 7.
6. Base and lower body from a jelly glass, decorated with mould-blown mesh design. Clear lead glass with medium weathering. Base diameter 56 mm. Early to mid eighteenth century. Ctx 395, pit 392, Phase 8.
7. Pushed-in base with pointed kick from a large bottle-shaped phial. Green mixed alkali glass with no weathering. Base diameter 80 mm. Early to mid eighteenth century. Ctx 396, pit 392.

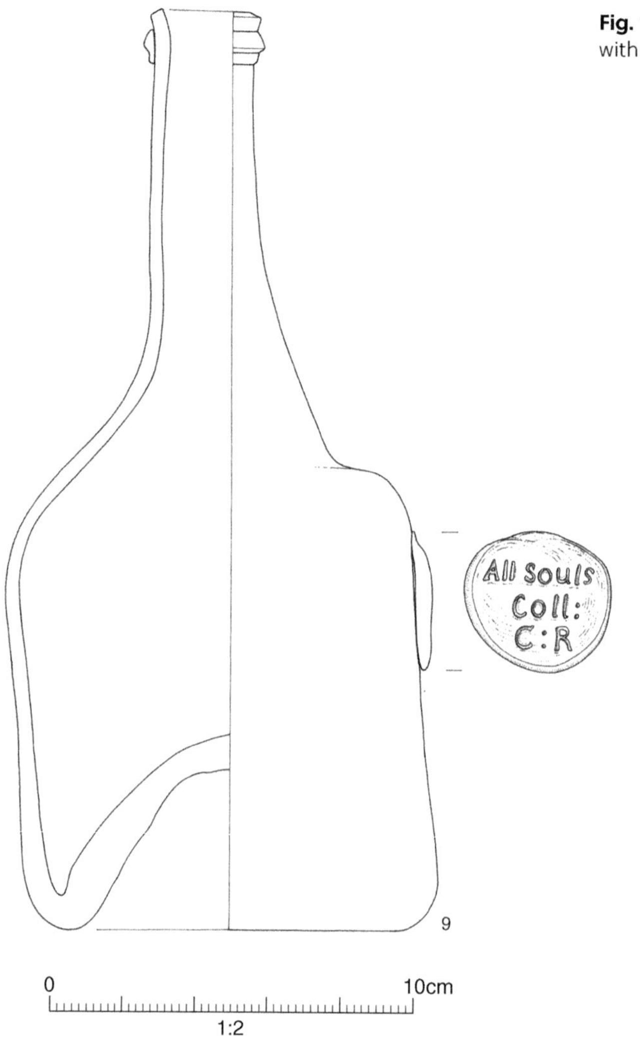

Fig. 11.19 Mallet wine bottle with seal of All Souls College.

8. Folded-out edge from a cloche. Green mixed alkali glass with light weathering. Eighteenth century. Ctx 397, pit 392, Phase 8.
9. Mallet wine bottle. Decorated with an applied seal from All Souls College. Green glass with little weathering. 1760s. Ctx 1350, pit 380, Phase 7.

CLAY TOBACCO PIPES by DAVID A. HIGGINS

The excavations produced 837 fragments of pipe, comprising 181 bowl, 630 stem and 26 mouthpiece fragments from 74 contexts. There is also one fragment of tobacco pipe kiln waste. The majority of the fragments date from the seventeenth or eighteenth century with only a very small quantity of nineteenth century material represented. Bowls dating from *c.*1620–50 (Fig. 11.20, nos. 1–2) onwards are represented, with the majority of the pipes dating from *c.*1620–1750. Only a summary of the pipe report is given here; the full digital version is available via the OA Library.

Recent studies have, to a large extent, been able to establish the nature and evolution of pipe styles in Oxford and surrounding areas.[63] The pipes from the present site generally follow the trends that have been established with, for example, groups of *c.*1640–60 being dominated by heel forms (pit 851), whereas by *c.*1650–90 spur forms dominate (e.g. Fig. 11.20, nos. 3–4). Heel forms regain the ascendancy by the start of the eighteenth century. The pit groups of 1720–50 (pit 380: Fig. 11.20, nos. 7–8 and Fig. 11.21, nos. 9–17; pit 371: Fig. 11.22, nos. 18–21) are particularly important since good-quality material of this date has not previously been studied and they now allow clear differences to be seen in the early eighteenth-century material. Early eighteenth-century pipes generally have bottered rims and burnished surfaces with few flared heels. By the second quarter of the century most rims are simply cut, burnishing is much rarer and the heels are more frequently flared. Later material is, once again, sparse from this site, particularly for the nineteenth century.

Marked Pipes

Twelve marked pipes were recovered, comprising two heel stamps, seven stem stamps and three moulded marks. These represent at least six different makers and make a valuable contribution to the relatively small number of marked pipes that are known from Oxford, especially since several previously unrecorded marks are present. There is also an important group of imported stem marks, all of which were found together in pit 380. The marks are described in alphabetical order by surname below.

ED/BEAS/TEN Five incuse stamped Edward Beasten marks dating from *c.*1700–30 were found in pit 380, three from context 381 (Fig. 11.21, no. 17) and two from context 382 (Fig. 11.21, no. 16). Cannon notes that the largest concentration of his marks has been found in the Newbury area, about 25 miles south of Oxford, suggesting that Beasten either worked there or at the neighbouring pipemaking centre of East Woodhay in Hampshire.[64]

RG/GR One pipe with the relief moulded heel mark RG was found (Fig. 11.22, no. 21) and another marked GR (Fig. 11.20, no. 6). Occasionally moulds were made with the initials transposed from the normal order, probably by mistake, and this seems likely to be the case here. There were two Oxford pipemakers named Robert Gadney, father and son. Both pipes date from the first half of the eighteenth century and so could have been made by either maker, since they were both working in 1722.[65]

MH A heel bowl was recovered from context 321 with a relief stamped MH mark on its heel, with stars above and below the initials (Fig. 11.20, no. 2). This can be attributed to Miles Higges (or Hickes), who is the earliest known Oxford pipemaker.[66] Pipes stamped MH can be dated to *c.*1630–50. The bowl was made in the same mould as an unmarked example from context 229, which shows that Higges did not always stamp his products.

GN One plain pipe with the relief moulded mark GN was recovered from pit 392 (Fig. 11.22, no. 22). This can be attributed to a member of the Norwood family, who were one of the principal pipemaking families in Oxford during the nineteenth century. At least five different patterns of marked pipe produced by this family were found during the excavations at St Ebbe's,[67] and a spur fragment marked GN was recovered from the Sackler Library site.[68] The initials GN here almost certainly refer to George (I) Norwood, documented as a pipemaker from 1826–63.

63 Cf. other pipe reports in this volume.

64 P. Cannon, 'Evidence of Tobacco Pipe Making in East Woodhay and District', *Transactions of the Newbury and District Field Club*, 14.1 (1991), pp. 16–27.

65 A. Oswald, 'Clay Pipes', in Hassall, 'St Ebbe's, Part II', p. 255.

66 R. Price, 'John Taylor of Oxford', *Society for Clay Pipe Research Newsletter*, 72 (2007), pp. 18–21.

67 Oswald, 'Clay Pipes', p. 258.

68 D.A. Higgins, 'Clay Tobacco Pipes', in Poore, *Beaumont*, fig. 19.9.

WP/WILL/PEARCE (Fig. 11.21, nos. 14–15) There is an incuse WP stem stamp from context 381 and an incuse WILL/PEARCE stem mark from 382, both of which are fills of pit 380 and seem likely to represent the same maker. Pearce is clearly identified from his marks, which date from *c.*1700–40, but has yet to be traced in the documentary record. WP marks have been noted from Marlborough and WILL/PEARCE marks from St Ebbe's, Marlborough and Queenhithe in London.[69]

TR (Fig. 11.20, no. 5) Pit 1159 produced a miniature pipe made of a fabric with fine sandy inclusions. Miniature pipes such as this are extremely rare and so this is an important addition to the known examples, particularly since it is not only associated with other datable pipes but also marked. On the heel are the incuse stamped initials TR, without any border or other decoration. Although very early maker's marks often consisted of unbordered incuse initials such as this, the style was rarely used later – except at Oxford, where a number of examples are known from the late seventeenth and early eighteenth centuries.[70] The sandy fabric suggests local production and the evidence points to the maker being Thomas Reeve, recorded as an Oxford pipemaker from 1667–1700.[71] This makes the present example one of only two miniature pipes that can not only be accurately dated but also attributed to a particular production centre and manufacturer. Despite its small size, this example has clearly been smoked, showing that these pipes were not only entertaining, but functional as well.

Coloured Pipes

The final point of note with regard to the pipes is that a number of them appear to have been coloured red originally. This is an extremely unusual phenomenon but there now appears to be compelling evidence that it was a regular practice on pipes produced in or near Oxford over quite a period of time (cf. an example from St Peter's College in chapter 5, above). Colouring occurs on eight stems ranging from thick pieces from adjacent to the bowl junction right down to thin pieces from near the tip of a pipe, so it appears that the whole stem length was coloured. No coloured bowl fragments were noted. The earliest pieces are probably from context 1037, where the associated bowls suggested a date of *c.*1650–90. Furthermore, the two pieces from this context are both made of a fine almost inclusion-free fabric, which predates the use of the later Thames Valley sandy fabric. All the other examples occur on stems made of this sandy fabric (which shows they were made locally), with the latest pieces occurring in context 374, a fill of pit 371, which dates from *c.*1720–50.

Kiln Furniture

One piece of pipe kiln furniture was recovered from context 137 (Fig. 11.22, no. 23). This comprises a small fired pipe clay roll with dished pipe bowl impressions on both sides. The roll would have been used damp to help secure the load when stacking the muffle kiln for firing. A date within the 1660–1750 range is most likely for this piece. There is no other evidence of pipe making from the site itself, but this piece of waste clearly indicates that it was taking place nearby.

Illustrations (Figs. 11.20–11.22):

1. Bowl of *c.*1620–50. Ctx 850, pit 851, Phase 6.
2. Bowl stamped MH for Miles Higges, *c.*1620–50. Ctx 321, pit 287, Phase 7.

3–5. Bowls ranging from *c.*1660–90, including a miniature stamped TR for Thomas Reeve. Ctx 1158, pit 1159, Phase 7.

[69] Oswald, 'Clay Pipes', fig. 52.15; A. Oswald, 'Pipe Stamp Index', unpublished copy of Adrian Oswald's archive index, held at the National Clay Tobacco Pipe Archive, which is currently housed at the University of Liverpool.

[70] D.A. Higgins, 'Clay Tobacco Pipes', in J. Munby et al., *From Studium to Station, Rewley Abbey and Rewley Road Station, Oxford*, Oxford Archaeology Occasional Paper, 16 (2007), pp. 46–7.

[71] Oswald, 'Clay Pipes', p. 262.

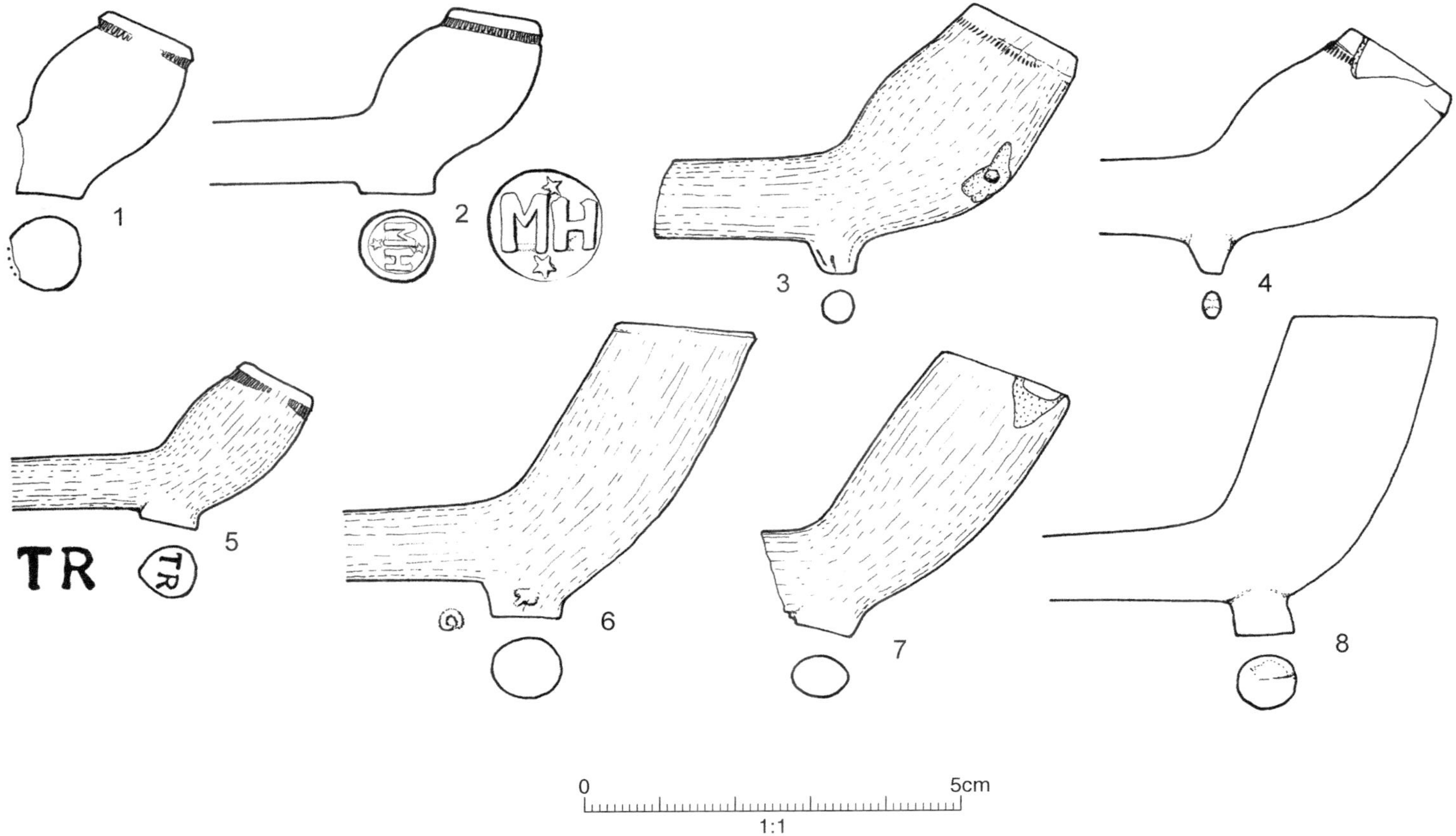

Fig. 11.20 Clay tobacco pipes, nos. 1–8. Relief marks are shown in outline and incuse marks in solid black. Burnished surfaces are indicated using a light broken line and damaged areas with a stippled finish. A complete outline is used if the entire fragment is shown, with a heavier line marking the profile and a lighter line the broken edges. Where a stem has been shortened to accommodate the page layout, the truncated end has been left open. Drawings by David A. Higgins.

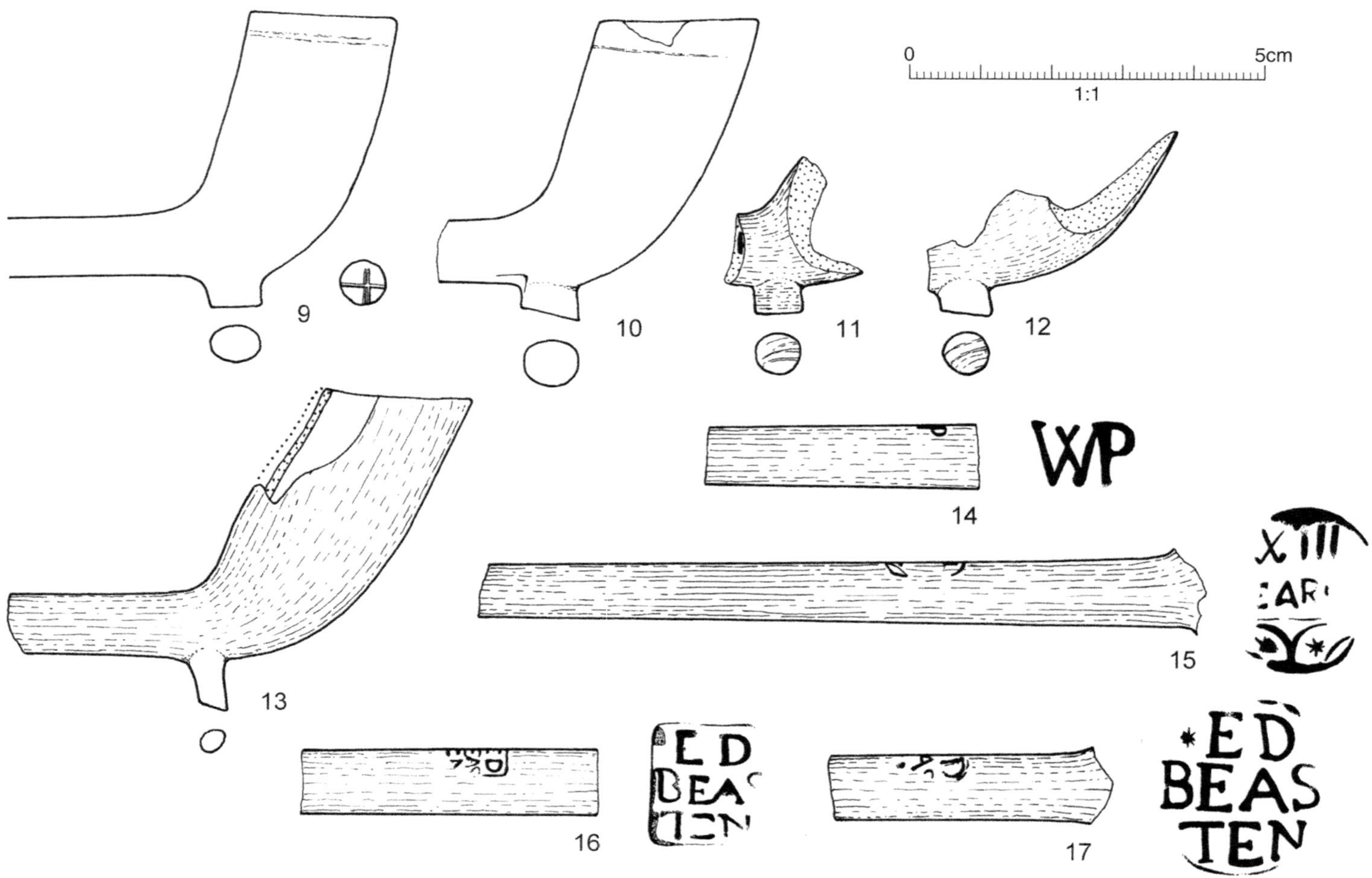

Fig. 11.21 Clay tobacco pipes, nos. 9–17. Drawings by David A. Higgins.

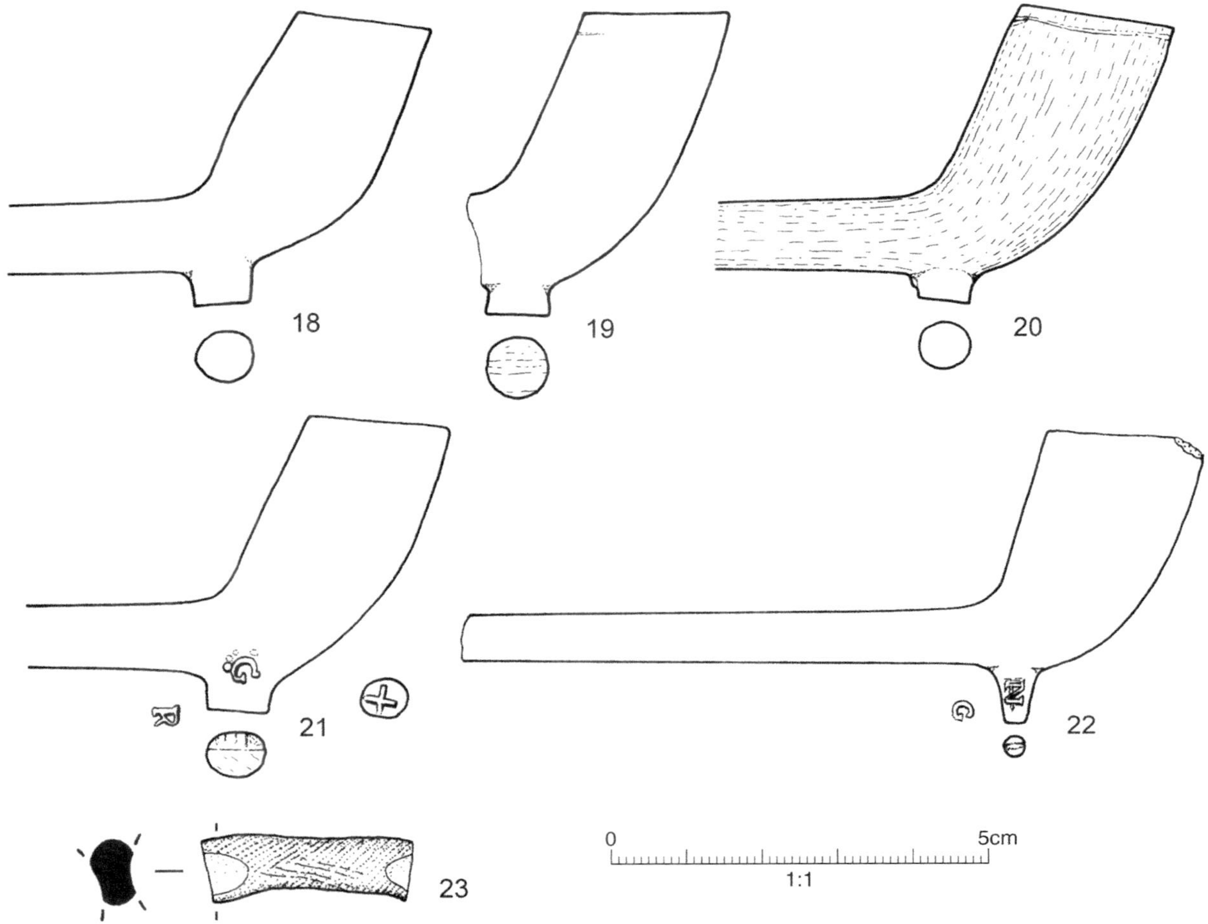

Fig. 11.22 Clay tobacco pipes and kiln furniture, nos. 18–23. Drawings by David A. Higgins.

6. Bowl of *c.*1700–50 marked GR. Ctx 260, Phase 7.
7–9. Bowls from a pit of *c.*1720–50. Ctx 730, pit 380, Phase 7.
10. Bowl of *c.*1720–50. Ctx 382 and 383, pit 380, Phase 7.
11–13. Bowls from a pit of *c.*1720–50. Ctx 382, pit 380, Phase 7.
14. Stem stamped WP, *c.*1720–50. Ctx 381, pit 380, Phase 7.
15–16. Stamped stems, *c.*1720–50. Ctx 382, pit 380, Phase 7.
17. Stamped stem, *c.*1720–50. Ctx 381, pit 380, Phase 7.
18. Bowl from a pit of *c.*1720–50. Ctx 372, pit 371, Phase 7.
19–20. Bowls from a pit of *c.*1720–50. Ctx 374, pit 371, Phase 7.
21. Bowl from a pit of *c.*1720–50. Ctx 372, pit 371, Phase 7.
22. Bowl of *c.*1820–70 marked GN for George Norwood. Ctx 396, pit 392, Phase 8.
23. Clay strip from a pipe kiln, perhaps *c.*1660–1750. Ctx 137, Phase 9.

Full catalogue descriptions are provided in the digital report.

METALWORK AND WORKED BONE by LEIGH ALLEN

A total of 886 metal objects and 7 worked bone objects were recovered from the excavations. Much of the ironwork was thickly corroded and fragmentary and, excluding unidentifiable fragments and nails, the remaining metal assemblage comprises 186 copper alloy objects (including 56 wire pins), 38 iron objects and 32 lead objects.

The majority of the objects from the excavation are late medieval or post-medieval in date. The assemblage includes a large number of wire pins and lace tags that occur in all areas of the site in all but the very earliest phases, personal and domestic items and objects associated with the structure of the properties and the furniture within; items of horsegear and a small number of military items also occurred.

Phase 3 (Twelfth Century)

A small writing lead (Fig. 11.24, no. 17) was recovered from ditch 1388; at Winchester writing leads of this form (class II) were recovered from thirteenth and fourteenth century contexts.[72] A large trapezoidal shaped iron buckle frame with a sheet metal roller came from rubbish pit 768. Heavy-duty buckles of this type were used to connect straps (or harness) of differing thickness. A late-medieval or post-medieval pin came from the upper fill of linear feature 673.

Phase 4 (Thirteenth and Fourteenth Century)

Most of the finds from this phase were recovered from rubbish pits and wells located at the eastern and western ends of Property 2, especially the well house (1402) and adjacent features. Smaller numbers of objects, predominantly nails, pins and lace tags, came from clusters of pits in the western end of Properties 1 and 3. Virtually no objects were recovered from the subsoil quarry pits at the centre of the site.

The 27 personal objects include 12 fine wire pins and 11 lace tags. Small, slender pins with wire wound heads are common finds on medieval and post-medieval sites; analysis of a large assemblage from Winchester established that this type of pin was first produced in the thirteenth century in this country.[73] They become more common from the fourteenth century onwards. They are often found in association with lace tags, which saw a similar increase in popularity in the late medieval/post-medieval period. The most interesting of the remaining four personal objects is a cast decorative bar mount from pit 473 (Fig. 11.23, no. 1). Bar mounts were used to

[72] M. Biddle and D. Brown, 'Writing Equipment', in M. Biddle, *Object and Economy in Medieval Winchester* (1990), p. 735, fig. 212, no. 2298.

[73] M. Biddle and K. Barclay, 'Sewing Pins and Wire', in Biddle, *Object and Economy*, pp. 560–71.

decorate belts, straps or harness. A small annular iron buckle for light clothing was found in pit 472, and two simple folded buckle plate fragments came from pit 477 and layer 219. The five household items comprise part of a needle, a bone bobbin and the remains of three whittle tang knives. The bobbin, from the backfill of well 1176, is probably a lace bobbin; it has a globular head and tapers very slightly along its length. It is decorated with bands of incised grooves and has a narrow axial perforation running the entire length. This form of bobbin dates from the twelfth to the fourteenth century.[74] Pit 543 contained a fragment of an eleventh to fourteenth century horseshoe, and three contemporary horseshoe 'fiddle key' nails came from layer 219, well 663 and pit 712.

Phase 5 (Fifteenth to Mid Sixteenth Century)

The personal objects comprise 22 pins, 7 lace tags, a loop fastener, a button and a buckle plate, and were all recovered from quarry or rubbish pits 355, 412, 448, 495, 815 and 821. The pins all have wire wound heads but a broad range of sizes are represented, including two very slender pins measuring in excess of 70 mm. This variation in size reflects the diverse uses of these items. Lace tags and a simple wire loop fastener (probably used to secure light clothing) were found along with the pins. A small, solid biconvex button with a simple looped shank was also recovered from pit 495 (Fig. 11.23, no. 2); this type of button was in common use in the thirteenth to fourteenth century, although it did continue into the early post-medieval period. A fragment from a simple folded buckle plate came from pit 815. A pair of tweezers (Fig. 11.23, no. 8) was recovered from pit 781. Tweezers of this form are generally found in early to middle Anglo-Saxon contexts, and this is an interesting find in view of the presence on the site of pottery of a similar date. The three household items recovered from this phase are all whittle tang knives but only SF 110 from pit 412 is complete (Fig. 11.23, no. 11). It has a long slender triangular blade and the tang is centrally placed. It is fourteenth to fifteenth century in date, and was probably a table knife. A fragment from a horsehoe and a horseshoe nail were recovered from pits 370 and 495. The horseshoe fragment is from the tip of the arm and has a countersunk circular nail hole and a calkin. The horseshoe nail is of 'fiddle key' form. The corroded remains of a key for a mounted lock were recovered from pit 1083. It has a kidney-shaped bow and a long stem, but all trace of the bit is missing. Keys with bows of this shape date to the late fourteenth to fifteenth century and beyond.[75] A possible arm from a steelyard weight was recovered from pit 370. The rectangular bar has a rounded end that is perforated, and on the lower edge there is a perforated lug.

Phase 6 (Late Sixteenth to Mid Seventeenth Century)

Objects from most of the functional categories were recovered from rubbish pits, cesspits and wells within Properties 1 and 2W, with a high concentration of objects coming from the backfill of latrine pit 1373 and adjacent rubbish pits. Objects from Property 1 are mainly limited to tools, horsegear and structural items.

The 23 personal objects include 13 pins, 5 lace tags, 4 buckle components and a hooked clasp. The pins are all small with wire wound heads; together with the tags they came from pits 375, 417, 702 and 835 and from the back fill of latrine pit 1373. A plain buckle came from pit 702; a second plain buckle and a very corroded hooked clasp came from latrine pit fill 1373. The plate of the clasp is highly decorated with filigree spirals and granulation similar to that seen on spherical headed dress pins from Norwich dating to the early post-medieval period.[76] The seven household items include a bone knife, a highly polished bone handle with swag decoration, a

[74] A. MacGregor, *Bone, Antler, Ivory and Horn: The Technology of Skeletal Materials since the Roman Period* (1985), pp. 183–5.

[75] I.H. Goodall, 'Locks and Keys' in Biddle, *Object and Economy*, p. 1008.

[76] S. Margeson, *Norwich Households: The Medieval and Post-Medieval Finds from Norwich Survey Excavations 1971–1978*, East Anglian Archaeological Report, 58 (1993), pp. 10–11, fig. 4, nos. 26–38.

blade fragment, a drape ring, a vessel fragment and the finger loop from a pair of scissors. The small bone knife recovered from pit 783 (Fig. 11.23, no. 9) was possibly a butter knife or letter opener. Scissors are known from the medieval period but they were not as popular as shears. They become more widely used in the sixteenth to seventeenth century. Two keys from pits 851 (Fig. 11.24, no. 15) and 1121 are both designed for mounted locks. They both have kidney-shaped bows, datable to the late medieval period and beyond (see above), moulded stems and complex bits. A near-complete horseshoe of late-medieval form was recovered from the upper fill of pit 937. The majority of the structural items are nails recovered in large numbers from pits 702, 815 and latrine pit 1373. A small number of structural fittings were also recovered; these include a hinge pivot, a rectangular staple and a long 'S'-shaped hook.

Phase 7 (Late Seventeenth to Eighteenth Century)

The great majority of objects from this phase came from soil layer 223. This spread of finds includes numerous weights, musket balls and book clasps, categories not represented in previous phases. Personal objects include buckle components (many from shoes), strap loops, five buttons, mounts, pins, a brooch, and a clog fastener. The buckle components include frames, plates and pins. The majority of the buckle frames are shoe buckles ranging in style from simple rectangular/sub-rectangular shaped frames with a central bar (Fig. 11.23, no. 3) to a more decorative double oval form with ornate outside edges (Fig. 11.23, no. 4). The two mounts were both recovered from context 223; one (Fig. 11.23, no. 5) is similar to an example from London dating to the late fourteenth to fifteenth century.[77] These mounts would have been used singly or in groups to decorate belts, straps or other leather items. A small, delicate annular brooch (Fig. 11.23, no. 6) from the same context has a pin with an expanded collet at the centre (from which the stone is missing). It is similar in form to a brooch from London from a mid fourteenth- to fifteenth-century context.[78] A small decorative open-work fitting from context 223 is an eighteenth-century clog fastening. The household items comprise three spoons, two thimbles, a skimmer/strainer fragment, a knife handle and a blade fragment. The complete spoon (Fig. 11.24, no. 13) comes from pit 393; it is of pewter, and has a fig-shaped bowl and simple 'slip-top' handle with a flattened oval section; there is a maker's mark at the top of the bowl. This type dates from the early sixteenth century onwards; two detached spoon handles were also recovered, one of the same date, the other of the late seventeenth century. The thimbles, both from context 223, are of two different forms. One (Fig. 11.23, no. 10) is an example of an open-topped thimble for heavy duty tailoring, whereas the other is a short squat thimble with hand applied indentations on the top and sides. The remains of a scale tang knife were recovered from pit 1077 (Fig. 11.23, no. 12).

The upper plates of three hooked and sprung book clasps were recovered (Fig. 11.24, nos. 18–20). These are sixteenth century or later in date and an identical example was recovered from the Beaumont Palace excavations.[79] A fourth clasp is a hinged open-work fitting also of post-medieval date. A second small writing lead identical to the one recovered from Phase 3 was recovered from context 261 (deposit overlying medieval pit 264); it dates to the thirteenth to fourteenth century. The items associated with furniture are drape rings, upholstery tacks, a drawer handle and a hinge plate. A set of spurs were recovered from pit 847 (Fig. 11.24, no. 22); the short straight arms would probably indicate a late-medieval/post-medieval date. A sexfoil mount (Fig. 11.24, no. 21) is highly decorated and resembles the small bosses or pendants used on harness.

77 G. Egan and F. Pritchard, *Medieval Finds from Excavations in London: 3. Dress Accessories c.1150–c.1450* (1991), pp. 198–200, fig. 125, no. 1078.

78 Ibid. p. 254, fig. 163, no. 1331.

79 M. Biddle and D.A. Hinton, 'Book-Clasps and Page Holder' in Biddle, *Object and Economy*, pp. 755–8; L. Allen, 'Metal and Worked Bone', in Poore, *Beaumont*, p. 59, fig. 18, no. 4.

Eleven weights of various forms were recovered from context 223; they include three disc or pan weights that would have been used with scales, and seven cylindrical or biconical weights that might have been used with fishing nets. A copper alloy coin weight (identified by Martin Allen) was recovered from context 223 (Fig. 11.24, no. 16). The weight, measuring *c.*12 mm square and weighing 2.23 g, is for a James I gold half angel and dates from 1612–25.[80] Coin weights were made to correspond to the weights of particular coin denominations; they were most commonly made of copper alloy and were generally produced for high-value pieces, gold rather than silver coins. Their purpose was to check the weight of coin in circulation and ensure that coin received was of good quality. Normally they would correspond to the lowest weight at which the coin remained legal tender. They could be used to guard against clipped, worn or counterfeit coin and to check the standards of foreign coin permitted in currency.

All the items associated with firearms came from this phase (context 223); they include 13 musket balls and a powder holder cover. The musket balls range in diameter from 10–17 mm; two examples still have traces of the pontil attached and therefore have probably not been used. The powder holder cover is cup-shaped with a flat bottom, straight sides and two small loops at the rim for attachment. It would have been connected to the bandolier by a cord running through the two cap loops and two loops on the body of the flask; the cap could therefore be removed without risk of loss.[81]

Phase 8 (1800–92)

The only three notable finds are a patten, a key and part of a composite button. The iron patten (Fig. 11.23, no. 7) would have been riveted to the sole of a wooden or leather overshoe to raise the wearer off the ground and away from the dirt and rubbish of the street or the cold of a stone floor. This form of patten dates from the seventeenth to eighteenth century.

Catalogue of Illustrated Metal and Worked Bone Objects (Figs. 11.23–11.24):

1. Bar mount, copper alloy, complete. 'V'-shaped section; pairs of expanded lobes at either end and one on either side at the mid point on the bar. There are three integral spikes on the back for attachment. L: 42 mm. SF 115, ctx 474, pit 473, Phase 4.
2. Button, copper alloy, complete. D: 11 mm. Ctx 742, pit 495, Phase 5.
3. Buckle, copper alloy, complete. L: 27 mm. SF 287, ctx 223, Phase 7.
4. Buckle, copper alloy, complete. L: 44 mm. SF 236, ctx 223, Phase 7.
5. Mount, copper alloy, complete. L: 19 mm. SF 227, ctx 223, Phase 7.
6. Brooch, copper alloy, complete. L: 17 mm. SF 292, ctx 223, Phase 7.
7. Patten, iron, incomplete. L: 134 mm. Ctx 236, construction cut 237, Phase 8.
8. Tweezers, copper alloy, complete. L: 66 mm. SF 131, ctx 778, pit 1017, Phase 5.
9. Knife, bone, incomplete. L: 80 mm. Ctx 782, pit 783, Phase 6.
10. Thimble, copper alloy, incomplete. L: 22 mm. SF 214, ctx 223, Phase 7.
11. Knife, iron, complete. L: 173 mm. SF 110, ctx 413, pit 412, Phase 5.
12. Knife handle, complete, bone scales secured to the tang by four copper alloy rivets. The handle expands towards the rounded butt end, which has a small decorative foot at the base. L: 78 mm. Pit 1077, Phase 7.
13. Spoon, pewter, complete. L: 58 mm. Ctx 400, pit 393, Phase 7.
14. Spoon handle, pewter, incomplete. L: 95 mm. SF 252, ctx 223, Phase 7.
15. Key, iron, complete. L: 145 mm. Ctx 850, pit 851, Phase 6.
16. Coin weight, copper alloy, complete. L: 13 mm. SF 298, ctx 223, Phase 7.

[80] P. Withers and B. Withers, *British Coin-Weights. A Corpus of the Coin-Weights Made for Use in England, Scotland and Ireland* (1993).

[81] P. Courtney, 'Finds Research Group 700–1700 Datasheet 11. Small Arms Accessories of the mid 17th Century' (1988), figs. 2–3.

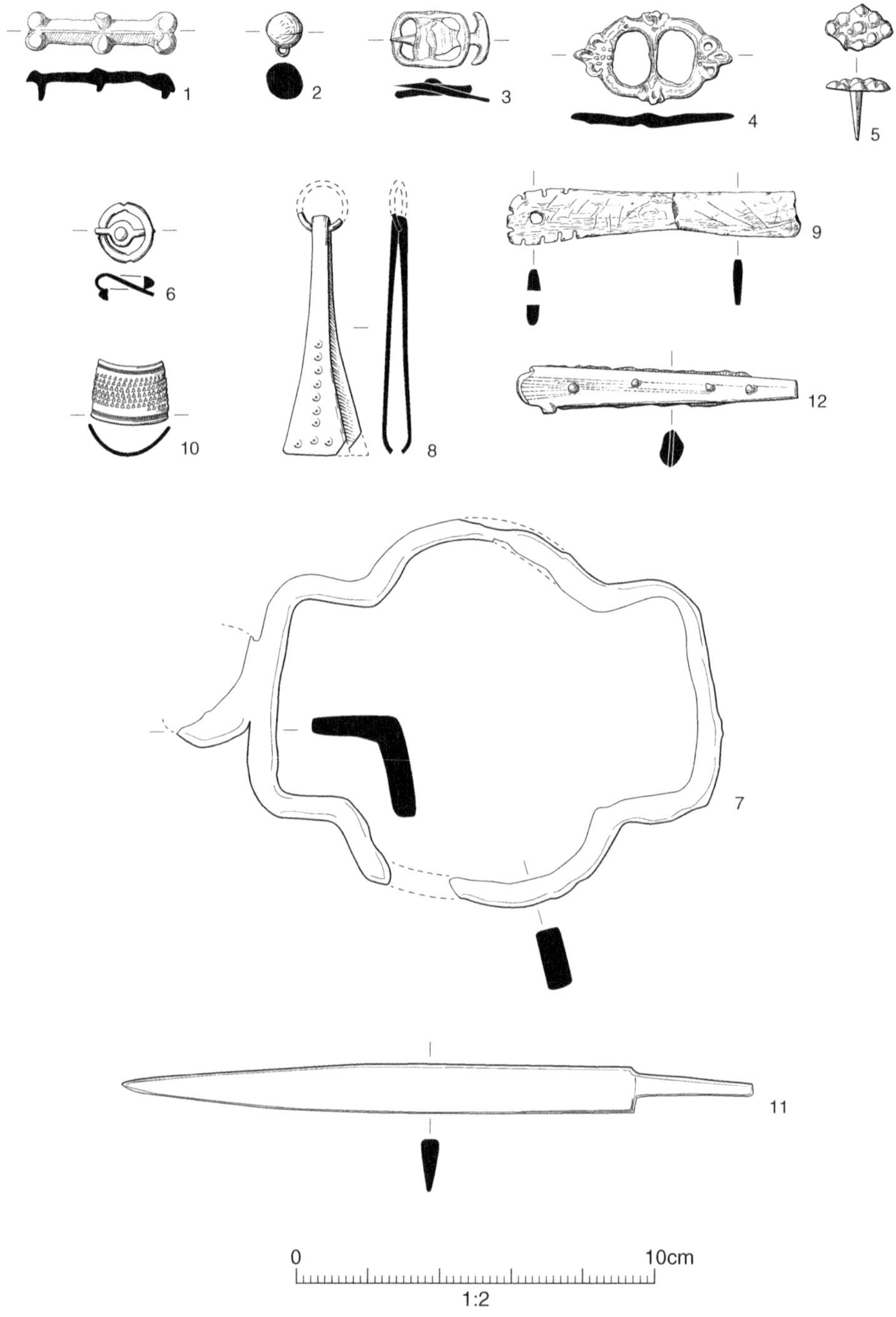

Fig. 11.23 Metalwork and worked bone, nos. 1–12.

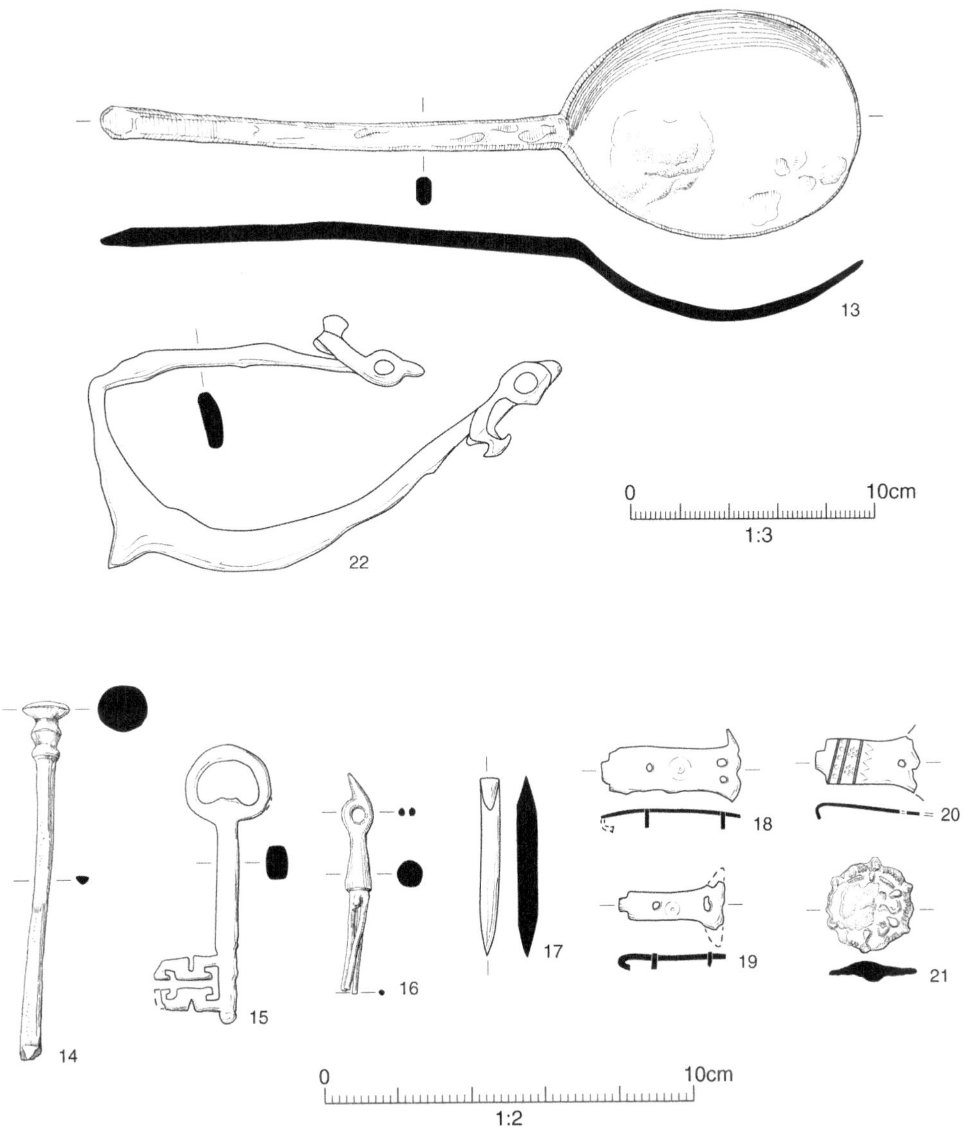

Fig. 11.24 Metalwork, nos. 13–22.

17. Stylus, lead, complete. L: 45 mm. Ctx 597, ditch 1388, Phase 3.
18. Hooked clasp, copper alloy, incomplete. L: 38 mm. SF 170, ctx 1035, pit 1034, Phase 7.
19. Hooked clasp, copper alloy, incomplete. L: 26 mm. SF 228, ctx, 223, Phase 7.
20. Hooked clasp, copper alloy, incomplete. L: 29 mm. SF 235, ctx 223, Phase 7.
21. Harness boss, copper alloy, complete. L: 23 mm. SF 291, ctx 223, Phase 7.
22. Spurs, iron, incomplete. L: 93 mm. Ctx 846, pit 847, Phase 7.

Table 11.2. Medieval coins.

No.	Context	Feature	Phase	Description	Date	Weight (g)	Condition
117	501	Unstratified	–	Henry I, silver penny, type 10, uncertain mint and moneyer	c.1117–19	0.99	
203	223	Garden soil	7	Richard I, silver penny, Short Cross class 2 or 3, uncertain mint and moneyer	c.1189–94	1.45	Bent double (reverse not visible)
207	223	Garden soil	7	Henry III, silver cut halfpenny, Short Cross class 7cC, uncertain mint, moneyer Nichole	c.1242	0.65	
160	1150	Well 663	4	Scotland, Short Cross and Stars coinage, silver cut halfpenny, inscriptions illegible	1195–c.1249	0.72	
182	1217	Pit 1210	4	Scotland, Short Cross and Stars coinage, silver cut halfpenny, inscriptions illegible	1195–c.1249	0.67	
190	223	Garden soil	7	Edward III, silver penny, Pre-Treaty series G, Durham mint	c.1356–61	0.72	Clipped
103	413	–	5	France, Charles VI, billon *double tournois* or *niquet*, Lafaurie 1951 no. 417	1421–2	1.99	

MEDIEVAL COINS AND POST-MEDIEVAL TOKENS AND JETONS by MARTIN ALLEN

The numismatic finds from the site include seven medieval coins, nine Nuremberg jetons of the sixteenth and seventeenth centuries, and seventeen seventeenth century farthing tokens. Table 11.2 provides details of the coins; a full listing of the jetons and farthing tokens is available from the OA Library. The earliest medieval coin is a silver penny of Henry I type 10, which can be dated to *c.*1117–19, and which was probably lost at the site no later than the 1130s, although coins of this type occur as a small residual element in a few coin hoards until the 1170s.[82] There are four coins issued between *c.*1189 and *c.*1249, which were probably deposited no later than the end of Henry III's complete recoinage of the English silver currency in 1247–50. These four finds include two coins of the Scottish Short Cross and Stars coinage, which circulated in England between *c.*1210 and the end of the recoinage in 1250.[83] There is one fourteenth century coin, an Edward III penny. This coin was issued *c.*1356–61, but it has been worn and clipped below the

[82] M. Allen, 'The Volume of the English Currency, *c.*973–1158', in B. Cook and G. Williams (eds.), *Coinage and History in the North Sea World, c.AD 500–1200. Essays in Honour of Marion Archibald* (2006), pp. 521–2.

[83] B. Cook, 'Foreign Coins in Medieval England', in L. Travaini (ed.), *Local Coins, Foreign Coins: Italy and Europe 11th–15th Centuries. The Second Cambridge Numismatic Symposium*, Società de numismatica Italiana collana di numismatica e scienze affini 2 (1999), pp. 242–3; M. Allen, 'Hoards and the Circulation of the Short

reduced standard weight of the English penny instituted in 1464 (0.78 g), and it was probably in circulation until the late fifteenth century or early sixteenth century. English pennies of the fourteenth century remained in circulation until the 1540s, although they were reduced to a small element of the currency by a recoinage of clipped coins in 1504–*c*.1506.[84] The remaining medieval coin is a French *double tournois* or *niquet* of Charles VI issued 1421–2. French coins were imported into England at this time, causing a complaint in a parliamentary petition of 1423.[85]

The absence of medieval jetons from a site with seven medieval coins can be contrasted with a survey of seven other sites in Oxford, which provided a total of thirty-four medieval jetons and only thirty-two medieval coins,[86] but the number of medieval coins from the present site may be too small to draw any definite conclusions from this. The jetons from the present site are all of common Nuremberg types often found in English excavations and as metal-detector and casual finds.

The seventeen farthing tokens of the seventeenth century, which are dominated by official issues of James I and Charles I (fifteen tokens), are typical of sites with activity in this period. The two unofficial tokens were both issued in Oxfordshire – one by the City of Oxford and one by the mercer Ralph Werge of Witney – providing evidence of the local circulation of these issues. The farthing tokens were probably deposited no later than the 1670s, as a royal copper coinage was introduced in 1672, and the circulation of tokens was suppressed by proclamation in 1672–4.[87]

WORKED STONE OBJECTS by RUTH SHAFFREY

The small assemblage of worked stone objects comprises three whetstones, one probable gaming counter and two pieces of marble (possibly decorative, but unphased and not described in detail here). A single unworked fragment of Norwegian Ragstone schist was recovered from well 663 (context 1150; Phase 4). Norwegian Ragstone was the most popular of the medieval whetstone materials and is commonly found on medieval sites both as whetstones and in raw material form, such as that seen here. Two whetstone fragments were recovered from Property 1 (Phase 5). These are made from schist, probably Norwegian Ragstone (pit 821) and a fine-grained sandstone (pit 412). Both are fragments and could be indicative of domestic or industrial activity. A single small circular object made from a flat piece of ironstone was recovered from Property 2E (261, Phase 7). This is almost certainly a gaming counter and could have been used with a multitude of games, for example Nine Men's Morris.

ANIMAL BONE by LENA STRID

The animal bone assemblage from Phases 2 to 6 was analysed, and is set out by phase in Table 11.3. Although the assemblage was in very good condition, particularly for the later part of the period, individual phase assemblages were generally small, with an unusually high component represented by the complete or partially complete articulated remains of single individuals.

In many respects, the assemblage is very characteristic of its urban medieval and post-medieval context, and consists largely of kitchen and butchery waste, with possible small-scale industrial

Cross Coinage', in J.P. Mass, *The J.P. Mass Collection of English Short Cross Coins, 1180–1247*, Sylloge of Coins of the British Isles, 56 (2001), p. 113.

84 M. Allen, 'The Interpretation of Single-Finds of English Coins, 1279–1544', *British Numismatic Journal*, 75 (2005), pp. 51–3, 57–9.

85 Cook, 'Foreign Coins', p. 263.

86 N.J. Palmer and N.J. Mayhew, 'Medieval Coins and Jettons from Oxford Excavations', in N.J. Mayhew (ed.) *Edwardian Monetary Affairs (1279–1344). A Symposium held in Oxford, August 1976*, BAR 36 (1977), pp. 81–95.

87 C.W. Peck, *English Copper, Tin and Bronze Coins in the British Museum 1558–1958*, 2nd edn (1964), pp. 105–6.

Table 11.3. Animal bone, identified species by phase. MNI (minimum number of individuals) in brackets. *a: articulated pig (133 fragments); *b: articulated dog (78 fragments); *c: articulated mouse (10 fragments); *d: one articulated dog (104 fragments); *e: articulated jackdaw (7 fragments); *f: articulated neonatal sheep/goat (7 fragments); *g: two articulated neonatal pigs (41, 46 fragments); *h: articulated horse (912 fragments); *i: two articulated dogs (7, 13 fragments); *j: articulated cat and kitten (58, 142 fragments); *k: articulated fowl (13 fragments); *l: articulated hedgehog (33 fragments).

	Phase				
Species	**2**	**3**	**4**	**5**	**6**
Cattle	9 (1)	54 (2)	317 (9)	142 (4)	259 (10)
Sheep/goat	7 (1)	57 (4)	208 (12)	131 (9)	207 (12)*f
Sheep	2	6	17	20	24
Goat			2		1
Pig	4 (1)	58 (3)	216 (4)*a	53 (5)	137 (4)*g
Horse		7 (1)	9 (1)	7 (1)	917 (2)*h
Deer sp.				4	
Fallow deer					1 (1)
Roe deer		1 (1)			
Dog		20 (2)	84 (2)*b	122 (3)*d	32 (3)*i
Cat		3 (1)	7 (2)	9 (2)	208 (4)*j
Rabbit			1 (1)	9 (2)	8 (2)
Hare		2 (1)			
Lagomorph		1			
Rodent					
Domestic fowl		3 (1)	28 (6)	14 (2)	36 (3)*k
Goose	1 (1)	3 (2)	1 (2)	7 (2)	9 (2)
Duck			4 (1)		8 (2)
Swan			1 (1)	4 (1)	12 (2)
Turkey					2 (1)
Peafowl				1 (1)	
Pigeon sp.			1 (1)		
Wood pigeon				2 (1)	
Raven			1 (1)		
Crow				4 (1)	
Rook					
Jackdaw				7 (1)*e	
Magpie				1	
Corvid (crow/rook size)				3	
Corvid (jackdaw/magpie size)				2	
Passerine			1	1	2
Indet. bird	2	16	44	65	273
Mouse			10 (1)*c		

	Phase				
Species	**2**	**3**	**4**	**5**	**6**
Rodent				1	
Hedgehog					33 (1)*I
Mole			1 (1)		
Frog		2 (1)	1 (1)	12 (3)	20 (6)
Toad					7 (1)
Amphibian	2	5	2	17	27
Microfauna		1		1	
Small mammal	1		7	9	16
Medium mammal	8	89	202	194	257
Large mammal	10	94	392	253	275
Indeterminate	81	453	890	1100	506
Total fragment count	127	875	2456	2195	3277
Total weight (g)	1223	6399	27,207	16,212	30,584

waste. The presence of primary butchery waste, particularly lower legs of cattle and sheep/goat, suggests that animals were either slaughtered at or near the site itself, or that entire carcass sections were bought from the butchers. Fragments from skull and mandibles suggest the utilisation of head meat. In Phase 6 (mid sixteenth to seventeenth century), cattle fragments from meat-rich body parts increase sharply in relation to fragments from head and lower legs, whereas there is no difference for sheep/goat or pig. This suggests that cattle butchery was not as common in the vicinity as previously, although whether this is the result of the increased status of the area (hinted at by an increase in high-status bird bone at this time), or whether it reflects the relocation of the butchery trade, is unclear. Both at the present site and at the Classics Centre cattle were mainly slaughtered as adults, although calves were present in all phases.[88] There was an increase in the number of juvenile cattle bones during the early post-medieval period, which may be connected to an increase in dairy production in the region. Contemporary dental ageing data sets from Ashmolean Forecourt (n:8) and the Classics Centre (n:5) both include a number of mandibles from calves,[89] and an increase in juvenile animals in the post-medieval period appears to be a general trend both in Oxford and elsewhere. Sheep were slaughtered at 3–6 years of age, which suggests a multi-purpose husbandry strategy. The slaughter age pattern for pigs is consistent throughout medieval and post-medieval Oxford: as is expected for an animal with high fecundity and no secondary products, pigs were slaughtered young, with few animals kept for more than 3 years. Deer, rabbit and hare contributed little to the diet, though rabbit, as well as swan (see below), increase noticeably in the two later phases. Rabbit was very expensive in the thirteenth to fourteenth centuries, but prices dropped slightly in the later medieval period and rabbit may have become more accessible to a larger part of the urban population.[90]

Domestic fowl and goose are the most numerous bird species not only in the present assemblage, but on most medieval and post-medieval Oxford sites. Fowl were probably kept in back yards and their eggs and feathers collected, whereas geese could graze on the fields and flood plains outside

88 K. Poole, 'Animal Remains', in Norton and Cockin, 'Classics Centre', pp. 189–92.

89 Ibid.; S. Hamilton-Dyer, 'The Animal Bone', in Andrews and Mepham, 'Ashmolean Museum Forecourt', pp. 212–16.

90 E.M. Veale, 'The Rabbit in England', *Agricultural History Review*, 5 (1957), pp. 89–90.

the city. The recovery of two immature turkey bones from Phase 6 (pit 1143) is noteworthy. The first British record of turkey, a New World species, dates from 1541 and turkey bones have been recovered from several sixteenth and seventeenth century sites in southern and eastern England, such as Norwich, Windsor and Hill Hall.[91] The only other Oxford sites with turkey are from the late sixteenth century at Jesus College, the seventeenth century at the former Greyfriars and the late seventeenth century at Corpus Christi College.[92] There is a small chance that the turkey bones may be from an immature peafowl, the bones from the two species being similar in size and shape. Peafowl is a rare bird in archaeological assemblages and associated with a high-status diet, whether from castles, manor houses, abbeys or wealthy urban households.[93] The single bone in Phase 5 that is positively identified as peafowl came from pit 815, which also contained a jeton dated to 1500–25. If the bone was contemporary with its context, it therefore probably came from a bird consumed on Property 1. The marked increase of swan, particularly in Phase 6, is interesting. Swan was associated with a high-status ideal during most of the medieval period and was very expensive to buy. During the late-medieval period the presence of swan increases markedly in urban assemblages, and it has been suggested that swanneries sold an increasing proportion of their birds to the urban market. Documents indicate that while expensive, swan may not have been exclusively connected to the urban rich, but also the aspiring middle classes.[94] The increase of bird taxa and number of unidentifiable bird bones in Phases 5 and 6 is consistent with a general increase in bird bones on archaeological sites from this period.[95]

Industrial Activity

There are small numbers of sheep horn cores which have been chopped away from the skull, as well as a number of metapodials with cut marks from pits in Properties 1 and 2 during Phases 3–6. These skeletal elements contain no meat and subsequently do not signify kitchen waste. They may be waste from a butcher's shop or from various industries, such as tanning, bone and horn working. Documents and pictorial sources from the sixteenth century onwards indicate that hides were often sold to tanneries with horns and metapodials intact. Prior to the tanning process, these elements were removed and discarded or sold as raw material to horn and bone workers. The presence of a small-scale butcher, tanner, bone or horn worker in the vicinity has been suggested by Poole, using the over-representation of cattle metapodials, horn cores and mandible from medieval and post-medieval phases at the Classics Centre as evidence.[96] Other animal remains from the present site that may be connected to the tanning industry include a roe deer metatarsal (Phase 3), a cattle skull (Phase 4) and a horse first phalanx (Phase 4), all with cut marks associated with skinning.

Articulated Remains

The assemblage contained 14 articulated or semi-articulated animal remains. Some, like mouse (Phase 4 well 663), jackdaw (Phase 5 pit 815) and hedgehog (Phase 6 latrine 1373), probably

[91] B. Fothergill, 'The Husbandry, Perception and Improvement of Turkeys in Britain, 1500–1900', *Post-Medieval Archaeology*, 48 (2014), pp. 207–28; S. Hamilton-Dyer, 'Animal Bones', in S. Preston (ed.) *Reading and Windsor, Old and New*, TVAS Monograph, 7 (2005), p. 126.

[92] L. Strid, 'Animal Bone', in R. Bashford and B.M. Ford, 'Eleventh-Century, Later-Medieval and Early Post-Medieval Evidence from Investigations at Jesus College and Market Street, Oxford', *Oxoniensia*, 79 (2014), pp. 229–31; B. Wilson, 'Medieval and Post-medieval Animal Bones and Marine Shells', in Hassall, 'St Ebbe's, Part II', p. 267; L. Broderick, 'Animal Bone', in 'Corpus Christi College, Oxford, New Sub-Main Works, Archaeological Watching Brief Report', unpublished OA report (2016), https://library.oxfordarchaeology.com/3527/.

[93] D. Serjeantson, *Birds* (2009), p. 311.

[94] N. Sykes, 'The Dynamic of Status Symbols: Wildfowl Exploitation in England AD 410–1550', *Antiquity*, 161 (2004), pp. 91–3.

[95] D. Serjeantson, 'Birds: Food and a Mark of Status', in C. Woolgar et al. (eds.), *Food in Medieval England: History and Archaeology* (2006), pp. 134–6.

[96] Poole, 'Animal Remains'.

represent natural mortalities of commensal species. Gnaw marks were not found on any of the articulated remains, suggesting a rapid and secure disposal of the animals.

An unusual find was the burial of an articulated pig in Phase 4 pit 562 (Fig. 11.8). The pit was truncated by a later wall and only the front half of the pig remained. The skull and mandible was highly fragmented and a dental analysis could not be carried out. However, the proximal humerus was fusing, suggesting the pig was approximately 3.5 years old when it died. As pigs were common food animals, it is very unusual to find adult pigs buried intact in medieval and post-medieval urban assemblages. Extensive exostoses were found on the distal part of the left metacarpals and lesser exostoses on the proximal first phalanges of the left foot. The joint surfaces are not affected, which would rule out septic arthritis. The presence of cloacae on the metacarpals suggests some form of osteomyelitis. However, osteomyelitis normally affects singular bones and not adjacent bones.[97] The aetiology is therefore somewhat uncertain. The infection would probably have been visible, not just from limping but also great swelling of the foot and discharging of pus. The pig may not have been considered suitable for consumption. Minor exostoses also occurred on the distal metaphysis on both left and right radius and ulna. This latter pathology is probably not directly related to the pathologies on the right foot. A similar case of burial of a diseased pig is recorded from post-medieval contexts on the Church Street excavations in Oxford.[98]

An almost complete skeleton of a horse had been deposited in Phase 6 pit 613. The distal femur was fusing, indicating an age at death of 3.5 years. It is very unusual for skeletally immature horses to be slaughtered, as their main worth during this period was as working animals. It may have died of an illness, or have been put down due to aggression. Pathological conditions included an area of woven bone on a distal metatarsal shaft, porosities on two tarsal bones and on one inter-vertebral epiphysis as well as a partially healed fractured rib. With exception of the broken rib, all other pathologies indicate infections. The burial also contained 11 fragments of calcified soft tissue from unknown body parts.

Neonatal and juvenile articulated remains from domestic food animals include one lamb (latrine 1373), two piglets (851, 1043) and one chicken (1045), but the level of articulation was not recorded during excavation for the neonatal animals, rendering it difficult to ascertain the possibility of discarded natural mortality versus kitchen waste. However, no cut marks were observed.

Four articulated dog skeletons (558, 773, 814, 1101) were recovered from pits in Phase 4, 5 and 6. No cut marks were noted, suggesting that the dogs represent dead pets rather than tannery waste. Withers' heights of 51.4 cm and 47.4 cm respectively could be calculated for the dogs from contexts 773 and 815, which is within the size range for a border collie. One dog (773) had small lesions on the rib joints of the eleventh and twelfth thoracic vertebrae. The dog from context 814 displayed several pathologies: exostoses around the joint surfaces of left and right distal calcaneus and the right distal radius, lipping at the joint surfaces of the left and right distal humerus and the right proximal ulna, bone growth indicative of infection on the proximal right femur, the distal left tibia and on the second and third left metatarsals, in addition to a healed rib fracture as well as a fractured dorsal process on its fifth thoracic vertebra. Fractures of ribs and vertebral processes are not unusual in historical dog populations and could have been the result of kicks or blows. A complete sub-adult cat from Phase 6 pit 702 and a semi-articulated kitten from Phase 6 latrine 1373 also lack cut marks, and therefore probably represent accidental mortalities or deliberate killings as a method of population control.

[97] J. Baker and D. Brothwell, *Animal Diseases in Archaeology* (1980), pp. 63–8, 123–6.

[98] B. Wilson, 'Medieval and Post-Medieval Animal Bones and Marine Shells', in Hassall, 'St Ebbe's, Part II', p. 267.

FISH REMAINS by REBECCA NICHOLSON

The fish remains discussed here were recovered predominantly from selected soil samples taken during the excavations in 2006. Unlike the mammal and bird bone which was in good condition in all phases, the fish remains from Phases 2–5 were only moderately, or in some cases poorly preserved, suggesting the possibility that significant amounts of fish bone have been lost through post-depositional decay. Apart from sample 155, the cesspit samples (e.g. thirteenth to fourteenth century pit fill 959) contained surprisingly few fish remains. By contrast, the bones from sample 155 (from the primary fill of Phase 6 latrine 1373) were extremely numerous and in very good condition; in some cases, bones were encrusted in cess. The condition and abundance of tiny bones and mineralised seeds is consistent with a primary cesspit fill. In most other samples a small proportion of the bones were burnt, indicating a component of kitchen waste and/or rubbish disposal.

The identified fish remains from each phase are set out in Table 11.4. The great majority came from deposits of Phase 6, late sixteenth to mid seventeenth century, most notably from primary deposit 1024 within latrine 1373. Around 1500 identifiable bones came from only half of the 4–2 mm residue in the case of sample 155 from this deposit. Species included the ubiquitous herring (in this case probably accompanied by sprat) and eel, together with abundant cyprinids, particularly dace but also chub, gudgeon and roach, bullhead, stickleback and, much less commonly, small pike, flatfish, rays and whiting. Measurements on the eel cleithrum suggest fish of 20–35 cm.[99] Fish bone preservation in this sample was extremely good and many bones were distorted in a manner consistent with chewing. Some of the larger bones were stained dark brown, possibly from cooking. A minimum of 87 individual cyprinids were represented by the robust and diagnostic pharyngeal bones in the sorted portion of 4–2 mm residue alone. While head bones and vertebrae were present for most of the commonly represented fish, clupeid head bones were almost completely absent, suggesting that in this case beheaded fish were cooked and eaten. A small number of smelt bones were also identified. The cessy deposit also included mineralised seeds, mineralised pupae, small crustacean fragments and tiny pieces of mineralised cloth, which probably represent the remains of wipes. Similar kinds of remains have been discovered in samples taken from Roman primary drain fills at Herculaneum (pers. observation). One eighth of the 0.5–2 mm residue from this sample was also sorted. This was not quantified but comprised very large quantities of tiny bones, mainly from fish already identified in the larger material: cyprinids, bullhead and clupeids (probably sprat). Occasional tiny ray dermal denticles were also present.

Despite its position, about as far away from the sea as it is possible to be in Britain, it is clear that sea fish were brought into Oxford on a fairly regular basis from at least the eleventh century (for example at Oxford Castle).[100] The fact that the fish represented in the early phases at the present site were herring and eel is no surprise, as these fish are typical for medieval and post-medieval inland sites, for example they were common at Eynsham abbey.[101] Herrings are likely to have been salted or pickled in brine and were widely traded in the early medieval period.[102] Both herrings and eels were relatively cheap, and commonly, but by no means only, eaten by the poorer sections of society in medieval times.

The sixteenth- to seventeenth-century samples, particularly sample 155, demonstrate the significance of riverine fishing in particular. Together with eels, small cyprinids, bullheads and

[99] J. Coy, 'The Provision of Fowls and Fish for Towns', in D. Serjeantson and T. Waldron (eds.) *Diet and Crafts in Towns. The Evidence of Animal Remains from the Roman to the Post-Medieval Periods*, BAR BS, 199 (1989), pp. 25–40.

[100] R. Nicholson, 'Fish Bone', in Munby, *Oxford Castle*.

[101] K. Ayres et al., 'Phases 2f–4a: The Medieval Abbey: Food Consumption and Production', in Hardy et al., *Aelfric's Abbey*, pp. 360–406.

[102] J.H. Barrett et al., 'Dark Age Economics Revisited – The English Fish Bone Evidence AD 600–1600', *Antiquity*, 78: 301 (2004), pp. 618–36.

Table 11.4. Numbers of identified fish remains, by phase.

	Phase					
	2	3	4	5	6	Total
Shark/Ray (Elasmobranchii)					3	3
Ray (Rajidae)					5	5
cf. Skate (*Raja batis*)					3	3
Thornback ray (*Raja clavata*)			1	1		2
Eel (*Anguilla anguilla*)	4	2	1	6	332	345
Conger eel (*Conger conger*)			1			1
Clupeid (Clupeidae)	1	3	6		495	505
Herring (*Clupea harengus*)	1		5	5	41	52
Smelt (*Osmerus eperlanus*)					13	13
Pike (*Esox lucius*)					10	10
Cyprinid (Cyprinidae)				1	286	287
Dace/Chub (*Leuciscus* sp.)					36	36
Dace (*Leuciscus leuciscus*)					101	101
Chub (*Leuciscus cephalus*)					3	3
Roach (*Rutilus rutilus*)					2	2
Gudgeon (*Gobio gobio*)					2	2
Gadid (Gadidae)			2		7	9
Cod (*Gadus morhua*)			2		9	11
Cod/Whiting					1	1
Whiting (*Merlangius merlangus*)				1	3	4
Gurnard (Triglidae)					2	2
cf. Perch/ruffe			1			1
Perch (*Perca fluviatilis*)					1	1
Bullhead (*Cottus gobio*)					116	116
3-spined Stickleback (*Gasterosteus aculeatus*)					26	26
Flatfish			1			1
Right-eyed flatfish (Pleuronectidae)				3	3	6
Plaice (*Pleuronectes platessa*)					2	2
Unidentified/unidentifiable fragments		7	19	59	392	477
Total	6	12	39	76	1894	2027

pike would have been caught in local rivers and streams. Smelt are inshore migratory fish which enter rivers in winter, to spawn in spring. They were common in the lower reaches of the Thames during the seventeenth and eighteenth centuries and were probably sold as salted or pickled fish.[103] In almost all cases the fish represented in sample 155 were under 15 cm, and in the case of the freshwater and migratory fish, were probably caught in fish traps or weirs laid across rivers.

Small pike were usually recorded as 'pickerel' in later medieval documents, while these tiny cyprinids were probably included with other small freshwater fish in the term 'minnows'. These small fish would have been sold together, cheaply. The fact that they were so very common in cess deposit 1024 suggests that the household of Property 2W ate considerable quantities of these small fish, together with small and tiny sprats and herrings; all were possibly cooked together as a type of whitebait. Since fish remains do not readily survive the human digestive process,[104] it is likely that the sample includes table waste as well as cess. Fish remains were also abundant in sixteenth to seventeenth century deposits from Merton College, although a wider range of fish were represented including several gadids, cyprinids, pike, salmon, smelt, flatfishes, gurnards and sea bream in addition to the ubiquitous herring and eel. At the Classics Centre, a very much smaller late-medieval and post-medieval assemblage included herring, eel, small freshwater fish and flatfish. A very similar assemblage to that recovered from sample 155 has been recorded from medieval cesspits at Abingdon West Central.[105]

CHARRED AND MINERALISED PLANT REMAINS by WENDY SMITH

Following assessment, eight samples were selected for full analysis. These were all from Property 2, with the exception of the twelfth century pit sample 119, which is from Property 1 and the sixteenth/seventeenth century latrine 1373 (sample 155) which is from Property 2W.

Results

Sample 102 from Phase 2 ditch 514 was not particularly rich, with just over 5 seeds per litre of sediment sampled generated. The majority of identifications (N = 139 or 69.2 per cent of the charred assemblage) were of charred free-threshing wheat (*Triticum* spp.) grains, but a few barley (*Hordeum* spp.) and rye (*Secale cereale* L.) grains were also identified. Three secure common vetch (*Vicia sativa* L.) seeds and an estimate of five possible common vetch seeds were identified. The absence of hila (the point where a pea/bean attaches to a pod) on these vetch seeds means that it was not possible to securely identify these as a crop (most likely a fodder crop) rather than a weedy variety. Low levels of charred cereal grains suggest small-scale food processing of whole grain to make edible cereal products such as groats, possibly parching of grain before hand-milling or grinding in a mortar and pestle. Sample 119, from Phase 3 pit 704, was also not particularly rich, and dominated by charred free-threshing wheat (*Triticum* spp.) grain, with small quantities of barley (*Hordeum* spp.) grain also present. Smaller sized vetch/vetchling (*Vicia* spp./*Lathyrus* spp.) seeds were recovered from this sample along with a range of common weeds of cereal crops such as black bindweed (*Fallopia convolvulus* (L.) Á. Löve), stinking chamomile (*Anthemis cotula* L.) and scentless mayweed (*Tripleurospermum inodorum* (L.) Sch. Bip.).

Five samples were analysed from Phase 4 deposits: pits 55 (evaluation), 493, 477 and 1166 and 1309 (samples 1, 118, 164, 165 and 170 respectively). All samples contained mixtures of charred

[103] A. Wheeler, *The Tidal Thames: A History of a River and its Fishes* (1979).

[104] R.A. Nicholson, 'An Investigation into the Effects on Fish Bone of Passage through the Human Gut: Some Experiments and Comparisons with Archaeological Material', *Circaea*, 10 (1993 for 1992), pp. 38–51.

[105] R. Nicholson, 'Fish Remains' in Poore, 'No. 4A Merton St.', pp. 306–11; R. Nicholson, 'Fishbone', in Norton and Cockin, 'Classics Centre', pp. 192–3; R.A. Nicholson, 'Fish Remains', in K. Brady and A. Smith 'Excavations at Abingdon West Central Redevelopment: Iron Age, Roman, Medieval, and Post-Medieval Activity in Abingdon', *Oxoniensia*, 72 (2007), pp. 187–90.

cereal grain and accompanying weeds of crop, but the relative proportions of these were highly variable. Cereal grain was only dominant in pit sample 164 (N = 382 or 68.7 per cent) and weed/wild plants were only dominant in pit sample 165 (N = 163 or 55.9 per cent). The three remaining samples were more even mixtures of grain and weed/wild plants with the pit samples (samples 1 and 118) having roughly two-thirds as much cereal grain to weed/wild plants and well sample 170 having two-thirds as much weed/wild plants as cereal grain. Free-threshing wheat (*Triticum* spp.) continues to dominate the cereal remains and several compact (small-sized) cereal grains were noted as well. In addition to free-threshing wheat, barley (*Hordeum* sp.) and rye (*Secale cereale* L.) grain are present in low numbers. Cereal chaff was only recovered in limited quantities (ranging from 0.3 per cent to 9.5 per cent of the charred assemblage) and often was too poorly preserved to be identified to species level. Barley and rye rachis nodes often were more frequently recovered than wheat rachis nodes, which does not agree with the grain data. This may suggest that barley and rye chaff was in use for other reasons (such as thatch, matting, kindling, floor litter or bedding) and was coming into contact with fire and subsequently entering the pit/well deposits through the disposal of hearth sweepings or other domestic refuse. Charred flax seeds/linseed (*Linum usitatissimum* L.) were recovered from pit sample 165 and well sample 170. Low levels of mineralised remains were recovered from samples 1, 118 and 170, suggesting that some cess may have also been deposited into these features.

Mineralised plant remains were recovered from all fractions of the heavy residue and from the flot of sample 155, taken from Phase 6 latrine 1373, Property 2W (Table 11.5). The sample was so rich that only a sub-sample of 1/8th of the flot and the various heavy residue fractions were analysed. A great deal of unquantifiable amorphous mineralised concretions was present, and cereal bran fragments were also recovered. In general, fruit stones/pips were most frequently observed, with fig (*Ficus carica* L.) and wild strawberry (*Fragaria vesca* L.) most abundant. Other fruit taxa recovered include apple (*Malus* sp.), bramble/blackberry (*Rubus* section Rubus), elder/elderberry (*Sambucus nigra* L.), grape (*Vitis vinifera* L.), hawthorn (*Crataegus monogyna* Jacq.), indeterminate pear/apple (*Pyrus* sp./*Malus* sp.) and quince (*Cydonia oblonga* Mill.). In total, fruit remains account for 79.5 per cent (N = 276) of all mineralised identifications made in the 1/8th sub-sample of sample 155. The bias toward fruit stones/pips is likely to reflect the fact that many of these taxa have thick seed coats; however, certain taxa are frequently preserved in situations of mineralisation (for example, fig and wild strawberry) and therefore may be more likely to survive than others.[106]

Small quantities of non-fruit foodstuffs were also noted, including wheat (*Triticum* sp.) grain and garden pea (*Pisum sativum* L. – identified from mineralised detached hilum). In addition to plant remains, mineralised insect remains were frequently noted, especially flies (Diptera – indet., *Thoracochaeta zosterae* (Hal.) and *Fannia scalaris* (L.)), woodlice (Isopoda of the suborder Oniscidea) and millipedes (*Julid* spp.). All of these are frequently associated with mineralised cess deposits.

Sample 156 (from context 1037, Phase 7 pit 1034, Property 2) was a fairly even mix of charred cereal grain (N = 43.9 per cent) and charred weed/wild plants (N = 65 or 43.9 per cent of all charred identifications). Most of the cereal grain that could be identified to genus level was identified as barley (*Hordeum* sp.), nine grains of which were clearly germinated. Several detached sprouts (coleoptiles) were also noted. These small numbers of sprouted grains are not sufficient to confirm that malting was taking place, although they occurred in the same context as numerous fragments of oast or malting kiln tiles. It is as likely that these are slightly spoiled grains, possibly discarded during hand cleaning of grain.

106 W. Carruthers, 'The Plant Remains: Comparing and Contrasting the Assemblages' in V. Birbeck et al. (eds.), *The Origins of Mid-Anglo-Saxon Southampton: Excavations at the Friends Provident St Mary's Stadium 1998–2000* (2005), pp. 183–5; A.R. Hall, 'A Brief History of Plant Foods in the City of York: What the Cesspits Tell Us', in E. White (ed.) *Feeding a City – York: The Provision of Food from Roman Times to the Beginning of the Twentieth Century* (2000), pp. 22–41.

Table 11.5. Charred and mineralised plant remains from sample 155, latrine pit 1373 (context 1024), Property 2W, Phase 6. (E): estimated; +: <5 items, ++: 5–25 items, +++: 25–100 items, ++++: 100–300 items, +++++: >300 items.

Sample volume (l)	**38**
Flot volume (ml)	**85 Combined 1/8 flot & >10–0.5 mm. HR fractions**
Seeds per litre of sediment	**73.9**
Charred plant remains	
Cereal grain	
Triticum spp. – free-threshing wheat	1
Weed/wild taxa	
Vicia spp./*Lathyrus* spp. – small sized – vetch/vetchling	1
Unidentified seed coat	1
Unidentified stalk	1
Indeterminate	++
Mineralised plant remains	
Cereal grain	
cf. *Triticum* sp. – possible wheat	1
Cereal – unidentified bran fragments	+++++
Pulses	
Pisum sativum L. – detached hilum – garden pea	1
Fruit	
Ficus carica L. – fig	113
Ficus carica L. – internal structure – fig	6
Rubus section Rubus – blackberry/bramble	3 (E)
Fragarius vesca L. – wild strawberry	115
Cydionia oblonga Mill. – quince	2 (E)
cf. *Cydonia oblonga* Mill. – internal structure	3 (E)
cf. *Cydonia oblonga* Mill. – fragments	++
Pyrus sp./*Malus* sp. – indeterminate internal structure – pear/apple	6
cf. *Pyrus* sp./*Malus* sp. – indeterminate	1
cf. *Purus* sp./*Malus* sp. – indeterminate mericarp	1
Malus sp. – apple	1
Crataegus monogyna Jacq. – hawthorn	1
Vitis vinifera L. – internal structure – grape	8
cf. *Vitis vinifera* L. (estimate from fragments)	5 (E)
Sambucus nigra L. (?mineralised) – elder/elderberry	10
Indeterminate nutshell/fruit stone fragments	1
Weed/wild	
Papaver somniferum L. (?MPR) – opium poppy	2

CARYOPHYLLACEAE – Pink family – unidentified large seeded	1
cf. *Malva* sp. – possible mallow – internal structure	1
cf. *Brassica* spp. – possible mustard – internal structure	2
Geranium sp. (?mineralised/?modern) – crane's bill	1
LAMIACEAE – Lamium type – dead nettle	1
cf. *Sagittaria sagittifolia* L./*Alisma* spp. – possible arrowhead/water plantain	1
Juncus spp. – rush	15
Carex spp. – 3-sided – sedge	6
POACEAE – small-sized caryopsis – Grass family	1
Unidentified	34
Unidentified bark/leaf fragments	1
Unidentified stalk fragments	3
Unidentified mineralised concretion	+++++
Other mineralised remains	
Thoracochaeta zosterae (Hal.) – 'seaweed' fly	++++
Fannia scalaris (L.) – 'latrine' fly	+
Diptera – unidentified puparia – indeterminate flies	+++
Isopoda of the suborder Oniscidea – indeterminate fragments – woodlouse	++
Julid spp. – fragments – millipede	+++
Coleoptera – unidentified fragments – beetle	+
Unidentified insect fragments	+
Animal dropping (?rodent)	5
?Crustacean shell fragments – ?crab/crayfish	++

Comparison with Other Oxford Sites

The eleventh- to twelfth-century deposits from the present site are consistent with other results of this period from Oxford, reflecting the predominance of free-threshing wheat (*Triticum* spp.) and barley.[107] The thirteenth-/fourteenth-century samples from the present site are also frequently dominated by cereal grain, although unlike those previously reported from the two ovens at the Ashmolean Forecourt they have a significant charred weed/wild component.[108] However, the grain-rich Ashmolean ovens are primary deposits. At the present site, the non-edible weed/wild plant remains are probably discarded refuse from small-scale domestic crop cleaning carried out repeatedly, probably in advance of parching or some other preparation of the grain.

Plant remains from the fifteenth century are not represented at the present site; however, the fruit-rich mineralised deposit from the Phase 6 cesspit/cellar backfill is so far unique for this area of Oxford. The sample was much richer and more diverse than thirteenth- to fourteenth-century

[107] R. Pelling, 'Charred Plant Remains', in Poore, *Beaumont*, pp. 82–4; R. Pelling, 'The Charred Plant Remains', in Z. Kamash et al., 'Late Anglo-Saxon and Medieval Occupation: Evidence from Excavations at Lincoln College, Oxford 1997–2000', *Oxoniensia*, 67 (2002), pp. 261–71; R. Pelling, 'Charred and Waterlogged Plant Remains', in Poore, 'No. 4A Merton St.', pp. 322–38; R. Pelling, 'The Charred and Mineralised Plant Remains', in Norton and Cockin, 'Classics Centre', p. 193.

[108] P. Hinton, 'The Charred Plant Remains from Ovens 166 and 167', in Andrews and Mepham, 'Ashmolean Museum Forecourt', pp 216–17.

garderobe remains from No. 4A Merton Street, or the sixteenth- to seventeenth-century remains from Abingdon West Central.[109] All the fruit taxa recovered, with the exception of quince (*Cydonia oblonga* Mill), were also recovered from No. 4A Merton Street and Abingdon, but not in such abundance. One major difference is that plum (*Prunus domestica* L.), smaller plums/bullace/greengage/damson (*Prunus domestica* ssp *insititia* (L.) Bonnier & Layens) and sloe (*Prunus spinosa* L.) were recovered at No. 4A Merton Street but are entirely absent from the present samples. Whether this suggests that such fruits regularly had their stones removed before consumption by the sixteenth/seventeenth century, or reflects a genuine absence of plums/bullace/damson and sloes in the general diet of this later period in Oxford, is not clear. It is unlikely that such fruit stones would not survive if present, since they are readily recovered from mineralised deposits elsewhere.

OTHER FINDS

Small amounts of iron smithing slag were recovered from medieval and post-medieval contexts, but the quantities were not sufficient to indicate that smithing took place on the site in any period. A flint strike-a-light is of probable post-medieval date. Some 516 fragments (3.2 kg) of marine shell were also recovered, mainly comprising oyster.

ACKNOWLEDGEMENTS

OA would like to thank Oxford University for funding the project, and Brian Durham, then Oxford City Council archaeologist, for monitoring the work. The project was managed for OA by Ben M. Ford. The site supervisor was Robin Bashford, who was assisted by Ceri Boston, Nick Croxson, Brian Dean, Jodie Ford, D. Gooney, Rebecca Griffin, Anna Hodgkinson, Paul Leader, Mark Littlewood, Alan Marshall, Toby Martin, Dave McNicol, Marta Perez, Emily Plunkett, Christopher Richardson, Jane Smallridge, Robert Tannahill, and Helen Webb. Thanks are also due to the staff that processed the finds under the management of Leigh Allen, processed the environmental samples under the management of Rebecca Nicholson, and prepared the archive under the management of Nicola Scott.

[109] Pelling, 'Plant Remains', in Poore, 'No. 4A Merton St.'; R. Pelling, 'The Charred, Mineralized and Waterlogged Plant Remains', in Brady et al. 'Abingdon West Central', pp. 190–202.

12.

A Seventeenth-Century Burial and Medieval to Post-Medieval Tenement Plots at St Cross College

ANDREW SIMMONDS, JULIAN MUNBY, KIRSTY SMITH and CARL CHAMPNESS

with contributions by LEIGH ALLEN, PAUL BLINKHORN, LEE BRODERICK, JOHN COTTER, DEIRDRE FORDE, REBECCA NICHOLSON, CYNTHIA POOLE, ALICE ROSE, IAN R. SCOTT and RUTH SHAFFREY

SUMMARY

Excavation was carried out in advance of completion of the West Quad at St Cross College. The area of the excavation was formerly the rear part of three adjacent tenements fronting onto St Giles' Street that were probably in continuous use from the twelfth century. Only limited evidence was found for activity earlier than the seventeenth century, by which time historic maps depict this part of the tenements as cultivated gardens. The most unusual feature was a burial of a young woman, dated by coin and radiocarbon evidence to c.1640–70, representing a rare instance of extra-cemetery interment during a period when burial within the parish graveyard was virtually universal. It is possible that the woman was a religious dissenter. Part of a wall that was believed to be the precinct wall of the medieval Beaumont Palace was also investigated and was found to be a later construction, probably no earlier than the seventeenth century, albeit perpetuating the line of the medieval boundary.

A programme of archaeological excavation at St Cross College was undertaken in advance of construction of a new building in the north-west corner of the college grounds to complete the northern and western sides of the West Quad. The investigations were commissioned by University of Oxford Estates Office in accordance with a condition attached to the planning permission for the development. They comprised a trial-trench evaluation in April 2013,[1] a survey of historic walls during January 2015, and an excavation in February to March 2015. The site encompassed the footprint of the new building, which was 'L'-shaped in plan and was situated within the junction of Pusey Street and Pusey Lane (formerly Nos. 57–61 St Giles' Street) at NGR SP 511 606 (Fig. 12.1). It covered a total area of 0.1 ha and was flat, lying at *c.*64 m OD.

[1] 'St Cross College Western Quad, Oxford: Archaeological Evaluation Report' (2013), unpublished OA report, https://library.oxfordarchaeology.com/3091/.

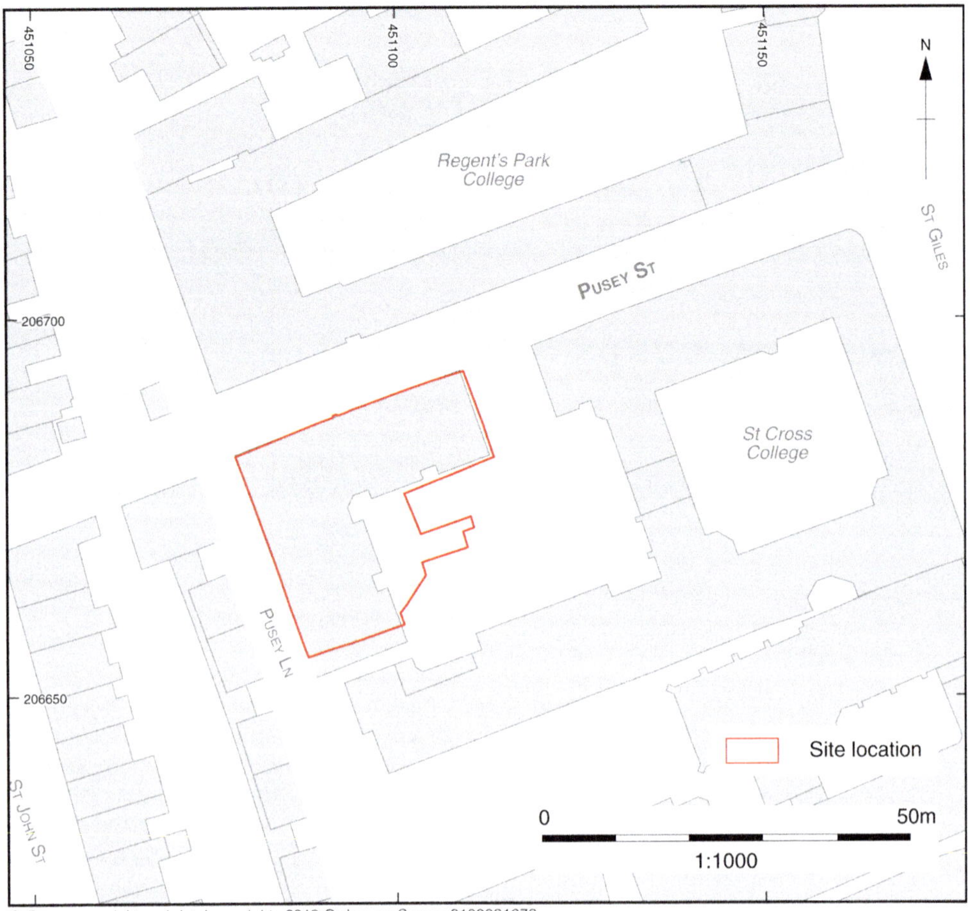

Fig. 12.1 Site location.

Full versions of the specialist reports, including data tables, are available via the OA Library.[2] The archive will be deposited with the Ashmolean Museum under accession code AN2015.2.

EXCAVATION METHODOLOGY

The excavation involved the stripping of the overburden, which comprised undifferentiated garden soils up to 0.7 m thick and areas of tarmac surface, using a mechanical excavator fitted with a toothless ditching bucket, under close archaeological control. This exposed a layer of loessic brickearth 0.25–0.40 m thick, which overlay the terrace gravel and into which the archaeological features were cut. Following machine excavation, the areas were cleaned as necessary and all archaeological features were recorded on plan. Hand excavation of the exposed features then proceeded, comprising half-sectioning of discrete features and excavation of a maximum of 20 per cent of each linear feature. A large number of features were encountered whose fills contained modern materials such as plastics and demolition rubble, or which were cut into the nineteenth-century garden soil. These features were not excavated.

2 https://library.oxfordarchaeology.com/5766/.

ARCHAEOLOGICAL AND HISTORICAL BACKGROUND

The site was situated north of the historic core of Oxford within the town's northern suburb, which developed during the twelfth and thirteenth centuries as a linear development on either side of the broad thoroughfare of St Giles' Street.[3] This comprised two extramural parishes centred on the churches of St Mary Magdalen and St Giles. The site encompassed the rear parts of three adjacent tenements that were later recorded as Nos. 57, 58/59 and 60 St Giles' Street, toward the northern end of the suburb, with the boundary between the two parishes passing between Nos. 57 and 58/59. The arrangement of the tenements is likely to have changed little by the time it was recorded on Loggan's 1675 map of Oxford (Fig. 12.2).

During the medieval period the western boundary of the site adjoined Gloucester Close, which is believed to have been part of the King's Houses, a minor royal residence built in 1132 by Henry I. Later known as Beaumont Palace, this was a resting place on the route from London or Windsor to the palace at Woodstock, which was used as a base for hunting in Wychwood Forest. During the twelfth and early thirteenth century the King's Houses were favoured by the crown but by the late thirteenth century it was rarely used, perhaps as a result of the waning importance of Oxford, and was gifted to the Carmelite friars in 1318, who retained it until the Dissolution.[4] The layout of the palace and subsequent friary are not well understood, but the main building complex was located in the south-western part, in the vicinity of the western end of Beaumont Street, and excavations in advance of construction of the Sackler Library revealed a plantation and one wall of a buttressed building that was interpreted as a possible monastic church.[5] The Grade II listed wall (list entry number 1047110) that defines the western boundary of the college grounds (and of the site) has been suggested to be the boundary wall of the palace.

The post-medieval period saw rapid development of the suburb, including building Beaumont Street and St John Street on the former site of Beaumont Palace. It was during this phase of development that Alfred Street and Alfred Lane (now Pusey Street and Pusey Lane) were constructed in 1828, passing along the north and west sides of the site respectively.

The property history of the college site is unfortunately less well known than many other Oxford properties for lack of documentation. What could be recovered of the early history was reported by David Sturdy in 1993 in a general and more detailed account,[6] while the more modern history of private and commercial occupation is given in Stephanie Jenkins' online history of St Giles' Street properties.[7] Given the particular interest in the owners and occupants of the northern part of the site (Nos. 57–9) in the seventeenth century (with regard to the burial discussed below), it is disappointing that neither can be traced in these poorly documented properties before the 1660s, beyond the general ownership of the Woodward and Cogan families. Their sub-tenants cannot easily be discovered, and moreover during the Civil War there were large numbers of 'strangers' billeted in the city whose names (except in St Aldate's parish) are quite unknown.[8]

A Quaker meeting house was built on the rear third of No. 60 St Giles' Street in *c.*1854 and in 1889 the front part of this tenement was incorporated into Pusey House, which had opened at No. 61 five years earlier. During the first two decades of the twentieth century, Pusey House acquired Nos. 57 and 58/59 and constructed the existing quad, into which St Cross College moved in 1981. An account of the buildings incorporated into the site of Pusey House is provided in David Sturdy's report, to which can be added an interesting coda from the time of the building of Pusey House Chapel in 1911. The college has a framed record drawing showing the elevation of the old buildings on St Giles' Street (Fig. 12.3), and this was certainly produced

3 Chapter 11, above for further discussion of the medieval development of the northern suburb.
4 Dodd, *Oxford*, p. 59.
5 Poore, *Beaumont*.
6 D. Sturdy et al., *A History of St Giles and the St Cross/Pusey House Site* (1993).
7 http://oxfordhistory.org.uk/stgiles/index.html (accessed Nov. 2017).
8 M. Toynbee and P. Young, *Strangers in Oxford: A Side Light on the First Civil War, 1642–1646* (1973).

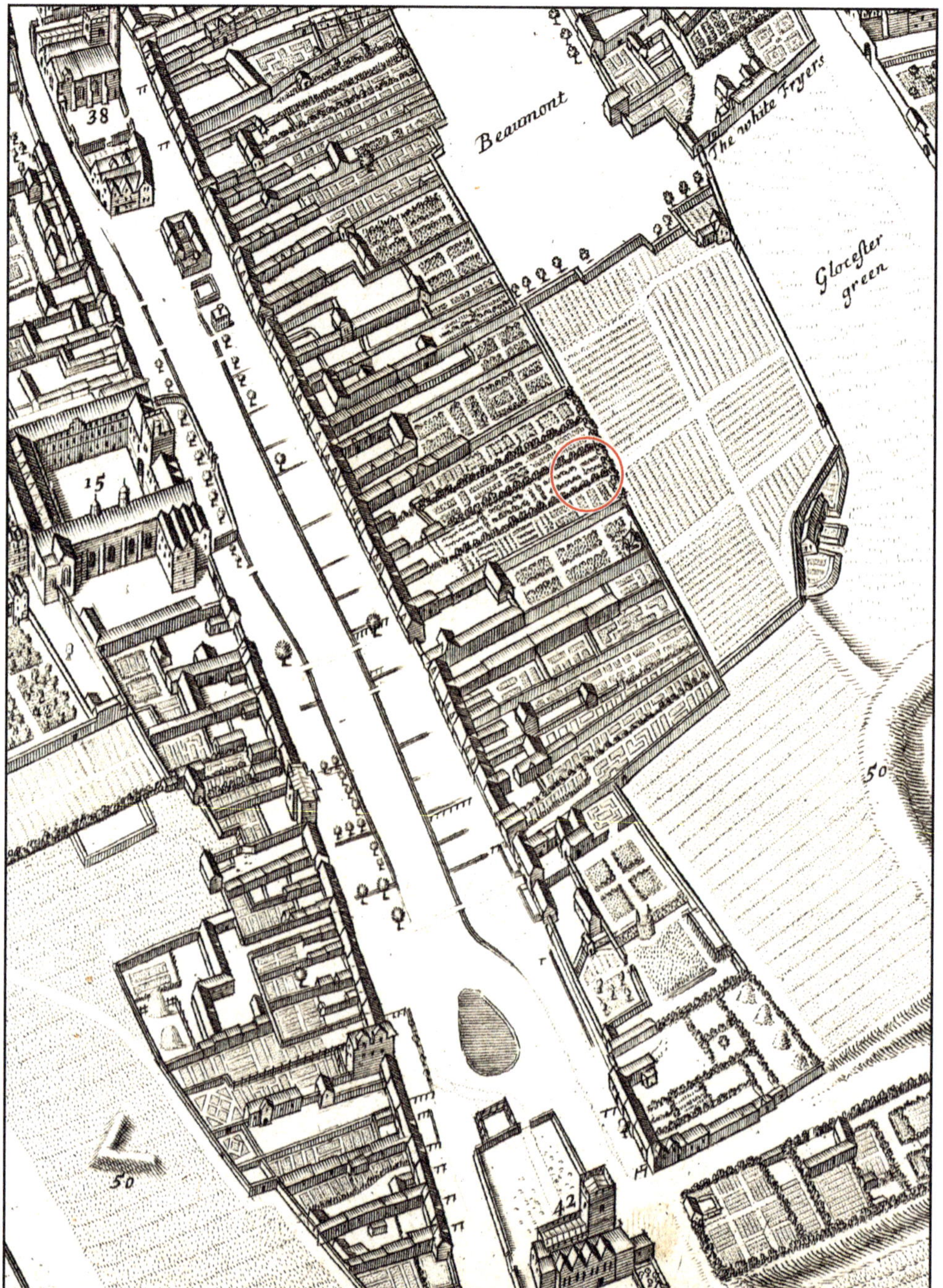

Fig. 12.2 Approximate location of the site on Loggan's 1675 map of Oxford (north to bottom).

Fig. 12.3 Record drawing of Nos. 57–59 St Giles', demolished in 1912.

at the instigation of the OAHS Committee for the 'Preservation of Old Houses in Oxford', presumably by the office of the architect Temple Lushington Moore (1856–1920). The Committee (a standing sub-committee of the Oxford Architectural and Historical Society) was established following Mrs Arnold Toynbee's protest in 1907 about the impending loss of the old houses by Elliston & Cavell in Magdalen Street. The earliest minute books record several discussions of the Pusey House proposals, and in June 1913 the plans of the 'recently demolished' houses on the site were shown to the committee. The drawing is of value as a record (in association with early photographs) and is an important document of the nascent conservation movement in the early twentieth century, and the growing realisation in Oxford (as in London and elsewhere) that progress and urban development were leading to the loss of large numbers of minor buildings of interest.

An archaeological evaluation and watching brief had previously been undertaken at St Cross when the south wing was built during the early 1990s. Pits dating from the medieval and post-medieval periods were recorded, as well as the south-east corner of the Quaker meeting house.[9]

DISCUSSION

The excavation uncovered evidence for the use of the rear parts of three adjacent tenements through the medieval and post-medieval periods, including the eastern boundary of the former Gloucester Close (believed to have formed part of the Beaumont Palace) and an unusual, extra-cemetery burial dated to the seventeenth century. Although historical evidence indicates that the tenements on St Giles' Street were probably laid out during the twelfth century and the road frontage was completely built up by 1279,[10] evidence for activity before the late seventeenth century was in fact very limited. The earliest evidence for occupation comprised a small pit (1174) that was dated to the thirteenth to fifteenth centuries, and the only other feature attributed to the medieval period was a similar pit (1147) that was dated to the mid fifteenth to sixteenth century. The ditch that defined the western end of the tenements may have originated during the sixteenth century, while the first half of the seventeenth century was represented only by the aforementioned burial. The absence of structures and sparseness of features is entirely consistent with the cartographic evidence for the use of these rear parts of the tenements as gardens, as shown on Loggan's 1675 Map of Oxford (Fig. 12.2). Material evidence for cultivation of the rear part of No. 60 was provided by the excavation of a series of parallel planting beds that extended laterally across the property. A few large pits were dug during the late seventeenth to eighteenth century, particularly at No. 57, after which the volume of pit digging increased substantially, resulting in the disturbance of large areas in all three tenements. These modern intrusions may have destroyed earlier features and were not excavated during the investigation.

The rear boundary of the tenements was contiguous with an area that, prior to the expansion of suburban development during the early nineteenth century, comprised a large field that adjoined the north side of the site of the former Beaumont Palace. Ralph Agas' 1578 map of Oxford depicts the field as a large open area surrounded by a wall, providing no indication of its use, but Loggan shows it under cultivation. The field is likely to be the 'Gloucester College Close' that was recorded as forming part of the palace when it was sold into private hands in 1542, since its size corresponds to the 3.5 acres specified in the deed and it was located adjacent to a small piece of common land known as Gloucester Green.[11] It is also likely to be identical

9 'St Cross College, Oxford: Archaeological Investigations in Advance of Redevelopment', unpublished OA report (1991); 'St Cross College, Oxford: Phase 2 Watching Brief', unpublished OA report (1992), https://library.oxfordarchaeology.com/3281/.

10 *VCH Oxon.* 4, pp. 25–6.

11 *VCH Oxon.* 2, p. 143.

with the 'Beaumont Close' that was previously leased out by the Carmelites in 1532, since this was also recorded as measuring 3.5 acres and as being located 'between St Giles Field and the Priory', in other words, north of the priory. Its size remained the same, and on the St Giles field map and terrier of 1769 it is divided into two closes labelled 'No. 20 – Wake – Beaumont Garden' of 3 acres, 2 roods and 16 perches.[12] Agas appears to show the boundary of the close as being a continuation of the boundary wall of the palace, and it was therefore assumed that the wall that stood at the western end of the site, fronting onto Pusey Lane, was the medieval boundary defining the precinct of the palace, albeit that the building survey had demonstrated that the above ground portion had been rebuilt during the nineteenth century reusing the original foundation. However, this is difficult to reconcile with the excavated evidence, which indicated a later date for the foundation. The excavation demonstrated that the existing structure (1176) was preceded by two phases of ditch. The earlier ditch was undated and had a steep-sided profile that would be consistent with a palisade trench, but interpretation is difficult as it was only recorded in a single intervention in the central part of the excavation. It may have been an intermittent boundary, or perhaps the feature was not in fact associated with the boundary at all. Ceramic evidence from the fills of the second ditch indicate that it was dug during the mid to late sixteenth century and infilled during the seventeenth century. A soil layer had accumulated over the infilled ditches before the substantial limestone rubble foundation was constructed, on which the wall was built. This sequence therefore indicates that the wall could not have been constructed before the seventeenth century. A solution to this apparent conundrum may be provided by Loggan, who differs from Agas in showing only the northern and southern ends of the boundary between the close and the tenements as a wall, with the central part, including the area of the site, defined by a hedge. If Loggan is correct, the wall may therefore be a late seventeenth- or eighteenth-century construction, as is suggested by the stratigraphic evidence. Loggan also shows the boundaries between Nos. 58/59 and 60 as hedgelines, and this might similarly explain the absence of excavated evidence for their form before the construction of the nineteenth-century walls that existed up until the current development.

The unexpected discovery of a burial beneath the college garden attracted much local interest and prompted speculation as to why she was buried in this location, some of which was of a rather melodramatic and lurid character.[13] The interment of this young woman in a location that appears at the time to have been a garden toward the rear of the tenement rather than within the parish cemetery is certainly unusual, as is the provision of two coins, and certainly demands further explication. It is worth emphasising, however, that many aspects of the burial appear to be fairly typical for the period. The grave pit itself was not in any way atypical, and the burial lay on an approximate west–east orientation. Furthermore, she had been interred in a supine position and contained within a shroud, as evidenced by the presence of shroud pins, coffins not becoming common until later in the century.[14] Ostensibly the individual's posture was somewhat unusual, being turned slightly to the right with the legs drawn up slightly and the arms flexed asymmetrically with the right elbow projecting toward the south-east edge of the grave. Importantly, however, the hands rested on the pelvis, as was the practice of the period. The unusual posture can perhaps be explained by the corpse having been lowered into the grave by inexpert hands, as could well have been the case for a burial that appears to have taken place outside the normal arrangements. The loose-fitting shrouds of the time, which typically comprised a bedding sheet wrapped around the body and tied at the top and bottom,[15] could easily allow such accidental disturbance of the corpse from its intended posture. Essentially, therefore, the form of the burial would not have appeared out of place in a typical

12 St John's College Archive, EST III.MP.41.

13 'Was it Murder or was Woman Buried Alive?', *Oxford Mail*, 6 March 2015; 'Did Plague Brought by Civil War Soldiers Kill Oxford's Lady of St Cross?', *Oxford Mail*, 13 May 2015.

14 J. Litten, *The English Way of Death. The Common Funeral Since 1450* (1991), p. 71.

15 Ibid.

seventeenth-century cemetery, and from this we might conclude that she was interred with the same reverence and dignity that accompanied any other burial of the time. There is certainly no indication that it represents the burial of someone who has been denied normal burial rites, such as a suicide or other outcast, or the illicit disposal of a murder victim.

The evidence of the coins places the burial sometime during or after 1640 and the radiocarbon date indicates that she is unlikely to have died later than the 1660s, providing a narrow window of only thirty years for the burial. This was a particularly turbulent period in the religious and social history or Britain, encompassing the final years of the reign of Charles I, the Civil War, the Commonwealth and the restoration of the monarchy. The upheavals during this period provided numerous possible reasons why an individual might be buried somewhere other than the parish cemetery, whether for reasons of conscience, compulsion or necessity. The largest group for whom burial at the parish church of St Mary Magdalen might have been problematic were Catholics, although other dissenter groups may also have buried elsewhere than the cemetery and an alternative explanation for the location of the burial might be provided by the large number of deaths caused by the outbreak of 'camp fever' that afflicted the city in 1643.

After Henry VIII broke with Rome and declared himself head of the Church of England in 1534, those who continued to practice the Catholic faith had become a persecuted minority, regarded with suspicion both for their religious differences and as a potential fifth column who owed allegiance to a foreign power. A series of laws were passed during the sixteenth and seventeenth centuries that restricted the rights of Catholics, making them subject to fines, confiscation of property and imprisonment. Some Catholics absented themselves from worship at the parish church and this practice, termed recusancy, comprised an indictable offence. The severity of persecution varied greatly over the thirty-year period to which the burial is attributed; Oxford had a reputation for tolerance toward Catholics, particularly during the Civil War when the court was based there, and persecution was at its greatest during the Commonwealth, only being subsequently relaxed following the restoration of the monarchy.[16] The fines and forfeiture of land arising from these offences appear in official records and provide us with an indication of the prevalence of recusancy. Recusants were certainly present in the parish of St Mary Magdalen, since a survey of the evidence by Davidson identified at least eleven individuals,[17] although it is likely that the number of recusants thus recorded significantly under-represents the true number of Catholics, most of whom probably continued to attend the parish church, if only to avoid being fined, and therefore would not appear in the records as dissenters. Burial of Catholics inevitably raised difficulties, since interment in the parish cemetery would have entailed a Church of England burial service administered by an Anglican priest. In some instances, recusants were refused burial due to their previous refusal to attend church, and equally some considered burial without the traditional liturgy unacceptable. In practice, an accommodation was usually reached and the majority of Catholics continued to be buried in their parish cemetery; instances are known from elsewhere of local priests turning a blind eye to surreptitious burials of recusants within the parish cemetery, a possible example of which from Oxfordshire is noted at Rotherfield Peppard, where Arthur Pitts, the son of a locally important recusant family, is recorded as having been buried in *c.*1634 but did not appear in the parish burial register, and Thomas and Mary Bullie were reported to have been buried by night in Dorchester-on-Thames churchyard in 1621.[18] It is possible that the individual buried at St Cross College is an exception, for whom no such compromise could be achieved. Evidence for such extra-cemetery burials is rare, but the imposition in 1606 of a £20 fine for any recusant who was buried other than in the parish cemetery clearly indicates that illicit burials were taking place and were an issue of some concern to the authorities. None are recorded in Oxford, but at Eynsham an excommunicated recusant

16 *VCH Oxon.* 4, p. 413.

17 A. Davidson, 'Roman Catholicism in Oxfordshire from the Late Elizabethan Period to the Civil War', University of Bristol Ph.D. thesis (1990), pp. 335–6.

18 Ibid. pp. 248, 362.

named George Prescott was buried illegally 'in a close called the park on the backside of Eynsham Abbey' in 1630, resulting in the further excommunication of those who conducted the burial.[19] Striking evidence for such illicit burials was found during excavations at Eynsham Abbey, which uncovered three graves that had been inserted into the ruins of the former refectory sometime between its abandonment at the Dissolution and the middle of the seventeenth century.[20] The abbey may have been chosen as an appropriate place for the burials due to its association with the old religion and the Stanley family, who owned the abbey after the Dissolution, were known to have Catholic sympathies and may have colluded in its use for such burials.[21] Two of the burials were of women and it may be relevant to the burial at St Cross College that examination of the church records for Oxfordshire and Berkshire has shown that the majority of individuals convicted for recusancy were women, perhaps because men, as head of the household, were under greater pressure to compromise and conform.[22] It is possible, therefore, that the burial at St Cross is one such woman who took her religion to the grave.

In addition to the schism between Protestants and Catholics, this was also a period of great dissent within the Protestant Church arising from the growth of puritan sentiment. Although their differences with the established church were very different to those of Catholics, protestant dissenters often likewise objected to attending church and the consequences regarding burial within the parish cemetery could be very similar. Quakers, Presbyterians and Baptists were all active in Oxford by the middle of the century, and certainly within the thirty-year period to which the burial has been assigned.[23] The most extreme of the new religious groups, such as the Quakers, disavowed the very concept of consecrated ground, and would therefore be expected to be buried elsewhere.

A further upheaval in the religious life of the seventeenth century occurred in 1645, when the Book of Common Prayer, which provided the liturgy for all church services, was outlawed by the puritan Parliament and replaced by the Directory of Public Worship. The new book made no provision for funeral services and, until a revised prayer book was instated in 1662 following the restoration of the monarchy, burials were officially conducted without a religious service since 'praying, reading and singing are in no way beneficial to the dead'. How widely these instructions were followed in uncertain, and the Prayer Book certainly continued to be used clandestinely in some places. During this period, however, the removal of burial from priestly authority allowed individuals to bury where and how they wished and may therefore provide a context for the burial at St Cross College.[24] However, although it is possible that the burial was interred here rather than at St Mary Magdalen due to her nonconformist beliefs, the provision of the coins would be inconsistent with puritan practice, which would have regarded the placing of such objects as an act of superstition with no religious validity.

An alternative explanation for burial within the tenement may be provided by the crisis that affected Oxford during 1643, when it was afflicted by an epidemic attributed to 'camp fever'.[25] During the Civil War Oxford received an influx of soldiers and non-combatants that may have almost doubled the population. Many of these people were billeted amongst the general population, including the billeting of a large number of ordinary soldiers in St Mary Magdalen parish, and the resultant overcrowded, insanitary conditions in the city contributed to the outbreak, which is generally attributed to typhus.[26] Thomas Willis, a physician who treated the

19 Bodl. MS. Top. Oxon, *c* 56, f. 29, quoted in E. Chambers, *Eynsham under the Monks* (1936), p. 41.

20 A. Hardy et al., *Aelfric's Abbey: Excavations at Eynsham Abbey, Oxfordshire, 1989–1992*, Thames Valley Landscapes Monograph, 16 (2003), pp. 153–4, 519–20.

21 Ibid. p. 519.

22 M. Gosling, 'Berkshire and Oxfordshire Catholics and the Lenten Assize of 1588', *Oxoniensia*, 58, pp. 258–9.

23 *VCH Oxon*. 4, pp. 415–24.

24 D. Cressy, *Birth, Marriage and Death: Ritual, Religion and Life-Cycle in Tudor and Stuart England* (1997), pp. 416–18.

25 R. Gilboy, 'Crisis Mortality in Civil War Oxford, 1642–1646', *Oxoniensia*, 82 (2017), pp. 83–104.

26 Ibid. p. 99.

Oxford victims of the outbreak, described its effect on the garrison: '[the King's] Foot being a great many together in straightened lodgings when they had filled all places with nastiness and filth, and stinking odours … fell sick many of them together, as it were in files; at length the fever reaching farther than the soldiery'.[27] Another physician, Edward Greaves, also recorded the outbreak in a leaflet entitled 'Morbus Epidemius', in which he described the symptoms as 'a great weakness without any manifest cause', 'a quick weak, creeping pulse, sometimes intermittent', fever, vertigo, vomiting or severe chills. Purple spots appeared on at least half of those affected. Greaves suggested that most people recovered from the disease, but many clearly did not, and parish records confirm that 210 died in the parish of St Mary Magdalen during the year, compared to only 32–49 in each of the preceding three years.[28] It is conceivable that such a large number of deaths could have overwhelmed the capacity of the parish cemetery and provide a context in which individuals may have been buried elsewhere. This certainly occurred during the outbreak of plague in London in 1665, when individual interments were replaced by mass burials in pits, some within existing cemeteries and others not, and a similar argument has been made for a group of Civil War mass burials at York.[29] Comparable overspill graveyards at Oxford may be represented by records of payments by the parishes of St Martin's and St Peter-le-Bailey for the burial of soldiers at the 'Jews' Mount' (land near the castle) and 'Bayleiffe Hills'.[30] However, against this it should be noted that in Roger Gilboy's research of the parish documents and churchwardens' accounts covering this period no mention was uncovered of the cemetery at St Mary Magdalen being closed or burial restricted.[31]

As noted above, the coins that were buried with this individual represent another unusual aspect of the burial. They comprise a silver shilling that was found near the left shoulder and a silver half groat that was recovered from a soil sample taken from the grave fill below the lower part of the body. The location of the shilling close to the head may indicate that the coins had originally been placed on the eyes but had become displaced, either accidentally during the burial or subsequently as a result of decomposition of the soft tissues, although the contrasting sizes of the pieces might argue against this. The placing of coins with burials, and particularly over the eyes or in the mouth, is commonly held to have been a widespread custom in Britain during the historic period, but the practice is in fact only rarely found in the archaeological record. Gilchrist's review of 8,000 late medieval burials, dating from the eleventh to sixteenth centuries, was able to provide only sixteen examples that contained coins, and a survey of post-medieval burials by Cherryson et al. listed only a further fourteen instances dating from the mid fifteenth to nineteenth centuries.[32] The location of the coins within the grave varied considerably and only in a small proportion of these burials were the coins placed on the eyes. None of the coins from medieval burials were recorded as being associated with the eyes, although in several instances they were near to the head and may have been displaced, and a thirteenth-century example from Tavistock Abbey may have been associated with the mouth.[33] Coins were placed on the eyes in four of the burials listed by Cherryson et al., including one example, at Fowlis Wester Church, Perthshire, that contained coins issued in 1642–50 and may therefore be contemporary with the burial at St Cross College.[34] In other instances the coins were located away from the head or the quantity of coins precludes an association with the eyes or mouth, and in some examples the coins were

[27] T. Willis, *The London Practice of Physick or the Whole Practical Part of Physick* (London, 1685), p. 607.

[28] Gilboy, 'Crisis Mortality in Civil War Oxford', table 3.

[29] A. Cherryson et al., *A Fine and Private Place: The Archaeology of Death and Burial in Post-Medieval Britain*, Leicester Archaeology Monograph, 22 (2012), p. 112; L.J. McIntyre, 'The York 113: Osteological Analysis of 10 Mass Graves from Fishergate, York', *Journal of Conflict Archaeology*, 11:2–3 (2016), pp. 115–34.

[30] Gilboy, 'Crisis Mortality in Civil War Oxford', p. 100.

[31] Personal communication from R. Gilboy, 2019.

[32] R. Gilchrist, 'Magic for the Dead? The Archaeology of Magic in Later Medieval Burials', *Medieval Archaeology*, 52 (2008), pp. 133–5; Cherryson et al., *A Fine and Private Place*, p. 73 and table 3.11.

[33] Gilchrist, 'Magic for the Dead?', table 3.

[34] Cherryson et al., *A Fine and Private Place*, table 3.11.

placed in a purse that still survives. The placing of these objects represents an enigmatic practice that we may never fully understand. There are records of a tradition of placing coins over the eyes to hold them shut during preparation of the corpse, and it is possible that in some instances the coins were forgotten and interred with the body accidentally.[35] However, this would entail a remarkable forgetfulness on the part of the undertaker (particularly in the instance of a valuable coin such as the silver shilling at St Cross College), and does not account for the occasions when coins were clearly placed in locations other than the eyes. It seems more plausible that in most cases the coins were placed deliberately by mourners for whom they held a definite significance, albeit one about which we can only speculate. Gilchrist has argued that coins may have had an apotropaic value and draws attention to their use in amulets and healing charms.[36]

Another possible explanation for the provision of coins may be provided by the seventeenth century antiquary John Aubrey, who recorded that during his childhood he heard of a practice of placing a coin in the mouth of the deceased for St Peter.[37] This explication surely owes its origins to the classical Greek tradition of providing the deceased with an obol to pay the fare across the Styx, often placed in the mouth; Christianisation of the tradition has simply transferred the recipient of the coin from Charon to St Peter. Logically this should involve only a single coin, but in Apuleius' Cupid and Psyche, Psyche takes two coins on her visit to the underworld so she can use the second coin pay for a return journey, and it is possible that in later centuries Christian mourners saw in this story an allegory for the resurrection. As a centre of learning, Oxford of all places would have contained people who would have understood such classical symbolism and it is possible that the provision of the coins therefore indicates that the deceased was the wife or daughter of an academic. They may also provide some evidence for the religious sympathies of the deceased and mourners, since St Peter played no part in protestant funerary traditions and the placing of such objects may therefore have been a clandestine statement of Catholic sympathies, or at least an example of a pre-reformation tradition that would only have been perpetuated by someone with conservative religious views. The practice would certainly have been considered idolatrous by the puritans. The final possibility in relation to the coins is that they were included because they bore portraits of Charles I and were intended as an expression of monarchist sympathies on the part of the deceased.

There are, therefore, a number of possible reasons why this individual may have been buried within the tenement at No. 58/59 St Giles' Street rather than the parish cemetery and it is unlikely that we will ever know the truth. The most likely explanation is that she was excluded from the cemetery (or chose not to be buried there) due to being a religious dissenter, probably a Catholic during the persecutions during the Commonwealth, although it is alternatively possible that she died during an outbreak of disease in the crowded and insanitary conditions that prevailed while Oxford was under siege during the Civil War. Whatever the case, such an extra-cemetery burial represents a very unusual practice for the period.

EXCAVATION RESULTS

The Tenement Boundaries

The excavation was delimited to west and north by walls 1176 and 1178 respectively, and walls 1098 and 1192 divided the site into the three historically-attested tenements, Nos. 57, 58–9 and 60 St Giles' Street (Fig. 12.4). The western wall, which defined the historical boundary between the tenements and Beaumont Palace, was preceded by a sequence of shallow ditches but no evidence was observed for the form of the other boundaries before the construction of the walls, which, at least in their surviving form, dated from the nineteenth century (see Building Survey, below).

35 Ibid. p. 73.
36 Gilchrist, 'Magic for the Dead?', pp. 133–5, 141.
37 J. Aubrey, *Remains of Gentilisme and Judaisme*, ed. John Buchanan-Brown (1972), p. 172.

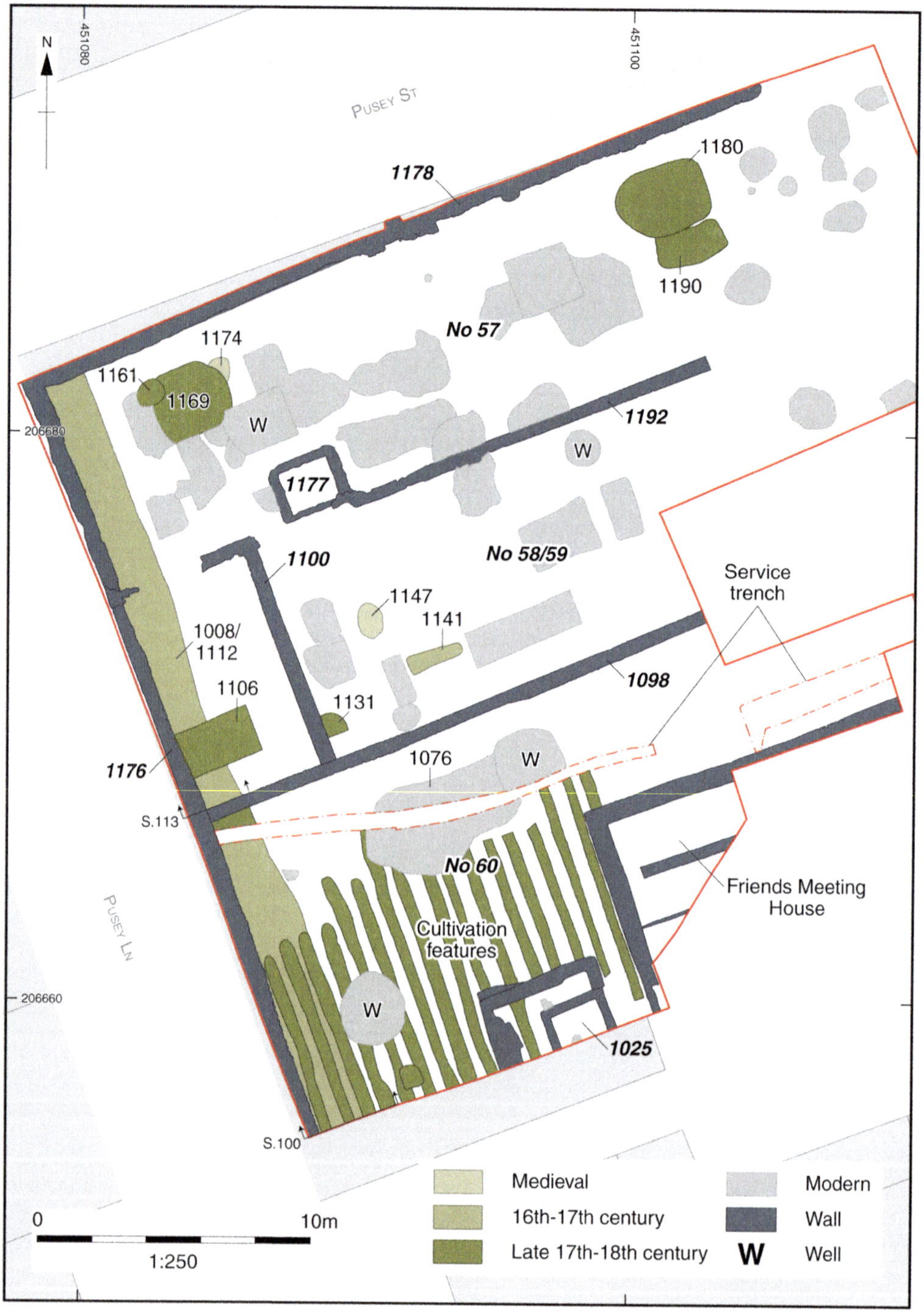

Fig. 12.4 Plan of archaeological features.

Medieval Period
The only features dated to the medieval period were pit 1174, toward the rear of tenement No. 57, and pit 1147, in a similar location within No. 58/59. Pit 1174 had been substantially cut away by a later feature but the surviving part was 0.55 m deep and contained a single small pottery sherd dating from the thirteenth to fifteenth centuries. Pit 1147 was oval in plan and measured 1.20 m x 0.85 m and 0.25 m deep. It had curved sides and a flat base and contained a fill of mixed sandy gravel (1148) that included mid fifteenth- to sixteenth-century pottery. Residual medieval pottery was also found in several later features.

Sixteenth to Seventeenth Century
The features attributed to this phase comprised the boundary ditches at the western end of the tenements, which predated the adjacent wall 1176, and burial 1141. The boundary ditch was investigated by means of two interventions, located in the middle and southern end of the excavation area. In the middle intervention, a possible early phase of the boundary was identified, represented by an undated ditch (1115; Fig. 12.5, section 113). It measured 1.1 m deep and 0.55 m wide with vertical sides and a flat base, a profile that might be consistent with an interpretation as a palisade trench. This boundary was recut as ditch 1008/1112, which had curved sides and a rounded base and was 1.6 m wide and 0.50 m deep. At the southern limit of the excavation, the ditch had a single phase and a more 'V'-shaped profile (Fig. 12.5, section 100). Pottery from the primary fill (1009, 1113) indicated that the feature was probably dug during the mid to late sixteenth century. It also contained a bosun's whistle (Fig. 12.9). The pottery from the subsequent fill dated from the seventeenth century. Following the accumulation over the ditch of a garden soil (1097) at least 0.40 m thick, a boundary wall was constructed on a foundation of large limestone rubble (1098) that was 0.7 m wide and 0.6 m deep.

Burial 1141 (Figs. 12.4 and 12.6) was situated in the rear part of No. 58/59, close to the boundary with No. 60. The grave cut (1138) was 2.0 m long and up to 0.20 m deep and tapered from west to east from 0.70–0.44 m wide. The grave contained the skeleton of a female of 18–23 years (1139). The skeleton was lying in the grave with the head at the western end, legs flexed, knees to the south with arms flexed and hands over the chest. A sample from a rib (SUERC-74447; Table 12.4) returned a radiocarbon date range of cal AD 1497–1666 (93.7 per cent) and 1785–94 (1.7 per cent). There was no evidence of a coffin but the skeleton was surrounded by copper alloy pins which would have been used to wrap the body in a shroud. The grave also contained a silver shilling dating to 1640–1 which was found next to the left shoulder, and a silver half groat dating to 1635–6 was recovered from an environmental sample collected from the grave fill beneath the body. The grave fill (1140) also contained a few sherds of residual pottery dated to the mid fifteenth to sixteenth century.

Late Seventeenth to Eighteenth Century
During this phase the three tenements began to develop differently. The digging of large rubbish pits first became a feature of No. 57, while No. 58/59 contained only two small pits of this date and the rear part of No. 60 was given over to cultivation features.

Two large pits (1169, 1180) were situated to the rear of No. 57. Pit 1169 was 2.35 m wide and was excavated to a depth of 1.2 m without reaching the bottom. It contained late-seventeenth- to early eighteenth-century pottery. A smaller rubbish pit (1161) truncated this large pit and contained eighteenth-century pottery. Pit 1180 was 3 m wide and was similarly more than 1.2 m deep. The earliest observed fill contained mid to late sixteenth-century pottery and brick inclusions. The upper fills contained gravels and redeposited brickearth. The pit was later truncated by a smaller pit (1190), which contained pottery of the late seventeenth to early eighteenth century.

Pits 1106 and 1131 were situated at the rear of No. 58/59. Pit 1106 was excavated to a depth of 1.10 m without reaching the base. It had vertical sides and produced pottery dating from the mid to late seventeenth century. Pit 1131 was only partly exposed, since it was situated beneath the wall of building 1100. It was similarly not bottomed but was more than 0.85 m deep. It had

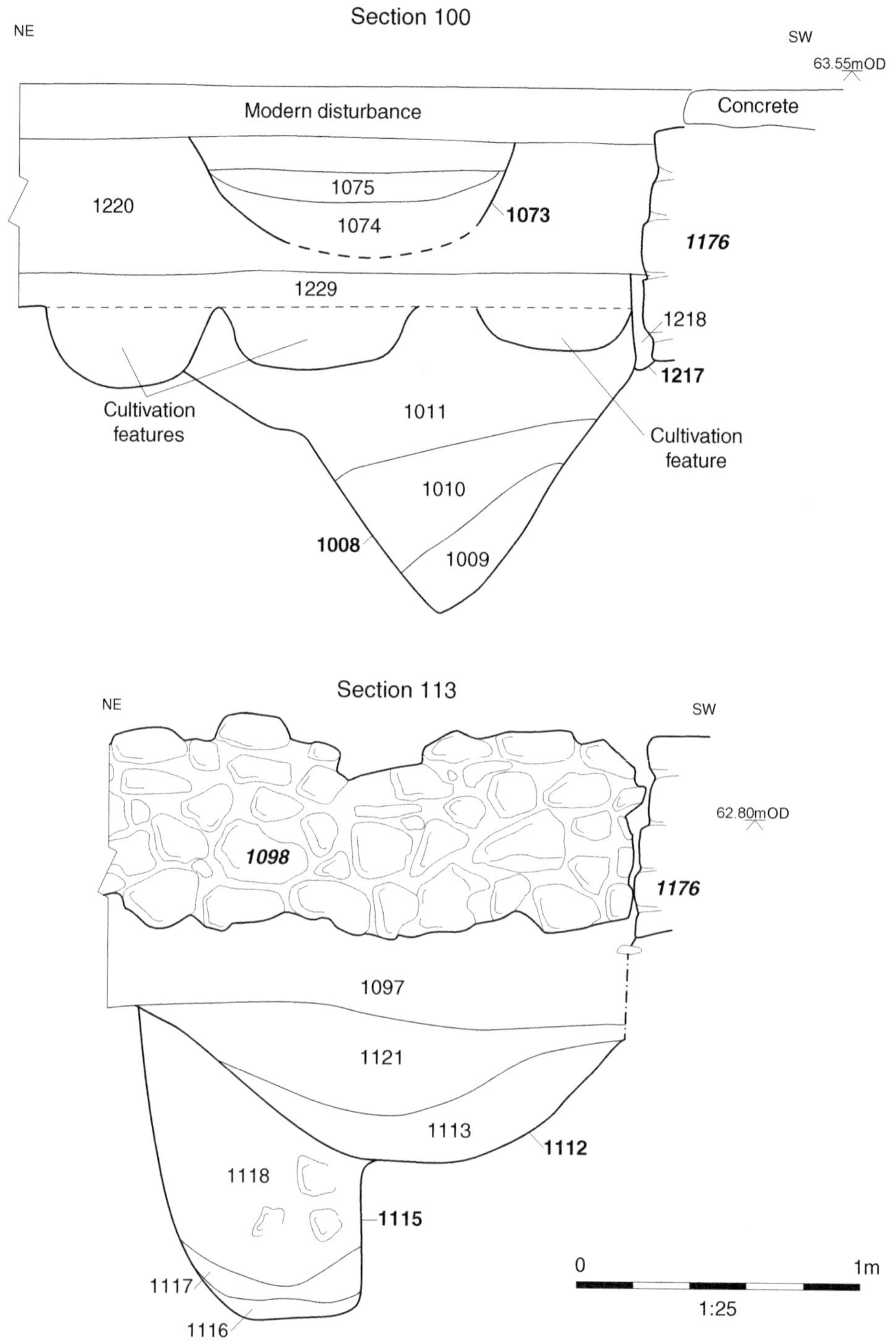

Fig. 12.5 Sections through boundary ditches defining the rear, western end of the tenements.

Fig. 12.6 Burial 1141, looking west. Scales: 0.5 m and 1 m.

vertical sides and may have been dug as a cesspit or rubbish pit. It has been backfilled with a single deposit (1137) that was dated by an eighteenth-century pipe stem.

The rear part of No. 60 was occupied by a series of at least seventeen cultivation features, comprising parallel linear gullies that produced a fairly large assemblage of late seventeenth- and eighteenth-century clay pipe fragments.

Nineteenth Century Onwards

The northern boundary wall (1178), which fronted onto Pusey Street, was built during the nineteenth century, as were the boundary walls that divided the tenements. The walls had been demolished prior to the excavation and only the foundations survived. Wall 1178 and the boundary between properties 57 and 58/59 (1192) were constructed from limestone rubble, with widths around 0.50 m, but the boundary between properties 58/59 and 60 (1098) had an extremely slight foundation. Walls 1098 and 1192 butted the western boundary wall.

A substantial number of pits dating from the nineteenth and twentieth centuries were situated within tenement No. 57, which also had a well and a small outbuilding (1177) inserted against the boundary with No. 58/59. A smaller number of pits were dug in No. 58/59, which also had a well, and an outbuilding (1100) was built at the western end. Part of No. 60 was occupied by the Friends Meeting House, to the rear of which was a smaller, brick-built outbuilding (1025). An extensive pit (1076) and two wells were also located within this property. All the walls and buildings are shown on the 1876–8 1:500 Ordnance Survey map.

The earlier features were sealed by a layer of undifferentiated garden soil that extended throughout the site, from which a small quantity of nineteenth-century pottery was recovered.

BUILDING SURVEY by DEIRDRE FORDE

The Grade II listed wall that formed the western boundary of the college, the boundary wall along Pusey Street and the wall between Nos. 57 and 58/59, which extended along part of the parish boundary, were recorded prior to demolition, following on from concerns and discussions about the age of the walls which were suspected of having medieval origins.[38] The survey included a photographic record, the enhancement of existing drawn records and a written descriptive record of each structure. In addition to this pre-demolition recording, a phase of intermittent watching brief was undertaken during the dismantling of the walls to record previously hidden evidence of their construction or other features of interest such as reused stones. The rear wall of No. 61 St Giles' Street had been removed in 1990, when the presence of reused medieval stonework was noted.[39]

End Wall of No. 60 St Giles' Street

Below ground level, the masonry and mortar of the western boundary wall was cobbled and irregular. The mortar is a rich yellow, sandy lime mortar with the foundation stones laid with brown earth. It was thought that this might be the original boundary wall of the Beaumont precinct shown on Agas' map of Oxford in 1578. The wall had been entirely rebuilt above ground using cementitious mortar, indicating a date after the middle of the nineteenth century. The masonry was small with irregular coursing, and on top of the wall is twentieth-century cement and red brick coping. Towards the south end was a Tudor-style arched doorway, which is a later insertion and not sewn into the masonry of the wall; it resembles the one on Pusey Lane and must be early twentieth century in date.

[38] The full report on the building survey appears in 'St Cross College West Quad Oxford, Watching Brief and Building Recording', unpublished OA report (2015), https://library.oxfordarchaeology.com/5557/.

[39] 'St Cross College, Oxford: Archaeological Investigations in Advance of Redevelopment'.

End Wall of Nos. 58–59 St Giles' Street
This section was constructed externally of large regular ashlar blocks, and internally of rubble masonry, and is distinct from the wall of No. 60, though it shares the same red brick coping. It was perhaps of eighteenth- or nineteenth-century date, and was rebuilt when the properties were united in 1914.

Walls of No. 57 St Giles' Street
The west wall had been removed for the insertion of garages. The other two walls both have relatively shallow foundations with masonry consistent with that above ground, suggesting that both, in their entirety, are much more recent. The north wall may have been built in 1828, when Pusey Street was formed, while the eastern section was rebuilt at the same time as the chapel of Pusey House (it shares the same damp course) and contains a Tudor style arch. Broken moulded stones as well as broken brick and tile were found in both this and the next wall, suggesting that debris from nearby buildings was used in their construction. The wall on the south side of the garden, unlike the street wall, was an historic property boundary, and also formed the boundary between the parishes of St Giles and St Mary Magdalen. The wall was constructed of random rubble masonry, and topped with twelve courses of Victorian red brick and a round coping course; the northward return at the east end was entirely of brick. The masonry included pieces of broken red brick and some broken tiles with sandy yellow striations, which were common in Oxford in the late sixteenth and seventeenth centuries.

POTTERY by PAUL BLINKHORN

The pottery assemblage comprised 553 sherds with a total weight of 16,858 g. The medieval material was recorded using the conventions of the Oxfordshire County type-series,[40] as follows:

OXAM Brill/Boarstall ware, 1200–1600. 49 sherds, 494 g.
OXBF North-East Wiltshire ware, 1050–1400. 14 sherds, 133 g.
OXBN Tudor green ware, late fourteenth–sixteenth century. 1 sherd, 1 g.
OXBX Late-medieval Brill/Boarstall ware, fifteenth–early seventeenth century. 32 sherds, 529 g.
OXY Medieval Oxford ware, 1075–1350. 23 sherds, 250 g.

The late-medieval and post-medieval wares were recorded using the conventions of the Museum of London Type-Series,[41] as follows:

BORDG Green-glazed Border ware, 1550–1700. 23 sherds, 962 g.
BORDY Yellow-glazed Border ware, 1550–1700. 6 sherds, 195 g.
CHPO Chinese porcelain, 1650+. 13 sherds, 205 g.
CSTN Cistercian ware, 1470–1600. 4 sherds, 64 g.
DERBS Derby stoneware, 1700–1900. 2 sherds, 33 g.
FREC Frechen stoneware, 1550–1750. 11 sherds, 297 g.
HORT Horticultural earthenwares, nineteenth–twentieth century. 13 sherds, 1,571 g.
LONS London stoneware, 1680+. 15 sherds, 651 g.
METS Metropolitan slipware, 1480–1900. 10 sherds, 231 g.
MPUR Midland purple ware, 1400–1700. 2 sherds, 33 g.

40 M. Mellor and G. Oakley, 'A Summary of the Key Assemblages …', in 'St Ebbe's, Part II', pp. 181–219; Mellor, 'Synthesis'.
41 A.G. Vince, 'The Saxon and Medieval Pottery of London: A Review', *Medieval Archaeology*, 29 (1985), pp. 25–93.

PMBL Post-medieval black-glazed redware, sixteenth–seventeenth century. 6 sherds, 138 g.
PMR Post-medieval redware, 1550+. 65 sherds, 2,883 g.
RAER Raeren stoneware, 1480–1600. 1 sherd, 87 g.
SIEG Siegburg stoneware, 1300–1500. 1 sherd, 10 g.
STMB Staffordshire-type mottled ware, 1680–1800. 7 sherds, 394 g.
STSL Staffordshire slipware, 1650–1800. 4 sherds, 43 g.
SWSG Staffordshire white salt-glazed stoneware, 1720–1800. 22 sherds, 525 g.
TGW Tin-glazed ware, 1600–1800. 57 sherds, 1397 g.
TPW Transfer-printed whiteware, 1830–1900. 169 sherds, 5612 g.
WEST Westerwald-type stoneware, 1590–1800. 3 sherds, 120 g.

The range of fabric types is typical of sites in the city of Oxford. The medieval assemblage is rather small, with the complete absence of fabric OXAC, a common Saxo-Norman ware, suggesting that there was no activity at the site before the Norman Conquest.

Chronology
Each stratified, context-specific pottery assemblage was given a ceramic phase (CP) date based on the range of ware and vessel types present, and adjusted according to the stratigraphic matrix. The chronology, defining wares and the amount of pottery per phase is shown in Table 12.1.

The bulk of the pottery (435 sherds, 15,186 g) dates to CP PM4 or later, broadly the eighteenth to nineteenth centuries. There was very little ceramic evidence of activity at the site in the medieval period, with just 25 sherds (273 g) occurring in features dated *c.*1200–1550, suggesting that the area generally had a somewhat marginal use during that time. Further medieval sherds were redeposited in post-medieval features and while these only amounted to 93 sherds weighing 1133 g, it suggests that what little evidence of medieval activity there was has been heavily disturbed by later activity. Certainly, the low mean sherd weight of the stratified CP M1 material (7.9 g) is entirely consistent with pottery which had been deposited in contexts which were repeatedly reworked, such as field or garden soils. As is typical for the city of Oxford, residuality is quite high in CP PM1–PM3, but lower in PM4–MOD (Table 12.2), although this seems likely to be due to the paucity of pottery dating to the earlier period.

Table 12.1. Ceramic phase chronology, occurrence and defining wares.

Phase	Defining wares	Date	No. sherds	Weight (g)	Mean sherd weight (g)
M1	OXAM	13th–15th C	19	150	7.9
M2	OXBX	15th–M 16th C	6	123	20.5
PM1	PMR, FREC, BORDY, BORDG	M–L 16th C	48	823	17.1
PM2	TGW, WEST, PMBL	E–M 17th C	28	391	14.0
PM3	STSL, TGW	M–L 17th C	17	185	10.9
PM4	LONS, STMB	L 17th–E 18thC	148	5420	36.6
PM5	SWSG	18th C	20	557	27.9
MOD	TPW	19th C	267	9209	34.5
Total			553	16,858	

Table 12.2. Pottery occurrence per ceramic phase by fabric type, expressed as a percentage of the total weight per phase, major fabrics only. Shaded cells: residual material.

Fabric	M1	M2	PM1	PM2	PM3	PM4	PM5	MOD
OXBF	39.3%	0	0	0	0	1.2%	0	0.1%
OXY	44.7%	0	2.6%	14.8%	15.1%	0.8%	0	0.4%
OXAM	16.0%	3.2%	15.7%	15.6%	0	2.9%	0	1.3%
OXBX	–	96.7%	21.6%	2.3%	48.6%	0.4%	0	1.2%
BORDG	–	–	8.6%	0.5%	4.9%	14.3%	0	1.1%
BORDY	–	–	9.2%	0	0	0.9%	0	0.8%
FREC	–	–	5.6%	3.3%	5.4%	3.9%	0	0.2%
PMR	–	–	36.6%	52.2%	7.0%	21.2%	2.2%	13.1%
METS	–	–	–	0	0	1.6%	5.9%	1.2%
TGW	–	–	–	8.7%	13.0%	24.4%	0	0.2%
WEST	–	–	–	0	0	1.8%	0	0.3%
PMBL	–	–	–	0	1.1%	2.5%	0	0.1%
STSL	–	–	–	–	0	0	0	0.5%
CHPO	–	–	–	–	1.1%	3.7%	0	0
LONS	–	–	–	–	–	11.0%	0	0.6%
STMB	–	–	–	–	–	7.1%	0	0.1%
SWSG	–	–	–	–	–	–	88.9%	0.3%
HORT	–	–	–	–	–	–	–	17.1%
TPW	–	–	–	–	–	–	–	60.9%
Total	150	123	823	391	185	5420	557	9209

Ceramic Phase M1, Thirteenth to Fifteenth Century (19 sherds, 150 g, EVE = 0.04) The small assemblage of pottery which dates to this period comprises unglazed body sherds from jars in OXY and OXBF and a few fragments of glazed jugs in OXAM. Just one rim sherd was present, from an OXBF jar. The only features which produced pottery of this date were 1179, a deposit above the natural, and 1174, the fill of a pit which produced just one sherd of pottery weighing 3 g, and thus could easily be of a later date.

Ceramic Phase M2, Fifteenth to Mid Sixteenth Century (6 sherds, 123 g, EVE = 0) Only two features produced pottery of this date: 1140, the fill of grave 1141, and 1148, the fill of pit 1147. Given the coin date from the former context, it would appear the pottery is probably residual, although the sherds of OXBX could date to the very end of the life of the industry and thus be broadly contemporary. The whole assemblage consisted of body sherds.

Ceramic Phase PM1, Mid to Late Sixteenth Century (48 sherds, 823 g) Over 18 per cent of the pottery from assemblages of this date consists of residual medieval material. Otherwise, the major ware is PMR (36.6 per cent), along with a smaller quantity of OXBX (21.6 per cent), with most of the rest of the assemblage made up of other utilitarian earthenwares in the form of Border wares (17.8 per cent), along with a small amount of Frechen stoneware (5.6 per cent). The only other pottery was a single small sherd (1 g) of OXBN. This is fairly typical of sites in the city at this time. Most of the assemblages of this date consisted of just a few sherds, other than fill 1137 of eighteenth-century pit 1131, which produced about half the pottery of this date (24 sherds, 411 g).

Ceramic Phase PM2, Early to Mid Seventeenth Century (28 sherds, 391 g) Just three contexts produced pottery of this date. Residuality is high, with around a third of the pottery being redeposited medieval material, including the only sherd of Siegburg stoneware from the site. As before, the assemblage is dominated by utilitarian earthenwares (PMR), along with small quantities of FREC (3.3 per cent), but also tablewares in the form of TGW, including a fragment of a fairly good quality polychrome dish from fill 1121 of ditch 1112.

Ceramic Phase PM3, Mid to Late Seventeenth Century (17 sherds, 185 g) Each of the five context-specific assemblages dating to this CP comprises a small number of fairly small sherds. Residuality is high, with nearly two-thirds of the pottery being redeposited earlier material. The majority of the small amount of contemporary pottery present consists of fragments of earthenware, porcelain and stoneware drinking vessels (FREC, PMBL, CHPO and TGW), with the two sherds of TGW being fragments of mugs with manganese sponged decoration typical of the mid to late seventeenth century.[42] The rest of the assemblage consists of PMR and BORDG. The only other pottery present was a single sherd of MPUR (5 g) and another of CSTN (2 g), with the latter also from a drinking vessel.

Ceramic Phase PM4, Late Seventeenth to Early Eighteenth Century (148 sherds, 5,420 g) The majority of the pottery from this phase came from the various fills of pit 1169 (78 sherds, 3,527 g). The fills produced sherds which cross-fit, indicating that they are all contemporary. The assemblage mainly consists of large fragments and appears to be a primary dump of domestic pottery. The tin-glazed earthenware assemblage comprises fragments of at least three chamber-pots and a fairly large plate, all plain white, a fragment of a small blue-painted plate and several from a fluted, footed bowl with similar decoration (Fig. 12.7, no. 1). The latter seems most likely to be Portuguese, as fluted bowls (Taça) were largely produced in that country in the eighteenth century. Such pottery is a rare find in Britain outside the ports.[43] Other imported wares include two partially complete Chinese porcelain tea-bowls with blue-painted decoration (Fig. 12.7, nos. 2 and 3), along with single sherds from two others and a few small fragments of another with polychrome Imari-style decoration. The only other imported sherds were German stonewares, in the form of the neck of a Frechen stoneware jug or bottle and a large sherd from the rim of a blue-painted Cologne/Westerwald jug. Other drinking pottery was present in the form of eight English stoneware brown-dipped mugs typical of the first two decades of the eighteenth century.[44] One small fragment was from a typical round-bodied 'tavern gorge', while the rest were straight-sided mug/tankard forms (Fig. 12.7, no. 4), one of which had somewhat unusual vertical fluting, and another with horizontal rouletting. Utilitarian earthenwares were relatively scarce. A few stray sherds of PMR and two bases, one from a METS bowl and another from a PMBL vessel, were noted but the only well-represented pottery of this type were three fragments of STMB bowls and four or five BORDG vessels. The latter consisted of fragments of three plates or shallow dishes, and another from a pipkin or porringer.

The rest of the CP assemblage largely consisted of small groups of single sherds from individual vessels, other than the group from context 1189, which had a fairly large group of large sherds of PMR bowls and jars (8 sherds, 969 g), a single large fragment of a BORD platter which was unusual in that it does not appear to have been glazed, and a few fragments of blue-painted CHPO tea-bowls. Overall, the pottery from this phase is typical of a reasonably well-to-do urban household of the period.

42 C. Orton, 'Post-Roman Pottery', in P. Hinton (ed.), *Excavations in Southwark 1973–76 and Lambeth 1973–79*, MoLAS and DGLA Joint Publication, 3 (1988), p. 321.

43 T.M. Casimiro, 'Portuguese Faience in London', *London Archaeologist*, 11:5 (2006), pp. 115–21.

44 For example, A.R. Mountford, *The Illustrated Guide to Staffordshire Salt-Glazed Stoneware* (1971), plate 15.

Fig. 12.7 Pottery.

Ceramic Phase PM5, Eighteenth Century (20 sherds, 557 g) Almost all the pottery dating to this phase (15 sherds, 539 g) comes from the fills of pit 1161, with the bulk consisting of a small group of well-represented SWSG vessels from fill 1163. It comprises fragments of a saucer, two hexagonal plates (Fig. 12.7, no. 5), two chamber pots, a slop-bowl and a small tankard. Again, this is a fairly typical assemblage from a well-to-do urban household of the period.

Ceramic Phase MOD, Nineteenth Century and Later (267 sherds, 9,209 g) This is the largest CP assemblage from the site, and makes up over half the overall pottery from it. Around 10 per cent of it is residual earlier material, with the bulk of the contemporary material comprising tablewares and utilitarian stonewares such as blacking bottles, along with a fairly large number of flower-pot fragments (17.1 per cent) and red earthenwares (13.1 per cent), with some of the latter perhaps being residual material. It appears to be entirely of a domestic nature.

Catalogue of Illustrated Pottery (Fig. 12.7):

1. Fabric TGW. Four non-joining fragments of a fluted bowl. Pale buff fabric, white tin-glaze with blue-painted decoration on both surfaces. Ctx 1171 and 1173, pit 1169.
2. Fabric CHPO. Full profile of a blue-painted tea-bowl. Ctx 1170, pit 1169.
3. Fabric CHPO. Base and lower body of a blue-painted tea-bowl. Ctx 1170, pit 1169.
4. Fabric LONS. Near-complete small tankard. Pale grey fabric with white salt-glaze over all and a brown-dipped rim. Ctx 1170, pit 1169.
5. Fabric SWSG. Hexagonal plate. White fabric with white salt-glaze on both surfaces. Ctx 1163, pit 1161.

BUILDING MATERIALS

Ceramic Building Material by Cynthia Poole

Sixty-nine fragments (5,749 g) of ceramic building material and fifty-three fragments (2,416 g) of nineteenth-century painted plaster were recovered. The assemblage was poorly preserved, comprising mostly small broken fragments with a mean fragment weight of 83 g. No complete objects were recovered and the only complete dimension was thickness. The assemblage is composed of roof, floor tile and brick ranging in date from twelfth/thirteenth century up to the nineteenth/twentieth century.

The roof tile was composed of flat tile fragments of fairly crude manufacture ranging in thickness from 10–19 mm, which included examples of both ridge and peg tile. A single example with remnants of thin amber glaze occurred in the early buff shelly limestone fabric IB, which dates to the late twelfth to early thirteenth century. This fabric was most commonly used for ridge tile. The peg tile was pierced by circular peg holes measuring 9, 11, 12 and 13 mm in diameter and one had a thickened halo of clay encircling the base. They can be broadly dated to thirteenth to fifteenth century, but were found in deposits of seventeenth to nineteenth-century date, suggesting the tile had remained in use for several hundred years.

A small quantity of flooring comprising three floor tiles and two brick paviours (1150 g) was all of post-medieval date. A single small fragment of floor tile was probably a 'Flemish type' floor tile of fifteenth- to sixteenth-century date. Two thicker unglazed quarry tiles and the paviours are probably of eighteenth to nineteenth century date.

All the brick recovered was very fragmentary with no complete dimensions surviving. None are closely dateable within the post-medieval period, but all are handmade and no evidence of frogs were present. The brick also points to improvements in the post-medieval phase, possibly with the insertion of chimneys suggested by the presence of burning on several bricks and the nineteenth-century firebrick.

Stone Roofing and Building Stone by Ruth Shaffrey
A total of sixty-five fragments (9.5 kg) of stone roofing was recovered. Seven fragments of stone roofing were recovered from medieval contexts. One fragment is made of fine-grained sandstone, but most of the roofing is made of shelly oolitic limestone probably from the Pusey Flags, a common roofstone type in Oxford.[45] Stone roofs occurred in Oxford from perhaps the late twelfth century and certainly from the thirteenth century.[46] Two fragments of stone roofing were found in late seventeenth- to eighteenth-century pit 1106. These are of a coarse shelly limestone and a sandy limestone, both typical of Oxford roofing. A post-medieval cultivation feature produced a small block of possible oolitic limestone, possibly Taynton stone. It is shaped but with no obvious tool marks and is presumed to be architectural.

Window Glass
A few sherds of window glass were recovered, some possibly of medieval date.

VESSEL GLASS AND BEAD by IAN R. SCOTT

An assemblage of 163 sherds of vessel glass was recovered. There was no glass that could be dated before the mid sixteenth century and overwhelming bulk of the material came from two nineteenth-century bottle dumps. Pit 1161 contained a dump of wine bottles that included twelve complete or almost complete bottles ranging in date from the very end of the seventeenth century to the mid eighteenth century. The only other glass of note from the pit was part of a stemmed wine glass probably of late seventeenth- or early eighteenth-century date.

A tiny opaque annular bead (D: 2.5 mm; L: 1.5 mm) was recovered from a soil sample taken from burial 1141. It is most likely to have been sewn onto clothing as decoration.

CLAY TOBACCO PIPES by JOHN COTTER

A total of 143 pieces of clay pipe (804 g) was recovered. Most of the pipe bowls, and one of the marks, can be paralleled with those published from excavations in St Ebbe's, Oxford and to a slightly lesser extent with those published in Oswald's simplified national typology.[47] The St Ebbe's pipe dates have been used in preference to the more general national dating. Other (mainly later) bowls are identified in the catalogue according to a series of codes based on Atkinson and Oswald's London pipes typology with bowl types assigned to an abbreviated code.[48]

The pipes are in a mixed condition with around two thirds of contexts producing a fairly worn and fragmentary assemblage, and the remaining third producing a much fresher assemblage with longer and more complete items. The more worn/fragmentary pipes mainly come from tenement No. 60 and from the parallel cultivation furrows in particular. These produced a fairly large assemblage of eighteenth-century pipes of which the latest datable pieces are *c.*1750–90, but with plentiful late seventeenth- and early eighteenth-century material as well. The fresher material is mainly from large pits and ditch fills in the central and northern areas of the site. Although the pipes here are of the same date as those from the southern area, they may have survived in better condition as they were not subjected to the cultivation activity seen in tenement No. 60.

45 W.J. Arkell, *Oxford Stone* (1947), pp. 149–50.
46 E.M. Jope, 'The Clarendon Hotel, Oxford, Part 1, The Site', *Oxoniensia*, 23 (1958), p. 78.
47 A. Oswald, *Clay Pipes for the Archaeologist*, BAR BS, 14 (1975); A. Oswald, 'Clay Pipes' in Hassall, 'St Ebbe's, Part II', pp. 251–62.
48 D. Atkinson and A. Oswald, 'London Clay Tobacco Pipes', *Journal of the British Archaeological Association*, 32 (1969), pp. 171–227.

Table 12.3. Quantification of clay tobacco pipe bowls by type and date.

Bowl type	Date	No. bowls
Oxford: B	1650–90	7
Oxford: B (Developed)	1680–1725	4
Oxford: C	1690–1720	5
Indeterminate	L 17th–E 18th C	1
Oxford: D	1750–90	8
London: AO25	1730–80	1
London: AO26	1730–1800	1
London: AO27	1780–1830	1
Total bowls		28

In total there are twenty-nine pieces of pipe bowl from a minimum of twenty-eight bowls (twelve complete, or nearly so), five pieces of mouth and 109 stem fragments. Four pieces bear maker's marks (below). A summary of the pipe bowl assemblage from the site is shown in Table 12.3.

Unusually for an Oxford assemblage of moderate size, there are no bowls from the first half of the seventeenth century. This may reflect the more remote location of the site, set back from the main thoroughfares of the city. The pipe bowls suggest a relatively sudden burst of activity only from the mid/late seventeenth century onwards, with a peak of activity from the late seventeenth through to the late eighteenth century (roughly *c.*1680–1780?). None of the later (post-*c.*1750) bowls bears a maker's mark and this might suggest that most of them predate *c.*1780, after which date heel/spur-marks become common. There are, likewise, no definite bowls of the nineteenth century; in fact, the only feature with pipes dating to the nineteenth century is a large pond or pit (1076) and the garden soil layer, these being dated only by slender late-looking stems. There is, however, a single bowl of *c.*1780–1830 from the fill of ditch 1008/1112.

The earliest bowls from the site are Oxford Type B (*c.*1650–90), with a barrel-shaped, sometimes biconical bowl and a short, stubby spur or conical heel.[49] These are usually the commonest seventeenth-century bowl type found in the city. More recent work, however, suggests that a slightly more 'chinned' development of this ('Developed' Type B) may have remained in production as late as *c.*1725/30.[50] These were joined by the taller, more slender, Type C bowl *c.*1690–1720. Together, the sixteen examples of these three types suggest considerable activity on the site during the later seventeenth and early eighteenth century. The eight examples of Type D (*c.*1750–90) show continued activity into the second half of the eighteenth century, but the smaller combined total of eleven pipes for this half century might suggest this was not so intense as the first half of the century. This could of course just reflect local changes in rubbish disposal at the turn of the eighteenth/nineteenth century, with rubbish carted off-site rather than disposed of in pits.

Most of the pipes are probably local Oxford or Oxfordshire products, even those made in the London style, but at least two early eighteenth-century pipes are distinguished by maker's

49 Oswald, *Clay Pipes for the Archaeologist*, fig. 51B.

50 J. Cotter, 'Clay Tobacco Pipes', in '33–35 George Street, Oxford: Archaeological Watching Brief Report', unpublished OA report (2012), https://library.oxfordarchaeology.com/1015/; D.A. Higgins, 'Clay Tobacco Pipes', in K. Brady et al., 'Excavations at Abingdon West Central Redevelopment: Iron Age, Roman, Medieval, and Post-Medieval Activity in Abingdon', *Oxoniensia*, 72 (2007), pp. 157–76.

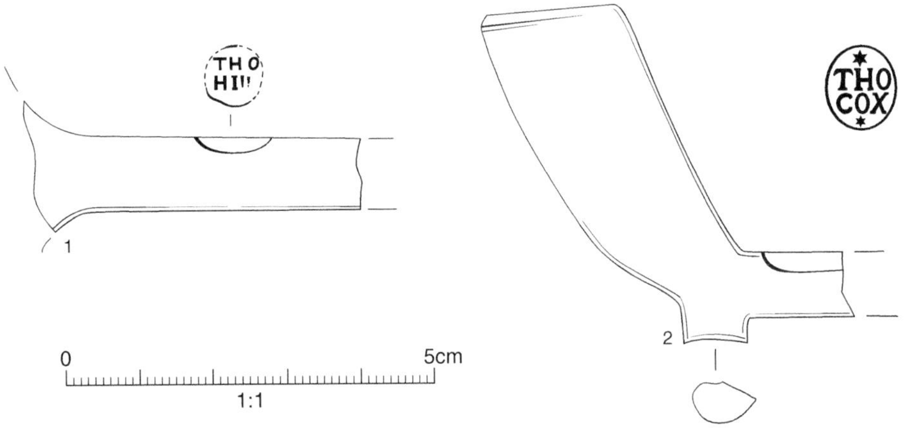

Fig. 12.8 Clay tobacco pipes.

marks as Wiltshire and Chester products (below). This ties in with Oswald's observation at St Ebbe's that the local pipe industry lost some of its dominance in the eighteenth century to outside competition from Wiltshire, Hampshire and Shropshire but regained its dominance in the nineteenth century.[51]

Four pieces have maker's marks, all on the upper side of the stem a short distance behind the bowl, a typical characteristic of 'West Country' pipes of the period *c.*1685–1750. These come from just two contexts and are described below:

Fill 1056 of cultivation feature 1055. Pipes datable c.1700–30

Two marked stems by different makers. The first is a burnished stem (69 mm long), yellower than usual. On the top is a faint oval mark largely obscured by subsequent burnishing, identifiable as the falcon mark attributed to the city of Chester. The only previous examples noted from Oxford are from St Ebbe's and Wadham College.[52]

The second piece is also a stem fragment (45 mm long), but with traces of a bowl attached (indeterminate type). It is weakly burnished. On the top, set back *c.*20 mm from the bowl, is a faint incuse maker's mark 'THO/HI[LL]' within a faint circle or cartouche possibly with a scalloped outline (Fig. 12.8, no. 1). Very probably by Thomas Hill of Salisbury (Wilts), died 1710.[53] The mark resembles very closely some of the many marks issued during the period *c.*1685–1720 by Thomas Hunt of Marlborough (Wilts)[54] but the first two letters of the surname here are clearly 'HI--' and the last two probably 'LL'. This appears to be the first example by this maker identified from Oxford.

Fill 1189 of pit 1180. Pipes datable c.1690–1720

This produced two marked pipes by the same Oxfordshire maker. The illustrated piece (Fig. 12.8, no. 2, combining both marks) is a complete fresh bowl similar to Oxford Type C (*c.*1690–1720) but more upright and slender, like a Type D. It has a bottered rim, a good quality burnish and

51 Oswald, 'Clay Pipes', p. 251.

52 Ibid. fig. 53.19B; J. Cotter, 'Clay Tobacco pipes', in 'Undergraduate Centre and Access Centre, Wadham College, Oxford, Archaeological Evaluation Report', unpublished OA report (2017), https://library.oxfordarchaeology.com/3536/.

53 Oswald, *Clay Pipes for the Archaeologist*, p. 198.

54 D.R. Atkinson, 'Clay Tobacco Pipes and Pipemakers of Marlborough', *Wiltshire Archaeological and Natural History Magazine*, 60 (1965), figs. 2.43–2.67.

a small teardrop-shaped heel (showing scorching). The stem bore diameter is *c.*2 mm. Only 15 mm of stem is still attached. On the upper side of this, just behind the bowl, is a faint but legible incuse maker's mark within a circle (diameter 10 mm) containing the name 'THO/ COX', with a small six-pointed star filler above and below the inscription. The second piece is a stem fragment (63 mm long) with exactly the same mark, but set back at least 40 mm from the bowl end. The colour of this piece is duller and the burnishing obscures some of the stamp detail. They clearly represent two separate pipes, both almost certainly by the maker Thomas Cox of Wheatley, active *c.*1691.[55] There is no published parallel from the city, so it is fairly remarkable to find two examples in the same pit. There is, however, an earlier pipe by this maker from Queen's College Nun's Garden.[56] This has a bowl of *c.*1680–1700 and a long piece of attached stem which is highly decorated in the 'Oxford style', with rouletted borders. In the centre of these is a circular mark with very neat lettering in relief, around a central rosette, reading 'THO: C[OX]. WHATELY'. Due to slight damage this was not recognised as a Cox product at the time but has since been re-identified as such (personal communication from David A. Higgins). The mark and pipe are completely different from the two relatively crude marks described here which almost certainly represent Cox's later production period (*c.*1700–20?), or perhaps that of his son.

One other noteworthy item, previously mentioned, is the 170 mm long stem fragment from fill 1110 of pit 1106. This has three parallel red streaks of pigment running down its entire length. Red pigment streaking, used as a deliberate decorative effect, has been noted on several other pipes from Oxford datable to the late seventeenth and eighteenth centuries.

METALWORK AND WORKED BONE by LEIGH ALLEN

A total of 159 metal objects and four worked bone objects were recovered from the excavation. The metalwork assemblage comprises 111 iron objects, 45 copper alloy objects and 4 lead objects. The assemblage includes a large number of miscellaneous unidentifiable fragments (85) and nails (22).

The majority of the finds were recovered from features dating to the late seventeenth–eighteenth century and only two objects were recovered from contexts dating earlier than the seventeenth century; a boatswain's call, pipe or bosun's whistle (Fig. 12.9) and a very damaged spur. Both objects came from the basal fill (1113) of the western boundary ditch. The whistle is complete but damaged. It is a non-diaphragm type whistle used on naval ships. The pipe consists of a hollow tube (the gun) which directs air over a metal sphere (the buoy) with a hole in the top. The player opens and closes the hand over the hole to change the pitch. Below the gun pipe is the 'keel', a decorative loop that helped to strengthen the pipe and would have held the 'shackle' or ring so that the pipe could be suspended from a chain. Historically the bosun used the pipe to pass commands to the crew when the voice could not be heard over the sounds of the sea or other activities.[57] This example has two rings or collars round the gun and is similar in design to a pipe recovered from Horncastle, Lincolnshire dated to the late-medieval or early post-medieval period.[58] The spur is incomplete and very corroded. Only a short length of one arm (with a 'D'-shaped section) and part of the neck survive.

Twenty-five corroded and mostly fragmentary shroud pins were recovered from burial 1141. They were located at the wrists, knees, shoulders and lower back. Only two pins are complete;

55 Oswald, 'Clay Pipes', p. 262.

56 J. Cotter, 'Clay Pipes' in S. Teague et al., 'Late Saxon, Medieval and Post-Medieval Archaeology at the Nun's Garden, The Queen's College, Oxford,' *Oxoniensia*, 80 (2015), fig. 11.2.

57 A. Strauss, *Boatswain's Call History, Timeline, Examples and More*, http://www.whistlemuseum.com/2014/02/28/american-bosun-pipes-bosun-whistles-and-more-astrauss.aspx.

58 Portable Antiquities Scheme, Unique ID DENO-8ADD43, https://finds.org.uk/database/artefacts/record/id/215974.

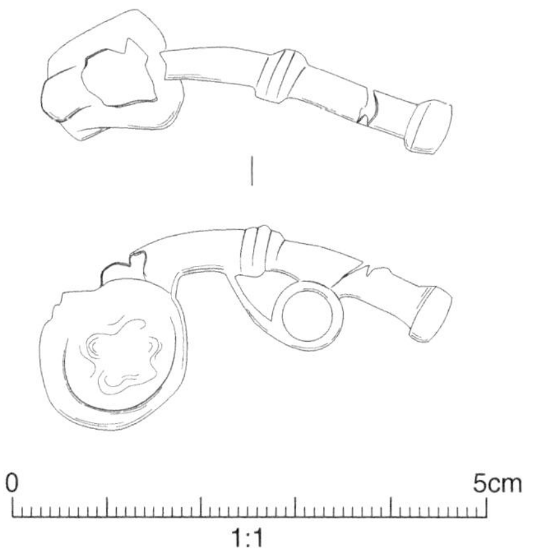

Fig. 12.9 Bosun's whistle.

they each have a wire wound head that has been crimped into a sphere, with a spiral groove visible around the head. The complete examples measure 25 mm and 27 mm. Two fragments have traces of textile surviving on the shank. Burial in a simple shroud was common practice for the vast majority of the population, only the wealthy being buried with clothing since an impoverished family was probably glad to keep a serviceable set of clothing. Shrouds of this period, rather than tightly swaddling the body, would have been loose, voluminous sheets (possibly the family bed sheet) three times the width of the body and twelve inches longer.[59] The shroud would have been tied at the head and foot and pins would have secured the edges of the shroud along its length.

A total of 33 objects were recovered from modern contexts. The only objects of note are a knife with a bone handle, two additional bone handles of the same type and an antler handle. The knife and handles are all examples of nineteenth-century table ware with parallel-sided blades with rounded tips and straight, simple rectangular handles. The red deer antler handle has been sawn flat at the butt end and has an internal chamfer at the socket end but is otherwise unworked; it retains the rough outside surface of the natural tine and is probably from a carving knife or fork.

COINS by IAN R. SCOTT

There are two coins, one jeton and a possible second jeton. The two coins were recovered from the fill of grave 1141 and were associated with the burial. Both of the coins are silver and were minted in the reign of Charles I prior to the Civil War. There is no reason to think that they were buried much later than the reign of Charles I. The Nuremberg jeton is of 'Galley de France' type of sixteenth-century date and was recovered from a modern feature. The possible jeton was recovered from pit 1169.

Coins from Burial 1141
Shilling, silver, Charles I, slightly worn and badly clipped. *Obverse*: L-facing bust with Roman numeral XII behind head. Legend 'CAROLVS . D:G . MAG . BRIT . FR . ET HI. REX' // *Reverse*: Square topped shield with Royal Arms. Legend: 'CHRIS|TO AVSPICE REGNO'. There is a misalignment of the legend and the inner circle between the S and T of Christo. Star mint mark on both sides: Tower Mint 1640–1. D: 30 mm x 29 mm. Context 1140, SF 132

[59] Cherryson et al., *A Fine and Private Place*, p. 23.

Half groat (two pence), silver, Charles I, worn and almost certainly clipped. *Obverse*: worn L-facing bust with Roman numeral II behind head. Legend reads: 'CAROLVS . D. G. [...] REX [...' // *Reverse*: oval garnished shield with Royal Arms. Legend reads 'IVSTITIA . T [. . .' Mint mark Crown on both sides: Tower Mint 1635–6. D: 15 mm. Context 1140, <109>

STONE ARTEFACTS by RUTH SHAFFREY

A single micaceous sandstone whetstone was recovered from late seventeenth to early eighteenth-century pit 1169; it has been used to sharpen large blades. The stone type is not distinctive enough for a provenance to be determined but it is slightly coarser grained than is typical for whetstones and may have been manufactured from an easily accessibly resource such as a river cobble.

HUMAN SKELETON by ALICE ROSE

Almost all elements of skeleton 1139 were present, with the exception of a few distal hand and foot phalanges, giving an overall completeness estimation of almost 100 per cent. Fragmentation was low, meaning less than 25 per cent of the bones present were fragmented. There was only slight, patchy surface erosion on the bones, consistent with McKinley's grade 1.[60]

All features of the skull, mandible and pelvis were observable for sex estimation and all exhibited morphology consistent with a female. All features of the skull, ribs and pelvis were observable for age estimation and indicated a young adult aged 18–23 years. Unfused and fusing epiphyses were observed (for example, medial and lateral clavicles, illiac crest and sternal rib heads), which provided a narrow age estimation. The skeleton appeared to be very gracile. Based on the maximum length of the complete left femur, stature was estimated to be 1.61 m (±3.27 cm), approximately 5 ft 3 ins.

Several cranial and post-cranial non-metric traits were observed in the skeleton. These may be genetically or environmentally induced and are not of pathological significance. There was no evidence of metabolic disease, specific infection or trauma, but congenital conditions, non-specific inflammation and Schmorl's nodes were present. Congenital conditions included evidence for border shifting in the spine, in the form of a cranial shift at the thoracolumbar border (where the transitional facets move to the eleventh thoracic vertebrae) and a cranial shift at the lumbosacral border (assimilation of the fifth lumbar vertebrae into the sacrum).[61] This had resulted in eleven thoracic vertebrae (instead of the usual twelve), comprising five lumbar vertebrae and six sacral vertebrae (instead of the usual five). Border shifting is not rare and is probably due to a delay in vertebral development *in utero*.[62] It is likely that the border shifting in this instance was asymptomatic. Another congenital condition was observed on a first sacral vertebra, which had a cleft neural arch, meaning that the arch had failed to fuse completely, but the cleft is very minor and is likely to simply be a small, asymptomatic developmental defect that is not attributable to spina bifida occulta. Very slight, inactive porosity was observed on the endocranial surface of the frontal bone in the skull, focused around the frontal crest, which appeared to be the result of a period of minor non-specific bone inflammation, of unknown cause, which had subsequently healed.[63] In addition, inflammation (spicules of dense new bone) was observed in the left and right maxillary sinuses, consistent

60 J.I. McKinley, 'Compiling a Skeletal Inventory: Disarticulated and Co-Mingled Remains', in M. Brickley and J.I. McKinley, *Guidelines to the Standards for Recording Human Remains*, IFA Paper 7 (2004), p. 16.

61 E. Barnes, *Developmental Defects of the Axial Skeleton in Palaeopathology* (1994), pp. 104–8.

62 Ibid. p. 79.

63 M. Lewis, 'Endocranial Lesions in Non-Adult Skeletons: Understanding their Aetiology', *International Journal of Osteoarchaeology*, 14 (2004), p. 13.

with maxillary sinusitis.[64] Maxillary sinusitis can result from dental disease, poor ventilation, air pollution or allergies.[65] Two small pieces of ossified material that were recovered from a sample taken around the upper body lacked a distinct morphology but may be ossified soft tissue from the pleura. Very shallow Schmorl's nodes were observed in the thoracic and lumbar spine. These are defects in the vertebral end plates caused by intervertebral disc herniation and are usually an age-related occurrence, but in younger individuals they are more likely to relate to activity or trauma.[66]

Three mandibular molars had been lost ante-mortem and the alveolus was largely remodelled, indicating that the teeth were probably lost more than *c.*12 months before death. Seventeen of the twenty-nine surviving teeth had dental calculus, which was most severe on the right posterior maxillary and mandibular teeth. This was probably due to ante-mortem tooth loss and a severe carious lesion seen in the right mandibular second molar, causing the individual to change the way she chewed her food. Other, smaller, carious lesions were also seen in the left mandibular third molar and the left maxillary first molar. The ante-mortem tooth loss was probably also caused by caries. Two tooth sockets exhibited mild periodontitis.[67]

ANIMAL BONE by LEE G. BRODERICK

The animal bone assemblage came from deposits dating from the medieval period to the eighteenth century. Specimens collected dating from the nineteenth century and later were not analysed. In all, 786 specimens were analysed, mostly recovered through hand-collection although a single environmental sample was taken.

There was a very small medieval component, which included each of the principal domesticates: cattle, caprine (definitely including sheep) and pig, as well as dog. These species were joined by cat and horse in the post-medieval deposits, in which the three principal domesticates continued to dominate. Domestic birds, comprising goose, duck and domestic fowl, were also present in this phase, with domestic fowl particularly common. If the composition of the environmental sample is anything to go by it seems likely that birds are underrepresented in the hand-collected material. The assemblage hints at some wider changes that we might suspect were taking place in society at the time – livestock 'improvement', the industrialisation of butchery and the urbanisation of wild species.

Each of the principal domesticates, as well as horse, were generally larger than is usually found on earlier sites and included specimens showing signs of butchery. There are indications that this was fairly standardised, with 50 per cent of the 42 vertebrae recovered having been chopped through axially, indicating that the carcass was suspended and halved lengthways. Twenty-two specimens have been gnawed by dogs, suggesting that scavenging activities may have played some role in assemblage formation; more generally, a large range in the condition of the specimens suggests that a wide variety of taphonomic pathways led to the assemblage, possibly including some residuality or redeposition. Although a majority of the specimens of all species were fused, unfused specimens of each were also present. This diversity was also observed among the domestic fowl bones, which included both males and laying females.

Common swift was identified in a late seventeenth- to eighteenth-century context. The common swift has only previously been identified from three Holocene archaeological sites in

64 A.C. Aufderheide and C. Rodríguez-Martín, *The Cambridge Encyclopedia of Human Paleopathology* (1998), p. 257.

65 M. Lewis et al., 'Comparative Study of the Prevalence of Maxillary Sinusitis in Later Medieval Urban and Rural Populations in Northern England', *American Journal of Physical Anthropology*, 98 (1995), pp. 497–506.

66 J. Rogers and T. Waldron, *A Field Guide to Joint Disease in Archaeology* (1995), p. 27; R.D. Jurmain, *Stories from the Skeleton: Behavioural Reconstruction in Human Osteology* (1999), p. 165.

67 Grade 2, after A. Ogden, 'Advances in the Palaeopathology of Teeth and Jaws', in R. Pinhasi and S. Mays (eds.), *Advances in Human Palaeopathology* (2008), p. 293.

Britain – Winterbourne Roman villa, medieval Middleton Stoney and Canterbury Cathedral.[68] The specimens identified here thus add considerably to the record of this species in the British Isles. Given that it relies on a free fall for take-off and that it nests today principally in the eaves of buildings it might be supposed that its numbers increased in the modern period alongside the numbers of taller buildings.

FISH REMAINS AND MARINE SHELL by REBECCA NICHOLSON

Four herring (*Clupea harengus*) vertebrae were recovered from a soil sample from the fill of grave 1141. The remains are likely to have been incorporated into the backfill incidentally.

Marine shell, virtually all oyster (*Ostrea edulis* L.) and weighing a total of 2.55 kg, was recovered by hand, the great majority of which is of post-medieval date. The shells were identified to species and side (left or right valves) and although shells were not individually recorded general notes were made by context of shell condition, completeness, shape and any visual evidence of encrustations or infestations, as described by Winder.[69] Typically individual contexts included only a small number of oyster shells (one to four valves). A single mussel (*Mytilus* cf. *edulis* L.) recovered from late seventeenth- to eighteenth-century pit 1106 is the only other shell type. The only assemblage with a significant number of oyster shells came from late seventeenth- to eighteenth-century pit 1180, with 63 left and 37 right oyster valves collected.

The oysters in pit 1180 include shells of a range of sizes, left valves with widths ranging under 50 mm to over 90 mm. The great majority are of the traditional rounded form, although elongated and irregularly-shaped shells are also present and hinge shape includes small and rounded as well as large and angled examples, suggesting that the shellfish came from more than one location. Several valves have distorted shapes consistent with growth on an irregular, hard substrate and a few oyster valves are fused to others, suggesting growth in crowded beds or the use of oyster cultch. In addition to occasional examples of epibont encrustation (barnacles and marine worm tubes), there are five example of shells disfigured by extensive holes consistent with those created by the sponge *Cliona celata* Grant, four of which could be considered to be 'rotten backs'.[70] Several valves exhibit 'V'-shaped notches on the margin opposite to the hinge, where they have been opened with a knife, and knife cuts are present on the interior of several valves from the removal of the meat.

The variety of oyster shells in pit 1180 and the inclusion of the extensively disfigured shells suggests a fairly unselective collection strategy and the purchasing of shellfish which would now not be marketed. This would be consistent with the industrialisation of oyster fishing and consequent consumption of shellfish by the poorer sectors of society.

RADIOCARBON DATING

A sample from a rib of skeleton 1139 was submitted to the Scottish Universities Environmental Research Centre (SUERC) AMS Facility, Glasgow, for radiocarbon dating and produced a result that was consistent with the dates of the coins (Table 12.4).

68 D.W. Yalden and U. Albarella, *The History of British Birds* (2009).

69 J.M. Winder, 'Oyster Shells from Archaeological Sites: A Brief Illustrated Guide to Basic Processing' (2011), https://oystersetcetera.files.wordpress.com/2011/03/oystershellmethodsmanualversion11.pdf.

70 Ibid.

Table 12.4. Summary of radiocarbon date.

Laboratory no.	Context	Feature	Material	δ^{13}C (‰)	Radiocarbon age (BP)	Calibrated date (95.4% confidence)
SUERC-74447	1139	1141	Human rib bone	−19.4	281 ± 30	Cal AD 1497–1505 (1.2%) Cal AD 1512–1601 (55.2%) Cal AD 1616–66 (37.3%) Cal AD 1785–94 (1.7%)

ACKNOWLEDGEMENTS

OA would like to thank University of Oxford Estates Office, who commissioned the investigations and funded the analysis and publication. Thanks are also owed to David Radford, Oxford City Council archaeologist, who monitored the archaeological fieldwork. The excavation was managed by Carl Champness and directed by Matt Fenn, who was assisted by Robin Bashford, Isobel Bentley, Sophie Bojadziev, Christof Heistermann, Conan Parsons, Alice Rose, and Charles Rousseaux. The post-excavation analysis was managed by Andrew Simmonds. Thanks are also due to the staff that processed the finds under the management of Leigh Allen, processed the environmental samples under the management of Rebecca Nicholson, and prepared the archive under the management of Nicola Scott. The authors would particularly like to thank Julian Litten for invaluable discussions regarding the interpretation of the burial.

13. Roman Settlement and the North-Eastern Civil War Defences of Oxford: Investigations at Mansfield College and the Tinbergen Building

ANDREW SIMMONDS, ROBIN BASHFORD, TOBY MARTIN, CHRIS PICKARD, RICHARD BROWN and KEN WELSH

SUMMARY

An excavation at the Hands Building, Mansfield College, uncovered further evidence for the known Roman settlement in this area and sectioned the inner line of the city's Civil War defensive ditch, while work at the Tinbergen Building, South Parks Road, recorded part of the outer line of the Civil War defences. New evidence was found for the sequence of construction, slighting and refortification of the inner defence, probably undertaken during August to November 1642, and for the elaboration of the outer defence by the provision of pitfalls.

In 2016 excavations were carried out at the Hands Building, Mansfield College (SP 5162 0673), and at the Tinbergen Building, Oxford University Department of Zoology, South Parks Road (SP 5182 0692; Fig. 13.1). The excavation at Mansfield College was undertaken in order to mitigate the construction of a new residential block, the Hands Building, in an area of the campus that was formerly garden, while the investigation at the Tinbergen Building was conducted in advance of replacement of single-storey buildings and hardstanding to the south of the main structure with a two-storey building.

Mansfield College and the University Science Area lie outside the historic core of the city but have nevertheless revealed important evidence for prehistoric and Roman activity predating the expansion of the city into this area and for the city's Civil War defences. An extensive complex of prehistoric funerary and ritual monuments has been identified in this part of the city and to the north and evidence for an extensive Romano-British settlement has been uncovered at the Institute for American Studies, the Chemistry Research Laboratory and Halifax House.[1] The precise character of the settlement is uncertain, but remains included at least one structure, a

1 G. Lambrick, 'Prehistoric Oxford', *Oxoniensia*, 78 (2013), pp. 14–18; P. Booth and C. Hayden, 'A Roman Settlement at Mansfield College, Oxford', *Oxoniensia*, 65 (2000), pp. 291–331; P. Bradley et al., 'Prehistoric and Roman Activity and a Civil War Ditch at the Chemistry Research Laboratory, 2–4 South Parks Road, Oxford, 2002', *Oxoniensia*, 70 (2005), pp. 141–202; S. Anthony, 'Prehistoric and Early Roman Field Systems at Halifax House, South Parks Road, Oxford', *Oxoniensia*, 70 (2005), pp. 129–39.

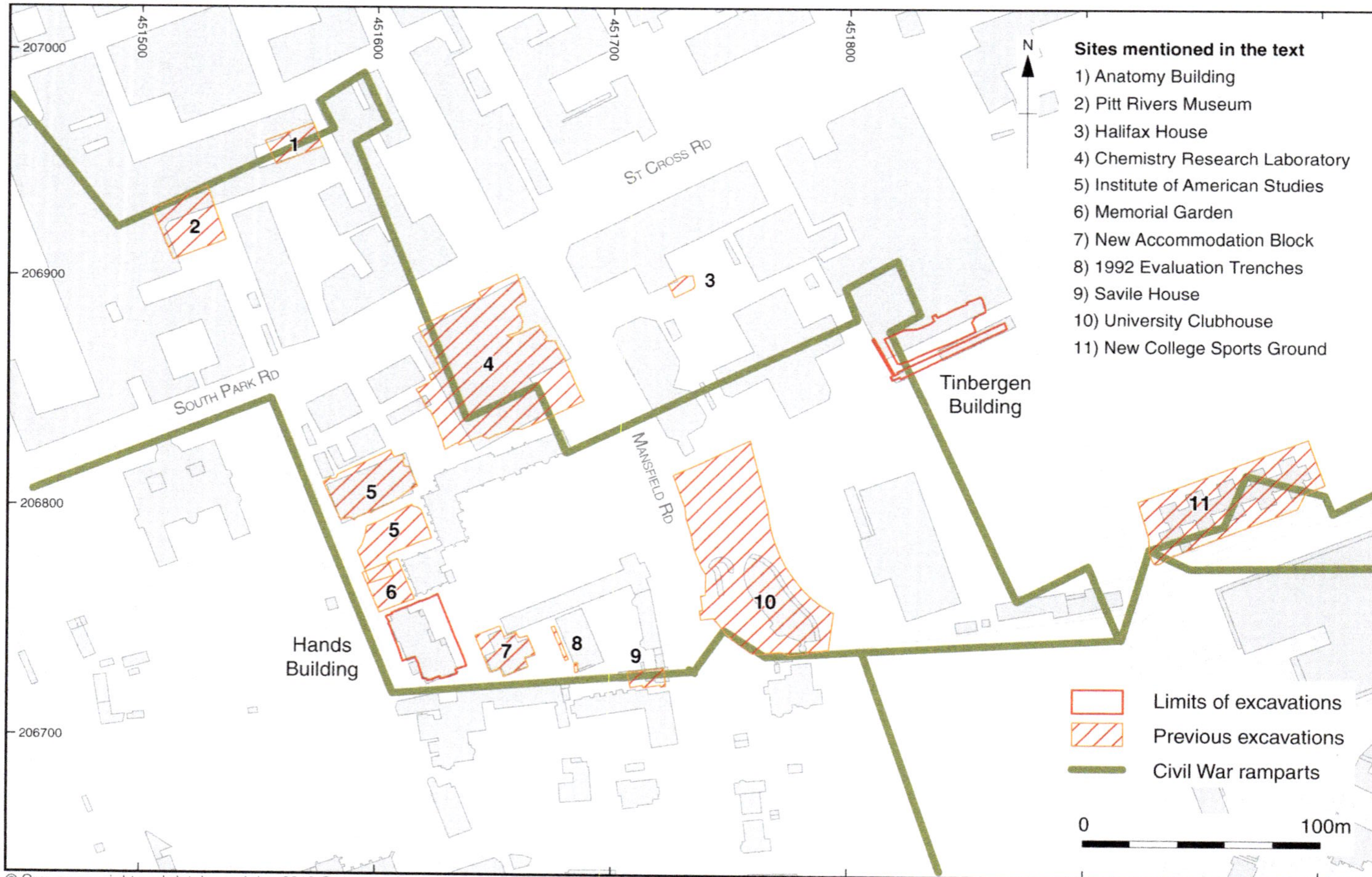

Fig. 13.1 Site locations.

sequence of ditched enclosures and a decapitated burial. Many centuries later, during the Civil War, the Royalist garrison constructed two lines of fortification around the northern side of the city: an earlier, inner, line begun in 1642, and an outer line built between 1644 and 1645. The location of the site at Mansfield College corresponded with a re-entrant angle in the inner line, and the footprint of the Tinbergen Building extended across the projected alignment the outer line.

The descriptions that follow are summaries of more detailed reports, including full finds reports, that can be found via the OA Library.[2] The archives will be deposited with Oxfordshire County Museum Service under the accession codes 2016.24 (Hands Building) and 2015.191 (Tinbergen Building).

DISCUSSION

Prehistoric Activity

Prehistoric activity was represented only by a small group of flintwork from the Hands Building. The small size of the assemblage of flint tools is likely to indicate that the site was peripheral to the activities represented by the early Neolithic pit excavated at the Institute for American Studies and the single late Neolithic pit at the Chemistry Laboratory. Indeed, it is notable that there is a clear drop-off in the number of flints recovered from north-east to south-west, with 303 from the Chemistry Laboratory, eighteen from the Institute for American Studies and only three from the Hands Building.[3] The recovery of only eight pieces of flint dated to the Neolithic/Bronze Age at Halifax House, a short distance east of the Chemistry Laboratory, may indicate that the activity was quite localised.[4]

Roman Settlement

The excavation at the Hands Building revealed a further area of the settlement that had been uncovered by previous investigations within the Science Area, particularly those at the Institute for American Studies, the Chemistry Laboratory and Halifax House. Occupation began during the second half of the first century AD, when an east–west-aligned boundary was established that was defined in successive phases by ditches 1092 and 1094, extending across the north-eastern corner of the excavation area. The absence of further early Roman features from the rest of the site may indicate either that the boundary represented the southern limit of occupation during this period or that this area was situated away from the focus of settlement.

No features or artefacts were found that certainly dated from the middle Roman period, and this is consistent with similar evidence for a hiatus in activity at the Institute for American Studies, which presumably indicates a relocation or shrinking of the settlement during the second and third centuries.[5] This was followed by a subsequent expansion of activity at both sites during the late third and fourth centuries, represented at the Hands Building by the digging of pit 1139 and the establishment of part of a rectilinear arrangement of boundaries indicated by ditches 1003 and 1138. Pit 1139 was unlike the features uncovered by the other nearby excavations, where pits were very shallow. Its substantially greater depth clearly indicates a special function and it is possible that it was dug as a well, although it lacked any evidence for a stone or timber lining or for the basal accumulation of water-lain sediment that usually characterises such

[2] 'Love Lane Building Mansfield College Oxford. Archaeological Excavation Report', unpublished OA report (2017), https://library.oxfordarchaeology.com/4634/; 'Tinbergen Building, South Parks Road, Oxford. Archaeological Strip, Map and sample Report', unpublished OA report (2016), https://library.oxfordarchaeology.com/4635/.

[3] H. Lamdin-Whymark, 'Flint', in Bradley et al., 'Chemistry Research Laboratory', p. 151; H. Lamdin-Whymark, 'Flint', in Booth and Hayden, 'Mansfield College', p. 318.

[4] Anthony, 'Halifax House', p. 132.

[5] Bradley et al., 'Chemistry Research Laboratory', p. 196.

features. It was subsequently used as a receptacle for the disposal of domestic refuse, hence the large quantities of pottery and animal bone that were recovered. The new arrangement of boundary ditches established during the fourth century, represented by ditches 1003 and 1138, evidently involved a change in orientation from the earlier arrangement represented by ditches 1092 and 1094. A similar change from an original arrangement of boundaries broadly aligned east–west and north–south to one based on a main boundary aligned north-east to south-west was observed at the Chemistry Laboratory, but at the Institute for American Studies the evidence for such a change in alignment was less certain.[6] Curving gully 1143 has a less regular form and lies on an oblique orientation to the other boundaries; comparable 'haphazard' alignments were recorded among the more regular boundaries at the Institute for American Studies and the Chemistry Laboratory.[7]

The precise extent and character of the settlement are still uncertain, although the Hands Building evidently lay on the periphery. Similarly, the features at the Institute for American Studies and Chemistry Laboratory appeared to peter out to the north, suggesting that these areas comprised paddocks and fields on the periphery of the settlement.[8] The greatest density of features was situated at the southern end of the excavation area at the Chemistry Laboratory and may indicate that the main focus of occupation lay in this vicinity, south-east of the excavated areas and extending beneath the main college buildings. Thus far, the only direct evidence for buildings is provided by the decidedly unprepossessing structure at the Institute for American Studies and a possible beamslot at the south-eastern limit of the Chemistry Laboratory; a piece from a box flue tile found at the former site may be an indication that a more substantial building lay somewhere nearby, but the tile could alternatively have been used in a structure such as a kiln or oven. The settlement certainly does not extend far east of the college, since a number of archaeological investigations undertaken east of Mansfield Road have recorded little or no Roman archaeology.[9] The artefactual evidence from the Hands Building is consistent with that from the previous excavations in indicating a low-status rural settlement; the pottery included a relative abundance of fine and specialist wares, including mortaria, amphorae, white-slipped wares and white wares, that might indicate that it attained a higher status during the later Roman period, although it is uncertain whether this is an accurate indication of the settlement's status or should instead be attributed to its proximity to production sites.[10]

The settlement is likely to have formed one element of a more extensive enclosed landscape, part of which has been recorded as cropmarks of boundaries and enclosures in the University Parks *c.*500 m to the north. Evidence for settlement foci in the intervening area has been provided by pottery, coins and at least one fibula found during construction of the University Museum, a substantial ditch excavated at the Radcliffe Science Library Extension and a quern found at No. 2 South Parks Road, since so bulky an object is unlikely to have been transported far from its place of use.[11] Further excavation of the Science Area would be required to establish whether these locations represent neighbouring farmsteads or part of a single more extensive settlement.

Civil War Defences

Between the Roman period and the construction of the city's Civil War defences, the sites lay beyond the city limits, in what was presumably agricultural land. The earliest map of the city, Ralph Agas' *Oxonia Antiqua Instaurata* (1578), shows the area lying in open ground beyond the

6 Ibid. p. 195.
7 Ibid.
8 Ibid.
9 Booth and Hayden, 'Mansfield College', p. 330.
10 E. Biddulph, 'Roman Pottery', in Bradley et al., 'Chemistry Research Laboratory', p. 164.
11 T.G. Hassall, 'Roman Finds from the Radcliffe Science Library Extension, Oxford, 1970–71', *Oxoniensia*, 37 (1972), pp. 38–50.

limits of the city. No features dating from this period were uncovered during the excavations and it is likely that the small assemblages of medieval pottery and probably pre-Civil War glazed bricks that were recovered from the Civil War ditches at the Hands Building derive from manuring during the medieval and early post-medieval period.

An initial line of Civil War defences around the northern side of the city was constructed by the Royalist forces in Summer 1642 but was slighted after only a few weeks when Oxford briefly fell into Parliamentarian hands. The Royalist garrison was restored in October 1642, and again built a line of defences around the northern side of the city, though whether this entirely followed the line of the earlier fortifications is unclear. A further, outer circuit was then constructed in 1644–5.[12]

The excavations extended across parts of both lines of defences, the ditch of the earlier, inner line being uncovered at the Hands Building and the ditch of the outer line at the Tinbergen Building. A contemporary depiction of the arrangement of the two lines of defences survives in a plan drawn in 1645 by the royalist engineer Sir Bernhard de Gomme, while David Loggan's 1675 map of Oxford (Fig. 13.2) records the condition of the earthworks thirty years after the war. The two sources are generally consistent as regards the general arrangement of the defences, but neither was surveyed to modern standards and consequently there remains considerable uncertainty regarding the precise alignment where this has not been confirmed by surviving earthworks or excavation of buried remains. Each line would have comprised a substantial earthen bank, fronted by a ditch, which followed a zig-zagging alignment to facilitate enfilading lines of fire. The top of the earthwork would have been further enhanced by the provision of a parapet, probably reinforced by gabions (earth-filled baskets). Projecting bastions would have provided platforms for cannon.

The earlier line is better understood than its successor, since part of its alignment survives as a north–south-aligned bank that extends along the west side of Love Lane, turning eastward at the southern end to define the south boundary of the college grounds and continuing to St Cross Road. The excavation area at the Hands Building was situated within this re-entrant angle and exposed the ditch that fronted the bank, but did not extend into the upstanding earthwork, which lies to the south and forms the boundary with the grounds of New College School. This area is now perhaps the best understood segment of the defensive line, at least as regards the ditch, as it has been recorded at several sites in advance of development, allowing the alignment to be reconstructed in some detail (Fig. 13.3). The ditch had previously been recorded to the east of the site at New College School in 1959,[13] and within the grounds of Mansfield College in an evaluation during 1992 and a watching brief in 2005, both in advance of construction of accommodation blocks, and at the University Clubhouse.[14] The accompanying bank was partly sectioned during the 2005 watching brief and at the University Clubhouse, and most recently at Savile House.[15] North of the re-entrant, the eastern edge of the ditch was exposed at the Rothermere Institute Memorial Garden and at the Institute for American Studies and further north the bank was sectioned at Rhodes House.[16]

The ditch at the Hands Building was found to be a steep-sided feature with a flat base and measured more than 7 m wide and up to 1.8 m deep, dimensions that correspond almost exactly with those recorded in the earlier investigations. The fills provided no certain

[12] A. Kemp, 'The Fortification of Oxford during the Civil War', *Oxoniensia*, 42 (1977), pp. 237–46.

[13] J. Munby and E. Simons, 'Oxford's Civil War Defences: The Northeast Sector', in Bradley et al., 'Chemistry Research Laboratory', p. 199.

[14] C. Bell, 'Oxford, Mansfield College, Civil War Defences', *SMidlA*, 23 (1993), p. 75; 'New Accommodation Block, Mansfield College, Oxford: Archaeological Watching Brief Report', unpublished OA report (2006), https://library.oxfordarchaeology.com/3567/; 'New University Clubhouse, Mansfield Road, Oxford: Archaeological Watching Brief Report', unpublished OA report (2003), https://library.oxfordarchaeology.com/4637/.

[15] S. Teague and B.M. Ford, 'The Civil War Earthwork and Earlier Remains at Savile House, New College, Mansfield Road, Oxford', *Oxoniensia*, forthcoming.

[16] Booth and Hayden, 'Mansfield College'; Munby and Simons, 'Oxford's Civil War Defences', p. 199.

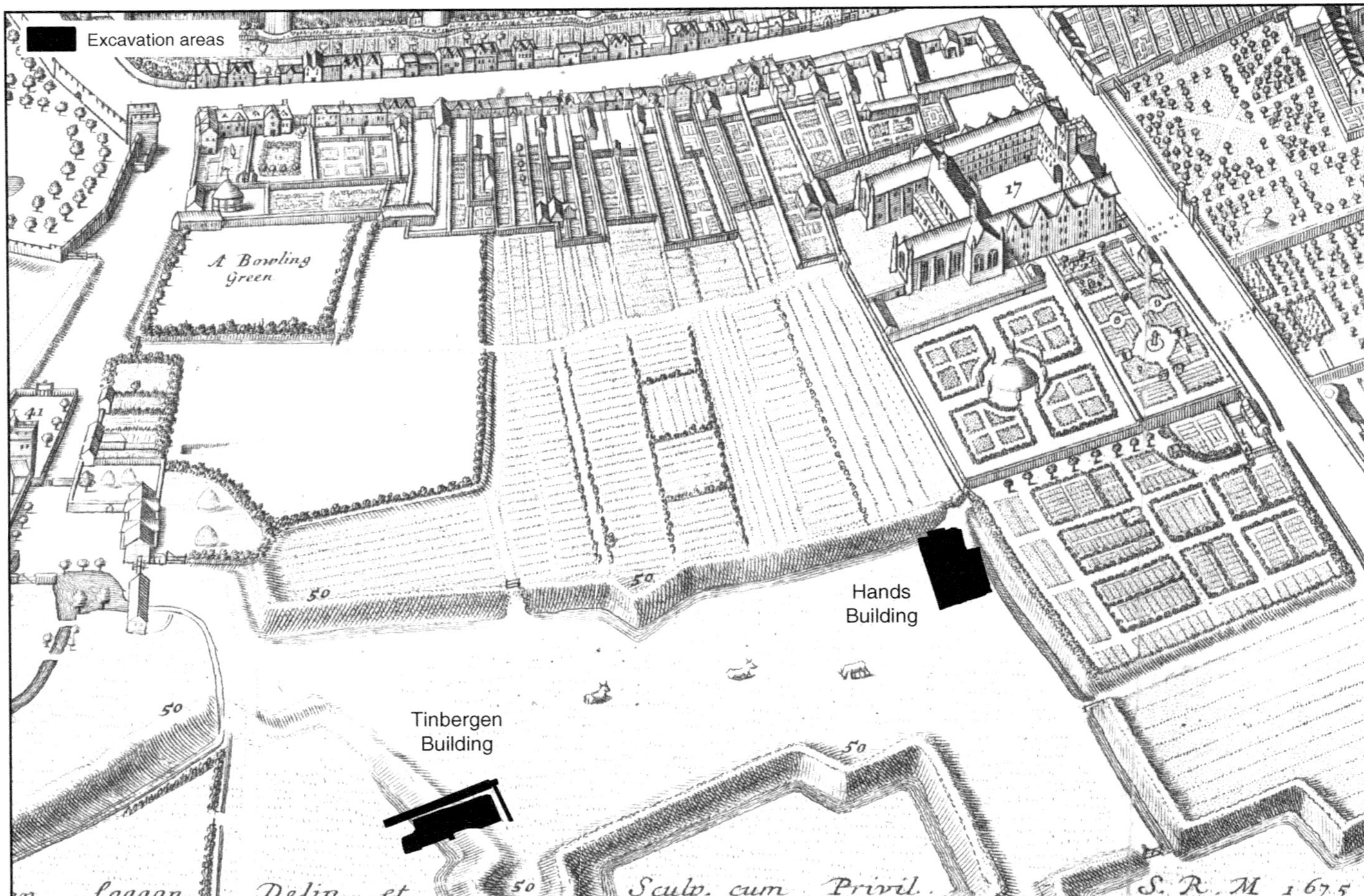

Fig. 13.2 Detail of the Civil War earthworks from Loggan's map of 1675, showing the approximate locations of the sites (north to bottom).

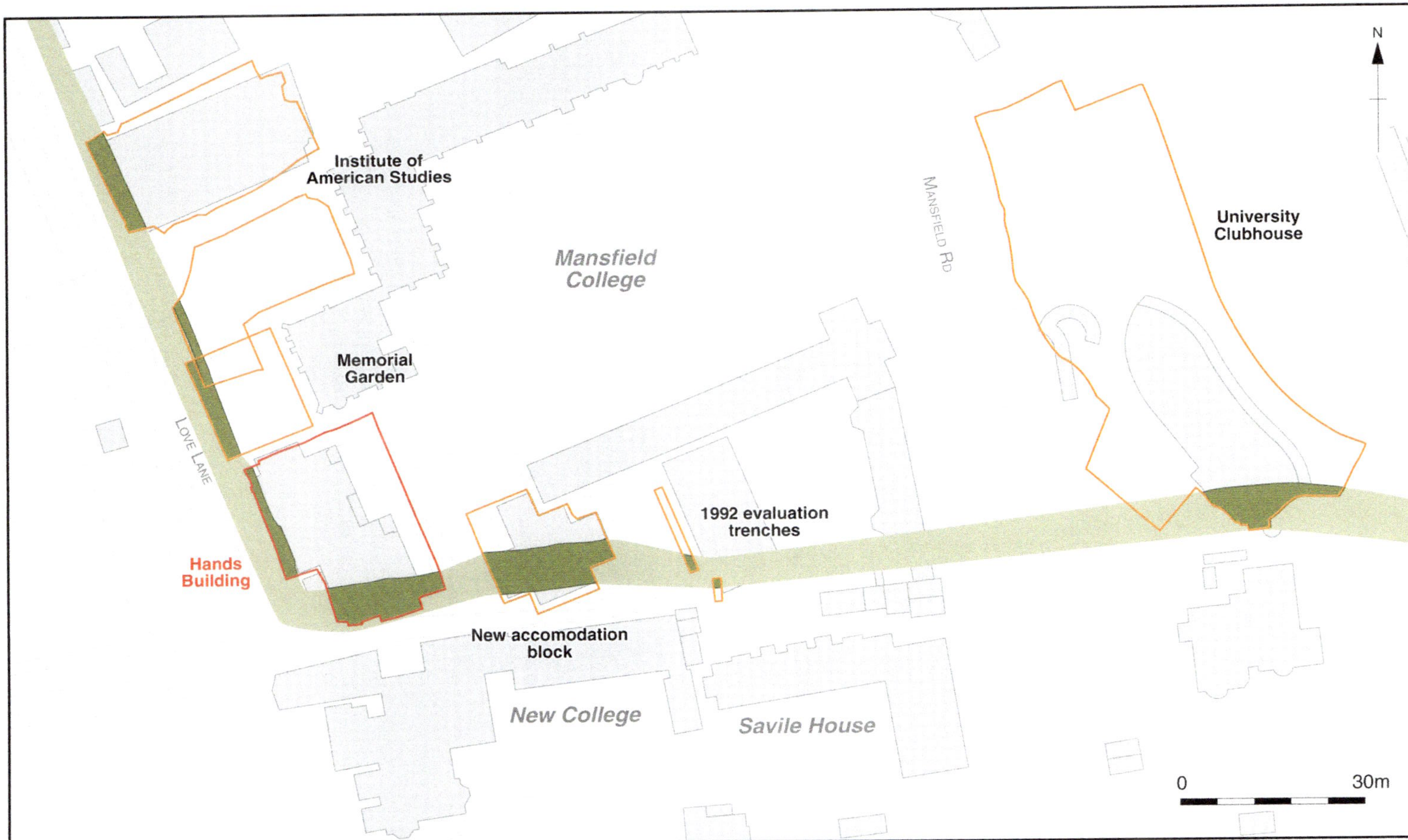

Fig. 13.3 The alignment of the ditch of the inner Civil War defences through the grounds of Mansfield College, as confirmed by excavations.

evidence that the ditch held water during its time as a fortification and it may therefore have been a simple dry ditch, although Loggan's depiction may be intended to indicate that it held water thirty years later (Fig. 13.2). The recutting observed in ditch 1141 represents a phenomenon that has previously only been seen at the University Clubhouse,[17] *c.*100 m east of the Hands Building, and may be significant in relation to the documented history of the defences, which indicates that the outer line was not instigated until after the second siege of the city, in 1645, and that the reinstated inner line was therefore the main defence during the first two sieges.[18] The sequence of digging, backfilling and recutting exhibited by ditch 1141 may therefore preserve the history of this part of the defences, representing respectively their construction in August 1642, slighting by Parliamentarian forces a few months later, and subsequent repair and refortification by the Royalist garrison. The absence of evidence for such a recut recorded by other investigations of this part of the ditch can probably be attributed to the limited nature of these investigations, most of which exposed only a small part of the ditch.

The earthwork may have been left to decay after the war. The artefactual material from the fills of the recut ditch suggest that it infilled over the course of the second half of the seventeenth century and the early part of the eighteenth century, the glass providing particularly important dating evidence, including a sherd possibly from a late seventeenth-century 'globe and shaft' wine bottle and three sherds from late seventeenth- or early eighteenth-century squat bottle forms. The molluscs from the ditch fills suggest the feature infilled in a grazed grassland environment, which is consistent with Loggan's depiction of the rampart reduced to a bare bank and water-filled ditch serving as a boundary between cultivated ground within the defences and pasture beyond.

None of the earthworks of the outer line of the defences survive and its arrangement is therefore known only from the depictions by de Gomme and Loggan, with the precise alignment verified in a few locations by the results of excavations. The north-eastern sector, between Banbury Road and the River Cherwell, had a more regular plan than the earlier line, comprising a geometric arrangement of four projecting bastions that alternated with intervening re-entrants. Only the westernmost bastion has been definitely located, its location being recorded on the 1st edition Ordnance Survey map and the ditch recorded when the University Physics Building was constructed at this location in 1909, as well as during subsequent building works in 1937–8 and 2015–16.[19] The second bastion should lie a short distance east of sections of the ditch that were recorded at the Human Anatomy Building in 1958 and near the Pitt Rivers Museum in 2005, and the re-entrant between the second and third bastions was excavated at the new Chemistry Laboratory in 2001,[20] but the excavation at the Tinbergen Building represents the first archaeological investigation of the part of the line between this and the fourth bastion, which was partly exposed during a watching brief at New College Sports Ground in 1998.[21] The ditch at Tinbergen extended from north-west to south-east and must be part of the defence immediately south of the third bastion. The ditch evidently extends through Merton College playing field parallel to and *c.*45 m west of St Cross Road (Fig. 13.1), placing it *c.*15 m further

17 Brossler, 'New University Clubhouse'.

18 F.J. Vardy, 'Further Notes on de Gomme's Plan of Oxford, 1644', *Oxoniensia*, 3 (1938), pp. 175–7.

19 R.T. Lattey et al., 'A Contemporary Map of the Defences of Oxford in 1644', *Oxoniensia*, 1 (1936), p. 171; R.T. Lattey, 'Note on the Royalist Defences of Oxford', *Oxoniensia*, 3 (1938), p. 177; J. Hart, 'Roman and Civil War Remains at the Oxford University Physics Building: Summary Report on Archaeological Investigations, 2015–2016', *Oxoniensia*, 84 (2019), pp. 205–15.

20 H. Case and D. Sturdy, 'Archaeological Notes', *Oxoniensia*, 24 (1959), p. 101; 'Land adjacent to the Pitt Rivers Museum', unpublished OA report (2005), https://library.oxfordarchaeology.com/482/; Bradley et al., 'Chemistry Research Laboratory'.

21 'New College Sports Ground, St Cross Road, Oxford: Archaeological Watching Brief Report', unpublished OA report (1999), https://library.oxfordarchaeology.com/876/.

west than indicated by previous projections.[22] The ditch was 4 m wide and 1 m deep, much less substantial than the dimensions of 9.5 m wide and 2.9 m deep recorded at the Physics Building and 11 m wide and 2.4 m deep at the Chemistry Research Laboratory.[23] This reduced size is most likely attributable to truncation of the upper part during the construction of the recently demolished buildings.

Five pits arranged into two off-set rows beyond the ditch are likely to represent 'pitfalls': mantraps dug as additional defences in front of the main defence in order to impede any attempt to storm the earthwork. There is a contemporary reference to pits forming part of the northern defensive line following a survey of the defences by Fairfax's council of war, which recorded that 'upon the outside of the Ditch round the Line it was strongly palisaded, and without that again, were digged several pits in the ground, so that a single footman could not without difficulty approach the brink of the ditch'.[24] At Newark-on-Trent, the pitfalls were described as 'two rows of holes ye height of a man in depth, and so near it might hinder their sudden assaulting the works'.[25] Both of these descriptions appear to correspond with the configuration of the features revealed by the excavation. If the interpretation of the relatively insubstantial dimensions of the ditch as indicating significant truncation is correct, then it would suggest that these pits would also have originally been considerably deeper than the surviving portion, perhaps amounting to as much as 2 m deep, a similar depth to pitfalls that were described at Newark.[26] The stakeholes in the base of the ditch may be evidence for further impediments to attack, such as iron or wooden stakes, which were a common feature of defences at this time.[27]

THE EXCAVATIONS

Hands Building, Mansfield College

A roughly rectangular area encompassing some 750 sq m was excavated (Fig. 13.4).

Roman Settlement Evidence for the Roman settlement that had been previously investigated to the north comprised a ditched boundary dating from the first century AD and subsequent late third- to fourth-century features.

The first-century ditch was partly exposed at the north-east corner of the site and had two phases (1092, 1094). The earlier ditch (1092) contained no finds but ditch 1094, which truncated it, yielded a modest amount of pottery indicating a date in the second half of the first century.

Following an apparent hiatus in activity, a large pit (1139) was dug south of the earlier ditches. The feature measured 4.3 x 4.0 m and 1.55 m deep and had steep, though somewhat irregular sides and a flat base (Fig. 13.5). There was no evidence that the pit had a lining or water-lain lower fills but the depth of the feature may indicate a function as a well or waterhole. The pit contained numerous fills, but there is little to suggest whether these were rapid or gradual. Large sherds of pottery dating from the fourth century were recovered, as well as a small number of potentially earlier sherds and some animal bone and shell.

Two ditched boundaries lying at right angles were subsequently established, ditch 1138 aligned north-east to south-west, cutting through the middle of pit 1139, and ditch 1003 extending into the site for a distance of 4.3 m from the south-west. Ditch 1138 was 0.65m deep but ditch 1003 measured only 0.18 m. Both ditches contained fourth-century pottery, including a necked bowl from ditch 1138 that dated from after AD 340. A further feature of probable late Roman date

22 Bradley et al., 'Chemistry Research Laboratory', fig. 14.
23 Hart, 'Roman and Civil War Remains', p. 209; Bradley et al., 'Chemistry Research Laboratory', p. 149.
24 F.J. Varley, *A Supplement to the Siege of Oxford* (1935), p. 115.
25 P. Harrington, *English Civil War Fortifications, 1642–51* (2003).
26 Ibid. p. 33.
27 Ibid.

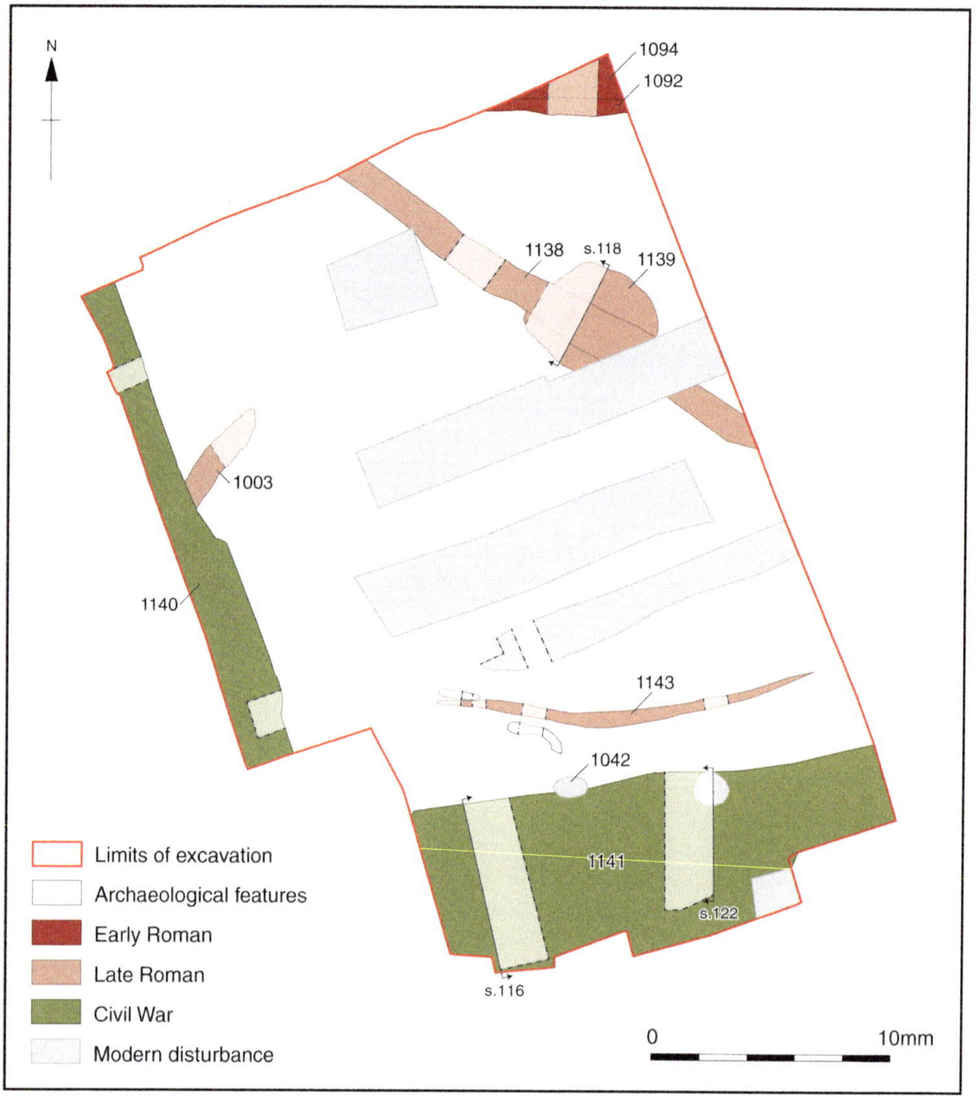

Fig. 13.4 Hands Building, site plan.

was represented by gully 1143, a slightly irregular, curving feature, 0.1 m deep, that lay in the southern part of the excavation area and contained a large sherd from a mortarium dated after *c.*AD 240, as well as a few other Roman sherds.

Civil War Defences The location of the site corresponded with a re-entrant angle in Oxford's Civil War defences, which appeared in the excavation as two substantial ditches that extended along the west and south edges of the trench (1140, 1141). Only the eastern edge of ditch 1140 was exposed within the excavation area. It contained small quantities of clay tobacco pipe and pottery with dates ranging between the sixteenth and eighteenth centuries, with the latest ceramics coming from the uppermost fill.

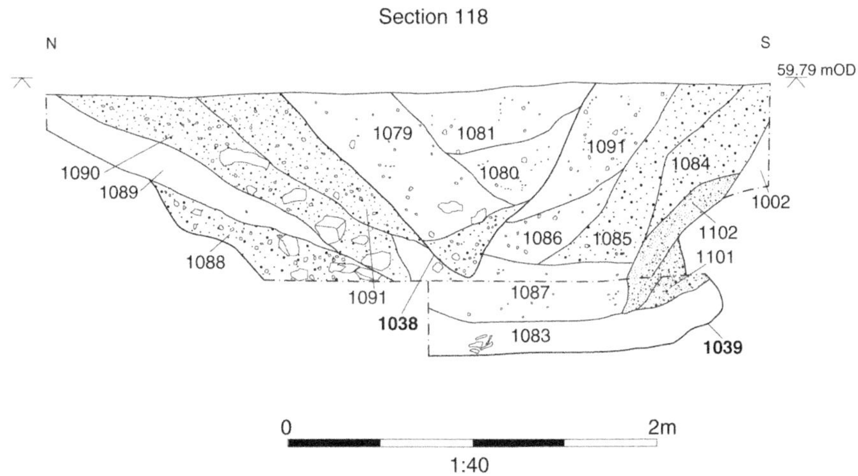

Fig. 13.5 Section through late Roman pit 1139 and ditch 1138 at the Hands Building.

Two interventions were dug through ditch 1141, the western one being dug by hand and the eastern one by machine. A much greater proportion of this ditch lay within the excavation area, allowing a more complete profile to be recorded, although the southern slope lay beyond the trench (Fig. 13.6). The ditch was more than 7 m wide and up to 1.8 m deep, with steep sides and a distinctly flat base. Following a series of side collapses and silty sedimentations (1057, 1058 in section 116; 1111, 1112 in section 122, Fig. 13.6), the ditch was backfilled with a series of deposits of soil and gravel, presumably representing the material that had been excavated when the earthwork was created. The composition of this material was quite variable; the sequence in the western intervention was notable for a large body of gravel (1162), whereas the fills in the eastern intervention, only 6 m away, were relatively stone-free. As with ditch 1140, the dating evidence was limited, comprising a modest quantity of mid sixteenth-century pottery and clay pipe from both interventions, as well as a very small amount of residual medieval and Roman pottery. The ditch was subsequently recut (1109 in section 122; 1137 in section 116, Fig. 13.6). The full dimensions of the recut ditch could be not established, since it extended beyond the southern edge of the site and in both sections the base was obscured by the stepped profile of the excavation. Nevertheless, the excavation demonstrated that it was at least 3.3 m wide and 1.25 m deep and that the north face lay *c*.2 m south of the corresponding slope of the original ditch. The recut yielded a small quantity of late seventeenth-century pottery and clay pipes as well as some residual sixteenth-century sherds.

Modern Features Two pits cut Civil War ditch 1141, one of which (1042) contained the articulated skeleton of cow. A shallow linear depression (1142) only 0.09 m deep, with much evidence for root activity, was probably the base of a flower bed or hedge line.

Finds Summary Prehistoric activity was represented only by three flint tools that were recovered from Roman and later features, comprising a borer, an awl or piercer and a notched flake or blade.

Some 558 sherds (16 kg) of Roman pottery were recovered from the site, the majority dating from the later part of the period. Oxfordshire white ware mortaria formed an unusually large proportion of the assemblage compared with contemporaneous assemblages elsewhere in the region, as was also the case at the adjacent site at the Institute for American Studies and at the

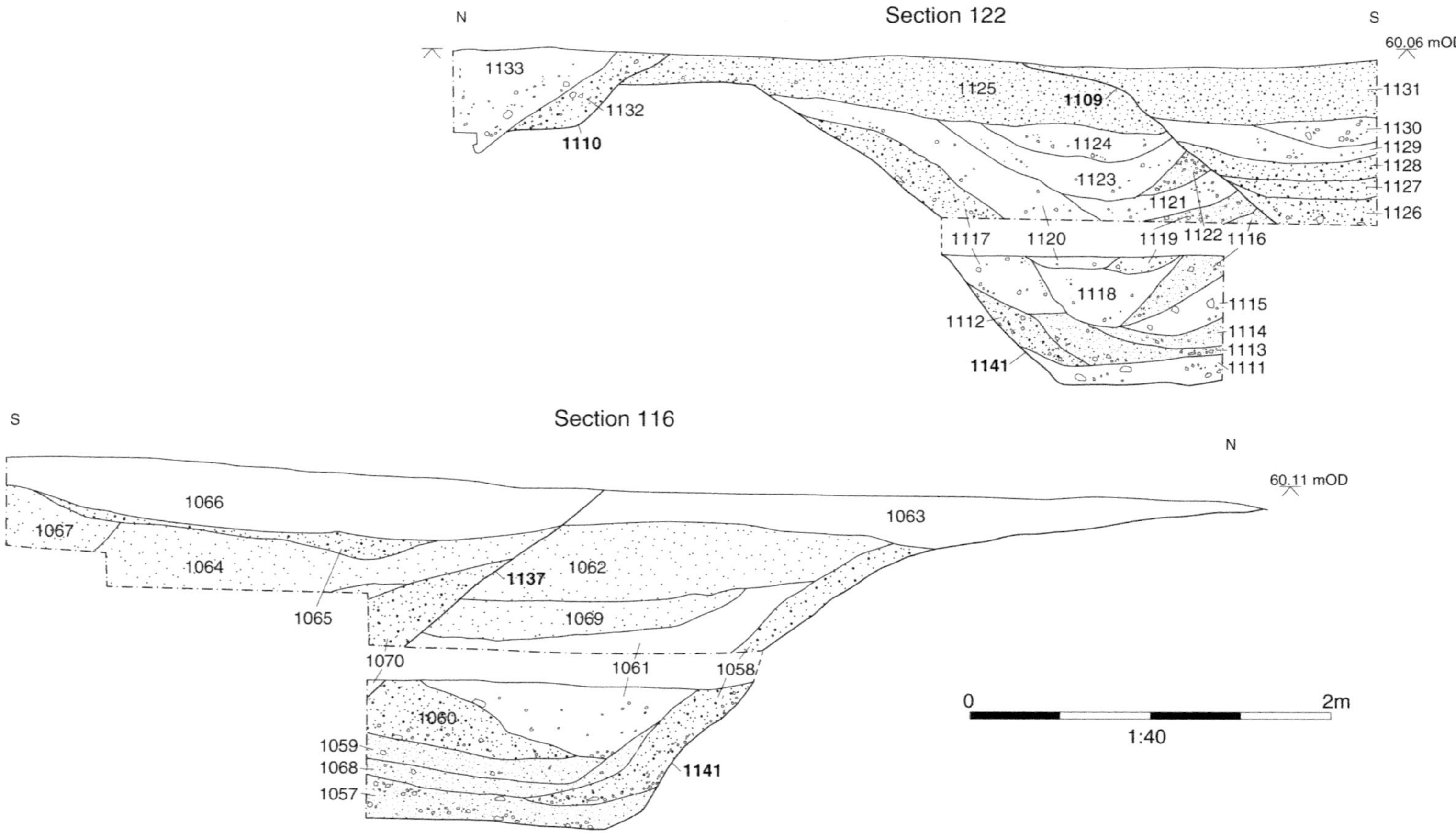

Fig. 13.6 Sections through Civil War defensive ditch 1141 at the Hands Building.

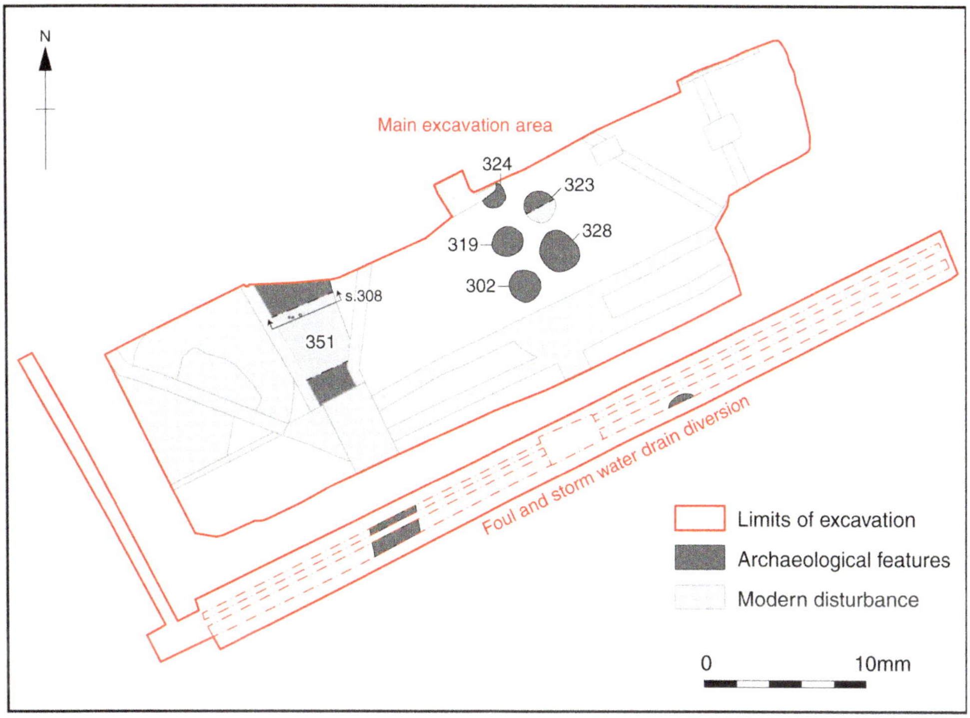

Fig. 13.7 Tinbergen Building, site plan.

Chemistry Research Laboratory.[28] This phenomenon may be explained by the presence of a nearby pottery production site, and although none of the mortaria at the current site displayed evidence of production damage, such as spalling or distortion, such damage was recorded on three other vessels – a necked bowl, a necked jar or bowl and a base sherd.

The post-Roman finds assemblage was small. The pottery (109 sherds, 1.6 kg) was mostly post-medieval and all the medieval pottery was residual in later deposits, suggesting that there was very little medieval activity at the site. Most of the finds dated from after the Civil War and derived from the infilling of the ditches after they had gone out of use. The clay pipe (22 pieces, 127 g) included a complete bowl of London Type A09, dating to *c.*1640–60, from ditch 1141 but otherwise the assemblage had a strong emphasis on the later seventeenth century and the first half of the eighteenth. The small assemblage of vessel and window glass provided useful dating evidence, including a sherd possibly from a late seventeenth-century 'globe and shaft' wine bottle and three sherds from late seventeenth or early eighteenth-century squat bottle forms from the Civil War ditch, and some pieces of ceramic building material were also recovered, including some probably pre-Civil War glazed bricks.

The Tinbergen Building, South Parks Road

The investigation at the Tinbergen Building comprised an excavation of a rectangular area encompassing 500 sq m following the demolition phase of the works, as well as the footprint of foul and storm water drain diversions (Fig. 13.7).

[28] P. Booth, 'Roman Pottery', in Booth and Hayden, 'Mansfield College', p. 313; E. Biddulph 'Roman Pottery', in Bradley et al., 'Chemistry Research Laboratory', table 5.

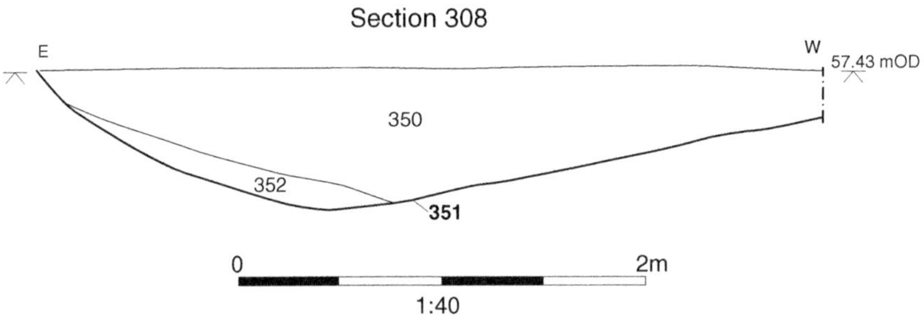

Fig. 13.8 Section through the Civil War defensive ditch at the Tinbergen Building.

The excavation revealed a roughly north–south-aligned ditch (351) that almost certainly represented the Civil War defensive earthwork (Fig. 13.8). The ditch was more than 4 m wide and was exposed for a total distance of 8 m, and was also seen in the service diversion trench to the south of the main excavation area. The full profile of the ditch was not exposed, having being truncated by modern services mainly to the west, but where it survived it was up to 1 m deep with a gently curving eastern edge and a rounded base. The primary fills appear to have accumulated through natural silting, presumably when the ditch was open. It was unclear whether the main fill represented further such accumulation or had been deliberately backfilled. At the base of the ditch was a group of three fairly ephemeral stakeholes.

A group of five substantial pits was located *c.*9 m east of the ditch, arranged in two parallel rows *c.*1 m apart and aligned roughly north–south. The western row comprised pits 302, 319 and 324 while pits 323 and 328 formed the eastern row. The pits were fairly uniform in size, each measuring *c.*2 m in diameter and 1 m deep, and had been deliberately backfilled with multiple layers of slightly gravelly sand. The uppermost fill of pit 319 contained a 'Rose' farthing of Charles I, minted 1636–44, and a stem fragment from a clay pipe dated to the seventeenth century was recovered from the bottom fill of pit 328. Pit 324 contained the partial remains of an articulated horse. The feature had been partially truncated by the foundations of the Tinbergen Building but the lower torso survived, as well as the rear legs and a disarticulated front hoof, each with a horse shoe. There was no indication that the pit was dug specifically to bury the animal and it is likely that the burial represents opportunistic use of a convenient receptacle after the defences had gone out of use.

Finds Summary The finds assemblage was very small, comprising 15 sherds (75 g) of pottery, 7 pieces (34 g) of clay pipe, 9 pieces (569 g) of ceramic building material and 9 metal finds comprising the farthing and horseshoes from the pits and as well as nails and miscellaneous fragments. The condition of all the material was poor. A total of 86 animal bones were recovered, 41 of which comprised the horse burial in pit 324. The latter was represented by the lower torso and back legs, with horseshoes attached. All the bones were fused, indicating that the horse was over four years old when it died, but there was no evidence to indicate its sex. No pathologies were visible on the bones and the cause of death is unknown. Several of the bones were complete, indicating an animal of between 1.47 and 1.54 m at the withers, equating to 14.5–15.2 hands. This size of horse is fairly typical for a modern riding horse or coach horse such as the Hackney horse. The horseshoe attached to the front hoof was substantially larger than the other two and was secured to the distal phalanx by a single nail in a position off-centre to the hoof, suggesting considerable lack of skill on the part of the farrier. Other bones included disarticulated fragments from sheep, caprines, pig, and fish.

ACKNOWLEDGEMENTS

OA would like to thank Mansfield College Developments, which commissioned the excavation at the Hands Building, and Oxford University Estates, which commissioned the work at the Tinbergen Building through CPC Project Services, and also David Radford, who monitored the work on behalf of Oxford City Council. The Mansfield College excavation was managed by Ken Welsh and directed by John Boothroyd and Robin Bashford, who were supported by Ashley Strutt and Jeremy Mordue. The Tinbergen Building excavation was managed by Richard Brown and undertaken by Robin Bashford and Vix Hughes; the client report was written by Robin Bashford and Chris Pickard. Julian Munby provided invaluable advice regarding the evidence for the city's Civil War defences. The Roman pottery was analysed and reported on by Edward Biddulph, the post-Roman pottery by Paul Blinkhorn (Mansfield College) and John Cotter (Tinbergen Building), the clay pipes by John Cotter, the metalwork and worked bone by Leigh Allen and Ian R. Scott, the glass by Ian R. Scott, the ceramic building material and fired clay by Cynthia Poole (Mansfield College) and John Cotter (Tinbergen Building), the flint by Michael Donnelly, the animal bone by Lee G. Broderick (Mansfield College), Rebecca Nicholson and Lena Strid (Tinbergen Building), the molluscs by Elizabeth Stafford, and the charred plant remains and charcoal by Sharon Cook. Thanks are also due to the staff that processed the finds under the management of Leigh Allen, processed the environmental samples under the management of Rebecca Nicholson, and prepared the archive under the management of Nicola Scott.

Index

All places within Oxford unless otherwise stated.